DATE DUE

NO 15'00			
DE 2'00			
MY 29'01			

DEMCO 38-296

Introductory
FOODS

Introductory
FOODS

10TH EDITION

MARION BENNION

Merrill,
an imprint of Prentice Hall
Upper Saddle River, New Jersey   Columbus, Ohio

OF CONGRESS CATALOGING-IN-PUBLICATION DATA

Marion.
oductory foods / Marion Bennion. — 10th ed.
   p.   cm.
Includes bibliographical references and index.
ISBN 0-02-308191-0 (h)
1. Food   2. Cookery   I. Title
TX354.B46 1995   94-3147
641.3—dc20   CIP

Cover art/photo: Barbara Maslen/SIS
Editor: Kevin M. Davis
Developmental Editor: Erin Haggerty
Production Editor: Patricia A. Skidmore
Text and Cover Designer: Susan E. Frankenberry
Production Buyer: Patricia A. Tonneman
Electronic Text Management: Marilyn Wilson Phelps, Matthew Williams, Jane Lopez,
    Karen L. Bretz

This book was set in Garamond, Humanist, and Swiss by Prentice Hall
Merrill is an imprint of Prentice Hall

© 1995 by Prentice-Hall, Inc.
A Simon & Schuster Company
Upper Saddle River, New Jersey 07458

Printed in the United States of America
10 9 8 7 6

ISBN: 0-02-308191-0

Prentice-Hall International (UK) Limited, *London*
Prentice-Hall of Australia Pty. Limited, *Sydney*
Prentice-Hall of Canada, Inc., *Toronto*
Prentice-Hall Hispanoamericana, S. A., *Mexico*
Prentice-Hall of India Private Limited, *New Delhi*
Prentice-Hall of Japan, Inc., *Tokyo*
Simon & Schuster Asia Pte. Ltd., *Singapore*
Editora Prentice-Hall do Brasil, Ltda., *Rio de Janeiro*

Preface

Change is constant in the area of food service and technology. Advances applied to food preparation and processing, along with shifting demographics and expanding knowledge of nutritional requirements, call for a text that can keep up with this fast-paced field. As with previous editions, the tenth edition of *Introductory Foods* has been written in order to provide the beginning student of foods with an introduction to the fundamental as well as some of the more innovative aspects of food science and technology.

TEXT ORGANIZATION

The first nine chapters of the book contain basic principles that the student may refer to throughout the entire course. The remaining chapters highlight specific types of foods and beverages. This edition has a chapter organization that allows you to choose the order in which you present chapters to fit the structure of your course. This is accomplished by the design and arrangement of chapters, so that each chapter functions both as an independent section and as part of a thematic unit. The chapter on beverages has been expanded to include drinks other than coffee, tea, and chocolate. It also has been placed earlier in the text so that it may be used in connection with a discussion of water and solutions.

Similarly, the chapters on sweeteners and frozen desserts which follow the beverages chapter also relate to solutions but, in addition, include crystallization and introduce carbohydrate-containing foods. These chapters are followed by starch, cereals, vegetables, fruits, and salads, which as a unit emphasize carbohydrates.

The chapter on fats and frying is placed after the carbohydrate-oriented chapters and is followed by a series of chapters that emphasize protein foods—eggs, milk, poultry, and fish. The next several chapters cover a unique group of products—batters and doughs. Finally, two chapters concerned with food preservation and packaging complete the text.

TOPICS NEW TO THIS EDITION

This edition covers new topics and innovations in food and discusses advances in biotechnology. Information concerning the 1990 nutrition labeling legislation and the food guide pyramid has been incorporated throughout the text. Food consumption data have been updated, and "light" products are addressed at several points.

The Hazard Analysis and Critical Control Point (HACCP) system is discussed in the chapter on food safety. A summary table on food infections and intoxications has been expanded to include additional organisms, and viruses are briefly discussed. Chapter 4, which is concerned with food regulations and standards, discusses food additives. Fat replacers are mentioned as food additives and are discussed further in the chapter on fats. Organic food standards also are briefly discussed.

Chapter 5, on food composition, includes information on water activity (use optional). The brief discussion of carbohydrates, fats, and proteins may be used as a review for students who have had chemistry courses or as an introduction for those who have not. A general discussion of browning reactions has been included with the section on carbohydrates.

A segment on forms for writing recipes has been added to the chapter on weights and measures. The discussion of heat conduction and radiation has been revised. Edible flowers are mentioned in the chapter on seasoning and flavoring materials. Biotechnology and vegetable production is an added topic in the chapter on vegetables. A short discussion of vegetarian diets is included along with material on plant proteins, particularly soybeans. The chapter on gelatin has been combined with the chapter on salads since gelatin is used in set salads. Safety precautions to consider in the handling of eggs and also of seafood have been expanded in these respective chapters. The discussion of food preservation by ionizing radiation has been updated. Aseptic packaging and modified atmosphere packaging of foods, including sous-vide processing, are addressed. The last chapter on food preservation by freezing and canning has been retained.

Definitions have again been placed in the margins for ready accessibility and additional definitions have been added. Cross-references have been noted at various points in the text in order to keep duplication at a minimum.

This text, as with previous editions, has been written for the beginning student of foods. A student who has not taken college chemistry should be able to read and understand the material presented. However, some background in science should be helpful in the student's attempt to grasp and apply the basic principles of food preparation.

ACKNOWLEDGMENTS

I express my appreciation for the insightful and constructive comments and suggestions that were offered by the reviewers of this edition: Jane Bowers, Kansas State University; Mary Wallace Kelsey, Oregon State University; Denise L. King, The Ohio State University; Carol M. Michael, Miami University; Elizabeth F. Reutter, University of Illinois at Urbana; Martha B. Stone, Colorado State University; and Anita Wilson, University of Wisconsin-Stout. The input of reviewers, in this and previous editions, has been invaluable.

Brief Contents

Contents

6
Weights and Measures   115

7
Heat Transfer in Cooking   125

8
Microwave Cooking   135

9
Seasoning and Flavoring Materials   149

10
Beverages   161

11
Sweeteners and Sugar Cookery   183

15
Vegetables and Vegetable Preparation   265

16
Fruits and Fruit Preparation   313

17
Salads and Gelatin   339

18
Fats, Frying, and Emulsions   355

19
Eggs and Egg Cookery   387

20
Milk and Milk Products*   421

21
Meat and Meat Cookery   461

25
Yeast Breads   589

26
Cakes and Cookies   611

APPENDIXES

A: Weights and Measures   685

B: Temperature Control   689

C: Nutritive Value of Selected Foods   691

D: Glossary   699

Index   705

Food Choices and Sensory Characteristics

1

The food choices that we make and the development of our habits concerning food are influenced by many interacting factors, such as income, culture, concerns about health, social values, and religion [7]. Yet, for most persons and in ordinary circumstances, foods must be palatable or have **appetite** appeal if they are to be eaten. A palatable food is one that is both acceptable to an individual and agreeable to his or her taste. Various **sensory** impressions or sensations, including odor, appearance, taste, and mouth-feel or touch, are involved in our judgment of palatability and food quality.

Learning to prepare foods with great appetite appeal includes learning to discriminate and evaluate the quality of food through the intensity of the sensations received when food is sampled. Individuals vary in their capacities to experience flavors and odors, but sensitivities to pleasurable encounters with food may be heightened as more is learned about food characteristics and quality. A taste or liking for many different foods may be acquired, and learning to like new foods can bring ample rewards by increasing enjoyment and enhancing aesthetic experiences. Eating a wide variety of foods is also an excellent practice from a nutrition and health point of view. You are, then, encouraged to develop a discriminating taste as you begin to learn basic reasons why foods behave as they do during preparation and/or processing.

• FACTORS AFFECTING PATTERNS OF EATING

Social and Cultural Effects

Humans, as biological beings, require food to sustain life. They eat to satisfy hunger and to meet a basic drive for food. But a person is also a social being. Humans have learned to live and work together and have organized themselves into societies. As infants grow and develop, they are incorporated into this society through a variety of experiences, and some of these experiences involve food.

Appetite a desire or craving either for food in general or for some specific food

Sensory having to do with the senses (sight, taste, smell, hearing, touch); connected with receiving and transmitting sense impressions

Our pattern of eating includes the foods deemed acceptable and the time periods and settings in which these foods are consumed. The family structure and interactions among family members are important influences on the development of our food habits, their rigidity, and the ease with which they may be changed [17]. The development of food patterns begins with the family but is modified as a child grows into adulthood and travels in ever-widening circles of contact with others [41]. It has been suggested that the family meal may be an endangered species in the United States [1]. Regular, shared meals are declining under the pressures of modern society. Nevertheless, the family meal plays an important role in human communication, communicating love and values as well as information. It can be especially effective in increasing the well-being of children.

Attitudes are considered an important link between knowledge of food and nutrition and the application of this knowledge to food habits or patterns of eating [18]. Contrary to the popular belief that dietary patterns are very stable and unyielding to change, patterns of eating by individuals and families are in a continuous process of change as their economic, social, and technological environments change [23].

Culture a way of life in which there are common customs for behavior and in which there is a common understanding among members of the group

The **culture** in which we develop determines, to a large extent, our food patterns or habits. Foods are eaten in combination with other foods in ways that are determined and perpetuated by our culture. Food patterns differ markedly from one culture to another. Grasshoppers, baked mouse, or roast dog may be delicacies in some parts of the world, whereas in other areas it would be unthinkable for humans to consume these products. Eggs are a staple breakfast food in certain cultures, whereas in others they are taboo, at least for some members of the group. Not everyone in a cultural group eats exactly alike, however. Within a culture, individual preferences differ and subgroups develop. Families tend to develop their own distinctive food patterns, and even individuals within a family have personal food preferences. Differences among cultural groups may be found not only in what specific foods are eaten but also in the number of meals eaten each day, the way the food is served, and the utensils used in the service. Each culture passes on its food habits and patterns by training children from infancy so that each child knows what is acceptable and not acceptable and patterns become familiar [25].

Ethnic pertains to basic divisions of mankind into groups that are distinguished by customs, characteristics, language, and so on

Cuisine a style of cooking or manner of preparing food

Demographic having to do with the statistical study of populations

The study of foods should help you understand and appreciate the food patterns of other cultures or **ethnic** groups as we move toward greater cultural diversity [3, 32]. Each ethnic group such as Mexican, Japanese, Korean, Italian, Armenian, Scandinavian, and so on, has developed a **cuisine** with its distinctive combination of flavorings for basic foodstuffs [27]. Ethnic restaurants have become popular in the United States and are widely distributed throughout the country. The food industry is accepting the challenges presented by **demographic** changes in the Americas and Western Europe, in particular, and recognizes the vital role played by ethnic tastes in the successful production and marketing of food [13]. Advances in food technology will likely enable the food industry to commercially produce many ethnic foods for the world market. We have open to us, therefore, a great variety of food choices. Fascinating experiences await the adventurer who learns to enjoy, and to prepare, the foods of many different cultures.

Availability of Food

Geography of an area and variations in climate influence the types of food that can be and usually are grown. Historically, this has had a profound influence on the availability of particular foods and, in turn, on the eating patterns of people in the area. Examples are the widespread use of pinto beans and chili peppers in the southwestern United States and the extensive use of seafood in coastal areas. With the development of rapid transportation and modern food-handling facilities, however, the influence of geography and climate on our food habits has decreased greatly. Now we have available in U.S. supermarkets, on a regular basis, fresh fruits from tropical areas and live seafood, even though we may live far from the tropics or the ocean.

The influence of ethnic groups is also seen in geographical areas where individuals from these cultures predominate. Food habits learned in other geographical areas of the world tend to continue whenever possible as an individual or group moves to a new location.

Economics

Whether or not we consume the variety of foods available to us in supermarkets and restaurants depends, to a considerable extent, on our purchasing power. Economics is a powerful factor in limiting or expanding our dietary patterns, although these changes may be transitory in some cases. When food budgets are restricted because of financial problems, less expensive foods must make up a larger share of the menus offered. When budgets are liberal, more convenience items and snack foods are often purchased, and "eating out" occurs more frequently. During a recent economic downtrend in the United States, store brand products, usually less expensive than highly advertised brands, gained in their share of supermarket revenue to nearly 20 percent of the total [19]. Consumers are expected to remain price-conscious and continue to purchase these types of products even with an improving economy.

Knowledge of Nutrition and Health Concerns

An interest in healthy lifestyles, including recognition of nutrition as an important part of the health improvement process, is flourishing among Americans. National nutrition objectives are included in the U.S. Public Health Service's broad-based initiative *Healthy People 2000: National Health Promotion and Disease Prevention Objectives* [16, 10]. Dietary guidelines for Americans, first published in 1980 by the U.S. Departments of Agriculture (USDA) and Health and Human Services, were revised in 1990 [36]. These guidelines focus on the promotion of general health and the prevention of certain chronic diseases. They recommend a diet low in fat, saturated fat, and cholesterol and high in vegetables, fruits, and grain products. Sugars and salt are to be used in moderation. Table 1.1 summarizes these guidelines.

The Food Guide Pyramid was introduced by the USDA to graphically illustrate the dietary guidelines [37]. This pyramid (Figure 1.1) places at the top those food groups that should be used sparingly. As one proceeds toward the bottom of the pyramid, the daily servings from the food groups are suggested

TABLE I.I
Dietary Guidelines for Americans

Guideline	Comments and Suggestions
1. Eat a variety of foods	Select foods from each of the major food groups. Adequate amounts of essential nutrients are present in a well-balanced diet containing foods from a variety of sources, and risk from overconsumption of any one food is minimized.
2. Maintain healthy weight	If you are too fat or too thin, your chances of developing health problems are increased. Obesity is associated with high blood pressure, increased blood lipids, heart disease, and certain cancers.
3. Choose a diet low in fat, saturated fat, and cholesterol	A high level of blood cholesterol increases the risk of having a heart attack. Populations with diets relatively high in fat, especially saturated fat, have an increased risk of heart attacks.
4. Choose a diet with plenty of vegetables, fruits, and grain products	Vegetables, fruits, and whole-grain products are emphasized especially for their complex carbohydrates, dietary fiber, and other components linked to good health.
5. Use sugars only in moderation	Sugars provide calories but few other nutrients. Large amounts should be avoided, especially by those with low caloric needs. Excessive snacking with sugary foods encourages dental decay.
6. Use salt and sodium only in moderation	Excess sodium is a major hazard to persons who have high blood pressure, although not everyone is equally susceptible.
7. If you drink alcoholic beverages, do so in moderation	Alcohol provides calories but not other nutrients, affects the absorption and utilization of some nutrients by the body, and stresses body organs, particularly the liver and brain.

Source: Reference 36.

in increasing amounts. The bread, cereal, rice, and pasta group forms the base of the pyramid with 6 to 11 daily servings recommended.

At the tip of the pyramid are fats, oils, and sweets, contained in such foods as salad dressings, cream, margarine, soft drinks, sweet desserts, and candies. These foods provide calories but few nutrients and should be used sparingly. The second level of the pyramid contains two food groups that come mostly from animal sources: the milk, yogurt, and cheese group and the meat, poultry, fish, dry beans, eggs, and nuts group. Important nutrients contained in these groups include protein, calcium, iron, and zinc.

The third level of the broadening pyramid consists of the vegetable and the fruit groups—plant food sources. The 5 to 9 recommended daily servings of fruits and vegetables are very important for the vitamins, minerals, and fiber that they supply to the diet. The base of the pyramid represents the foundation of the diet, which comes from breads, cereals, and pasta. Whole-grain products are particularly recommended. These supply additional vitamins, minerals, and fiber, along with complex carbohydrates and some protein. With the food pyramid as a guide, people can easily follow the recommended diet.

Information about nutrition and the effects of various diets on health may encourage those responsible for food purchasing and preparation to adjust food patterns in accordance with public health suggestions on diet. Patterns of "eating out" may also be influenced. U.S. food consumption has changed dramatically in the last 20 years [29]. Americans have shifted away from meat or animal products as the main entree to a mixture of animal products, vegetables, fruits, nuts, and grains. Based on two USDA surveys of women and young children, the average fat intake of the women fell from 42 percent of calories in

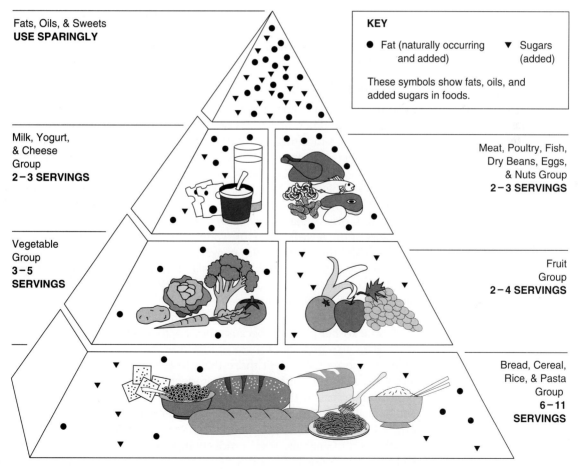

FIGURE 1.1
The Food Guide Pyramid (Courtesy of the U.S. Department of Agriculture)

1977 to 37 percent in 1985 [40]. Some of this difference could be attributed to a shift from whole milk to low-fat milk. Correspondingly, carbohydrate intake increased from 41 percent of calories in 1977 to 46 percent in 1985 with a rise in the consumption of grain products. At the same time, there was also an increase in the consumption of carbonated beverages containing sugar.

Government and professional groups have attempted to educate the public about the adverse health effects associated with diets high in fat. Apparently their message is getting through [28]. Increased awareness of diet-health relationships has been documented, but this awareness was not distributed evenly across the population studied. Women with more education had a higher diet-health awareness than did less educated women.

Increased awareness appears to have some impact on dietary behavior, as indicated by the USDA surveys showing decreases in fat intake. However, the more educated women with higher diet-health awareness decreased their fat intake by approximately the same degree as did women with less education. The women with more education consumed less red meat, thus substantially reducing their fat intake from this source, but they had larger increases in fat intake from other food sources. They were thus simply trading sources of dietary fat. These findings suggest that along with programs for increasing public awareness of diet-health relationships, there is a need for the dissemination of more specific information about food composition.

Religious Beliefs

Food has significance in relation to many religious beliefs. Among the sets of rules governing different aspects of religious life are food laws. These may set strict guidelines dictating the types of food to be consumed, the procedures for processing and preparing foods, the complete omission of certain foods, and the frequency of eating other foods. In order to take advantage of the large markets available in the religious communities, the food industry must serve the needs of these various groups.

The kosher dietary laws, *kashruth*, are observed to varying degrees by members of the Jewish faith [30]. These laws include a prohibition against eating blood and thus dictate rules concerning the slaughter of animals as well as their further processing. Milk products and meat products must be kept separate. Only certain species of animals are considered to be suitable for consumption. Pork and shellfish, among others, are prohibited. Kosher laws also extend to ingredients that are used in food processing. Even many non-Jewish individuals choose kosher products because they see them as clean, high-quality foods.

Islam also prescribes a set of food laws [9]. As a general principle, all foods are permitted except those that are specifically prohibited. Prohibited foods include swine and all their by-products, intoxicants of all types, birds of prey, land animals without ears such as snakes, flowing or congealed blood, and animals killed in a manner which prevents their blood from being fully drained from their bodies. There are, therefore, strict requirements for the slaughtering of animals. Food products may be certified by the Islamic Food and Nutrition Council of America.

A number of religions advocate vegetarianism, although vegetarianism may be chosen for ecological, health, or other reasons as well. Chinese Buddhists advocate vegetarianism because they believe in compassion [21]. A vegetarian diet is recommended by the Seventh-Day Adventist church but is not required for membership [6].

In the United States there are an estimated 7 million vegetarians. The majority of these are **lacto-ovo-vegetarians**. The remainder are strict vegetarians or **vegans** [14]. The food industry has made available a number of products of special interest to vegetarians, including high-quality plant-protein foods prepared from wheat and soy, soy milk, and cereal products free of animal fats. Vegetarian entrees are being offered with increasing frequency in many foodservice establishments. (Vegetarianism is discussed further in Chapter 15.)

Technological Developments

The food-processing industry is sharing in the many ideas, innovations, and technological developments that are bringing about major changes in our society. The industry's growth and continued development keep an ever-increasing supply of convenience foods on the market and affect the purchasing habits of the consumer and the types of meals served both at home and in foodservice establishments [26]. Advertising through television, radio, newspapers, and magazines assures that the consumer not only is aware of the new types of foods available but also is enticed to try them. The development of technological expertise in transportation and in food preservation extends the seasons of food availability. Irradiation may decrease bacterial contamination on poultry and increase the shelf life of fresh fruits. Aseptic packaging decreases processing time and results in more flavorful food products. New-generation refrigerated foods offer fresh and flavorful entrees that may be stored under refrigeration for several weeks before reheating and service.

Sous vide [2] refers to one method of producing refrigerated foods that involves vacuum sealing fresh food in impermeable plastic pouches, cooking at length at low temperatures in circulating water, then chilling and holding at refrigerated temperatures. This method of food processing was developed in France and has the potential to consistently deliver superior cuisine on a large scale to the foodservice industry [31]. There are concerns, however, that sous vide foods could pose a potential public health hazard in terms of microbiological safety if proper controls are not maintained throughout the processing and delivery operations.

Conventional breeding and selection of plants and animals over the centuries has been used to improve food supplies. Now, with a group of genetic tools that falls under the heading of **biotechnology**, the variety, productivity, and efficiency of food production can be targeted in less time and with greater predictability and control than was possible with traditional methods [15]. Genetic engineering may be used to increase crop yields and disease resistance and to produce faster-maturing, drought-resistant varieties. Biotechnology could be used to improve the nutritional quality of the food supply or improve flavor and texture of vegetables. There is a need, however, for public education about biotechnology so that people will acquire a base of knowledge with which to make judgments about these new tools as they make choices in food purchasing [8].

Lacto-ovo-vegetarians those who consume milk, eggs, and products derived from them as well as vegetable foods

Vegans those who exclude from their diet all products that are not of plant origin

Sous vide literally means "under vacuum"

Biotechnology the collection of industrial processes or tools that involve the use of biological systems, i.e., plants, animals, and microorganisms

Refrigeration and freeze-processing within the modern home allow patterns of cooking and eating that cannot exist in still-technologically-developing societies in which methods for keeping foods fresh are not readily available. Cooking equipment, including the microwave oven, has markedly affected patterns of eating.

The proliferation of food-vending machines in technologically developed countries and the ready availability of fast-food restaurants are also changing food habits for many of us. An increasingly larger share of the U.S. consumer's food dollar is spent for meals away from home.

Even the social aspects of food may be influenced by developments in food technology as we need to rely less on other family members to prepare the food we eat. Almost anyone in the household can retrieve an entree from the freezer and quickly heat it in the microwave oven.

Emotional and Psychological Effects

With all of today's technological influences, it is important that the meanings of food, other than the biological and economic ones, be considered (Figure 1.2). Food means security, hospitality, and even status. Infants learn about security when mothers respond to their crying by giving them food. Familiar foods bring back memories of home and family and make one feel secure. Feeling full and physically satisfied and knowing that there is more food available for other meals bring security. Food is a symbol of hospitality and is used to show that one cares about others and is a friend. Gifts of food are given in times of both happiness and sorrow.

•SENSORY CHARACTERISTICS OF FOOD

Flavor

Flavor   a blend of taste, smell, and general touch sensations evoked by the presence of a substance in the mouth

Olfactory   having to do with the sense of smell

Tactile   having to do with the sense of touch

Pungency   a sharp, biting quality

Taste   sensations perceived through stimulation of taste buds on the tongue; primary tastes are sweet, salty, sour, and bitter

Aroma   an odor detected by the olfactory sense

Millions of flavor sensations are experienced in a lifetime. **Flavor** is an important attribute of a food. It involves the complex integration of sensations from the **olfactory** center in the nasal cavity, the taste buds on the tongue, **tactile** receptors in the mouth, and the perception of **pungency**, heat, cooling, and so on when a food is placed in the mouth [22]. However, much of what we call flavor is a blending of **taste** and **aroma**. Other sensory factors may also affect our total experience with food, including its visual appearance and even the sounds of crunching crisp foods such as raw carrots and celery and the sizzle of fajitas when they are brought to the table.

Taste and Aroma

Sometimes the words *flavor* and *taste* are used synonymously. In a strict sense, however, taste is only one part of flavor. Taste involves the sensations produced through stimulation of the taste buds on the tongue. It is generally accepted that there are only four primary taste sensations: sweet, sour, bitter, and salty. But the perceived flavor of a food involves, to a considerable extent, the sense of smell along with the taste sensations. It is influenced by other senses as well.

Mexican women chat while they roast chili peppers. (Photograph by Kay Franz)

A brother and sister can get to know each other over ice-cream cones. (Photograph by Roger P. Smith)

Eating spaghetti requires real concentration. (Photograph by Chris Meister)

FIGURE 1.2

Papillae   small, nipplelike projections of various shapes on the surface of the tongue

Taste receptor   tiny ends of the taste cells that come in contact with the substance being tasted

Taste pore   a tiny opening from the surface of the tongue into the taste bud

Taste bud   a group of cells, including taste cells, supporting cells, and nerve fibers

Taste buds are found in small elevations, called **papillae**, on the surface of the tongue (Figure 1.3). The actual taste sensations are produced when bitter, salty, sweet, or acid substances in a solution contact **taste receptors** in the **taste pore** leading to the **taste bud**. Figure 1.3 also shows a diagram of a taste bud. A message is sent to the brain from the taste cells by way of nerve fibers with endings in the taste cells. The brain interprets and identifies the specific taste.

The olfactory center is found at the top of the nasal cavity, as shown in Figure 1.4. To stimulate the olfactory center, substances must be in gaseous form. The gaseous molecules enter the nose as food is placed in the mouth and are drawn toward the olfactory center where they stimulate nerve endings. Nerve impulses are thus sent to the brain to be interpreted. The sense of smell is estimated to be about 10,000 times as sensitive as the sense of taste in detecting minute concentrations, and it can differentiate hundreds, or possibly thousands, of distinct odors.

Temperature may affect the blending of primary tastes as well as other factors contributing to flavor. Within the temperature range at which most food is eaten, from ice cream to hot chocolate, there are marked changes in the apparent intensity of some of the primary tastes. The same amount of sugar seems sweeter at higher temperatures than at lower temperatures. Just the

FIGURE 1.3
Drawing of the tongue, showing papillae on the surface. Taste buds are located on the sides and at the base of many of the papillae. Taste buds near the tip are more sensitive to sweet and salt, those on the sides are more sensitive to sour, and those near the back are more sensitive to bitter.

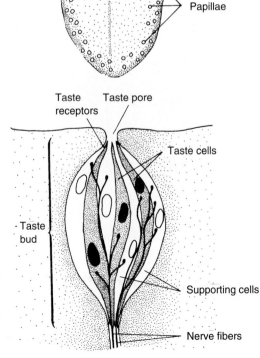

Diagram of an individual taste bud containing tiny taste receptors that come in contact with the substance being tasted, taste cells, and nerve fibers that carry the message from the taste bud to the brain for interpretation.

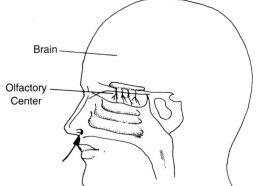

FIGURE 1.4
Gaseous molecules enter the nose and stimulate the olfactory center from which nerve fibers send messages to the brain concerning the odor of food.

Brain

Olfactory Center

reverse seems to be true of salt. Furthermore, extremes of temperature may create pleasant sensations or cause actual pain or injury to body tissues. Some substances such as menthol feel cool; certain receptors in the mouth and throat are sensitized so that they exaggerate the feeling of coolness. Conversely, some foods such as red peppers contain molecules that irritate the mucous membranes lining the mouth and produce a hot or biting sensation. The compound primarily responsible for the "hotness" of red peppers is called *capsaicin*. To the uninitiated, this hot sensation is often so strong that it is painful.

Countless numbers of molecules contribute to our perception of aroma (odor) and taste. One single flavor may be produced from the interaction of many different chemical molecules. Did you know, for example, that more than 200 different compounds are used to make artificial banana flavor? Many of the odorous substances in foods occur in such vanishingly small concentrations that it is difficult to show that they are even present. With the development of analytical tools such as the gas chromatograph, tracings from which are shown in Figure 1.5, the chemist has been able to separate, isolate, and identify many of the molecules that are responsible for aroma and taste in such foods as onions, strawberries, and beef. Another analytical tool used to great advantage by the flavor researcher is high-performance liquid chromatography or HPLC [24]. It is especially useful for studying **nonvolatile** and/or **labile** flavor components. Among other things, it can be used to test for adulteration of flavoring materials from natural sources (see Figure 1.6).

Continuing research about flavor is important in order to learn more about flavor molecules and how the flavor of food is perceived by humans. The aroma and taste of food seem to be the complex result of many simultaneous responses to odor and taste stimuli. As food markets continue to expand on a global basis, more knowledge is needed concerning the diverse tastes of people from different cultures. If flavor research is to be applied in a real-life setting, then cultural, economic, and environmental factors must be integrated with information about the chemical components of odor and taste.

Nonvolatile   lacking the ability to readily change to a vapor or to evaporate

Labile   unstable

FIGURE 1.5

The geographic origin of a spice may be identified by examining the gas chromatographic tracing of its flavor components. Each peak on the tracing represents a different flavor substance. Oregano grown in Greece contains various flavor components in different amounts than does the oregano grown in Mexico. (Courtesy of the R.T. French Company)

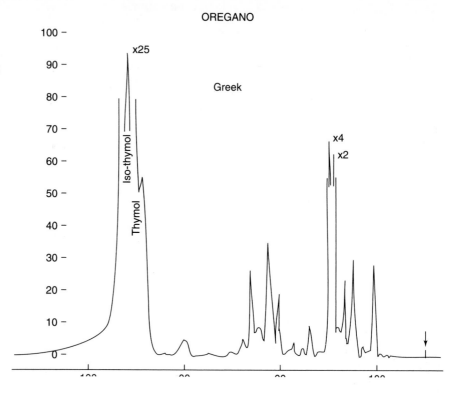

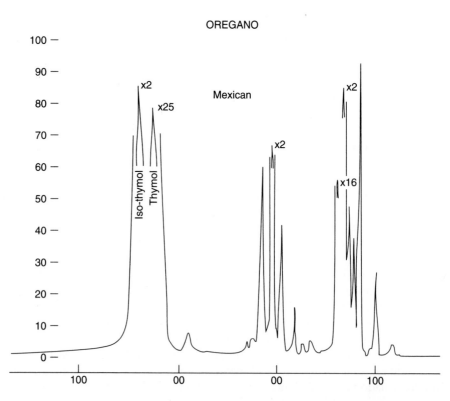

Types of Flavors

The flavors of some foods are readily perceivable in the raw "natural" state, whereas cooking other foods produces flavors from nonflavor substances called flavor **precursors**. For example, strawberries, peaches, and other fresh fruits contain a natural, unique flavor bouquet composed of many volatile substances that stimulate the nasal olfactory center in combination with sweet and acid components that stimulate the taste buds. Raw vegetables, meats, and fish also present their own characteristic flavors. The flavor of raw meat and fish is appreciated by some people, whereas others prefer the change in flavor that is produced when these foods are cooked. Incidentally, raw meat and fish are made safer by proper cooking to destroy any pathogenic organisms that may be present.

The chemical changes that occur during heating in the presence of air are apparently very complex and are not completely understood for most foods. For example, different flavors are produced when meat is cooked in water from those produced when it is roasted in an oven where it is surrounded by dry heat. Some flavor precursors are present in the lean portion of meats such as beef, pork, and lamb, whereas other precursors are present in their fat. The tantalizing odors that develop during the baking of bread are additional examples of flavor substances produced by heating. Many of the volatile substances that waft from the oven where bread is baking are initially the products of **yeast fermentation**. Crust formation occurs as the outer layers of the bread are dehydrated and subjected to very high temperatures. Browning of the crust contributes to both an attractive appearance and a pleasant flavor.

Precursor   something that comes before; in flavor study, it is a compound that is nonflavorful but can be changed, usually by heat or enzymes, into a flavorful substance

Yeast fermentation   a process in which enzymes produced by the yeast break down sugars to carbon dioxide and alcohol, and also produce some flavor substances

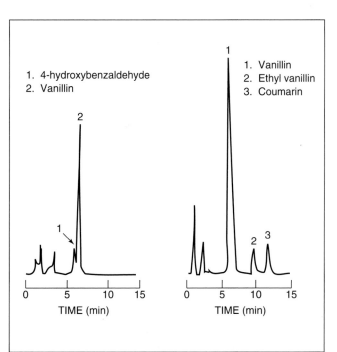

FIGURE 1.6
High-performance liquid chromatography may be used in testing vanilla for adulteration. The tracing on the left is from a true vanilla-bean extract and the one on the right is from a sample that has been adulterated with coumarin, a substance banned as a flavor source in the United States. (From Kenney, B.F. "Applications of high-performance liquid chromatography for the flavor research and quality control laboratories in the 1990s." *Food Technology* 44, 76 (No. 9), 1990. Copyright © Institute of Food Technologists.)

Enzymatic reactions   those that are *catalyzed* by enzymes, which are special proteins produced by living cells; a catalyst changes the rate of a reaction without itself undergoing permanent change

Synthetic compounds   those produced by chemically combining two or more simple compounds or elements in the laboratory

Flavors may also be produced during processing by **enzymatic reactions**, as is cheese flavor, or by microbial fermentation, as is butter flavor. Flavor substances that occur naturally or that are generated during heating, processing, or fermentation are considered to be "natural" flavors [22].

Biotechnology can be used to generate "natural" flavor substances from enzymatic or microbial reactions. These and other "natural" flavors may be added to fabricated foods to improve or create desirable flavor bouquets. Since there are not enough natural flavorings to flavor all of the foods that are produced by the food industry, these natural flavors are simulated as closely as possible through the production of **synthetic compounds**. Synthetic compounds that are added to foods either individually or as part of a mixture are considered in the United States to be "artificial" or "synthetic" flavors. Both natural and artificial flavorings are combined in many foods.

Knowledge of flavor chemistry and ways of simulating natural flavors is especially important as the world population increases and new protein foods are required. The protein may be derived from soybeans, fish meal, or algae, but it will have no nutritional value if it is not eaten by the people who need it. It must be flavored so that it is acceptable. To apply the science of flavor successfully to the development of new products and the improvement of old ones, the flavor researcher must first identify the substances that are responsible for the acceptable flavor and the mechanism by which people eating the food experience flavor. Then new food-flavor ingredients can be developed and foods can be processed in a manner that results in more desirable flavors [4, 20].

Texture

Texture   arrangement of the parts of a material showing the structure; the texture of baked flour products such as a slice of bread may be fine and even or coarse and open; the texture of a cream sauce may be smooth or lumpy

The physical properties of foods, including **texture**, consistency, and shape, involve the sense of touch or feeling, also called the *tactile* sense. When food is contacted, pressure and movement receptors on the skin and muscles of the mouth and tongue are stimulated. Sensations of smoothness, stickiness, graininess, brittleness, fibrous qualities, or lumpy characteristics may be detected [34]. The tingling feeling that comes from drinking a carbonated beverage is an attribute of texture. Terms describing extremes of texture and consistency may include *dry* or *moist*, *solid* or *fluid*, *thick* or *thin*, *rough* or *smooth*, *coarse* or *fine*, *tough* or *tender*, *hard* or *soft*, and *compact* or *porous*.

The sound that is made when a food is eaten is also part of palatability and the enjoyment of eating. We often evaluate crispness by the sound it makes as well as by its tactile sensations in the mouth. Try to imagine how crisp carrot and celery sticks would "taste" without the accompanying sound of crunching.

Texture is an important attribute that affects consumer attitudes toward and preferences for different foods. Textural characteristics of food have both positive and negative connotations for the consumer [35]. Those textures that are universally liked are crisp, crunchy, tender, juicy, and firm. Those generally disliked are tough, soggy, crumbly, lumpy, watery, and slimy.

Appearance

Such qualities as color, form, size, and design or arrangement contribute to what may be called "eye appeal" of foods. Without an attractive and appealing appearance, foods may be rejected without being tasted. For the commercial vendor of prepared foods, the appearance of the food is extremely important because this is the first opportunity to impress the potential buyer with the quality and desirability of the product.

•SENSORY EVALUATION OF FOOD

When the quality of a food is judged or evaluated by the senses (taste, smell, sight, touch, and hearing), it is said to be a sensory evaluation. Since food is prepared for the primary purpose of being eaten and enjoyed through the senses, sensory evaluation is most appropriate. No machine has yet been devised that can totally substitute for the human senses in evaluating the quality of human food. However, the human instrument used in sensory evaluation is very complex, and many problems need to be managed as data are collected and analyzed. Computers are generally used to analyze data from sensory evaluations and may also be used to collect information firsthand [5, 39].

Flavor perceptions are difficult to characterize verbally. For example, think about how a strawberry tastes; then try to describe it to someone else. In food research, small groups of trained individuals, called judging panels or sensory panels, are commonly used to determine differences among food samples [11]. These panels often consist of from 5 to 15 individuals who have had training and experience in testing the particular food products being evaluated.

Sensory evaluation of foods and flavors has a long history in the food industry. It is an important part of quality assurance for the food processor. It may sometimes be desirable to do a complete analysis of all of the flavor components, such as sweet, buttery, burnt, fragrant, grainy, and metallic, in a particular food. Such a **flavor profile** of the food, giving a picture of its palatability, may be determined by a panel of trained judges working together. Aroma and taste are studied separately to complete the total flavor analysis. Various types of scoring, ranking, or difference tests are used by sensory panels.

Flavor profile an outline of the major flavor components and their intensities that are blended to form the overall flavor sensation created by a food

As new food products are developed, food manufacturers need to know if they can capture a large enough share of the market to warrant the cost of development and marketing. Many new products are introduced and fail each year. Sensory-evaluation professionals, along with marketing personnel, may conduct consumer tests to obtain information on product quality and preference. Consumers and producers may not always agree on quality or preference and, therefore, consumer input is important from the very beginning of the development process [33].

The character of a taste or aroma may be described using a wide variety of terms. Often, the terms used to describe the flavor of a food indicate that the flavor is similar to that of some other familiar food product. For example, a prepared cereal may be described as being nutty, starchy, haylike, floury, oily, or buttery. The primary tastes—sweet, sour, salty, and bitter—are relatively easy to describe. Other terms used to describe flavors in foods include caramel, stale, rancid, metallic, cardboardlike, musty, fragrant, flowery, fruity, sharp, pungent, tart, chalky, branny, burnt, spicy, astringent, sulfury, diacetyl (butterlike), malty, effervescent, earthy, chemical, putrid, yeasty, fishy, grassy, bland, toasted, and **aftertaste**. You may enjoy the challenge of finding new descriptive words for flavor evaluation.

Aftertaste a taste that remains in the mouth after a food has been swallowed

(a)

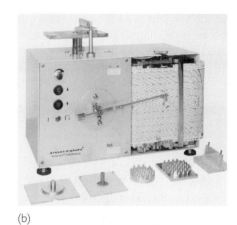

(b)

(c)

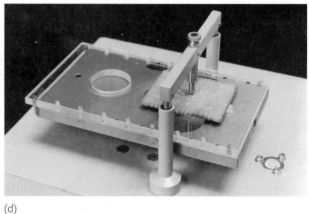

(d)

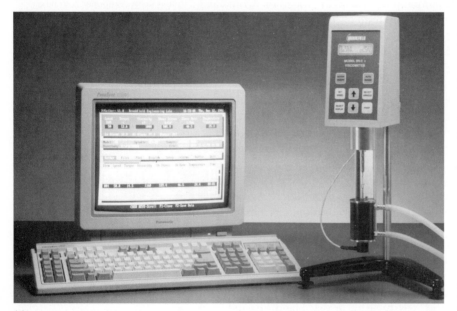

(e)

FIGURE 1.7
A variety of instruments are used in the objective measurement of food quality. (a) The Armour Tenderometer gives an indication of meat tenderness when the needles on the probe are pushed into raw muscle. (Reproduced from *Objective Methods for Food Evaluation*, 1976, with permission from the National Academy Press, Washington, DC) (b–d) The Brabender® Struct-O-Graph® may be used for testing mechanical parameters of foods that describe texture and structure. For example, textural characteristics of crackers and cookies may be measured. (Courtesy of C. W. Brabender Instruments, Inc., South Hackensack, New Jersey) (e) The Brookfield DV-II+ is a calculating digital viscometer; a plot of the viscosity may be generated on a computer screen. (Courtesy of Brookfield Engineering Labs, 240 Cushing Street, Stoughton, Massachusetts)

In addition to a description of the character of the taste or aroma, the intensity of the flavor should be described. It may be weak, moderate, strong, or someplace in between.

Aroma, taste, and texture change as we eat and drink, especially for foods such as chocolate that melt in the mouth. These dynamic aspects of taste may be examined by using a time-intensity curve. Through the use of a computer mouse, the taster may record the changing intensity of a particular flavor attribute over a 30-second to 2- or 3-minute period [38].

In some cases, particularly in consumer preference testing involving large groups of people, an **hedonic** scale is used without a description of the flavor components. An example of such a scale follows:

Hedonic having to do with pleasure; a hedonic scale indicates how much a person likes or dislikes a food

___ Like extremely well
___ Like very much
___ Like moderately well
___ Like slightly
___ Neither like nor dislike
___ Dislike slightly
___ Dislike moderately
___ Dislike very much
___ Dislike extremely

•OBJECTIVE EVALUATION OF FOOD

Objective evaluation of food involves the use of laboratory instruments to determine certain characteristics that may be related to eating quality. Devices and the objective measurements that may be made in the laboratory include a viscometer to measure viscosity (thickness or consistency) of a tomato paste or a starch-thickened pudding, a gelometer to measure the firmness or strength of a gelatin gel or a fruit jelly, a pH meter to measure the acidity of lemon juice, a color difference meter to measure the color of tomato catsup, a compressimeter to measure the compressibility or softness of a slice of bread, and a shear or cutting apparatus to measure the tenderness of a sample of meat (Figure 1.7). These types of tests do not directly involve the human senses and thus are not part of sensory evaluation.

The use of judging panels to evaluate food is often time consuming and expensive. Therefore, the use of laboratory instruments that give useful information with less time and expense is desirable whenever the information thus collected correlates well with sensory characteristics. Objective tests can usually be reproduced with reasonable precision. In the overall evaluation of the quality of a food product, sensory and objective methods complement each other.

Objective evaluation having to do with a known object as distinguished from existing in the mind; in food science, measurement of the characteristics of food with a laboratory instrument such as a pH meter to indicate acidity or a viscometer to measure viscosity or consistency

STUDY QUESTIONS

1. a. What is meant by *palatability*?
   b. Why is it important for the student of food science to be able to evaluate the palatability and quality of foods?
2. Discuss at least six factors that are likely to affect the kind of eating patterns that an individual develops.

3. a. Define and distinguish among the terms *flavor*, *taste*, and *odor*.
   b. List four primary tastes.
4. Briefly describe how the eating of food produces the sensations of taste and smell in humans.
5. Give examples of (a) flavors that occur preformed in foods, and (b) flavors that are produced by heating.
6. What effect does the temperature of a food have on your perception of its flavor? Discuss this.
7. a. Of what practical importance to humanity is research on flavor chemistry?
   b. Discuss recent technological developments affecting flavor chemistry and their potential influence on the future of food processing.
8. Give an example of how the appearance of a food may influence your evaluation of its flavor or other quality characteristics.
9. Which human sense perceives the texture and consistency of a food?
10. Food quality may be evaluated by sensory or objective methods.
    a. Give examples of each type of evaluation.
    b. Describe several situations or conditions under which quality evaluation of specific food products may be desirable or necessary.

REFERENCES

1. ADA works to bridge the gap between culinary and health professionals. April 1993. *ADA Courier 32*, 1 (No. 4).
2. Baird, B. 1990. Sous vide: What's all the excitement about? *Food Technology 44*, 92 (No. 11).
3. Bartholomew, A. M. 1990. Food frequency intakes and sociodemographic factors of elderly Mexican Americans and nonHispanic whites. *Journal of the American Dietetic Association 90*, 1693.
4. Beauchamp, G. K. 1987. Recent developments in flavor research. *Food Technology 41*, 74 (No. 6).
5. Billmeyer, B. A. and G. Wyman. 1991. Computerized sensory evaluation system. *Food Technology 45*, 100 (No. 7).
6. Bosley, G. C. and M. G. Hardinge. 1992. Seventh-Day Adventists: Dietary standards and concerns. *Food Technology 46*, 112 (No. 10).
7. Brown, E. L. 1976. Factors influencing food choices and intake. *Geriatrics 31*, 89.
8. Bruhn, C. M. 1992. Consumer concerns and educational strategies: Focus on biotechnology. *Food Technology 46*, 80 (No. 3).
9. Chaudry, M. M. 1992. Islamic food laws: Philosophical basis and practical implications. *Food Technology 46*, 92 (No. 10).
10. Danford, D. E. 1991. Healthy people 2000: Development of nutrition objectives. *Journal of the American Dietetic Association 91*, 1517.
11. Ennis, D. M. 1990. Relative power of difference testing methods in sensory evaluation. *Food Technology 44*, 114 (No. 4).
12. Foley, C., A. A. Hertzler, and H. L. Anderson. 1979. Attitudes and food habits: A review. *Journal of the American Dietetic Association 75*, 13.
13. Ganguly, A. S. 1991. Developments and opportunities in the global food industry. *Food Technology 45*, 24 (No. 8).
14. Hardinge, F. and M. Hardinge. 1992. The vegetarian perspective and the food industry. *Food Technology 46*, 114 (No. 10).
15. Harlander, S. K. 1991. Biotechnology: A means for improving our food supply. *Food Technology 45*, 84 (No. 4).

16. Healthy people 2000: Nutrition objectives. 1991. *Journal of the American Dietetic Association 91*, 1515.

17. Hertzler, A. A. and C. E. Vaughan. 1979. The relationship of family structure and interaction to nutrition. *Journal of the American Dietetic Association 74*, 23.

18. Hertzler, A. A., N. Wenkam, and B. Standal. 1982. Classifying cultural food habits and meanings. *Journal of the American Dietetic Association 80*, 421.

19. Hollingsworth, P. 1993. Private label power. *Food Technology 47*, 88 (No. 3).

20. Horton, H. W. 1987. Consumer reaction to flavor innovations. *Food Technology 41*, 80 (No. 6).

21. Huang, Y. and C. Y. W. Ang. 1992. Vegetarian foods for Chinese Buddhists. *Food Technology 46*, 105 (No. 10).

22. Institute of Food Technologists' Expert Panel on Food Safety & Nutrition. 1989. Food flavors. *Food Technology 43*, 99 (No. 12).

23. Jerome, N. W. 1982. Dietary patterning and change: A continuous process. *Contemporary Nutrition* (General Mills Nutrition Department) 7 (No. 6).

24. Kenney, B. F. 1990. Applications of high-performance liquid chromatography for the flavor research and quality control laboratories in the 1990s. *Food Technology 44*, 76 (No. 9).

25. Lowenberg, M. E. 1974. The development of food patterns. *Journal of the American Dietetic Association 65*, 263.

26. Lund, D. 1989. Food processing: From art to engineering. *Food Technology 43*, 242 (No. 9).

27. Pangborn, R. M. 1975. Cross-cultural aspects of flavor preferences. *Food Technology 29*, 34 (No. 6).

28. Putler, D. P. and E. Frazao. 1991. Diet/health concerns about fat intake. *Food Review 14*, 16 (No. 1).

29. Putnam, J. J. 1991. Food consumption, 1970–90. *Food Review 14*, 2 (No. 3).

30. Regenstein, J. M. and C. E. Regenstein. 1979. An introduction to the kosher dietary laws for food scientists and food processors. *Food Technology 33*, 89 (No. 1).

31. Rhodehamel, E. J. 1992. FDA's concerns with sous vide processing. *Food Technology 46*, 73 (No. 12).

32. Sills-Levy, E. 1989. U.S. food trends leading to the year 2000. *Food Technology 43*, 128 (No. 4).

33. Stone, H., B. J. McDermott, and J. L. Sidel. 1991. The importance of sensory analysis for the evaluation of quality. *Food Technology 45*, 88 (No. 6).

34. Szczesniak, A. S. 1963. Classification of textural characteristics. *Journal of Food Science 28*, 385.

35. Szczesniak, A. S. 1990. Texture: Is it still an overlooked food attribute? *Food Technology 44*, 86 (No. 9).

36. U.S. Department of Agriculture and U.S. Department of Health and Human Services. November 1990. *Nutrition and your health: Dietary guidelines for Americans*, 3rd ed. Home and Garden Bulletin No. 232.

37. U.S. Department of Agriculture. August 1992. *The food guide pyramid*. Home and Garden Bulletin No. 252.

38. van Buren, S. 1992. Analyzing time-intensity responses in sensory evaluation. *Food Technology 46*, 101 (No. 2).

39. Winn, R. L. 1988. Touch screen system for sensory evaluation. *Food Technology 42*, 68 (No. 11).

40. *Women 19–50 years and their children 1–5 years, 1 day*. 1985. NFCS, CSFII Report No. 85-1. Washington, DC: Department of Agriculture.

41. Zifferblatt, S. M., C. S. Wilbur, and J. L. Pinsky. 1980. Understanding food habits. *Journal of the American Dietetic Association 76*, 9.

Food Economics and Convenience

2

Economics has been defined as the efficient use of resources to achieve a desired goal [29]. Food economics, then, is our wise use of all available resources to obtain food that is acceptable, enjoyable, and healthful to an optimal extent. To achieve our goal we use not only money but also time, energy, knowledge, skills, equipment, and even our values or philosophy.

We are all consumers. Throughout our lives we exchange money for goods and services. The responsibility for spending an individual's or a family's income is tremendous, and the cost of food is usually the second largest expenditure for a household. Thus, the responsibility for food purchasing is a major one, and the choices made can have significant impact on resources available for other expenses. For those involved in purchasing food for a foodservice establishment, financial responsibility is even greater.

Today's consumers occupy a key position in the economic world. *Consumerism* has become popular. To increase the power of separate individuals, groups of consumers have become organized, and the influence of many of these groups is being felt in the world of food marketing. Consumers are also making an impact on legislation related to food safety and nutritional quality as well as cost.

To be most effective in the economic world, both the individual consumer and the professional in foods and nutrition need some knowledge of trends in food consumption. An understanding of some of the factors that affect the cost and quality of food is also important.

•TRENDS IN FOOD USE

What do people eat? And how much? Answers to these questions are important to those who work in the various fields of food and nutrition. Information on food consumption of populations and of individuals may be collected in different ways using various sources.

Food Disappearance Data

One method of obtaining information on the food consumption or food use of populations is to measure directly (or to estimate through sampling and statistical procedures) the quantities of food that "disappear" into the nation's food distribution system. First, to calculate the total available food supply, three components are measured: total food production, total imports of food, and beginning-of-the-year inventories. From this total of available food is subtracted food that was exported, used by nonfood industries, used for seed by farmers, and year-end inventories. Food consumption calculated in this manner is called a *residual component*, that is, what is left over when other uses are subtracted from the available total supply. Therefore, the data are subject to various errors resulting from sampling, incomplete reporting, and techniques that may be used in estimating. These limitations should be kept in mind when the information is interpreted and used [34]. The U.S. Department of Agriculture (USDA) has periodically collected data for up to 350 commodities, such as beef, eggs, wheat, various fruits and vegetables, and so on, since 1909 [45].

Food consumption on a per capita basis is calculated from the primary figures using various conversion factors that account to some degree for further processing, trimming, shrinkage, or loss occurring during marketing. The data are national averages for the entire population and do not differentiate such factors as age, sex, ethnic background, region, or income level. Nutrient content is calculated from the food consumption data [35].

According to these figures for food use [34], Americans are now eating more food overall, more poultry and less beef, fewer eggs, more fruits and vegetables, more grains, and more caloric sweeteners than they did 10 to 20 years ago (Figure 2.1). Fat and oil consumption has decreased in recent years but is still 15 percent higher than in 1970. There is, however, an increased consumption of fried foods in foodservice outlets.

Food Consumption Surveys

Periodic surveys of food consumption involving individual and household interviews and record keeping constitute a check on the accuracy of food disappearance data. The USDA conducts a Nationwide Food Consumption Survey at periodic intervals. The most recent one, conducted in 1987 and 1988, is the seventh since 1936. In the 1987–88 survey, food-use information covering a 7-day period was collected from 9,600 households. Also, 3-day food intakes for about 25,000 individuals were compiled. Considerable time is required for the compilation and analysis of these large amounts of data.

The response rate for the 1987–88 USDA survey was lower than that for similar studies done previously, and, for this reason, the results may not be applicable for the entire U.S. population. However, data from this survey indicated that 30 to 50 percent of the participants ate meat on all three of the days surveyed. Less than 10 percent reported eating no meat on any of the three days. Men reported consuming a mean number of about 3.5 servings of meat in the three-day period while women reported consuming 2.5 to 3.0 servings. Although many different meat cuts were available, ground beef was the most frequently mentioned in the survey. Ground-beef mixtures, such as burgers, tacos, and chili, were commonly consumed [36]. As compared with the 1977 USDA survey, the 1987–88 data indicated that Americans were consuming less red meat and using meat as an ingredient with a mixture of other foods more often [34].

Calculated energy intake levels (kcal/day) were generally lower than recommended levels, suggesting that the food intake was underreported [26, 27]. The energy level, however, was a strong negative predictor of the number of low-intake nutrients (protein, vitamins, and minerals), that is, those that were at a level of less than two thirds of the 1989 **Recommended Dietary Allowances**. This means that the lower the energy level reported, the larger the number of nutrients that were below suggested levels. With higher energy intakes, however, the percent of energy coming from fat tended to increase, particularly for younger men. In general, it appears that many of the adult participants in this survey were not meeting the dual dietary goals of consuming a low percentage of kilocalories from fat and an adequate intake of nutrients—in other words, they did not have a "balanced" diet.

Recommended Dietary Allowances   standards of nutrient intake that serve as a goal for good nutrition for people of different ages in the United States; published by the Food and Nutrition Board. National Research Council, National Academy of Sciences

Rapidly Increasing Poultry Consumption is Behind the Higher Meat Consumption[1]

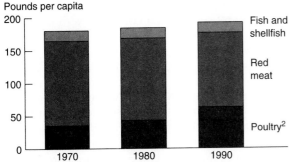

Pounds per capita

Fish and shellfish

Red meat

Poultry[2]

[1]Includes quantities sold to renderers and pet food processors.
[2]Includes skin, neck meat, and giblets.

Grains Consumption Jumped 50 Pounds per Person Since 1970, But a Decreasing Share Comes From Wheat[1]

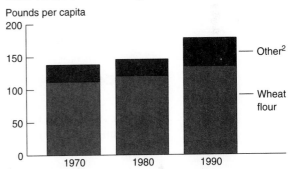

Pounds per capita

Other[2]

Wheat flour

[1]At the processing level. Excludes alcoholic beverages, corn sweeteners, feed, seed, fuel, and industrial uses.
[2]"Other" includes rice, corn, oat, rye, and barley products.

Americans Are Eating More Fresh Fruit

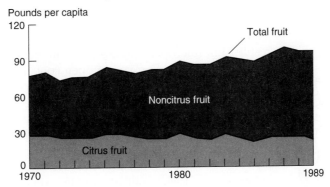

Pounds per capita

Total fruit

Noncitrus fruit

Citrus fruit

FIGURE 2.1

U.S. Food Consumption (Courtesy of the U.S. Department of Agriculture. *Food Consumption, Prices, and Expenditures, 1968–89*, SB-825, ERS, May 1991.)

24-hour dietary recall the recollection by a survey participant of all food and beverages consumed over the previous day and an estimation of the amounts eaten

The National Center for Health Statistics (NCHS) also periodically collects food and nutrition information in its health surveys. The second National Health and Nutrition Examination Survey (NHANES II) was conducted from 1976 to 1980 and included a single **24-hour dietary recall** on a nationwide sample of civilian, noninstitutionalized persons in the United States. When these data were evaluated for the consumption of items from food groups—dairy, meat, grain, fruits, and vegetables—it was found that only a third of the participants surveyed reported consuming food from all of the food groups on the day they were surveyed. Less than 3 percent of the participants reported consuming foods from all food groups in at least the recommended amounts. There was a trend toward greater variety in dietary intake with increasing levels of education and income [19]. These findings suggest that typical U.S. diets are not in compliance with current dietary guidelines.

Although our food habits may be quite firmly established, they are receptive to change with sufficiently compelling reasons for the changes. Public nutrition-education campaigns may help to bring about desirable change. Continuing surveys of food intakes by individuals, conducted by the USDA in 1985 and 1986, reveal substantial increases in the intakes of fish and shellfish, low-fat or skim milk, and legumes, nuts, and seeds when compared with intake data from the 1977–78 nationwide survey [23, 46].

Consumer Food Waste

Trends toward increasing food prices, coupled with growing concerns about conservation of resources, have focused attention on food loss or waste. It is important to know how much food is generally being wasted by consumers to attack this problem sensibly and try to change wasteful practices.

What is food waste? Different definitions may be used. In a broad sense, however, any food that was once usable but has since been discarded and not eaten by humans may be considered waste. Food eaten by animals and birds that are household pets may be counted as waste if this food was originally prepared for human consumption [16].

Food loss may occur at different stages of the handling and preparation processes. As food is taken home from the market and transferred to cabinets, refrigerators, and freezers, it should be handled so as to minimize any potential losses. While food is in storage, even on a very temporary basis, waste may result from microbial spoilage, contamination by insects and rodents, and spilling as a result of broken or open containers. If food is held or stored too long, particularly with improper packaging or temperature control, it may be discarded simply because it is not fresh or has dried out.

Additional waste may occur during preparation as a result of discarding edible portions of the food before cooking [6], improper cooking procedures such as scorching or overcooking, preparing too much for the number of people to be served, and spoilage because of inappropriate holding of the food before service. Lack of utilization of leftovers also creates waste. Plate waste, or food left on plates by individual diners (Figure 2.2), accounts for a significant portion of total food loss.

One study of garbage discarded by 200 to 300 households in the United States suggested that 9 to 10 percent of food, by weight, was wasted in these homes [16]. Six percent, by weight, of food available for eating in 243 Oregon

FIGURE 2.2

Plate waste. (Courtesy of the U.S. Department of Agriculture)

households was estimated to have been discarded [43]. The cost of the wasted food in the Oregon study was estimated to average $2.88 per week with a range among households of 0 to $32.48. The annual cost of food waste would thus average $150, with a range of 0 to $1,689. This money could certainly be more wisely spent.

Major reasons why the Oregon householders discarded foods were that they judged the food to be unsafe to eat, that the quality had deteriorated, that the food was left over, that the expiration or pull date on the package was past, or that the food was left on the plate (plate waste). Not all of these reasons for discarding food were necessarily valid or justifiable in all cases. In other words, educational programs to help consumers, especially those under 35 years of age, make wiser decisions should be useful.

Plate waste of edible food served in commercial establishments may also be substantial. In one hospital food service that used a cook-freeze production system, plate waste for all food served averaged 21.3 percent [13]. In a university dining hall study published in 1983, plate waste per person averaged 8.8 ounces per day [20]. The cost of this waste was 26.5 cents per person, but when considering all of the students served, the total cost was estimated to be $26,400 per semester. A more recent report [28], in 1991, confirms that plate waste is a continuing problem in university dining halls. In a study of a dining hall serving 850 male and 490 female students on board plans, an average of 17 percent of the food items selected was wasted. It was suggested that reduction of food costs through control of plate waste could be achieved with strict portion control during preparation and service and elimination of second servings. Another solution might be to charge students for each item selected.

•SOME FACTORS INFLUENCING FOOD COSTS

Rising food prices are a reality in the United States (Figure 2.3), although U.S. food costs are among the lowest in the world. Lower food costs allow Americans to spend a smaller percentage of their incomes on food and more on other goods and services, or on savings. In 1989, 9.8 percent of the total personal consumption expenditures of Americans went for food at home [39]. Additional expenditures were made for food consumption away from home. In addition to the general effects of inflation, a number of factors affect the cost of food.

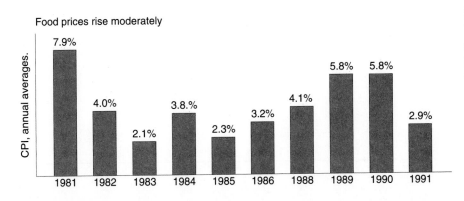

FIGURE 2.3

The percentage of increase in annual retail food prices is shown for several years. (Courtesy of the U.S. Department of Agriculture)

Farm-value share   the proportion of the retail price of food that is received by the farmer

Crop Production

Food production is costly, yet farmers receive a relatively small percentage of the consumer food dollar (Figure 2.4). In 1991, the **farm-value share** of food purchased in grocery stores was 27 percent [31]. Substantial initial investments must be made by farmers in property and equipment before they can even begin to produce crops. More and more, farmers have become dependent on such things as fuel to operate their equipment, and fertilizers, herbicides, and insecticides that they must purchase. Recent years have brought substantially increased costs for both farm machinery and wages for farm workers. Today, farming is a highly technical enterprise requiring large capital investment and skilled management.

Poor weather conditions often reduce the size of crops of fruits, vegetables, and grains. The weather is not controllable, and efficient management of commodity production thus becomes very difficult. When there are crop shortages, prices rise.

Trade Policies

The United States presently enjoys a competitive advantage, particularly for grains and oilseeds, in world agricultural trade [44]. Abundant natural resources and technological developments have contributed to this country's becoming a net exporter of agricultural products. However, changing world demand for certain commodities and government policies concerning production or international sales can change trade advantages and affect prices. Sound policy decisions help control wide fluctuations in export sales.

Food Processing and Packaging

Much of the food on supermarket shelves has been processed to some degree. Even the trimming of retail meat cuts and the packaging of fresh vegetables are types of processing, though minimal, that increase the cost of the food items

FIGURE 2.4
Farmer's share of consumers' food dollar. (Courtesy of the U.S. Department of Agriculture. Parlett, R. 1992. 1991 rise in retail food prices was the smallest since 1985. *Food Review* 15, 2 [No. 2].)

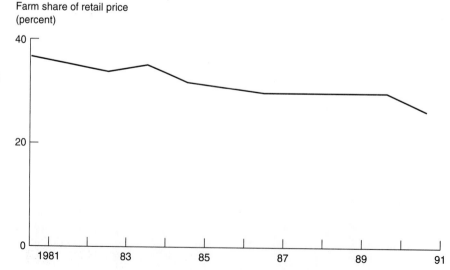

offered to the consumer. Examples of highly processed foods include fabricated breakfast cereals, meat substitutes produced from textured vegetable proteins, and frozen ready-to-eat entrees of various descriptions.

Food processing, as well as food production, is costly. A large investment in equipment and facilities is essential. Labor costs are high. Additional costs include packaging materials and labeling to meet governmental regulations. Many new, expensive packaging materials have recently been developed (see Chapter 28), and as a result, packaging costs are sometimes substantial in proportion to the cost of the food itself.

Technological developments have made possible many new food products scarcely dreamed of a century ago. During 1991, over 11,000 new food products were introduced into U.S. retail stores [17]. Most new products are extensions of existing lines, offering new flavors, sizes, packages, and so on. Because of changing demographics, many ethnic-style foods are being introduced. For example, Americans now use more salsa than catsup. Also, processed foods are increasingly being marketed on an international basis.

The research and development necessary to produce new food products is costly. Once new foods are developed, they require extensive promotional campaigns and test-marketing procedures. Losses to the manufacturer due to a new product's lack of success in the marketplace are reflected in increased prices at the consumer level.

Many of today's foods have built-in "maid service" with partial or complete preparation having been accomplished before the food is purchased. These so-called **convenience foods** must include the costs of preparation in their prices. In foodservice institutions, informed decisions must be made regarding the cost advantages of buying preprepared and partially prepared food products versus paying labor costs to completely prepare the foods in the institutional kitchen. There will be more discussion about convenience foods later in this chapter.

Convenience foods foods that are partially or completely prepared by the food processor, with little or no additional food preparation required of the consumer

Marketing

The USDA calculates marketing costs for food purchased by consumers in the United States, including food purchased both in retail markets and in foodservice establishments. These marketing expenses include the cost of food processing, packaging, transportation, advertising, energy use, and other costs incurred in bringing food from the farmer to the consumer (Figure 2.5). In 1991, marketing expenses accounted for 78 percent of the cost of a food product [12].

Types of Food Stores

There are a number of different types of stores through which food is marketed on a retail basis. For foodservice institutions, a variety of vendors supply different types of food products, generally on a wholesale basis. *Specialty stores*, such as bakeries and fish markets, offer only one type of food. *Food cooperatives*, or *co-ops*, are organized by groups of consumers to purchase food on a wholesale basis. *Farmers' markets* are open seasonally as outlets for local farm produce. *Convenience stores*, almost miniature supermarkets, carry a limited stock of merchandise that has high turnover. They are often part of a large chain of stores and usually remain open 24 hours a day. This type of store has become very popular in the United States in recent years. It usually offers fast service but somewhat higher prices. *Warehouse* or *discount markets* forgo some consumer services such as individual item pricing and bagging of groceries. They generally buy in very large quantities and pass some of their cost savings on to the customer.

The largest volume of retail food sales in the United States, however, is handled by *supermarkets*. These stores stock thousands of food items and, usually, other merchandise as well, including beauty aids, pharmaceutical supplies, kitchen tools, flowers, and plants. Foodservice offerings in supermarkets are increasing in number and complexity. Even catering is offered by some. The concept of supermarkets as full-service centers is growing. They may include florist shops, bakeries, ethnic food take-out services, delicatessens, tortillerias, sushi bars, pharmacies, photo-finishing shops, and even branch banks and post offices.

Prices are influenced by services offered. You should evaluate the various kinds of markets in terms of the services and benefits you desire and what you are willing to pay for them. The following items may be considered in this evaluation:

1. Quality and variety of merchandise carried
2. Layout and organization of the market

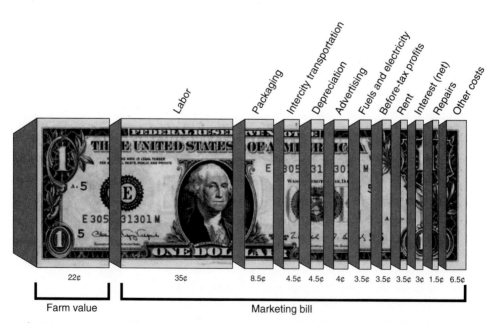

Labor Packaging Intercity transportation Depreciation Advertising Fuels and electricity Before-tax profits Rent Interest (net) Repairs Other costs

22¢ 35¢ 8.5¢ 4.5¢ 4.5¢ 4¢ 3.5¢ 3.5¢ 3.5¢ 3¢ 1.5¢ 6.5¢

Farm value Marketing bill

[1]Includes food eaten at home and away from home. Other costs include property taxes and insurance, accounting and professional services, promotion, bad debts, and miscellaneous items.

FIGURE 2.5

Over three-quarters of every dollar spent on food goes to pay marketing costs.[1] (Courtesy of the U.S. Department of Agriculture. Elitzak, H. 1992. Marketing bill is the largest chunk of food expenditures. *Food Review 15*, 12 [No. 2].)

3. Pricing policies, such as specials, discounting, advertising, availability of in-store brands and **generic** or unbranded products, coupons, trading stamps, and games
4. Location of market
5. Sanitation
6. Customer services, such as bagging, carryout, express checkout and rapid service, and availability of printed information on nutrition and food preparation

Generic a class of packaged food products that do not carry a specific brand name

Shopping Aids

Food manufacturers and retailers offer the consumer a number of conveniences to facilitate efficient shopping for food. These include unit pricing, open-date labeling, nutrition labeling, and computerized checkout systems. Some of these aids involve additional labor and skill in producing and/or marketing food products and may thus increase the cost of food to the consumer.

Unit Pricing. The cost per pound or ounce for products sold by weight or the cost per quart, pint, or fluid ounce for products sold by volume is printed on a label that is usually attached to the edge of the shelf where the products are displayed. This allows the shopper to compare prices per unit for different-sized packages of the same product. The most economical size to buy can thus be readily determined. Generally, the smaller package sizes and individual-size convenience items are more expensive per unit because of the basic package cost. Unit pricing is mandatory in some states but voluntary in others.

Open-Date Labeling. A date code is placed on each packaged food product for the customer to read and interpret. The date may appear in different forms on different packages. It may represent the last recommended day of retail sale, the end of the period of optimum quality, or the date of processing or final packaging. Open-date labeling provides some information for the shopper, but the conditions, particularly of temperature, under which the products are handled and stored greatly affect the quality.

Nutrition Labeling. There are certain basic requirements for *all* food labels; these include net weight of contents, manufacturer's or distributor's name and address, and ingredient declaration. Regulations governing the labeling of food products are prepared by the U.S. Food and Drug Administration (FDA). In the early 1970s, the FDA completed a major revision of labeling requirements which included regulations governing **nutrition labeling**. Under these regulations, nutrition labeling was voluntary, except when the products contained added nutrients or when nutrition claims were made.

Nutrition labeling a special type of food labeling, in addition to basic requirements concerning net contents and manufacturer, that gives information about the nutrient and caloric content of the food on a per-serving basis

Nutrition labeling was designed to help consumers choose diets that are well-balanced and health-promoting and to do this at the lowest cost. When a product carries nutrition labeling, information in addition to the basic labeling requirements listed earlier must be included. This additional material details the nutrient content of the product in the package.

In November of 1990, the President of the United States signed into law the Nutrition Labeling and Education Act. Regulations to implement this legislation were issued by the FDA and finalized by the end of 1992. A new era in food labeling had begun [24].

Under the new legislation, most foods are required to carry nutrition labels. Exemptions include food sold by small businesses; food sold in foodservice establishments; ready-to-eat foods prepared on-site for later consumption; foods that contain insignificant amounts of nutrients, such as tea and spices; medical foods; and meat and poultry products produced or packaged at retail, such as sliced bologna. However, if a nutrition or health claim is made for any of these foods, they must have nutrition labeling. Fresh fruits and vegetables and raw fish also do not require nutrition labeling. However, the FDA has a *voluntary* program in which nutrition information about these products is displayed at the point of purchase in retail food markets [33].

The Food Safety and Inspection Service of the USDA is responsible for regulating the labeling of meat and poultry products. Nutrition labeling is *mandatory* for most meat and poultry products except raw, single-ingredient items. Labeling of these exempted products is encouraged, however, either by package labeling or by presenting nutrition information at the point of purchase.

Restaurants and other foodservice establishments may make certain health and nutrition claims for items they prepare. When they do so, they must explain how the food meets the FDA criteria for that claim and must have a reasonable basis for believing that the food meets the criteria. This information must be provided to the customer on request [25].

Required nutrition information is presented on a label under the heading of Nutrition Facts, and, on a per-serving basis, includes calories, calories from fat, and grams of total fat, saturated fat, cholesterol, sodium, total carbohydrates, dietary fiber, sugars, and protein. (Serving sizes have been standardized by the FDA and the USDA.) Vitamin A, vitamin C, calcium, and iron are presented as percent of **Daily Values** based on a 2,000 calorie diet. Some additional information is optional. Figure 2.6 gives an example of how the required information is presented.

Daily Values nutrient standards used for labeling purposes; they include Daily Reference Values (DRVs) and Reference Daily Intakes (RDIs)

Daily Values are dietary standards used for labeling purposes, and include two types. *Daily Reference Values* (DRVs) refer to fat, carbohydrates (including fiber), protein, cholesterol, sodium, and potassium. These are listed on the label for 2,000 and 2,500 calorie intakes. *Reference Daily Intakes* (RDIs) are for other nutrients. RDIs replace the U.S. recommended daily allowances (U.S. RDAs) that were previously used.

The FDA has defined certain descriptive terms to be used on food labels. Some of these terms and their definitions are listed in Table 2.1. Standardized definitions are established with the aim of decreasing consumer confusion when such terms as *high*, *low*, *reduced*, and *less* are used with food products.

Certain health claims are also allowed on labels. The following relationships between a nutrient or food and the risk of a disease have been approved for labeling purposes with some specific requirements governing their use.

Calcium and osteoporosis

Fat and cancer

Saturated fat and cholesterol and coronary heart disease

Fruits, vegetables, and grain products and cancer

Fruits, vegetables, and grain products and coronary heart disease

Sodium and hypertension

Serving sizes are stated in both household and metric measures.

Nutrition Facts

Serving Size ½ cup (114g)
Servings Per Container 4

Amount Per Serving

Calories 90	Calories from Fat 30

Calories from fat are shown on the label to help consumers meet dietary guidelines that recommend people get no more than 30 percent of their calories from fat.

% Daily Value*

Total Fat 3g	5%
Saturated Fat 0g	0%
Cholesterol 0mg	0%
Sodium 300mg	13%
Total Carbohydrate 13g	4%
Dietary Fiber 3g	12%
Sugars 3g	
Protein 3g	

% Daily Value shows how a food fits into the overall daily diet.

The list of nutrients covers those most important to the health of today's consumers, most of whom need to worry about getting too much of certain items (fat, for example), rather than too few vitamins or minerals, as in the past.

Vitamin A	80%	•	Vitamin C	60%
Calcium	4%	•	Iron	4%

* Percent Daily Values are based on a 2,000 calorie diet. Your daily values may be higher or lower depending on your calorie needs:

	Calories	2,000	2,500
Total Fat	Less than	65g	80g
Sat Fat	Less than	20g	25g
Cholesterol	Less than	300mg	300mg
Sodium	Less than	2,400mg	2,400mg
Total Carbohydrate		300g	375g
Fiber		25g	30g

Calories per gram:
Fat 9 • Carbohydrates 4 • Protein 4

Daily values are something new. Some are maximums, as with fat (65 grams or less); others are minimums, as with carbohydrates (300 grams or more). The daily values on the label are based on a daily diet of 2,000 and 2,500 calories. Individuals should adjust the values to fit their own calorie intake.

FIGURE 2.6

An example of the nutrition labeling panel that should appear on almost all packaged foods. (Courtesy of the U.S. Food and Drug Administration)

Nutrition labeling gives consumers much more information about the foods they buy than they would have without this feature. For those on diets modified because of health reasons, nutrition labeling is especially useful. Education is needed, however, if the typical consumer is to make the most effective use of nutrition labeling [21]. The cost to manufacturers for nutrition labeling may be appreciable because they are required to perform laboratory analyses of samples of their food for nutrient content. In addition, new labels had to be designed to meet the requirements of the 1990 nutrition-labeling legislation. This expense ultimately affects the cost of food to the customer.

TABLE 2.1

Nutrient Content Descriptors Used on Food Labels*

Descriptor	Definition
Free	No amount or an amount that is of no physiological consequence based on serving size
Calorie-free	Less than 5 calories
Sodium-free	Less than 5 milligrams
Fat-free	Less than 0.5 gram of fat and no added fat
Cholesterol-free	Less than 2 milligrams
Sugar-free	Less than 0.5 gram
Low	Would allow frequent consumption of a food low in a nutrient without exceeding the dietary guidelines
Low-calorie	Less than 40 calories
Low-sodium	Less than 140 milligrams
Very low-sodium	Less than 35 milligrams
Low-fat	Less than 3 grams
Low in saturated fat	Less than 1 gram and less than 15% of calories from saturated fat
Low in cholesterol	20 milligrams or less with less than 2 grams of saturated fat
Reduced	Nutritionally altered product containing 25% less of a nutrient or 25% fewer calories than a reference food
Less	Contains 25% less of a nutrient or 25% fewer calories than a reference food
Light	33% fewer calories or 50% of the fat in a reference food; if 50% or more of the calories comes from fat, reduction must be 50% of the fat; or
	Sodium content of a low-calorie, low-fat food has been reduced by 50%: thus the term "light in sodium" may be used; or
	Describes such properties as texture and color, as "light brown sugar" or "light and fluffy"
High	20% or more of the Daily Value for a nutrient
Good source	Contains 10–19% of the Daily Value for a particular nutrient

Source: Reference 24.

* Per serving basis

Computerized Checkout Systems. Computer-assisted electronic cash register systems are commonly used in supermarkets. The cost of the items in the customer's shopping cart is tabulated by using a laser optical scanner to read Universal Product Code (UPC) symbols, which are affixed to each food package. The scanner is connected to a computer that then retrieves the necessary information from its storage and prints the name and price of each item on a screen for the customer to see. It also prints this information on the sales receipt. The computer must be properly programmed at all times with current price information.

The UPC symbol contains a series of dark lines and spaces of varying widths, as shown in Figure 2.7. The left half of the symbol identifies the manufacturer, and the right half identifies the product. A large proportion of the items on supermarket shelves carries a UPC symbol.

Use of a computerized system allows pricing of items to be done on the display shelves only and not on each individual product. It also speeds up checkout time and reduces errors at the cash register. Additional advantages are a meaningful record of purchases for the customer and improved inventory control for the retailer. However, a disadvantage is not having cost information readily available on the item itself for later reference.

FIGURE 2.7
Universal Product Code.

Manufacturer
identification
number   Item code

•AVAILABILITY AND USE OF CONVENIENCE FOODS

Convenience foods have been defined as fully or partially prepared foods for which significant preparation time, culinary skills, or energy use have been transferred from the consumer's kitchen to the food processor and distributor [40]. Most of the foods in a modern supermarket have had some preparation treatment and thus, in a sense, are convenience foods. However, as commonly used, this term applies to foods that have undergone a comparatively large amount of processing or market services and may be served with a minimum of effort and skill. Other names for these types of foods are *service ready*, *prefabricated*, *ready prepared*, or *efficiency* foods.

Many different processes are used by the food industry in the preparation of convenience foods. These include dehydrating the food to variable moisture levels by freeze-drying and other methods, compressing the food to decrease bulk, precooking and freezing, and using various flexible packaging materials or pouches that withstand both high and low temperatures. A **retort pouch** has been developed that may be used even at the temperatures well above boiling that are necessary for canning low-acid meats and vegetables [42]. Unfrozen, prepared entrees that can be stored on the shelf and heated in the microwave oven in 2 minutes or less are now on the market [38] (Figure 2.8).

The production of convenience foods actually began many years ago with the development of canning. A number of canned products are now well-established convenience foods. With the widespread availability and use of home freezers, many frozen convenience foods entered the market. Also plentiful are dehydrated convenience items.

The real convenience food era began in the 1950s. It is interesting to note that the development of certain convenience foods has had an apparent snow-

Retort pouch   a flexible laminated package that withstands high-temperature processing in a commercial pressure canner called a *retort*

balling effect. For example, potato flakes were developed by the Eastern Regional Research Laboratory, U.S. Department of Agriculture, to encourage a wider use of potatoes. The marketing of potato flakes and granules for making instant mashed potatoes was soon followed by numerous other commercial potato products, such as frozen scalloped, hashed brown, and french-fried potatoes, which require only a brief heating period, and a wide variety of packaged dehydrated potato mixes containing convenient sauce and seasoning packets. The quality of these potato products in relation to the prepared fresh product may vary, depending on both the type of product and the manufacturer. Many of them have been very well accepted and have become established convenience foods. If new products are not well-accepted, which is true in many cases, they disappear from the market in a short period.

Some convenience foods are designed for the snack shelf, but the majority are for regular use in food preparation both in the home and in foodservice establishments. Among the convenience foods sold are a growing number of products that are reduced in fat and caloric content. Also popular are a number of ethnic dishes. The aging of the population, the focus on health and fitness, the increasing number of women in the workforce, and the increasing numbers of Hispanics and Asians in the population have fragmented the consumer market. There are many different groups whose needs must be met [9, 14]. Food processors are producing a variety of convenience items to supply the

FIGURE 2.8

Breast of Chicken Acapulco is one of the varieties of entrees that represent the beginning of the "freezer freedom" era. It can be stored on the shelf and then heated quickly in the microwave oven. (Reprinted from *Food Technology* Vol. 41, No. 4, p. 102, 1987. Copyright © by Institute of Food Technologists. Photograph courtesy of Hormel Company.)

needs of all. Cookbooks also reflect the convenience food market, with many convenience items included in recipes.

Industry, as well as the consumer, benefits from storage and transportation savings. Dehydrated fruit and tomato juices, which can be shipped and stored without refrigeration and reconstituted with water before use, are examples of products that create great savings in transportation costs and storage space. Industry also has the advantage of knowing about and being able to obtain and use ingredients that are well-suited to prolonged storage. Suitable packaging aids in the retention of desirable qualities in the final product.

Space-Age Convenience Foods

Travel into space brought special requirements with regard to food for the astronauts. The demanding specifications for weight, volume, and ease of preparation were met by convenience-type foods [4]. Because the astronauts have much work and experimentation to do in space, the time required to prepare and eat must be kept to a minimum. Foods must be stable to store at temperatures up to 38°C (100°F). Their packaging must be flexible and able to withstand extremes of pressure, humidity, temperature, and vibration that could cause breakage or cracking. Packages of food must also be convenient to handle.

Many changes have been made in space foods since space exploration began. Much had to be learned about how foods could be handled in a state of weightlessness. During the *Mercury* flights, it was learned that a person could chew and swallow while weightless. Early space foods were either pureed so they could be forced into the mouth through tubes or compressed into compact, bite-sized pieces that were coated to avoid any loose crumbs that would float in zero gravity (see Figure 2.9). During the *Apollo* flights, a spoon, rather than a tube, was used to eat moist foods. During the *Skylab* program, astronauts had knives and forks available to them and ate from a food tray with cavities to hold containers of food. Beverages were still sent as dry powders and were rehydrated by putting water through a one-way valve into a special container.

A new era in the exploration of space began with the space shuttle. It can carry up to seven persons, and a galley has been designed for their foodservice needs. The galley has hot and cold water, an oven, and a small refrigeration unit but no freezer. Food packaging has been simplified to some degree compared with that used for previous space ventures. The food includes dehydrated, thermostabilized, irradiated, and intermediate-moisture items. Many foods are dehydrated because water is produced onboard as a by-product of the spacecraft's fuel cells [3].

Plans for the launching of a space station, called *Freedom*, bring new challenges to the designers of foodservice in space [3]. The tour of duty for astronauts on *Freedom* will be 90 days, and food will be an important factor affecting the way the crew responds to the psychological as well as the physiological stresses encountered. The basic goal is to provide food that is as "Earthlike" as possible. The space station will have a galley with microwave–convection ovens and a refrigerated storage area for individually packaged foods (Figure 2.10 and Plate XV). A wardroom will also serve as a dining area.

Challenges encountered in the development of foods for a 28-day-cycle menu include controlled and modified packaging of fresh fruits and vegetables, development of an acceptable milk-based beverage with an extended shelf life, storage and preparation of shell-less eggs in zero gravity, and determination of the optimum storage method for bread (controlled-atmosphere packaging, frozen dough, or ingredients to make from scratch) [3]. Foods will be pack-

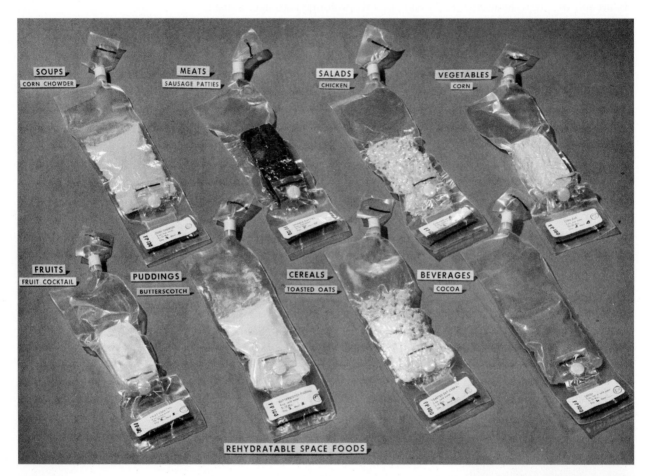

FIGURE 2.9
Foods developed in the early years of space travel included bite-sized portions (*bottom*) and rehydratable items. (Courtesy of U.S. Army)

aged individually and served on a tray (Plate XV), the width of all packages being the same in order to interface with storage and heating facilities. As development and testing of space foods and packages to contain them continues, spinoffs from this work may benefit all of us as a greater number and variety of convenience-type foods become available.

Military rations for battlefield foodservice have also undergone many changes in recent years. The old combat rations, C-rations, have been replaced by space-age-type MREs, meaning meals, ready-to-eat [1]. MREs are single meals packaged in flexible plastic and foil pouches that do not require refrigeration and have a shelf life as long as seven years. They may be eaten cold or hot, heated, if desired, by using an electrochemical sleeve that is activated by an ounce or so of water. At the beginning of Operation Desert Shield, in the Saudi Arabian desert, MREs were used almost exclusively by the U.S. military until field kitchens were able to use B-rations, which are traditional field fare packed in No. 10 cans or dehydrated. The development of the retort pouch by the food industry was an important breakthrough contributing to the subsequent development of MREs.

Cost of Convenience

How much does convenience cost? In making cost comparisons between various convenience foods and similar home-prepared products, some difficulties may be encountered. The proportions of ingredients contained in convenience foods are not identified on the labels and, therefore, home-prepared products may not contain the same amounts of component ingredients. The eating quality of the two products may also be very different. Nevertheless, a number of cost comparisons have been made with these limitations in mind.

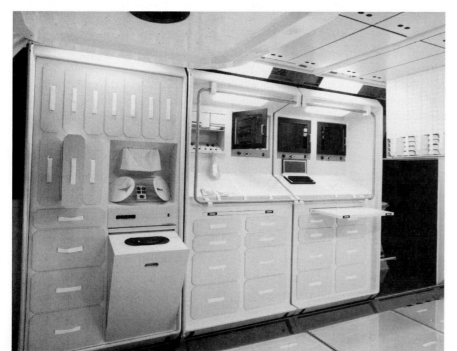

FIGURE 2.10

Full-scale mockup of space station *Freedom*'s galley at the Johnson Space Center. Restrained food packages, suspended from an overhead refrigerated storage rack, are shown in the upper right. (Reprinted from *Food Technology* Vol. 43, No. 2, p. 76, 1989. Copyright © by Institute of Food Technologists. Photograph courtesy of the National Aeronautics and Space Administration (NASA) Johnson Space Center.)

Five frozen-prepared plate dinners (TV dinners) and 12 frozen entrees, such as lasagna, chicken à la king, cheese pizza, fried chicken, and crabcakes, were purchased in the Washington, DC area and compared with home-prepared foods [18]. The frozen dinners cost from 13 to 105 percent more than the comparable home-prepared products. Frozen entrees were also more expensive than the home-prepared items, with the exception of crabcakes and deviled crab. These dishes, however, contained substantially less crabmeat than the home-prepared products. The cost increases ranged from 9 percent for chicken pie to 127 percent for lasagna.

A major study to provide more information about 166 convenience foods considered not only the cost of food, but also, for 41 products, the cost of fuel used in preparation and, for 115 products, the cost of the preparer's time [40, 41]. Food cost comparisons were based on price information from supermarkets in Philadelphia, Milwaukee, San Francisco–Oakland, and New Orleans. When only the cost of the food was considered, 59 percent of the 166 convenience foods were at least 1 cent more expensive per item than their home-prepared or fresh counterparts, about 25 percent were at least 1 cent less expensive, and about 16 percent cost approximately the same as their counterparts.

When the cost of fuel used and the consumer's time, calculated at the minimum wage rate, were added to the food cost for 41 convenience products, nearly one-half of the convenience items were at least 1 cent *less* expensive than their home versions.

Consumer Reports periodically evaluates convenience foods and compares them with similar homemade products. In a comparison of fried chicken, they found that homemade chicken cost 9 cents per edible ounce, frozen prepared chicken cost from 12 to 21 cents per edible ounce, and fast-food-restaurant fried chicken cost 23 to 29 cents per edible ounce [15]. Pancake mixes and frozen pancakes were also evaluated by *Consumer Reports*. Frozen pancakes cost as much as 53 cents per serving and were generally tough and chewy. Standard mixes, which called for added eggs, oil, and milk, were of better quality and cost between 14 and 26 cents per serving, including the cost of the added ingredients [30].

It may be concluded that most convenience products have a higher food cost than home-prepared products; however, when fuel and time costs are also considered, the total cost for many of them may be less than that of the home-made counterpart.

Eating Quality

Convenience foods vary widely in quality, but many compare quite favorably with home-prepared products. In a USDA study published in 1978, twenty-two convenience foods and their home-prepared counterparts were evaluated by a trained taste panel [41]. A 5-point evaluation scale was used, with 5 being the optimum score. All home-prepared foods and about 80 percent of the convenience products rated 4 points or higher in overall quality. However, compared with their corresponding convenience products, 19 of 22 home-prepared foods rated higher in texture, 18 rated higher in appearance and overall quality, and 15 rated higher in flavor.

Half of 24 canned or frozen beef stew samples were rated by a *Consumer Reports* panel as being "good" [2]. A variety of cakes made from commercial mixes also were evaluated by a *Consumer Reports* panel [8]. A few cakes were rated "very good." Most of the rest were rated "undistinguished" with artificial flavorings predominating. Despite these ratings, the panel felt that a flavorful frosting could cover up many of the defects in the cakes.

A variety of meatless and meat-flavored spaghetti sauces and spaghettis were evaluated by *Consumer Reports* as well. Their panel found that inexpensive brands often tasted as good or better than higher-priced brands. Four spaghetti and two spaghetti sauce samples were rated both high in quality and very low in price. Dry-mix packets for making spaghetti sauce that were also evaluated were reported to be only fair in eating quality. Although the packets themselves were fairly inexpensive, the extra ingredients that must be added made the finished sauce more costly than those sauces purchased ready-made [37].

Nutritive Value

Nutritive value of convenience foods should be an important consideration in purchasing. In commercial products, the more expensive components, particularly meat, fish, and poultry, may be present in somewhat lower quantities than in home-prepared dishes.

During dehydration of potato products, there is usually substantial loss of vitamin C, but instant potatoes are often fortified with this vitamin to make them more comparable to the fresh product. Many canned and dehydrated soups contain very small amounts of protein or other nutrients. Soups made at home vary greatly in the amount and type of ingredients used and thus in nutritional value, so comparisons with commercial soups are difficult to make. Extra ingredients may be added to purchased soups to make them more hearty and nutritious.

Saving of Time and Effort

A major consideration for many in the purchase of convenience foods is the promise of reduced preparation time and effort, including fewer cleanup chores such as dishwashing. The USDA reported that less than 10 minutes of active preparation time was needed to prepare four servings each of most of the 95 tested convenience items that contained meat, fish, poultry, or cheese [22].

Male food preparers, particularly those living alone, were reported to spend more money on complex and manufactured convenience foods than did other food preparers [32]. More money per household member was also spent on food at home in households with male food preparers. Thus, the male preparers appeared to be willing to pay for the convenience.

From annual supermarket sales figures it is obvious that households rely heavily on convenience foods. They are undoubtedly here to stay. Some of them, such as frozen orange juice and gelatin or pudding mixes, have become so well established and widely used that they are probably not considered to be convenience foods in the same sense as frozen entrees. There are both advantages and disadvantages to the use of convenience foods. Personal preferences vary from one household to another. We need to consider several factors when deciding to purchase or not to purchase convenience foods: time, equipment, and storage space available; comparative costs; aesthetic appeal; our ability to cook and the joy and pride that we, and others around us, may feel when we cook "from scratch"; and concerns regarding nutrition and health.

Preparing Your Own Basic Mixes

An incredible variety of mixes are numbered among the convenience foods found on supermarket shelves and many are also available to foodservice institutions. There are many dry flour mixes for preparing such items as cakes, cookies, gingerbread, brownies, piecrusts, muffins, cornbread, coffee cakes, biscuits, pancakes, and hot rolls. Seasoning mixes such as taco mix, meatloaf mix, and a variety of salad dressing mixes are widely used. Pudding mixes, canned fruit pie fillings, and many, many others are available.

Although commercial mixes are convenient and timesaving, do-it-yourself mixes may also provide convenience. Considerable time is saved by making mixes, as compared with cooking from "scratch," because the basic ingredients for a large number of prepared items are mixed at one time. The time for preparing the mix may also be scheduled during less busy periods, thus making more effective use of time.

Eliason, Harward, and Westover [10, 11] have published two cookbooks on how to make your own mixes. They have suggested that the convenience of cooking with mixes may be combined with the quality advantages of cooking "from scratch" when mixes are made. They present three types of master mixes, from each of which several recipes may be prepared. One type consists of dry mixes that contain only dry ingredients with no shortening. These may be stored at room temperature for 6 to 8 months. Examples of this type of mix include hot-roll mix, pancake mix, and pudding mix.

Another type of master mix includes semidry mixes, which contain vegetable shortening, butter, or margarine. Because of the fat content, these mixes keep for shorter periods of time than do the dry mixes. If stored in a cool, dry place they should keep well for 10 to 12 weeks. Examples of this type are basic cake mix, cornmeal mix, muffin mix, oatmeal mix, and gingerbread mix.

The third type of master mix is a freezer-refrigerator mix, which is moist and more perishable than the other master mixes. These mixes require freezer or refrigerator storage in well-sealed containers and keep well for about 3 months. Examples are braised-beef-cube mix, chicken mix, Mexican meat mix, and moist piecrust mix.

•BUYING FOOD

Since a substantial portion of all household budgets is used to buy food, the use of wisdom in food purchasing will pay dividends. For the foodservice professional purchasing food, wise decisions are imperative for the financial success of the business operation. Here are a few general guidelines to follow:

1. Compare prices for specified quality items; use unit pricing; consider cost of packaging; watch advertised specials.
2. Buy only quantities that can be utilized well; do not overbuy in terms of storage facilities available.

TABLE 2.2
Examples from a Guide for Calculating Amounts of Food to Buy and Making Cost Comparisons

Description of Food as Purchased	Size of Market Unit	Description of Food as Prepared after Purchase	Servings or Measures per Market Unit	Size of Serving or Measure	Amount-to-Buy Factor
Applesauce, canned	16 oz. (454 g)	As purchased	3½	1/2 c	0.28
Bananas, fresh	Pound (454 g)	Peeled			
		Sliced	4	1/2 c	0.24
		Whole	2½	1 medium	0.39
Beans, pinto					
Canned	15½ oz (439 g)	Heated, drained	3	1/2 c	0.32
Dry	16 oz. (454 g)	Cooked, drained	12¾	1/2 c	0.08
Beef steaks, round, with bone	Pound (454 g)	Cooked	3	3 oz cooked lean meat without bone	0.33
Carrots, fresh, without tops	Pound (454 g)	Uncooked: Strips Cooked, drained: Diced	6¼ 5	1/2 1/2	0.16 0.20
Cereals, ready-to-eat, bran flakes	16 oz (454 g)	As purchased	13¼	1 c	0.07
Orange juice, frozen concentrate	6 fluid oz. (177 ml)	Reconstituted	6	1/2 c	0.17
Rice, white, regular, long grain	16 oz (454 g)	Cooked	17½	1/2 c	0.06

Source: Reference 7.

3. Buy staples in quantity but store them properly.
4. Buy in-store brands or generic items whenever the quality is acceptable for a particular use.
5. Make reasonable substitutions when desired items are too expensive or unavailable.
6. Plan ahead and purchase on a regular basis; use specifications or a written list; avoid impulse buying.
7. Choose vendors or markets that generally have reasonable pricing.

A guide for buying food in household quantities has been published by the USDA [7]. Examples of information from this booklet are found in Table 2.2. From the number of servings typically derived from a market unit, an "amount-to-buy" factor has been calculated by dividing the number of servings into 1. To determine the amount, or number of market units, to buy, multiply the amount-to-buy factor by the number of servings of the food that are needed.

Comparisons of cost per serving may also be made using these figures. The price per market unit should be multiplied by the amount-to-buy factor to give the cost per serving. Be certain, however, that the serving sizes are equal for the foods being compared.

STUDY QUESTIONS

1. Describe two different methods that have been used by the USDA to obtain information on what and how much food is eaten in the United States. Evaluate the advantages and inaccuracies that may be associated with each method.
2. a. Describe several findings from food consumption surveys that give us information concerning the types and amounts of food being consumed in the United States.
   b. What types of information collected from these surveys may be useful to professionals working in the areas of food and nutrition?
3. What is *food waste* and how may food be wasted at the household level?
4. List at least six factors that are likely to influence food cost to the consumer and briefly explain how they exert their influence.
5. Describe what is meant by *unit pricing* and *open-date labeling* and explain their possible usefulness to the consumer.
6. What is required when a food product is given nutrition labeling and what is the purpose of this type of labeling?
7. Define the term *convenience foods* and give several examples.
8. Explain how the widespread availability of convenience foods may affect food preparation techniques used in the home.
9. Convenience foods are sometimes compared with similar home-prepared products. Discuss how they generally compare in these factors:
   a. Cost (both food cost alone and cost that includes energy use and preparer's time)
   b. Eating quality
   c. Nutritive value
   d. Preparation time and effort
10. Discuss advantages and disadvantages of making your own mixes at home.
11. Suggest several useful guidelines to follow when purchasing food.

REFERENCES

1. Baird, B. 1991. Hot meals in a hot spot. *Food Technology 45*, 52 (No. 2).
2. Beef stews. 1981. *Consumer Reports 46*, 267.
3. Bourland, C. T., M. F. Fohey, V. L. Kloeris, and R. M. Rapp. 1989. Designing a food system for space station *Freedom. Food Technology 43*, 76 (No. 2).
4. Bourland, C. T., M. F. Fohey, R. M. Rapp, and R. L. Sauer. 1982. Space shuttle food package development. *Food Technology 36*, 38 (No. 9).
5. Bourland, C. T., R. M. Rapp, and M. C. Smith, Jr. 1977. Space shuttle food system. *Food Technology 31*, 40 (No. 9).
6. Brittin, H. C., and S. S. Miles. 1987. Yield and waste of food prepared using a spatula. *Journal of the American Dietetic Association 87*, 639.
7. *Buying Food*. 1978. Home Economics Research Report No. 42. Washington, DC: U.S. Department of Agriculture.
8. Cake mixes. 1982. *Consumer Reports 47*, 120.
9. Courington, S. M. 1989. Who is the American food consumer? *Food and Nutrition News* (National Live Stock and Meat Board) *61*, 25.
10. Eliason, K., N. Harward, and M. Westover. 1978. *Make-a-Mix Cookery*. Tucson, AZ: H. P. Books.
11. Eliason, K., N. Harward, and M. Westover. 1980. *More Make-a-Mix Cookery*. Tucson, AZ: H. P. Books.
12. Elitzak, H. 1992. Marketing bill is the largest chunk of food expenditures. *Food Review 15*, 12 (No. 2).
13. Frakes, E. M., B. H. Arjmandi, and J. F. Halling. 1986. Plate waste in a hospital cook-freeze production system. *Journal of the American Dietetic Association 86*, 941.
14. Frank, G. C., M. Zive, J. Nelson, S. L. Broyles, and P. R. Nader. 1991. Fat and cholesterol avoidance among Mexican-American and Anglo preschool children and parents. *Journal of the American Dietetic Association 91*, 954.
15. Fried chicken. 1982. *Consumer Reports 47*, 362.
16. Gallo, A. E. Fall 1980. *Consumer Food Waste in the United States. National Food Review* NFR-12, p. 13. Washington, DC: U.S. Department of Agriculture.
17. Gallo, A. E. 1992. Record number of new products in 1991. *Food Review 15*, 19 (No. 2).
18. Isom, P. 1979. Frozen-prepared plate dinners and entrees—cost vs. convenience. *Family Economics Review* (U.S. Department of Agriculture) *18* (Summer).
19. Kant, A. K., G. Block, A. Schatzkin, R. G. Ziegler, and M. Nestle. 1991. Dietary diversity in the U.S. population, NHANES II, 1976–1980. *Journal of the American Dietetic Association 91*, 1526.
20. Kelley, S. M., G. E. Jennings, K. Funk, C. T. Gaskins, and G. B. Welch. 1983. Edible plate waste assessment in a university dining hall. *Journal of the American Dietetic Association 83*, 436.
21. Levy, A. S., S. B. Fein, and R. E. Schucker. 1992. More effective nutrition label formats are not necessarily preferred. *Journal of the American Dietetic Association 92*, 1230.
22. *Meat, Fish, Poultry, and Cheese: Home Preparation Time, Yield, and Composition of Various Market Forms*. 1965. Home Economics Research Report No. 30. Washington, DC: Agricultural Research Service, U.S. Department of Agriculture.
23. *Men 19–50 Years, 1 Day*. 1985. Nationwide Food Consumption Survey, Continuing Survey of Food Intakes by Individuals, NFCS, CSFII Report No. 85-3. Washington, DC: U.S. Department of Agriculture.
24. Mermelstein, N. H. 1993. A new era in food labeling. *Food Technology 47*, 81 (No. 2).
25. Mermelstein, N. H. 1993. Nutrition labeling in foodservice. *Food Technology 47*, 65 (No. 4).

26. Mertz, W. 1992. Food intake measurements: Is there a "gold standard"? *Journal of the American Dietetic Association 92*, 1463.

27. Murphy, S. P., D. Rose, M. Hudes, and F. E. Viteri. 1992. Demographic and economic factors associated with dietary quality for adults in the 1987–88 Nationwide Food Consumption Survey. *Journal of the American Dietetic Association 92*, 1352.

28. Norton, V. P., and C. Martin. 1991. Plate waste of selected food items in a university dining hall. *School Food Service Research Review 15*, 37 (No. 1).

29. Paarlberg, D. 1977. Food and economics. *Journal of the American Dietetic Association 71*, 107.

30. Pancakes. 1992. *Consumer Reports 57*, 56.

31. Parlett, R. 1992. 1991 rise in retail food prices was the smallest since 1985. *Food Review 15*, 2 (No. 2).

32. Pearson, J. M., O. Capps, Jr., and J. Axelson. 1986. Convenience food use in households with male food preparers. *Journal of the American Dietetic Association 86*, 339.

33. Pennington, J. A. T., and V. L. Wilkening. 1992. Nutrition labeling of raw fruit, vegetables, and fish. *Journal of the American Dietetic Association 92*, 1250.

34. Putnam, J. J. 1991. Food consumption, 1970–90. *Food Review 14*, 2 (No. 3).

35. Raper, N. 1991. Nutrient content of the U.S. food supply. *Food Review 14*, 13 (No. 3).

36. Smicikias-Wright, H., L. E. Giles, and M. Q. Wang. 1993. Meat as consumed in the U.S. *Food and Nutrition News* (National Live Stock and Meat Board) *65*, 1 (No. 1).

37. Spaghetti and spaghetti sauce. 1992. *Consumer Reports 57*, 322.

38. Staff article. 1987. New product offers "freezer-freedom." *Food Technology 41*, 102 (No. 4).

39. Traub, L. 1992. Per capita food expenditures declining around the world. *Food Review 15*, 19 (No. 1).

40. Traub, L. G., and D. D. Odland. 1979. *Convenience Foods and Home-Prepared Foods*. Agricultural Economic Report No. 429. Washington, DC: U.S. Department of Agriculture.

41. Traub, L. G., and D. D. Odland. September 1978. *Convenience Foods vs. Home-Prepared: Costs, Yield, and Quality. National Food Review* NFR-4, p. 30. Washington, DC: U.S. Department of Agriculture.

42. Tuomy, J. M., and R. Young. 1982. Retort-pouch packaging of muscle foods for the Armed Forces. *Food Technology 36*, 68 (No. 2).

43. Van Garde, S. J., and M. J. Woodburn. 1987. Food discard practices of householders. *Journal of the American Dietetic Association 87*, 322.

44. Vollrath, T. L. 1992. U.S. farm trade complements world trade. *Food Review 15*, 7 (No. 1).

45. Welsh, S. O., and R. M. Marston. 1982. Review of trends in food use in the United States, 1909 to 1980. *Journal of the American Dietetic Association 81*, 120.

46. *Women 19–50 Years and Their Children 1–5 Years, 1 Day*. 1986. Nationwide Food Consumption Survey, Continuing Survey of Food Intakes by Individuals. NFCS, CSFII Report No. 86-1. Washington, DC: U.S. Department of Agriculture.

Food Safety

3

•PREVENTING FOOD-BORNE ILLNESS

Everyone along the food-handling chain—the processor, the packager, the wholesaler, the retailer, the foodservice manager, and the consumer—should recognize potential health hazards related to food and know how to control them. Why is this so important? It has been estimated that between 24 and 81 million-plus cases of food-borne diarrheal disease occur each year in the United States, costing between $5 billion and $17 billion in medical care and lost productivity [20]. Furthermore, the true incidence of food-borne disease is undoubtedly underreported.

The food-processing industry utilizes a variety of measures to limit potential food hazards. It **pasteurizes, sterilizes**, uses specialized packaging, freezes, refrigerates, dehydrates, and applies approved antimicrobial preservatives to various food products. These processes help to ensure that the American food supply remains the safest and most wholesome in the world.

One concept being used by the food industry and governmental regulatory agencies to assure **food safety** is the Hazard Analysis and Critical Control Point (HACCP) system [21, 38]. This is a preventative system in which safety is built into the entire process of food manufacture. HACCP operates on a set of basic procedures: (1) the analysis of **hazards** and assessment of **risks**; (2) the determination of **critical control points** in the process for each hazard where loss of control may result in an unacceptable health risk; (3) the monitoring of each critical control point on a set schedule; (4) the establishment of clearly defined corrective action to be taken if a deviation occurs at a critical control point; and (5) the keeping of adequate records so that the source of problems can be effectively traced. The HACCP system is an important part of food processors' overall quality-assurance programs and helps to assure the safety of their products. According to the federally operated Centers for Disease Control, over a five-year period only 3 percent of reported cases of food-borne disease were attributed to food-processing plants [20].

What about the other 97 percent? Of total cases reported, about 77 percent involved foodservice establishments and about 20 percent were caused in homes. It is probable that many additional cases occurring in homes

Pasteurize   to treat with mild heat to destroy pathogens—but not all microorganisms—present in a food product

Sterilize   to destroy essentially all microorganisms

Food safety   a judgment of the acceptability of the risk involved in eating a food; if risk is relatively low, a food substance may be considered safe

Hazard   a source of danger, long- or short-term, such as microbial food poisoning, cancer, birth defects, and so on

Risk   a measure of the probability and severity of harm to human health

Critical control point   any point in the process where loss of control may result in a health risk

45

Cross-contamination   contamination of one substance by another; for example, cooked chicken is contaminated with *Salmonella* organisms when it is cut on the same board used for cutting the raw chicken

were not reported. Clearly, both food handlers and consumers have a tremendous responsibility to maintain proper control measures to prevent food-borne illness.

Well over 500,000 foodservice establishments serve the American public. Many of them use the HACCP system as part of their quality-assurance program [4], which is highly recommended. Workers in the foodservice industry, including those employed in fast-food and carryout restaurants, delicatessens, self-service food counters, mobile refreshment stands, family and gourmet restaurants, schools, hospitals, and other establishments, *must* be educated about potential food safety hazards. This is vitally important so that they fully understand the need to continuously carry out sanitary procedures that ensure microbial quality and safety in the food served to the public. The primary responsibility of foodservice managers and dietetic practitioners is to supply consumers with safe products that are as free as possible from pathogenic microorganisms and other health hazards [33].

The following safeguards are essential for safe foodservice: prevention of contamination and **cross-contamination** in preparation, thorough cooking and thorough cooling of foods that are recognized as high-risk items, prevention of recontamination during storage, the use of appropriate storage conditions, and rapid, thorough reheating (to at least 75°C [165°F]) of these products for subsequent service to customers [6]. At each of these critical control points in production, a schedule for monitoring should be established and followed precisely. If monitoring reveals a potential hazard, the corrective action to be taken must be clearly defined.

It has been suggested that the concept of HACCP should be extended to the consumer at home [1]. Consumer dissatisfaction with commercial food products, as well as development of food-borne illness, may result from consumers' failure to handle the products properly on the way home from the market, to store and/or prepare the food properly, to keep kitchen equipment clean and sanitary, or to practice good personal hygiene. National surveys have indicated a need for more consumer education concerning the proper handling of food [40]. Labels on food products could aid in customer education by supplying more information about proper storage of foods after they have been prepared and by providing better directions for proper handling before and during preparation [42].

It may seem an unsurmountable task to protect food from contamination, since pathogenic microorganisms are widespread in air, dust, soil, insects, and even in about half of the foodservice workers themselves. However, the recognition of the potential risk of mishandling various foods, the following of proper programs for food and equipment sanitation, and the use of a little common sense can go a long way toward averting possible problems [33].

Some pathogens, such as *Listeria monocytogenes*, have been known to survive even the minimum high-temperature, short-time pasteurization process for milk. This organism, as well as some others such as *Yersinia enterocolitica*, can also grow at refrigerator temperatures. For this reason and others, sanitary handling procedures must be used to minimize opportunities for contamination, particularly post-processing contamination. Following simple rules of sanitation, such as washing hands before handling food, putting clean bandages on cuts and sores before working with food, wearing plastic gloves, and maintaining proper temperatures when holding food, can prevent numerous outbreaks of illness [11].

All dishes and equipment used in food preparation should be carefully cleaned. Machine-washed dishes, both in the home and in commercial foodservice establishments, may be almost if not entirely sterile because hot water and strong sanitizing agents are used in machine washing. In homes where infectious diseases exist, it is important to keep all dishes used by patients separate from other dishes until they are sterilized.

Precautions should always be taken in preparing, cooking, and storing foods. It cannot be overemphasized that cold foods should be kept cold (below 5°C [40°F]) and hot foods should be kept hot (above 60°C [140°F]). Perishable foods should be at room temperature for no more than two to three hours' total time, including preparation and serving time. Any temperature between 5° and 60°C (40° and 140°F), a critical temperature zone, permits growth of food-poisoning bacteria.

Cross-contamination among raw foods, particularly meat and poultry, and ready-to-eat foods, including fruits and vegetables to be eaten raw, must be avoided. *Escherichia coli* 0157:H7 has been found in ground beef [33], and *Campylobacter jejuni* is often spread by cross-contamination from raw meat, poultry, or seafood. The latter organism is found primarily as part of the intestinal microflora of mammals and birds. Appropriate internal temperatures must therefore be attained in the cooking of meat, poultry, and fish. Temperature requirements for food preparation in commercial foodservice establishments may vary somewhat, depending on state and local public health departments. It is the foodservice manager's responsibility to know and follow the regulations that apply to his or her facility.

Since the most common food-related illnesses result from growth and/or toxin production in foods of certain microbes, we will briefly review some of the basic characteristics of microorganisms. Then we will discuss the two general types of bacterial food-borne disease that are recognized: intoxications and infections. **Food intoxication** occurs when microorganisms have grown and produced a toxin in food, and the toxin-laden food is consumed. **Food infection** results when live microorganisms that can cause illness (called *pathogens*) are present, often in large numbers, in food that is eaten and they continue to grow in the gastrointestinal tract.

Food intoxication   illness produced by microbial toxin production in a food product that is consumed; the toxin produces the illness

Food infection   illness produced by the presence and growth of pathogenic microorganisms in the gastrointestinal tract; they are often, but not necessarily, present in large numbers

•CHARACTERISTICS OF MICROORGANISMS

The microorganisms with which we are primarily concerned in food science include bacteria, molds, and yeasts. These tiny organisms perform some extremely useful functions in food preparation and processing. We should not always think of them in terms of the undesirable effects of food spoilage and illness. For example, the delightful flavors and characteristic textures of a variety of cheeses result from the activity of various bacteria or molds. Sauerkraut and pickles are made by using bacterial **fermentation**. Baker's yeast leavens bread and other baked products, as well as contributes flavor. Those who enjoy Oriental foods with soy sauce are indebted to molds used in its manufacturing process. Various bacteria and molds are also used in industries that manufacture such things as citric acid and a great number of different enzymes.

Fermentation   the transformation of organic molecules into smaller ones by the action of microorganisms; for example, yeast ferments glucose to carbon dioxide and alcohol

Spore   an encapsulated, resistant form of a microorganism

Molds

Molds are multicellular, filamentous microbes that appear fuzzy or cotton-like when they grow on the surface of foods. The growth may be white, dark, or various colors. Mold **spores**, by which molds can reproduce, are small, light, and resistant to drying. They easily spread through the air and can contaminate any food on which they settle.

Molds may grow readily on relatively dry foods like bread or stored cereal grains because they require less moisture than most other microorganisms. They thrive at ordinary room temperatures but, given sufficient time, can also grow under cool conditions in refrigerators. Some molds can grow even at relatively high temperatures.

Yeasts

Yeasts are one-celled organisms that are often spherical in shape. They usually reproduce asexually through budding, by which process new daughter cells are pinched off from the parent cell (see Figure 25.4). Unlike molds, most yeasts grow best with a generous supply of moisture. They also grow in the presence of greater concentrations of sugar than do most bacteria. The growth of many yeasts is favored by an acid reaction (**pH** 4.0 to 4.5), and they grow best in the presence of oxygen. Thus, yeasts thrive particularly in acidic fruit juices, where they can ferment the sugar, producing alcohol. The range of temperature for the growth of most yeasts is, in general, similar to that for molds, with the optimum around 25° to 30°C (77° to 86°F).

pH   expression of the degree of acidity on a scale of 1 to 14, 1 being most acid, 7 neutral, and 14 most alkaline

Bacteria

Tiny one-celled microbes smaller than either molds or yeasts, bacteria may be rod-shaped (bacilli) or round (cocci). There are many different families of bacteria involved in food spoilage and food poisoning.

Generally, bacteria require more moisture than either molds or yeasts. They grow best where concentrations of sugar or salt are low and where the pH is about neutral (neither acid nor alkaline). Some bacteria love the cold; these are called psychrophilic and thrive at refrigerator temperatures. Others are heat-loving (thermophilic) and may create particular hazards in cooked foods. Many others, however, are mesophilic, meaning that they do best at moderate temperatures.

Some bacteria are able to form spores or endospores (see Figure 3.3) that have special protective coatings, making them very resistant to destruction by heating. These spores are especially resistant in low-acid environments. Vegetables and meats are generally considered to be low-acid foods.

Bacteria also vary in their need for oxygen or air. Aerobic bacteria must have oxygen, anaerobic bacteria can grow only in the absence of oxygen, and facultative bacteria can grow either with or without free oxygen.

•FOOD-BORNE INFECTIONS AND INTOXICATIONS

Tremendous technological progress has been made in recent years in the entire system of food processing and distribution. Improved methods of preservation have been developed, and techniques for the chemical and bacteriological identification of injurious agents in food have been improved. Despite such progress, however, food-borne infections and food intoxications are still too common and continue to create a great deal of unnecessary human misery.

Outbreaks of food-related illness in the United States, as well as in other countries, are inadequately reported or not reported at all. When outbreaks are reported, information about them is often incomplete and does not allow a specific cause to be assigned to the incident. To increase knowledge about food-borne illness and its effective control, a better system of reporting and investigating is essential. Many different causative microbial agents of food-borne illness have been identified. In recent years, a number of new bacteria have been added to the list of microorganisms involved [12, 31]. Many of these so-called *new* food-borne disease agents are well-known pathogens of domestic animals. What is new about them is the recognition that they can be transmitted to humans via food and may produce illness. Whenever an outbreak of food poisoning occurs, a search should be made for the causative organisms.

Out of 2,279 food-borne disease outbreaks (involving variable numbers of cases) reported to the Centers for Disease Control over a five-year period, 1,285 occurred in foodservice establishments, 327 in homes, 52 in food processing plants, and 615 in other or unknown places [31]. In 46 percent of the outbreaks involving homes and restaurants, the probable cause was improper cooling of food. Other significant factors in the outbreaks were the lapse of time between preparing and serving food, and the touching of cooked foods by persons carrying pathogenic bacteria.

Some pathogenic microbes may be carried by food even though they do not grow in the food itself. Others are able to grow in foods, increasing dramatically in numbers when held under certain conditions, particularly warm temperatures. In yet other cases, microbes grow and produce toxins that cause illness when consumed. The contamination of foods by pathogens may occur through food handlers, air, soil, water, flies, roaches, and rodents, and from animals or birds that produce milk or eggs or are used for meat. Food utensils used for eating, drinking, or food preparation may become contaminated when used by persons who are carrying potential disease-producing organisms. Examples of pathogens most often transmitted by food contaminated by infected persons who handle food are the Hepatitis A virus, *Salmonella typhimurium*, and *Staphylococcus aureus*. Pathogens that are usually transmitted by contamination at the source of the food, in food processing, or by non-food-borne routes are *Campylobacter jejuni*, enteropathogenic *Escherichia coli*, and *Yersinia enterocolitica*.

Common Food Infections

Salmonella

Salmonella bacteria are one of the leading causes of food-borne illness on a worldwide basis. There are about 2,000 different strains of *Salmonella*, and any of these is capable of causing infection in humans. The organisms, which appear under the microscope as short rods (Figure 3.1), usually enter the body orally in contaminated food or water and may produce a food-poisoning syndrome as they multiply in the intestinal tract. It has been assumed that large numbers of salmonellae growing in food are necessary to cause illness, but a

FIGURE 3.1

Salmonella is a rod-shaped bacterium, shown here as clusters. (Courtesy of the U.S. Department of Agriculture. *The Safe Food Book*. Home and Garden Bulletin No. 241, 1985.)

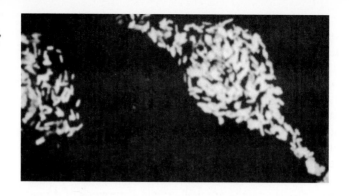

Salmonellosis illness produced by ingestion of *Salmonella* organisms

number of outbreaks in recent years have led to the conclusion that even small numbers can cause initiation of infection [31].

The primary signs and symptoms of **salmonellosis** are nausea, diarrhea, abdominal pain, and fever. These symptoms usually appear within 12 to 18 hours after the contaminated food has been eaten. In most cases, recovery occurs within 2 or 3 days. However, some individuals develop complications that persist for weeks or even months. Although information on mortality from salmonellosis is incomplete, death may sometimes occur with this disease, especially among the very young, the aged, and the infirm. The Centers for Disease Control in Atlanta, Georgia, estimate an annual incidence of two million clinically significant *Salmonella* infections in the United States, of which 2,000 may be fatal [20]. The major factors involved in salmonellosis are summarized in Table 3.1.

Salmonellae are found in many animals, both wild and domestic. We are particularly concerned about the presence of these organisms in meat and poultry, because these appear to be the most important sources of human salmonellosis. As present processing methods cannot ensure that raw meat, poultry, and eggs are free of salmonellae, there is a constant introduction of contaminated animal products into the food supply. It is not unusual to find that 25 percent of a particular lot of broiler chickens are carrying salmonellae [13]. Turkeys, swine, and eggs may be contaminated with the microorganisms. During slaughtering, microorganisms may be spread from one carcass to another.

In 1992, the U.S. Department of Agriculture (USDA) approved a new process designed to reduce the incidence of *Salmonella* during the processing of chicken [14]. Using specialized equipment installed in the processing line, a solution of trisodium phosphate is applied to the poultry carcasses. Little or no residue is left on the finished poultry. It has been suggested that this process removes a fat coating on the surface of the poultry, thus allowing bacteria to be more effectively washed from it. Also, the U.S. Food and Drug Administration (FDA) has approved the irradiation of poultry to destroy *Salmonella* and to increase the shelf life of the product.

Humans who have had salmonellosis may carry the infecting organisms in their digestive tracts for some time after the symptoms of the disease have disappeared and may contaminate foods that they handle improperly. Household pets can also carry salmonellae and thus should not be fed from plates and utensils used by humans.

TABLE 3.1

Food Infections and Intoxications

Disease/ Organism	Cause of Illness	Incubation Time	Nature of Illness	Foods Involved	Control Measures
Salmonellosis	Infection with *Salmonella* species	12–24 hours	Nausea, diarrhea, abdominal pain, fever, headache, chills, prostration	Meat, poultry, and egg products; milk products	Cook thoroughly; no cross-contamination; use sanitary practices
Staphylococcus poisoning	Toxin produced by certain strains of *Staphylococcus aureus*	1–6 hours	Severe vomiting, diarrhea, abdominal cramping	Custard- or cream-filled baked goods, ham, tongue, poultry, dressing, gravy, eggs, potato salad, cream sauces, sandwich fillings	Refrigerate foods; use sanitary practices
Botulism	Toxin produced by *Clostridium botulinum*	12–36 hours	Nausea, vomiting, diarrhea, fatigue, headache, dry mouth, double vision, muscle paralysis, respiratory failure	Low-acid canned foods, meats, sausage, fish	Properly can foods following recommended procedures; cook foods properly
Clostridium perfringens poisoning	Toxin released in intestine	8–24 hours	Diarrhea, abdominal cramps, chills, headache	Meat, poultry, and other foods held for serving at warm but not hot temperatures	Cool foods rapidly after cooking; hold hot foods above 55° C (131° F)
Campylobacter jejuni	Infection, even with low numbers	1–7 days	Nausea, abdominal cramps, diarrhea, headache: varying in severity	Raw milk, eggs, poultry, raw beef, cake icing, water	Pasteurize milk; cook foods properly; prevent cross-contamination
Escherichia coli 0157:H7	Strain of enteropathic *E. coli*	2–4 days	Hemorrhagic colitis, possibly hemolytic uremic syndrome	Ground beef, raw milk, chicken	Thoroughly cook meat; no cross-contamination
Yersiniosis	Infection with *Yersinia enterocolitica*	1–3 days	Enterocolitis, may mimic acute appendicitis	Raw milk, chocolate milk, water, pork, other raw meats	Pasteurize milk; cook foods properly; no cross-contamination; use sanitary practices
Listeriosis	Infection with *Listeria monocytogenes*	2 days– 3 weeks	Meningitis, septicemia, miscarriage	Vegetables, milk, cheese, meat, seafood	Pasteurize milk; cook foods properly; no cross-contamination; use sanitary practices

Source: Reference 33.

The specific foods most commonly involved in the development of salmonellosis are various kinds of meat and poultry products; eggs and foods made with eggs, such as cream or custard fillings; milk and milk products, such as ice cream, cream, and custard-filled confectionery; and fish and shellfish. The most vulnerable foods are those that are lightly cooked and subject to much handling, especially if they are unrefrigerated for long periods.

A 1985 outbreak of salmonellosis was caused by the presence of *Salmonella typhimurium* in pasteurized low-fat milk from a large modern dairy located in a Chicago suburb. The milk had apparently been recontaminated by raw milk after pasteurization. By the time the outbreak was over, there were almost 20,000 laboratory-confirmed cases of salmonellosis, with estimates of the total number of victims approaching 200,000 [12, 20, 31].

During recent years, *Salmonella enteritidis* has become a main cause of salmonellosis. Most of the outbreaks of illness traced to this organism have been associated with eggs and have occurred in the northeastern part of the United States. The eggs involved typically were held at improper temperatures during preparation, allowing the microbe population to increase markedly. For example, in one case hundreds of eggs were cracked into large containers and held for many hours at temperatures that permitted organisms to grow. The eggs were then either undercooked before being served or used uncooked in foods such as mousse. The ovarian tissue of some hens is apparently contaminated with *Salmonella enteritidis*, and these hens produce eggs with contaminated yolks in the intact egg. Precautions must therefore be taken to properly refrigerate eggs from the time they are laid [8].

The consumer or foodservice worker cannot control contamination of animal products with salmonellae that occurs before the food is brought into the kitchen. Proper cooking and careful handling practices after the products have been received, therefore, are the only protection against illness. Salmonellae are sensitive to heat and are destroyed by normal conventional cooking of foods and pasteurization of milk. In one study, however, poultry cooked in a microwave oven to an internal temperature of 85°C (185°F) was not sufficiently heated to destroy *Salmonella* organisms in five out of six contaminated birds. Because of uneven heating in microwave-cooked products, internal temperature cannot be used as an exclusive means of determining the safety of these products [26]. Salmonellae also survive for long periods in dried or frozen foods and in moist foods held at room temperature.

Milk should be pasteurized before drying, and eggs should be pasteurized before freezing or drying. Fresh meats, poultry, and eggs should be refrigerated at 2° to 4°C (35° to 40°F) or frozen and held at −18°C (0°F). Poultry should be cooked to a well-done stage. Eggs should be cooked; raw eggs should not be used in foods, such as ice cream, egg nog, and mayonnaise, that do not receive heat treatments sufficient to kill salmonellae.

Cooked meat or poultry and leftovers should be tightly covered and stored immediately in the refrigerator or freezer. Perishable foods should be kept chilled when they are carried on a trip or a picnic. Cutting boards used for cutting up raw poultry should be disinfected by washing with a dilute solution (1 tablespoon per quart) of sodium hypochlorite (household bleach) before being used for the cutting of other foods, such as the slicing of potatoes for salad. This prevents cross-contamination from an infected food to a noninfected one.

Eradication of salmonellae from animals seems unlikely. Therefore, the only truly effective way to reduce the incidence of salmonellosis is to educate foodservice workers and consumers about the proper handling of foods, particularly raw meat, poultry, and eggs.

Campylobacter Jejuni

During the 1980s, *Campylobacter jejuni* ceased to be a pathogen encountered mainly in veterinary science and became one of the leading causes of acute bacterial **gastroenteritis** in humans in the United States. This occurred after the development of procedures for detecting the organism in stool specimens. It is estimated that there are more than two million cases of *Campylobacter*-caused illness in the United States annually, making it approximately equal to salmonellosis in incidence [8, 20].

Gastroenteritis inflammation of the gastrointestinal tract

Campylobacter is often found in the intestinal tract of cattle, swine, sheep, chickens, and turkeys, where it does not cause harm. Therefore, the most likely sources of human infection are raw or inadequately cooked foods of animal origin. Raw meats and poultry become infected during processing when intestinal contents come into contact with meat surfaces. A 1985 survey of retail fresh red meat and poultry showed that 30 percent of poultry, 4 to 5 percent of pork, 3 to 5 percent of beef, and 8 percent of lamb contained *C. jejuni* and/or *Campylobacter coli*, a closely related pathogen [20].

Undercooked poultry and ground beef have been suspected in several outbreaks of illness due to *Campylobacter* infection. Cake that was likely contaminated by a *C. jejuni*-infected food handler was the cause of illness in another outbreak. Unchlorinated water may also spread the organism [3, 20, 31].

A number of *Campylobacter* outbreaks have implicated raw milk as the source of infection. Between 1981 and 1990, twenty outbreaks of illness associated with the consumption of raw milk during youth activities occurred and were investigated by health departments in the eleven states involved. Among 1,013 persons who drank raw milk, 458 cases of *Campylobacter* infection developed [41]. This type of information should be useful in educating young people and school personnel about the dangers of drinking raw milk.

Symptoms and signs of illness caused by *Campylobacter* infection include nausea, abdominal cramps, headache, diarrhea, and sometimes fever. If the diarrhea is severe, it may be bloody. Symptoms usually last 2 to 7 days but may last longer with complications [3]. The infectious dose of *C. jejuni* can be quite low, with illness resulting from the ingestion of only a few hundred cells. Therefore, growth of the organism in foods held improperly is not necessary for food to serve as a vehicle for illness [8].

C. jejuni is relatively fragile, being sensitive to drying, normal atmospheric concentrations of oxygen, storage at room temperature, acidic conditions, and high heat. It cannot grow at temperatures below 30°C (86°F), grows slowly even under optimal conditions, and does not compete well with other bacteria. It grows at temperatures between 30° and 47°C (86° and 117°F) and is preserved by refrigeration, but it is readily destroyed by heat sufficient to cook foods. Therefore, *C. jejuni* is not likely to be a problem in properly cooked foods or in processed foods that have been pasteurized or dehydrated. It is most often transmitted by foods of animal origin that are eaten raw or are inadequately cooked, and by foods that are contaminated after cooking through contact with *C. jejuni*-infected materials. Illness can be prevented by thorough cooking of poultry and meat, pasteurization of milk, and proper handling of foods both before and after preparation for service [8, 20].

Escherichia Coli

Escherichia coli is a normal inhabitant of the human intestinal tract and occurs in high numbers in fecal material. It was long considered to be harmless to human health, even though its presence in food or water indicated fecal contamination. In recent years, however, certain strains of *E. coli* have been identified as the causative factors in several food poisoning outbreaks in the United States and Canada.

Enteropathogenic causing illness in the intestinal tract

Hemorrhagic colitis bleeding and inflammation of the colon or large intestine

A subgroup of *E. coli* called **enteropathogenic** *E. coli* may produce foodborne illness. One particular strain of this subgroup, *E. coli* 0157:H7, is hardier than other strains, is more difficult to detect, and can be deadly [27]. The *E. coli* 0157:H7 organism produces a toxin that causes **hemorrhagic colitis**, producing bloody diarrhea and severe abdominal pain. It can also cause a rare disease called *hemolytic uremic syndrome*, the leading cause of acute kidney failure in children, as well as damage to the central nervous system.

An unfortunate example of this organism's deadly power received national attention in January 1993 when more than 475 people in the northwestern United States became seriously ill after eating hamburgers at a chain of fast-food restaurants. Three children subsequently died. Investigations into the cause of the food poisoning outbreak revealed that the hamburgers had been contaminated with *E. coli* and served undercooked. The hamburgers had been cooked to a minimum internal temperature of 60°C (140°F), according to company policy and as recommended by the FDA. Company personnel were apparently unaware that the Washington State Health Department had set a minimum internal temperature requirement of 68°C (155°F). The FDA is now recommending that hamburgers in foodservice establishments be cooked to a minimum internal temperature of 68°C (155°F). It also recommends that consumers cook ground meat to an internal temperature of 70°C (160°F). In both cases, the center of the meat should be light gray or brown and the juices should run clear, with no trace of pink [27].

While *E. coli* 0157:H7 is generally associated with dairy cattle and their products, beef and milk, *E. coli* food poisoning has also been associated with water and apple cider. The organism can survive freezer storage as well as refrigeration [27].

To avoid illness caused by *E. coli*, foods should be adequately cooked and postcooking contamination avoided. Food may be contaminated by contact with contaminated equipment, water, or infected food handlers. Foodservice establishments, particularly, should carefully monitor adequacy of cooking, holding times, temperatures, and personal hygiene of food handlers [20]. Industry groups have recommended to the USDA and the FDA that livestock slaughter operations and ground beef producers, food processors, and the foodservice and retail industries handling food utilize the HACCP system to ensure safety.

Yersinia Enterocolitica

An infection caused by *Yersinia enterocolitica*, known as yersiniosis, may cause gastroenteritis. Pigs are the primary animal source of this organism. Foods involved in outbreaks of yersiniosis have included chocolate milk, pasteurized milk, and tofu that was packed in unchlorinated spring water. The precise manner by which the organism contaminated these foods was not determined, but in each case there was thought to be a lack of good sanitary practice. *Y. enterocolitica* can grow at refrigeration temperatures, but is sensitive to heat. Therefore, to control illness from this cause, it is important to eliminate the organism from foods by pasteurization or cooking. Care should be taken to avoid cross-contamination of processed, ready-to-eat foods with pork and porcine wastes [20].

Listeria Monocytogenes

The importance of *Listeria monocytogenes* as a causative agent in the development of food-borne illness has been recognized only in recent years. This organism is normally present in the environment and frequently contaminates many foods, being found most often in dairy, meat, and seafood products. It may also be present in some vegetables. Soil is a common reservoir of *Listeria monocytogenes*, which may be carried in the intestinal tracts of a variety of animals, including humans. Home environments are often contaminated with *L. monocytogenes* [8].

Because *L. monocytogenes* is able to grow at refrigerator temperatures, there is concern for potential problems with the increasing number of refrigerated ready-to-eat foods, salads, and minimally processed foods that are being marketed [34]. It is of paramount importance that refrigerator storage temperatures be carefully controlled when these products are held since fluctuations in temperature are likely to affect the growth of this and other organisms. *L. monocytogenes* can grow well at temperatures as low as 0°C (32°F) but is sensitive to heat and is destroyed by pasteurization. In 1985, more than 100 cases of listeriosis occurred in Southern California and were traced to Mexican-style soft cheese manufactured at one particular plant in the area [20]. It is presumed that the cheese was contaminated after pasteurization of the milk.

This organism can be responsible for a variety of health problems, including meningitis, **septicemia**, and miscarriage. Illness occurs principally in individuals whose immune system is compromised in some way by such conditions as cancer, cirrhosis, AIDS, pregnancy, or transplantation of organs. In these cases, the mortality rate is high. Healthy individuals are usually able to overcome the infection with considerably fewer problems. Most people do not appear to be susceptible to listeric infection even though many foods contain low levels of the organism. Public health authorities in some countries advise pregnant women and immunosuppressed individuals to avoid eating low-acid soft cheeses, which have been identified as primary sources of listeriosis [8].

Septicemia   the presence of pathogenic microorganisms in the blood

Other Food Infections

Microorganisms of the *Shigella* species may be carried by food and cause gastrointestinal symptoms, including diarrhea, vomiting, fever, and abdominal cramps. Relatively small numbers of the organisms can cause disease. The major cause of shigellosis is infected food handlers who are carrying the organism in their intestinal tracts and practice poor personal hygiene. Most outbreaks result from contamination of raw or previously cooked foods during preparation in the home or in foodservice establishments. The best preventive measure is education of the food handler, with an emphasis on good personal hygiene [20].

The most common cause of food-borne illness in Japan is *Vibrio parahaemolyticus*, which is, almost without exception, derived from contaminated seafood. Some outbreaks of illness caused by this organism have also been reported in the United States [2].

The growth of *V. parahaemolyticus* is slowed or arrested at refrigeration temperatures. Most important with respect to human infections is prevention of their multiplication in uncooked seafoods and employment of hygienic handling procedures to avoid the recontamination of cooked foods. Consumption of raw seafoods should be avoided, particularly during the warmer months of the year when the *Vibrio* organisms tend to increase in numbers [22].

Common Food Intoxications

Staphylococcus Food Poisoning

Certain strains of *Staphylococcus aureus* produce a potent toxin that is recognized as a common cause of food poisoning. It is called an *enterotoxin* because it produces gastroenteritis or inflammation of the lining of the stomach and intestines. The symptoms of staphylococcal poisoning, severe vomiting and diarrhea, appear between 1 and 6 hours after the food is consumed, and usually disappear a few hours later. Complete recovery normally takes 1 or 2 days. The mortality rate for this type of food poisoning is essentially zero, but it could be fatal in severely malnourished infants or in infirm adults [13]. *Staphylococcus* organisms are shown in Figure 3.2.

The food-poisoning strains of *S. aureus* may be present in the nasal passages of many people. Boils and some wounds may also be infected with them. Food may be contaminated with these potentially dangerous organisms when transfer occurs from the nasal passage or a sore on the hands of the food handler to the food being prepared.

If foods contaminated with staphylococcal organisms cool very slowly or are held without refrigeration, these organisms grow and produce the toxin that is responsible for illness. Because the toxin is preformed, the gastrointestinal symptoms occur relatively quickly. Once it has formed in the food, the staphylococcal toxin is not easily inactivated or destroyed. Since it is stable in heat and may withstand boiling for 20 to 60 minutes, it is important to prevent the formation of the toxin. This can be done by the sanitary handling of food during preparation and by proper refrigeration of prepared foods.

Because staphylococci usually get into food by way of human handlers, contamination can be controlled by such simple rules as washing hands before preparing food and rewashing hands after using a handkerchief or tissue. Rubber or plastic gloves should be worn if cuts or sores are present on the hands. This not only keeps staphylococci from being transferred to the food from the cuts, but also prevents additional bacteria from getting into the sores.

A wide variety of foods may provide excellent media for the growth of staphylococcal bacteria. Cooked poultry, baked ham, tuna, egg products, potato salad, and custard- or cream-filled baked goods are often involved.

FIGURE 3.2

Staphylococcus bacteria are tiny, round cells that cluster together. (Courtesy of the U.S. Department of Agriculture. *The Safe Food Book*, Home and Garden Bulletin No. 241, 1985.)

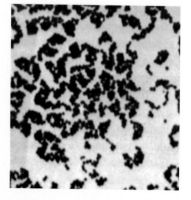

These foods, in particular, should be refrigerated at 2° to 4°C (35° to 40°F). Failure to refrigerate foods that have been contaminated with the microorganisms, thus allowing toxin to form, is the usual reason for an outbreak of the disease. The toxin does not necessarily affect the taste of the product and thus individuals consuming such foods are not aware that they are eating "spoiled" food.

In 1989, several outbreaks of staphylococcal food poisoning occurred in the United States as a result of people consuming canned mushrooms imported from the People's Republic of China [16]. More than 100 people became ill. Canned food is not usually associated with this type of poisoning because the staphylococcal organism is easily destroyed by heat, so a team of specialists went to China to investigate the cause. The conclusion was that the toxin had been produced during the period when the fresh mushrooms were packed in nonpermeable polyethylene bags as they were being shipped to the processing plant. Since the mushrooms used up the oxygen in the bags through respiration, the carbon dioxide level became elevated and inhibited the growth of competing microorganisms. The staphylococcal organisms thus grew and produced the heat-stable toxin that was not destroyed in the canning process. This emphasizes the importance of careful control at *all* phases of food production, processing, packaging, and delivery in order to assure safety in the final product.

An accurate figure for the number of cases of staphylococcal food poisoning in the United States is not available because, as with most food-borne illness, so many cases are not reported. Usually, only outbreaks that involve large groups of people, such as those at conventions or company picnics, are reported. A large proportion of all cases of food poisoning are probably of this type, and many of us encounter them several times during our lives. Table 3.1 summarizes the major factors involved in staphylococcal food poisoning.

Clostridium Perfringens

The symptoms associated with *Clostridium perfringens* food poisoning include severe abdominal cramps and pronounced diarrhea. Nausea and vomiting are rare. The symptoms appear 8 to 12 hours after eating the contaminated food and the illness lasts no more than 24 hours. It is usually not serious. Foods responsible include beef, chicken, turkey, stews, meat pies, and gravy that have been mishandled. These foods may have been cooled too slowly after cooking, kept several hours without refrigeration, or kept on a serving line steam table at a temperature below 55°C (131°F) for an extended period. *C. perfringens* organisms multiply rapidly under these conditions.

The mechanism causing illness seems to involve the ingestion of large numbers of live vegetative cells of *C. perfringens*. These cells then form encapsulating spores in the intestinal tract and release an enterotoxin. The toxin produces the characteristic symptoms [18]. Thus, this microorganism exhibits characteristics of both a food infection and a food intoxication.

Clostridium Botulinum

Botulinum food poisoning is the most feared of all food-borne diseases. At one time, the death rate of those contracting this disease was 50 to 60 percent. In recent years, however, the mortality has dropped to about 20 percent. This is probably the result of early diagnosis and improved treatment of the illness.

Botulism is a condition that results from the action of a potent toxin on the neurological system of the body, causing paralysis. The toxin is produced by the bacterium *C. botulinum*. Symptoms include nausea, vomiting, diarrhea, double vision, difficulty in swallowing, inability to talk, and finally, respiratory paralysis and death. The signs of disease usually appear about 12 to 36 hours after eating food that contains the active toxin [13].

C. botulinum is able to form spores, as shown in Figure 3.3, that are very resistant to destruction by heat in a low-acid environment. It is also *anaerobic*, meaning that it can grow and produce toxin only in the absence of free oxygen. The organism itself and its spores are not pathogenic or disease producing in adult humans, but the toxin that it produces in such foods as inadequately heated canned meats, low-acid vegetables, low-acid tomatoes, and some processed fish is one of the most potent known. Toxin production has also occurred in such foods as fresh mushrooms kept in tight plastic bags, baked potatoes wrapped in foil and left at room temperature for several days before being used to make potato salad, and seasoned cooked onions that were kept warm for extended periods of service [31]. Spoiled foods containing the toxin may have off-odors and gas and appear to be soft and disintegrated. However, cases of botulism have been reported from eating foods that had little or no abnormal appearance or odor. Because of this, and because the toxin can be inactivated by boiling temperatures, the USDA has recommended that home-canned low-acid foods (including low-acid tomatoes) that have not been processed using recommended procedures be boiled for 10 to 15 minutes before being tasted.

Although adults can apparently consume the *C. botulinum* cells themselves without ill effect, this may not be the case with infants up to about 12 months of age. *C. botulinum* is apparently able to colonize, grow, and produce toxin in the colon of certain infants, causing typical signs of neurological distress. Possibly, because infants' intestinal bacteria are colonized after birth, *C. botulinum* organisms may grow before other bacteria that inhibit their growth have become well-established [31]. *C. botulinum* spores may be found in honey, which has been implicated in some cases of infant botulism.

The extent of botulism outbreaks in the United States resulting from commercially canned foods has been very small considering that more than 10 billion cans of commercially processed low-acid canned foods are consumed each year. Between 1899 and 1976, home-processed foods accounted for 72 percent of outbreaks of botulism. Commercially processed foods were involved in only 8.6 percent, and unknown foods were responsible for 19.8 percent of outbreaks. Some more recent outbreaks have been associated with food prepared in foodservice establishments [20]. From 1899 to 1981, 522 outbreaks of botulism involving home-canned foods and 55 outbreaks involving commercially canned foods were reported. Between 1973 and 1981, there were six incidents with botulism toxin in commercially canned products. These involved peppers, marinated mushrooms, tuna, beef stew, and salmon. In some of these cases, the problem was the use of imperfect cans [35]. Some outbreaks have also involved vacuum-packed smoked fish.

Inadequate processing of home-canned foods that are low in acid, particularly vegetables, low-acid varieties of tomatoes, and meats, creates the greatest problem with respect to botulism. If spores of this bacterium are present, boiling will not destroy them unless the solution is sufficiently acid or unless boiling is continued for 6 to 10 hours. Various strains of the organism vary in their temperature relations, but low-acid foods are never safe unless they are heated at temperatures considerably above the boiling point of water, 100°C (212°F). It is recommended that temperatures no lower than 114° to 119°C (237° to 246°F) be used for low-acid vegetables. These temperatures can be achieved by processing in a pressure cooker at 10 to 15 pounds pressure. Low-

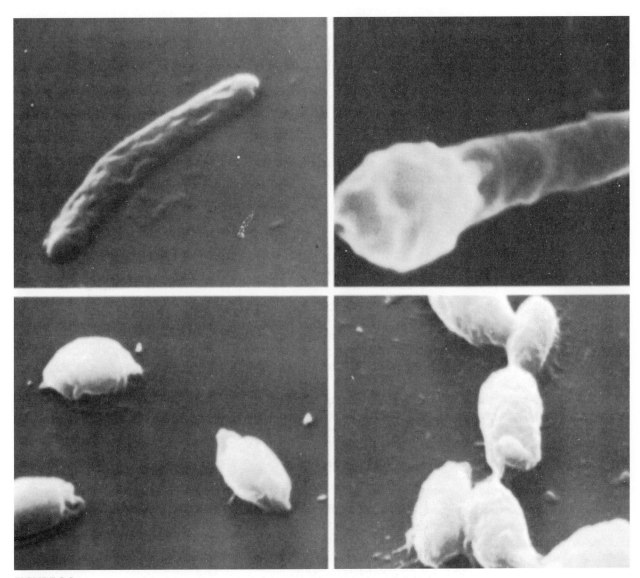

FIGURE 3.3

Scanning electron photomicrographs of (*top left*) a cell of *Clostridium botulinum*, type A, prior to formation of a spore and (*top right*) another type A cell during actual sporulation. At the bottom are spores of type B (*left*) and type E (*right*). (Courtesy of the U.S. Department of Health and Human Services, Food and Drug Administration. Kautter, D. A., and R. K. Lynt, Jr. 1971. Botulism. *FDA Papers*, Vol. 5, No. 9, p. 16.)

acid foods should never be processed in a boiling water bath. Because the botulinum toxin is so deadly, procedures recommended by the USDA [39] or by established companies that manufacture home-canning equipment should always be carefully followed in the home canning of low-acid foods to guard against any possibility of the toxin's developing.

Mycotoxins

It was discovered in 1960 that toxins produced by molds growing on cereal grains were responsible for the deaths of thousands of young turkeys that were fed the grain. These toxins were called *aflatoxins*, because it was found that they had been produced by certain strains of the mold *Aspergillus flavus*. Aflatoxins have been detected in peanuts and cottonseed and in meals made from them. Other toxins produced by molds, including some species of *Penicillium*, have also been identified and are generally called **mycotoxins**. These toxins are capable of causing damage to humans, including cancer, if mold-contaminated foods are eaten over an extended period [30].

Mycotoxins toxins produced by molds

Generally, foods that develop mold growth in the home should be discarded; however, solid cheeses may be trimmed of mold and the nonmoldy portion used if the cheese has been kept under refrigeration. Studies indicate that aflatoxins do not develop under refrigeration and that other toxins may be produced only in very small amounts or not at all [30]. In the holding or storing of foods, precautions should always be taken to minimize mold growth by such practices as adequate refrigeration and use of foods within a reasonable time.

Animal Parasites

In some parts of the world, infestation by such parasites as roundworms, flatworms, and certain species of **protozoa** may be common problems, and food or water may be carriers of these infecting agents. Protozoa include *Entamoeba histolytica*, the cause of amoebic dysentery, which is spread principally by fecal contamination of water, food, and diverse objects. Food handlers can spread this parasite. *Ascaris lumbricoides* is a roundworm or nematode that is spread fecally and is resistant to sewage treatment. It may survive for years in the soil and contaminate vegetables. *Trichinella spiralis*, another nematode, becomes encysted in meat and may be spread by this route. Certain tapeworms (flatworms) may also be encysted in meat, while other types may be acquired from the eating of raw or insufficiently cooked fish [19, 25].

Protozoa one-celled animals

In the United States, problems with animal parasites are infrequent; however, there is a continuing, though small, risk from the tiny roundworm, *Trichinella spiralis*. About one hog per one thousand in the United States may be infected with this parasite [29]. *Trichinella* may also occur in some wild game such as bear, boar, and rabbit. When the meat from these animals is consumed before it has been sufficiently cooked to destroy the larvae in it, trichinosis results. The larvae are freed in the digestive tract after consumption of the meat and enter the small intestine, where they develop into mature worms. Their offspring (newborn larvae) migrate throughout the body via the circulatory system and invade striated muscles. Here they become encysted and may persist for years. In the first few weeks after ingestion of trichinae, symptoms include nausea, vomiting, diarrhea, sweating, and loss of appetite. Later, after the larvae reach muscles in the body, muscular pains, facial edema, and fever may occur. The incidence of trichinosis in the United States has declined in recent years but continues to be a public health concern, as well as an economic burden to the American swine industry [36].

The USDA has recommended a procedure for processing cured pork products so that any trichinae present are destroyed. Therefore, these pork products should be free of trichinae. Poultry products that contain pork are subject to the same requirements concerning treatment for trichinae as are meat products containing pork. Thorough cooking of fresh pork to an internal temperature of at least 58°C (137°F) should also ensure the destruction of any trichinae that might be present. Cooking pork to an internal temperature of 77°C (170°F) as recommended by the National Live Stock and Meat Board allows a margin of safety. Precautions must be taken when cooking pork by microwaves to ensure that a final temperature sufficient to destroy any trichinae is achieved throughout the meat. Microwaves may heat unevenly. The microwave cooking of pork is discussed in Chapter 21.

Viruses

Viruses are now recognized as important causes of food-borne disease in the U.S. and the United Kingdom [24]. **Hepatitis** A was known in the 1940s as a food-borne viral disease and was first associated with shellfish. When symptoms occur, they often include fever, malaise, anorexia, nausea, and abdominal discomfort, followed in a few days by **jaundice**. After a few weeks the illness usually subsides, but may produce debility that lasts for months.

The hepatitis A virus is transmitted by the fecal-oral route in which food or water may serve as a vehicle. Infection often results from mishandling of food by infected persons. Viral transmission via food is largely the result of avoidable fecal contamination.

Gastroenteritis, characterized by vomiting and diarrhea, may be caused by Norwalk-like viruses that are shed in the feces. Although food is not the only means by which these viruses can be spread, it is a very effective one. Viruses cannot multiply in foods and can be inactivated by cooking. Therefore, it is important to avoid contamination of ready-to-eat foods that will not be cooked. Sanitary personal hygiene habits among food handlers are extremely important in avoiding the spread of these viruses via food.

Hepatitis inflammation of the liver

Jaundice a condition in which the skin and eyeballs become abnormally yellow due to the presence of bile pigments in the blood

•ENVIRONMENTAL CONTAMINANTS

Toxic substances may contaminate the environment in which people, plants, and animals live. These substances include both inorganic elements, such as arsenic, cadmium, mercury, and lead, and organic substances, such as various chemicals used in pesticides. When contaminants persist in the environment, they may accumulate along the food chain in amounts that are toxic to humans when various animals and plants are consumed. For example, fish taken from water contaminated by the industrial use of mercury contain high levels of mercury, which may cause illness in humans if consumed in large amounts [28].

Lacquered cans cans with an inner lacquer or enamel coating; the coating is of variable composition and overlies the basic tin-coated steel, protecting certain canned foods from discoloration

Metals may enter foods from certain utensils. Galvanized containers are not suitable for foods because the zinc used for galvanizing is toxic. Cadmium and brass are also undesirable metals for use as food containers. Tin-coated cans are used in food processing, but only very small amounts of tin are generally found in most foods. Acid fruits and fruit juices packed in **unlacquered tin-coated cans** and stored in the opened cans in the refrigerator were found to contain increased amounts of both tin and iron [15]. Food stored in opened tin-coated cans may also change in color or develop a metallic taste. Although these changes are undesirable, illness will not result from the canning materials currently used in the food-processing industry.

Small quantities of aluminum are dissolved from utensils in many cooking processes. This is apparently not harmful, but scientists are continuing to study the effects of aluminum in the diet. The element copper is nutritionally essential, yet certain salts of copper are toxic. Cooking green-colored foods in copper containers to get bright green color is no longer practiced because of the danger of toxicity.

Foods are packaged in various types of containers from which certain chemical molecules may migrate to the food contained inside. The FDA is responsible for approving food-grade packaging materials to ensure that the type and amount of material that may migrate into the food will not be harmful to the consumer.

For many consumers, pesticide residues on fresh produce are a major food safety concern. A 1990 survey of 1,860 shoppers at 24 stores in Raleigh, North Carolina revealed that 60 percent of the participants had high levels of concern when asked to rate the seriousness of health risks from chemicals in the food supply [10]. Food scientists, on the other hand, consider the predominant risk in the food supply to be microbiological, not chemical. Evidence from the scientific community and from governmental agencies generally supports the premise that the level of pesticides in the American food supply is very low and represents a negligible health risk [9]. According to the FDA, 65 percent of the domestically grown foods it tested (7,394 samples) in 1989 showed no pesticide residues at all and 34 percent contained residues that were well within the limits set by the Environmental Protection Agency (EPA). However, research on pesticide residues will continue in order to ensure a safe food supply.

The Federal Fungicide, Rodenticide, and Insecticide Act is administered by the EPA, whereby it approves pesticides for specific uses and, after careful study, sets tolerances for residues on foods. These tolerances may be zero. Foods grown in other countries and imported into the United States are regulated under provisions of the law just like foods grown domestically. The FDA regularly monitors pesticide residues on foods, including in its program the completion of a yearly Total Diet Study [32]. Representative foods that might be consumed by various age and sex groups are purchased from grocery stores across the United States and analyzed in FDA laboratories for pesticide residues, as well as for other contaminants and some nutrients.

Pesticides are widely used in the intensified agriculture practiced today in the United States. They are intentionally added to agriculture crops although they are not intended to become part of the consumed food. Pesticides may also get into foods unintentionally as they move through soil, water, and air in the environment. Pesticides aid in preventing food destruction during growth and storage; however, they also constitute hazards when misused. For this reason, pesticides today are being increasingly used in combination with non-chemical control practices, including biological control methods and selective plant breeding. The Institute of Food Technologists encourages implementation of such procedures to further enhance the quality of the American food supply and to contribute to a more ecologically favorable agricultural production system [23].

In spite of much scientific evidence supporting the safety of our food supply, many in the public sector continue to be concerned about chemicals. There is thus a need for a constructive process by which experts, policy makers, and the public may effectively communicate and understand each other's perceptions about risk and food safety [37].

The first food-processing aid produced by a genetically engineered microorganism (so-called biotechnology) was approved by the FDA in March 1990: it is the enzyme *rennet*. Other enzymes, crops, processing aids, and food ingredients are under development. A growth hormone (BST) given to cows to increase milk production is derived through the use of new techniques in biotechnology. Implants of hormones to enhance growth and feed utilization in beef cattle have been used for many years. The entire area of biotechnology may cause safety concerns for many people. If biotechnology is to be used to its full potential to ensure a safe, abundant, and affordable food supply, it must be accepted by the public. The public's concerns must therefore be addressed and satisfied by the scientific community [17].

•NATURALLY OCCURRING TOXIC SUBSTANCES IN FOODS

Although the term *natural* is always associated with safety in the minds of some, certain plants and animals may contain *natural* constituents that are toxic, thereby producing gastrointestinal disturbances or even death when they are consumed in sufficient quantities. Poisonous varieties of mushrooms, mistaken for edible kinds, are a well-known example of toxic plants. Oxalic acid is a constituent of plants such as spinach and beet greens. In large amounts, these may be responsible for oxalic acid poisoning in certain individuals. A very high content of oxalic acid is found in leaves of the rhubarb plant.

Solanine is a water-soluble toxin that may be present in potatoes and increases during sprouting or exposure to light. This toxin is found principally in the skin and in the green-colored portion directly underneath the skin, which may be removed by paring. Recently, potato-peel products have increased in popularity. A wide range in solanine content of both raw and cooked potato peels has been reported for 12 different varieties of potatoes [5]. The upper ranges in these analyses exceeded the upper safety limit of 20 milligrams per 100 grams of whole potato established for use in releasing new potato varieties. It has been recommended, therefore, that potato varieties with low solanine concentrations be chosen for use in the preparation of commercial peel products.

Some tropical fish contain poisonous substances. Ocean mussels and clams may contain a poisonous alkaloid compound at certain seasons of the year.

Goitrogen   a substance that is capable of causing enlargement (goiter) of the thyroid gland in the neck area

Protease   an enzyme that breaks down or digests proteins

Agglutination   the sticking together as with glue

Many toxic substances are found in tiny amounts in plant foods as normal components. Plants often manufacture toxins to protect themselves from environmental predators. It has been suggested that we ingest thousands of times more "natural pesticides" than we do man-made pesticides. Vegetables of the cabbage family contain substances called **goitrogens** that can depress the activity of the thyroid gland. Legumes contain **protease** inhibitors that may interfere with the digestion of proteins. These inhibitors are destroyed by cooking. Substances called hemagglutinins, which cause **agglutination** of red blood cells, are found in soybeans, peanuts, kidney beans, and wax beans. Most of these substances are destroyed or inactivated in the human digestive tract. Seeds of the Senecio genus, which grow among and may contaminate the harvest of grains, contain substances that are toxic to the liver.

Many foods doubtless contain small amounts of naturally occurring substances that could cause toxicity if eaten in excess. However, the amounts of oxalic acid, solanine, and several other natural toxins in foods have not been shown to be toxic in the amounts usually eaten. These toxins, therefore, represent only minor hazards [7, 22].

STUDY QUESTIONS

1. Name three general types of potential hazards that are associated with food.
2. Explain the difference between a *food infection* and a *food intoxication*. Give examples of each.
3. For each type of food poisoning listed below, (a) indicate if it is an infection or an intoxication, (b) list the usual symptoms, (c) list the types of food most likely to be involved, and (d) suggest measures that should prevent the occurrence of an outbreak of illness.
   Salmonellosis
   Campylobacter jejuni poisoning
   Escherichia coli 0157:H7 poisoning
   Yersiniosis
   Listeriosis
   Staphylococcal poisoning
   Clostridium perfringens poisoning
   Botulism
4. Describe some other types of bacterial food poisoning.
5. Why is it extremely important that food handlers observe appropriate sanitary procedures when working with food? Explain.
6. What is *trichinosis*? How is it caused? How might it be prevented?
7. Describe examples of food-related illness resulting from
   a. environmental contaminants.
   b. naturally occurring toxicants.
   c. mycotoxins.

REFERENCES

1. Beard, T. D. 1991. HACCP and the home: The need for consumer education. *Food Technology 45*, 123 (No. 6).
2. Beuchat, L. R. 1982. *Vibrio parahaemolyticus*: Public health significance. *Food Technology 36*, 80 (No. 3).
3. Blaser, M. J. 1982. *Campylobacter jejuni* and food. *Food Technology 36*, 89 (No. 3).

4. Bryan, F. L. 1990. Application of HACCP to ready-to-eat chilled foods. *Food Technology 44*, 70 (No. 7).

5. Bushway, R. J., J. L. Bureau, and D. F. McGann. 1983. Alpha-chaconine and alpha-solanine content of potato peels and potato-peel products. *Journal of Food Science 48*, 84.

6. Chipley, J. R. and M. L. Cremer. 1980. Microbiological problems in the foodservice industry. *Food Technology 34*, 59 (No. 10).

7. Crocco, S. 1981. Potato sprouts and greening potatoes: Potential toxic reaction. *Journal of the American Medical Association 245*, 625.

8. Doyle, M. P. 1991. A new generation of food-borne pathogens. *Contemporary Nutrition* (General Mills Nutrition Department) *16*, No. 6.

9. Dunaif, G. E. and E. P. Krysinski. 1992. Managing the pesticide challenge: A food processor's model. *Food Technology 46*, 72 (No. 3).

10. Eom, Y. S. 1992. Consumers respond to information about pesticide residues. *Food Review 15*, 6 (No. 3).

11. *Food Safety for the Family*. 1982. Washington, DC: U.S. Department of Agriculture, Food Safety and Inspection Service.

12. Foster, E. M. 1989. A half century of food microbiology. *Food Technology 43*, 208 (No. 9).

13. Foster, E. M. 1978. Food-borne hazards of microbial origin. *Federation Proceedings 37*, 2577.

14. Giese, J. 1993. *Salmonella* reduction process receives approval. *Food Technology 47*, 110 (No. 1).

15. Greger, J. L. and M. Baier. 1981. Tin and iron content of canned and bottled foods. *Journal of Food Science 46*, 1751.

16. Hardt-English, P., G. York, R. Stier, and P. Cocotas. 1990. Staphylococcal food poisoning outbreaks caused by canned mushrooms from China. *Food Technology 44*, 76 (No. 12).

17. Harlander, S. K. 1991. Social, moral, and ethical issues in food biotechnology. *Food Technology 45*, 152 (No. 5).

18. Hatheway, C. L., D. N. Whaley, and V. R. Dowell, Jr. 1980. Epidemiological aspects of *Clostridium perfringens* food-borne illness. *Food Technology 34*, 77 (No. 4).

19. Higashi, G. I. 1985. Food-borne parasites transmitted to man from fish and other aquatic foods. *Food Technology 39*, 69 (No. 3).

20. Institute of Food Technologists' Expert Panel on Food Safety and Nutrition. 1988. Bacteria associated with food-borne diseases. *Food Technology 42*, 181 (No. 4).

21. Institute of Food Technologists' Expert Panel on Food Safety and Nutrition. 1992. Government regulation of food safety: Interaction of scientific and societal forces. *Food Technology 46*, 73 (No. 1).

22. Institute of Food Technologists' Expert Panel on Food Safety and Nutrition and the Committee on Public Information. 1975. Naturally occurring toxicants in foods. *Food Technology 29*, 67 (No. 3).

23. Institute of Food Technologists. 1990. Organically grown foods. *Food Technology 44*, 26 (No. 6).

24. Institute of Food Technologists' Expert Panel on Food Safety and Nutrition. 1988. Virus transmission via foods. *Food Technology 42*, 241 (No. 10).

25. Jackson, G. J. 1990. Parasitic protozoa and worms relevant to the U.S. *Food Technology 44*, 106 (No. 5).

26. Lindsay, R. E., W. A. Krissinger, and B. F. Fields. 1986. Microwave vs. conventional oven cooking of chicken: Relationship of internal temperature to surface contamination by *Salmonella typhimurium*. *Journal of the American Dietetic Association 86*, 373.

27. Mermelstein, N. H. 1993. Controlling *E. coli* 0157:H7 in meat. *Food Technology 47*, 90 (No. 4).

28. Munro, I. C. and S. M. Charbonneau. 1978. Environmental contaminants. *Federal Proceedings 37*, 2582.

29. Murrell, K. D. 1985. Strategies for the control of human trichinosis transmitted by pork. *Food Technology 39*, 65 (No. 3).

30. Mycotoxins and food safety. 1986. *Food Technology 40*, 59 (No. 5).

31. New bacteria in the news. 1986. *Food Technology 40*, 16 (No. 8).

32. Pennington, J. A. T. 1983. Revision of the total diet study list and diets. *Journal of the American Dietetic Association 82*, 166.

33. Ryser, E. T. and E. H. Marth. 1989. "New" food-borne pathogens of public health significance. *Journal of the American Dietetic Association 89*, 948.

34. Saguy, I. 1992. Simulated growth of *Listeria monocytogenes* in refrigerated foods stored at variable temperatures. *Food Technology 46*, 69 (No. 3).

35. Schaffner, R. M. 1982. Government's role in preventing food-borne botulism. *Food Technology 36*, 87 (No. 12).

36. Schantz, P. M. 1983. Trichinosis in the United States: 1947–1981. *Food Technology 37*, 83 (No. 3).

37. Scherer, C. W. 1991. Strategies for communicating risks to the public. *Food Technology 45*, 110 (No. 10).

38. Sperber, W. H. 1991. The modern HACCP system. *Food Technology 45*, 116 (No. 6).

39. U.S. Department of Agriculture. 1989. *Complete Guide to Home Canning*. Agriculture Information Bulletin No. 539. Washington, DC: U.S. Government Printing Office.

40. Williamson, D. M., R. B. Gravani, and H. T. Lawless. 1992. Correlating food safety knowledge with home food-preparation practices. *Food Technology 46*, 94 (No. 5).

41. Wood, R. C., K. L. MacDonald, and M. T. Osterholm. 1992. *Campylobacter* enteritis outbreaks associated with drinking raw milk during youth activities: A 10-year review of outbreaks in the United States. *Journal of the American Medical Association 268*, 3228.

42. Woodburn, M. and C. Raab. 1993. Product care directions on food labels: Status and needs. *Food Technology 47*, 97 (No. 2).

Food Regulations and Standards

4

There are thousands of different food items on the supermarket shelves from which to choose. As we make our selections, we all like to feel that we are getting our money's worth. But how can we be assured that we are receiving the quality and safety for which we are paying?

Most food processors and manufacturers work hard to establish and maintain reputations for good quality in their products: they want to keep customers coming back again and again. The government also plays an important role in assuring quality and safety in the foods we purchase. Government intervention in this area is not new. Throughout history, civilized societies have established various controls over the integrity of their food supplies [6]. English laws concerning food were brought to America with early settlers and later enacted as state laws. Since the passage of the first Pure Food and Drug Act of 1906, the role of the federal government in this area has expanded. Various federal agencies now have responsibilities to regulate the food supply including the setting of standards, control of adulteration and misbranding, promotion of **Good Manufacturing Practices** (GMPs), approval of **food additives**, **inspection**, and **grading**. By setting standards and regulations, the government is attempting to implement the constitutional mandate to "promote the general welfare."

•FOOD AND DRUG ADMINISTRATION

The U.S. Food and Drug Administration (FDA) is housed in the U.S. Department of Health and Human Services and includes a Center for Food Safety and Applied Nutrition with responsibility for all policy and enforcement having to do with human food. The federal Food, Drug, and Cosmetic Act of 1938 and its several amendments are administered by the FDA, which regulates all food except red meats, poultry, and eggs. These are the responsibility of the U.S. Department of Agriculture (USDA). Much activity in the FDA is also devoted to the Fair Packaging and Labeling Act and to implementation of the 1990 Nutrition Labeling and Education Act (discussed in Chapter 2). Sanitation in food

CHAPTER OUTLINE

FOOD AND DRUG
ADMINISTRATION
DEPARTMENT OF AGRICULTURE
DEPARTMENT OF COMMERCE
FEDERAL TRADE COMMISSION
STATE AND LOCAL AGENCIES
INTERNATIONAL STANDARDS

Good Manufacturing Practices recommended rules for maintaining sanitation, safety, and quality assurance to be followed in a food processing plant

Food additive a substance, other than usual ingredients, that is added to a food product for a specific purpose, for example, flavoring, preserving, stabilizing, thickening

Inspection the examining of food products or processes carefully and critically in order to assure proper sanitary practices, labeling, and/or safety for the consumer

Grading the examining of food products and classifying them according to quality, such as Grade A, B, or C, based on defined standards

processing plants, restaurant operations, and interstate travel facilities also comes under the jurisdiction of the FDA.

Under the Food, Drug, and Cosmetic Act, the FDA sets three kinds of mandatory standards for products being shipped across state lines: standards of identity, standards of minimum quality, and standards of fill of container.

Standards of Identity

The basic purpose for setting standards of identity for food products is to "promote honesty and fair dealing in the interest of consumers." Standards of identity define what a food product must be or must contain if it is to be legally labeled and sold by its common or usual name. The standard also lists optional ingredients that may be used but are not required. For example, the standard of identity for mayonnaise specifies the ingredients it must contain—oil, egg, and an acid component—and requires that at least 65 percent oil be included in the finished dressing.

Standards of identity have been established for a large number of food products, including bakery and cereal products, cacao products, canned fruits and vegetables, fruit butters and preserves, fish and shellfish, eggs and egg products, margarine, nut products, dressings for foods, cheeses and cheese products, milk and cream, frozen desserts, macaroni and noodle products, and tomato products. Only after many public hearings and much discussion were the standards set. Both food industry representatives and consumers had ample opportunities for input.

Since 1970, the FDA has not promulgated any new standards of identity. In fact, in order to permit the use of new approved food additives, such as emulsifiers, thickeners, and so on, without amending existing standards each time, the FDA has increased the flexibility of many standards. It has done so by modifying the requirement to specifically list certain processing aids so that *any* "safe and suitable" functional ingredient is permitted [7]. The FDA has also defined *imitation* solely in terms of nutritional inferiority. That is, it must be labeled "imitation" only if it is not nutritionally equal to the food that it is imitating or replacing. The FDA has emphasized that a new food product, rather than being called "imitation," should have its own descriptive name. Essentially, all foods, including those with a standard of identity, are subject to nutrition labeling under the 1990 Nutrition Labeling and Education Act.

Standards of Minimum Quality

Standards of minimum quality have been set for a number of canned fruits and vegetables specifying minimum requirements for such characteristics as tenderness, color, and freedom from defects. If a food does not meet the minimum standard, it must be labeled "below standard in quality; good food—not high grade." Other words may be substituted for the second part of the statement to show in what respect the product is substandard, such as "below standard in quality; excessively broken." The consumer seldom sees a product with a substandard label at retail stores. Standards of minimum quality, as well as other grade standards, are indications of quality characteristics and are not concerned specifically with safety. Both lower and higher grade products are safe to eat.

Standards of Fill of Container

Standards of fill of container state, for certain processed foods, how full a food container must be. These standards aim to avoid deception by preventing the selling of air or water in place of food. They are needed especially for products that are made up of a number of pieces packed in a liquid, such as various canned vegetables, or for products, such as nuts and ready-to-eat cereals, that shake down after filling.

Sanitation Requirements

One of the basic purposes of the Food, Drug, and Cosmetic Act is the protection of the public from articles that may be deleterious, that are unclean or decomposed, or that have been exposed to unsanitary conditions that may contaminate the article with filth or render it injurious to health [15]. The law requires that foods be protected from contamination at all stages of production and that they be produced in sanitary facilities. Foods may not be distributed if they contain repulsive or offensive matter considered to be filth, whether or not it poses actual physical danger to an individual. Filth includes rodent hair and excreta, insects or insect parts and excreta, maggots, larvae, pollution from the excrement of humans and animals, or other materials that, because of their repulsiveness, would not be eaten knowingly.

The Food, Drug, and Cosmetic Act declared any food prepared, packed, or held under unsanitary conditions to be adulterated [14]. Therefore, the FDA has produced directives called *current Good Manufacturing Practices* (GMPs). These establish regulations regarding many facets of the food-manufacturing process, including requirements for cleanliness; education, training, and supervision of workers; design and ease of cleaning and maintenance of buildings, facilities, and equipment; and adequate record keeping to assure quality control. The current Good Manufacturing Practices also indicate errors to be avoided to ensure sanitary products.

Labeling

The FDA shares responsibility with the Federal Trade Commission for enforcing fair packaging and labeling laws. The USDA is also involved for some foods.

If a food is packaged, the following must appear on the label:

1. Name and address of the manufacturer, packer, or distributor.
2. Accurate statement of the net amount of food in the package—weight, measure, or count.
3. Common or usual name of the product, i.e., peaches, and the form, i.e., sliced, whole, or chopped.
4. Ingredients listed by their common names in order of their predominance by weight.
5. Nutrition information, with few exceptions, as mandated by the 1990 Nutrition Labeling and Education Act (discussed in Chapter 2).

Food additives are required to be listed as ingredients. Spices and flavors may be simply mentioned as such, without each specific item being named. The

Certified colors   synthetic colors tested on a batch-by-batch basis and certified by the FDA as having met set standards

Protein hydrolysate   the resulting mixture when a protein is broken down or hydrolyzed, by an enzyme or other means, to smaller units called peptides and amino acids

Caseinate   a protein salt derived from milk

presence of any artificial colors or flavors must be indicated as such. **Certified colors**, such as FD&C Yellow No. 5, commonly known as tartrazine, must be listed by name. The original source of **protein hydrolysates** must be stated. **Caseinate** must be identified as a milk derivative in foods that claim to be nondairy, such as coffee whiteners. Beverages that are claimed to contain juice must have the total percentage of juice identified on the label [12].

Food Additives

The use of chemical additives in foods is not new, but their roles have become more prominent in recent years as the production of processed convenience foods has increased. At the same time, several issues concerning food safety have been raised, particularly by consumer groups. The popular press and television news programs have paid particular attention to such alleged hazards in the U.S. food supply as pesticide residues on fruit crops and animal drug residues in meat and poultry. Scientific issues that previously were discussed only in journals and other scholarly publications today often make headlines, with the scientific terminology translated into the vernacular. If such information is effectively reported from a sound scientific basis, it provides the advantage of educating consumers so that they can make informed choices. At the same time, it also creates challenges for food professionals both in industry and governmental regulatory agencies [19]. It is important that accurate information reach the public and that scientifically unjustified concern and fear not be created.

Definitions

What is a food additive? Under a broad definition, it is any substance that becomes part of a food product either when it is added *intentionally* or when it *incidentally* becomes part of the food. Examples of incidental additives are pesticide residues that may remain on farm produce and substances that may migrate from the packaging material into a food. In either of these cases, the amount of additive involved is extremely small [1].

The legal definition of *food additive* extends only to those substances that must receive special approval from the FDA after they have been thoroughly tested for safety and before they can be used in food. In addition to these specially tested and approved additives, the FDA maintains an official list of other substances added to foods that are "generally recognized as safe" (GRAS) for human consumption by experts in the field. Although GRAS substances do not require the detailed clearance for safety that is specified for legally defined food additives, they are evaluated and reevaluated for safety by the FDA on a case-by-case basis. Occasionally, substances may be removed from the GRAS list as more sophisticated analytical tools and methodologies for evaluation of safety are developed. It should be emphasized that there is an ongoing process of reassessment and evaluation by the FDA on all issues of food safety, including additives.

Justifiable Uses

An additive is intentionally used for one or more of the following general purposes.

1. To maintain or improve nutritional quality. Vitamins and minerals are used to fortify some foods when these nutrients may have been lost in processing or when they might be otherwise lacking in the usual diet.

2. To enhance the keeping quality with consequent reduction in food waste. Freshness may be maintained by the use of additives to retard spoilage, preserve natural color and flavor, and retard the development of rancid odors in fats.
3. To enhance the attractiveness of foods. Many additives will make food look and taste better. Natural and synthetic flavoring agents, colors, and flavor enhancers serve this purpose.
4. To provide essential aids in processing or preparation. A large variety of additives are used to give body and texture to foods as stabilizers or thickeners, to distribute water-soluble and fat-soluble particles evenly together as emulsifiers, to control the acidity or alkalinity, to retain moisture as humectants, to leaven or make rise many baked products, to prevent caking or lumping, and to perform other functions.

Legislation

The federal Food, Drug, and Cosmetic Act governs the use of additives in food entering interstate commerce. However, state and local governments are responsible for regulations concerning the safety and quality of foods produced and sold within a state.

There is an interesting history behind the passing of legislation dealing with food additives and food safety. Harvey Wiley, the chief chemist of the USDA, was an early pioneer, in the late 1800s and early 1900s, involved in the struggle for adequate laws to protect the public's food supply (Figure 4.1). Wiley tried various tactics over many years, including feeding measured amounts of chemical preservatives to twelve young volunteers in a so-called "poison squad" experiment, to convince Congress and the president of the need for pure food legislation. Finally, in 1906, the first Pure Food and Drug Act was passed. It was a beginning.

The original act was completely revised in 1938 and renamed the Food, Drug, and Cosmetic Act. Among other things, the 1938 law required truthful labeling of additives. Several amendments to the Food, Drug, and Cosmetic Act

FIGURE 4.1
Dr. Harvey W. Wiley climaxed 20 years of scientific investigation with his "Poison Squad" experiment in 1903. He fed weighed amounts of chemical preservatives to 12 young volunteers. This project caused nationwide concern and helped to dramatize the need for pure food legislation. (Courtesy of the U.S. Department of Health and Human Services, Food and Drug Administration)

have been passed to strengthen the law and keep up with changes in food technology and medical science.

Pesticide Amendment.   The Miller Pesticide Amendment of 1954 was passed to establish a procedure for setting safe levels or tolerances for pesticide residues on fresh fruits, vegetables, and other raw agricultural commodities. Growers were using many new pesticides to produce more and better crops, and some of these chemicals left a residue on the food even at harvest. The safety of these incidental residues had to be determined and regulations set.

Pesticides are now regulated, and tolerances for residues on raw agricultural products are set by the Environmental Protection Agency (EPA). It establishes maximum allowable levels for pesticide residues after careful consideration of the risks and benefits. The EPA also operates under the more recently passed Federal Fungicide, Rodenticide, and Insecticide Act.

When a pesticide residue has been shown to concentrate in a processed food to levels higher than those found on the original agricultural product before processing, the EPA treats the residue as a food additive. For example, when grapes are dried and become raisins, any pesticide residue present on the fresh grapes may be concentrated. As food additives, these pesticide residues are subject to the Delaney clause in the Food Additives Amendment that was passed in 1958. The Delaney clause is discussed later in this section.

Food Additives Amendment.   The 1958 Food Additives Amendment was designed to protect the public by requiring approval of new additives *before* they can be used in foods. The responsibility for proving the safety of additives rests with the manufacturer, which must file a petition with the FDA showing the results of extensive tests for safety. The FDA must approve the additive as safe before it can be marketed. The FDA also prescribes the types of foods in which the additive can be used and specifies labeling directions. Additives in meat and poultry products are under the jurisdiction of the USDA.

Color Additives Amendment.   All coloring substances added to foods are regulated under the Color Additives Amendment, passed in 1960. Rules regarding color additives were made stronger under this amendment, and previously approved certified colors were retested.

Delaney Clause and Safety.   Included in the Food Additives Amendment is a special clause carrying the name of Congressman James J. Delaney, who sponsored it. A similar provision is contained in the Color Additives Amendment. The Delaney clause provides "that no additive shall be deemed to be safe if it is found to induce cancer when ingested by man or animal, or if it is found, after tests which are appropriate for the evaluation of the safety of food additives, to induce cancer in man or animals" [21].

The Delaney clause has created a great deal of discussion and disagreement in the years since the legislation was passed. Science, in relation to the study of cancer and carcinogenesis (cancer development), has changed, and the causes and nature of cancer have become better understood. Many think that an absolute prohibition of carcinogens under the Delaney clause is unnecessarily restrictive. No distinction is made between cancer in humans or experimental animals nor is there a specification on the amount of the substance to be consumed. As an alternative to strict enforcement, the FDA could estimate the risk that might result from exposure of humans to chemicals that show a carcinogenic effect in animals. In this assessment, the FDA could conclude that in some cases the estimated risk to the public is insignificant, if it exists at all [13, 20]. This would be a policy applying a negligible risk standard to decisions concerning the approval of food additives, including pesticide residues on foods. Some scientists have suggested that the debate about the Delaney clause should be viewed as a statutory issue, having to do only with the fine points of the law, rather than a true food safety issue, since the health benefits provided by a strict interpretation of the clause would appear to be trivial [21].

Actually, there is no way in which the *absolute* safety of a food additive, either a legally defined or GRAS substance, can be guaranteed [8]. Clearance through the FDA should ensure that the risk of adverse effects is minimal. However, benefits from the use of additives must also be considered— improved shelf life for many foods and reduced distribution costs, increased aesthetic qualities and convenience, and improved nutritional value. Risk versus benefit must be evaluated. Better ways to do this are being investigated by government, industry, and consumer groups [18, 20].

Food Biotechnology. The FDA has developed a food biotechnology policy for foods derived from genetically modified plants. This policy is science-based and reflects the FDA's understanding that changes in food composition can be accomplished using new genetic engineering techniques. In many cases, the changes in plants involve familiar substances—proteins, carbohydrates, and fats that raise no new safety questions. However, if substances that have no history of safe use in foods are produced, they will be subject to the same careful testing and approval used to ensure the safety of all food additives [9].

Additives Used

Each approved additive must serve a useful purpose. It cannot be placed in food to conceal damage or spoilage or to deceive the consumer. There are many different, specific functions of food additives but most additives may be grouped into classes based on similar function. Some of the more important classes or types of additives follow. Examples of each class are given in Table 4.1.

Nutrient Supplements. Vitamins and minerals are often added to processed foods either to restore or to improve their nutritive value. Examples include the enrichment of bread and cereals, the addition of iodine to salt, and the fortification of milk with vitamin D. Some vitamins—for example vitamins C and E—also play functional roles such as acting as **antioxidants**.

Preservatives. Antioxidants are a group of preservatives. Fatty foods are particularly susceptible to spoilage as **rancidity** develops with unpleasant off-odors. Some antioxidants retard the development of rancidity. Another type of antioxidant may prevent **enzymatic oxidative browning** in fresh fruits and vegetables. Vitamin C is an effective antioxidant in this regard.

Antimicrobial agents are another group of preservatives. These additives prevent or inhibit spoilage caused by such microorganisms as molds and bacte-

Antioxidant   a substance that can stop an oxidation reaction

Rancidity   a special type of spoilage in fats that involves oxidation of unsaturated fatty acids

Enzymatic oxidative browning the browning of cut surfaces of certain fruits and vegetables catalyzed by enzymes in the presence of oxygen

Antimicrobial agents   substances that prevent or inhibit the growth of microorganisms

TABLE 4.1
Additives in Use for Various Types of Foods

Type or Class	Additive	Food in Which Used
Nutrients	Thiamin Niacin Riboflavin Iron	Flour, breads, and cereals in enrichment process
	Vitamin C	Fruit juices, fruit drinks, and dehydrated potatoes
Antioxidants	Butylated hydroxyanisole (BHA) Butylated hydroxytoluene (BHT) Tertiary butylated hydroxyquinone (TBHQ)	Animal fats such as lard, ready-to-eat cereals, crackers, and potato chips to retard rancidity
	Ascorbic acid (vitamin C)	Frozen peaches and apples to prevent browning
Antimicrobial agents	Propionates	Bread to retard molding and development of "rope"
	Benzoates	Carbonated beverages, fruit drinks, and margarine
Coloring agents	ß-carotene Certified colors: Citrus Red No. 2, Red No. 3, Green No. 3, and Yellow No. 6 Annato	Margarine, butter, and cheese Limited to use on skins of oranges Candies, cereals, soft drinks, and bakery goods Cheese
Flavoring agents	Benzaldehyde Vanilla Monosodium glutamate (MSG)	Almond flavoring Ice cream, baked goods, and candies Soups and Chinese foods as a flavor enhancer
Emulsifiers	Mono- and diglycerides Lecithin	Margarines and shortenings Bakery products, chocolate, and frozen desserts
Stabilizers and thickeners	Alginates Carrageenan Pectin Modified starches	Ice cream Evaporated milk, sour cream, and cheese foods Fruit jellies, confections, and sherbets Puddings and pie fillings
Sequestrants	Ethylenediamine tetraacetic acid (EDTA)	Wine and cider
Humectants	Glycerine Sorbitol	Marshmallows, flaked coconut, and cake icings
Anticaking agents	Calcium silicate Magnesium carbonate	Table salt, powdered sugar, and baking powder
Bleaching and maturing agents	Chlorine Chlorine dioxide Benzoyl peroxide (bleaches only)	Cake flour All-purpose flour All-purpose flour
Acids, alkalies, and buffers	Citric acid and its salts	Soft drinks
	Acetic acid Sodium bicarbonate Sodium hydroxide	Processed cheese Baking powders Dutch processed cocoa, pretzels (glazing)
Alternative sweetners	Aspartame	Lemonade and cocoa mixes, ready-to-eat cereals, and many other foods
	Acesulfame-K	Dry beverage mixes and chewing gum
Fat replacers	Sucrose polyester (as Olestra)* Microparticulated protein (as Simplesse®)†	Ice cream, sour cream, salad dressing, and margarine
	Hydrocolloids such as gums and starch derivatives†	Salad dressings, frozen desserts, beverage mixes, and many other foods
Bulking agents	Polydextrose	Baked goods, confections, puddings, and other foods

* FDA approval pending   † GRAS substances

ria. The effectiveness of such preservation methods as refrigeration may be enhanced by the judicious use of certain antimicrobial agents.

Coloring Agents. Proper use of color makes foods more visually appealing and corrects natural variations and irregularities. Artificial colors must be certified to meet specifications set by the FDA on a batch-by-batch basis. Some natural pigments, such as **carotenoids**, are available for use in foods, although they are generally less stable than artificial colors.

Flavoring Materials. A wide variety of substances are used to improve the flavor of processed foods. These include natural extractives and **essential oils** as well as synthetic or artificial flavorings. Flavor enhancers are also used. Flavorings, which include herbs and spices, make up the largest group of intentional additives.

Emulsifiers. **Emulsifiers** are substances widely used to mix fat and water-soluble substances uniformly together in the making and stabilizing of **emulsions**. They are also used to stabilize foams and suspensions.

Stabilizers and Thickeners. Texture and body are important characteristics of many foods. A variety of stabilizers and thickeners are used to achieve desired smoothness and consistency, including many vegetable gums, such as carrageenan, as well as a number of starch products.

Sequestrants. **Sequestrants** are used to bind (chelate) small amounts of metals, such as iron and copper, that may have undesirable effects on flavor or appearance.

Humectants and Anticaking Agents. **Humectants** are used to retain moisture and keep certain foods soft. Some humectants are added to finely powdered or crystalline foods to prevent caking as moisture is absorbed.

Bleaching and Maturing Agents. The baking properties of wheat flours are improved by the addition of certain oxidizing agents (**maturing agents**). Many of these also have a bleaching effect.

Acids, Alkalis, and Buffers. Acidity or alkalinity is very important in many processed foods. Acids, alkalis, and **buffers** are used to adjust and control the pH. The alkaline salt, sodium bicarbonate or baking soda, is also used to produce carbon dioxide gas to leaven baked products.

Alternative Sweeteners. A sweet tooth has apparently always been part of the human anatomy. The harvesting of honey and sugar cane has a very long history. Substitutes for the taste of caloric sweeteners, including sucrose (table sugar), honey, and corn syrups, have been developed; however, only in this century. Three alternative sweeteners presently have approval from the FDA: saccharin, aspartame, and acesulfame-K. Sucralose has been approved in Canada, and a petition to the U.S. FDA for its approval is pending. Because of

Carotenoids yellow-orange-red, fat-soluble pigments found in some plant materials such as fruits and vegetables

Essential oils concentrated flavoring oils extracted from food substances, such as oil of orange or oil of peppermint

Emulsifier a substance that acts as a bridge between two immiscible liquids and allows the formation of an emulsion

Emulsion the dispersion of one substance within another with which it ordinarily does not mix (is immiscible)

Sequestrant a substance that binds or isolates other substances; for example, some molecules can tie up trace amounts of minerals that may have unwanted effects in a food product

Humectant a substance that retains moisture

Maturing agent a substance that brings about some oxidative changes in white flour and improves its baking properties

Buffer a substance that resists change in acidity or alkalinity

increased health and nutrition concerns, the market for reduced-calorie foods has expanded greatly in recent years, thus increasing the demand for new alternative sweeteners.

Fat Replacers.   Professional groups' and public health agencies' current stress on the important relationship between high fat intake and the risks of developing coronary heart disease and some cancers has generated much interest in low-fat substitutes for many traditional high-fat food products. Millions of consumers are trying to change their high-fat consumption habits. The food industry is thus motivated to develop substances that can replace fat but leave flavor and texture unchanged or minimally changed. Some of the approved fat replacers are GRAS (generally regarded as safe), while others require special approval by the FDA as food additives.

Carbohydrate-based fat replacers include cellulose, various gums such as xanthan gum and carrageenan, dextrins, and modified starches. Microparticulated protein, whose trade name is Simplesse®, is a protein-based fat replacer produced from whey protein or milk and egg protein. Some emulsifiers can also replace part of the fat in a food product [5].

Sucrose polyesters (Olestra) are nonabsorbable and thus noncaloric fat replacers. They may be used in cooking oils and shortenings, commercial frying, and snack foods [5]. Their approval by the FDA is pending.

Bulking Agents.   Polydextrose contains only one calorie per gram and helps to add texture and body when fat and sugar are reduced in some food products. Some of the modified starches also add body and texture to low-fat products. When used to provide texture and body in reduced-fat or reduced-sugar food products, these substances are called *bulking agents*.

•DEPARTMENT OF AGRICULTURE

The USDA is involved with food processing and marketing in a number of different ways. Under the auspices of the Food Safety and Inspection Service, the USDA inspects meat and poultry products for wholesomeness and truthful labeling, administering the Federal Meat Inspection Act and the Poultry Products Inspection Act (see Figure 4.2).

The Agricultural Marketing Service is responsible for administering the Egg Products Inspection Act, which requires inspection of all plants that process liquid, dried, or frozen egg products. It also offers grading services for meat, poultry, fruits, vegetables, and dairy products.

Official certification that a particular food product meets a predetermined standard of quality is available through grading services. These services are generally voluntarily requested but are sometimes required on a local level or for a particular industry program. They are performed by USDA inspectors but paid for by the manufacturer requesting the service. Grading may be done for meat, poultry, eggs, dairy products, some fish, nuts, rice, and fresh fruits and vegetables. The grading of each of these products is discussed in more detail in other chapters. Only a general discussion of grading and inspection is given here.

Grade standards were originally established to aid in wholesale food trading, but recently many consumer grades have become useful. These consumer grades apply to small units of food that are usually sold in a retail market. The quality of the food at the time it was graded is indicated by the grade on the package, but no allowance is made for changes in quality that may occur during the handling and storage involved in the marketing process. At any rate, graded foods offer us a choice of quality and enable us to pick the one that is most suitable for the intended use.

Grade a symbol, such as Grade A or No. 1, that indicates that the food product carrying this label has met specified predetermined standards

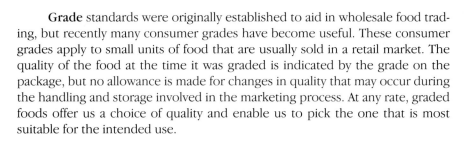

FIGURE 4.2
U.S. Department of Agriculture meat inspectors, under regulations of the Federal Meat Inspection Act, examine beef animals before slaughter (*top*) and beef carcasses (*bottom*) for wholesomeness and freedom from disease. (Courtesy of the U.S. Department of Agriculture)

Grade standards are defined to cover the entire range of quality of a food product. Some products are more variable in quality than are other products and therefore may require more grades. For example, there are eight grades for beef but only three for chicken. Most federal grades for consumers are preceded by the letters *U.S.* and are enclosed in a shield-shaped mark (Figure 4.3).

Since the grade standards for various products were developed at different times, there is variance in the naming systems. For instance, the top-quality grade for cantaloupes is U.S. Fancy; for beets, it is U.S. No. 1; for carrots, it is U.S. Grade A; and for celery, it is U.S. Extra No. 1. U.S. Grades A, B, and C are used on poultry and on canned fruits and vegetables. To help achieve a more uniform grading system, the USDA issued a policy statement that when future standards for fresh fruits, vegetables, and nuts are issued, revised, or amended, only the classifications U.S. Fancy and Grades 1, 2, and 3 may be used.

Even though a product may have been officially graded, the law still does not require that a designation of grade appear on the label. If the grade shield is used on a food product, however, the food must have been officially graded.

Foods are *inspected* for grade determination, or it might be said that they are "inspected for grade." However, the term *inspection* has different meanings when applied to various commodities. The USDA administers a mandatory *inspection* program for meat and poultry that is sold in interstate commerce and in those states that do not have an inspection program of their own that is equal to the federal program. This inspection is for wholesomeness (safety) and proper labeling; it not for grading. The meat and poultry must be from healthy animals or birds, be processed under strict sanitary conditions, and be truthfully labeled. All meat and poultry must be inspected before it can be graded. The inspection determines wholesomeness; the grading determines quality.

Food grading aids foodservice managers as they write specifications for the purchasing of various food products. The required quality of the product being ordered can be easily specified by grade, since the grade standards are known to both purchasers and vendors. Food grading is also an aid available to retail shoppers to help them more effectively meet their needs and desires. However, the results of two national surveys [2, 15] of U.S. households in 1970 and 1980 showed that although there was a general awareness of the food grading program and its purpose, only 10 to 25 percent of the respondents knew specific details. The 1980 respondents were less knowledgeable about

Butter

Instant
nonfat
dry milk

Eggs

Poultry

Fresh fruits
& vegetables

Meat

FIGURE 4.3

Shield-shaped marks used by the U.S. Department of Agriculture in grading food products.
(Courtesy of the U.S. Department of Agriculture)

the system and more often confused regarding grading versus inspection than were their 1970 counterparts. These consumers would find the system more useful if it were simpler and more uniform and if information about it were more readily available. More consumer education concerning food quality standards and grades would undoubtedly be helpful.

National **organic food** standards were established under the provisions of the 1990 Farm Bill [11]. Under these standards, growers cannot generally use synthetic materials or natural materials that are harmful to human health in production. A National Organic Standards Board proposes allowable and prohibited substances. These proposals are reviewed and submitted for public comment, resulting in a national list of exemptions and prohibitions. The board may also make recommendations concerning residue testing in the foods and allowable tolerance levels. Standards define for consumers what organic foods are and help them decide whether they want to pay a premium price for these products. With annual sales of $1 billion, the organic food industry has become an important component of the U.S. food system.

Organic foods foods grown and/or produced under conditions that replenish and maintain soil fertility, use only nationally approved materials in their production, and have verifiable records of the production system

•DEPARTMENT OF COMMERCE

The National Marine Fisheries Service in the U.S. Department of Commerce offers voluntary, fee-for-service inspections to fishery product processors [17]. Plant sanitation inspection, inspection of fish products for wholesomeness, and grading of fish are included in this service. Such products as frozen fish fillets and steaks, frozen raw breaded and precooked fish portions, and fish sticks are covered by grade standards.

•FEDERAL TRADE COMMISSION

The Federal Trade Commission (FTC) is an independent law enforcement agency charged with promoting free and fair competition in the marketplace. One of the major activities of the FTC is ensuring that fair and honest competition is allowed in the marketing of food products. The FTC attempts to protect the consumer from false or misleading advertising and misbranding, and shares with the FDA responsibility for enforcing labeling laws.

•STATE AND LOCAL AGENCIES

The legislation and regulations previously discussed in this chapter are federal, and they apply only in interstate commerce. Within each state and within cities, there are also many laws and regulations dealing with food processing, quality, and marketing. Each state has its own unique problems and attempts to solve them in individual ways, but federal laws and regulations are often used as models. States are usually organized with their own departments of agriculture and health and their own food and drug commissions. Assurance of sanitation, milk quality, inspection of meat and poultry, and protection of vegetable crops are some of the activities conducted by state organizations.

State and local governments provide for the inspection of foodservice establishments to protect the public who eat in restaurants, cafeterias, and other places where foodservice is offered. This is usually the responsibility of state, county, and city health departments, which assess cleanliness and sanitary practices. In many cases, those working with food served to the public are required to obtain food-handling permits, sometimes involving both a physical examination and education.

•INTERNATIONAL STANDARDS

In our rapidly shrinking world, international trade in food is accelerating. Particularly over the past decade, the U.S. food industry has become more and more internationalized. An ever-growing number of food products made outside the United States are appearing on our supermarket shelves, probably because consumers' attitudes toward eating are changing. Most consumers today are more open and eager to try new foods and new **cuisines**. They are buying more specialty products and becoming familiar with imported items [4].

Cuisine   a style of cooking or manner of preparing food

Increased international trade in foods has created an even greater need for international standards to safeguard the consumer's health and ensure fair food trade practices. The Codex Alimentarius Commission was established by a joint effort of the United Nations' Food and Agriculture Organization (FAO) and the World Health Organization (WHO) in 1963 to meet this need. Any nation that is a member of the FAO or the WHO may become a member of the Commission. The international standards are quite comprehensive and include a description of the product; composition requirements; additives that may be allowed, if any; sanitary handling practices; fill of container, weight, and measure or count of units; labeling provisions; and methods of analysis and sampling necessary to determine that the standard is being met [10].

After the Commission develops a recommended international standard, it sends it to the member nations for consideration of adoption. Individual members may or may not adopt the standard for themselves.

Continuing international conferences on food standards and trade help nations recognize and attempt to reduce barriers to international trade. Adjustments are being made in how the Commission standards are accepted and applied in member countries in order to increase the effectiveness of the process in influencing international food regulation [3].

STUDY QUESTIONS

1. Which agencies of the federal government are particularly involved in setting standards and regulations for food? How is each involved? Discuss this.
2. What are the distinguishing characteristics of each of the following standards?
   a. Standards of identity
   b. Standards of fill of container
   c. Standards of minimum quality
   d. U.S. grade standards
3. What sanitary requirements for food processors are included in the federal Food, Drug, and Cosmetic Act? Why does the FDA outline current Good Manufacturing Practices (GMPs) for food processors?

4. a. Define *food additives* in a general sense.
   b. What is the legal definition of *food additives*?
   c. What are *GRAS* substances?
   d. Give examples of intentional and incidental food additives.
5. Describe four justifiable uses for food additives.
6. Discuss implications for foods resulting from each of the following federal laws or amendments:
   a. 1906 Pure Food and Drug Act
   b. 1938 Federal Food, Drug, and Cosmetic Act
   c. 1954 Miller Pesticide Amendment
   d. 1958 Food Additives Amendment
   e. 1960 Color Additives Amendment
7. What is the Delaney clause and why is it important to both the food processor and the consumer?
8. How can a consumer know that a food additive is safe? Discuss this.
9. List at least ten different types or groups of food additives and give examples of specific additives for each group. Also, indicate the foods in which these additives are generally used.
10. Four pieces of information are required to be listed on food package labels. Describe these.
11. What are *organic foods*? How can a consumer know that he is truly getting organic food after he pays for it?
12. How is grading of food products useful to the wholesaler, the retailer, and the consumer? Discuss this.
13. Describe differences between *inspection* and *grading* of meat and poultry as applied to USDA regulations.
14. What is the Codex Alimentarius Commission, and what functions does it perform?

REFERENCES

1. *A Primer on Food Additives*. 1988. DHHS Publication No. (FDA) 89-2227. Washington, DC: Department of Health and Human Services.
2. *Consumer's Knowledge and Use of Government Grades for Selected Food Items*. 1970. Marketing Research Report No. 876. Washington, DC: U.S. Department of Agriculture.
3. Crawford, L. M. 1992. International food safety regulations: Improving the Codex Alimentarius process. *Food Technology 46*, 98 (No. 2).
4. Dziezak, J. D. 1987. International foods: A growing market in the U.S. *Food Technology 41*, 120 (No. 9).
5. *Fat Replacers*. 1992. Calorie Control Council, Suite 500-G, 5775 Peachtree-Dunwoody Road, Atlanta, GA 30342.
6. Hutt, P. B. 1989. Development and growth of the Food and Drug Administration. *Food Technology 43*, 280 (No. 9).
7. Hutt, P. B. 1989. Regulating the misbranding of food. *Food Technology 43*, 288 (No. 9).
8. Institute of Food Technologists' Expert Panel on Food Safety and Nutrition. 1988. The risk/benefit concept as applied to food. *Food Technology 42*, 119 (No. 3).
9. Kessler, D. A. 1992. Reinvigorating the Food and Drug Administration. *Food Technology 46*, 20 (No. 8).
10. Kimbrell, E. F. 1982. Codex Alimentarius food standards and their relevance to U.S. standards. *Food Technology 36*, 87 (No. 6).
11. Lynch, L. 1991. Congress mandates national organic food standards. *Food Review 14*, 12 (No. 1).

Chapter 4

12. Mermelstein, N. H. 1993. A new era in food labeling. *Food Technology 47*, 81 (No. 2).

13. Middlekauf, R. D. 1985. Delaney meets de minimis. *Food Technology 39*, 62 (No. 11).

14. Middlekauff, R. D. 1989. Regulating the safety of food. *Food Technology 43*, 296 (No. 9).

15. Reidy, K. Fall 1980. *Solving the Mysteries of the Food Grading System. National Food Review* NFR-12, p. 19. Washington, DC: U.S. Department of Agriculture.

16. *Requirements of Laws and Regulations Enforced by the U.S. Food and Drug Administration*. 1981. Washington, DC: U.S. Department of Health and Human Services, Public Health Service, Food and Drug Administration.

17. Sackett, I. D., Jr. 1982. Quality inspection activities of the National Marine Fisheries Service. *Food Technology 36*, 91 (No. 6).

18. Schramm, A. T. 1984. Future trends in risk analysis. *Food Technology 38*, 119 (No. 10).

19. Shank, F. R. 1992. Science in the marketplace. *Food Technology 46*, 78 (No. 2).

20. Smith, M. V. 1984. Use of risk assessment in regulatory decision making. *Food Technology 38*, 113 (No. 10).

21. Winter, C. K. 1993. Pesticide residues and the Delaney clause. *Food Technology 47*, 81 (No. 7).

Food Composition

5

Foods contain different chemical molecules that are put together in a variety of ways. It is obvious, simply by looking, that some food products are not homogeneous. From casual observation of a sliced tomato, for example, you may note skin, seeds, and soft tissues, each with a different structural appearance. Even foods that appear to be homogeneous, such as cheddar cheese, are composed of an ultrastructure that may be seen by examining a sample of the food under a microscope. With the aid of even the finest microscope, however, there are molecules and structures that still cannot be seen. Thus, foods are, indeed, very complex materials.

Determination of the amount of each of the chemical components in a food, called its chemical composition, may be made in the laboratory. Water, carbohydrates, fats, and proteins are the chemical substances found in largest amounts in foods. Enzymes are special types of proteins that are found in small amounts in unprocessed plant and animal tissues. Minerals, vitamins, acids, and many flavor substances, as well as pigments that give color, are also present in foods in very small amounts.

Comprehensive tables of food composition have been produced by compiling the results of numerous analyses of food samples done in laboratories. The U.S. Department of Agriculture (USDA) has published a series of handbooks (No. 8). Each book in the series contains information on the composition of a class of food products, for example, Dairy and Egg Products (8-1), Spices and Herbs (8-2), Baby Foods (8-3), Fats and Oils (8-4), Poultry Products (8-5), Soups, Sauces, and Gravies (8-6), Sausages and Luncheon Meats (8-7), Breakfast Cereals (8-8), and Fruits and Fruit Juices (8-9). An abbreviated bulletin on food composition is also published by the USDA [7].

It is important for us, as we study food science, to have some knowledge about the characteristics and properties, as well as the quantities, of the major chemical substances in foods. Changes may occur in these components as a food is processed and prepared. For example, water is removed in large quantities from fruits, vegetables, and meats when they are dehydrated. Fat melts and is found in the drippings when meat is roasted. Oil and water or vinegar separate from each other when the **emulsion** in mayonnaise is broken. Addition of fresh pineapple to a gelatin mixture prevents setting of the gelatin, because the

Emulsion   the dispersion of one liquid in another liquid with which it usually does not mix (is immiscible), such as oil and water

83

Peptide a variable number of amino acids joined together

Amino acids small molecules, each having both an organic acid group (—COOH) and an amino acid group (—NH₂), that are the building units for protein molecules

gelatin, which is a protein, is broken down to **peptides** or **amino acids** by an enzyme in the pineapple.

In this chapter, we briefly describe some of the chemical characteristics of the major components of foods. This information is useful for those who have not previously studied chemistry and increases understanding of the nature of foods as discussed in other chapters of this text.

•WATER

All foods, even those that appear to be quite dry, contain at least some water. Amounts present range from as low as 1 or 2 percent to as high as 98 percent, although most foods contain intermediate amounts. Table 5.1 gives the water content of selected foods. Examples of foods that are high in water are raw vegetables and juicy fruits. Fresh greens contain about 96 percent water, and watermelon has about 93 percent. Crackers, an example of low-moisture food, usually contain only 2 to 4 percent water.

TABLE 5.1
Water Content of Selected Foods

Food	Water Content %
Lettuce, iceberg, raw	96
Celery, raw	95
Broccoli, cooked	90
Carrots, raw	88
Milk, whole	88
Orange juice	88
Oatmeal, cooked	85
Apples, raw	84
Creamed cottage cheese	79
Eggs, raw, whole	75
Bananas	74
Chicken breast, cooked	65
Ice cream	61
Beef roast, lean, cooked	57
Pork, ham, cooked	53
Pizza, cheese, baked	46
Potatoes, french-fried	38
Cheddar cheese	37
Bread, whole wheat	38
Bread, white	37
Cake, white layer	24
Butter	16
Raisins	15
Brownies	10
Cookies, chocolate chip	4
Popcorn, popped, plain	4
Cornflakes	3
Peanuts, roasted in oil	2

Source: Reference 7.

Much of the water in plant and animal tissues is held inside the cells (intracellular). In many cases it is held within the cells as a hydrate, which means that it does not flow from the cells when the tissues are cut or torn. For example, by visual observation, lean broiled beef-steak does not appear to contain about 60 percent water, and a sliced stalk of celery does not appear to be 94 percent water. The ability of a food to hold water in this way is called its *water-holding capacity*. Although much of this water is held as a hydrate, it still retains the properties of pure water; that is, it can be frozen or act as a **solvent** to dissolve other molecules.

Some of the water in foods is held in an extremely tightly bound form called **bound water**. Bound water actually becomes part of the structure of large molecules, such as proteins and **complex carbohydrates**, has reduced mobility, and does not have the same properties as free water; that is, it does not readily freeze or boil and cannot easily be pressed from the tissue. Some water is bound by interacting with **ions** and small molecules.

The more water that is bound in a food, the less the activity of the water. Water activity (a_w) is defined as the ratio of the **vapor pressure** of water in a food (p) at a specified temperature to the vapor pressure of pure water (p_o) at the same temperature, that is, p/p_o. The presence of **nonvolatile** substances in a food lowers the vapor pressure of the water present. Therefore, the water activity value of a food will be less than 1.0.

The perishability of a food is related to its water content, the food being generally more perishable with higher water content. However, there is an even closer relationship between the water activity and perishability. Water activity can be reduced by drying a food. In this case, water is removed by vaporization, thus causing the substances that are dissolved in the water to become more concentrated and the vapor pressure to be lowered. Water activity can also be reduced by freezing, because water is removed from the system when it forms ice. The addition of sugar or salt also lowers the water activity of a food since water is bound by these substances; that water is then unavailable for use by microorganisms. Intermediate-moisture foods normally have water activity between 0.7 and 0.9 and are not susceptible to microbial growth, although they are soft enough to eat without rehydration. Fresh meats, fruits, and vegetables have water activity values of 0.95 to 1.00.

Uses of Water in Food Preparation

Water plays a number of very important roles in food preparation, affecting both the sensory characteristics of food [6] and the processes by which heat is transferred and foods are cooked.

Water has been called a *universal solvent*, indicating that it can dissolve many different substances. It acts as a solvent or a dispersing medium for most of the chemical substances in foods. For example, many of the flavor molecules in beverages such as coffee and tea are dissolved in water; sugars are dissolved in fruit juices and in syrups; and starch granules may first be dispersed in cold water and then, as they are heated, absorb large amounts of water to produce a thickened mixture, as a pudding or sauce. A negative aspect of water when it is used in cooking is that it may leach out and dissolve some important nutrients, particularly vitamins and minerals, found in vegetables. If the cooking water is not consumed, then some major nutrient losses occur.

Solvent   a liquid in which other substances may be dissolved

Bound water   water that is held so tightly by another molecule (usually a large molecule such as a protein) that it no longer has the properties of free water

Complex carbohydrates   carbohydrates made up of many small sugar units joined together, for example, starch and cellulose

Ion   an electrically charged (+ or −) atom or group of atoms

Vapor pressure   the pressure produced over the surface of a liquid as a result of the change of some of the liquid molecules into a gaseous state and their escape from the body of the liquid

Nonvolatile   not able to vaporize or form a gas at ordinary temperatures

Latent heat   the heat or energy required to change the state of a substance, that is, from liquid to gas, without changing the temperature of the substance

Freezing mixtures   mixtures of crushed ice and salt that become very cold, below the freezing point of plain water, because of the rapid melting of the ice by the salt and the attempt of the system to reach equilibrium; freezing mixtures are used to freeze ice creams in ice cream freezers

In cooking, water is an important medium for applying heat. It may be used for this purpose both in its liquid form as hot or boiling water and in its vapor form as steam. When water boils, the forces of attraction between water molecules are overcome and the water molecules become gaseous. They leave the container in bubbles of steam. At sea level, the temperature of boiling water is 100°C (212°F). Making water boil very rapidly does not increase this temperature. Steam that is not under pressure has the same temperature as boiling water. However, a certain amount of energy, called **latent heat** or *heat of vaporization*, is necessary to change the state of water from its liquid form to its vapor form as steam. This heat is absorbed by the steam but does not register on a thermometer. When steam condenses on a cooler surface and returns to its liquid form, the latent heat is released and helps to cook the food. For example, steamed vegetables are cooked both by the heat of the steam itself and also by the release of latent energy from the steam as it condenses on the surface of the vegetables and changes back to its liquid water form.

Water is involved in the preparation of **freezing mixtures** that may be used to freeze ice creams and other frozen desserts, particularly those made at home. When crushed ice (water in its solid form) is mixed with salt, the salt dissolving on the surface of the ice increases the melting rate. As ice changes from its solid form to liquid water, heat is absorbed. This energy is called *latent heat of fusion*. The same amount of heat is given off when water freezes to ice. Water freezes at 0°C (32°F).

Water also performs an important function as a cleansing agent both for food itself and for utensils and equipment used in the preparation and serving of food. It removes soil particles and many microorganisms as well. Cleaning agents, such as soaps and detergents, increase the cleaning capacity of water.

Water promotes chemical changes in certain cases. Some mineral salts become ionized in solution, that is, they break apart, and each part develops either a positive (+) or a negative (–) charge. For example, common table salt is known chemically as sodium chloride or NaCl. When this salt is placed in water it dissolves and ionizes as follows:

$$NaCl \longrightarrow Na^+ + Cl^-$$

Ionization often causes other chemical reactions to occur. As long as baking powder remains dry, for example, no chemical reactions take place; however, when it dissolves in water, some of the chemicals that it contains ionize and then react with each other to produce new chemical substances. Among these products is carbon dioxide (CO_2) gas, which rises in tiny bubbles and makes a baked product light or leavened.

Water also affects the reactions of acids and bases (or alkalies). The chemical phenomenon that characterizes an acid substance is the ionization of a hydrogen atom, producing a positively charged hydrogen ion (H^+). This hydrogen ion, among other things, stimulates our taste buds to give us the impression of sourness. The ion that is characteristic of bases or alkalies is a negatively charged hydroxyl ion (OH^-).

The degree of acidity or alkalinity affects the characteristics of many foods and food mixtures during preparation. The color of fruit juices and of vegetables during cooking, as well as the color of chocolate in baked products, is affected by the acidity. To simplify the quantification of degrees of acidity, the pH scale was developed. This scale runs from 1 at the most acid end to 14 at the most alkaline end. A pH of 7, in the middle, indicates an essentially neutral solution (neither acidic nor basic).

Pure water that has an equal number of hydrogen (H^+) and hydroxyl (OH^-) ions has a pH of 7. However, tap water usually has small amounts of other ions that affect its acidity or alkalinity, thus changing the pH from 7. For example, the harder the tap water, the more calcium and magnesium ions it contains. The presence of these ions increases the alkalinity of hard water, so its pH is above 7. This alkaline or basic pH will affect the color of some vegetables cooked in the water. The pH values of selected foods are given in Table 5.2.

Water is very much involved in a special type of chemical reaction called *hydrolysis*. Hydrolysis refers to the breaking of a linkage between units of a larger or more complex molecule to yield smaller molecules. If a complex molecule is completely hydrolyzed, all of the linkages between the small building blocks that make up the larger molecule are broken. In this process, a water molecule actually becomes part of the end product. For example, starch is a complex carbohydrate molecule made up of hundreds of small glucose (a simple sugar) molecules. When starch is hydrolyzed, the chemical linkages between the glucose units are broken. For each linkage that is broken, one molecule of water enters into the reaction and becomes part of the glucose molecules:

Part of a starch molecule   Hydrolysis $+ 2H_2O$ → (Two linkages broken)   glucose   glucose

Food	pH
Limes	2.0
Lemons	2.2
Vinegar	2.9
Strawberries	3.4
Pears	3.9
Tomatoes	4.2
Buttermilk	4.5
Bananas	4.6
Carrots	5.0
Bread	5.4
Meat, ripened	5.8
Tuna	6.0
Potatoes	6.1
Corn	6.3
Egg yolk	6.4
Milk	6.6
Egg white	7.0–9.0

TABLE 5.2
pH of Selected Foods

Source: Reference 4.

Covalent bond   a strong chemical bond that joins two atoms together

Polar   having two opposite natures, such as both positive and negative charges

The Nature of Water

Water is a small molecule containing two hydrogen atoms and one oxygen atom (H_2O) bonded strongly together by what are called **covalent bonds**. It is very interesting to note, however, that water does not behave in the same manner as do most other molecules of similar size with regard to such characteristics as boiling point, freezing point, and vapor pressure. Water is a unique molecule, fortunately for all of us living on Planet Earth who depend so much on water for our very existence.

Water is unique chiefly because of what is called its **polar** nature [1]. Although the hydrogen and oxygen atoms of water are joined together by strong covalent bonds, the positive and negative charges are not evenly distributed over the whole molecule. Figure 5.1 is a representation of a water molecule with a negative (−) charge on the oxygen side and positive (+) charges on the hydrogen sides. The water molecule has positive and negative poles and may be said to be *dipolar*. Since opposite charges attract each other, the negative part of one water molecule is attracted to the positive part of another water molecule, causing these molecules to cluster together, as demonstrated in Figure 5.2. The attraction between the negatively charged oxygen and the positively charged hydrogen is a type of bonding in itself, although much weaker than covalent bonding. This special bond is called a *hydrogen bond* (see Figure 5.3).

Because water molecules have such a special attraction for their fellow molecules, considerable energy is necessary to separate them from each other. This is apparent when water is boiled and its state is changed from the liquid to the gaseous molecules of steam or water vapor. The boiling point of water (100°C [212°F] at sea level) is really very high, considering the small size of this molecule.

The *vapor pressure*, which is the pressure produced by those water molecules that have already become vapor and are close to the surface of the liquid water even at room temperature (see Figure 5.4), is comparatively low. This means that water does not readily change to a gaseous state. Therefore, a considerable amount of heat must be applied to the water to overcome the special attraction of the molecules for each other and raise the vapor pressure before the water will boil. The amount of heat or energy required to change water from the liquid state to a gaseous state (called latent heat of vaporization) at its boiling point is 540 calories (0.54 **kilocalories**) for each gram of water that is

Kilocalorie   one kilocalorie is equal to 1000 small calories; the small calorie is used in chemistry, whereas the kilocalorie is used in nutrition

FIGURE 5.1
The water molecule is called a *dipolar molecule* because part of it is positively charged and another part is negatively charged.

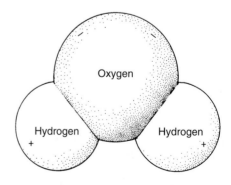

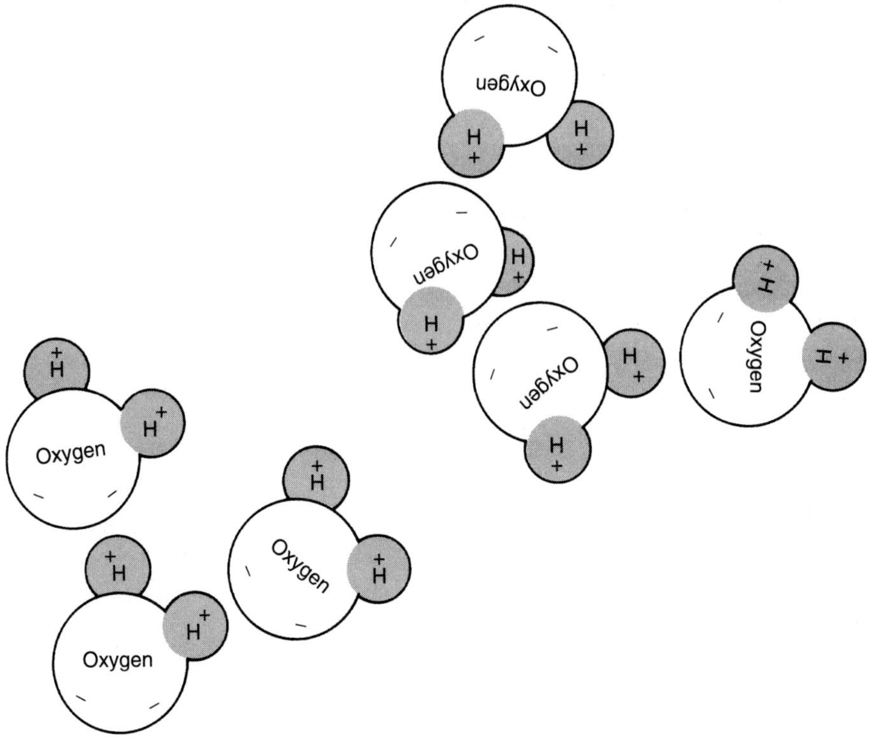

FIGURE 5.2
Water molecules cluster together because the positive charge on one molecule is attracted to the negative charge on another molecule, forming a weak bond.

changed to steam. The temperature of the steam itself is the same as the temperature of the boiling water. The boiling point of water is discussed in more detail in connection with boiling sugar solutions in Chapter 11.

Water Hardness

Water is generally classified as being soft or hard to various degrees. What is it that makes water hard? Basically, it is the presence of various mineral salts.

 There are two general types of hard water. One is called *temporarily hard water* because the calcium, magnesium, and iron bicarbonates that it

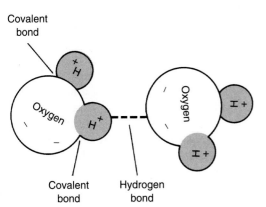

FIGURE 5.3
A hydrogen bond forms as water molecules are attracted to each other.

FIGURE 5.4

Vapor pressure is the pressure produced over the surface of a liquid, such as water, as a result of the escape of some of the liquid molecules into the vapor or gaseous state. This process causes water to gradually disappear or evaporate from an open container even at room temperature.

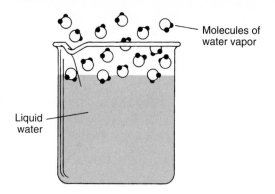

Molecules of water vapor

Liquid water

contains precipitate as insoluble carbonates when the water is boiled. These mineral deposits may accumulate as *scale* in hot water heaters and kettles used over a long period primarily for boiling water. *Permanently hard water* contains calcium, magnesium, and iron sulfates that do not precipitate on boiling. They form insoluble salts with soap and decrease its cleaning capacity.

The mineral salts of hard water may affect food preparation in various ways. Calcium retards the rehydration and softening of dried beans and peas during soaking and cooking. Hard water is often fairly alkaline and may thus affect the color of some of the pigments in cooked vegetables. Iced tea may be cloudy because some compounds in the tea (polyphenols) precipitate with the calcium and magnesium salts in hard water. Water that is naturally soft contains very few mineral salts.

Hard water may be softened by several different processes. In one method, water-softening agents, such as washing soda and polyphosphates, may be added to water to precipitate the calcium and magnesium salts. Another method uses an ion-exchange process in which calcium and magnesium ions are exchanged for sodium ions. A resinous material may be contained in a water-softening tank through which the hard water flows. Sodium ions held by the resin are exchanged for calcium and magnesium in the hard water until the resin has exhausted its sodium supply. At this point, the resin may be recharged with sodium by flushing it with a strong salt solution. Water softened in this manner is higher in sodium than it was originally.

•CARBOHYDRATES

What comes to mind when you hear the word **carbohydrate**? Probably, you think of sugars and starch. Possibly, you also include fiber. Sugars are *simple carbohydrates*, consisting either of one basic sugar unit or of a few of these small units linked together. Starch and fiber belong to a class of carbohydrates called *complex* because they may have thousands of basic sugar units linked together to form very large molecules. Thus, carbohydrates are either sugars or more complex substances, such as starch, which are formed by combining many sugars together.

Carbon (C), hydrogen (H), and oxygen (O) are the elements that make up carbohydrates. The ratios of these elements to each other form a pattern:

One molecule of water (H_2O), containing the hydrogen and oxygen, is present for each atom of carbon. *Hydrated carbon* is suggested by the ratio $[C_x(H_2O)_y]$ and from this the name carbohydrate has been derived.

Carbohydrates are formed in green plants through *photosynthesis,* by which process energy from the sun is harnessed to convert carbon dioxide (CO_2) from the atmosphere and water (H_2O) from the soil into the simple sugar, glucose ($C_6H_{12}O_6$). Oxygen (O_2) is given off by the plant during this photosynthetic process. Thus begins the cycle of nature on which animal life depends.

High-carbohydrate foods, including various cereal grains, legumes, and starchy roots or tubers, are staples in the diets of millions of people throughout the world. Foods classified as largely carbohydrate include the following:

Sugars	Jellies and jams
Syrups	Flours
Molasses	Dried fruits
Honey	Legumes
Candies	Cereal products

Chemical Classification

Carbohydrates are classified according to the number of basic sugar units that are linked together. They may thus be grouped in the following way.

Monosaccharides: simple sugars with one basic unit

Disaccharides: simple sugars with two basic units

Oligosaccharides: intermediate-size molecules containing approximately ten or fewer basic units

Polysaccharides: complex carbohydrates with many basic units (up to thousands)

Monosaccharides

The simplest sugar carbohydrates are called *monosaccharides. Saccharide* refers to their sweetness and *mono* to the fact that they are a single unit. Those with which we are most concerned in food preparation contain six carbon atoms and are thus called **hexoses**, although some five-carbon sugars, called **pentoses**, are important components of certain fibers and **vegetable gums**.

Three important hexose monosaccharides are glucose, fructose, and galactose. Another name for glucose is *dextrose*, and fructose is sometimes called *levulose*. Each sugar has the same number of elements, $C_6H_{12}O_6$, but slight differences in position of the chemical groups produce differences in properties, including sweetness and solubility. Chemical structures for these sugars are shown in Figure 5.5, and some sources are given in Table 5.3. Sugars are discussed in more detail in Chapter 11.

Glucose

The most widely distributed monosaccharide in foods is glucose, which is present in at least small amounts in all fruits and vegetables. The sugar that circu-

Hexose   a simple sugar or monosaccharide with six carbon atoms

Pentose   a simple sugar or monosaccharide with five carbon atoms

Vegetable gums   polysaccharide substances that are derived from plants, including seaweed and various shrubs or trees, have the ability to hold water, and often act as thickeners, stabilizers, or gelling agents in various food products; for example, algin, carrageenan, and gum arabic

lates in the bloodstream is also glucose. A number of complex carbohydrates, including starch, have glucose as their basic sugar unit. Glucose is a major component of corn syrup, which is produced by the breakdown or hydrolysis of the complex starch molecule. Crystalline glucose, as well as corn syrup, is widely used in bakery products and in other manufactured foods. Glucose is also present in honey along with relatively large amounts of fructose.

Fructose

Probably the sweetest of all the common sugars is fructose. It contributes much of the sweetness to honey and is found in many fruits, sometimes being called fruit sugar. Because it is very soluble, fructose is not easily crystallized.

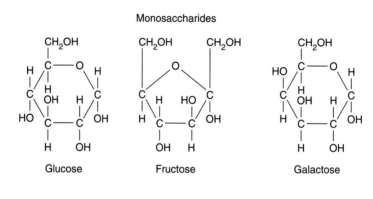

FIGURE 5.5

Chemical structures for monosaccharides and disaccharides of importance in food preparation.

TABLE 5.3
Sugars, Their Sources, and Products of Hydrolysis

Sugar	Common Sources	Products of Hydrolysis
Monosaccharides, $C_6H_{12}O_6$		
Glucose or dextrose	Fruit and plant juices. Often present with other sugars. Honey. Formed by hydrolysis of sucrose, lactose, and maltose.	
Fructose or levulose	Fruit and plant juices. Often present with other sugars. Honey. Formed by hydrolysis of sucrose.	
Galactose	Does not occur free in nature. Formed by hydrolysis of lactose or galactans.	
Disaccharides, $C_{12}H_{22}O_{11}$		
Sucrose	Present with other sugars in many fruits and vegetables. Sugar cane and sugar beets are rich sources. Maple sugar and syrup. Used in many processed foods.	One molecule each of glucose and fructose. A mixture of equal amounts of glucose and fructose is called *invert sugar*.
Lactose	Milk and whey.	One molecule each of glucose and galactose.
Maltose	Malted or germinated grains. Corn syrup. Formed by hydrolysis of starch.	One molecule yields two molecules of glucose.
Oligosaccharides		
Raffinose (a trisaccharide)	The seed coats of legumes, nuts, and dried beans.	One molecule each of galactose, glucose, and fructose.
Stachyose (a tetrasaccharide)	Legumes, nuts, seeds, and dried beans.	One molecule of raffinose plus galactose.

Technology has made possible the production of a high-fructose corn syrup by employing a special enzyme, called *glucose isomerase*, to change glucose to fructose. This syrup is widely used in processed foods, particularly soft drinks.

Galactose

Although galactose is generally not found free in natural foods, it is one of the two building blocks of milk sugar (lactose). Some is formed from the breakdown or **hydrolysis** of lactose when fermented milk products, such as yogurt, are made. Galactose is also present in some oligosaccharides, such as raffinose, and a derivative of galactose (galacturonic acid) is the basic unit of pectic substances. Galactose is a basic building block of a number of vegetable gums, which are complex carbohydrates.

Hydrolysis   the breaking of a chemical linkage between basic units of a more complex molecule to yield smaller molecules; water participates in the reaction and becomes part of the end products

Disaccharides

Monosaccharides are the building blocks of disaccharides, which consist of two monosaccharides linked together. Disaccharides of particular interest in the study of foods are sucrose, lactose, and maltose. Their chemical structures are shown in Figure 5.5, and some sources are listed in Table 5.3.

Sucrose

Sucrose is table sugar and is widely used in crystalline form for food preparation. It is usually extracted from sugar cane or the sugar beet. Sucrose is composed of one molecule of glucose and one of fructose. These two monosaccharides are linked together through their most reactive chemical groups, the aldehyde group ($HC = O$) of glucose and the ketone group ($C = O$) of fructose.

When sucrose is hydrolyzed, the linkage between glucose and fructose is broken and a molecule of water is added in the reaction. The resulting mixture, containing equal molecular amounts of glucose and fructose, is sometimes called *invert sugar* and is important in controlling sugar crystallization during the process of making crystalline candies (see Chapter 11). Sucrose may be hydrolyzed by an enzyme called *sucrase* or *invertase*.

Lactose

Lactose, commonly called milk sugar, is found naturally only in milk and milk products. The two monosaccharides that make up lactose are glucose and galactose. Whey, produced during cheese making, is a rich source of lactose and is sometimes used in processed or manufactured foods.

Maltose

Two molecules of glucose link together to form maltose. Maltose is one of the products of hydrolysis when the complex carbohydrate starch is broken down. Therefore, it is present in germinating or sprouting grains, where starch hydrolysis provides energy for the grain growth. It is also an important component of corn syrups, which are made by breaking down corn starch.

Oligosaccharides

The term *oligosaccharide* may be used to refer to carbohydrate molecules containing ten or fewer monosaccharide units. (*Oligo* is a Greek word meaning "few.") This category includes the trisaccharide (three sugar units) raffinose and the tetrasaccharide (four sugar units) stachyose. These carbohydrates are not digested by humans and may be broken down by bacteria in the intestinal tract, resulting in some gas formation. They are present in dried beans.

Polysaccharides

Polysaccharides are complex carbohydrates containing monosaccharide units numbering from about 40 to several hundred thousand. These basic units are linked together in various ways. Linkages may produce long, straight chains in some cases and branched-type molecules in other instances.

Starch and Dextrins

Starch is the basic storage carbohydrate of plants and is, therefore, found in abundance in seeds, roots, and tubers. Hundreds or even thousands of glucose molecules join together to make a starch molecule. Basically, there are two kinds of starch molecules, sometimes called *fractions of starch*. One is a long chain or linear type of molecule called *amylose*. The other is a highly branched, bushy type of molecule referred to as *amylopectin*. Most natural starches are mixtures of these two fractions, each contributing its own properties in relation to thickening and gelling. The chemical structures of amylose and amylopectin are shown in Figure 5.6.

As starch molecules are produced in a growing plant, they are placed in a tightly organized formation called a *granule*. **Starch granules** are large enough to be seen under an ordinary microscope. When starch granules are heated in water, they swell tremendously in a process called *gelatinization*. The swollen starch granules are responsible for the thickening that occurs when starchy puddings and sauces are cooked. Starch and gelatinization are discussed in more detail in Chapter 13.

Starch granule   a particle formed in the plant seed or root when starch is stored; composed of millions of starch molecules laid down in a very organized pattern; the shape of the granule is typical for each species

FIGURE 5.6
Portions of starch molecules, of which there are two types: (a) amylose, the linear fraction, and (b) amylopectin, the branched fraction. Each small unit represents one molecule of glucose.

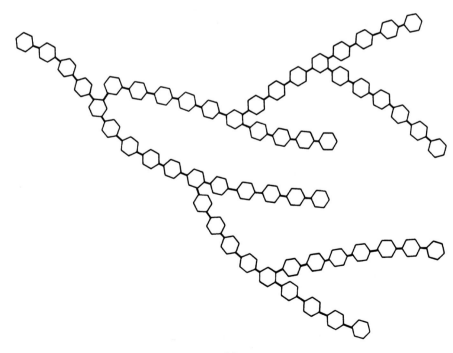

(a)

(b)

Dextrins are produced when starch molecules are partially broken down by enzymes, acid, or dry heat. We might think of dextrins as large chunks of broken starch molecules. They are formed from starch when corn syrup is made, when bread is toasted, and when flour is browned. They have less thickening power than starch.

Glycogen

Glycogen, a polysaccharide, is sometimes called *animal starch* because it is found in animal tissues. It is similar in structure to the amylopectin or branched fraction of starch. When completely hydrolyzed, it yields only glucose. The liver stores glycogen on a short-term basis until it is hydrolyzed to help maintain a normal blood sugar level. The muscles also temporarily store glycogen.

Plant Fiber Components

Dietary fiber, sometimes called *roughage* or *bulk*, is indigestible by humans, since no enzymes that can hydrolyze the molecules that make up plant fiber are present in the digestive tract. Dietary fiber is a complex mixture that includes *cellulose*, *hemicelluloses*, *beta-glucans*, and *pectins*, which are all polysaccharides. A noncarbohydrate molecule called **lignin** may also be part of the fiber complex, particularly in woody portions of vegetables. These polysaccharide fiber components are found in or around the cell walls of plants and play important structural roles, while some other polysaccharides, including various vegetable gums, are nonstructural. In recent years, various public health agencies have emphasized the importance of fiber in our diets for the prevention or control of several chronic disorders, including colon cancer, cardiovascular disease, and diabetes [5]. The bran layers of cereal grains and fresh fruits and vegetables contain relatively large amounts of dietary fiber, many of whose components have the capacity to absorb water and swell.

Lignin   a woody, fibrous, noncarbohydrate material produced in mature plants; component of the fiber complex

Cellulose.   Cellulose has many glucose units linked together, as does the linear fraction of starch; however, the glucose molecules in cellulose are linked in a different way than are the glucose units in starch, and form long, strong fibers. The cell walls of plant tissues contain cellulose in tiny fibrils, helping to give structure to these tissues.

Cellulose may be chemically modified to make it more soluble and able to form gels. Examples of modified cellulose include methylcellulose and carboxymethyl cellulose, which are used to thicken, stabilize, gel, and provide bulk in various processed foods [3].

Hemicelluloses.   Also found in plant cell walls are hemicelluloses. These are a heterogeneous group of polysaccharides that contain a variety of different monosaccharide building blocks. In many cases these molecules have branching sidechains. Hemicelluloses, along with cellulose, play important structural roles in plants. Xylose and arabinose, which are pentoses (monosaccharides with five carbon atoms), are common components of hemicelluloses.

Beta-glucans. Beta-glucans are polysaccharides made up of glucose building blocks that are linked together differently from the glucose components of cellulose. Beta-glucan molecules are less linear than are cellulose molecules and more soluble in water. Oats and barley are rich sources of beta-glucans [5].

Pectic Substances. Pectic substances are polysaccharides found in the spaces between plant cells as well as in the cell walls, and aid in cementing plant cells together. **Galacturonic acid**, a derivative of the sugar galactose, is the basic building block of pectic substances. The largest of the pectic molecules, sometimes called the parent, is *protopectin*. It is present in largest amounts in unripe fruit and is hydrolyzed by enzymes in the tissues to the less complex *pectinic acid*, also called *pectin,* as the fruit ripens. *Pectic acid* is produced from pectin by additional hydrolysis of special chemical groups on the molecule called **methyl esters**. Pectin is the substance responsible for forming gels in various jams, jellies, and preserves; it also occurs naturally in many fruits.

Vegetable Gums. A group of polysaccharides called *vegetable gums* or **hydrocolloids** is increasingly being used to perform important functions in food processing. These compounds are long-chain **polymers** of monosaccharides that dissolve or disperse in water, producing a thickening or texture-building effect. Gums may help to retain water, reduce evaporation rates, modify ice crystal formation, and produce other desired changes in the consistency and flow characteristics of various foods. The preparation of low-calorie and reduced-fat foods often requires the ingenious use of hydrocolloids; for example, gums can thicken and stabilize low-calorie salad dressings made with reduced amounts of oil or with none at all. Various hexose and pentose sugars and their derivatives are the basic building blocks of hydrocolloids.

The U.S. Food and Drug Administration (FDA) regulates gums, classifying them as either food additives or GRAS (generally regarded as safe) substances [3]. Vegetable gums include the following:

Source	*Examples*
Seaweed extracts	Agar
	Alginates
	Carrageenan
Plant seed gums	Guar gum
	Locust bean gum
Plant exudates	Gum arabic
	Gum tragacanth
	Gum karaya
Modified materials	Methyl cellulose
	Sodium carboxymethyl cellulose
Microbial derivatives	Xanthan gum
	Gellan gum

Browning

Chemical reactions that cause browning of foods often occur during preparation and storage. In some cases this is desirable, while in other cases it is not. It

Galacturonic acid a chemical molecule very similar to the sugar galactose and containing an organic acid (carboxyl) group in its chemical structure

Methyl ester of galacturonic acid ester is the chemical word used to describe the linkage between an organic acid group (—COOH) and an alcohol group (—OH); in this case, the alcohol is methanol (which contains only one carbon atom) and the acid is galacturonic acid

Hydrocolloids large molecules, such as those that make up vegetable gums, that form colloidal dispersions, hold water, and often serve as thickeners and stabilizers in processed foods

Polymer a giant molecule formed from smaller molecules that are chemically linked together

Plant exudates materials that ooze out of certain plants; some that ooze from certain tree trunks and branches are gums

Catalyze   to make a reaction occur at a more rapid rate by the addition of a substance, called a catalyst, which itself undergoes no permanent chemical change

Caramelization   the process by which a brown colored and characteristically flavored substance is produced when dry sugar is heated to very high temperatures

Carbonyl group   a ketone (-C = O) or an aldehyde (HC = O) group

Amino group   a chemical group (NH$_2$) characteristic of all amino acids

is important to be able to control browning so that it can be inhibited or encouraged as needed. Some browning reactions are **catalyzed** by enzymes. Those involved in the browning of fresh fruits and vegetables are discussed in Chapter 15. Other browning results from nonenzymatic reactions, some of which involve carbohydrates.

When sugars are heated to temperatures above their melting points, they undergo a series of chemical reactions that begin with dehydration and end with polymerization, which produces brown compounds. This process is called **caramelization**. If this operation is not too extensive, a desirable caramel flavor and a light brown color result. As heating is continued, however, many bitter compounds are produced and the color becomes very dark.

Browning produced by the *Maillard reaction* also involves a carbohydrate in its initial step. The **carbonyl group** of a sugar combines with the **amino group** of an amino acid or protein with the removal of a molecule of water. After this, a series of chemical reactions occurs, including fragmentation and then polymerization, with the eventual formation of brown pigments. The specific compounds involved and the conditions of temperature, pH, moisture, and so on, under which the reaction occurs, all affect the final flavor and color. The browning of a loaf of bread during baking is due mainly to the Maillard reaction. The flavor and color, in this case, are desirable. However, the browning and off-flavor that may develop when nonfat dry milk solids are stored for long periods of time are not.

•LIPIDS OR FATS

The term *lipids* is used to describe a broad group of substances with similar properties or characteristics of insolubility in water and a greasy feel. The lipid classification includes at least three major groups with which we are particularly concerned in the study of food and nutrition: neutral fats known as triacylglycerols or triglycerides, phospholipids, and sterols.

Triglycerides (Triacylglycerols)

Approximately 95 percent of the fatty substances in foods fall into this group. Thus, when we talk of fats in food, we are really talking about triglycerides or triacylglycerols. For our discussions in this text, we use the older term *triglyceride*, rather than triacylglycerol; both refer to the same kind of chemical molecule.

Triglycerides are made up of three *fatty acids* combined with one molecule of an alcohol called *glycerol.* Glycerol has three carbon atoms and three hydroxyl groups (— OH). Fatty acids are commonly composed of

chains of carbon atoms with an organic acid group (— $\overset{\overset{\textstyle O}{\|}}{C}$ —OH) on the end. The fatty acids are joined to the glycerol molecule by what is called an *ester linkage,* as shown in the following, where *R* represents the chain of carbon atoms.

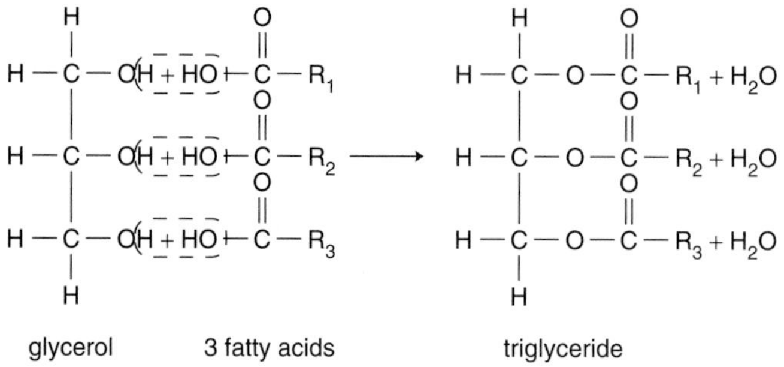

glycerol   3 fatty acids   triglyceride

Fatty Acids

Most fatty acids in foods are not free fatty acids but are combined in triglycerides. There may be different fatty acids joined with the glycerol in the same triglyceride molecule. Fatty acids vary in two important ways—they differ in length of the chain of carbon atoms, and different amounts of hydrogen atoms are attached to the carbons.

The carbon chain in fatty acids may be as short as 4 carbons or as long as 24 or more carbons. Generally, however, the fatty acids in foods have an even number of carbons. Names of some of the common fatty acids and the lengths of their carbon chains are listed in Table 5.4.

Some fatty acids have all of the hydrogen atoms with which the carbon atoms can bond. There are no *double bonds* between carbon atoms, which might be broken to allow bonding with more hydrogens. These types of fatty acids are called *saturated*. Other fatty acids contain double bonds between some carbon atoms and are *unsaturated* in terms of the amount of hydrogen

TABLE 5.4

Fatty Acids Found in Foods

Fatty Acid Common Name	Systematic Name	Number of Carbon Atoms
Saturated		
Butyric	Butanoic	4
Caproic	Hexanoic	6
Caprylic	Octanoic	8
Capric	Decanoic	10
Lauric	Dodecanoic	12
Myristic	Tetradecanoic	14
Palmitic	Hexadecanoic	16
Stearic	Octadecanoic	18
Arachidic	Eicosanoic	20
Monounsaturated		
Palmitoleic	Hexadecenoic	16
Oleic	*Cis*-Octadecenoic	18
Polyunsaturated		
Linoleic	Octadecadienoic	18
Linolenic	Octadecatrienoic	18
Arachidonic	Eicosatetraenoic	20

they contain. Examples of saturated fatty acids are butyric acid, which is present in butter, and stearic acid, which is a major component of beef fat. Palmitic acid, a saturated fatty acid with 16 carbon atoms, is widely distributed in meat fats, vegetable oils, and cocoa butter.

$$H-\overset{\displaystyle H}{\underset{\displaystyle H}{C}}-\overset{\displaystyle H}{\underset{\displaystyle H}{C}}-\overset{\displaystyle H}{\underset{\displaystyle H}{C}}-COOH$$

(butyric acid; 4 carbon atoms)

$$H-C-C-C-C-C-C-C-C-C-C-C-C-C-C-C-C-C-COOH$$

(stearic acid; 18 carbon atoms)

$$H-C-C-C-C-C-C-C-C-C-C-C-C-C-C-C-COOH$$

(palmitic acid; 16 carbon atoms)
Saturated Fatty Acids

Oleic acid contains one double bond. It is thus a *monounsaturated* fatty acid. Linoleic, linolenic, and arachidonic acids contain two, three, and four double bonds, respectively. Fatty acids with more than one double bond are often called *polyunsaturated*. Polyunsaturated fatty acids that have a double bond between the third and fourth carbon atoms from the left (as you look at the following chemical structures) are called ω-3 polyunsaturated fatty acids. Some ω-3 fatty acids appear to be of importance in body metabolism related to the prevention of coronary heart disease. Fish, particularly fatty fish, contain ω-3 fatty acids.

$$H-C-C-C-C-C-C-C-C=C-C-C-C-C-C-C-C-COOH$$

(oleic acid; 18 carbon atoms)

$$H-C-C-C-C-C-C=C-C-C=C-C-C-C-C-C-C-C-COOH$$

(linoleic acid; 18 carbon atoms)
Unsaturated Fatty Acids

The body is not able to make linoleic acid with its two double bonds. Linoleic acid is, therefore, considered to be an essential fatty acid for both infants and adults because it must be obtained in the diet. Skin lesions and poor growth have been reported in infants receiving a diet limited in fat, and these symptoms disappeared after a source of linoleic acid was added to the diet. It has been suggested by the Food and Nutrition Board of the National Research Council—National Academy of Sciences that a linoleic acid intake equivalent to 2 percent of the total dietary kilocalories for adults and 3 percent for infants is probably satisfactory to avoid any deficiency. The average American diet apparently meets this recommendation.

Good food sources of linoleic acid include seed oils from corn, cottonseeds, and soybeans (50 to 53 percent linoleic acid) and special margarines and peanut oil (20 to 30 percent). Corn oil contains more than six times as much linoleic acid as olive oil, and chicken fat contains up to ten times as much as the fat of **ruminant animals** such as cattle. The fat from an avocado is about 10 percent linoleate.

Cis–Trans Configuration

The shape of a fatty acid is changed by the presence of a double bond since the double bond limits the rotation of the carbon atom at this point. The particular molecular shape produced by a double bond is dependent upon the configuration of the bond. It may be either cis or trans. A cis configuration has the hydrogen atoms on the same side of the double bond, as illustrated below.

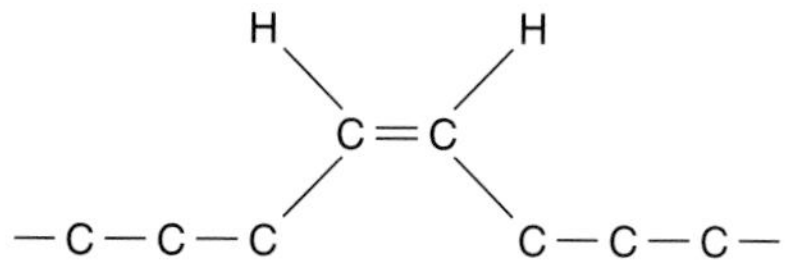

In a trans configuration, the hydrogen atoms are on opposite sides of the double bond.

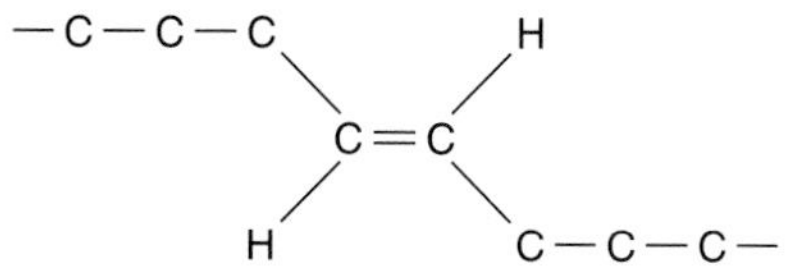

Since it is part of a triglyceride molecule, the fatty acid's shape affects the melting point of the triglyceride. An unsaturated fatty acid with a trans configuration has a higher melting point than the same size molecule with a cis configuration. This is apparently because the bending of the chain in the cis fatty acid does not allow the triglyceride molecules to pack as closely together when they crystallize in a solid state. Thus, less energy is required to separate them when they melt and therefore they melt at a lower temperature.

Types of Triglyceride Molecules

A triglyceride molecule may be formed with three of the same kind of fatty acids, for example, three palmitic acid molecules. In this case the triglyceride would be called a *simple* triglyceride and could be named tripalmitin. More commonly, however, triglycerides in foods are *mixed*, that is, they contain different fatty acids—either all three different or two alike and one different.

Ruminant animal   an animal with multiple stomachs, one of which is called a *rumen*, where bacterial action occurs on the food that has been eaten; the animal—for example, a cow—"chews its cud" (material regurgitated and chewed a second time)

Phospholipids

Phospholipids are present in foods in relatively small amounts but play some important roles, chiefly as **emulsifying agents**. Lecithin is a phospholipid that is used as a food additive in various processed foods, including margarines. Phospholipids are present in buttermilk, resulting from the churning of cream. Certain baked products made with dried buttermilk may benefit from the emulsifying action of the phospholipids present. Egg yolk is a good source of phospholipids.

Structurally, phospholipids are much like triglycerides. They contain glycerol attached through an ester linkage to two fatty acids; however, they differ from triglycerides in that instead of a third fatty acid, there is a phosphoric acid group joined to the glycerol. A **nitrogen base**, such as choline, is also linked with the phosphoric acid.

$$
\begin{array}{l}
\quad\quad\quad\ \ H\quad\quad O \\
\quad\quad\quad\ \ | \quad\quad\ \ \| \\
H-C-O-C-R_1 \quad\text{(fatty acid No. 1)}\\
\quad\quad\quad\ \ | \quad\quad\quad O \\
\quad\quad\quad\ \ | \quad\quad\quad \| \\
H-C-O-C-R_2 \quad\text{(fatty acid No. 2)}\\
\quad\quad\quad\ \ | \\
H-C-O-\text{phosphoric acid + nitrogen base}\\
\quad\quad\quad\ \ | \\
\quad\quad\quad\ \ H
\end{array}
$$

In a mixture, the fatty acid portions of the phospholipid molecules are attracted to other fat substances, whereas the phosphoric acid–nitrogen base portion is attracted to polar molecules such as water or vinegar. Thus, the phospholipid may act as a bridge between fat and water and allow them to be mixed in an emulsion. The phospholipid functions as an emulsifying agent.

Sterols

Cholesterol is probably the most widely known sterol and is found only in animal foods—meat, fish, poultry, egg yolks, and milk fat. Cholesterol is an essential component in the cells of the body, but too high a level of cholesterol in the bloodstream is one factor associated with an increased incidence of coronary heart disease. Vitamin D is also a sterol.

Plants do not manufacture cholesterol, but plant oils do contain some other sterols, generally called *phytosterols*. These sterols, however, are not well-absorbed from the human digestive tract and may actually interfere with the absorption of cholesterol. The chemical structures of sterols are complex and quite different from those of the triglycerides.

Fats in Food Preparation

Several important roles are filled by fats in food preparation. They act as primary tenderizing agents in baked products. For example, contrast the marked tenderness of a croissant, which contains a high proportion of fat, with the chewiness of a bagel, which is made with very little fat.

Oils are major components of salad dressings and mayonnaise. Fats may be heated to high temperatures and act as a medium of heat transfer in the frying of foods. High-fat products such as butter and margarine are used as table spreads. A number of flavor compounds are fat-soluble and are carried in the fat component of many food products. The properties and processing of fats are discussed in Chapter 18.

Foods high in fat include the following (see also Table 18.1):

Butter	Deep-fat fried foods
Cream	Chocolate
Lard	Cheese
Oils	Nuts
Margarine	Fat meats
Hydrogenated shortening	

•PROTEINS

Proteins are complex molecules found in every living cell. The name protein is derived from the Greek word *proteos*, meaning "of prime importance" or "to take the first place." Thus, all foods that were once living animal or plant tissues, including meats, vegetables, and cereal grains, contain some protein. Protein is an essential nutrient for human life and growth. In food preparation, proteins play important functional roles, for example, binding water, forming **gels**, thickening, producing **foams**, and aiding browning. In addition, enzymes, which are special kinds of protein molecules, catalyze a number of reactions that affect the characteristics of prepared foods.

Gel   a gel forms when the material can be molded; that is, it holds its shape when turned out of a container

Foam   the dispersion of a gas in a liquid, such as a beaten egg-white mixture

Structure of Proteins

Proteins are unique because, in addition to the elements carbon, hydrogen, and oxygen, they also contain nitrogen. Often, sulfur is present as well. Proteins are large molecules made up of hundreds or thousands of small building blocks called *amino acids,* which are joined together in a special chemical linkage called a **peptide linkage**. These linkages produce long chains that are said to constitute the *primary structure* of proteins.

The *secondary structure* of proteins results from the springlike coiling of the long peptide chains (see Figure 5.7). The characteristic coil is called an *alpha helix*, and special bonds, called **hydrogen bonds**, help to hold the helix in place.

The secondary coils of peptide chains may fold back on themselves, usually in an irregular pattern, to form more compact structures. This folding, which is characteristic for each particular protein, produces what is called the *tertiary structure* of a protein molecule. The long chains of amino acids, when coiled and folded, often produce a globular shape for the protein. A still higher level of organization, called the *quaternary structure*, may result when some globular proteins combine with others, and each forms subunits in a more complex whole. The structure of many protein molecules is indeed very intri-

Peptide linkage   linkage between two amino acids that connects the amino group of one and the acid (carboxyl) group of the other

Hydrogen bond   the relatively weak chemical bond that forms between a hydrogen atom and another atom with a slight negative charge, such as an oxygen or a nitrogen atom; each atom in this case is already covalently bonded to other atoms in the molecule of which it is part

FIGURE 5.7
Representation of an alpha-helix.

cate, but the final shape of the protein is often of critical importance to its function in a living cell or in food preparation.

Amino Acids

About twenty-two different amino acids are used as building blocks for proteins. Each of these amino acids has two chemical groups that are the same for all of the amino acids—an amino group ($-NH_2$) and a carboxyl or acid group.

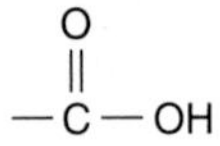

$$
\begin{array}{c}
\text{O} \\
\parallel \\
-\text{C}-\text{OH}
\end{array}
$$

The remainder of the molecule differs specifically for each amino acid. A general formula for amino acids is written as follows, with the R representing a side chain of variable structure.

The side chains or R groups give a protein its particular characteristics.

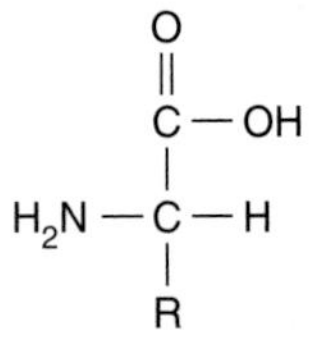

$$
\begin{array}{c}
\text{O} \\
\parallel \\
\text{C}-\text{OH} \\
| \\
\text{H}_2\text{N}-\text{C}-\text{H} \\
| \\
\text{R}
\end{array}
$$

Some R groups have short carbon chains, some contain sulfur, some have additional amino or acid groups, and some have a cyclic structure. A few of the side chain structures are shown in Table 5.5.

The peptide linkage is between the amino group of one amino acid and the acid or carboxyl group of another. Protein molecules are formed as hundreds of these linkages are made. The following hypothetical protein molecule shows several amino acids joined together by peptide linkages.

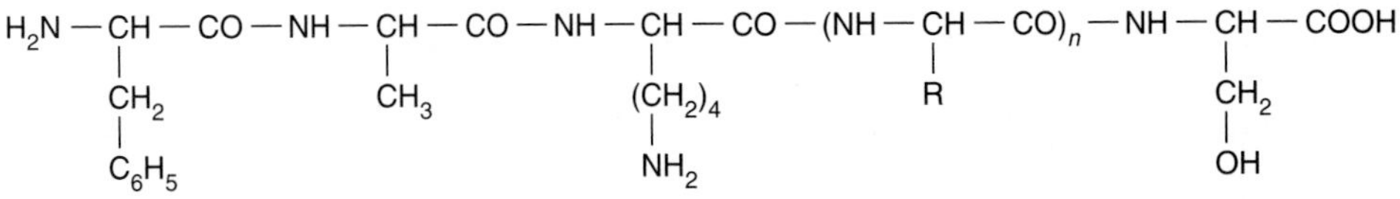

$$
\text{H}_2\text{N}-\text{CH}-\text{CO}-\text{NH}-\text{CH}-\text{CO}-\text{NH}-\text{CH}-\text{CO}-(\text{NH}-\text{CH}-\text{CO})_n-\text{NH}-\text{CH}-\text{COOH}
$$

CH$_2$	CH$_3$	(CH$_2$)$_4$	R	CH$_2$
C$_6$H$_5$		NH$_2$		OH
phenylalanine	alanine	lysine		serine

TABLE 5.5

Side Chain (R) Groups for Selected Amino Acids

Amino Acid	Structure for Side Chain (R Group)
Glycine	$-$H
Alanine	$-$CH$_3$
Serine	$-$CH$_2$OH
Cysteine	$-$CH$_2-$SH
Glutamic acid	$-$CH$_2-$CH$_2-$C($=$O)$-$OH
Lysine	$-$CH$_2-$CH$_2-$CH$_2-$CH$_2-$NH$_2$
Methionine	$-$CH$_2-$CH$_2-$S$-$CH$_3$
Tyrosine	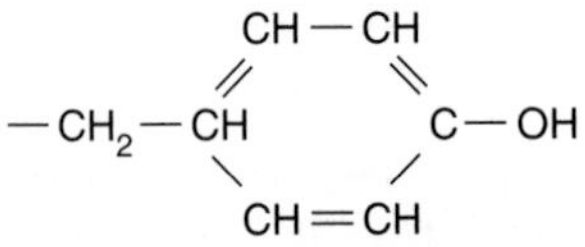 $-$CH$_2-$CH (ring: CH$=$CH, CH$=$CH, C$-$OH)

Protein Quality

At least eight amino acids, and possibly nine, are considered nutritionally essential for tissue maintenance in the adult human, in the sense that the diet must furnish them in suitable amounts. These essential amino acids are isoleucine, leucine, lysine, methionine, phenylalanine, threonine, tryptophan, valine, and possibly histidine. Histidine has been shown to be essential in the diet of infants. The other amino acids, considered nonessential, may be synthesized in the body if nitrogen sources are available.

The balance of essential amino acids in a protein determines the biological value of that protein. Proteins of high biological value contain adequate amounts of the essential amino acids to promote the normal growth of animals and are sometimes called *complete proteins*, whereas proteins of low biological value do not. Because the amino acid requirement for growth is more rigid than that for the maintenance of tissues, some proteins that are inadequate for growth may function satisfactorily for maintenance or repair of body tissues. Specific examples of proteins of high biological value are those found in milk, cheese, eggs, meat, poultry, and seafood.

Vegetable sources of protein are often lacking to some degree in one or more of the essential amino acids and have a lower score for biological value. In addition, the total amount of protein in relation to the total calories found in certain vegetable products, such as cereal grains, is low. An exception among plant protein foods is the soybean, which contains a relatively large amount of high-quality protein. Some protein foods of relatively low biological value may be combined with other protein sources that complement them, one supplying more of an essential amino acid(s) that may be limited in the other.

Cereals or legumes are more valuable in the diet if they are combined with even a small amount of protein from an animal source, such as milk, cheese, egg, meat, fish, poultry, or soy protein, that furnishes amino acids that cereals and most legumes lack. Cereals and legumes also complement each other to improve protein quality. For example, a peanut butter sandwich contains a better quality protein mixture than the bread or peanut butter eaten separately.

Table 5.6 lists the common names of several food proteins, their sources, and their general biological value.

Food Sources

Protein is present in many foods but in varying amounts. Since it is an essential substance for living cells, one would expect to find it in both plant and animal tissues. Foods that are relatively high in protein (20 to 30 percent) include meats, fish, poultry, eggs, cheese, nuts, and dry legumes. Even after dry legumes are rehydrated and cooked, they make an excellent contribution to dietary protein requirements. Although milk contains only about 4 percent protein, it is an excellent source of good-quality protein because of the amounts usually consumed on a regular basis. Cereal grains contain lesser amounts of protein; however, in the quantities of cereal grains that are often eaten, they make an important contribution to protein needs.

TABLE 5.6
Sources and Qualitative Values of
Some Common Proteins

Protein	Source	Biological Value
Casein	Milk or cheese	High
Lactalbumin	Milk or cheese	High
Ovovitellin	Egg yolk	High
Ovalbumin	Egg white	High
Myosin	Lean meat	High
Gelatin	Formed by hydrolysis from certain animal tissues	Low
Gliadin	Wheat	Low
Glutenin	Wheat	High
Hordein	Barley	Low
Prolamin	Rye	Low
Glutelin	Corn	High
Zein	Corn	Low
Glycinin	Soybean	High
Legumelin	Soybean	Low
Legumin	Peas and beans	Low
Phaseolin	Navy beans	Low
Excelsin	Brazil nut	High

Properties and Reactions

Buffering

Amino groups act as bases or alkalies, whereas carboxyl groups act as acids. As both of these groups are present on the same amino acid or protein structure, amino acids and proteins may act as either acids or bases, and are said to be *amphoteric*. This is an important characteristic for many aspects of food preparation where the degree of acidity or alkalinity affects the quality of a food product. Proteins may combine with either acid or base within a limited range and resist any change in acidity. Because of this characteristic, they are called **buffers**.

Buffer   a substance that resists changes in pH

Denaturation and Coagulation

The large complex protein molecules may undergo changes in their structures when they are subjected to the various conditions commonly encountered in food processing and preparation. If the protein molecule unfolds to some degree yet still retains all of the peptide linkages between the amino acids that make up the molecule, it is said to be *denatured*. The process of *denaturation* is illustrated in Figure 5.8. Some of the properties of the protein change when it is denatured. For example, it usually becomes less soluble. If it is an enzyme, it loses its ability to function as such. The extent of denaturation may be limited or it may be extensive. If the conditions causing denaturation persist, additional changes may occur in the protein. The unfolded parts of the molecule recombine in different ways to produce a new molecular shape, and protein molecules may bond together to form a continuous network. The term *coagulation* has been used to describe some of the later stages of protein denaturation in which denatured protein molecules bind together and produce a gel or a solid mass. The coagulation of egg white upon being heated is an example of this process.

Applying heat in the cooking of food produces denaturation and/or coagulation of proteins. An example is the roasting of meat, which denatures the meat proteins. Proteins may also be denatured by mechanical beating. For example, when egg whites are whipped to produce a foam, denaturation and coagulation of the egg white proteins occur. Changing the degree of acidity, changing the concentration of mineral salts, and freezing may also cause denaturation.

Enzymes

Enzymes are protein molecules with a special function. Produced by living cells, they act as *catalysts* to change the rate of a chemical reaction without actually being used up in the reaction itself. Enzymes catalyze a wide range of reactions in living matter, from the digestion of foods in the digestive tract of animals to most of the complex processes occurring in plant and animal metabolism. Enzymes in plant and animal tissues do not stop functioning when the animal is slaughtered or the plant tissue harvested. Thus, we must deal with enzymatic activity when we handle foods from these sources. Enzymes and enzymatic action in foods are mentioned frequently throughout the text.

Nomenclature. Names of enzymes often include the substrate or substance on which they act, joined with an *-ase* ending. For example, *lactase* is an enzyme that works on lactose to bring about its hydrolysis, and *maltase* catalyzes the hydrolysis of maltose to yield glucose. Sometimes an enzyme is named for the product that results from its action. Sucrase, for example, is sometimes called *invertase* instead, because its action to hydrolyze sucrose produces an equimolecular mixture of glucose and fructose, which is commonly called *invert sugar*. In other cases, the name describes the reaction catalyzed; **oxidase**, for example, is the name of an enzyme involved in an **oxidation reaction**. Still other names, such as *papain* and *bromelin*, do not provide any information about the substrate, end products, or reaction.

A systematic nomenclature program that attempts to describe both the substrate and the type of reaction has been established. However, the names

Oxidase an enzyme that catalyzes an oxidation reaction

Oxidation reactions chemical reactions in which oxygen is added or hydrogen is removed or electrons are lost

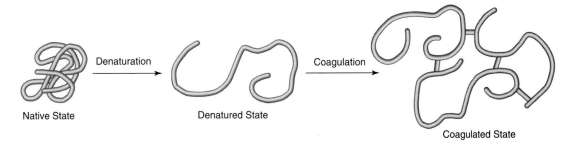

FIGURE 5.8
Denaturation of a protein involves unfolding of the molecule. The denatured molecules may bond together again to form a coagulated mass.

are often cumbersome and difficult to use on a practical basis. Numerical codes are sometimes used, but they are also difficult to use.

Mechanism of Action.   It has been suggested that enzymes function somewhat like a lock and key. They first combine with the substrate on which they will act, forming an intermediate compound sometimes referred to as the *enzyme-substrate (E-S)* complex. This complex formation undoubtedly involves a specific catalytic site on the enzyme. When the reaction is complete, the enzyme separates from the product and is free to react with another molecule of substrate. This process may be depicted as

$$\text{enzyme (E)} + \text{substrate (S)} \longrightarrow \text{E-S} \longrightarrow \text{E} + \text{product (P)}$$

Some Types of Enzymes.   Enzymes may be classified into groups according to the type of reaction they catalyze. For example, some enzymes catalyze hydrolysis reactions (*hydrolytic enzymes*) and some catalyze **oxidation-reduction reactions**. Hydrolysis is a chemical reaction that involves the breaking or cleaving of a chemical bond within a molecule. Water plays an essential role in this reaction, and the hydrogen and oxygen atoms of water are added to the two new molecules formed. Within the classification of hydrolytic enzymes, some are designated *proteases*, or *proteinases*, because they hydrolyze or digest proteins; *lipases* hydrolyze fats, and *amylases* act on starch. *Sucrase* breaks down sucrose into two simpler sugars. Some enzymes that catalyze oxidation-reduction reactions are commonly called oxidases or **dehydrogenases**.

Reduction reactions   chemical reactions in which there is a gain in hydrogen or in electrons

Some hydrolytic enzymes occur in plant tissues and have importance in food preparation. For example, the enzyme bromelin, which occurs in pineapple, is a protease and causes gelatin (a protein product) to liquefy when fresh or frozen uncooked pineapple is added to gelatin. It is necessary to destroy bromelin by heating the pineapple before adding it to a gelatin mixture if the gelatin is to set. Bromelin has been used as a meat tenderizer because of its proteolytic action. Papain, which is obtained from the papaya plant, also acts on proteins to hydrolyze them. It forms the basis of some tenderizing compounds applied to less tender meats. Enzymes used as meat tenderizers do not penetrate very far into the meat and may tenderize only on the surface. Certain oxidases in plant tissues are involved in the darkening of cut or bruised surfaces of many fresh fruits and vegetables. *Rennin* or chymosin is an enzyme that brings about the clotting of milk and is used in the manufacture of cheese.

Dehydrogenase   an enzyme that catalyzes a chemical reaction in which hydrogen is removed, similar to an oxidation reaction

Enzyme Activity.   There are optimal conditions under which each enzyme acts. Temperature, degree of acidity or pH, amount of substrate, and amount of enzyme are all important. In general, the rate or speed of an enzymatic reaction increases as the temperature increases until a critical level is reached, at which point denaturation or coagulation of the enzyme by heat stops the activity. There is an optimum temperature at which activity is greatest and denaturation does not occur. For example, the optimum temperature for the activity of papain is 60° to 70°C (140° to 160°F). When it is used as a meat tenderizer, it does not begin to hydrolyze meat proteins to any significant extent until this temperature range is reached during the cooking process. The enzyme is then inactivated as the temperature rises above 70°C (160°F).

There is also an optimal pH for the activity of each enzyme. Often, this is a very narrow range, outside of which activity does not occur. For example, rennin clots milk most effectively when the pH is about 5.8. Clotting does not occur if the pH is strongly alkaline.

The rate of an enzymatic reaction increases with increasing substrate up to a certain point and then remains constant. The rate of an enzymatic reaction also increases with increasing amounts of enzyme. Enzyme activity in foods may thus be at least partially controlled by controlling the conditions under which the food is held or handled.

•SOLUTIONS AND DISPERSIONS

Foods are usually mixtures of the various chemical substances that we have discussed—sugars, starch, fiber, fats, proteins, minerals, vitamins, water—and also air. To complicate things still further, some of these substances may be in different states—solid, liquid, or gas. Substances combined with other substances are often spoken of as *dispersion systems*. One (or possibly more) substance called the *dispersed phase* is scattered or subdivided throughout another continuous substance called the *dispersion medium* (Figure 5.9). For example, table sugar or sucrose may be dispersed in water; the individual molecules of sucrose are the dispersed phase and the water surrounding each of the sucrose molecules is the dispersion medium or continuous phase.

Dispersion systems may be classified on the basis of the state of matter in each phase. According to this classification, a food system may have a gas dispersed in a liquid (air in whipped egg whites [a foam]), a liquid dispersed in a liquid (oil dispersed in vinegar to make mayonnaise [an emulsion]); or a solid dispersed in a liquid (proteins such as **casein** dispersed in milk or **ovalbumin** dispersed in egg white).

Casein   a major protein found in milk

Ovalbumin   a major protein found in egg white

Another classification of dispersion systems is according to the size of the dispersed particles (see Table 5.7). In this classification, the very smallest molecules or particles dispersed in a liquid are said to form true solutions. Particles of intermediate size, although still very small, form colloidal dispersions. Comparatively large particles, such as corn starch granules dispersed in cold water, form suspensions. In line with this classification, small molecules or ions such as sugars, salts, and vitamins are usually found in true solutions; large molecules such as proteins, pectic substances, cellulose, hemicelluloses, and cooked starch are usually colloidally dispersed; and clumps of molecules such

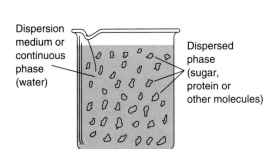

Dispersion medium or continuous phase (water)

Dispersed phase (sugar, protein or other molecules)

FIGURE 5.9
A dispersion system.

Solution   the resulting mixture of a solute dissolved in a solvent

Solute   a dissolved or dispersed substance

Solvent   the liquid in which another substance is dissolved

Kinetic motion   the very rapid vibration and movement of tiny molecules or ions dispersed in true solution

Crystallize   to form crystals, each of which consists of an orderly array of molecules in a pattern characteristic of that particular substance

as fat globules and uncooked starch granules are usually suspended and readily separate from the dispersion medium on standing. In true **solutions**, the dispersed phase is called the **solute** and the dispersion medium is referred to as the **solvent**. In food systems, water is the most common solvent or dispersion medium; however, in a few cases, such as those of butter and margarine, fat is the dispersion medium and small droplets of water form the dispersed phase.

Characteristics of Solutions

Solutions are common phenomena with respect to food systems. Sugars are in water solutions in fruits, fruit juices, and vegetables. In fact, in all foods containing sugars or salts and water, a solution is formed.

The solutes in solutions are always very small molecules or ions. These tiny particles are in constant **kinetic motion** but are evenly distributed throughout the solvent; therefore, the mixture is homogeneous. Because solutions are very stable, they remain unchanged indefinitely unless water evaporates and the solute becomes so concentrated that it **crystallizes** out of solution. The solute is so finely dispersed that it passes through most membranes and filters and cannot be seen under a microscope. True solutions do not usually have the capacity to form gels.

Characteristics of Colloidal Dispersions

The colloidal state is intermediate between a true solution and a coarse suspension, with dispersed particles that are either very large molecules, such as proteins or pectin, or clumps of smaller molecules, such as very tiny globules of fat containing groups of triglyceride molecules. Because colloidal particles are larger than those in true solution, they do not have as much kinetic energy and do not move as rapidly in the dispersion medium. Therefore, they are not as homogeneous and not as stable. They do, however, remain dispersed under usual conditions of food preparation and storage.

Three major factors are responsible for the stabilization of colloidal dispersions: (1) The colloidal particles are moved back and forth by the smaller, faster-moving water molecules of the dispersion medium in what is called *Brownian movement,* (2) there are similar net electric charges on the dispersed particles—either all positive or all negative—and like charges repel each other, keeping the colloidal particles separated, and (3) the colloidal particles often bind water closely around them (called water of hydration), forming a somewhat protective shell.

A unique characteristic of many colloidal systems is the ability to form gels, which are more or less rigid systems. A colloidal dispersion in a liquid,

TABLE 5.7
Particle Size in Various Types of Dispersion Systems

System	Particle size
True solutions	Less than 1 nm[a] in diameter
Colloidal dispersions	1 nm to 0.1 or 0.2 μm[b] in diameter
Suspensions	Greater than 0.2 μm in diameter

[a] A nanometer (nm) is one thousandth of a micrometer.
[b] A micrometer (μm) is one millionth of a meter.

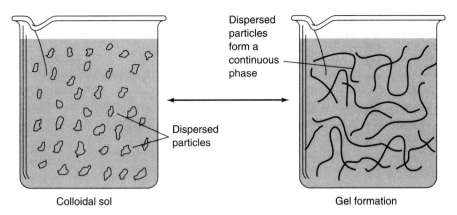

Dispersed particles form a continuous phase

Dispersed particles

Colloidal sol

Gel formation

FIGURE 5.10

A representation of gel formation. This is sometimes called *sol-gel transformation* and is typical of colloidal dispersions.

pourable condition is called a *sol*, distinguishing it from a true solution in which the dispersed particles are smaller. The sol, under proper conditions of temperature, pH, and concentration, may be transformed from a pourable mixture into a somewhat rigid solid called a *gel*. It has been suggested that during gel formation, the relatively large colloidal particles loosely join together to form a continuous network, sometimes called a brush-heap structure, trapping the liquid dispersion medium in its meshes. Figure 5.10 suggests how this might happen. Gel formation in foods may involve proteins, such as egg and gelatin gels, or carbohydrates, such as pectin jams or jellies and starch-thickened pies or puddings.

Characteristics of Suspensions

Suspensions are generally very unstable. The dispersed particles are composed of large groups of molecules, and the force of gravity tends to cause separation of the particles from the dispersion medium. The particles are large enough to be seen under an ordinary microscope. Examples of suspensions in food preparation include French dressings without added emulsifying agents. When the mixture is shaken, the oil becomes dispersed in the vinegar; however, the two phases separate immediately on standing. When corn starch and cold water are mixed together in the preparation of a starch-thickened pudding, the starch granules are suspended in the water; however, on standing only a short time, they settle to the bottom of the container. Tiny crystals of sugar in a crystalline candy such as chocolate fudge also represent an example of a suspension. In this case, the system is more stable; however, larger crystals may form and the candy may become "sugary" if it stands too long in a dry atmosphere where moisture is evaporated from the product.

STUDY QUESTIONS

1. The chemical composition of food can be determined in the laboratory. List the major components and the minor components that are present in foods.
2. Give examples of foods that are high, intermediate, and limited in water content. What is meant by *water activity*? Explain.
3. Describe four or five important functions of water in food preparation.
4. What is the *pH scale* and what does it indicate? Place several common foods on the scale.

5. Describe some unique characteristics of the water molecule.
6. a. Name two types of hard water and the types of mineral salts contained in each.
   b. Describe two methods of softening permanently hard water.
7. a. What are *carbohydrates*? *Simple carbohydrates*? *Complex carbohydrates*?
   b. In the following list of carbohydrates, indicate which are monosaccharides, which are disaccharides, and which are polysaccharides.
      (1) Starch
      (2) Glucose (dextrose)
      (3) Lactose
      (4) Cellulose
      (5) Maltose
      (6) Fructose (levulose)
      (7) Galactose
      (8) Dextrins
      (9) Glycogen
      (10) Sucrose
   c. Identify the monosaccharide building blocks for each of the disaccharides and polysaccharides listed in question b.
   d. What are *oligosaccharides*? Give examples.
   e. Give several examples of vegetable gums and describe some of their uses in food processing.
   f. Name two fractions of starch and describe the major differences in their chemical structures.
   g. List at least four chemical components of dietary fiber. Indicate which are carbohydrates.
8. a. Describe in words the chemical structure of a triglyceride.
   b. Distinguish among saturated, unsaturated, and polyunsaturated fatty acids.
   c. For each of the fatty acids listed below, indicate if it is saturated, monounsaturated, or polyunsaturated.
      (1) Palmitic acid
      (2) Linoleic acid
      (3) Butyric acid
      (4) Stearic acid
      (5) Oleic acid
   d. Distinguish between *cis* and *trans* fatty acids.
   e. What is a *simple triglyceride*? A *mixed triglyceride*?
   f. In the following list of foods, check those that are rich sources of fat.

Whipped cream	Lard	Pork spareribs
Spinach	Walnuts	Potato chips
Pinto beans	Cheddar cheese	Shortening
Corn tortillas	Chocolate	White bread
Margarine	Corn oil	Apples

   g. How do phospholipids differ from triglycerides in chemical structure? What useful role do phospholipids play in food preparation?
   h. List several food sources of cholesterol.
9. a. What chemical groups characterize amino acids?
   b. How are amino acids joined to make proteins?
   c. What is meant by the *side chains* or *R* groups of a protein? Explain why proteins may act as buffers in foods.
   d. What is an *essential amino acid* and how many amino acids are so designated for the human adult?
   e. From the following list of amino acids, identify those that are nutritionally essential.

Methionine	Threonine	Glutamic acid	Phenylalanine
Isoleucine	Cystine	Tryptophan	Glycine
Leucine	Serine	Alanine	Valine
Lysine	Tyrosine		

   f. Explain the meaning of *biological value* in relation to proteins. Why do some protein foods, such as eggs and milk, have high biological value while others, such as kidney beans and wheat flour, have lower biological value?

g. How can proteins supplement each other to improve the net nutritional value? Explain this.

h. Name several food sources that are relatively high in protein.

i. Describe, in general, the primary, secondary, tertiary, and quaternary structure of proteins.

10. a. Describe what probably happens when a protein is denatured and list at least four treatments, likely to be applied to foods, that can cause protein denaturation.

b. Explain what probably happens when proteins are coagulated and describe some examples of coagulation in foods.

11. a. What is a *catalyst*? What are *enzymes* and how do they act as catalysts?

b. Suggest a general mechanism of action for enzymes.

c. Give examples of hydrolytic enzymes.

d. Explain why enzymes are of importance in food processing and preparation.

12. a. Describe what is meant by *dispersion system*, *dispersed phase*, *dispersion medium*, *solution*, *solute*, and *solvent*.

b. Give examples from foods of types of dispersion systems classified according to the state of matter in each phase.

c. Describe three types of dispersion systems classified on the basis of size of dispersed particles.

d. Describe what probably happens during a sol-gel transformation in a food product. What types of dispersion systems are likely to show this phenomenon?

REFERENCES

1. Buswell, A. M. and W. H. Rodebush. 1956. Water. *Scientific American 194*, 2 (No. 4).

2. *Composition of Foods*. Agriculture Handbook No. 8 Series. Washington, DC: U.S. Department of Agriculture.

3. Dziezak, J. D. 1991. A focus on gums. *Food Technology 45*, 116 (No. 3).

4. *Handbook of Food Preparation* 9th ed. Washington, DC: American Home Economics Association, 1993.

5. Institute of Food Technologists' Expert Panel on Food Safety and Nutrition. 1989. Dietary fiber. *Food Technology 43*, 133 (No. 10).

6. Katz, E. E. and T. P. Labuza. 1981. Effect of water activity on the sensory crispness and mechanical deformation of snack food products. *Journal of Food Science 46*, 403.

7. *Nutritive Value of Foods*. 1991. Home and Garden Bulletin No. 72. Washington, DC: U.S. Department of Agriculture.

Weights and Measures

6

Correct proportions of ingredients are vital to success in the preparation of many food products. These proportions are best achieved when the measuring or weighing of each individual ingredient in a recipe is done accurately and consistently. In the United States, recipes generally call for volume measurements, whereas in other countries ingredients may be more commonly weighed than measured. A change in the United States from the U.S. customary system of weights and measures to the metric system was recommended and became public policy with passage by the U.S. Congress of the Metric Conversion Act of 1975. Although conversion presently remains voluntary, many food labels carry metric units along with the customary ones.

Weighing is generally more accurate than measuring, particularly for ingredients such as flour that may pack down in the container [5]. Weight and volume relationships also vary with certain chopped foods, such as onions, depending on the fineness and uniformity of chopping before measuring. Because of these differences in **density**, the use of standardized measuring techniques and equipment is particularly important.

CHAPTER OUTLINE

THE METRIC SYSTEM
MEASURING EQUIPMENT
MEASUREMENT OF STAPLE
 FOODS
RECIPES

Density weight per unit of volume

•THE METRIC SYSTEM

During the French Revolution, France's lawmakers asked their scientists to develop a system of measurement based on science rather than custom. The result was the metric system, which has since been adopted by most of the nations of the world. The United States will benefit by a changeover from the U.S. customary to the metric system as it participates in international trade, since most of the rest of the world already uses the metric system in conducting business.

The metric system is a decimal system based on multiples of ten. The basic unit of length is the meter, which is slightly longer than a yard. When the meter is divided by 10, it produces 10 decimeters; a decimeter divided by 10 produces 10 centimeters; and a centimeter divided by 10 results in 10 millimeters. In other words, 1 meter equals 1000 millimeters or 100 centimeters or 10 decimeters. The same prefixes are combined with the basic unit of mass or

TABLE 6.1

The Metric System—Prefixes and Symbols

	Prefix	Mass	Symbol	Volume	Symbol	Length	Symbol
0.000001	micro-	microgram	μg	microliter	μL	micrometer	μm
0.001	milli-	milligram	mg	milliliter	mL	millimeter	mm
0.01	centi-	centigram	cg	centiliter	cL	centimeter	cm
0.1	deci-	decigram	dg	deciliter	dL	decimeter	dm
1.0		gram	g	liter	L	meter	m
10	deka-	dekagram	dag	dekaliter	daL	dekameter	dam
100	hecto-	hectogram	hg	hectoliter	hL	hectometer	hm
1000	kilo-	kilogram	kg	kiloliter	kL	kilometer	km

weight (gram) and the basic unit of volume or capacity (liter) to indicate designated amounts. Prefixes and symbols for mass, volume, and length are shown in Table 6.1. Other units and symbols associated with the metric system are given in Table 6.2.

Conversion to Metric

While using containers or packages for food that were designed for use with U.S. customary measurements, such as the ounce and the quart, many food manufacturers list the net contents of the package in both U.S. customary and metric units. For example, the label on a one and one-half quart bottle of fruit juice may read "48 oz. (1½ qts.) 1.42 L." Packaged food products are now commonly labeled with dual measurements. This type of conversion to the metric system is called *soft conversion*.

Hard conversion to the metric system is occurring more gradually. This involves actually designing containers and packages to hold a certain number of metric units of food. For example, a number of soft drinks are now being marketed in 2-liter bottles rather than in the 32-ounce bottles that were previously used. More containers will be designed in this manner as the conversion from U.S. customary to metric becomes more comprehensive.

Hard and soft conversion to the metric system is occurring with food-measuring equipment as well as with food containers. Most standard liquid measuring cups are stamped with both metric and U.S. customary quantity indicators. In a one-cup measure, the graduations are usually marked at 1/4, 1/3, 1/2, 2/3, and 3/4 cup. The metric scale is usually marked at 250, 200, 150, 100, and 50 milliliters. One cup or 8 fluid ounces of liquid converts precisely to

TABLE 6.2

Some Metric Units and Symbols

	Unit	Symbol
Energy	Joule	J
Temperature	Degree Celsius	°C
Pressure	Pascal	Pa
Frequency	Hertz	Hz
Power	Watt	W

236.59 milliliters while one-half cup converts to 118.29 milliliters, with neither of these quantities fitting exactly the markings for milliliters on the cup. Separately designed metric measures use hard conversion; they are standardized at 250 milliliters, approximately equal to 1 cup; 125 milliliters, approximately equal to 1/2 cup; and 50 milliliters, approximately equal to 1/4 cup. Measuring spoons are available to measure 1, 2, 5, 15, and 25 milliliters.

Some adjustment will undoubtedly be necessary in converting recipes made with U.S. customary measures to metric measurements in order to make the converted recipe practical. For example, as indicated, one cup will convert to 237 milliliters. However, a metric measure will not be available for exactly this quantity; rather, it will be more practical to use the 250 milliliter measure. Depending upon the recipe, these small differences may or may not affect the final product. Standardization of each converted recipe will therefore be necessary.

The use of the metric system will affect Americans in all types of jobs as well as consumers in the marketplace. Particularly involved will be foodservice managers and workers. Not only must recipes be converted to metric units for measuring and/or weighing, but purchasing also will be done in metric units. It is likely that measuring rather than weighing will commonly be used in home food preparation, whereas the foodservice worker may use a combination of scales and volume-measuring devices when preparing recipes [4, 6].

Information about conversion between U.S. customary units and metric units is found in Appendix A. Conversion formulas and charts for changing Fahrenheit and Celsius temperatures are given in Appendix B.

•MEASURING EQUIPMENT

Standard U.S. customary measures are available in various sizes. Gallon measures (4 quart or 16 cup capacity), half-gallon or 2-quart measures, and quart measures are commonly used in quantity food preparation. The measuring cup has a half-pint or 8-fluid-ounce capacity (Figure 6.1). Metric measures are available in various equivalents of one liter as well as 500- and 250-milliliter capacities.

For more accurate measurement of dry or solid ingredients, it is best to use measuring containers that are filled and leveled at the top. Fractional cups, as well as one-cup measures, are available (Figure 6.1).

FIGURE 6.1

Household measuring utensils include a glass cup for measuring liquids, fractional-cup measures for measuring dry ingredients, and measuring spoons.

Measuring spoons are commonly available in sets that measure 1 tablespoon, 1 teaspoon, 1/2 teaspoon, and 1/4 teaspoon. One tablespoon measures 1/16 cup; there are 16 tablespoons in 1 cup. Three teaspoons are equal to 1 tablespoon.

The American Home Economics Association and the American Standards Association have published a set of standards and tolerances for household measuring utensils [2]. A deviation of 5 percent from the precise measure indicated on the measuring cup or spoon is allowed. Not all measuring utensils on the market meet the tolerance of 5 percent, however.

A scale or balance can be used to weigh foods. To be accurate, the scale must be of good quality. Such scales are usually relatively expensive. Weighing is often more practical than measuring, in terms of time and convenience, when large quantities are involved. Although weighing is also generally more accurate than measuring volumes, particularly for foods that tend to pack down as do flours and chopped ingredients, scales are not usually available in U.S. homes.

•MEASUREMENT OF STAPLE FOODS

Even though accurate measuring equipment is available, measuring problems still exist. Inaccuracies may occur through the manner in which the equipment is used. Most recipes allow small deviations in the amounts of ingredients used, which result from differences in measuring techniques, and acceptable products are still produced. However, the quality of some products, such as shortened cakes, may be adversely affected by different methods of measuring the flour [3]. Accurate and consistent measurement of ingredients is very important in producing uniform products of high quality time after time [1]. Some common measurements and symbols used in food preparation are found in Appendix A.

Flour

White wheat flour is one of the most difficult ingredients to measure consistently because it is composed of tiny particles of different sizes that tend to pack [3]. For this reason, it is generally recommended that white flour be sifted once before measuring. Graham or whole wheat flours are usually not sifted before they are measured because the bran particles may be sifted out. Finely milled whole-wheat flour may be sifted, however. Instantized flour, which contains agglomerated particles of quite uniform size, does not require sifting before being measured.

To measure sifted or unsifted flour, spoon tablespoons of the flour lightly into a dry-measure cup until the cup is heaping full. Do not pack the flour by shaking the cup while filling or hitting it with the spoon. Then level the top of the filled cup with the straight edge of a spatula (Figure 6.2). Quantities of less than 1 cup should be measured in the smaller fractional cups.

When measuring with a tablespoon or teaspoon, the spoon should be heaped full by dipping into the flour and then leveled with the straight edge of a spatula. Fractional spoons should be used to measure half and quarter spoon-

(a) Sift flour once   (b) Spoon lightly into cup   (c) Level top with straight edge

FIGURE 6.2
A recommended procedure for measuring white flour.

fuls. If these are not available, half spoonfuls may be measured by using a straight edge to divide the flour in half lengthwise and scrape out half. Quarter spoonfuls may be measured by dividing a half spoonful crosswise into two portions as nearly equal as possible and scraping out half.

The mass or weight of equal measures of white and whole-wheat flour are not the same. One cup of whole-wheat flour weighs approximately 132 grams while one cup of white flour weighs about 115 grams. Also, there is a difference in the mass of sifted and unsifted white flour, since unsifted flour is generally more tightly packed. If unsifted white flour is substituted for sifted flour in a recipe previously standardized with the use of sifted flour, the amount of flour may be adjusted by removing 2 level tablespoons from each cup of unsifted flour measured [5]. This adjustment should give satisfactory results in baking.

Solid Fats

Solid fats should be removed from the refrigerator long enough before they are measured so that they will be **plastic**. Very hard fats are difficult to measure accurately except in the case of sticks of butter or margarine that have measurements marked on the wrapper. In this case they may be cut, as marked, with a sharp knife. To measure plastic fats, press the fat into the cup with a spatula or knife so that air spaces are forced out. Then level the cup or fractional cup with a straight edge. For measurements up to 1/4 cup, level tablespoons may be used.

As an alternative, a water displacement method may be used if the water that clings to the fat does not affect the product. Pour cold water into a cup up to the measure that will equal 1 cup when added to the amount of fat to be measured. Then add enough fat to bring the water up to 1 cup when the fat is completely submerged in the water. Finally, drain off the water.

Plastic able to be molded into various shapes without shattering as a force is applied; plastic fats can be mixed or creamed

Sugar

Sifting is not necessary before measuring sugar unless the sugar becomes lumpy. Simply spoon granulated sugar into a cup and level the top with the straight edge of a spatula.

For brown sugar, any lumps should first be rolled out before the sugar is pressed into the cup firmly enough that it holds its shape when turned out of the cup. Measured in this way, 1 cup of brown sugar is approximately equal in mass to 1 cup of granulated sugar.

For the measurement of confectioners' or powdered sugar, sifting is followed by spooning of the sugar into a cup, as for flour. One cup of confectioners' sugar is slightly heavier than 1/2 cup of granulated sugar. About 1¾ cups of confectioners' sugar is equal in mass to 1 cup granulated sugar.

Syrups

To measure syrups or molasses, place the cup or fractional cup on a flat surface and fill completely. Because it is thick, the liquid may tend to round up higher than level full. It should be cut off level with the straight edge of a spatula. Measure spoonfuls by pouring syrup into the spoon and cutting off level with the straight edge of a spatula. Care should be taken to keep syrups from sticking to the measuring cup or spoon.

Liquids

For the measurement of liquids, a cup that extends above the largest measure mark should be used to increase ease and accuracy of measurement. The cup should have a lip for pouring. Only liquids are measured accurately in liquid measuring cups; these cups should not be used for measuring dry ingredients. Place the cup on a flat surface and fill to the desired measure mark. The eye should be at the level of the measure mark when reading the contents. In clear liquids, a **meniscus** can be seen at the upper surface as a curved concave line. The eye should read the lowest point of this meniscus (Figure 6.3).

Meniscus   the curved upper surface of a column of liquid

FIGURE 6.3
When measuring clear liquids, read the meniscus at the lowest point.

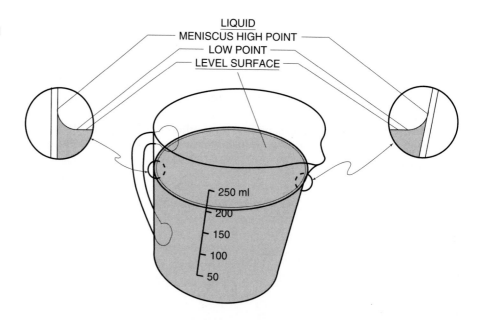

LIQUID
MENISCUS HIGH POINT
LOW POINT
LEVEL SURFACE

250 ml
200
150
100
50

Recipe Styles

A recipe lists the ingredients and the procedure for preparing a food product. To be effective, it must be written simply and clearly so that it cannot be misunderstood. There are four general styles of written recipes [1]. A description and an example of each style follow.

Standard style. Ingredients are listed first, in the order in which they will be used, followed by the method of combining ingredients in either step or paragraph form. For example:

1 cup sifted all-purpose flour

2 Tbsp granulated sugar

1 tsp baking powder

1/4 tsp salt

1/4 cup shortening (at room temperature)

(And so on.)

1. Preheat oven to 350°F.
2. Sift dry ingredients together into mixing bowl.
3. Add shortening.
4. (And so on.)

Action style. The narrative describing the action or method is combined with the listing of ingredients in order of the steps involved in the procedure. For example:

Measure and sift together in a mixing bowl:

1 cup sifted flour

2 Tbsp sugar

1 tsp baking powder

1/4 tsp salt

Add:

1/4 cup shortening

(And so on.)

Descriptive style. Each ingredient, followed by the modification for that ingredient, is listed in one column. The amount of each ingredient is listed in a separate column, and each step in the procedure is listed in a third parallel column. For example:

Flour, all-purpose, sifted	1 cup	Sift dry ingredients together in mixing bowl.
Sugar, granulated	2 Tbsp	
Baking powder	1 tsp	
Salt	¼ tsp	
Shortening	¼ cup	Add to dry ingredients.
(And so on.)		

Narrative style. The amounts of ingredients and the method are combined in narrative. This may be difficult to follow unless the recipe is short or has few ingredients. For example:

Sift all-purpose flour once. Measure 1 cup sifted flour, 2 Tbsp granulated sugar, 1 tsp baking powder, and 1/4 tsp salt. Sift all of the dry ingredients together in a mixing bowl. Add 1/4 cup shortening. (And so on.)

This last style is more easily used for a recipe with few ingredients. For example:

Thaw two pounds of frozen fish fillets. Cut into serving-size pieces. Place on broiler rack. Brush with melted butter or margarine. (And so on.)

Standardization

A recipe is considered standarized only after it has been tried and evaluated for quality, and any necessary adaptations or adjustments have been made. Equipment, types of ingredients available, and skills of the person preparing the recipe differ from one situation to another. Therefore, each recipe must be adapted and standardized for use in a particular situation. Once a recipe has been standardized for a particular setting, it is useful in making out market orders and in calculating food costs. Recipes that are standardized for inclusion in cookbooks generally use the methods for measuring ingredients outlined earlier in this chapter. Recipes with eggs are generally standardized using large-size eggs.

STUDY QUESTIONS

1. Discuss why accurate measurements are important in the preparation of quality food products.
2. a. What is the metric system of measurement and where did it originate?
   b. Why is it important for the United States to convert from the U.S. customary to the metric system?
   c. Name the basic metric units for length, volume or capacity, and weight or mass. What is indicated by the prefixes *deci-*, *centi-*, *milli-*, and *micro-*?
   d. What is meant by *soft conversion* and *hard conversion* to the metric system?
3. What type of measuring cups should be used to measure liquids? What type should be used to measure dry ingredients?
4. How many tablespoons are there in 1 cup? How many teaspoons are there in 1 tablespoon?
5. Describe appropriate procedures for measuring flour, liquid, solid fat, sugar, and syrups.
6. What is a *standardized recipe*? What advantages are there to the use of standardized recipes?
7. Describe several styles of written recipes and discuss the advantages of each.

REFERENCES

1. American Home Economics Association. 1993. *Handbook of Food Preparation*, 9th ed. Washington, DC: American Home Economics Association.
2. American Standards Association. 1963. *American Standard Dimensions, Tolerances, and Terminology for Home Cooking and Baking Utensils*. New York: American Standards Association, Inc.

3. Arlin, M. L., M. M. Nielsen, and F. T. Hall. 1964. The effect of different methods of flour measurement on the quality of plain two-egg cakes. *Journal of Home Economics 56*, 399.

4. *Handbook for Metric Usage in Home Economics*. 1977. Washington, DC: American Home Economics Association.

5. Matthews, R. H. and O. M. Batcher. 1963. Sifted versus unsifted flour. *Journal of Home Economics 55*, 123.

6. Miller, B. S. and H. B. Trimbo. 1972. Use of metric measurements in food preparation. *Journal of Home Economics 64*, 20.

Heat Transfer in Cooking

7

Heat is a form of energy that results from the rapid movement or vibration of molecules within a substance. This movement of molecules is called *kinetic energy*. With the use of a thermometer, we can measure the average intensity of the heat resulting from the molecular movement within a substance. We record it as *temperature*.

As the molecules move, they constantly collide with other molecules in the same substance or with molecules of another substance with which they come into contact. And, as molecules collide, their speed of movement may be changed. Rapidly moving molecules striking slower-moving molecules transfer some of their energy to the slower-moving ones. Thus, heat is transferred from a warmer substance to a cooler one.

Cooking results when heat is transferred to or produced in a food and is distributed from one part of the food throughout the whole. Heating or cooking produces many changes in foods that, when the cooking is properly done, increase their palatability and appetite appeal.

•EFFECTS OF COOKING FOOD

There are several important reasons for cooking food. Probably the major one is to make certain foods edible and increase their palatability. Some basic staple foods, such as dry legumes and whole grains, are not in an edible form when they are harvested. These products must be **rehydrated** and softened so that the raw starch is made more palatable. A remarkable transformation occurs when flour mixtures are baked or cooked, with many new flavors and color changes contributing to their increased palatability and appeal. Meat, poultry, and seafood, although consumed raw in some instances and particularly within certain cultures, are also generally more aesthetically pleasing and palatable when they have been cooked. Moreover, proper cooking destroys **pathogenic microorganisms** that may be present in these raw products.

Cooking improves the sanitary quality of other foods as well. The extent of destruction of microorganisms in food is dependent on time and temperature relationships. For example, the threat posed by potentially pathogenic microorganisms in milk is eliminated by **pasteurization**, a heat process.

CHAPTER OUTLINE

EFFECTS OF COOKING FOOD
HEAT INVOLVED IN CHANGE OF STATE
TYPES OF HEAT TRANSFER
MEDIA FOR HEAT TRANSFER
THERMOMETER SCALES

Rehydrate to add water to replace that lost during drying

Pathogenic microorganisms microbes capable of causing disease

Pasteurization a mild heat treatment that destroys microorganisms that may cause disease but does not destroy all microorganisms in the product

125

Starch granules starch molecules are organized into tight little bundles, called granules, as they are stored in the seeds or roots of plants; the granules, with characteristic shapes and sizes, can be seen under the microscope

Texture the arrangement of the particles or constituent parts of a material that gives it its characteristic structure

Blanch to heat for a few minutes by immersing in boiling water, surrounding with steam, or applying microwaves

Digestibility and nutritive value may, in some cases, be increased by cooking. Starch in cooked grain products and legumes becomes more readily available to digestive enzymes than that in compact raw **starch granules**. Some antidigestive factors in dry beans and peas are also destroyed by heating. Of course, cooking may bring about decreases in nutritive value as well. For instance, some loss of vitamins and minerals occurs when vegetables and meats are cooked. By avoiding overcooking and improper cooking methods, we can minimize these losses.

The keeping quality or shelf life of some foods is extended by cooking. For example, very perishable fresh peaches or other fruits keep somewhat longer if they are cooked. When cooked and canned, they keep for a considerably longer period.

Finally, we must not forget that food is to be enjoyed. Cooking foods makes possible the creation of many new delectable dishes, greatly increasing variety and interest in dining.

Flavor, **texture**, and color of foods are affected in various ways by the cooking process. Some new flavors are formed by heating, as meats are browned, breads are baked, and caramels are cooked, for example. Flavor may also be lost or undesirable flavors may be produced by cooking, as is the case when vegetables are overcooked or toast is burned.

Texture is often softened by cooking; the fiber of vegetables becomes limp and the connective tissue of meat is tenderized. However, some foods become crisp on cooking, for example, bacon, potato chips, and other fried foods. Eggs, both whites and yolks, become more firm on heating. The entire character of a texture may be changed by cooking. Note the great difference in texture between a cake batter and the finished cake or between bread dough and the baked loaf. A starch-thickened pudding or sauce also undergoes a remarkable change in texture after sufficient heating.

Color changes occur during cooking as well. Bright green vegetables turn dull and drab when they are overcooked or cooked with acid, whereas a short **blanching** period may actually enhance the color of fresh green peas. Rich brown gravy is made from drippings that have browned during the roasting of meat. Light brown crusts on baked goods enhance their eye appeal, as well as improve flavor and texture characteristics. The effects on food of cooking are truly diverse and, in many cases, highly desirable.

•HEAT INVOLVED IN CHANGE OF STATE

A substance may exist as a solid, a liquid, or a gas. When it changes from a solid to a liquid or from a liquid to a gas, we say that there is a *change of state*. The physical state of the matter—solid, liquid, or gas—has changed. Energy is involved in this change of state. Let us use water as an example, because water is commonly employed as a medium for applying heat in food preparation.

The solid form of water is ice. In a piece of ice, the water molecules have formed an ordered crystalline pattern and are held in a fixed arrangement. In a solid such as ice, the molecules may vibrate in place but do not move around freely.

When heat is applied to ice, the water molecules vibrate more rapidly and push against each other. When sufficient heat has been applied, the ice melts and becomes liquid water. In a liquid, the molecules have broken away from each other and are free to move about; however, they remain together and take the shape of the container in which they are placed.

A special kind of heat or energy is used to bring about the change from solid ice to liquid water. It is called *latent heat*, that is, heat required to change the physical state without changing the temperature as measured by a thermometer. Heat measured by use of a thermometer is called *sensible heat*.

In the case of water, the latent heat involved is 80 **calories** for each gram of ice that changes to liquid water. This energy is *absorbed* by the melting ice and is used to break up the ordered molecules of water in the ice structure. Actually, the same amount of energy—80 calories per gram—was *released* from the liquid water as it froze and formed solid ice crystals. This heat that is absorbed during a change from solid to liquid state and released during a change from liquid to solid state is called *latent heat of fusion or solidification*. We take advantage of the latent heat of fusion when we freeze ice cream using an ice and salt mixture. As the ice melts, the heat necessary for bringing about this change of state is taken from the ice cream mixture to be frozen, thus making it colder. Pure water freezes to ice at 0°C (32°F), and ice melts at this same temperature.

Latent heat is also involved when liquid water forms water vapor or steam, which is a gas. The molecules in a gas are widely separated and move freely in space. When liquid water stands in an open container, some of its molecules vaporize, even at room temperature. These gaseous molecules hovering over the surface of liquid water create a pressure called *vapor pressure*. As heat is gradually applied to liquid water, the vapor pressure increases to a point just greater than the atmospheric pressure. At this point, bubbles in the liquid break at the surface and boiling ensues, equalizing the vapor pressure and the atmospheric pressure. At sea level, the boiling point of water is 100°C (212°F).

When liquid water changes to steam, latent heat is absorbed. In this case, it is called *latent heat of vaporization*. For each gram of water vaporized at the boiling point, 540 calories are absorbed, but the temperature of the newly formed steam is the same as that of the boiling water, 100°C (212°F). The energy of latent heat is necessary to bring about the wide separation of water molecules from each other as they form a gas. In the reverse process, the condensation of steam to liquid water, the same amount of energy is given off as the *latent heat of condensation*. We take advantage of this released heat when we steam foods. As steam touches the cooler surface of the food, it condenses to liquid and releases the 540 calories per gram, energy that may be absorbed by the food, thus actually aiding in the cooking process.

Liquid water itself has a relatively large capacity to absorb heat. It is used as a standard for measuring the heat capacities of other substances. Water has been assigned a heat capacity of 1.00, called its *specific heat*, which indicates that 1 calorie is required to increase the temperature of 1 gram of water 1°C. Thus, to take 100 grams of water (about 2/5 cup) from 0°C to boiling at 100°C, 10,000 calories of heat or energy (1 calorie per gram per degree = 1 calorie x 100 grams x 100° = 10,000 calories) are required.

Calorie   a unit of heat measurement; in this chapter, we are referring to the small calorie used in chemistry; the kilocalorie (1 kilocalorie is equal to 1000 small calories) is used in nutrition

•TYPES OF HEAT TRANSFER

Conventional cooking methods transfer heat energy from its source to the food by means of conduction, convection currents, and radiation. In most methods, more than one means of heat transfer is involved.

Conduction

In the case of conduction, heat is transmitted from one molecule or particle to the next one in direct contact with it. Heat moves from the heated coil of an electric unit, the touching flame of a gas unit, or other heat source to the saucepan placed on it and from the saucepan to the first layer of food, water, or fat in contact with the bottom and sides of the pan. Then heat is conducted throughout the mass of the food in the pan the same way, particle by particle (Figure 7.1). Because fat can be heated to much higher temperatures than can water, it is possible to bring more heat into the pan during the frying process. Using a pan with a flat bottom that comes in close contact with the heat source conserves heat and utilizes it most efficiently.

Materials used in the construction of cooking utensils vary in their ability to conduct heat efficiently. Metals that are good conductors include aluminum, cast iron, steel, and copper. Pans are commonly made of either cast aluminum or aluminum formed from sheets. Cast-iron skillets and dutch ovens are heavy cooking utensils that distribute and hold heat well. Stainless steel is an alloy of iron with a small percentage of carbon and other metals, such as chromium and nickel. It is a very durable, easily cleaned metal, but it does not conduct heat uniformly. Because so many of its other properties are desirable for cooking utensils, however, it is often combined in various ways with other metals to improve heating efficiency and eliminate "hot spots." For example, the heating base of a stainless steel pan may be clad with copper or aluminum, or a core of iron or other high-conductivity metal may be placed between the sheets of stainless steel used to form the pan. Cooking utensils are also made of heat-resistant glass, ceramic materials, and metal coated with a porcelain-type substance. Nonstick finishes such as teflon may also be applied to the inner surfaces of pans and skillets.

Ideally, pans should be sturdy and warp-resistant even with extended use. It is important that the bottom of the pan maintain contact on a flat heating surface so that heat conduction will be efficient. The durability of a metal is determined to a great extent by its thickness, which is measured by its *gauge*. Gauge may be defined as the number of metal sheets of this particular thickness required to equal one inch. For example, ten sheets of 10-gauge stainless steel or aluminum would equal a thickness of one inch; in other words, each sheet is one tenth of an inch thick. Ten-gauge metal will produce a sturdy pan. Pans should be cared for in a manner that will prevent warping. For example, hot pans or skillets should never be placed immediately in cold water.

Convection Currents

An aid to heating by conduction for liquid and gaseous substances is convection. When gases and liquids are heated, they become lighter or less dense and tend to rise. The colder portions of these gases and liquids are more dense or

FIGURE 7.1

Conduction. Heat is transferred from an electric heating unit or from a gas flame that touches the bottom of the pan, through the pan, to the layer of the food that is next to the pan, and then throughout the food mass.

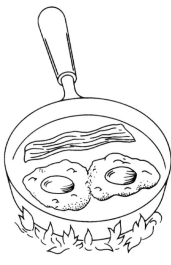

Heat source

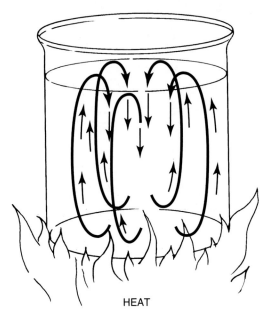

FIGURE 7.2
When liquids and gases are heated they become lighter (less dense) and rise, whereas cooler molecules of the liquid or gas move to the bottom of a container or closed compartment. These movements create convection currents that aid in distributing heat throughout the liquid or gas.

HEAT

heavier and move to the bottom to replace the heated portions that have risen. Circular convection currents are thus set up, as illustrated in Figure 7.2.

Convection currents move the molecules around in their enclosed space and tend to distribute the heat uniformly throughout. Examples of the usefulness of these currents include cooking in a saucepan or other container with food particles dispersed in water (as is done with soups and stews), deep-fat frying, and baking in an oven. When foods are cooked in water, convection currents move the heated water molecules up and around the larger particles of food, transferring heat to the surfaces of the food. This heat can then be transferred into the particles by the process of conduction. In deep-fat frying, the molecules of fat are moved upward and around the surfaces of the foods being fried in them. During cooking on a gas surface burner, heat is also transferred to the outside surface of the pan partially by convection.

In conventional-oven baking, heated gas molecules of air rise from the energy source in the bottom and move around the surfaces of the baking containers. This particularly aids in the browning of the tops of baked products and other foods. Placement of containers in the oven is important to take full advantage of convection currents in cooking and browning. When it is necessary to use two racks, the pans should be staggered so that one is not directly underneath the other (see Figure 7.3). A convection oven employs a mechanical fan that increases air movement in the oven during baking, thus increasing the efficiency of heat transfer and decreasing cooking time.

Radiation

Energy can be transmitted as waves or rays that vibrate at high frequency and travel very rapidly through space. An example of radiant energy is sunlight, which travels at the rate of 186,000 miles per second. Radiant waves go directly

FIGURE 7.3
Convection currents move heated air around cake surfaces to aid in baking and browning.

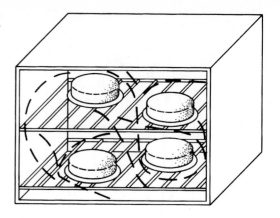

from their source to the material they touch without any assistance in the transfer of energy from the air molecules in between.

When radiant waves or rays reach the exterior parts of a food mass, energy is absorbed on the surface of the food and produces heat by increasing the vibration of the molecules in the food. Since the waves cannot penetrate below the surface, the interior is heated by conduction as the surface energy is transferred from one molecule to the next until it reaches the center of the food mass. Therefore, a combination of radiation and conduction is responsible for the heating of food in this manner.

The broiling, barbecuing, and toasting of foods all utilize radiant energy for cooking. The glowing coals of a fire, the red-hot coils of an electric heating unit, and the burning of a gas flame give off waves of radiant energy that travel from their source in a straight line to the surface of food that is placed in close proximity.

Radiant energy is an important factor in baking in an oven. The waves of energy reach the exposed surface of the food and the outer surface of the utensil that holds the food. The utensil absorbs the energy and becomes hot. Heat is then transferred by conduction from the utensil to the food that is in it. The characteristics of the utensil being used affect the amount of energy absorbed by it from the radiant waves. Dull, dark, rough surfaces absorb radiant energy readily, whereas bright, shiny, smooth surfaces tend to reflect the waves and absorb less energy, thus slowing down cooking and browning. Sometimes shiny aluminum bakeware is desirable, for example, in order to produce a light crust to layer cakes and cookies. Ovenproof glass dishes transmit radiant waves more effectively. Therefore, when glass bakeware is used, the oven temperature should be about 25°F less than that used with aluminum bakeware.

Air molecules in the oven absorb some of the radiant energy coming from the heating unit and become less dense or lighter. The lighter air rises and is replaced by colder, heavier air, thus setting up convection currents. These convection currents help to distribute the heat uniformly throughout the interior oven space, although they are separate from the radiant waves. The radiant energy continues to travel from its source in a straight line, with some fanning out as the distance from the source increases.

Although microwave cooking utilizes a form of radiant energy, microwaves are different from radiant waves. They are both high-frequency electromagnetic waves, but microwaves have longer wavelengths and are somewhat lower in frequency than are visible-light and infrared waves in the electromagnetic spectrum (see Figure 8.1). Microwaves cook food somewhat differently from the way radiant waves cook. Microwave cooking is discussed in Chapter 8.

Induction Heating

Induction cooking utilizes a high-frequency **induction coil** that is placed just beneath the cooktop surface. The cooktop is made of a smooth, ceramic material. A magnetic current is generated by the coil, and **ferrous** metal cooking utensils placed on the cooktop are heated with magnetic friction. The cooking surface itself remains cool. Only the cooking utensil gets hot. The hot utensil rapidly transmits heat to the food.

Flat cooking utensils made of cast iron, magnetic stainless steel, or enamel over steel are required for use on induction cooktops; utensils made of nonferrous materials cannot be heated. Heating by induction is rapid, and numerous power settings are available. Another advantage of the induction cooktop is the ease of cleaning. Since there is no exposed heating unit and the surface does not get hot, spills do not burn onto the unit.

Induction coil a coiled apparatus made up of two coupled circuits; interruptions in the direct current in one circuit produce an alternating current of high electrical potential in the other

Ferrous iron-containing

•MEDIA FOR HEAT TRANSFER

Media for transferring heat to food include air, water, steam, and fat. Combinations of these media may be employed.

Air

Roasting, baking, broiling, and cooking on an outdoor grill are methods employing heated air as the cooking medium. These are generally considered to be dry-heat cookery methods, because the surface of the food comes into contact with dry air; however, in the interior of most foods, water participates in the transfer of heat. Also, where part of the product is in direct contact with a pan or cookie sheet, the heat from the air is conducted through the pan to the food. In convection ovens, a blower circulates the heated air and the food heats more rapidly. When the surface of a food is dehydrated, temperatures higher than the boiling point of water may be attained, aiding in browning.

Water

Simmering, boiling, **stewing**, **braising**, and **poaching** are methods that use water as the primary cooking medium. For obvious reasons, these are called *moist-heat* cookery methods. When water is the cooking medium, the highest temperature attainable is that of boiling, 100°C (212°F) at sea level. Simmering and poaching use temperatures just below boiling. At altitudes higher than sea level, the boiling point of water is decreased 1°C for each 900 feet of elevation.

Stew to simmer in a small to moderate quantity of liquid

Braise to cook meat or poultry slowly in a small amount of liquid or in steam in a covered utensil

Poach to cook in a hot liquid, carefully handling the food to retain its form

Water is a better conductor of heat than is air; therefore, foods cooked in water cook faster. Heat is transferred or conducted directly from the hot water to the food with which it comes into contact. Convection currents are also set up in hot water and help to distribute heat uniformly throughout the food mass.

Steam

Steaming is also a moist-heat method of cooking. Foods are steamed when they are placed on a rack above boiling water in a covered container that holds in the steam. Steaming also occurs when a food containing water is closely wrapped and baked in the oven, such as a baked potato or a cut of meat wrapped in aluminum foil or placed in a cooking bag. Cooking a covered casserole in the oven involves cooking with steam, because the steam produced when the liquid boils is contained in the dish.

Heat is transferred from the steam to the surface of the food it touches. Since the food is often cooler than the steam, the steam condenses on the surface, releasing the latent heat absorbed when the steam was formed from boiling water. This aids in cooking and also explains why a steam burn is likely to be more severe than one caused by boiling water.

In a pressure canner, steam is the cooking medium; however, because the close containment of the steam within the canner raises the vapor pressure, the boiling point of the water producing the steam is increased. Therefore, the temperature of cooking within the pressure canner is elevated above the boiling point of water at atmospheric pressure and cooking is much more rapid. In a pressure saucepan, an adjustable gauge on the pan regulates the pressure and thus the temperature by releasing some steam during the cooking process.

Fat

Fat is the cooking medium in sautéing, panfrying, and deep-fat frying. To *sauté* means to cook quickly in a small amount of hot fat. It is a partial cooking process. Panfrying is cooking to doneness, also in a small amount of fat, but at a more moderate temperature [2]. Cooking a food immersed in fat at a controlled temperature is deep-fat frying. In all these methods of cooking, heat is transferred by conduction from the energy source through the pan to the fat. Convection currents are set up in the heated fat to aid in distributing the heat. The heated fat then conducts heat to the food it touches.

Fat can be heated to a much higher temperature than the boiling point of water. Since some fat is also absorbed by the food, the flavor is changed to a considerable degree. Frying is discussed in more detail in Chapter 18.

•THERMOMETER SCALES

Two thermometer scales may be used to indicate the temperature of a substance. Using the Fahrenheit scale (F), water at sea level freezes at 32°F and boils at 212°F. Although the Celsius scale is used for scientific research and in most of the world, the Fahrenheit scale has been commonly used in the United

States in previous years, in connection with the U.S. customary system of weights and measures. With the current movement for the United States to change to the metric system, however, the Celsius (or Centigrade) scale (C) is being used more often in the U.S. On this scale, water freezes at 0° and boils at 100°. The usual room temperature of 72°F is 22° on the Celsius scale. As long as the two scales are in use, it is sometimes necessary to convert from one to the other. Formulas that may be used for the conversion, as well as a partial conversion chart, are found in Appendix B. Conversion tables may also be found in Reference 1.

STUDY QUESTIONS

1. List and explain five reasons for cooking food.
2. Give examples of changes in flavor, texture, and color of foods that may occur during cooking.
3. a. Define and compare *latent heat* and *sensible heat*.
   b. How much energy is involved in the latent heat of fusion for water? The latent heat of vaporization at boiling?
   c. What is *vapor pressure* and how is it related to the boiling point of water?
   d. What is meant by the *specific heat* of water?
4. Describe how heat is transferred in food preparation by (a) conduction, (b) radiation, (c) convection currents, and (d) induction heating.
5. a. Name four different media commonly used for transferring heat to food and give examples of several cooking methods using each medium.
   b. What types of heat transfer are generally used in each method that you cited in question a?
6. Compare the Fahrenheit and Celsius thermometer scales.

REFERENCES

1. *Handbook of Food Preparation*, 9th ed. 1992. Alexandria, VA: American Home Economics Association.
2. Mizer, D. A. and M. Porter. 1978. *Food Preparation for the Professional*. San Francisco: Canfield Press.

Microwave Cooking

8

Since the 1950s, microwave ranges have been available for heating and cooking foods. The first manufactured models of microwave ovens were large, heavy, specially wired, and very expensive. The microwave oven of today is very different: it is convenient, attractive, and available in varying sizes, wattages, and prices.

Microwave ovens have had a tremendous impact on food preparation practices. The commercial foodservice microwave market was developed first, and it has grown to include convenience stores, lounges, taverns, hospitals and other institutions, snack bars, and restaurants of all sizes [8]. The consumer microwave oven market developed later and expanded greatly during the 1970s, after advances in technology made it possible to produce reliable ovens at an affordable cost. Microwave ovens are now common household appliances.

In 1969, there were an estimated 40,000 microwave units in use in the United States. This figure had increased to more than 9 million by 1978. In 1988, almost 75 percent of American households had microwave ovens [10, 22]. By 1992, it was estimated that 92 percent of homes had at least one microwave oven and 40 percent had two [13]. The use of microwaves also continues to increase in both the commercial food production and the food processing industries.

The widespread use of microwave ovens in homes and foodservice establishments has created a major challenge for food processors. Microwavable convenience foods of all types are in demand. These foods must reproduce the appearance, texture, and flavor of foods prepared by conventional-oven cooking. In order to accomplish this, reformulation of conventional recipes is generally required [2]. Directions for both microwave and conventional heating and cooking are found on many food packages. In view of these trends and challenges, it is important for students in food science to understand the principles of microwave cookery. While the cooking of vegetables, meats, eggs, and some starch and flour mixtures by microwaves is discussed in the various chapters about those foods, general principles of microwave cookery are included in this chapter.

•FOOD-RELATED USES OF MICROWAVES

As has been indicated, microwave heating of food is useful in institutional foodservice, in households, and also in the food industry for processing. Heavy-duty commercial units are often installed in foodservice establishments. These units have high-output capabilities and are designed to withstand rough treatment. They are currently employed primarily for reheating. For example, hospital foodservices often use microwaves as part of a system in which individual plates of chilled menu items are reheated, one meal at a time, just prior to service to the patient [14, 19]. Microwave tunnel ovens are also used for continuous microwave heating of cooked portioned foods [8]. Defrosting and primary cooking currently consume a relatively small proportion of total use time for microwaves in foodservice, but there is potential for expansion, particularly in the area of primary cooking.

Several surveys have indicated that the majority of consumers in U.S. homes use their microwave ovens much of the time for reheating or defrosting, although excellent meals can be prepared from scratch using microwaves [12, 18]. With continuing consumer education, the microwave oven is likely to be used more frequently for basic meal preparation.

Although industrial uses of microwave energy for food processing have developed relatively slowly, they are becoming more attractive, particularly in terms of equipment design and energy cost [15]. Microwave equipment can be custom-designed and tailored to the needs of a particular food product,

FIGURE 8.1

A microwave pasteurization unit with a continuous conveyer passing through a microwave field.
(Reprinted from *Food Technology* Vol. 46, No. 9, p. 121, 1992. Copyright © by Institute of Food Technologists.)

process, or package [13]. Conveyer belts are often used to move products through a microwave field (Figure 8.1), resulting in more uniformity in the distribution of energy throughout the food products.

One important industrial application of microwave energy is in the **tempering** of frozen foods. As the foods are tempered, they are brought to a temperature just below the freezing point of water, where they are not frozen but are still firm. Conventional thawing of these foods may take several days, whereas microwave tempering can be completed within minutes, with less drip loss and reduced microbial growth [13].

A combination of microwave and conventional heating is often used for drying pasta, saving both time and energy as compared with conventional drying. Microwave drying is also used for fruit juice concentrates, herbs, bread crumbs, potato chips, and snack foods [13, 25]. Microwave cooking is successfully being applied to produce industrially precooked bacon, which is supplied, for the most part, to foodservice establishments.

Fresh pasta, bread, granola, yogurt, meat products, and prepared meals can be **pasteurized** using microwave energy. **Sterilization** can be achieved with microwaves using overpressure conditions to produce temperatures of 110–130°C (230–266°F) when proper packaging materials are used. The **proofing** of yeast-leavened products can also be accomplished in a short time with the use of microwaves. Microwaves are also used for baking bread, pizza, cake, and pastry products, often in combination with conventional baking methods [13, 24].

•ACTION OF MICROWAVES IN HEATING

Microwaves are high-frequency electromagnetic waves of radiant energy. They can be described as radio waves of very short wavelength, falling between television and infrared frequencies on the electromagnetic spectrum (see Figure 8.2). In comparing wavelengths, radio waves are measured in kilometers, television frequencies in meters, microwaves in centimeters, and infrared waves in microns [8]. Microwaves are generated in a vacuum tube called a *magnetron*, which converts alternating electric current from a household circuit into electromagnetic energy radiation. Microwaves radiate outward from their original source and can be absorbed, transmitted, or reflected. In most microwave ovens, a stirrer blade in the top of the oven helps to distribute the waves (Figure 8.3). In other ovens, foods are rotated by turntables as a means of uniformly distributing energy.

Tempering   holding a substance at a specified temperature to give it the desired consistency; frozen foods may be tempered by holding them just below 0°C (32°F)

Pasteurization   the process of heating a food to 60–82°C (140–180°F) to destroy pathogenic organisms of public health significance

Sterilization   the process of heating a material sufficiently to destroy essentially all microorganisms

Proofing   The last rising of yeast-leavened dough after it is shaped and placed in a baking pan

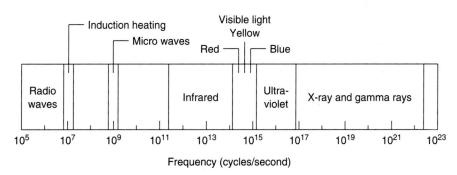

FIGURE 8.2
The electromagnetic spectrum, showing the frequency of microwaves located between the frequencies of radio waves and infrared-visible light.

FIGURE 8.3

Microwaves are produced by a magnetron, from which they enter the oven. A stirrer deflects the microwaves and distributes them to various parts of the oven. They are reflected back from the metal walls of the oven. The food in the oven absorbs the microwave energy, and heat is created in the food as a result of the friction produced between the rapidly moving molecules.

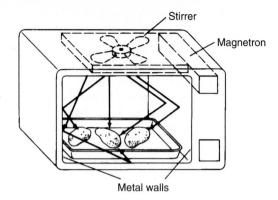

The short, straight microwaves are reflected by metals. The metal walls of a microwave oven reflect and thus contain the microwaves within the oven cavity. Microwaves reach the food that is to be cooked both directly from the magnetron unit and indirectly by reflection from the metal walls.

The Federal Communications Commission has assigned certain frequencies for microwave cooking to avoid interference with communication systems that operate in closely associated frequencies. These assigned frequencies are 915 and 2,450 megahertz (million cycles per second). The higher the frequency, the shorter the wavelength and the more shallow the depth of penetration of the waves into the food being cooked. At a frequency of 2,450 megahertz, the wavelength is approximately 4.8 inches, whereas at a frequency of 915 megahertz, the wavelength is about 13.5 inches. The shorter wavelengths produce more uniform heating and better results for small items being cooked. Thus, although microwave cooking can be satisfactorily accomplished at either frequency, only the 2,450 megahertz frequency is used in the microwave ovens being manufactured today for commercial foodservice and home use [8].

Some manufacturers have combined a conventional electric oven with a microwave oven in the same compartment, whereas others have provided conventional electric ovens as part of a cooking center. A microwave–convection oven combination is also available.

Variable cooking power outputs are made possible in a microwave oven by varying the design of the magnetron tube. Microwave ovens for consumer use usually have an output capability of 600 to 700 watts, whereas commercial units often have a higher wattage. The design assumption for the heavy-duty units is that they will be used hundreds of times per day [19]. Microwave ovens with lower power—400 to 500 watts—are also available for home use. These units cost less than those with higher wattages and although they heat more slowly than the units with higher wattages, they have sold well in the United States, representing 35–50 percent of total microwave oven sales [8].

High-speed cooking can be slowed down in most microwave ovens presently being manufactured, allowing cooking on various medium and low speeds. The reduced-power settings actually give full power intermittently, with on–off cycling. This reduces localized overheating and helps to protect sensitive foods. Variable settings have increased the adaptability of the oven for many different products.

Automatic features also add to the greater efficiency of today's microwave ovens. For example, some ovens automatically determine the cooking time and power level when the weight of a roast of meat or poultry is entered into the program. Some sensor programs can automatically determine doneness and then turn off the oven, or, alternatively, the product can be cooked and then held warm for a period. In addition, defrost cycles are often automatic.

Since 1971, the U.S. Food and Drug Administration (FDA) has regulated the manufacture of microwave ovens in terms of performance standards and design safety. A radiation safety standard enforced by the FDA limits the amount of microwaves that can leak from an oven throughout its lifetime [11]. The limit is 5 milliwatts of microwave radiation per square centimeter at a distance of 5 centimeters (2 inches) from the oven surfaces. This is far below the level known to harm people, and the exposure decreases as one moves away from the oven. It is generally recognized that the harmful consequences of microwave radiation are due solely to thermal effects, that is, effects produced by contact with materials heated to very high temperatures [15].

How do microwaves produce heat to cook food? Microwaves in themselves are not heat. However, they contain energy that is absorbed directly by the food in the oven. As the microwaves enter the product, they interact with electrically **polarized molecules** in the food, including water, proteins, and some carbohydrates. These polarized molecules act like tiny magnets and line up in the microwave electromagnetic field. The field alternates billions of times each second, causing the polarized molecules in the food to rapidly rotate due to forces of attraction and repulsion between the oppositely charged regions of the field. Heat is produced by the friction that is created between the rapidly moving molecules, thereby cooking the food. Positive and negative ions of dissolved salts in the food also migrate toward oppositely charged regions of the electric field and generate additional heat by their movement [13, 15].

Microwaves generally penetrate about 1 to 2 inches into the food, the depth varying with the frequency of the microwaves and the composition of the food. Further distribution of the heat, particularly toward the center of a relatively large mass of food, occurs by conduction, as it does in conventional heating.

Both microwave heating and the radiant heating used in conventional broiling and baking produce heat by increasing the motion of the molecules as energy is absorbed. Microwaves do not, as is sometimes supposed, cook from "the inside out." Microwave cooking is faster, however, because microwaves penetrate farther into food than do the infrared radiant waves used in conventional cooking and, therefore, deposit more energy at greater depths in the food. Since the air inside the oven is cool, the surface of the food does not become hot enough to develop a brown, dry, and crusty surface as do the surfaces of conventionally baked products [3].

The composition of a food affects the rapidity of heating. Fats and sugars have low **specific heats** compared with water; therefore, foods high in fat or sugar heat more rapidly than do foods high in water. Foods with less **density** also heat more rapidly than high-density foods when similar weights of these products are heated. Dense foods limit the depth of penetration of the microwaves. For example, a dense brownie batter heats more slowly than a light, porous cake.

Polarized molecules   molecules that have both (+) and negative (−) charges on them, creating two poles

Specific heat   the number of calories needed to raise the temperature of 1 gram of a given substance 1°C; the specific heat of water has been set at 1.0 and other substances are related to this figure; fats and sugars have lower specific heats, thus requiring less heat than does water to raise their temperature an equal number of degrees

Density   weight per unit of volume

•ADVANTAGES OF MICROWAVE COOKING

One of the great advantages of using a microwave oven is the speed with which cooking can be accomplished—two to ten times faster than conventional methods. The actual time required for cooking depends on the volume and type of food being cooked. Microwave ovens are not generally designed for quantity cookery, and the time of cooking must be lengthened as the quantity of food to be cooked is increased. One potato, for example, cooks in 4 to 6 minutes in a microwave oven, whereas four potatoes require 16 to 19 minutes to cook.

In microwave cooking, the oven walls and surrounding air do not become hot. Only the food is heated. If the cooking period is sufficiently long, some heat is conducted to the container that holds the food; however, the likelihood of receiving severe burns from the handling of cooked food is less than that of conventional cooking methods.

Microwave cooking has special advantages in reheating precooked foods and in thawing frozen foods, both individually packaged and packaged in meals. A survey of microwave owners found that they generally preferred their microwave ovens to conventional appliances for cooking convenience meat items, casseroles, and all types of vegetables [9]. The microwave oven not only reheats precooked foods more quickly than do conventional methods, but also avoids the reheated or warmed-over flavor [6]. Another advantage is that a minimum amount of water is needed to cook vegetables, thus conserving soluble nutrients.

The microwave oven has a real advantage in the saving of energy when compared with conventional ovens, particularly for cooking up to about six servings at one time. When larger amounts of food are cooked, the energy/cost comparisons may change. On tests with a variety of food types and menus cooked in a microwave oven and on the surface units and oven of a conventional electric range, it was shown that the microwave oven consumed less energy in 100 of 127 tests [20]. In other comparisons, energy use for rangetop cooking and microwave cooking was comparable, whereas broiling and baking by conventional oven cooking used more energy [23]. In cooking pork sausage links, the microwave oven had the lowest energy requirement, followed by the convection oven, with the still-air oven requiring the most energy [17]. Additional savings of energy from microwave use comes from the lesser amount of dishwashing that is generally required. Containers used for microwave cooking are usually suitable for serving as well.

In the food processing industry, the gap between the cost of conventional and microwave equipment appears to be closing. A number of applications lend themselves to the use of microwaves, and environmental concerns may make the saving of energy desirable. In addition to energy savings, advantages of microwave cooking may come from the speed of operation, precise process control, and faster start-up and shut-down times [13].

•LIMITATIONS OF MICROWAVE COOKING

As noted earlier, foods cooked for short periods in a microwave oven do not become brown on the surface as do many foods that are baked or roasted in a conventional oven or cooked in a skillet. For many products, however, particularly baked ones, a browned surface is desirable. A loaf of bread without a crisp, golden-brown crust does not have the same appeal as one that possesses these characteristics. The lack of browning of microwave-cooked products is due to the cool air temperature inside a microwave oven as compared with the high temperatures in a conventional oven, and to the cooling effects of moisture evaporation at the surface of foods cooked with microwaves; the temperature inside the microwave-cooked food is actually higher than it is at the surface [8].

In order to overcome to some degree the problems created by the lack of browning in microwave cooking, a special browning dish can be used to sear chops, meat patties, steaks, and similar products. A special coating on the bottom of the dish absorbs the microwave energy and becomes very hot (450° to 550°F). The dish is preheated according to the manufacturer's directions, the food is added, and cooking is continued according to the recipe being used.

Special disposable packaging employing **heat susceptors** is often used for such products as microwave pizza, french-fried potatoes, and some filled pastry products in which crispness and browned surfaces are desirable characteristics. Susceptors may consist of metallized paperboard, which strongly absorbs energy and becomes very hot. The metal itself does not absorb the microwave energy but it readily absorbs the heat produced by the other materials in the packaging. While microwave-interactive containers have increased the options for microwave cooking, there is a need for careful analysis of degradation products that might result from their use and adulterate the foods they come in contact with [4]. Components that may migrate from packaging materials to food are considered to be indirect food additives and require approval as food additives by the FDA. As new packaging materials are developed, careful consideration must be given to possible interactions with microwave energy.

Foods that need long cooking periods at simmering temperatures to tenderize or to rehydrate are not as satisfactorily prepared in a microwave oven as they are in conventional ovens. Some flavors do not have an opportunity to develop well in the short cooking periods of microwave ovens.

It is relatively easy to overcook foods in the microwave oven, because heating is rapid. Caution must be exercised to avoid the dehydrating effects that may result from only a few seconds, in some cases, of overheating.

Unevenness of cooking is a major disadvantage in the use of the microwave oven. This lack of uniformity in heat distribution raises some questions about the microbiological safety of certain foods heated with microwaves. For example, it has been reported that the usual procedures followed in cooking chicken by microwaves may not destroy all of the *Salmonella* organisms that may be present [16]. Concern has also been expressed in regard to the destruction of *Trichinella spiralis* in pork prepared in the microwave oven (discussed in more detail in Chapter 21). It is important to ensure the safety of these foods by checking the final temperature in several locations within the product. Visual examination of pork should also be made to verify that the flesh is not pink.

Problems may be caused by heating several menu items on a single plate because of variations in the rate of heating each item that result from differences in composition and density. When individual portions of meat loaf (beef), mashed potatoes, and green beans were heated in a microwave oven during

Heat susceptors   materials that intensify localized heating in microwavable packaged food products

Salmonella   a bacterium that may cause food poisoning

Trichinella spiralis   a tiny parasite that may be present in some fresh pork and, if not destroyed by cooking, causes a disease called *trichinosis*

Hydrocolloids colloidal materials, such as vegetable gums, that bind water and have thickening and/or gelling properties

Microcrystalline cellulose a purified nonfibrous form of cellulose (a complex carbohydrate) that is physically broken into very tiny particles

one study that simulated procedures used in cook–chill foodservice systems, a wide range (up to 83°F [46°C]) of endpoint temperatures was observed [7].

It is a challenge to the food processor to develop microwavable food products that reproduce the appearance, texture, and flavor of foods prepared by conventional oven cooking. The use of **hydrocolloids**, such as xanthan gum, carrageenan, and **microcrystalline cellulose**, which have high water-binding capabilities, may help to stabilize many microwavable products and prevent dry spots due to uneven heating and loss of moisture [5]. Custom-made flavors may also help to overcome the problems with flavor that can occur when cooking times are shortened.

•PACKAGING MATERIALS AND COOKING UTENSILS

The commercial packaging of microwavable foods serves several functions. It protects the product in storage and distribution, controls the heating of the product, may function as a serving dish, and also helps to sell the product [8].

Microwaving requires that only certain types of containers be used. Generally, materials that are transparent to microwaves should be used; the waves pass through these materials, as light passes through a window, and heat the food inside the container. Heat-resistant or ovenproof glass utensils can be used in both conventional and microwave ovens. This type of container can also be used for freezing foods and can be taken from freezer to oven without danger of breakage. Unglazed glass-ceramic dishes are highly recommended for microwave use. These are sold under the trademark name Corningware. Ceramic products, which include pottery, earthenware, fine china, and porcelain, vary somewhat in microwave absorption characteristics, but in general, they all can be used in the microwave oven. Some ceramic dishes, however, may become too hot to handle before the contents have reached their serving temperature [8]. Such dishes should not be used in microwave cooking, nor should utensils with metal trim or screws in lids or handles. The use of dinnerware with gold or silver trim also is not recommended. Ceramic mugs or cups with glued-on handles should be avoided, since the handles may come unglued [21]. Some utensils that are acceptable for use in the microwave oven are shown in Figure 8.4.

If one is not certain that a container is microwave-oven safe, it should be tested. Place the container in the oven along with a heat-resistant glass cup containing 1/2 to 1 cup water and turn on the oven with high power for 1 to 2 minutes. If the dish remains cool, it is suitable for microwaving. If it becomes hot, it has absorbed some microwave energy and should not be used.

Paper products, such as paper towels, can be used in the microwave oven either under or over a food to absorb moisture and splatters during cooking. Plastic films and cooking bags hold in steam and speed cooking, but slits must be made in the bags or film to prevent pressure buildup.

Microwave plastics are designed especially for microwave cooking. Many conventional plastics are unacceptable, because although plastics are transparent to microwaves, some are sensitive to heat from the food and melt or distort when used to cook foods that reach high temperatures [21]. Some plasticizers used in flexible packaging films may migrate into the food during microwaving, depending on cooking time, the temperature achieved, and the contact of the plastic film with the food being heated. Levels of migration have been found to be highest when there is direct contact between the film and foods with a high fat content [15]. Efforts are being made to produce plastic packaging materials from which plasticizers do not migrate. With many new packaging materials being developed for microwavable foods, it is important to follow the instructions on the label so that overheating will not occur.

Some paper dishes are made from formed or pressed paperboard and coated with a highly heat-resistant polyester resin. Others are molded from

FIGURE 8.4
Utensils for use in a microwave oven must be chosen carefully. Metal utensils should generally be avoided. (Photographs by Chris Meister)

Appropriate materials for microwave heating and cooking include heat-resistant glass such as the amber pie pan, the quart Pyrex measure, and the rectangular glass dish; glass ceramic (pyroceram), such as the rectangular casserole at the top and the small shallow baking dish used for individual servings; porcelain soufflé dishes, such as the white one in the center front; and microwave plastics, such as the rectangular roasting rack on the right which is designed to elevate meats and allow drainage of drippings. This rack is especially useful for cooking bacon in the microwave oven. The bacon is placed between paper towels or on a nonwoven, melt-blown polypropylene pad to absorb the fat lost in cooking.

Light plastic materials, such as dishwasher-safe containers and foam plates, may be used for heating in the microwave oven; however, they melt or distort at cooking temperatures. Paper products, including paper plates and paperboard trays, can be used for heating or as light covers to absorb moisture and prevent spattering.

pulp and coated with polyester. These containers are usable in both microwave and conventional ovens [8].

A variety of wide-mouth, heat-resistant glass containers in which various commercially prepared foods such as spaghetti sauce and baked beans were packaged were tested for reheating in the microwave oven [26]. The test results indicated that consumer microwave reheating of these foods in the wide-mouth glass containers in which they were packaged is feasible. Closures should be removed before heating and the jar opening covered with plastic wrap or waxed paper to avoid splattering. To ensure uniform heating, the contents should be stirred at least once midway through heating.

Since metal reflects microwaves, its use has not been recommended in the past. However, it can be used under certain circumstances. Some coated aluminum pie pans and coated steel cans are being used to package microwavable food products. Arcing may occur when there is metal-to-metal contact, for example, when an aluminum container is placed against the oven wall or against another container [8]. The Aluminum Foil Container Manufacturers Association has suggested a method that may be used to satisfactorily heat frozen foods packaged in aluminum foil containers [1]. This procedure involves (1) removing the foil container from the carton and taking off the lid; (2) returning the container to the carton, leaving one end-flap partially open to eliminate the risk of arcing; and (3) placing the carton in the microwave oven and heating.

•GENERAL COOKING SUGGESTIONS

Browning

Large pieces of food, such as meat roasts and whole poultry, brown during cooking in a microwave oven because cooking time is relatively long, but smaller quantities of food cooked for short periods need to be browned by some means other than the use of microwave energy. Small cuts of meat and poultry may be broiled conventionally after microwave cooking to develop browned color and flavor. Bacon is easily cooked in a microwave oven, however, and does brown. The fat on the surface of the bacon aids in browning. The optimum time for cooking should not be extended to increase the likelihood of browning. Foods dry out very rapidly with only slight overcooking when using microwaves.

Creative use of dark-colored toppings, sauces, crumbs, and spices can compensate for lack of browning in many dishes. Melted cheese and gravies also may be used to improve the appearance of casseroles and meat dishes.

Some formulated products are available for use in coating the surfaces of meats to encourage browning. Their major ingredient may be salt, which, when applied to a wetted surface, increases the electrical conductivity of the surface. Electrical conductors absorb microwave energy avidly and produce higher temperatures on the surface [8].

Stirring and Turning

Power is unevenly distributed in the microwave oven; therefore foods need to be turned around, turned over, stirred, or relocated in the oven at various times during cooking. Multiple items such as individual potatoes, pieces of fish, and custard cups should be placed in a circle. Some microwave ovens are equipped with a turntable whose rotation automatically distributes power more evenly; turntables can also be purchased separately. Thin or sensitive parts of a food may be shielded with small strips of aluminum foil to prevent overcooking.

Standing Time

A food continues to cook several minutes after it is removed from the microwave oven. This should be taken into account when cooking time is determined. Some foods may be cooked in the microwave oven directly from the frozen state; however, for frozen foods of large volume, such as whole poultry, a short thawing period in the microwave oven should be followed by a few minutes of standing out of the oven to allow the temperatures to equalize throughout the food before cooking is continued. Wrapping individual potatoes in foil *after* they have been cooked in the microwave oven and allowing them to stand for several minutes will complete the cooking process with limited danger of overcooking.

Defrosting

One of the benefits of a microwave oven is the ease of defrosting. Most ovens have a defrost setting with a low to medium power input. The oven cycles on and off. During the off periods, the heat produced in the food is distributed or equalized throughout.

As defrosting proceeds, some attention to the product improves the outcome. Ground meat, stew meat, whole poultry, or whole fish should be turned. As soon as possible during the defrosting process, small pieces of meat, poultry, or fish should be broken apart and separated in the oven while defrosting is completed.

Combining Microwave and Conventional Cooking

Many foods can be prepared most efficiently if they are cooked partly by microwaves and partly by conventional methods [21]. Bread can be toasted conventionally and then combined with sandwich fillings prepared by microwaves. Cheese placed on top of a sandwich is easily melted in the microwave oven. A casserole can be cooked in the microwave oven, then a crumb topping placed on it, and the topping finished by broiling in a conventional oven. Chicken can be browned on a grill after it is cooked in a microwave oven. Sauces for pasta can be cooked in the microwave while the pasta is prepared conventionally. Since microwave energy does not increase the water-absorption rate of the starch granules in most cereal products, microwave cooking does not generally save time for such foods.

The microwave oven can increase efficiency in food preparation in other ways. For example, syrup for pancakes can be warmed by microwaving while it is in the serving pitcher. Sprinkling a few teaspoons of water over raisins, covering tightly, and microwaving 1/2 to 1 minute will plump the raisins. Baking chocolate can be melted in its paper wrapper in the microwave oven, and butter or margarine is also easily melted. Brown sugar can be softened by placing an apple slice in the bag, closing tightly, and microwaving 1/4 minute or until lumps soften.

Heating Meals

Microwave ovens are widely used, in both homes and institutions, to reheat fully cooked, plated meals. Individual meal items should be chosen and grouped so that they are compatible in terms of rapidity and uniformity of heating. Placement on the plate is also important for optimal heating and maintenance of quality in the heated meal. Dense meal items, including baked potatoes, mounded mashed potatoes, lasagna more than 1/2 inch thick, cabbage rolls, stuffed peppers, and thickly sliced meat or fish, heat slowly. Therefore, such foods should be thinly portioned. Examples of meal items that heat more rapidly and easily are piped, mashed potatoes or mashed potatoes with the center pressed down and a butter pat placed in the depression; thinly sliced meats, centered on the plate with gravy draining over them; and thinly portioned fish without sauce. Denser items should also be placed toward the outside of the plate, where heating is faster. Subdivided vegetables or loose rice and pasta may be placed in the center.

STUDY QUESTIONS

1. What are *microwaves* and how do they produce heat when they are absorbed by food?
2. Discuss several advantages and several limitations to the use of microwave equipment in home cooking, institutional foodservice, and industrial food processing.
3. What types of containers should be used to hold food during cooking in the microwave oven and why?
4. Why should foods be stirred or turned at intervals during cooking in a microwave oven? Of what value is standing time after cooking? Explain.
5. What precautions should be taken when reheating fully cooked, plated meals in a microwave oven and why?
6. Why are *on* and *off* cycles used for defrosting in a microwave oven?
7. Give several suggestions for using the microwave oven in combination with conventional methods of cooking.

REFERENCES

1. AFCMA promotes microwave cooking in aluminum foil containers. 1981. *Food Technology 35*, 99 (No. 11).
2. American Home Economics Association. 1993. *Handbook of Food Preparation*, 9th ed. Dubuque, Iowa: Kendall/Hunt Publishing Co.
3. Bakanowski, S. M., and J. M. Zoller. 1984. Endpoint temperature distributions in microwave and conventionally cooked pork. *Food Technology 38*, 45 (No. 2).
4. Booker, J. L., and M. A. Friese. 1989. Safety of microwave-interactive paperboard packaging materials. *Food Technology 43*, 110 (No. 5).
5. Carroll, L. E. 1989. Hydrocolloid functions to improve stability of microwavable foods. *Food Technology 43*, 96 (No. 6).
6. Cipra, J. S., and J. A. Bowers. 1971. Flavor of microwave- and conventionally-reheated turkey. *Poultry Science 50*, 703.
7. Dahl, C. A., and M. E. Matthews. 1980. Effect of microwave heating in cook/chill foodservice systems. *Journal of the American Dietetic Association 77*, 289.
8. Decareau, R. V. 1992. *Microwave Foods: New Product Development*. Trumbull, Connecticut: Food & Nutrition Press, Inc.

9. Drew, F., K. S. Rhee, and A. C. Stubbs. 1977. Microwave ovens. *Journal of Home Economics 69*, 31 (No. 1).

10. Dziezak, J. D. 1987. Microwavable foods—Industry's response to consumer demands for convenience. *Food Technology 41*, 52 (No. 6).

11. Food and Drug Administration. 1982. *Microwave Oven Radiation*. HHS Publication No. (FDA) 80-8120. Washington, DC: U.S. Department of Health and Human Services.

12. Gast, B., G. J. Seperich, and R. Lytle. 1980. Beef preparation expectations as defined by microwave user survey—A marketing opportunity. *Food Technology 34*, 41 (No. 10).

13. Giese, J. H. 1992. Advances in microwave food processing. *Food Technology 46*, 118 (No. 9).

14. Hoffman, C. J., and M. E. Zabik. 1985. Current and future foodservice applications of microwave cooking/reheating. *Journal of the American Dietetic Association 85*, 929.

15. Institute of Food Technologies' Expert Panel on Food Safety & Nutrition. 1989. Microwave food processing. *Food Technology 43*, 117 (No. 1).

16. Lindsay, R. E., W. A. Krissinger, and B. F. Fields. 1986. Microwave vs. conventional oven cooking of chicken: Relationship of internal temperature to surface contamination by *Salmonella typhimurium. Journal of the American Dietetic Association 86*, 373.

17. Mandigo, R. W., and T. J. Janssen. 1982. Energy-efficient cooking systems for muscle foods. *Food Technology 36*, 128 (No. 4).

18. Markov, N. 1985. The microwave oven market: An overview. *Microwave World 6*, 6 (No. 1).

19. Matthews, M. E. 1985. Microwave ovens: Effects on food quality and safety. *Journal of the American Dietetic Association 85*, 919.

20. McConnell, D. R. 1974. Energy consumption: A comparison between the microwave oven and the conventional electric range. *Journal of Microwave Power 9*, 341.

21. Methven, B. 1978. *Basic Microwaving*. Minnetonka, MN: Cy DeCasse Inc.

22. Ready-to-eat foods usage tied to microwave ovens. 1988. *Food Engineering International 13*, 23 (No. 4).

23. Rhee, K. S., and F. Drew. 1977. Energy consumption and acceptability comparison of cooking methods and appliances for beef patties. *Home Economics Research Journal 5*, 269.

24. Rosenberg, U., and W. Bogl. 1987. Microwave pasteurization, sterilization, blanching, and pest control in the food industry. *Food Technology 41*, 92 (No. 6).

25. Rosenberg, U., and W. Bogl. 1987. Microwave thawing, drying, and baking in the food industry. *Food Technology 41*, 85 (No. 6).

26. Shapiro, R. G., and J. F. Bayne. 1982. Microwave heating of glass containers. *Food Technology 36*, 46 (No. 2).

Seasoning and Flavoring Materials

9

We eat with our senses. A prepared dish may entice us to taste it because of its attractive appearance or perhaps because of its delicious aroma. Once we taste it, we relish its *flavor*—that complex combination of taste, aroma, and mouth-feel that is characteristic of that particular dish. We thus enjoy the experience of eating and desire to repeat this experience. The natural flavors of many foods—fresh fruits, for example—are enticing in themselves. But the judicious use of seasonings and flavoring materials can greatly enhance the natural flavors of many foods alone and combined in a recipe. Flavorful food is always the ultimate goal of the cook. Attainment of this goal requires the proper use of seasonings and flavorings.

Seasonings are those substances that enhance the flavor of a food or combination of foods without being perceived or detected as themselves. They may bring out hidden flavors. Examples of seasoning are salt and pepper. Some seasonings, called *flavor enhancers*, act somewhat differently. A flavor enhancer does not itself bring flavor to a dish. Instead it acts to heighten the diner's perception of flavor, possibly by affecting the taste buds [11]. Examples of flavor enhancers include monosodium glutamate and some other substances called **5'-ribonucleotides**.

Flavorings are substances that are added for their own distinctive flavors, such as extracts of lemon or peppermint oil. Still other substances called *flavor builders* may be added at the beginning of cooking to blend with and enhance other flavors in the dish, producing a total *flavor bouquet* in which individual flavors cannot be distinguished. Most dried herbs and spices are used to build flavor [11].

• BASIC SEASONINGS

Salt

Salt, one of the most widely used seasonings and also found naturally in some foods, is a **crystalline** substance with the chemical name *sodium chloride* (NaCl). It is obtained from salt beds or extracted from brine and is purified

CHAPTER OUTLINE

BASIC SEASONINGS
FLAVOR ENHANCERS
SPICES AND HERBS
FLAVOR EXTRACTS
ALCOHOL

5'-Ribonucleotides compounds similar to the RNA found in all body cells; certain ones have been shown to act as flavor enhancers

Crystalline the aggregation of molecules of a substance in a set, ordered pattern, forming individual crystals

149

Iodized salt   table salt to which small amounts of a stabilized iodide compound have been added to increase dietary iodine and prevent goiter (enlargement of the thyroid gland); its use is encouraged particularly in areas where the soil is deficient in iodine

before being marketed for food use. An anticaking agent may be added to it, and it may be **iodized** for nutritional purposes.

The optimal amount of salt depends on the food product being prepared and the preferences of the persons who will consume the food. However, a certain amount of caution is necessary so that salt will not be overused. A large amount of salt in food is undesirable from a health as well as a flavor standpoint. Because of the possible relationships between a high sodium intake and hypertension (high blood pressure), governmental and professional organizations encourage Americans to reduce their intakes of salt. From a study of the acceptability of various dishes prepared with no added salt, it was concluded that dietitians and/or foodservice managers can produce quantity food recipes that are reduced in sodium and acceptable to customers [12]. The recipes tested included two dessert items, nine entrées, six vegetables, four starch items, six salads, and one bread item. Only six of the twenty-eight recipes with no added salt were rated significantly less acceptable than the control recipes in which salt was added.

For most cooked dishes, salt and other seasonings should be added in small increments, with a tasting after each addition, until the most desirable taste is achieved. In foods that are cooked to concentrate, such as tomato juice cooked to paste, salt should be added at the end of the cooking period. In liquids, generally, salt should be added at the end of the cooking period.

Some interesting flavor profiles for various soups prepared both with and without the addition of salt have been reported [3]. Salt enhanced the sweetness as well as the saltiness of soups and decreased bitterness. It also affected the mouth-feel of the soup, giving the impression of increased thickness and fullness, as if the product were less watery and thin. The addition of salt produced an overall flavor balance that was more "rounded out" and "fuller." Figure 9.1 compares the flavor profile for tomato soup to which salt was added with those for soup to which dill seed or onion powder was added.

The usual amount of salt consumed varies from one population to another as well as from one individual to another. The food industry is making serious attempts to reduce the level of sodium in processed foods, offering consumers a variety of low-sodium and lightly salted products, such as lower salt bacon, unsalted peanuts and potato chips, and canned vegetables without added salt.

A number of people are following low-sodium diets for specific health purposes. As the reduction of dietary sodium becomes desirable or necessary, the judicious use of herbs and spices, as well as fresh lemon juice, may make foods acceptable with little or no added salt [10, 17].

"Hot" peppers   peppers that contain a substance known as capsaicin, which gives them the highly pungent characteristic called "hot"; this substance also stimulates the flow of saliva; "hotter" peppers contain more capsaicin, concentrated mainly in the thin tissues or veins where the seeds are attached to the spongy central portion

Pepper

Pepper was the first Oriental spice to arrive in Europe and today remains the most widely used spice in the world [9]. Not all pepper is the same. Black pepper is the dried unripe berry of a climbing vine. White pepper is the kernel of the ripe berry. Red peppers come from plants of the genus *Capsicum*, and while they are hot, they also have their own distinctive flavors. **"Hot" peppers** originated in the New World and were taken back to Europe by Christopher Columbus. Commonly called *chilies*, they come in many different varieties

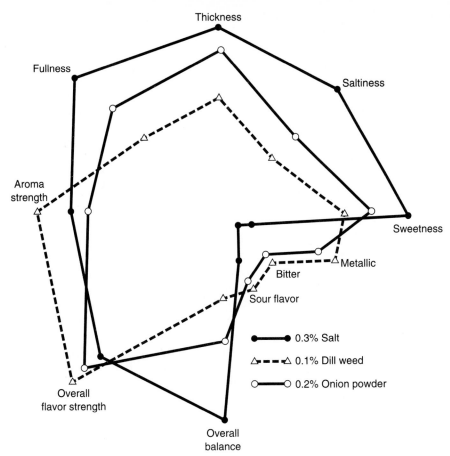

Thickness

Fullness

Saltiness

Aroma
strength

Sweetness

Metallic

Bitter

Sour flavor

●——● 0.3% Salt

△–––△ 0.1% Dill weed

○——○ 0.2% Onion powder

Overall
flavor strength

Overall
balance

FIGURE 9.1

Aroma and flavor profiles for tomato soup with (1) 0.3 percent salt, (2) 0.1 percent dill weed, or (3) 0.2 percent onion powder. The farther away a point is placed from the center point, the more pronounced is the attribute. (Reprinted from Gillette, M. Flavor effects of sodium chloride. *Food Technology* Vol. 39, No. 6, p. 47, 1985. Copyright © by Institute of Food Technologists.)

varying in hotness, color, and flavor and are basic to many **cuisines** of India, Asia, and Africa, as well as the New World. Although peppers in ground form are often used to season food without altering the natural flavor of the food, certain cuisines use peppers in amounts large enough to convey their own distinctive flavors.

We commonly think of "heat" in reference to our sensory reaction to peppers. However, the effect is really not thermal but rather a chemically-induced irritation that stimulates the endings of the trigeminal nerve—quite different from the sense of taste or the sense of touch [9]. The chemical responsible for this stimulation in black pepper is called *piperine*, while the active agent in red pepper is *capsaicin*. Capsaicin is about 100 times more potent than piperine. Even when handling chili peppers, "burning" of the hands can occur if latex gloves are not used.

Black table-ground pepper is used as a seasoning only in dark-colored foods; it spoils the appearance of light-colored foods. Light peppers, white and red, are used in both light and dark menu items. Ground white pepper is good for all-around seasoning. It blends well, both in appearance and in flavor, in white dishes, and it has the necessary strength to season dark dishes. Very little is usually needed [11]. Red peppers are the most difficult to use well. As many of them are quite hot, they can easily be overused [11].

Cuisine   a style of cooking or manner of preparing food

•FLAVOR ENHANCERS

Monosodium Glutamate

Monosodium glutamate (MSG) is a crystalline material that looks something like salt. Chemically, it is the sodium salt of an amino acid called *glutamic acid*. Glutamic acid occurs naturally in a variety of foods, including tomatoes and mushrooms, and also is a component of some protein molecules present in such foods as meat, fish, poultry, legumes, and cereal grains. In past years, MSG was often manufactured from wheat gluten or corn protein, but today it is usually made in a **fermentation** process that starts with molasses or some other carbohydrate food material.

The history of MSG as a flavor enhancer is a long and interesting one. Many hundreds of years ago, Oriental cooks used a dried seaweed called *sea tangle* to make a stock. Dishes prepared from foods cooked in this stock had a remarkably full and rich flavor. Much later, in 1908, a Japanese professor in Tokyo discovered that it was the glutamate in the seaweed that was responsible for flavor enhancement. The Japanese began producing glutamate almost immediately, and about thirty years later it was manufactured in North America [7].

MSG is generally considered to be a flavor enhancer or intensifier, bringing out the flavors of other foods. At the levels ordinarily used in cooking, MSG does not have a taste of its own; however, when used in sufficiently large amounts, it may add its own flavor. It seems to have the greatest flavor effect in low-acid foods such as vegetables, meats, poultry, and fish. It does not improve the taste of high-acid foods, including fruits and fruit juices; neither does it enhance the flavor of milk products or sweet doughs. Approximately one-half teaspoon for each pound of meat or four to six servings of vegetables is generally recommended for use.

In the past, there has been controversy over the safety of the widespread use of MSG in foods. Extensive study of its effects on a variety of animal species, however, has led to the conclusion that, in the amounts commonly used, there is no hazard to the health of the public [6, 7]. Some persons do, however, report adverse reactions to MSG. It is possible that a small percentage of the adult population, 1 to 2 percent, may react negatively to large doses of MSG, with such symptoms as tingling, warmth, and a feeling of pressure in the upper part of the body [8, 13]. Although MSG is commonly used in a number of manufactured food products, processed foods marketed primarily for babies and small children do not now include this flavor substance as an ingredient. MSG must be included on the label when it is added to foods as a separate ingredient.

5'-Ribonucleotides

A group of compounds called *5'-ribonucleotides* are present naturally in some foods, such as beef, chicken, fish, and mushrooms. They apparently act as flavor enhancers. In crystalline form, they are available to the food processor for use in flavoring various snack foods and other dishes. Commercially they are usually prepared from yeast extracts or **yeast autolysates**. These flavor enhancers are widely used in Japan, and various combinations of the ribonucleotides, such as a 50/50 ratio of **disodium 5'-inosinate** to **disodium 5'-**

Fermentation   the breakdown of more complex molecules to simpler ones by the action of microorganisms

Yeast autolysate   the preparation of yeast in which the cells have been destroyed; contains many flavorful substances

Disodium 5'-inosinate and disodium 5'-guanylate   two of the 5'-ribonucleotides that appear to have the greatest strength as flavor enhancers

guanylate, have been marketed by Japanese companies for a number of years. The inosinate and guanylate compounds appear to have the strongest flavor effects of all the ribonucleotides.

The 5'-ribonucleotides appear to act synergistically with MSG. Synergism refers to cooperative action among two or more substances so that the total effect of the mixture is greater than the sum of the individual effects. Even a very small amount of the ribonucleotides increases the flavor-enhancing properties of MSG. Some studies have strongly suggested that the effectiveness of MSG and 5'-nucleotides in flavoring is more than simple enhancement of natural basic flavors. In fact, they may provide a fifth basic taste, in addition to sweet, sour, salty, and bitter. This new taste is called *umami* in Japanese ("tastiness") [7].

•SPICES AND HERBS

History

Spices have played an important role in shaping human history [2]. In ancient times, spices were valued for many nonfood purposes, as ingredients of incense, perfumes, cosmetics, embalming preservatives, and medicines. After the first century A.D., spices were increasingly utilized to improve the bland qualities of many foods. The ancient Greeks seasoned their foods with spices, using, for example, caraway and poppy seeds in bread, fennel seed in vinegar sauces, and mint in meat sauces. Spices became valuable commodities imported from India, China, and Southeast Asia, with the Arabians controlling the spice trade for many years.

The quest for tropical spices was instrumental in encouraging exploration. Marco Polo went to the Far East in search of spices as well as precious stones, and Columbus was searching for a new trade route when he discovered America. Spices were so important, costly, and scarce, even being accepted as currency in the late 13th century, that wars were fought over them. The United States is now the world's largest importer of spices and herbs, which come mainly from the Orient, the Mediterranean area, and Central and South America.

Classification and Use

The term *spice* is used to describe a wide variety of dried aromatic vegetable products that are used in building the flavors of prepared foods. True spices are defined as parts of aromatic plants, such as bark, roots, buds, flowers, fruits, and seeds, that are grown in the tropics. Allspice, anise, cardamom, cayenne pepper, cinnamon, cloves, cumin, ginger, mace, nutmeg, paprika, and turmeric are all spices. Some spices are sweet, some are spicy sweet, and some are "hot."

The term *herb* usually refers to leaves and stems of soft-stemmed plants that grow in temperate climates. However, some woody-stemmed plants also produce culinary herbs, such as sage. Bay leaves come from an evergreen tree, the laurel [2]. Other herbs include basil, marjoram, mint, oregano, rosemary, savory, tarragon, and thyme.

Seeds used in cooking may sometimes be classified separately, because they come from plants cultivated in both tropical and temperate regions. Caraway, celery, sesame, and dill seeds are examples.

Mixtures of several true spices, herbs, seeds, and/or dehydrated vegetables are also marketed as spice blends for use in food preparation, for example, curry powder, chili powder, poultry seasoning, and mixed pickling spice.

In practical use it is difficult to separate spices and herbs [15]. They are both generally used as flavor builders in the cooking process so that their separate flavors merge indistinguishably with the total flavor as it develops. Some herbs and spices, however, have very distinctive flavors and, when used in quantities large enough to taste, become major flavors for prepared foods rather than blending into the total flavor. These special flavored spices and herbs include basil, with a warm sweet flavor that blends well with tomato dishes; oregano, with a strong bittersweet taste commonly associated with spaghetti sauce; tarragon, anise, and fennel, with a licorice-like flavor; and sage, with a pungent, fragrant flavor that permeates many stuffings for poultry or meat.

A mixture of spices in a cheesecloth bag, or *bouquet garni*, can be cooked with prepared dishes; the bag is removed before serving. Some herbs and spices are shown in Figure 9.2. The description and use for a number of herbs and spices are given in Table 9.1. As you use herbs and spices, your ability to identify each one by its particular aroma, color, and appearance will increase.

FIGURE 9.2

Many herbs and spices can be judiciously used in seasoning to enhance the flavor of food. (FPG)

Storage

Spices are sold whole or in ground forms. Whole spices retain flavor strength quite well, although quality gradually decreases during long storage. The flavor of ground spices and herbs is lost much more readily because of their greatly increased surface area.

Both spices and herbs should be stored in a cool, dry place in airtight containers. Under favorable conditions they should keep their aroma and flavor for several months. Storage may be extended by refrigerating or freezing in airtight containers if the space is available. Since ground spices release their flavor immediately when added to prepared dishes, they should usually be used near the end of the cooking period. Whole spices are added at the beginning of long cooking periods so that their full flavor can be extracted. They may be tied in a cheesecloth bag so that they can be easily removed. Crumbling whole herbs just before use helps to release their flavor. The flavor of seeds may be enhanced by toasting.

Fresh Herbs

Many herbs can be successfully grown in backyard or windowbox gardens. In the summer, you can gather them fresh and use them to enhance the flavors of grilled meats and fish, fresh garden vegetables, and even some desserts and beverages. In the fall, you can dry or freeze them to be used all winter long. Or you can move the windowbox garden indoors. A few examples of useful herbs to grow include mint, tarragon, many different varieties of basil, rosemary, chives, oregano, parsley, and cilantro.

Fresh herbs are used in a variety of ways. In cooked recipes, the amount of fresh minced herb used is approximately twice that called for with the dried product. Placing a few sprigs of fresh tarragon in a bottle of red wine vinegar and setting the bottle aside in a warm place for a month will produce tarragon vinegar for use in salad dressings. Fresh basil has a special affinity for tomato dishes; for example, it gives spaghetti sauce a delightful flavor. Any stuffing recipe for poultry is enhanced by a combination of such fresh herbs as sage, thyme, and oregano [16].

Fresh marjoram, oregano, cilantro, chives, and other herbs make a pleasant-flavored garnish for salads, tomato slices, and freshly cooked vegetables. Minced fresh herbs add delicious flavor to stir-fried or broiled garden vegetables, for example, snow peas sautéed with snipped fresh tarragon and spearmint in a small amount of oil, or broiled zucchini brushed with oil containing minced marjoram and topped with grated Parmesan cheese [16]. Many combinations are possible with a little experimentation.

Edible Flowers

The growing of edible flowers has become a thriving business for some enterprising entrepreneurs. The appearance of edible flowers on dining tables was once relatively common, and the custom is now being revived [18]. In selecting flowers, be sure that they have been grown to be eaten and have not been subjected to various insecticide sprays. Also, you should be aware that all flowers are not edible. Some, like lily of the valley and daffodils, are poisonous. Rose petals, nasturtiums, Johnny jump-ups, and pinks are good for eating.

Some suggestions for using edible flowers include nasturtium blossoms stuffed with crab meat, with each blossom affixed to a small cracker with a tiny amount of cream cheese mixture. These make a colorful dish when served on a bed of deep-green nasturtium leaves. Or sprinkle the top of an iced white cake with coconut and calendula petals before the icing has set. Edible flowers can be sugared by painting them with a light coat of slightly beaten egg white, dipping them in granulated sugar, and placing them on waxed paper to dry. Sugared flowers can be used to garnish rose petal sorbet or other desserts [18].

TABLE 9.1

Characteristics and Uses of Some Spices and Herbs

Spice/Herb	Description	Flavor Characteristics	Applications
Allspice	Dried berry of tree grown in West Indies and Latin America	Resembles mixture of nutmeg, cloves, cinnamon, and pepper	Pickling, meats, fish, cakes, soups, vegetables, chili sauce
Anise seed	Dried greenish-brown seed of annual herb of the parsley family	Strong licorice-like flavor and odor	Beverages, baked goods, confections, lunch meats, soups
Basil	Leaves and tender stems from annual herb of the mint family	Pungently aromatic, sweet, spicy flavor	Tomato paste, tomato sauce, vegetables, pizza, chicken dishes, salad dressings
Bay leaves	Leaves of evergreen member of the laurel family	Aromatic, bitter, spicy, pungent flavor	Bouillons, meats, fish, barbecue sauces, soups, vegetables
Capsicum, red pepper	Dried pod of member of nightshade family	Intensely pungent, biting, hot, sharp taste	Chili powder blends, meat seasonings, condiments, soups, beverages, baked goods
Caraway seed	Fruit of biennial herb of the parsley family; long curved seeds tapered at one end	Warm, biting, acrid but pleasant, slightly minty, medicinal flavor	Rye breads, baked goods, cheese, goulash, vegetables
Cardamom	Seeds from the fruits of a perennial herb of the ginger family	Sweet, pungent, highly aromatic, camphoraceous flavor	Baked goods, Indian curry dishes, lunch meats, pickles
Chervil	Leaves of an annual of the parsley family	Highly aromatic; resembles mixture of anise, parsley, caraway, and tarragon	Instant soups, fish dishes, condiments, baked goods
Chives	Leaves of a perennial of the onion family	Delicate onion flavor	Soups, salad dressings, dips
Cinnamon	Dried inner bark of an evergreen tree of the laurel family	Warm, spicy, aromatic, pungent flavor	Confections, ice cream, cakes, pies, cookies, beverages, soup bases, processed meats
Cloves	Dried flower buds from evergreen of the myrtle family	Warm, spicy, astringent, fruity, slightly bitter flavor	Pickling, beverages, baked goods, confections, spiced fruits, processed meats, pudding mixes
Cumin seed	Dried ripe fruits of an annual herb of the parsley family	Aromatic, warm, heavy, spicy, bitter flavor	Chili powder, chili con carne, curry powder, salad dressings
Fennel seed	Seeds of a perennial of the parsley family	Anise-like flavor	Sausage, pizza, processed meats, baked goods

FLAVOR EXTRACTS

Extracts and essential oils from aromatic plants, dissolved in alcohol, are often used to flavor baked products, puddings, sauces, and confections. These include extracts of vanilla [14], lemon, orange, and almond, and oils such as peppermint and wintergreen. Only small amounts of these flavorful materials are required but they add their own distinctive flavors to the final products. The extraction solvent is often alcohol and, thus, very volatile. Consequently,

Ginger	Rhizome (underground stem) of perennial tropical plant	Aromatic, biting, fragrant, pungent, warm, camphoraceous flavor	Baked goods, beverages, gingerbread, cookies, sauces, condiments, processed meats
Marjoram	Leaves and floral parts of a perennial of the mint family	Warm, aromatic, sweet-minty, slightly bitter flavor	Gravies, soups, stews, poultry, fish, processed meats
Nutmeg	Seed of a fruit of the evergreen nutmeg tree	Sweet, warm, pungent, highly spicy flavor	Sauces, custards, puddings, baked goods, dehydrated soup mixes, processed meats
Oregano	Leaves of a perennial of the mint family	Strong, pungent, aromatic, bitter flavor	Tomato dishes, pizza, meats, omelets, soups, vegetables
Parsley	Leaves of a biennial	Grassy, herbaceous, bitter flavor	Chicken and tomato soup bases, lasagna, salad dressings, potato chips
Rosemary	Narrow leaves of small evergreen shrub of mint family	Sweet, fresh, spicy, peppery	Soups, stews, vegetables, beverages, baked goods
Saffron	Dried stigmas of crocuslike flower of iris family; bright yellow; very expensive	Earthy, bitter, fatty, herbaceous flavor	Baked goods, rice dishes
Sage	Leaves of a perennial semi-shrub of the mint family	Fragrant, warm, astringent, camphoraceous flavor	Sausages, poultry seasonings, fish, meat loaf, condiments
Savory	Leaves of an annual of the mint family	Spicy, peppery taste	Meats, fish sauces, chicken, eggs, dry soup mixes, baked goods
Sesame seed	Seeds of an annual herb	Nutty flavor	Breads, rolls, crackers, cakes, salad dressings, confections
Tarragon	Flowering tops and leaves of a perennial herb	Minty anise-like flavor	Salad dressings, vegetables, meats, fish, soup bases, condiments
Thyme	Leaves and flowering tops of a shrublike perennial of the mint family	Biting, sharp, spicy, herbaceous, pungent	Fish, meat, poultry, vegetables, fresh tomatoes, poultry stuffing, canned soups
Turmeric	Rhizomes of tropical perennial herb	Mild, peppery, mustard-like, pungent taste	Curry powders, mustards, condiments

Source: References 2 and 15.

Encapsulate   to enclose in a capsule; flavoring materials may be combined with substances such as gum acacia or modified starch to provide an encapsulation matrix and then spray-dried

the flavorings should be stored in tightly closed containers and kept in a cool place. In puddings and other products cooked on surface units, the flavorings should be added at the end of the cooking period. In baked products, they should be added to the fat during preparation to reduce volatilization.

Many different flavor extracts are produced from botanical materials for use in the food-processing industry [4]. These extracts may be in solid or liquid form. Some flavoring materials are added to processed foods in **encapsulated** forms. Flavors are encapsulated for a number of reasons: the process helps to retain flavor in food products during storage, protects the flavor from undesirable interactions with the food, minimizes oxidation, and allows the controlled release of flavors.

Vegetable gums, or hydrocolloids, are often used in the industrial preparation of food. Many of these substances modify the perception of flavor, taste, and aroma. Flavors may be suppressed in systems thickened with hydrocolloids. Perceived sweetness is decreased as is the sour (acid) taste. Aroma intensities may also be decreased. These and other effects should be considered when formulating new food products [5].

•ALCOHOL

Wines, liqueurs, and distilled spirits can be used in preparing main dishes, sauces, and desserts, creating new and interesting flavors. It has generally been assumed that, because of its low boiling point, the alcohol is evaporated from the foods during cooking. However, a recent study [1] of six alcohol-containing recipes found that from 4 to 85 percent of the alcohol was retained in the food. For a pot roast that was heated over two hours the retention was 4 to 6 percent. For a sauce to which Grand Marnier was added when the sauce was boiling, the alcohol retention was 83 to 85 percent. Flamed cherries jubilee retained 77 to 78 percent of the alcohol. The presence of alcohol in significant amounts affects the energy value of a food since alcohol contributes approximately 7 kilocalories per gram.

STUDY QUESTIONS

1. Distinguish among seasonings, flavorings, and flavor builders.
2. Describe the basic effects or roles of salt and pepper when properly used in cooking.
3. What is a *flavor enhancer*? Give examples.
4. What is *MSG*? How was it discovered? With which types of food is it most effectively used?
5. In a strict classification, what are *spices* and what are *herbs*?
   a. Give examples of each.
   b. Describe their basic roles in cooking.
   c. Give suggestions for proper storage.
   d. Suggest uses for fresh herbs.

REFERENCES

1. Augustin, J., E. Augustin, R. L. Cutrufelli, S. R. Hagen, and C. Teitzel. 1992. Alcohol retention in food preparation. *Journal of the American Dietetic Association 92*, 486.
2. Dziezak, J. D. 1989. Spices. *Food Technology 43*, 102 (No. 1).

3. Gillette, M. 1985. Flavor effects of sodium chloride. *Food Technology 39*, 47 (No. 6).

4. Glazer, M. 1989. A flavor odyssey. *Food Technology 43*, 38 (No. 7).

5. Godshall, M. A. 1988. The role of carbohydrates in flavor development. *Food Technology 42*, 71 (No. 11).

6. Institute of Food Technologists. 1992. Monosodium glutamate. *Food Technology 46*, 34 (No. 2).

7. Institute of Food Technologists' Expert Panel on Food Safety and Nutrition. 1987. Monosodium glutamate (MSG). *Food Technology 41*, 143 (No. 5).

8. Kerr, G. R., M. Wu-Lee, M. El-Lozy, R. McGandy, and F. J. Stare. 1979. Prevalence of the "Chinese restaurant syndrome." *Journal of the American Dietetic Association 75*, 29.

9. Lawless, H. 1989. Pepper potency. *Food Technology 43*, (No. 11).

10. Miller, R. W. 1983. *How to Ignore Salt and Still Please the Palate. Department of Health and Human Services Publication* No. (FDA) 82-2165. Washington, DC: Department of Health and Human Services.

11. Mizer, D. A., and M. Porter. 1978. *Food Preparation for the Professional*. New York: Harper & Row.

12. Norton, V. P., and J. M. Noble. 1991. Acceptance of quantity recipes with zero added salt by a military population. *Journal of the American Dietetic Association 91*, 312.

13. Reif-Lehrer, L. 1977. A questionnaire study of the prevalence of Chinese restaurant syndrome. *Federation Proceedings 36*, 1617.

14. Riley, K. A., and D. H. Kleyn. 1989. Fundamental principles of vanilla/vanilla extract processing and methods of detecting adulteration in vanilla extracts. *Food Technology 43*, 64 (No. 10).

15. Rosengarten, F., Jr. 1969. *The Book of Spices*. Wynnewood, PA: Livingston Publishing Company.

16. Shaudys, P. 1986. *The Pleasure of Herbs*. Pownal, VT: Storey Communications, Inc.

17. Shimizu, H. H. 1984. Do yourself a flavor. *FDA Consumer 18*, 16 (No. 3).

18. Tolley, E., and C. Mead. 1989. *Cooking with Herbs*. 201 East 50th Street, New York, NY 10022: Clarkson N. Potter, Inc.

Beverages

10

The pattern of beverage consumption in the United States has changed markedly in recent years. Americans now drink more commercially produced beverages than ever before. Since 1970, the increase in per capita consumption of soft drinks, fruit juices, and alcoholic drinks has more than offset decreases in per capita consumption of milk and coffee. Per capita consumption of bottled water increased from 3.4 gallons per person in 1983 to 8 gallons in 1990. Of this, 7.2 gallons was nonsparkling water and 0.8 gallon was sparkling [14].

Consumption of beverages such as canned or bottled iced coffee, iced tea, and noncarbonated fruit drinks is increasing, while the growth of soft drink consumption has slowed [8]. A recent trend is the marketing of "clear" beverages, with the introduction of both caffeinated and caffeine-free clear cola drinks. These join a variety of transparent, sweetened, flavored sparkling water drinks with different exotic-sounding flavor names [10]. Of course, the "clear" beverages still include the traditional bottled water, often labeled as purified mountain spring water. The labels frequently indicate that these are purified by reverse osmosis.

• CARBONATED BEVERAGES

Carbonated soft drinks are still the most widely consumed beverage in the United States, even though the growth of their consumption has slowed recently. Carbonation is the process of saturating the beverage with carbon dioxide, giving unique zest to the drink. The carbonation also provides protection against bacterial spoilage during storage [8].

The first step in the production of carbonated soft drinks is the preparation of a syrup for sweetening. To this are added flavoring, coloring, acid, and a preservative, with continuous mixing and blending. Finally, the syrup is diluted to the finished beverage level, which is carbonated in a pressurized carbon dioxide vessel, or carbo-cooler. The carbonated beverage is then pumped to the filler, which meters the liquid into a sterile container, and the container is

Aspartame an alternative sweetener whose trade name is Nutrasweet®

then closed [8]. Many carbonated drinks are made without sugar, using alternative sweeteners such as **aspartame**. They are often labeled "diet" drinks.

Sparkling water beverages contain carbon dioxide, a low level of sweetener, which is often fructose, and flavoring. Enticing names such as *summer strawberry*, *wild mountain berry*, *Mexican lime*, *fiesta orange*, and *orchard peach* are often attached to these flavored waters. Club soda is carbonated water with sodium bicarbonate and potassium carbonate added. The original seltzer is simply carbonated water, but seltzers are also sold with sweetener and flavor ingredients added.

•SPORTS OR ISOTONIC BEVERAGES

Sports beverages are designed to prevent dehydration during vigorous exercise and to give a quick energy burst. They should have the same osmotic pressure as human blood so that they can be rapidly absorbed. Typically they have a low level of carbonation and a carbohydrate content of 6 to 8 percent (compared with soft drinks, which have 10 to 12 percent). The sweeteners added to sports drinks are usually glucose, maltodextrins, and sucrose. For electrolyte replacement, sports drinks contain such ingredients as monopotassium phosphate, sodium chloride, sodium citrate, and potassium chloride [8]. The ideal beverage for fluid replacement in athletes during training and competition appears to be one that tastes good, does not cause gastrointestinal discomfort when consumed in large volumes, promotes rapid fluid absorption and maintenance of extracellular fluid volume, and provides energy to working muscles [4].

•NONCARBONATED FRUIT BEVERAGES

Fruit beverages contain fruit or juice (1.5 to 70 percent) and water, as well as sweeteners, flavoring, coloring, and preservatives. These are different from fruit juices, although fruit may be a predominant ingredient. They can be either low-calorie or high-calorie. Added acids are normally used, and the blending of fruit flavors and juices is common. The addition of flavoring substances strengthens the flavor of the fruit juice in the drink [8]. A line of concentrated pink grapefruit flavors derived from pink grapefruit grown in the Mediterranean is available, for example. Whey-based fruit beverages that contain a stabilizer system are advertised as healthful products.

Fermentation the transformation of organic molecules, such as sugar, into smaller ones by the action of microorganisms

Pasteurization the process of heating to a temperature below the boiling point of water but high enough to destroy pathogenic microorganisms

Aseptic free from disease-producing microorganisms; filling a container that has been previously sterilized without recontaminating either product or container is an aseptic process

Fruit beverages are susceptible to microbial spoilage and **fermentation**. They therefore require protection by **pasteurization** or added preservatives. Pasteurization is accomplished by heat or microfiltration, with the product often being heated in-line and then placed in **aseptic** packaging. The approval of hydrogen peroxide as a packaging sterilant in 1984 made possible the packaging of many beverages in laminated boxes, which are available in various sizes. Alternatively, the beverage may be pasteurized by filling the package, closing, and then heating it. A hot-filling method, involving filling the package with the hot product and turning the package so that all sides contact the product, may also be used [8].

•ALCOHOLIC BEVERAGES

The French have a saying that "a meal without wine is a day without sunshine." A meal accompanied by wine must be eaten slowly since the wine must be sipped; and, there should be long pauses between sips so that the bouquet of the wine can linger on the palate. Wine may aid the digestive processes by the simple fact that it prevents eating in a hurry [19].

Epidemiologic studies of important factors in the development of coronary heart disease have revealed that French subjects who have intakes of saturated fatty acids and risk factors similar to U.S. subjects show a much lower incidence of death from heart disease. The intake of wine was different between the two groups studied and showed a negative correlation with coronary heart disease. Alcohol consumed in wine appears to be superior to alcohol from other beverages, such as beer. Thus, components in wine other than alcohol may be important factors. It has been suggested that antioxidant substances in wine are responsible for these effects, as may be similar substances found in fruits and vegetables [12].

The process of making wine involves the chemistry of fermentation, as does the making of all alcoholic beverages. The process of fermentation is simple in that yeast acts on sugar, converting it into alcohol and carbon dioxide gas. If, at this point, the mixture is not protected from the air, then the alcohol turns into acetic acid, producing vinegar. The complete process of making wine, however, is very complicated, involving the selection of the right kinds of grapes and consideration of where they are grown. The grapes are crushed and their pulp and juice fermented. The wine is slowly aged in closed oak casks and sampled periodically for quality. Some impurities may be removed from the wine before it is bottled by a process called *fining*. The neck of the wine bottle is closed with a cork. When the bottle is tilted on its side, the cork is moistened by the wine and permits only a minuscule amount of air to enter the bottle; a larger amount of air would quickly turn the liquid to vinegar [19]. The wine then continues to age slowly.

•COFFEE

The coffee plant is apparently native to Ethiopia and other parts of tropical Africa. It was introduced into the Middle Eastern countries in the fifteenth century, and, later, both the growing of the plant and the custom of coffee drinking spread throughout the eastern hemisphere. Coffee was introduced into Java by the Dutch in the seventeenth century and later into South America. Since that time, Brazil has become the largest coffee-producing country in the world. Central America, Colombia, Hawaii, and Puerto Rico also have climatic conditions favorable to the growth of a fine grade of mild coffee.

The Coffee Plant

The coffee plant grows 6 to 20 feet high, depending on the species, the country in which it is grown, and the local custom of pruning. There are many varieties of coffee, but only a few are grown for commercial use. The original

FIGURE 10.1
Flowers and fruit of the coffee tree. (Courtesy of the American Can Company)

Pectic enzymes   enzymes such as pectinase that hydrolyze the large pectin molecules

Chlorogenic acid   polyphenolic organic acid

species native to Ethiopia and the one that is most commonly grown is *Coffea arabica*, but when grown in different soils, altitudes, and climates, this species takes on different characteristics. Arabica, which is now grown chiefly in Central and South America, has a fine full flavor and aroma. A second hardy variety commonly grown in Africa is *Coffea robusta*. Robusta coffee shrubs are best suited to low elevations (about 1000 feet), and the beans are not as flavorful or as acid tasting as those from arabica coffee plants.

The evergreen coffee plant bears white flowers, from which the fruit develops. When ripe, the fruit resembles a small cherry with the dark red pulp covering two oval beans, growing with the flat sides together (Figures 10.1 and 10.2). The bean or seed is the part used to make the coffee beverage.

Preparation and Blending of Beans

In the curing process that prepares the coffee beans for market, the cherries may be either dried for 2 to 3 weeks in the sun, or soaked, depulped, washed, and dried by machine. One curing process—the washed coffee process—makes use of **pectic enzymes** on selectively picked cherries to replace spontaneous fermentation.

The skin, pulp, parchment, and silverskin are all removed, leaving the cleaned beans, which are light green or blue-green. The green beans are then classified into six different sizes and graded. Unripened and discolored beans, sticks, small stones, and other foreign matter are eliminated. Next the beans are packed into jute or fiber bags and shipped to various markets. Green coffee may be stored for prolonged periods with no adverse effects.

Each variety of coffee has its own flavor and other characteristics. Coffee that is available to the consumer may be a blend of as many as five or six different varieties of coffee beans. The blends are controlled for flavor, aroma, color, and strength or body of the beverage from the roasted bean. Blending is done by "creative artists" of the coffee world, who choose beans that combine to produce desirable brews and yet are not too expensive. Once a blend combination has been developed, it is continuously produced so that one brand of coffee always has the same flavor and aroma.

Roasting

Green coffee beans have little flavor and aroma until they are roasted. Naturally occurring sugars, plant acids (including **chlorogenic acid**), proteins, and other minor nitrogen-containing compounds react at high roasting temperatures to form a majority of the desirable flavor constituents [9]. The beans expand to half again their original size and become more porous. The dull green changes to brown. Coffee roasts are classified according to the color of the roasted bean

FIGURE 10.2
Coffee berry with half of the fruit pulp removed. (Courtesy of the American Can Company)

Bean
Sliverskin
Parchment covering
Fruit pulp

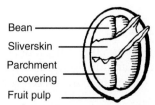

into light roast, medium roast, dark roast, and Italian or French roast, which is very dark. Other names may be given to the various roasts such as *cinnamon*, *high*, *New York*, *Chicago*, and *New Orleans*.

Moisture is lost during roasting, carbon dioxide gas is formed, and sugar is decomposed. Changes in the sugar, possibly in combination with other substances, contribute much to the color of the beverage produced from the roasted beans. Modern roasting equipment allows careful control of time and temperature so that the flavor is constant from batch to batch.

Carbon dioxide gas appears to be lost gradually from roasted coffee on standing but is better retained in the bean than in ground coffee. Carbon dioxide is a desirable constituent of coffee from the standpoint of both the keeping quality and the retention of flavor and aroma substances. Flavor and aroma substances may be in some way tied up with the gas, or the presence of the gas may tend to prevent undesirable oxidation reactions on certain coffee constituents. At any rate, the loss of carbon dioxide is closely associated with loss of flavor and aroma.

Composition of Coffee

The constituents of coffee that are of significance in the making of the beverage include acids, volatile substances, bitter substances, and caffeine. Caffeine is desired by those who seek stimulation from the beverage. It is not desirable for others who enjoy the flavor but not the stimulating effect of coffee.

Organic Acids

Several organic acids are present in aqueous coffee extracts, including acetic, pyruvic, caffeic, chlorogenic, malic, citric, and tartaric acids. The predominant acid is chlorogenic, which is somewhat sour and slightly bitter. It has been suggested that, in general, the more acid tasting the coffee, the better are the aroma and flavor [17]. Coffee acidity is apparently affected by many factors including variety, altitude at which the plant is grown, processing of the fruit, age of the beans, and the degree of roasting of the beans.

Volatile Substances

Many of the volatile constituents contributing to the aroma of coffee have been identified [18]. Sulfur compounds and **phenolic compounds** are among the main contributors to the characteristic aroma. Many of the flavor substances in coffee beverage are volatile or are changed by heat. Therefore, an extended heating period at a high temperature can remove or destroy the desirable aroma and flavor. Long heating even at a low temperature may have the same effect. Reheating coffee beverage has been shown to decrease organoleptic acceptance by a judging panel at the same time that a loss of volatile substances was shown by gas chromatographic techniques [15].

Phenolic compound an organic compound containing in its structure an unsaturated ring of carbon atoms with an —OH group

Bitter Substances

Bitterness in coffee becomes more pronounced as the **polyphenol** content increases. Polyphenol solubility apparently increases with temperature, and a boiling temperature releases polyphenols readily from the coffee bean. Caffeine contributes to bitterness. Coffee also contains other substances that produce distinctly bitter tastes.

Polyphenol a phenol compound with more than one —OH group attached to the unsaturated ring of carbon atoms; some produce bitterness in coffee and tea

Caffeine

Pharmacologists classify caffeine as a mild stimulant of the central nervous system and consider it one of the world's most widely used drugs [11]. Caffeine is one of a group of chemical compounds called *methylxanthines*, which occur naturally in the parts of many species of plants, including coffee beans, tea leaves, cocoa beans, and cola nuts. Theobromine, a somewhat milder stimulant than caffeine, is also a methylxanthine. It is found in chocolate and cocoa.

Table 10.1 gives the caffeine content of some common foods and beverages. While caffeine is added to some soft drinks, manufacturers of soft drinks also market caffeine-free cola beverages. Decaffeinated coffee and tea are produced as well.

Decaffeinated Coffee

Certain people want the flavor of the coffee beverage but not the stimulating effect of the caffeine it contains. By a chemical process, usually involving solvent extraction, most of the caffeine can be removed from the green coffee beans to yield *decaffeinated coffee*. Methylene chloride is the solvent most commonly used in the United States. The U.S. Food and Drug Administration (FDA) allows a residue of not more than 10 parts per million of this solvent to remain in the decaffeinated bean. A water soaking process of decaffeination is

TABLE 10.1

Caffeine Content of Selected Foods and Beverages

	Caffeine (mg)
Coffee (5-oz cup)	
Drip method	110–150
Percolated	64–124
Instant	40–108
Decaffeinated	2–5
Instant decaffeinated	2
Tea (5-oz cup)	
1-minute brew (black)	21–33
3-minute brew (black)	35–46
5-minute brew (black)	39–50
Instant	12–28
Iced tea (12-oz can)	22–36
Chocolate products	
Hot cocoa (6-oz cup)	2–8
Milk chocolate (1 oz)	1–15
Soft drinks (12-oz can)	
Coca-Cola	65
Dr. Pepper	61
Mountain Dew	55
Tab	49
Pepsi-Cola	34
Diet RC	33

Source: References 17 and 2.

also available, although it is more costly and not widely used in the United States at the present time.

Although decaffeinated coffee generally has good flavor, there is a slight loss of the usual coffee flavor during processing.

Instant Coffee Products

Instant or soluble coffee is very convenient. It is composed of dry, powdered, water-soluble solids produced by dehydrating very strong, brewed coffee, which is often percolated under vacuum to minimize the loss of flavor substances. Some carbohydrate may be added. The flavor of instant coffee is similar to that of freshly brewed coffee, but the aroma is usually somewhat lacking in comparison with the fresh-brewed beverage.

Some soluble coffees are freeze-dried. In this process the strong, brewed coffee is first frozen and then dried by vaporization in a vacuum. Like instant coffees produced by other methods, the freeze-dried products are reconstituted by adding boiling water according to directions on the package. Soluble coffees should be kept packaged in water- and airtight containers because they are **hygroscopic**, tending to absorb moisture.

Hygroscopic tending to attract or absorb moisture from the atmosphere

Instant coffee beverage is available in dry form, containing instant coffee, flavorings, and coffee creamer. Gourmet flavors to be added to brewed coffee are also marketed. The wide assortment of flavored and instant coffee products offered to the consumer can make choosing one a real challenge.

Cappuccino Coffee

Espresso coffee is prepared from a French roast coffee and heated by steam. Special equipment is available for its preparation. Cappuccino coffee is similar, but it is prepared with cream or milk products. Instant cappuccino may contain sugar, hydrogenated fat, corn syrup solids, coffee, nonfat milk solids, sodium caseinate, and emulsifiers. It may also contain additives to aid the dissolving process (dipotassium phosphate) and to prevent caking (silicon dioxide). Flavors such as hazelnut, almond, and chocolate may be added. Iced cappuccino coffee is marketed in bottles to be served cold. Freeze-dried espresso coffee is also marketed as an instant product.

Coffee Substitutes

Parched ground cereals and/or roots are used as coffee substitutes. Their flavor is due largely to various products formed during the heating process. **Chicory** is sometimes added to coffee substitutes for a somewhat bitter taste. Chicory can also be blended with coffee. This mixture is preferred over coffee alone by some people. A darker color results from the addition of chicory, but the characteristic coffee flavor and aroma are decreased. The coffee substitutes do not generally produce a stimulating effect as does the caffeine in coffee.

Chicory a plant whose root is roasted and ground for use as a coffee substitute

Storage and Staling

One of the most important factors affecting the quality of the coffee beverage is the freshness of the coffee used. Coffee is best when it is freshly roasted. It deteriorates on standing. Because ground coffee becomes flat or stale more rapidly than coffee in the bean, and because coffee exposed to air changes more rapidly than coffee not so exposed, the chief cause of staleness has been assumed to be the oxidation of certain coffee constituents. However, the oxidation theory seems to be inadequate in explaining all of the changes brought about in stale coffee. The fat of coffee apparently does not become rancid in the short time required for coffee to become stale.

Moisture has a very pronounced effect in decreasing the storage life of coffee. Tests on volatile substances extracted from coffee show that if the substances are sealed in a vacuum tube, changes are retarded; if the substances are exposed to air, changes occur rapidly; and if the substances are exposed to moisture, the changes are still more pronounced.

The effect of oxygen on roasted coffee is very rapid during the first 3 weeks and is thought to affect mainly the flavor constituents. After 3 weeks, the oxygen probably combines with the oils of the coffee, which results in the development of true rancidity several months later.

Proper sealing of roasted—especially ground—coffee is fundamental. The vacuum type of package from which air is removed before sealing affords more protection than other types of packages. Flavor deterioration in vacuum-packed coffee depends on the extent to which air is removed from the container. Another development involves the use of carbon dioxide gas under pressure in cans after the air is removed. It has been suggested that vacuum-packed roasted and ground coffee in cans at a moisture content of 5 percent or less can be expected to have a storage life of at least 2 years [1]. Because of the rapid loss of flavor after grinding and exposure to air, many markets have facilities for grinding coffee at the time of purchase.

After a container of vacuum-packed coffee is opened, it should be stored, tightly covered, in a cool place, preferably at a temperature as low as 4°C (40°F), to retard staling. Moisture is particularly detrimental to the maintenance of coffee freshness, and therefore contact with moist air should be kept to a minimum.

Preparation of Coffee Beverage

Grind and Quality

Coffee may be ground to differing degrees of fineness. Any grind, however, contains particles of many sizes. Ground coffees differ basically in the proportion of each size of particles. A *regular grind* contains a higher proportion of coarse particles than a *drip* or *medium grind*; a *fine grind* contains no coarse particles. It is also possible to pulverize coffee but neither institutional nor home-type brewing equipment is designed for pulverized coffee. Its use in such equipment would result in a very bitter tasting beverage.

Consistency in the grind is important in maintaining consistent quality. As the percentage of large particles in the coffee grind is increased, the brewed beverage is weaker. A foodservice manager should know if the supplier actually measures the grinds and is consistent in the grind provided.

Good grades of coffee are characterized by a sharp, more desirable flavor as compared with the flat, neutral flavor of poor grades. A middle grade of coffee, purchased and used fresh, yields a better beverage than a high grade that is stale.

Methods

Instant coffee has gained wide acceptance because of its convenience, but it has not replaced brewed coffee. Good coffee may be brewed by several methods (Figure 10.3). In each method, important factors include control of the water temperature and control of the time that the coffee is in contact with the water. The temperature of the water should be at least 85°C (185°F) to extract a desirable amount of soluble solids; however, it should not be hotter than 95°C (203°F) to avoid extraction of excessive amounts of bitter substances and loss of many volatile flavor substances.

The amount of coffee used in relation to the water determines the initial strength of the brew. One to three tablespoons of coffee per cup (8 ounces) of water yields brews ranging from weak to very strong. Use of 1⅓ to 1½ tablespoons of coffee per cup of water gives a medium-strength brew.

Filtration. In the drip or filtration method, the water filters through the coffee into the lower compartment of the coffeemaker. In institutional foodservice, an urn is used to make drip or filtered coffee. The upper part of a drip coffeemaker is perforated and holds the coffee grounds, and the lower com-

FIGURE 10.3
Types of coffeemakers.

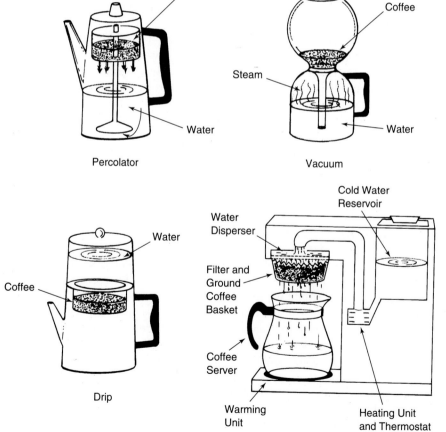

Percolator

Vacuum

Drip

Automatic Drip-filter Coffee Maker

partment receives the filtered beverage. The perforations of the upper compartment are covered with thin filter paper or cheesecloth to prevent the passage of coffee into the beverage. If the perforations are too small, the rate of filtration is too slow to yield a desirable beverage.

The drip method probably extracts less of the bitter substances than do other methods. If it is not allowed to boil and is not kept hot too long, coffee made by the drip method retains more of the flavor constituents than coffee made by other methods. Probably all methods extract a high percentage of the caffeine.

Another type of pot for the filtration method is the vacuum coffeemaker. The upper compartment, which holds the coffee, has an open tube that extends almost to the bottom of the lower compartment. Coffee is usually prevented from passing into the lower compartment by a cloth-covered disk, which is held in place over the tube opening. In some models, a glass rod that fits the tube opening is used instead of the disk. Water is placed in the lower compartment and the pot is heated until most of the water rises into the upper compartment. The pot is then removed from the source of heat until the water filters through the coffee and passes back into the lower compartment. The upper compartment is removed, and the beverage is carefully reheated to a desirable temperature for serving. The chief difficulties in the use of this method are that the coffee may not be hot when served, and that, in being kept hot it may boil, thus losing much of the flavor and aroma.

Percolation.   When coffee is percolated, heated water is forced upward through a tube into the coffee compartment. The water filters through the coffee several times before the beverage is of desirable strength. The water is probably not at the boiling point when it is in contact with the coffee, but the beverage is close to the boiling point when it is ready to be served. Unless the construction of the pot is good and the time of percolating is carefully controlled, much of the flavor and aroma may be lost by this method. The time required varies with the speed of percolation and with the quantity of coffee made. Usually 6 to 8 minutes is adequate to make 4 to 6 cups of coffee.

Steeping.   Although steeped coffee is sometimes described as *boiled*, the beverage made by heating the coffee and water together is more desirable in flavor if it is not allowed to boil. Steeping (extracting flavor below the boiling point) extracts much less of the bitter substances from coffee than does boiling. Coffee boiled for 1 minute is distinctly more bitter than coffee heated from 85° to 95°C (185° to 203°F). This method may be convenient for use on picnics and camping excursions. If egg white is mixed with the coffee before the water is added, the temperature must rise high enough to coagulate the dilute solution of egg in order to clarify the beverage. Boiled coffee made with egg is more bland than that made without egg because of the combination of egg albumin with the polyphenol compounds. The length of steeping varies with the temperature of the water that is mixed with the coffee and with the fineness of the coffee grind. Hot water is preferable because less time is required to make the beverage than when cold water is used. Short infusion periods usually yield better flavored coffee than do longer periods.

Iced Coffee

An iced beverage that possesses the maximum flavor is made by pouring a freshly made, strong coffee infusion over crushed ice in a glass. Strong infusions, whether combined hot or cold with ice, are made with a larger-than-usual amount of coffee per cup of water rather than by longer-than-usual infusion periods. Long infusion periods decrease flavor and aroma and increase bitterness. Iced coffee is also available in bottles to be refrigerated and served cold.

Other Factors

Material from Which the Pot Is Made.   Tin is the least desirable of metals for coffee pots, but even silver has an influence on the flavor of the beverage. Some metals form compounds with caffeine and probably with other constituents of coffee. Metallic pots impart a metallic flavor to coffee. Pots made of glass, earthenware, or enamelware are good choices. Stainless steel is resistant to attack and, therefore, its effect on the flavor of coffee is negligible. Chrome and nickel plating show no staining or corrosion when used in a coffee pot.

Water.   The water used to brew coffee should be free of any undesirable elements picked up in pipelines, boilers, or water tanks. You should never brew coffee with water you would not drink. Soft water or water of low hardness gives coffee a more desirable flavor than does very hard or alkaline water. Water having a high carbonate or bicarbonate content and water that has passed through an ion-exchange softening system (and thus is high in sodium ions) will not filter through coffee in a drip or vacuum pot as rapidly as naturally soft water. This means an increase in both the time of contact with the coffee and the amount of material extracted, which can be objectionable. Experimental coffee was prepared using solutions of eight minerals each at 750 parts per million [13]. Those containing carbonates were the least desirable, having flat, insipid characteristics. Coffee prepared from distilled water was excessively sour. Changes in the visual characteristics of the coffee were observed with the various kinds of water used.

Temperature.   Probably 85° to 95°C (185° to 203°F) is optimum for brewing a good coffee beverage. Boiling gives a distinctly bitter beverage. Polyphenol substances are more soluble at boiling than at 95°C (203°F). The longer the heating period, even at lower temperatures, the higher the percentage of bitter substances dissolved and the greater the loss of flavor substances. Nearly all the caffeine is dissolved at 85° to 95°C (185° to 203°F) and the flavor substances are not lost as much as at higher temperatures. Boiling water may be used to start the preparation of coffee because the temperature drops once the water comes in contact with the coffee and the pot.

Cleanliness of Pot.   A clean coffee pot is essential to making a good coffee beverage. The pot should be washed with hot soapy water or scoured as necessary to remove the oily film that collects on the inside. Thorough rinsing is essential. A pot that retains a stale coffee odor is not a clean pot and will mar the flavor of the best-made coffee. Regular cleaning schedules should be employed for coffee-making equipment used in foodservice establishments.

•TEA

Tea is a widely used beverage produced from the dried shoots of an evergreen shrub of the genus *Thea*, chiefly *Thea sinensis*. The principal tea-producing areas of the world are India, Sri Lanka, China, Indonesia, and Japan. Teas vary according to the age of the leaf, the season of plucking, the altitude, the soil, and climatic conditions, as well as the method of processing.

The Tea Plant

The tea plant is pruned and cultivated to produce many young shoots. Pluckings extend over a period of several months, with spring and early summer leaves yielding better tea than late summer and autumn pluckings. Grades of tea are determined largely by the location and size of the leaf. The young unopened leaf buds at the tip of the shoot rank first in quality. Quality decreases as the size of the leaf increases, toward the lower end of the shoot (Figure 10.4). The quality of tea is also influenced by the climate and soil where the tea is grown and by the processing.

Processing

There are three principal types of tea, differentiated by the method by which the leaves are processed: green, black, and oolong. Any size leaf may be made into any one of these.

FIGURE 10.4
Tea shoots, showing buds and leaves. (Copyright © *Tea and Coffee Trade Journal*)

Black Tea

Most of the tea consumed in the United States is black tea. In its manufacture, the leaves are withered and rolled to break tissues and release juices. They are then held and allowed to undergo oxidative changes catalyzed by enzymes in the leaves. After this they are heated and dried. The process of holding is called *fermentation*. During fermentation, polyphenolic substances are oxidized and some new phenolic products are produced. The color of the leaf changes to black. The beverage made from black tea has an amber color, is less bitter and astringent than green tea, and has a rich aroma and flavor.

Generally, the best grade of black tea is Broken Orange Pekoe. Other grades are Broken Pekoe (used as a filler in blends), Orange Pekoe, Pekoe, Souchong, Fannings, and Dust. Teas from various countries are blended to give uniform flavor, strength, and color.

Green Tea

Green tea is produced by first steaming the leaves to inactivate the enzymes and then rolling and drying. The leaf retains much of its original green color, especially the finer leaves. Older leaves often are a blackish gray color. The beverage made from green tea is greenish yellow and is distinctly bitter and astringent. It has little aroma and flavor as compared with black tea because the preliminary steaming destroys the enzymes that produce flavor substances during the fermentation of black tea. Less than 5 percent of the world's tea is made into green tea. Grades of green tea include Gunpowder, Young Hyson, Hyson, and Imperial.

Oolong Tea

Oolong tea is a partially fermented tea. The fermentation period is too short to change the color of the leaf completely; it is only partially blackened. The flavor and aroma of this beverage is intermediate between those produced from green and black teas.

Composition and Nutritive Value

The alkaloid substance that gives tea its stimulating property was formerly designated *theine*, but the substance has been shown to be identical to caffeine. The tea beverage contains somewhat less caffeine than does coffee, but the content depends on the method of brewing. Longer brewing results in higher caffeine content. Table 10.1 provides information about caffeine content of brewed tea. Tea also contains small amounts of theobromine.

Tea has been reported to contain a significant amount of folacin [3]. A person could obtain up to 25 percent of the Recommended Dietary Allowance (RDA) for folacin by drinking five cups of tea per day. Tea appears to have a negative effect on iron absorption when it is consumed with a meal [6].

The flavor of tea is influenced by the presence of considerable quantities of polyphenolic substances, which are particularly responsible for **astringency**. Some of the polyphenols are changed in the **oxidation** process that takes place when black tea is fermented. They contribute to the characteristic aroma and

Astringency   the puckering, drawing, or shrinking sensation produced by certain compounds in food

Oxidation   a chemical change that involves the addition of oxygen; for example, polyphenols are oxidized to produce different flavor and color compounds

flavor of this tea. Degradation of other substances, including **linolenic acid**, amino acids, and **carotenes**, during the manufacture of black tea may also contribute to flavor and aroma.

Linolenic acid   polyunsaturated fatty acid

Carotenes   yellow-orange, fat-soluble pigments

Market Forms

A wide variety of teas are available on the market. Much of the tea sold for consumer use is in the form of tea bags for convenient brewing. Many scented and flavored teas are marketed. These teas contain such flavorings as oils of peppermint, strawberry, orange, or lemon; spices such as cinnamon or cloves; blackberry leaves; almond; and licorice root.

As with coffee, decaffeinated tea is available. The decaffeinated product is also sold with various flavors added, such as blackberry and almond.

Instant teas are dried products prepared from brewed teas. These teas are particularly useful for preparing iced tea. One simply disperses the tea in cold water, adds ice, and serves. Instant tea mixes may contain sugar, citric acid, maltodextrins, and flavoring such as lemon. There are also low-calorie tea products sweetened with aspartame or saccharin.

A variety of herbal teas are available. They contain dried leaves of various plants other than tea. Often they are made up of a mixture of several dried plant materials such as strawberry leaves, apples, hibiscus flowers, rose hips, peppermint, ginger, nutmeg, cinnamon, chamomile, and alfalfa. Various flavors may be added as well. Herbal teas contain no caffeine but often contain substances that have soothing, stimulating, or euphoric effects. Some potential health hazards are associated with their misuse. For example, long-term use of ginseng may produce hypertension, nervousness, sleeplessness, and edema [10].

Preparation of Tea Beverage

Water

Soft water is preferable to hard alkaline water for making tea just as it is for making coffee. The polyphenol substances in tea may interact with certain salts in hard water to produce an undesirable precipitate. Water should be freshly boiled with enough oxygen still in it to prevent the flat taste that results from the loss of dissolved gases by boiling.

Teapot

Metallic pots impart a metallic taste to the tea beverage. Glass, earthenware, enamelware, or other vitrified ware is recommended for making tea because of the large amount of polyphenolic substances in it.

Temperature

Temperatures slightly under boiling are less likely to volatilize flavor and aroma substances than is boiling temperature. Boiling water is quickly reduced in temperature, however, when poured over tea leaves. A lid on the teapot helps to retain heat and prevent the escape of volatile substances. The optimum time of contact between hot water and tea varies somewhat with the temperature of the water. A steeping period of 2 to 6 minutes is appropriate between 85° and 93°C (185° and 199°F).

Methods

The soluble substances of the tea leaves are extracted in the beverage. Because the polyphenol content of tea is fairly high, excessive steeping, especially at or near the boiling point, extracts more bitter polyphenol substances than is desirable. These substances are more soluble in boiling water than in water under the boiling temperature. Flavor substances and caffeine are readily extracted by short infusion periods. The aim in making tea is to extract the maximum flavor with a minimum of polyphenol compounds. Strong beverages of good flavor require more of the beverage-making constituents rather than long infusion periods.

What constitutes a desirable strength of tea beverage? This is largely a matter of individual opinion. The usual proportion of tea per cup of water is about 1 teaspoon. However, when steeping periods are prolonged or when the quantity of beverage made is larger, as little as 1/2 to 3/4 of a teaspoon produces a better beverage.

Tea Balls. The tea ball method, in which boiling or almost boiling water is poured over tea in a cheesecloth or paper bag, or in a silver ball, is one of the most desirable methods of making tea. The ball or bag remains in contact with the water until the desired strength is obtained, after which it is removed. A modification of this method can be used to make tea in large quantities. The measured tea is placed in a wire strainer and the hot water is poured once through the tea. In many foodservice establishments, a pot of hot water with the tea bags separate is served to those who order tea.

Steeping. To steep tea, the measured tea is placed in a preheated pot, and boiling water is poured into the pot. The pot is then covered and allowed to stand in a warm place until the desired strength is obtained. Steeping periods usually range from 2 to 4 minutes, depending on the temperature and the strength desired. If the maximum quantity of tea is used, 4 minutes may produce a somewhat bitter beverage. The tea should be poured from the grounds immediately to avoid excess bitterness in later portions of tea served from the pot.

Iced Tea

Iced tea, a favorite drink in the United States, is best made from a larger proportion of tea to water than is usually used for hot tea because melting ice dilutes the beverage. Lenthy steeping to brew a beverage strong enough to stand dilution extracts too many polyphenol substances. It is believed that a cloudy beverage may result from a complex formed between caffeine and some of the polyphenol substances. This complex may form more readily in iced tea than in hot tea. Its formation is encouraged when larger amounts of polyphenol substances are present. Diluting strong infusions while they are hot helps to prevent cloudiness.

Tea is lightened by the addition of lemon because the oxidized polyphenolic compounds change color in an acid medium. These substances tend to be dark in an alkaline medium.

For sweetening iced tea with sugar, an extrafine granulation that is quickly soluble is desirable. If mint flavor is desired in iced tea, the mint leaves can be crushed and added to the tea leaves before the boiling water is added, or a sprig of mint can be served in the glass of iced tea.

In addition to regular, decaffeinated, sweetened, and low-calorie instant iced tea mixes, bottled iced tea drinks with a variety of flavors are also marketed. Commercial iced tea drinks may contain water, high fructose corn syrup, tea, citric acid, and flavoring.

•COCOA AND CHOCOLATE

The cacao tree (*Theobroma cacao*) requires very exacting growing conditions and is cultivated only in an area within 20 degrees of the equator. Much of the world cacao crop now comes from West Africa; however, cocoa originated in Latin America, where Brazil and Ecuador are still large producers.

The cultivated cacao tree is deliberately kept pruned to a height of about 19 feet (6 meters) so that the fruits can be harvested with a long stick. A ladder is not necessary. The fruits grow directly on the stem or thick branches of the tree. Full-grown fruits are about 8 inches (20 centimeters) long and 4 inches (10 centimeters) across in an oblong shape. Botanically, the leathery fruits are giant berries. Each berry, or pod, contains 30 to 40 seeds or beans occurring in rows and embedded in a white or pinkish pulp (Figure 10.5).

Processing

Cocoa and chocolate are made by grinding the seeds of the cacao tree. To decrease the bitter taste, the seeds are first fermented. One by one, the ripe pods are cut from the tree with a cleaver and chopped open. The seeds, surrounded by the gelatinous pulp, are piled into large heaps or put into special

FIGURE 10.5

Cacao pods have a semiwoody shell that does not readily yield to the blow of a cutlass. One or two well-aimed blows from an expert, or perhaps three or four from a less experienced worker, are usually required before the contents of the pod are laid bare. One pod carries anywhere from 20 to 50 beans. (Courtesy of the Nestle Company)

boxes and covered with a layer of leaves. Fermentation then begins; the fruit pulp is digested as the temperature rises. This process is completed within 5 to 7 days; the cocoa flavor has begun to develop. The bean has become dark brown and its shell thinner. Now, the beans can be dried easily, preferably outdoors in the sun. After they are dried, the beans are bagged and shipped to the cocoa processor.

There are many varieties of cacao beans, and the great variation in flavor, color, and other characteristics that exists in cocoa and chocolate products is explained, to a large extent, by the characteristics of the various seeds used to make these products. Usually, there is some blending of the beans of different varieties.

The processor cleans the beans and removes impurities and irregularities. They are then roasted to further develop flavor characteristics. The beans next go to a winnowing machine, which cracks them and separates the shell from the bean. The cracked kernels are called *nibs*. The nibs go to grinders and various mills that reduce the particle sizes so that they cannot be detected on the tongue. Heat from this process melts the fat, converting the nibs into a suspension of cocoa solids in cocoa butter. This is called *chocolate liquor* [7].

For the making of cocoa, the liquid mass is pumped into presses from which much of the cocoa butter is squeezed out under high pressure. The remaining solids are formed into a cocoa cake, which is further processed. Eventually it is broken up to form a powder.

Cocoas may be divided into two main classes: natural-processed and dutch-processed. Some chocolate is also dutch-processed. Dutch processing consists of treating the nibs with alkali, the object being to increase the reddish color and the solubility. The latter effect is accomplished only to a slight degree. Dutch-processed cocoa is distinctly darker than natural-processed cocoa. It also has a reddish tinge. The characteristic chocolate flavor is diminished by the alkali treatment. The pH of dutch-processed cocoa is 6.0 to 8.8, and that of natural-processed cocoa is usually 5.2 to 6.0. The color of such products as chocolate cake may range from cinnamon brown to deep mahogany red as the pH changes from acid to alkaline (see Chapter 26).

A number of instant cocoa mixtures are marketed. They contain sugar, flavorings, emulsifiers, and sometimes nonfat dry milk. The beverage is made simply by adding the dry mixture to hot or cold milk, or to water if nonfat milk is an ingredient in the dry mix. Instant cocoa mixes sweetened with aspartame and/or saccharin are also produced for the low-calorie market.

If chocolate is to be produced from the roasted nibs, the ground liquid mass is refined to a smooth, velvety texture and then subjected to a process called *conching*. This involves heating the liquid chocolate at a carefully controlled temperature while constantly stirring. The mixture is aerated, some volatile acids and moisture are driven off, and flavor is developed. Additional cocoa butter, emulsifiers, sugar, milk solids, and flavorings may be added at this stage before the liquid mass is molded. Chocolate must be carefully tempered at a controlled temperature while it cools to ensure that a desirable texture results from the proper type of crystallization of the fat in the finished product.

Chocolate liquor can be solidified without the addition of sugar to form unsweetened chocolate, mixed with sugar and fat to produce sweet chocolate, or processed with sugar and milk to produce milk chocolate.

Chapter 10

Composition

Fat

According to the FDA standard of identity, bitter chocolate contains not less than 50 percent and not more than 58 percent by weight of cacao fat. The high fat content of chocolate produces a beverage richer than that made from cocoa. Cocoas vary in fat content. Breakfast cocoa is a relatively high-fat cocoa and must contain at least 22 percent cacao fat.

When cocoa is substituted for chocolate, particularly in baked products, approximately 3 tablespoons of cocoa plus 1 tablespoon of fat are considered to be equivalent to 1 ounce of chocolate.

The fat of chocolate contributes much to its eating quality because it has a sharp melting point that is close to body temperature. This results in rapid melting of the chocolate in the mouth with a smooth, velvety feel and the release of flavor substances.

Starch

Cocoa contains about 11 percent starch and chocolate contains about 8 percent starch. In preparing a beverage from cocoa and chocolate, a method that cooks the starch results in a more homogeneous beverage in which there is less tendency for the cocoa or chocolate to settle out than does a method in which no heat is applied.

The thickening effect of starch must be taken into account when cocoa and chocolate are used in flour mixtures, and the amount of flour must be adjusted accordingly. If cocoa is substituted for chocolate directly, on the basis of weight, it thickens more than does chocolate.

Flavor Substances

Many flavor substances in chocolate and cocoa have not been identified. Volatile compounds make up a large part of the flavor bouquet. Marked changes in the flavor of chocolate and cocoa occur when these products are heated to high temperatures, especially in the absence of water. Bitter, disagreeable flavors develop, and scorching occurs easily.

Phenolic Substances

Both flavor and color are affected by the phenolic compounds present in the cacao bean. These substances undergo oxidation to form various reddish-brown compounds that are insoluble in water. Some of the astringent phenolic compounds in the fresh unfermented bean have an extremely bitter taste. These undergo a change during fermentation and are present to a small extent in the fermented bean.

Theobromine and Caffeine

Considerably more theobromine than caffeine is found in cocoa and chocolate. Both substances are methylxanthines, but theobromine is a milder stimulant than caffeine. The theobromine and caffeine contents of various foods containing cocoa or chocolate are listed in Table 10.2.

TABLE 10.2

Theobromine and Caffeine Content of Cocoa Products

	Theobromine (mg/serving)	Caffeine (mg/serving)
Dark sweet chocolate, 1 oz	123.5	15.1
Milk chocolate, 1 oz	38.1	5.4
Chocolate fudge topping, 2 Tbsp	62.7	3.5
Brownies, 1 oz	29.4	2.8
Chocolate chip cookies, one serving	17.6	2.1
Chocolate cake with chocolate frosting, 1/12 cake	161.2	15.8
Chocolate pudding, 1/2 cup	87.5	7.0

Source: Reference 5.

Nutritive Value of Chocolate Beverages

Because cocoa and chocolate beverages are usually made with milk, they have a food value similar to milk in proportion to the amount of milk used. Unlike tea leaves and coffee grounds, which are strained from the beverages, cocoa and chocolate remain in the beverage, thus adding fat and starch to the milk and increasing the caloric value.

Storage

Heat and moisture rapidly destroy the gloss on the surface of a cake of chocolate. A mottled or gray surface known as *bloom* then develops. The bloom probably occurs because some of the fat melts and recrystallizes in a different physical form at the surface of the cake of chocolate. The use of proper tempering temperatures and time periods during the manufacturing process and the use of emulsifiers and modifiers retard bloom formation. However, the avoidance of high storage temperatures is still essential in maintaining the quality of chocolate.

The ideal conditions for storing cocoa are a temperature around 16° to 21°C (61° to 70°F) and 50 to 65 percent relative humidity. Cocoas tend to lump and lose their brown color if they are stored in too moist an atmosphere or at too high a temperature. Although the flavor of chocolate products is usually not impaired by bloom or lumping, the products appear stale and the mouthfeel of solid sweetened chocolate may be granular. Milk chocolate absorbs flavors and odors and should be stored where this cannot occur.

Melting Chocolate

When chocolate is melted, care must be used to avoid overheating, which may produce a firm, lumpy mass that does not blend with other ingredients. A low to moderate temperature should be applied to chocolate that has been shaved or chopped into pieces. Heating the chocolate over hot water lessens the danger of overheating. Chocolate can also be easily melted in the microwave oven. The use of chocolate in coating confections is discussed on pages 210–211.

Methods for Making Cocoa Beverage

The quick method, in which hot liquid is poured over a cocoa-sugar mixture in the cup, does not cook the starch sufficiently to prevent the cocoa from settling out. With instant cocoa mixes, the addition of a stabilizer or emulsifier may help keep the particles dispersed. Preparation of the beverage by either a syrup or a paste method produces more desirable body and flavor than usually results from simply pouring hot liquid over a cocoa-sugar mixture.

SYRUP METHOD

Cocoa

2 tsp to 1 Tbsp cocoa
2 tsp to 1 Tbsp sugar
1/4 c water

Chocolate

1/3 oz chocolate, shaved fine
1 to 1½ Tbsp sugar
1/3 c water

Make a syrup by boiling the ingredients in either of these two lists for 1 or 2 minutes. Evaporation reduces the volume. Add 3/4 cup of hot milk. The syrup can be made in quantity and stored in the refrigerator.

PASTE METHOD

1/2 Tbsp cornstarch
1/3 c water

1 oz chocolate (or 3 Tbsp cocoa)
2 Tbsp sugar

Boil for 1 or 2 minutes. Combine with 2 c of hot milk. The purpose of the cornstarch is to produce a beverage with more body and to most satisfactorily prevent any tendency of the cocoa to settle.

Because milk is a prominent constituent of cocoa or chocolate beverages, scum formation may occur. It can be retarded by covering the pan or by beating the mixture to produce a light foam. High temperatures, which may scorch both milk and chocolate, should be avoided (see Chapter 20.)

STUDY QUESTIONS

1. a. Describe recent trends in beverage consumption in United States.
   b. How are carbonated soft drinks usually processed?
   c. What roles do sports drinks play in the beverage market?
   d. How do fruit drinks differ from fruit juices?
   e. How is wine produced?
2. From what is coffee made and how is it processed to make it ready for use in preparing a beverage?
3. List the constituents of coffee that contribute to its quality as a beverage and describe the contributions each constituent makes.
4. Describe conditions that will aid in preserving freshness in coffee, both in the bean and in the ground.
5. a. Describe three methods for preparing coffee.
   b. What types of material are preferable for coffee pots and why?
   c. How does the type of water used affect coffee quality?

d. Why should coffee not be boiled? Explain.

e. How is instant coffee produced?

6. Describe differences in processing and characteristics of black, green, and oolong teas.

7. a. Describe two appropriate procedures for the preparation of tea.

   b. Discuss the importance of the type of water, the teapot, and the temperature in the preparation of tea of good quality.

   c. Discuss several factors that are important in the preparation of iced tea.

8. What is the source of chocolate and cocoa and how are they processed?

9. a. How do natural-processed and dutch-processed cocoa differ?

   b. How do chocolate and breakfast cocoa differ in fat and in starch content?

   c. How might cocoa be appropriately substituted for chocolate in a recipe?

10. What is responsible for the development of a whitish or gray mottled surface on chocolate that has been stored? Explain.

11. Suggest a satisfactory method for preparing cocoa beverage and explain why this is a good method.

REFERENCES

1. Adinolfi, J. 1981. How long is coffee's shelf life? *Food Technology 35*, 42 (No. 6).

2. Bunker, M. L., and M. McWilliams. 1979. Caffeine content of common beverages. *Journal of the American Dietetic Association 74*, 28.

3. Chen, T., C. K. F. Lui, and C. H. Smith. 1983. Folacin content of tea. *Journal of the American Dietetic Association 82*, 627.

4. Coleman, E. 1991. Sports drink research. *Food Technology 45*, 104 (No. 3).

5. Craig, W. J., and T. T. Nguyen. 1984. Caffeine and theobromine levels in cocoa and carob products. *Journal of Food Science 49*, 302.

6. Disler, P. B., S. R. Lynch, R. W. Charlton, J. D. Torrance, and T. H. Bothwell. 1975. The effect of tea on iron absorption. *Gut 16*, 193.

7. Dziezak, J. S. 1989. Ingredients for sweet success. *Food Technology 43*, 94 (No. 10).

8. Giese, J. H. 1992. Hitting the spot: Beverages and beverage technology. *Food Technology 46*, 70 (No. 7).

9. Hughes, W. J., and T. M. Thorpe. 1987. Determination of organic acids and sucrose in roasted coffee by capillary gas chromatography. *Journal of Food Science 52*, 1078.

10. Hollingsworth, P. 1993. Clear conscience. *Food Technology 47*, 44 (No. 5).

11. Institute of Food Technologists' Expert Panel on Food Safety and Nutrition. 1987. Evaluation of caffeine safety. *Food Technology 41*, 105 (No. 6).

12. Kinsella, J. E., E. Frankel, B. German, and J. Kanner. 1993. Possible mechanisms for the protective role of antioxidants in wine and plant foods. *Food Technology 47*, 85 (No. 4).

13. Pangborn, R. M., I. M. Trabue, and A. C. Little. 1971. Analysis of coffee, tea and artificially flavored drinks prepared from mineralized waters. *Journal of Food Science 36*, 355.

14. Putnam, J. J. 1991. Food consumption, 1970–90. *Food Review 14*, 2 (No. 3).

15. Segall, S., C. Silver, and S. Bacino. 1970. The effect of reheat upon the organoleptic and analytical properties of beverage coffee. *Food Technology 24*, 54 (No. 11).

16. Siegel, R. K. 1976. Herbal intoxication. Psychoactive effects from herbal cigarettes, tea, and capsules. *Journal of the American Medical Association 236*, 473.

17. Sivetz, M. 1972. How acidity affects coffee flavor. *Food Technology 26*, 70 (No. 5).

18. Vitzthum, O. G., and P. Werkhoff. 1974. Oxazoles and thiazoles in coffee aroma. *Journal of Food Science 39*, 1210.

19. Waugh, A. 1968. *Wines and spirits*. New York: Time-Life Books.

Sweeteners and Sugar Cookery

Sweeteners have been used for food since prehistoric times, probably beginning with the discovery of honey. From drawings in Egyptian tombs we learn that, as early as 2600 B.C., bee keeping was practiced for honey production. It is doubtful, however, that the honey was available to anyone but the rich and powerful. Today, some type of sweetener is found in most people's diets [13].

•TRENDS IN SWEETENER CONSUMPTION

From so-called **disappearance data**, published by the U.S. Department of Agriculture (USDA), it is apparent that the consumption of refined (cane and beet) sugar in the United States rose through 1925 and then remained relatively stable at about 100 pounds per person per year until 1970 [4]. During the 1970s, a decline occurred in refined sugar consumption, accompanied by a rise in the use of corn sweeteners, particularly high-fructose corn syrup. By 1985, the consumption of refined sugar was approximately equal to that of corn sweeteners, on a dry-weight basis, at 62–65 pounds per person per year for each type of sweetener. High-fructose corn syrup has largely replaced sugar in soft drinks [26].

Disappearance data indicate that the consumption of refined sugar has increased 4 pounds per person per year since 1986, reversing a long downward trend. Higher consumption of bakery and cereal products has contributed to this increase, these industries now being the largest industrial users of refined sugar. America's taste for candy has also returned, as indicated by the graph in Figure 11.1 [26].

Disappearance rates of sugar, however, are only indications of *availability*. Sugar can "disappear" in a number of ways without being consumed in the human diet. For example, some is used in pet foods and in fermentation processes such as breadmaking and distilling, and some is wasted. Dietary survey data give much lower levels of sugar consumption, at approximately 43 pounds or 20 kilograms per person per year [7].

Disappearance data the amount of food going into the national supply, calculated from beginning inventories, annual production, imports, and exports

FIGURE 11.1

Candy consumption in the United States has been increasing in recent years. (Courtesy of the U.S. Department of Agriculture. *Food Consumption, Prices, and Expenditures, 1968–89,* SB-825, USDA, ERS, May 1991.)

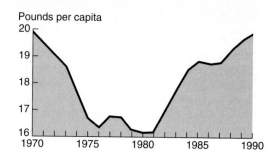

Consumption of low-calorie, high-intensity or alternative sweeteners has increased in the United States in recent years. In 1950, their level of use was 2.9 pounds per person; by 1970, it was 5.8 pounds; and in 1988, it was reported to be 20 pounds, with aspartame accounting for 14 pounds of this total [13, 26].

•NUTRITIVE VALUE

Sugar provides only energy for the body; the dry product is essentially 100 percent carbohydrate. Therefore, foods that contain relatively large amounts of sugar generally have low nutrient density. Increasing the consumption of sugar-rich foods may contribute to an unbalanced diet by proportionately decreasing the consumption of protein, minerals, and vitamins. In addition, disguising many natural food flavors by adding excessive amounts of sugar to foods results in a loss of variety and appreciation for individual food flavors. The Dietary Guidelines for Americans recommend that sugars be used only in moderation.

Molasses, which contains the natural ash of the plant juices from which it is made, furnishes some nutrients other than carbohydrate, such as a small amount of calcium and iron; however, the less refined sugars and syrups, including honey, are still essentially energy foods and, on the whole, cannot be relied on to furnish other nutrients in significant amounts.

A position paper of the American Dietetic Association points out that, on the basis of present research evidence, dietary sugars are not an independent risk factor for any particular disease, nor do they appear to be responsible for behavioral changes. Sugars can, however, contribute to acid production in the mouth and promote dental cavities [1]. Sugars have their proper place in food preparation, providing variety and satisfying the apparently inborn desire for sweet taste. However, the total caloric need, as well as the requirements for protein, vitamins, and minerals, must be carefully considered when adding sugar-rich foods to the diet.

Monosaccharide   a simple sugar with a single basic unit

Disaccharide   two monosaccharides linked together

•PROPERTIES OF SUGARS

The chemical classification of sugars as **monosaccharides** and **disaccharides**, along with a description of some of the common sugars, is provided on pages 91–94.

Solubility

In the natural state of foods, sugars are in solution. **Crystallization** of sugar occurs from a sufficiently concentrated sugar **solution**, and use is made of this fact in the commercial production of sugar from sugar cane and beets.

The common sugars vary in their solubilities. Sucrose is the most soluble of the dissaccharides, and lactose is the least soluble. Fructose is the most soluble of the monosaccharides and is more soluble than sucrose. At room temperature, the relative solubilities in water of the common sugars are fructose (most soluble), followed by sucrose, glucose, maltose, and lactose. The solubility of all sugars in water is increased by heating. At 20°C (68°F), 203.9 grams of sucrose may be dissolved by 100 grams of water, whereas at 70°C (158°F) and 100°C (212°F), 320.5 grams and 487.2 grams of sucrose, respectively, may be dissolved by the same amount of water.

When small amounts of sugar are added to water and the mixture is stirred, the sugar dissolves and the solution appears to be transparent. We call this solution *unsaturated* because it will dissolve more sugar if it is added. The solution becomes *saturated* when it is dissolving all of the sugar that can be dissolved at that particular temperature. The only way that you can know if a solution is truly saturated is by adding sufficient solute (the dispersed substance, which is sugar in this case) so that some remains undissolved in the bottom of the container and is in contact with the solution.

A solution is *supersaturated* when it holds more solute than is usually soluble at a particular temperature. To produce a supersaturated sugar solution, more sugar than can dissolve at room temperature is added to water and the mixture is heated to the boiling temperature, at which point all of the sugar dissolves. As this solution is carefully cooled to room temperature without being disturbed, the solution gradually becomes saturated and then supersaturated.

Only by careful cooling and the avoidance of factors that promote crystallization can a solution be held in the supersaturated state. Because supersaturation is such an unstable state, crystallization eventually occurs and all excess solute beyond saturation is precipitated or crystallized. Some substances require more time to crystallize from a supersaturated solution than others, unless agitation or seeding (adding a few already formed crystals) starts the process of crystallization. The sugars that are the most soluble, such as fructose, are the most difficult to crystallize; those that are the least soluble, such as lactose, crystallize readily. In the making of candies, close attention is given to the solubility and ease of crystallization of sugars.

Melting Point and Decomposition by Heat

With the application of sufficient dry heat, sugars melt or change to a liquid state. Heating beyond the melting point brings about a number of decomposition changes. As sucrose melts at about 160°C (320°F), a clear liquid forms that gradually changes to a brown color with continued heating. At about 170°C (338°F), caramelization occurs with the development of a characteristic caramel flavor along with the brown color.

Caramelization is one type of browning, called *nonenzymatic browning* because it does not involve enzymes. It is a complex chemical reaction, involving the removal of water and eventual **polymerization**, and is not very well

Crystallization the formation of crystals from the solidification of dispersed elements in a precise orderly structure

Solution ions or small molecules, called the *solute*, dispersed in a liquid, called the *solvent*

Polymerization the formation of large molecules by combining smaller chemical units

understood. Caramel has a pungent taste, is often bitter, is much less sweet than the original sugar from which it is produced, and is noncrystalline. It is soluble in water. The extent and the rate of the caramelization reaction are influenced by the type of sugar being heated. Galactose and glucose caramelize at about the same temperature as sucrose, but fructose caramelizes at 110°C (230°F) and maltose caramelizes at about 180°C (356°F).

Granulated sugar, when heated dry in a heavy pan, caramelizes. When hot liquid is added, the caramelized sugar dissolves and can be used to flavor puddings, ice creams, frostings, and sauces. Caramel is also produced during the cooking of such foods as peanut brittle and caramel candy.

Absorption of Moisture

That sugars absorb moisture is clearly shown in many ways. Crystalline sugars become caked and lumpy unless they are stored in dry places. Baked flour mixtures that are rich in sugar take up moisture when surrounded by a moist atmosphere in tightly closed containers. Because of this tendency to absorb moisture from the atmosphere, sugars are said to be *hygroscopic*. Fructose is more hygroscopic than the other sugars commonly found in food. Therefore, higher moisture absorption occurs in products containing fructose, such as cakes or cookies made with honey, molasses, or crystalline fructose. These baked products remain moist noticeably longer than similar products made with sucrose. Exactly how the water is associated with sugars in food systems has not been clearly defined. At least in systems in which the sugar is dissolved, the water surrounding the sugar molecule does not appear to be tightly bound. It is still mobile [10].

Fermentation

Fermentation the transformation of organic molecules into smaller ones by the action of microorganisms; enzymes produced by the microbes catalyze each of the many steps in the process

Most sugars, except lactose, may be **fermented** by yeasts to produce carbon dioxide gas and alcohol. This is an important reaction in the making of bread and other baked products; the carbon dioxide leavens the product and the alcohol is volatilized during baking. The spoilage of canned or cooked products containing sugar may occur by fermentation.

Acid Hydrolysis

The disaccharides are hydrolyzed by weak acids to produce their component monosaccharides. Sucrose is easily hydrolyzed by acid, but maltose and lactose are slowly acted on. The end products of sucrose hydrolysis are a mixture of glucose and fructose. This mixture is commonly called *invert sugar*. The monosaccharides are not appreciably affected by acids.

Cream of tartar the acid salt of tartaric acid; a weak acid substance commonly added to fondant to produce variable amounts of invert sugar from the hydrolysis of sucrose

The extent of acid hydrolysis in a sugar solution is variable, depending on whether or not the solution is heated, the kind and concentration of acid used, and the rate and length of heating. Application of heat accelerates the reaction, and long, slow heating tends to bring about more hydrolysis than does rapid heating for a shorter period. The higher the acidity, the greater the rate and extent of decomposition. Hydrolysis may occur incidentally, as in the cooking of acid fruits and sugar, or it may be brought about purposely as a means of improving the textures or consistencies of certain sugar products, such as fondant, for which it is often produced by the addition of **cream of tartar**, an acid salt.

Enzyme Hydrolysis

Enzymes also hydrolyze disaccharides. The enzyme *sucrase*, also called *invertase*, is used in the candy industry to hydrolyze some of the sucrose in cream fondant to fructose and glucose. This is done to produce soft, semifluid centers in chocolates. The enzyme is commonly added to the fondant layer around the fruit in chocolate-coated cherries. It must be added after the sugar solution is boiled and cooled so that the enzyme is not destroyed. The addition is usually made during beating or when the fondant is molded for dipping. The fondant must be dipped in chocolate as soon as it is made, and chocolate coatings must completely cover the fondant to prevent leakage as the enzyme acts on the sucrose. Because the enzyme acts best in an acid medium, the fondant is acidified.

Decomposition by Alkalies

The decomposition of sugars by alkalies also has significance in sugar cookery. Alkaline waters used in boiling sugar solutions may bring about some decomposition of sugars. The monosaccharides, which are only slightly affected by weak acids, are very markedly affected by alkalies. Both glucose and fructose are changed into many decomposition products both by standing and by being heated in alkaline solutions. The stronger the alkali solution, the more pronounced are the effects on sugars. Sucrose, one of the disaccharides, is the least affected by alkalies, but the invert sugar formed by the hydrolysis of sucrose is readily decomposed. The decomposition products of glucose and fructose are brownish, and, when the process is extensive, the flavor may be strong and bitter.

Fondant made with glucose or corn syrup is usually less white than fondant made with cream of tartar, at least partly because the fondant mixture is more alkaline without the addition of cream of tartar and some decomposition of monosaccharides may occur. When hard water, which is alkaline, is used, the effect is more pronounced.

Other examples of cooked products may be cited to illustrate the color and flavor changes resulting from the decomposition of glucose and fructose: baked beans are more brown in color and have a more caramelized flavor if they are made with glucose- or fructose-containing sweeteners, such as corn syrup, rather than table sugar; and cakes and cookies made from honey and baking soda invariably have a darkened color and strong flavor. These are complex food products, and browning may occur not only as a result of sugar decomposition by alkali but also because of the Maillard-type browning reaction. This reaction begins with the interaction of sugars and amino groups from proteins.

Sweetness

The flavor of purified sugars is described as being sweet. We humans love sweetness, as do virtually all mammals. This has been so since history began, with honey, dates, and figs providing early sources of sweetness [6]. The degree of sweetness that we perceive is affected by several factors, including genetic variation among individuals as well as concentration of the sweetener, temperature, viscosity, pH, and the presence of other substances with the sweetener [24]. It is therefore sometimes difficult to make consistent and reproducible comparisons of sweetness among the various sweeteners, including the common sugars.

In general, it appears that, of the sugars, lactose is the least sweet, followed by maltose, galactose, glucose, and sucrose, with fructose being the most sweet [20]; however, these orders of sweetness do not hold at all temperatures nor in all products. For example, fructose was reported to give a sweeter lemonade than did sucrose when added in equal weights. But sugar cookies, white cake, and vanilla pudding were sweeter when made with sucrose as compared with fructose [16]. A maximum sweetness from fructose is most likely to be achieved when it is used with slightly acid, cold foods and beverages.

•CRYSTALLINE FORMS OF SUGAR

Crystals will form in a concentrated, supersaturated sugar solution, thus changing the physical state of the sugar molecules. From their dispersion in a liquid solution, the molecules pack closely together in a precise, organized, set pattern to form a solid substance. The crystals take a shape that is characteristic for each substance crystallized.

The size of the crystals formed depends on a number of factors, including concentration, temperature, agitation, and the presence of other substances that interfere with crystal formation. The factors are carefully controlled both in the crystallization of commercial sugars and in the making of candies.

Granulated Sugar

Granulated sugar or crystalline sucrose, called *table sugar*, plays a variety of roles in food systems. To the food scientist, sucrose is much more than a sweetener. For example, it affects the texture of many baked products, it improves the body and texture of ice creams, it is fermented by yeast to produce carbon dioxide gas, which leavens breads, and it preserves jams and jellies by retarding the growth of microorganisms.

Table sugar is produced commercially from both sugar beets (about 37 percent of total world sugar production) and sugar cane. The product, refined sucrose, is chemically the same from both sources.

In the production of table sugar, the plant material is crushed or sliced, and the high sugar content is pressed or leached out [22]. The juice is filtered, clarified, and evaporated under a vacuum to form a concentrated sugar syrup, from which the sugar is crystallized. At this stage, a number of impurities are still present and the product is called *raw sugar*. Raw sugar is further refined through a series of steps involving dissolving, purifying, and recrystallizing to produce granulated sugar. The crude raw sugar, containing about 3 percent of various impurities, is not suitable for human consumption at this stage. A by-product of the manufacture of sugar from beets is sugar beet fiber. It is available in varying particle sizes to food processors who desire to increase the fiber content of certain manufactured foods.

Many grades and granulations of refined sugar are available, finer granulations being more desirable for many culinary uses because they are more rapidly soluble. Fine Granulated is the principal granulated sugar of commerce, but other classes, each more finely granulated than the preceding one, are Extra-Fine Granulated, Berry or Fruit or Fruit Powdered (this sugar is not powdered), and Coating. Sanding sugar is coarsely granulated sugar used for decorating purposes. In addition to Sanding sugar, other grades of coarsely granulated sugars are available, each more finely granulated than the preceding one: Coarse, Standard, Medium, and Manufacturers' Grade. These grades of sugar are for use when high temperatures must be obtained in cookery, such as for clear hard candies.

Loaf sugars are prepared by the pressing of wet sucrose crystals into a cake. When it is hard, the cake is cut into cube or tablet form, which is commonly designated *lump sugar*.

Other Crystalline Sugars

A white crystalline form of glucose, 75–80 percent as sweet as sucrose, is produced by the complete hydrolysis of corn starch. It can be obtained in various particle sizes, including powdered and pulverized, but is used chiefly in the food industry. The crystals sometimes found in honey are mostly glucose; the fructose remains in the syrup.

Crystalline fructose that is more than 99 percent pure is available but, like crystalline glucose, it is used mainly by food processors. When used in combination with sucrose, the sweetness is greater than when an equal amount of either sugar is used alone, thus allowing less sugar to be used. Compared with sucrose, fructose produces more rapid development of viscosity and increased gel strength in starch-thickened pies and puddings [28]. Crystalline lactose, which is about one-sixth as sweet as sucrose, and maltose are also available for special uses.

Maltodextrins, which are derived from corn starch, are available as dry products and as concentrated solutions. The starch in maltodextrins is less completely hydrolyzed to glucose than are corn syrup solids, and therefore, they are less sweet and have a very bland flavor. They also contribute chewiness, binding properties, and viscosity to candy [12].

Powdered Sugars

Powdered sugars are machine-ground from the granulated sucrose obtained from sugar cane or sugar beets. Powdered sugars range from Coarse Powdered through Standard Powdered to a series of fine powdered sugars variously labeled according to the manufacturer but all using the letter *X*. Some labels seen on packages are XXXX or Confectioners'; 6X or Special XXXX, which is extra-fine powdered sugar; and Confectioners' 10X Powdered, which is still finer. Powdered sugars usually contain small amounts of corn starch to prevent caking.

Brown Sugars

Brown sugar is obtained from cane sugar during the late stages of refining. It is composed of clumps of sucrose crystals coated with a film of molasses.

Molasses is a by-product of the sugar production process; it is the liquid remaining after most of the sugar crystals have been separated from it. Some invert sugar, which is an equal molecular mixture of fructose and glucose, is present in molasses and thus in brown sugar. A small amount of ash, an organic acid, and flavoring substances are also present in brown sugar, contributing to the characteristic pleasant caramel flavor and light yellow to dark brown color. The lighter the color, the higher the stage of purification and the less pronounced the flavor. Brown sugar is available in a free-flowing form for use in pre-mixes and also in a liquid form for use in continuous-process systems [12]. A one-half measure of the liquid is roughly equivalent to one measure of the crystalline product.

Cocrystallized Sucrose

An interesting new process known as *cocrystallization* can be applied to the crystallization of sucrose, resulting in a number of new functions for this product in the food industry. In the cocrystallization process, spontaneous crystallization of a purified supersaturated sugar solution is accomplished by rapid agitation, resulting in the production of aggregates of microsized crystals as cooling proceeds. The aggregates have a sponge-like appearance, with void spaces and an increased surface area (Figure 11.2). In the presence of a second ingredient, an infinite dispersion of this ingredient follows over the entire surface area of the sucrose aggregate. This cocrystallization process may be defined as one whereby a second ingredient is incorporated in or plated onto a microsized sucrose crystal by spontaneous crystallization [3]; there is no settling out of the second ingredient. The resulting sugar product is homogeneous and readily dispersed in food ingredients. The second ingredient may be flavorings such as honey, fruit juice, maple, peanut butter, chocolate, and alternate sweetener–sugar combinations. The incorporation of mixtures of ingredients into a crystallized sugar matrix is also used to make instant-type products with improved functions in gelling, aeration, and emulsification, for example, pudding mixes, gelatin dessert mixes, flavored drink mixes, and icing mixes.

•SYRUPS, MOLASSES, AND HONEY

Corn Syrups

Regular corn syrups contain about 75 percent carbohydrate and 25 percent water; however, the proportions of the various sugars present in the carbohydrate portion may vary greatly, depending on the manufacturing process and the proposed use of the product. In Europe, a similar syrup is called *glucose syrup* since it is produced from starches other than corn [12].

Corn syrup has traditionally been produced in the United States by using acid and high temperatures to hydrolyze corn starch. The carbohydrate of the resulting product comprises from 10 to 36 percent glucose and from 9 to 20 percent maltose, the remainder consisting of higher sugars and **dextrins** [23]. With the additional use of selected enzymes, a corn syrup that contains a much

Dextrins polysaccharides, somewhat smaller in size than starch, resulting from the partial hydrolysis of starch

Glucoamylase an enzyme that hydrolyses starch by breaking off one glucose unit at a time, thus producing glucose immediately

ß-amylase an enzyme that hydrolyzes starch by breaking off two glucose units at a time, thus producing maltose

Reducing sugar a sugar with a free-aldehyde or ketone group that has the ability to chemically "reduce" other chemical compounds and thus become oxidized itself; glucose, fructose, maltose, and lactose, but not sucrose, are reducing sugars

higher proportion of glucose and/or maltose may be prepared. The use of **glucoamylase** yields more glucose, whereas the use of **ß-amylase** yields more maltose. High-glucose syrups have lower viscosity and higher sweetening power.

The extent of conversion of starch to glucose is described by the term *dextrose equivalent* or *DE*. DE is defined as the percent of **reducing sugar** calculated as dextrose (glucose) on a dry-weight basis. Dextrose or glucose thus has a DE of 100. Corn syrups are available with different sugar compositions having DEs of 20–95 [12].

Dried corn syrups or corn syrup solids are produced by the spray or vacuum drying of refined corn syrup. The dried product is useful in such foods as dry beverage mixes, instant breakfast mixes, cereal bars, and sauce mixes.

Ordinary sugar crystals at 35x magnification.

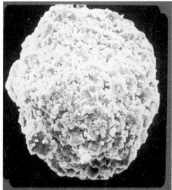

Cocrystallized sugar aggregates of microsized sucrose crystals at 175x magnification.

Surface structure of cocrystallized sugar aggregates at 1,750x magnification.

FIGURE 11.2

A new generation of sucrose products can be made by cocrystallization. (Reprinted from *Food Technology* Vol. 47, No. 1, p. 147, 1993. Copyright © by Institute of Food Technologists. Photographs courtesy of Ahmed Awad, PhD, Domino Sugar Corporation.)

Glucose isomerase an enzyme
that changes glucose to fructose

High-Fructose Corn Syrup

A high-glucose corn syrup is used as the basis for production of a high-fructose corn syrup (HFCS) by use of the enzyme **glucose isomerase** [25]. This enzyme catalyzes the chemical reaction that changes about half of the glucose in the mixture to the sweeter fructose. HFCS containing about 42 percent of the carbohydrate as fructose was produced in the early 1970s [27]. Syrups containing up to 90 percent fructose have since been prepared by a fractionation process that removes much of the glucose from a 42 percent HFCS. To produce a syrup of 55 percent fructose content, a stream of 90 percent fructose syrup is blended into a stream of 42 percent fructose syrup [25].

HFCSs are widely used in the manufacture of soft drinks. They are also used in a variety of other products, including prepared cereals, chocolate products, icings, canned and frozen fruits, frozen desserts, confections, and sauces.

Molasses and Sorghum

Molasses is the residue that remains after sucrose crystals have been removed from the concentrated juices of sugar cane or beet. It contains not more than 25 percent water and not more than 5 percent mineral ash. The sugar, which may be present in amounts up to 70 percent, is a mixture of sucrose, glucose, and fructose, but is chiefly sucrose.

Molasses differs in sugar and mineral content depending on the stage of the crystallization process from which it is derived. After the first crystallization of sucrose, the molasses is high in sugar and light in color. After the final process, a dark and bitter product with a relatively high mineral content, called *blackstrap molasses*, remains. Most molasses sold on the market is a blend of different types.

Sorghum is made from sorghum cane and is similar to molasses in appearance. Its total sugar content is about 65 to 70 percent.

Maple Syrup

Maple sugaring has been an early-spring tradition in some parts of the United States ever since Native Americans first discovered that sap from the maple tree cooked over an open fire produced a sweet syrup. Vermont is particularly well known for its delicious pure maple syrup.

Maple syrup is probably the most highly prized of all syrups used for culinary and table purposes. It is made by evaporation of the sap of the sugar maple to a concentration containing no more than 35 percent water. The special flavor that gives maple syrup its economic importance is not in the sap as it comes from the tree. It is developed in the processing or cooking down of the sap into syrup. Organic acids present in the sap enter into the flavor-developing process by heat. It has been found that evaporating the sap at low temperatures through distillation or freeze-drying results in a syrup that is practically flavorless and colorless. Approximately 40 gallons of sap are necessary to yield a single gallon of maple syrup.

Honey

Honey is flower nectar that is collected, modified, and concentrated by the domesticated European honeybee. Honey contains about 17 percent water and

82.5 percent carbohydrate, with small amounts of minerals, vitamins, and enzymes. The carbohydrate portion of honey includes fructose (38%), glucose (31%), maltose (7%), and sucrose (2%). As specified by the U.S. Food and Drug Administration (FDA), honey may not contain more than 8 percent sucrose; a higher percentage is taken as an indication of adulteration. The addition of any other sugar substances—such as high-fructose corn syrup—to honey is also considered to be adulteration.

The flavor of honeys differs according to the characteristic flavoring compounds present in the nectar of different flowers. Over half of the honey produced in this country is mild-flavored sweet clover, clover, or alfalfa honey. Honeys also come from orange and other citrus blossoms, wild sage, cultivated buckwheat, and the tulip tree. Much of the honey on the market is a blend of different floral types.

The color of honey may vary from white to dark amber. The color of fresh honey is related to its mineral content and is characteristic of its floral source. Grades of honey are independent of color, but darker-colored honey generally has a stronger flavor than the white or light-colored product.

Honey is stored in the comb by bees and in that form is marketed as comb honey. If the comb is uncapped and centrifuged, the honey is extracted. Extracted honey may optionally be pasteurized by a mild heat treatment to destroy yeasts and to delay crystallization. Honey may then be strained to remove wax particles and foreign matter. It may also be filtered to remove pollen, air bubbles, and other fine particles. Controlled crystallization produces a product called *crystallized honey*. A process has also been developed for producing dried honey. This product has a color and flavor that are quite close to those of the original honey. It is granular in form, is free flowing, and has a long shelf life. Whipped honey may have part of the fructose removed, leaving a higher proportion of glucose, which crystallizes to some degree. A thickened mixture results.

The USDA has set standards for grades of honey, including comb honey and extracted honey (filtered and strained; liquid and crystallized). The grades are based on moisture content, minimum total solids, flavor, aroma, clarity, and absence of defects.

Honey is a supersaturated solution and, with storage, glucose tends to crystallize out of solution, producing granulation. Granulation is reversed by heating.

Table 11.1 lists some sugar and syrup substitutions that can be made in food preparation. Adjustment must be made for the liquid present in syrups.

•SUGAR ALCOHOLS

Sorbitol, mannitol, xylitol, and maltitol are sugar alcohols. When tasted in the dry state, they give a pleasant cooling sensation because of their negative heat of solution. When consumed in excess, however, they may produce a laxative

---

TABLE 11.1

Substitution Among Sugar and Syrup Products

1 c brown sugar = ½ c liquid brown sugar
1 c honey = 1¼ c sugar + ¼ c liquid
1 c corn syrup = 1 c sugar + ¼ c liquid

effect. Their uses in foods depend on the specific alcohol but generally include candy for diabetics, chewing gum, and hard candies. The sugar alcohols contribute 4 kilocalories per gram, the same as sucrose, but they are **noncariogenic** since they are not fermented by bacteria [12].

Sorbitol is about half as sweet as sucrose. It has been used in dietetic cookies and candies for many years. Sorbitol is more slowly absorbed from the intestinal tract than are the common sugars and may, therefore, have a lesser effect in raising the level of sugar in the blood after these foods are eaten.

Xylitol has about the same relative sweetness as sucrose. It appears to be the best nutritive sweetener with respect to caries prevention. Mannitol is about 65 percent as sweet as sucrose and is sometimes used in chewing gum. Maltitol is about 75 percent as sweet as sucrose, resists crystallization, and is useful as a humectant [12].

•HIGH-INTENSITY OR ALTERNATIVE SWEETENERS

Sugar has been used to sweeten foods for many decades. However, concerns about caloric excess in the diet and tooth decay, particularly in the Western world, have sparked a desire for alternatives. The food industry has responded with a variety of reduced-sugar products. To produce acceptable products with little or no sugar, high-intensity sweeteners and/or low-calorie bulking agents must be used.

The American Dietetic Association has taken the position that there is an appropriate use for nonnutritive, as well as nutritive, sweeteners when they are consumed in moderation and within the context of a diet consistent with the Dietary Guidelines for Americans [2]. It is interesting to note that the use of alternate sweeteners does not necessarily decrease the amount of sugar in the diet, however. A recent study of college students revealed a higher incidence of use of high-intensity sweeteners than was reported in 1980, with 61 percent of the women and 31 percent of the men surveyed using alternative sweeteners regularly [9]. But there was no evidence that this use was associated with a biologically significant reduction in sugar intake.

Sweeteners may be classified into two groups: bulk sweeteners that provide calories (sometimes called *nutritive sweeteners*), and alternative sweeteners that have a sweet taste but are essentially noncaloric (sometimes called *nonnutritive sweeteners*) [15, 21]. The alternative sweeteners are often called *high-intensity sweeteners* because they are more potent than bulk sweeteners and therefore can be used in much smaller quantities to achieve a similar degree of sweetness.

Three alternative sweeteners are currently approved as food additives in the United States. They are saccharin, aspartame, and acesulfame-K. Cyclamates were considered **GRAS** by the FDA at one time but are now banned from use. The FDA is currently considering a petition, submitted in 1982, to approve cyclamates as food additives [15]. A number of other substances have been developed but most do not presently have regulatory approval. Combinations of different alternative sweeteners, called *sweetener blends*, offer promise for improved taste and stability [31].

Saccharin

Saccharin was first synthesized in 1878, when it was accidentally discovered that it has a sweet taste. It has been used in the United States since 1901 for both food and nonfood purposes. Intensely sweet, 300 to 700 times as sweet as sucrose, it is stable in a wide variety of products under extreme processing conditions [5]. It can be synthesized with relatively few impurities and is inexpensive. One of the major disadvantages of saccharin is its perceived bitter aftertaste at higher concentrations; however, when used in combination with other nonnutritive sweeteners such as aspartame or cyclamate, sweetness is enhanced and bitterness decreased.

Saccharin has been the only approved nonnutritive sweetener used in the United States during certain periods. Some concern about its safety, however, has been expressed since it was first used. Because an increase in bladder tumors in laboratory rats was found to be associated with the ingestion of high levels of dietary saccharin, the FDA proposed banning this GRAS substance in 1977. Strong public protest influenced Congress to impose a moratorium against any action to ban saccharin. The moratorium was extended periodically to allow continued use of saccharin as further research clarified saccharin's role in the **carcinogenic** process [11]. It has been found to be a carcinogen only in rats and only if administered over two generations. **Epidemiological** studies in humans have not shown the risk of developing bladder cancer to be increased with exposure to saccharin. In December 1991, the FDA officially withdrew the proposed federal ban on saccharin [15].

Aspartame

Aspartame is made by joining two amino acids, aspartic acid and phenylalanine, and adding methyl alcohol to form a methyl **ester** (see Figure 11.3). Aspartame is a white, odorless, crystalline powder that has a clean, sugarlike taste and a sweetness potency 180 to 200 times that of sucrose [19]. No bitter aftertaste is associated with aspartame. The registered trade name for aspartame as a food ingredient is NutraSweet®. Equal is a tabletop low-calorie sweetener containing NutraSweet®. Another tabletop sweetener is Spoonful®, which consists of

Carcinogen a cancer-causing substance

Epidemiology the study of causes and control of diseases prevalent in human population groups

Ester a special chemical linkage involving an alcohol and an organic acid

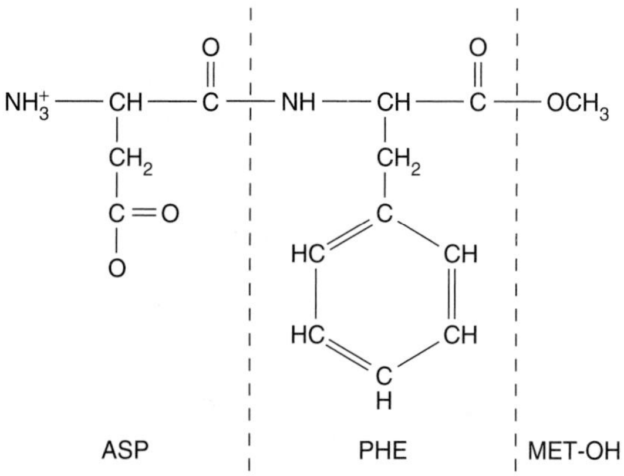

FIGURE 11.3
Chemical structure of aspartame. ASP, aspartic acid; PHE, phenylalanine; MET-OH, methyl alcohol.

aspartame and maltodextrin. It is designed to measure like sugar [15]. Aspartame can be utilized as an energy source in the body. However, it is used in such small amounts that its caloric value is insignificant.

In 1981, aspartame was approved by the FDA for use in several foods. It is now approved for use in many countries and has applications in more than 3,000 products throughout the world, including carbonated soft drinks, refrigerated flavored milk beverages, yogurt-type products, cold cereals, powdered soft drinks, chewing gum, instant coffee and tea, dry pudding mixes and gelatins, ready-to-serve gelatin desserts, refrigerated or frozen drinks with and without juice, frozen novelties on a stick, breath mints, and ready-to-drink tea beverages and concentrates [18].

Since aspartame is not stable to heat but changes chemically and loses sweetness, it has not been useful in such foods as baked layer cakes [17]. However, its instability to heating can be corrected by encapsulating a core of granulated aspartame with a water-resistant coating of polymer and/or a layer of fat. After the outer layer melts, the core layer slowly hydrates, releasing the aspartame in the final stages of baking. The use of low-calorie bulking agents along with aspartame is also necessary to produce the effects on volume and texture that sugar provides in many baked products.

Rigorous testing has been done to ensure the safety of aspartame. Although some have questioned the wisdom of its use, particularly in soft drinks kept at high temperatures, research from several sources has documented the safety of aspartame use by healthy adults and children, as well as by individuals with diabetes [1, 29]. Aspartame-containing foods should not, however, be used by individuals with **phenylketonuria** (PKU) because phenylalanine is released during its metabolism.

The stability of aspartame in fruit preparations used for yogurt has been assessed [14]. About 60 percent of the original aspartame remained after 6 months of storage. It was estimated that the shelf life for the fruit preparations was 1.5 months when stored at 21°C (70°F). Enhancement of fruitiness has been reported in aspartame-sweetened fruit-flavored systems at low flavor levels [32].

Phenylketonuria a genetic disease characterized by an inborn error in the body's ability to metabolize the amino acid phenylalanine

Acesulfame-K

Acesulfame is a synthetic derivative of acetoacetic acid (see Figure 11.4). It is apparently not metabolized in the body and is excreted unchanged. This sweetener is characterized by a rapid onset of sweetness. It has little undesirable aftertaste, although at high concentrations it does exhibit lingering bitter and metallic flavor attributes. Acesulfame-K, the potassium salt of acesulfame, is up to 200 times sweeter than a 3-percent sucrose solution [13].

Acesulfame-K was inadvertently discovered by a German chemist in 1967. In 1988, the FDA approved this compound for use as a tabletop sweetener and in dry beverage mixes, instant coffee and tea, puddings, gelatins, chewing gum, and dairy product analogs. It is marketed under the brand name Sunette®. In mixtures of acesulfame-K and aspartame (1:1 by weight) there is a strong **synergistic** enhancement of sweetness. Blends were found to be 300 times sweeter than sucrose solutions, while individually they were only 100 times sweeter [15].

Synergism an interaction in which the effect of the mixture is greater than the effect of the sum of component parts

Acesulfame-K is heat stable. It does not decompose under simulated pasteurization or baking conditions [13]. It thus has potential for use in cooked and baked products. Baked custard made with half sucrose and half acesulfame-K was equally as acceptable to a taste panel as custard made with sucrose alone or with fructose, even though the crust was less smooth and tender [30]. Custards made with half aspartame and half saccharin, however, were significantly less acceptable and more bitter than the custard made with sucrose.

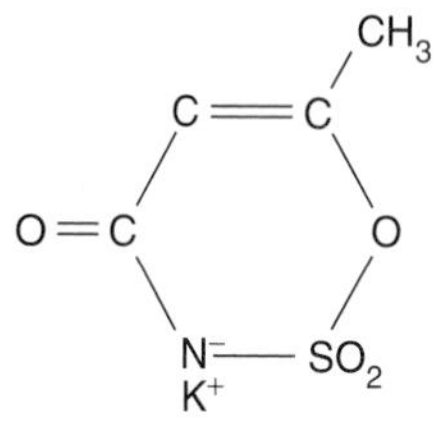

Cyclamates

Cyclamates are 30 times sweeter than sucrose, taste much like sugar, and are heat stable. The sweetness has a slow onset and then persists for a period of time. Cyclamate was discovered in 1937 and was used in the United States for a number of years. In 1958, with the passage of the Food Additives Amendment, cyclamates were classified as GRAS substances. In 1970, however, they were removed from the GRAS list and their use banned because of some questions about their possible carcinogenicity. A petition for their approval is presently pending.

Sucralose

Sucralose is a white, crystalline solid produced by the selective addition of chlorine atoms to sucrose (see Figure 11.5). It is 600 times sweeter than sugar and has no bitter aftertaste. It is very soluble in water and stable at high temperatures, and therefore can be used in baked goods. Sucralose does not interact with any other food components.

A food additive petition for the approval of sucralose is pending with the FDA. In the fall of 1991, the use of sucralose was approved in Canada, where it is marketed under the brand name Splenda® [15].

Other Alternative Sweeteners

A number of other high-intensity or nonnutritive sweeteners that are being studied have potential for future use after sufficient testing and approval by regulatory agencies. These include a peptide called *alitame*, which is up to 2,000 times sweeter than a 10-percent solution of sucrose. Thaumatins are sweet proteins obtained from the fruit of a West African plant. Some of these are marketed under the trade name Talin®. Its use is permitted in the U.S. as a flavor enhancer in chewing gum, but it is expensive. Glycyrrhizin, another alternative sweetener, is found in the root of the licorice plant [15].

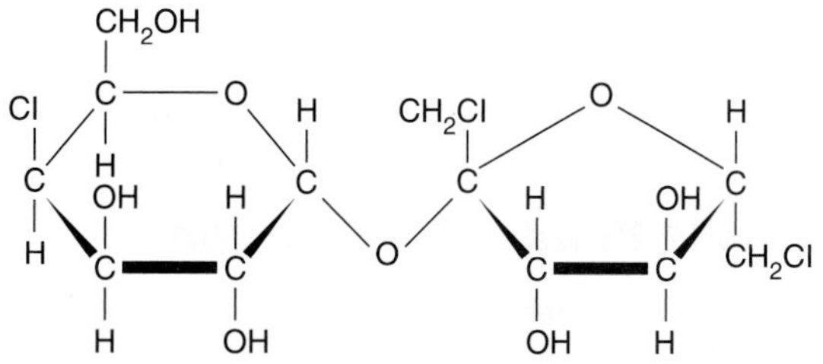

FIGURE 11.4
Chemical structure of acesulfame-K.

FIGURE 11.5
Chemical structure of sucralose.

Structure of sucralose

Bulking Agents

Many consumers today are looking for foods that are low in calories or "lite" but are still good-tasting. Often, good-tasting is synonymous with sweet. Although it is relatively easy, with the approved nonnutritive sweeteners, to make a low-calorie product sweet, it is more challenging to match the other functions provided by sugar in the formulation [13]. One way to do this is to use a bulking and bodying agent—something that is low in calories but provides volume, texture, and a thickened consistency. Bulking agents are also called *macronutrient substitutes*.

Polydextrose is a bulking agent that has been shown to be safe through extensive testing. It is an approved food additive used—often with an artificial sweetener—in such products as frozen desserts, puddings, baked goods, frostings, and candies. Polydextrose contributes 1 kilocalorie per gram, only one-fourth of the calories that sucrose or other sugars provide. Therefore, when used with aspartame and/or saccharin, it can reduce the caloric content of an item by 50 percent or more [13]. The materials used in the production of polydextrose are a 89:10:1 mixture of dextrose, sorbitol, and citric acid. One polydextrose product is marketed under the brand name Litesse™ [15].

Other bulking agents include cellulose and maltodextrins. Maltodextrins consist of glucose units with a dextrose equivalent (DE) of less than 20, and contribute 4 kilocalories per gram. Some fat-free products in which bulking agents may or may not be used, such as fat-free cookies and granola bars, contain concentrated fruit juices and dried fruits as substitutes for added sugar.

Cookie dough intended to be frozen and then baked at the point of purchase was developed using acesulfame-K as the sweetener, with polydextrose, powdered cellulose, or soy fiber used as bulking agents [8]. In one taste test, cookies made with polydextrose received the highest ratings by college students with a mean rating of 4.4 on a seven-point **hedonic scale**. Cookies made with cellulose were rated 3.3, and those with soy fiber 2.8. For cookies made with alternative sweeteners and bulking agents to attain maximum hedonic scores, additional development will be needed. Both the bulking agent and the alternative sweetener should be chosen carefully.

Hedonic scale   a rating scale indicating the degree of liking, usually involving a range from 1 for "dislike extremely" to 7 for "like extremely"

•SUGAR COOKERY

Sucrose, or table sugar, is the mainstay of the enormous worldwide chocolate and sugar confectionery industry. Sugar makes up 44 percent of the net weight of all confectionery shipments in the United States.

In the preparation of concentrated sugar products, such as candies and frostings, many of the chemical and physical properties of sugar are of particular importance. The foundation for cooked frosting and candies is a boiled sugar solution. Some properties of solutions, therefore, are discussed here.

Boiling Points and Solutions

Boiling Pure Liquids

The boiling point of a liquid may be defined as the temperature at which the vapor pressure of the liquid is equal to the atmospheric pressure resting on its surface. At the boiling point, the vapor pressure of the liquid pushes against the atmospheric pressure to the extent that bubbles of vapor break and are released. Once boiling occurs, the temperature of the boiling liquid does not increase: an equilibrium is established.

The boiling point of a liquid varies with altitude, because atmospheric pressure is lower at high altitudes and higher at low altitudes. The boiling point of water at sea level, where atmospheric pressure is about 15 pounds per square inch or barometric pressure is 760 millimeters of mercury, is taken as a standard. At sea level, water boils at 100°C (212°F). At higher altitudes, water boils below this temperature. For each 960 feet above sea level the boiling point of water drops 1°C (1.8°F). In mountainous areas, the low boiling point of water seriously interferes with many cooking operations, and thus methods and formulas usually require modification for use at high altitudes.

The boiling point of water may be lowered artificially by creation of a partial vacuum. This is accomplished by withdrawal of part of the air and steam above a boiling liquid, thus lowering the air and steam pressure. Similarly, the boiling point may be elevated by an increase in air or steam pressure. The pressure cooker, which is a tightly closed utensil, increases pressure by preventing the vapor above the liquid from escaping. The pressure of the accumulated steam is thus added to that of the atmosphere above the liquid.

Boiling Solutions

Anything that decreases the vapor pressure of a liquid increases its boiling point. Substances in true solution, such as sugar or salt, that do not become volatile or gaseous at the boiling point of water will decrease the **vapor pressure** of the water in which they are dissolved. This occurs because these molecules displace water molecules on the surface of the liquid. The boiling point is thus increased because it takes more heat to raise the lowered vapor pressure to the point where it is equal to atmospheric pressure (Figure 11.6). When dissolved substances ionize in solution, as does salt, they decrease the vapor pressure and, therefore, raise the boiling point of the water to an even greater degree. The extent is dependent on the number of particles or ions formed. The larger the number of particles of solute in the solution, the more the vapor pressure is lowered and the higher the temperature of boiling.

Boiling sugar solutions do not reach a constant boiling point as does water alone. As water evaporates and the remaining solution thus becomes more concentrated, the boiling temperature increases. This process continues until all of the water is evaporated or the solubility of the sugar is exceeded. The boiling point of some pure sucrose solutions of various concentrations is given in Table 11.2. These figures are for sucrose solutions alone and do not apply to mixed sugar solutions such as sucrose solutions containing corn syrup, glucose, or molasses, which are more commonly used in making candy than are pure sucrose solutions. Candy mixtures are, however, predominantly sucrose.

Calibrating and Reading the Thermometer

The first step in candy making is to calibrate the thermometer by taking the temperature of boiling water. If the thermometer does not show the proper temperature for the altitude, an adjustment is made by adding or subtracting,

Vapor pressure   the pressure produced over the surface of a liquid as a result of a change in some of the molecules from a liquid to a vapor or gaseous state

FIGURE 11.6

Pure water boils at 100°C (212°F) at sea level because its vapor pressure is equal to atmospheric pressure at this point: an equilibrium is established. When sugar or other nonvolatile solute is dissolved in water, some of the nonvolatile sugar molecules displace water molecules on the surface. The vapor pressure of the solution is, therefore, decreased. Heating to 100°C does not increase the water vapor pressure enough to be equal to the atmospheric pressure at this point. More heat must be put into the solution to vaporize more water and increase the vapor pressure enough to equal the atmospheric pressure. Therefore, a sugar solution boils at a higher temperature than does pure water. The higher the concentration of sugar or other nonvolatile solute, the higher the boiling point of the solution.

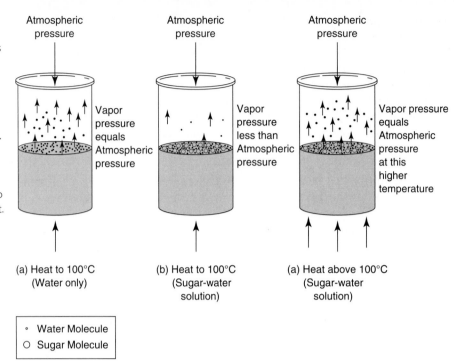

(a) Heat to 100°C (Water only)

(b) Heat to 100°C (Sugar-water solution)

(a) Heat above 100°C (Sugar-water solution)

- Water Molecule
- Sugar Molecule

as appropriate, the difference in degrees between the expected and observed temperatures.

In taking the temperature of boiling sugar solutions, the bulb of the thermometer should be completely immersed in the solution but should not touch the bottom of the pan. In reading the scale, the eye should be on a level with the top of the mercury column.

Inversion of Sucrose

The hydrolysis of some sucrose to produce equal amounts of glucose and fructose, a mixture called *invert sugar*, helps control sugar crystallization in candy making. Thus, it deserves some special consideration in our discussion.

Because a mixture of invert sugar and sucrose is more soluble than a sucrose solution alone, and thus less easily crystallized, the mixture allows the process of crystallization to be more easily controlled than when invert sugar is

TABLE 11.2

The Boiling Points of Sucrose Solutions of Various Concentrations

Percent Sucrose	10	20	30	40	50	60	70	80	90.8
Boiling point									
°F	212.7	213.1	213.8	214.7	215.6	217.4	223.7	233.6	266.0
°C	100.4	110.6	101.0	101.5	102.0	103.0	106.5	112.0	130.0

Source: Browne's *Handbook of Sugar Analysis*. Reprinted by permission of John Wiley & Sons, Inc.

not present. Desirably small sugar crystals can therefore be produced in crystalline candies such as fondant and fudge. Although a small amount of invert sugar is formed by the long, slow heating of a plain sucrose solution, the reaction is accelerated by the presence of a weak acid. Cream of tartar, an acid salt, is probably the preferable acid to use in most candy making, because its composition is fairly uniform and measurements are usually quite accurate. In addition, fondant made with cream of tartar is snowy white.

The amount of inversion that occurs when sucrose is heated with water and acid varies greatly and is difficult to control. The rate of heating, the length of heating, and the quantity of cream of tartar used all affect the amount of invert sugar formed. If too much acid is used, or if the period of heating is too long, too much inversion occurs, with the result that the fondant is extremely soft or fails to crystallize at all. It has been found that the presence of 43 percent invert sugar prevents crystallization completely.

Usually, about 1/4 teaspoon of cream of tartar is used with 2 cups of sugar in making fondant. It has been reported [33] that in fondant cooked to 115°C (239°F) in 20 minutes, approximately 1/8 teaspoon cream of tartar with 200 grams (1 cup) sugar produced about 11 percent invert sugar in the finished fondant.

Glucose, fructose, or invert sugar may be added directly to sucrose solutions in candy making rather than producing invert sugar during cooking by the addition of cream of tartar. Direct addition of these substances makes control of their quantity easier than trying to regulate the amount of invert sugar produced by sucrose hydrolysis. Corn syrup, which contains a high proportion of glucose, is sometimes used instead of cream of tartar in fondant mixtures. The glucose in the sucrose solution has an effect similar to that of invert sugar in increasing the solubility of the sucrose and allowing better control of the crystallization process so that small sugar crystals are produced in the final product.

Classification of Candies

Boiled sugar solutions may be treated to produce either *crystalline* or *noncrystalline* candies. Crystalline candies are generally soft. If properly made, they are so smooth and creamy that the tiny sugar crystals that make up their microscopic structure cannot be felt on the tongue. The principal crystalline candies are fondant, fudge, and panocha. Divinity, with added egg white, is also a crystalline candy.

Noncrystalline candies are sometimes called *amorphous*, which means "without form." In their preparation, by use of various techniques, crystallization of sugar is prevented. Noncrystalline candies may be chewy, such as caramels, or hard, such as butterscotch, toffees, and brittles.

Crystalline Candies

Fondant

Fondant is the soft, smooth candy that results from the cooking of a sucrose solution to a certain range of temperatures, after which the solution is cooled and beaten until crystallization occurs. A simple sucrose and water solution sometimes makes good fondant; however, more satisfactory results are gener-

FIGURE 11.7

Complete solution of sugar. Wipe all sugar crystals from the sides of the pan as the candy mixture begins to boil. a. Roll a small strip of moistened paper towel or cheesecloth around the tines of the fork. b. Dip the covered fork in and out of a cup of clean water as the sides of the pan are wiped free of sugar crystals. The extra water on the wrapped fork goes into the boiling sugar solution.

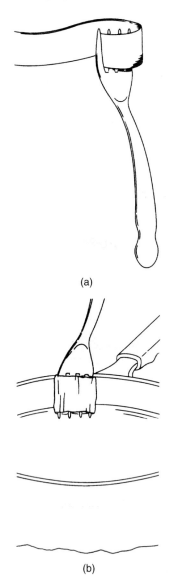

(a)

(b)

ally obtained by the addition of acid to accelerate inversion or by the direct addition of invert sugar, glucose, or corn syrup to aid in keeping crystals small. Use of milk or cream as the liquid increases the creamy character of fondant.

Essential steps in the making of fondant include (1) complete solution of the crystalline sugar; (2) concentration of the solution to the desirable stage; and (3) prevention of crystallization until conditions are favorable for the formation of fine crystals.

Solution. Complete solution of sugar is accomplished by adding sufficient liquid to dissolve the amount of sugar used, stirring, and covering the pan at the beginning of cooking to allow steam to dissolve any crystals that may remain on the sides of the pan. Instead of covering the pan, the sides of the pan may be washed down with a small piece of moistened paper towel or cheesecloth wrapped around a fork (see Figure 11.7).

Undissolved crystals cause seeding while the solution is cooling and start crystallization before it is desirable. The pan cannot remain covered throughout the cooking period as evaporation must occur to bring about the necessary concentration within a reasonable time period. Stirring the solution during cooking does not start crystallization. Stirring and vigorous boiling may, however, splash syrup on the sides of the pan above the level of the liquid. Here it may dry, drop into the cooling syrup, and start premature crystallization. The spoon used for stirring may also introduce dried crystals unless it is well rinsed between stirrings. It is best to wash down the crystals from the sides of the pan again during the boiling period if more crystals form after the initial washing.

Concentration. Table 11.3 gives the temperatures and tests of doneness for candies of various types. As may be seen, the temperature range for the final cooking of fondant mixtures at sea level is 112° to 115°C (234° to 240°F). The lower temperature gives a very soft fondant, and the upper temperature gives a firmer, drier fondant for easier molding. A temperature of 112°C (234°F) may be a little low except for fondants for special uses (remelting) or for fondants containing corn syrup. When corn syrup is used in candy, definite stages of firmness are reached at slightly lower temperatures than when it is not used. For general use, 113° and 114°C (235° to 237°F) are the most satisfactory temperatures for fondants. The higher the temperature, the lower the water content and consequently the drier the fondant. When the humidity is high, higher temperatures are desirable, because more water is absorbed by fondant in damp weather. At altitudes above sea level, the final boiling temperatures should be lowered to the extent that the boiling point of water is decreased below 100°C (212°F).

Testing the doneness of candy mixtures by measuring the temperature of the boiling solution is a method of estimating the concentration of sugar in the mixture. The final concentration of sugar is related, in general, to the consistency of the candy when it is completely prepared—the more concentrated the sugar solution, the firmer the consistency of the finished candy. Another method of measuring doneness in candy making is to drop a small portion of the boiling syrup into very cold water, allow the syrup to cool, and evaluate its consistency. The results of the cold water tests of doneness are compared with the temperatures of cooking in Table 11.3.

TABLE 11.3

Temperatures and Tests for Syrup and Candies

Product	Final Temperature of Syrup at Sea Level*		Test of Doneness	Description of Test
	°C	°F		
Syrup	110–112	230–234	Thread	Syrup spins a 2-in. thread when dropped from fork or spoon.
Fondant	112–115	234–240	Soft ball	Syrup, when dropped into very cold water, forms a soft
Fudge				ball that flattens on removal from water.
Panocha				
Caramels	118–120	244–248	Firm ball	Syrup, when dropped into very cold water, forms a firm
				ball that does not flatten on removal from water.
Divinity	121–130	250–256	Hard ball	Syrup, when dropped into very cold water, forms a ball
Marshmallows				that is hard enough to hold its shape, yet plastic.
Popcorn balls				
Butterscotch	132–143	270–290	Soft crack	Syrup, when dropped into very cold water, separates into
Taffies				threads that are hard but not brittle.
Brittle	149–154	300–310	Hard crack	Syrup, when dropped into very cold water, separates into
Glacé				threads that are hard and brittle.
Barley sugar	160	320	Clear liquid	The sugar liquefies.
Caramel	170	338	Brown liquid	The liquid becomes brown.

* For each increase of 500 feet in elevation, cook the syrup to a temperature 1°F lower than the temperature called for at sea level. If readings are taken in Celsius, for each 960 feet of elevation, cook the syrup to a temperature 1°C lower than that called for at sea level.

The desired rate of cooking fondant mixtures depends partly on the proportions of ingredients used. Faster boiling is necessary if a high proportion of water is used in order to avoid too long a cooking period and consequently too great inversion in acid solutions. Violent boiling is usually to be avoided because of the larger amount of syrup that is splashed on the sides of the pan.

When the syrup is boiled to the desired degree of doneness, it may be poured onto a smooth flat surface, such as a marble-topped counter, on which it can later be beaten. Alternatively, it may be cooled in the pan in which it was cooked. In this case, the cooling period is considerably extended. As the hot syrup cools, it becomes saturated and then supersaturated because it is holding in solution more solute (sugar) than is normally soluble at the lower temperatures. As has been discussed previously, this is an unstable condition and the product must be handled carefully to avoid premature crystallization. The syrup should be poured quickly, taking care not to scrape the pan. Scraping, prolonged dripping from the pan, or jostling of the poured syrup usually start crystallization. Uneven cooling may start crystallization in those portions of the syrup that first become supersaturated. If a thermometer is placed in the syrup to determine when the syrup is ready for beating, it should be read without its being moved in the syrup.

Crystallization. An important aim in making crystalline candies is to produce a very smooth texture. For this to be achieved, many fine crystals, rather than few large crystals, must be formed. For small-crystal structure, conditions must be conducive to the formation, within the supersaturated solution, of many nuclei or small clumps of molecules. These act as centers around which crystal formation may begin. Some substances readily crystallize from a water solution with only a slight degree of supersaturation. With other substances, such as sugar, there must usually be a high degree of supersaturation before formation of nuclei and crystallization start.

The presence of substances that interfere with crystallization of sucrose in fondant and other candies is desirable, but at an optimum level. Glucose, corn syrup, or invert sugar, either added directly or formed by acid hydrolysis, affect crystallization because they make the sugar solution more soluble and, therefore, decrease the ease of crystal formation. Other substances, including fats from milk, cream, butter, margarine, and chocolate, and proteins from milk and egg white, do not themselves crystallize. They physically interfere with the

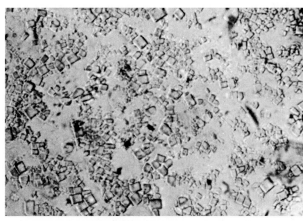

Crystals from fondant made with sugar, water, and cream of tartar, boiled to 115°C (239°F) and cooled to 40°C (104°F) before beating.

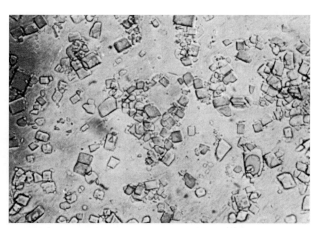

Crystals from fondant made with sugar and water with 7 percent glucose added, boiled to 115°C (239°F), and cooled to 40°C (104°F) before beating.

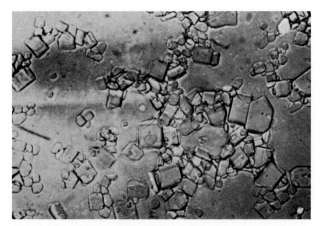

Crystals from fondant made with sugar and water only, boiled to 115°C (239°F) and cooled to 40°C (104°F) before beating.

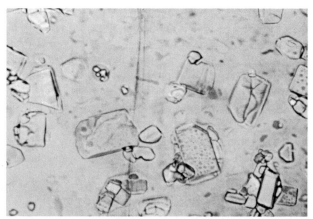

Crystals from fondant made with sugar and water only, boiled to 115°C (239°F) and beaten immediately.

FIGURE 11.8

Comparison of sugar crystal size with various methods of making fondant. (Courtesy of Dr. Sybil Woodruff and the *Journal of Physical Chemistry*)

FIGURE 11.9
Fondant is manipulated with a spatula after it has cooled to 40°C (104°F). Some form of agitation is needed until crystallization is complete. The fondant is then quickly formed into a ball and kneaded until smooth. (Courtesy of General Foods, Inc.)

process of sugar crystallization, retarding the growth of crystals. All of these interfering substances aid in fine crystal formation and smooth texture in crystalline candies.

The temperature at which crystallization occurs affects the size of crystals, primarily because it affects the rate of crystallization. In general, the higher the temperature at which crystallization occurs, the faster the rate of crystallization and the more difficult it is to keep the crystals separated, resulting in larger crystals. Cooling the mixture to about 40°C (104°F) before starting to beat it favors the formation of more nuclei and finer crystals. The viscosity of the solution is also greater at lower temperatures. High viscosity is a further aid in the production of fine crystals because it retards crystallization. Figure 11.8 shows the sizes of crystals formed in fondant beaten at different temperatures. The syrup may be cooled to so low a temperature that beating is impossible. Too low a temperature may also hinder the formation of many nuclei.

Agitation or stirring favors the formation of finer crystals than are produced spontaneously. Therefore, it is important to stir a crystalline candy, not only until crystallization starts, but until it is complete. As crystallization proceeds, the candy stiffens and becomes moldable. It can be kneaded in your hands (see Figure 11.9). It is important to work rapidly to prevent hardening and crumbling of the fondant before kneading is started. It is usually possible to see when the fondant is about to set in a more stiff mass. Its shiny appearance becomes dulled, and it seems to soften temporarily. The softening is the result of the heat of crystallization being given off as the crystals form.

Ripening. As crystalline candy stands after crystallization is complete, it becomes somewhat more moist and smooth and kneads more easily, because some of the very small crystals dissolve in the syrup. Changes that occur during the initial period of storage are called *ripening*. Adsorbed substances that interfere with crystallization aid in retarding the growth of crystals during storage.

PROPORTIONS FOR FONDANT

I. With Cream of Tartar

2 c (400 g) granulated sugar
1/4 tsp cream of tartar
1 c (237 mL) water

II. With Corn Syrup

2 c (400 g) granulated sugar
1 to 1½ Tbsp (21 to 39 g) syrup
1 c (237 mL) water

Combine sugar, salt, cream, milk, corn syrup, and margarine in a heavy saucepan.

Cook over medium heat, stirring constantly, until sugar is dissolved and mixture boils.

Continue cooking, stirring occasionally, until temperature reaches 114°C (238°F) or until a small amount dropped into very cold water forms a soft ball that flattens on removal from the water. Remove from heat and cool without stirring.

Beat until fudge begins to thicken and lose its gloss. Fold in nuts. Immediately spread into a buttered pan.

Cut into squares when cold. Chocolate fudge is made by adding unsweetened chocolate to the ingredients in the saucepan before starting to cook.

FIGURE 11.10
Preparation of blonde fudge. (Courtesy of Best Foods)

Fudge

The principles of making fudge do not differ from those of making fondant. Usually, the butter or margarine, the fat of chocolate, and the milk furnish the substances that interfere with crystallization. Acid is sometimes used, and corn syrup may be used. If brown sugar replaces part or all of the white sugar, some invert sugar, as well as some acid, is introduced to help invert sucrose. Therefore, brown sugar fudge (panocha) crystallizes less rapidly than white sugar fudge. When crystallization is almost complete, the initially glossy fudge becomes dull, and the whole mass softens slightly, as it does for fondant (Figures 11.10 and 11.11).

Noncrystalline Candies

Sugar does not crystallize in noncrystalline candies. The crystallization is prevented by cooking to very high temperatures so that the finished product hardens quickly before the crystals have a chance to form, adding such large amounts of interfering substances that the crystals cannot form, or combining these methods.

Brittles

Brittles are cooked to temperatures that are high enough to produce a hard, brittle candy that solidifies before it has a chance to crystallize. The brown color and characteristic flavor of brittles result from nonenzymatic browning reactions, probably both the Maillard-type and the caramelization of sugar. The development of caramel also helps to prevent crystallization of sugar in the brittles because it is noncrystalline.

Some brittles are made merely by melting and caramelizing sucrose. Soda is sometimes a constituent of brittles and is added after cooking is completed. It neutralizes acid decomposition products and forms carbon dioxide gas, which gives the candy a porous texture. The flavor is also made milder and less bitter by the use of soda. The degree of bitterness in a brittle depends on the extent of decomposition of the sugar. Brittles include butterscotch, nut brittles, and toffee (see Figure 11.12).

FIGURE 11.11
Fudge should be beaten to the correct consistency before it is poured out to harden. (Courtesy of Best Foods)

Fudge that has been beaten too long and has hardened in the pan.

Fudge beaten to the correct stage for pouring into a dish to harden.

Caramels

Caramels are firm noncrystalline candies containing large amounts of interfering substances. They are cooked to temperatures between those for crystalline candies and those for hard brittle candies. The added substances that interfere with crystallization are usually butter or margarine and viscous corn syrup or molasses, which contain glucose, fructose, or invert sugar. Corn syrup also contains dextrins, which do not crystallize. Acid hydrolysis may be used to produce invert sugar, but more inversion is necessary for caramels than for fondant. Fats and proteins in milk or cream also aid in preventing crystallization. The final cooking temperature varies with the kind and proportion of ingredients. The brown color of caramels results chiefly from the Maillard reaction. The color and flavor of caramels develop better with long, slow heating than with rapid cooking. The characteristic flavor of plain caramels may be modified somewhat by the addition of chocolate or molasses.

Taffy

Taffy can be made from a simple sucrose syrup with the addition of cream of tartar, vinegar, or lemon juice to invert part of the sucrose and prevent crystallization. Flavoring extracts may be added when the solution has cooled sufficiently for pulling. Glucose, corn syrup, or molasses can be used instead of acid. Taffies are harder than caramels and therefore require higher cooking temperatures.

Fondant Confections

There are many possible uses of fondant. It may be made into bonbons, which are fondant centers dipped in melted fondant, or into fondant loaves, which have fruit and nut mixtures added. Centers for chocolates are commonly made from fondant. Fondant patties are made from melted fondant that is flavored and colored as desired. Candy cookbooks suggest many specific combinations of fondant with other ingredients.

Fondant Dipping

Fondant centers are prepared ahead of time from fondant of a suitable texture for molding. The molded centers are allowed to stand on waxed paper until firm and slightly hardened on the outside. The fondant for melting may or may not be of softer consistency than that used for molding.

Only a small quantity—about 1 cup—of fondant should be melted at one time. In a container of appropriate size, this quantity provides sufficient depth to coat the centers easily yet not enough to become too coarse and granular before it can be used.

The fondant is best melted over hot water. While melting, the solid fondant is broken up or turned frequently but with a minimum amount of stirring. Formation of coarse crystals by the stirring of a hot solution is as important here as in the making of the original fondant. While the fondant is melting, food colors in liquid or paste form may be applied on the point of a toothpick. Care should be taken to avoid adding too much color. Food flavors, if they are in the form of oils, must be added with equal care to avoid too strong a flavor. Extracts are more dilute.

After the fondant is melted, colored, and flavored, it must be cooled slightly to such a consistency that it clings to the molded fondant during dipping. The molded pieces of fondant are quickly dipped into the melted fondant and are then placed on waxed paper in a cool environment to set. The following colors and flavors are often used together:

Color	Flavor
Red	Oil of cinnamon or cloves
Green	Oil of lime
White	Oil of peppermint
Pink	Oil of wintergreen
Yellow	Oil of lemon
Orange	Oil of orange

Fondant Patties

Fondant patties are also made from melted fondant. After the melted fondant is colored and flavored, it is dropped on waxed paper from a teaspoon. One-half to one teaspoonful may be used according to the size of patty desired. Speed is necessary to dip and pour the fondant before it begins to harden. If the melted fondant becomes too stiff to flow into a smooth patty, it should be remelted or a very small amount of hot water should be added to it.

Chocolate Dipping

The chocolate used for ordinary culinary purposes is not generally suitable for dipping candies. Dipping chocolate should be of fine quality and contain sufficient cocoa butter to promote hardening with a smooth, glossy finish.

Centers to be coated with chocolate should be prepared several hours before dipping so that they are firm enough to handle easily. An exception is fondant centers to which invertase enzyme has been added; this type of fondant becomes softer the longer it stands.

Successful chocolate dipping depends largely on the use of a suitable chocolate; the control of temperatures and avoidance of a humid atmosphere; and thorough stirring or hand manipulation of the chocolate while it is melting and cooling, and, so far as possible, while dipping. Manipulation of the chocolate ensures uniform blending of the cocoa butter with the other chocolate constituents and produces a more even coating.

Temperatures and Techniques

Room temperature and humidity are well controlled in commercial chocolate dipping rooms. The temperature should be 15° to 20°C (60° to 70°F). A clear, cool day of low relative humidity is desirable. Drafts should be avoided, as uneven cooling affects the gloss and color of chocolates.

Even melting of the chocolate is facilitated by grating, shaving, or fine chopping. The chocolate should be melted over hot (not boiling) water; higher temperatures may allow the cocoa butter to separate out. While the chocolate is melting, it should be stirred continuously. Stirring prevents uneven heating and overheating and maintains a uniform blend.

After the chocolate has melted, it should be taken to a temperature of about 49°C (120°F) for tempering. It should then be continuously stirred while being cooled to about 29°C (85°F). At this point the chocolate is ready for dipping. The range of temperatures at which chocolates can be satisfactorily dipped is narrow; hence rapid dipping is necessary. Fondant centers may be dropped into the chocolate, coated, and lifted out with a wire chocolate dipper or a two-tined fork. The coated chocolate is inverted on waxed paper. Another method of dipping chocolates is to pour the melted chocolate onto a marble-topped surface and stir it with the hand. Fondant centers may be rolled in the melted chocolate; the surplus chocolate is removed by tapping the fingers lightly on the marble surface, and then the coated chocolate is dropped quickly onto waxed paper (see Figure 11.13).

Defects of Dipped Chocolates

The chief defects of dipped chocolates are gray or streaked surfaces, a broad base on the dipped chocolate, or sticky spots on the surface. Gray surfaces are caused by unfavorable room temperatures, incorrect temperatures, direct drafts, excessive humidity, insufficient stirring of the chocolate, and not rapid enough

Chocolate is mixed until it reaches the correct temperature for dipping.

A fondant center is rolled in the chocolate and then placed on waxed paper in a cool room. The chocolate should set up or harden immediately.

FIGURE 11.13
Chocolate dipping. (Photographs by Roger P. Smith and Ava Winterton)

cooling of the chocolate. The surface of a defective chocolate appears dull and gray because the fat of the chocolate has not crystallized in a stable form.

A broad base on the dipped chocolate results from dipping at too high temperatures or from failure to remove excess chocolate after dipping. Sticky spots result from leakage of the centers because of incomplete coating with chocolate. These spots are particularly likely to occur in chocolates made from fondants that liquefy on standing.

STUDY QUESTIONS

1. Sugars have many properties that are of importance in the preparation of candies and other sugar-containing foods.
   a. List the common sugars in order of their solubilities in water at room temperature and describe how the solubility of sugars is affected by temperature.
   b. Describe a saturated and a supersaturated solution and explain the significance of a supersaturated solution in making crystalline candies.
   c. What happens when sugar is heated in a dry state above its melting point? Why is this reaction important in food preparation?
   d. What is meant by *hygroscopic*? Which is the most hygroscopic sugar?
   e. Name the two monosaccharides that result from the hydrolysis of sucrose. What catalysts may cause sucrose hydrolysis? Describe examples of the importance of this reaction in food preparation, particularly in candy making.
   f. Describe examples from food preparation of the effect of sugar decomposition by alkali.
   g. Compare the common sugars for relative sweetness and discuss several factors that affect these comparisons. Under what conditions is fructose likely to taste most sweet?
2. Various types of sugars and syrups are available on the market. Describe the major characteristics of each of the following.
   a. Fine-granulated sugar (sucrose)

b. Powdered sugar

c. Brown sugar

d. Corn syrup

e. High-fructose corn syrup

f. Molasses

g. Honey

h. Maple syrup

3. Describe how sweetener consumption has changed in the United States since 1970.

4. List some sugar alcohols and describe their possible uses in foods.

5. a. Give several examples of nonnutritive, high-intensity, or alternative sweeteners.

   b. What is the present legal status of saccharin and cyclamates in the United States? Discuss.

   c. What is the chemical nature of aspartame? Of acesulfame-K? Of sucralose?

   d. Discuss some advantages and limitations to the use of alternative sweeteners in manufactured foods.

   e. Give examples of bulking agents and describe their role in the production of reduced-sugar foods.

6. a. What is the effect of sugar on the boiling point of water? Explain.

   b. Describe what happens as one continues to boil a sugar solution.

7. a. Name two major classifications for candies and describe the general characteristics of each type.

   b. Classify caramels, toffee, fondant, taffy, butterscotch, fudge, brittles, and panocha into the appropriate groups described in question a.

8. Describe the basic steps involved in the preparation of crystalline candies such as fondant and fudge. Explain what is happening in each step and how crystallization is controlled.

9. Describe the basic steps involved in the preparation of brittles and caramels. Explain how crystallization is prevented in each case.

10. Suggest several uses for basic fondant.

11. Describe and explain several precautions that must be observed for successful dipping of chocolates.

REFERENCES

1. American Dietetic Association. 1987. Position of the American Dietetic Association: Appropriate use of nutritive and non-nutritive sweeteners. *Journal of the American Dietetic Association 87*, 1689.

2. American Dietetic Association. 1993. Position of the American Dietetic Association: Use of nutritive and nonnutritive sweeteners. *Journal of the American Dietetic Association 93*, 816.

3. Awad, A., and A. C. Chen. 1993. A new generation of sucrose products made by cocrystallization. *Food Technology 47*, 146 (No. 1).

4. Bailey, L., L. Duewer, F. Gray, R. Haskin, J. Putnam, and S. Short. 1988. Food consumption. *National Food Review 11*, 1 (No. 2).

5. Bakal, A. I. 1987. Saccharin functionality and safety. *Food Technology 41*, 117 (No. 1).

6. Bartoshuk, L. M. 1991. Sweetness: History, preference, and genetic variability. *Food Technology 45*, 108 (No. 11).

7. Black, R. M. 1993. Sucrose in health and nutrition—facts and myths. *Food Technology 47*, 130 (No. 1).

8. Bullock, L. M., A. P. Handel, S. Segall, and P. A. Wasserman. 1992. Replacement of simple sugars in cookie dough. *Food Technology 46*, 82 (No. 1).

9. Chen, L. A., and E. S. Parham. 1991. College students' use of high-intensity sweeteners is not consistently associated with sugar consumption. *Journal of the American Dietetic Association 91*, 686.

10. Chinachoti, P. 1993. Water mobility and its relation to functionality of sucrose-containing food systems. *Food Technology 47*, 134 (No. 1).

11. Cohen, S. M. 1986. Saccharin: Past, present, and future. *Journal of the American Dietetic Association 86*, 929.

12. Dziezak, J. D. 1989. Ingredients for sweet success. *Food Technology 43*, 94 (No. 10).

13. Dziezak, J. D. 1986. Sweeteners and product development. *Food Technology 40*, 112 (No. 1).

14. Fellows, J. W., S. W. Chang, and W. H. Shazer. 1991. Stability of aspartame in fruit preparations used in yogurt. *Journal of Food Science 56*, 689.

15. Giese, J. H. 1993. Alternative sweeteners and bulking agents. *Food Technology 47*, 114 (No. 1).

16. Hardy, S. L., C. P. Brennand, and B. W. Wyse. 1979. Fructose: Comparison with sucrose as sweetener in four products. *Journal of the American Dietetic Association 74*, 41.

17. Hess, D. A., and C. S. Setser. 1986. Comparison of aspartame- and fructose-sweetened layer cakes: Importance of panels of users for evaluation of alternative sweeteners. *Journal of the American Dietetic Association 86*, 919.

18. Homler, B., A. Kedo, and W. R. Shazer. 1987. FDA approves four new aspartame uses. *Food Technology 41*, 41 (No. 7).

19. Homler, B. E. 1984. Properties and stability of aspartame. *Food Technology 38*, 50 (No. 7).

20. Inglett, G. E. 1981. Sweeteners: A review. *Food Technology 35*, 37 (No. 3).

21. Institute of Food Technologists' Expert Panel on Food Safety and Nutrition. 1986. Sweeteners: Nutritive and non-nutritive. *Food Technology 40*, 195 (No. 8).

22. Iverson, C., and H. G. Schwartzberg. 1984. Developments in beet and cane sugar extraction. *Food Technology 38*, 40 (No. 1).

23. Koivistoinen, P., and L. Hyvönen. *Carbohydrate Sweeteners in Foods and Nutrition*. New York: Academic Press, 1980.

24. Noble, A. C., N. L. Matysiak, and S. Bonnans. 1991. Factors affecting the time-intensity parameters of sweetness. *Food Technology 45*, 121 (No. 11).

25. Pszczola, D. E. 1987. American Fructose unveils new technologies in HFCS plant. *Food Technology 41*, 50 (No. 10).

26. Putnam, J. J. 1991. Food consumption, 1970–90. *Food Review 14*, 2 (No. 3).

27. Saussele, H., Jr., H. F. Ziegler, and J. H. Weideman. 1976. High-fructose corn syrups for bakery applications. *Baker's Digest 50*, 32 (February).

28. Staff. 1987. Crystalline fructose: A breakthrough in corn sweetener process technology. *Food Technology 41*, 66 (No. 1).

29. Steginck, L. D. 1987. Aspartame: Review of the safety issues. *Food Technology 41*, 119 (No. 1).

30. Thielen, T. F., and D. R. McComber. 1993. Effect of alternative sweeteners on egg-thickened mixtures. *Journal of the American Dietetic Association 93*, 814.

31. Verdi, R. J., and L. L. Hood. 1993. Advantages of alternative sweetener blends. *Food Technology 47*, 94 (No. 6).

32. Wiseman, J. J., and M. R. McDaniel. 1991. Modification of fruit flavors by aspartame and sucrose. *Journal of Food Science 56*, 1668.

33. Woodruff, S., and H. Van Gilder. 1931. Photomicrographic studies of sucrose crystals. *Journal of Physical Chemistry 35*, 1355.

Frozen Desserts

12

Frozen desserts are among the most popular desserts in the United States, especially during the warm months of the year, when something cold and sweet is particularly inviting. However, they are served and enjoyed year-round. Old favorites among frozen desserts include ice cream, ice milk, sherbet, frozen yogurt, and fruit ices. These are often sold in bulk, and many of them are also sold as novelty items.

A great variety of novelty frozen dessert items are now marketed. These include frozen pudding on a stick, frozen cheesecake, chocolate-covered ice cream bars with caramel and nut centers, small chocolate-covered ice cream bonbons, and many different fruit-flavored bars, both creamy and noncreamy. Another frozen dessert product is *sorbet*, which contains fruit puree along with sweeteners and stabilizers. Like fruit ice, sorbet contains no fat. Tofutti is the brand name of a nondairy frozen dessert that resembles ice cream in appearance, texture, and flavor. It contains tofu or soybean curd along with sweeteners, stabilizers, and a fat component such as corn oil. A "light" tofutti is also marketed, containing no fat and less than half the kilocalories of regular tofutti. Other nondairy frozen desserts are produced with a number of different plant protein sources, including pea protein isolate [3].

Reduced-calorie or reduced-fat frozen desserts are among the "light" dairy products that consumers seem to want and the food industry is attempting to supply [12]. Low-fat and non-fat frozen yogurts are one of the fastest growing segments of the frozen dessert industry, with many other modified-fat frozen desserts with ice cream-like characteristics being marketed as well. Ingredients for both fat and sugar replacement are available to the food industry for the development of reduced-calorie frozen desserts. One fat replacer that was introduced in recent years in frozen desserts resembling ice cream is a microparticulated protein with the trade name Simplesse®. It is produced in a patented process using heat and shear to form spheroidal particles so tiny that they are below the perceptual threshold of the tongue, creating the rich, creamy mouth-feel characteristic of fats [5]. Also included in today's freezer cases are such items as frozen-fruit and juice bars sweetened with aspartame and frozen-drink bars that contain only 14 calories each.

CHAPTER OUTLINE

COMMERCIAL ICE CREAM
  PROCESSING
"LIGHT" FROZEN DESSERTS
TYPES OF FROZEN DESSERTS
NUTRITIVE VALUE
CHARACTERISTICS OF FROZEN
  DESSERTS
PREPARATION OF FROZEN
  DESSERTS

•COMMERCIAL ICE CREAM PROCESSING

Most of the ice cream used in this country is commercially manufactured, although some ice cream is still prepared at home. Electrically operated ice cream freezers are available for home use. These include equipment for operation inside a home freezer as well as traditional ice cream makers that utilize crushed ice and rock salt. Commercial ice creams differ from products made at home. They generally contain more emulsifiers and stabilizers and have a greater increase in volume when they are frozen. The increase in volume during freezing that results from the beating of air into the mixture is called *overrun*.

In the making of commercial ice creams and other frozen desserts, mixes are first prepared. The ingredients are assembled, weighed or metered, and mixed. The mix is then **pasteurized** to destroy pathogenic organisms. Pasteurization also aids in the blending of ingredients, makes a more uniform product, and improves flavor and keeping quality. The mix is **homogenized** by forcing the liquid through a small orifice under conditions of temperature and pressure suitable to finely divide the fat globules, which are reduced to about one-tenth of their usual size. The texture and palatability of ice cream are improved by homogenization. The homogenized mix is cooled and usually aged for a few hours before freezing. During this time, the fat globules solidify, and the viscosity increases [1].

During agitation or stirring of the ice cream mix as it is frozen, some of the fat globules **agglomerate** into a form similar to a bunch of grapes. If this agglomeration process is too extensive, however, with extended freezing time and agitation, actual churning may take place and clumps of butter will result. Commercial ice cream manufacturers add emulsifiers, such as mono- and diglycerides, to the ice cream mix. These help to control the degree of agglomeration and thus decrease freezing time, improve whipping quality, and produce a dry ice cream with a fine, stiff texture that melts slowly and uniformly [2]. Various stabilizers, including a number of vegetable gums such as alginate and carrageenan, also aid in fine ice-crystal formation. All of these additives contribute to a smooth texture in frozen desserts.

The commercial freezing process usually involves two stages. The mix is rapidly frozen so that small ice crystals are quickly formed while agitation incorporates air into the mixture. When the ice cream is partially frozen to a certain consistency, it is drawn from the freezer into packages and quickly transferred to cold storage rooms. Here the freezing and hardening process is completed without agitation. Processing procedures in commercial ice cream manufacture are fully mechanized. Many phases of the process are automatically controlled [1].

Soft-serve ice cream and frozen yogurt are popular items in many fast-food and buffet-type foodservice establishments. These products are similar in composition to their harder frozen counterparts, but they are served directly from the ice cream maker and therefore do not undergo the hardening process. Additional stabilizers or emulsifiers may be used in soft-serve ice cream, yogurt, and ice milk products. State regulations vary regarding the sale of soft-serve products.

Even though commercial and homemade ice creams differ considerably in quality characteristics, the basic principles involved in their preparation are

Pasteurize   to subject to a mild heat treatment that destroys vegetative bacteria but does not completely destroy microorganisms

Homogenize   to subdivide particles, usually fat globules, into very small, uniform-sized pieces

Agglomerate   to gather into a cluster, mass, or ball

similar. Although one may not often prepare ice cream at home, a better understanding of the various factors that influence the quality of ice creams may still be profitable. Also useful in making wise purchasing decisions is a recognition of the standards of identity and composition for frozen desserts.

•"LIGHT" FROZEN DESSERTS

The process of producing acceptable frozen desserts with useful reductions in sugar and fat is complex. Fat contributes greatly to the flavor and richness that consumers have come to expect in frozen desserts that are similar to ice cream. The smooth mouth-feel of fat may be only partially replaced by the addition of low-calorie texturizers such as vegetable gums. Sugar also has important functions in frozen desserts beyond its sweetening power. For example, the freezing point of the mixture is markedly increased when sugar is replaced by a high-intensity sweetener such as aspartame. This increases the amount of water frozen at any given temperature below the freezing point of the mixture and thus affects the texture and body of the frozen dessert [10]. It also affects the overrun of the finished product, which modifies its usual characteristics.

So-called **bulking agents** have been used to replace some of the non-sweetening functions of sugar in frozen desserts. These include **polydextrose**, **maltodextrins**, and **sorbitol**. However, these ingredients have certain disadvantages. Some have the same caloric value as sucrose, some contribute off-flavors, and some may cause gastrointestinal distress [6].

Another adjustment sometimes made in light frozen desserts is an increase in the nonfat milk solids. This increase is normally limited, however, because of the insolubility of lactose, which may produce a sandy texture. If the enzyme lactase is added to the mix before processing, lactose is hydrolyzed to glucose and galactose. These products are more soluble and sweeter than lactose and allow an acceptable light product to be made with increased milk solids [7].

As fat replacers in frozen desserts, a maltodextrin product and a microparticulated protein product were compared with ice milk containing 4.8 percent fat [9]. It was reported that, overall, the protein-based fat replacer resulted in a product containing 2.1 percent fat that had quality characteristics more similar to the ice milk containing 4.8 percent fat than did the carbohydrate-based fat replacer. Microparticulated proteins, one marketed as Simplesse®, appear to be relatively successful fat replacers in frozen desserts.

Major changes in the composition of frozen desserts are necessary in order to achieve reduced calories and/or fat and attain "light" status. A "light" product has been defined by the U.S. Food and Drug Administration (FDA) as one containing either 33 percent fewer calories than or 50 percent of the fat in a reference food, and, if 50 percent or more of the calories come from fat, the reduction must be 50 percent of the fat. Understanding the role of ingredients available for the production of acceptable light frozen desserts is, therefore, essential. Consumer demand for light frozen desserts, as well as for a variety of other light food products, is high. With continued research and development, more quality products will be created.

Bulking agent   a substance used in relatively small amounts to affect the texture and body of some manufactured foods made without sugar or with reduced amounts; it compensates to some degree for the non-sweetening effects of sugar in a food product

Polydextrose   a bulking agent made from an 89:10:1 mixture of glucose, sorbitol, and citric acid; in body metabolism it yields one kilocalorie per gram

Maltodextrins   a mixture of small molecules resulting from starch hydrolysis, having a dextrose equivalent (DE) of less than 20

Sorbitol   a sugar alcohol similar to glucose in chemical structure but with an alcohol group $(-\overset{|}{\underset{|}{C}}-OH)$ replacing the aldehyde group $(H-\overset{|}{\underset{|}{C}}=O)$ of glucose

•TYPES OF FROZEN DESSERTS

The classification of frozen desserts, particularly those made in home kitchens, is somewhat difficult because of the large variety of recipes and combinations of ingredients used. Commercial frozen desserts, however, are subject to state regulations and to federal regulations if they enter interstate commerce. These regulations were specifically designed to control the milkfat content.

There are four main types of frozen desserts: ice creams, ice milks, sherbets, and water ices [4]. Some ice creams contain enough egg yolk solids to be considered a custard-type ice cream. A number of ice creams also contain bulky flavoring ingredients such as fruits, nuts, chocolate syrup, cookie pieces, and peanut butter mixtures. Table 12.1 summarizes the distinguishing characteristics of and regulatory limitations for the basic types of frozen desserts.

TABLE 12.1

Classification of Frozen Desserts

Type	Distinguishing Characteristics	Regulatory Limitations
Plain ice cream	Medium to high in milkfat and milk-solids-not-fat. With or without small amounts of egg products. Without visible particles of flavoring materials. With the total volume of color and flavor less than 5 percent of the volume of the unfrozen ice cream mix.	Not more than 0.5 percent edible stabilizer. Not less than 10 percent milkfat. Not less than 20 percent total milk solids.
Frozen custard	High in egg yolk solids, cooked to a custard before freezing. Medium to high in milkfat and milk-solids-not-fat. With or without fruits, nuts, bakery products, candy, or similar materials.	Not more than 0.5 percent edible stabilizer. Not less than 1.4 percent egg solids for plain and 1.12 percent for bulky flavors. Not less than 10 percent milkfat. Not less than 20 percent total milk solids.
Composite ice cream or bulky flavors	Medium to high in milkfat and milk-solids-not-fat. With or without small amounts of egg products. With the total volume of color and flavor material more than 5 percent of the volume of the unfrozen ice cream mix, or with visible particles of flavoring materials.	Not more than 0.5 percent edible stabilizer. Not less than 8 percent milkfat. Not less than 16 percent total milk solids.
Ice milk	Low in fat. With or without small amounts of egg products. With or without chocolate, fruits, nuts, or other flavor materials.	Not more than 0.5 percent edible stabilizer. Not less than 2 percent nor more than 7 percent milkfat. Not less than 11 percent total milk solids.
Sherbet	Low in milk-solids-not-fat. Tart flavor.	Not less than 0.35 percent acidity. Not less than 1 percent nor more than 2 percent milkfat. Not less than 2 percent nor more than 5 percent total milk solids.
Ice	No milk solids. Tart flavor.	
Imitation ice cream	Proper labeling required. Mellorine types have milkfat replaced by another fat (not less than 6 percent fat). Parevine types contain no dairy ingredients.	

Source: Reference 1.

Commercial ice creams made according to traditional formulations contain milkfat, milk solids, sweeteners, flavorings, and small amounts of emulsifiers and stabilizers. The emulsifiers and stabilizers permitted under federal ice cream standards include mono- and diglycerides, polysorbates, sucrose–fatty-acid esters, lecithin, gelatin, sodium carboxymethylcellulose, agar, algin, carrageenan, gum acacia, and several other vegetable gums. Whey can make up part of the nonfat milk solids in ice cream.

Commercial water ices are water-sugar syrups combined with fruits, fruit juices, or other flavoring materials; a small amount of gelatin, vegetable gum, or other stabilizer is added to produce body and a smooth texture. Commercial sherbets have ingredients similar to those of water ices except that they contain some amount of a dairy product, such as milk or cream.

Mellorine is similar to ice cream except that the milkfat has been replaced with a nondairy substance such as a vegetable fat. Mellorine is less expensive to produce than ice cream and generally sells for less. *Parevine* contains no dairy products but has characteristics similar to those of ice cream and mellorine.

A frappé is a dessert that is frozen to a mush. A high percentage of salt is used in the freezing mixture to produce a coarse granular texture.

Mousse is sweetened and flavored whipped cream. It may contain a small amount of gelatin and is usually frozen without stirring. Biscuit is similar to mousse but is frozen in individual forms.

•NUTRITIVE VALUE

The higher the percentage of milk constituents in frozen desserts, the more important is the contribution of protein, minerals, and vitamins. Desserts with a high butterfat content are obviously of higher caloric value and higher vitamin A content than are those with a low percentage of fat. Frozen desserts, to taste desirably sweet, must have a higher sugar content than most other types of desserts because of the dulling effect of cold temperatures on taste sensations. Fruit ices and sherbets, because of their acidity, also require a fairly high sugar content. Vitamins are probably unaffected by freezing.

•CHARACTERISTICS OF FROZEN DESSERTS

Frozen desserts are generally complex food systems. They are foams with air cells dispersed in a continuous liquid phase that contains ice crystals, emulsified fat globules, proteins, sugars, salts, and stabilizers. For a high-quality ice cream product, desirable characteristics are a smooth, creamy, somewhat dry and stiff texture with tiny ice crystals, enough body so that the product melts slowly and uniformly, and a sweet, fresh characteristic flavor.

Crystal Formation

All types of frozen desserts are crystalline products in which water is crystallized as ice. The aim in preparation is generally to obtain fine crystals and produce a smooth mouth-feel. However, some differences in crystal size and creamy texture are apparent among products, depending on the fat content and the use of stabilizers. For example, fruit ices containing no fat usually have a more crystalline texture than high-fat, creamy ice creams. Many of the same general factors that tend to produce fine crystals in crystalline candies, in which the crystals are sugar, also produce fine ice crystals in frozen desserts. Both fat and nonfat solids such as proteins interfere mechanically with crystal formation and growth. Many stabilizers, including vegetable gums, are hydrocolloids that bind large amounts of water, increase viscosity, and interfere with crystallization.

Overrun or Swell

Ice cream, being a partly frozen foam, typically contains 40 to 50 percent air by volume [2]. This means that, during freezing, the volume of the ice cream mix increases by 80 to 100 percent. Homemade ice creams usually have no more than 30 to 40 percent overrun. The higher percentage of overrun in commercial ice creams in comparison with homemade products results from a better control of freezing conditions, such as the rate of freezing and the stage of hardness at which the freezing is discontinued. Homogenization increases the viscosity of the mix, which favors retention of air.

Too little overrun produces a heavy, compact, coarse-textured frozen dessert, whereas too great an overrun results in a frothy, foamy product. Better ice creams are often sold by weight, and federal standards suggest a minimum weight of 4.5 pounds per gallon.

Body

The term *body* as used in connection with frozen desserts implies firmness or resistance to rapid melting. Homemade ice creams usually have less body than commercial ice creams because stabilizers used in the commercial products often add body. Homemade ice creams generally melt faster in the mouth and give the impression of being lighter desserts, although they may actually be richer mixtures than many commercial ice creams.

Texture

Texture refers to the fineness of particles, smoothness, and lightness or porosity. The size and distribution of ice crystals is a major factor influencing the texture of frozen desserts. Substances that interfere with large-crystal formation, such as fat and certain stabilizers, help to produce a fine, smooth texture in frozen desserts. Preference tests show that consumers generally like smooth, fine-grained ice cream.

•PREPARATION OF FROZEN DESSERTS

Commercial ice cream mixes are pasteurized and homogenized. The latter process finely divides the fat particles, thus producing a more homogeneous and smooth mixture. When homemade ice cream is prepared from pasteurized products, the mixture does not require pasteurization, although heating in a double boiler for 15 to 20 minutes at 63°C (145°F) blends ingredients thoroughly and may be an extra precaution from a health standpoint. After it is heated, the mixture should be cooled quickly to 13°C (55°F) or below. A smoother ice cream and improved flavor result from aging or holding the mix for 3 or 4 hours at low temperature before freezing.

If gelatin is used in a frozen dessert, it may be mixed with the sugar and added to the liquid when the latter has reached a temperature of 43°C (109°F). The entire mixture is then heated further. If egg yolks are used, they may be mixed with the sugar to form a smooth paste, which is then mixed with the liquid and heated enough to cook the egg. Unpasteurized raw eggs should not be used to make ice cream because of the possible danger of *Salmonella* infection in the eggs. Flavoring and coloring are added just before freezing.

Both sweetened and unsweetened fruit are used in ice creams, but sweetened fruit gives the better flavor. Two pounds of strawberries require about 1 pound of sugar for good flavor. Other fruits may require different amounts of sugar, depending on the acidity of the fruit. To avoid hard particles of frozen fruits in ice cream, the fruit should be finely crushed or run through a strainer.

Effect of Ingredients on Quality Characteristics

Milkfat

An optimum amount of milkfat gives desirable flavor to ice cream and also improves body and texture, resulting in a firm, smooth product. The amount of milkfat influences the viscosity of the mix and affects the incorporation of air. A moderate viscosity is desirable. A very viscous mixture resists the incorporation of air, as does a very thin, nonviscous mixture. The air cells are desirably small and the texture is smooth in a mixture with optimum viscosity.

Homemade ice creams with a high milkfat content may have a tendency to churn, producing agglomerated particles of butter. The homogenization of commercial ice cream mixes helps to avoid this problem. Commercial ice creams usually contain 10 to 14 percent milkfat.

Nonfat Milk Solids

Homemade ice creams usually are not reinforced with milk solids, although some may be added. Unless they are reinforced, homemade ice creams probably contain not more than 6 percent milk serum solids as compared with an average of about 9 or 10 percent in commercial ice creams. A relatively high percentage of milk solids reduces the free water content of ice cream. This improves its texture by encouraging finer ice crystal formation. Commercial ice creams can be reinforced with milk solids by the use of evaporated skim milk or nonfat dry milk.

Too high a percentage of nonfat milk solids gives a sandy ice cream as a result of the crystallization of lactose at the low temperature of holding. About 11 percent nonfat milk solids is close to the upper limit for prevention of a sandy product, unless the enzyme *lactase* is added to hydrolyze the lactose. In this case, a higher level of nonfat milk solids can be used without the development of sandiness. Too low a percentage of nonfat milk solids encourages high overrun, which creates fluffiness and poor body.

Sweeteners

Sweeteners, of course, affect flavor. Consumer preference generally is for a fairly sweet ice cream (one containing about 14 or 15 percent sugar or approximately one-sixth by weight) [8]. Sugar also lowers the freezing point and affects the amount of water frozen at the usual holding and serving temperatures for ice cream. If too much sugar is added, the freezing point is lowered excessively and freezing is retarded. If too little sugar is used, the freezing point is high enough that much of the water is frozen, adversely affecting the texture of the ice cream [10].

Although table sugar is the usual sweetener in homemade frozen desserts, various sweeteners are used in commercial products. These include corn syrups and high-fructose corn syrups, as well as sugar. The use of corn sweeteners is increasing. A comparatively large amount of high-fructose corn syrup, which produces a lower freezing point, was reported to contribute to the development of iciness on storage of ice cream [13].

Stabilizers and Emulsifiers

Stabilizer a water-holding substance, such as a vegetable gum, that interferes with ice crystal formation and contributes to a smooth texture in frozen desserts

Emulsifier a substance that aids in producing a fine division of fat globules; in ice cream, it also stabilizes the dispersion of air in the foam structure

A number of different **stabilizers** and **emulsifiers** are used in commercial frozen desserts in amounts up to 0.5 percent. The emulsifiers affect the fat-globule structure and the agglomeration of these globules during freezing. This contributes to improved whipping quality and texture. Stabilizers interfere somewhat with ice crystal formation, helping to keep the crystals small. They also give body to the mixture [11]. Some of the water in frozen desserts is bound by the stabilizers; this inhibits ice crystal growth, particularly during distribution and storage [13].

The Freezing Process

Freezing Points of Liquids

Pure liquids have characteristic freezing points at constant pressure. The freezing point is the temperature at which the vapor pressures of the pure liquid and its pure solid substance are equal and the liquid and solid forms remain together in equilibrium. The melting point and freezing point are identical. Because a liquid can be supercooled to a temperature below its freezing point before freezing occurs, it is not altogether accurate to describe the freezing point as the temperature at which the liquid changes to a solid.

Water freezes at 0°C (32°F) at a pressure of 760 millimeters of mercury. After freezing, the temperature of ice may be lowered below 0°C (32°F). If the temperature of the surroundings is lower than 0°C (32°F), the ice as well as the air eventually reaches the lower temperature. Water expands during freezing to occupy more space than it did in the liquid form. The swelling or increased volume of frozen desserts results partly from the expansion of watery mixtures on freezing; however, the incorporation of air as the mixture is agitated during freezing is the major reason for the increase in volume.

Solution a mixture resulting from the dispersion of small molecules or ions (called the *solute*) in a liquid such as water (called the *solvent*)

Substances dissolved in a liquid to form a true **solution** cause the freezing point of the solution to be lower than the freezing point of the pure liquid. A sugar solution, which is the basis for frozen desserts, has a lower freezing point than pure water. The higher the concentration of the solution, the lower the freezing point. Ices and sherbets that contain acid fruit juices have a higher percentage of sugar than ice creams. Therefore, they freeze at a lower temperature.

Freezing Mixtures

The freezing mixture used in an ordinary ice cream freezer is a mixture of crushed ice and a salt. The salt is usually coarse sodium chloride (NaCl), called *rock salt*. The greater the proportion of salt to ice in the mixture, the lower the temperature of the mixture. This holds true until no more salt will dissolve in the water coming from the melting ice, that is, until a **saturated salt solution** is produced. The lowest temperature possible in a brine from a salt and ice mixture is about $-21°$ or $-22°C$ ($-6°$ to $-8°F$). Few dessert mixes require a temperature lower than $-8°$ to $-10°C$ ($14°$ to $18°F$) to freeze.

When ice and salt are mixed, the surface of the ice is usually moist and dissolves some of the salt. The vapor pressure of the concentrated salt solution that is formed on the surface of the ice is lower than that of the ice itself. In an attempt by the system to establish equilibrium, more ice melts. More salt then dissolves, and the process is repeated.

As ice melts, it absorbs heat, and the rapid melting of ice that occurs when salt is added to it increases the rate of heat absorption. Some heat is also absorbed as the salt dissolves in the film of water on the surface of the ice. The heat that is absorbed in both of these processes is taken from the brine, from the air, or from the mixture to be frozen. Because cold is really the absence of heat, as heat is removed, the temperatures of the brine and of the mixture to be frozen are lowered. When the mixture to be frozen reaches its freezing point, ice crystals begin to form and precipitate out.

The removal of some water as ice causes the remaining unfrozen mixture to become more concentrated, with a freezing temperature lower than that of the original dessert mixture. Thus, as freezing proceeds, the freezing temperature is gradually lowered, just as the evaporation of water that occurs in the boiling of a sugar solution produces a gradual increase in the boiling temperature of the mixture.

When freezing is accompanied by stirring, a proportion of salt to ice that is efficient for home freezing is about one part coarse salt to six parts crushed ice by weight. This is equivalent to about one to twelve by measure. For faster freezing, a proportion of about one part salt to eight parts ice, by measure, is also satisfactory. The higher the percentage of salt, the shorter the time required for freezing; however, if freezing is too rapid, not enough time is available to keep the ice crystals separated and small while stirring, and the crystals of ice formed may be large enough to produce a granular texture.

If desserts are frozen without stirring, that is, packed in the freezing mixture, the proportion of salt to ice is about one to two by measure. Mixtures frozen without stirring require a longer time and a colder temperature to freeze than do stirred mixtures. Removal of heat from the center of the mass may be difficult in unstirred frozen desserts because they are high in fat and have air beaten into the heavy cream that is usually used as the basis of the mixture. Both cold fat and air are poor conductors of heat.

The fineness of the division of salt and ice is also a factor influencing the rate of freezing in the preparation of frozen desserts. Finely crushed ice has

Saturated solution   a solution containing all of the solute that it can dissolve at that temperature

more surface exposed to the action of salt than does coarsely chopped ice and hence melts faster. Fine salt dissolves more rapidly, but because of its lumping and collecting in the bottom of the freezer, it is less desirable to use than coarse salt.

Ice Cream Freezers

Construction.   Figure 12.1 illustrates the structure of an ice cream freezer. The outer container of the freezer is usually made of a material that conducts heat poorly, such as wood or plastic foam. This minimizes the absorption of heat from the air. The goal is to have the melting ice absorb heat from the mixture to be frozen.

The container that holds the ice cream mix inside the outer container is made of metal, which conducts heat readily and permits the rapid absorption of heat from the ice cream mix. A paddle or dasher inside the metal can agitates the ice cream mixture as the freezer is turned, thus incorporating air. The dasher scrapes the mixture from the side walls, thus permitting a new layer of mixture to come in contact with the can. Agitation also tends to form many nuclei on which ice crystals may form, which favors small crystal formation.

FIGURE 12.1
Structure of an ice cream freezer.

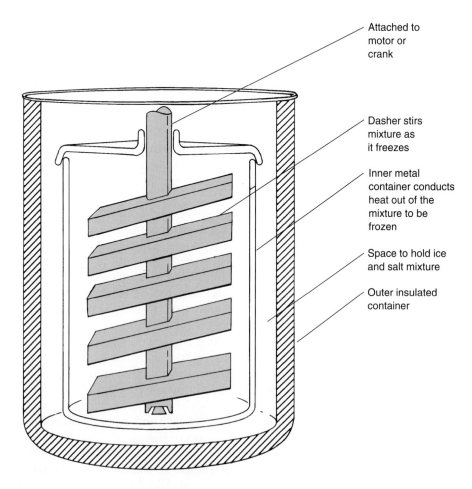

Attached to motor or crank

Dasher stirs mixture as it freezes

Inner metal container conducts heat out of the mixture to be frozen

Space to hold ice and salt mixture

Outer insulated container

Rate of Turning the Freezer. Slow agitation of the ice cream mixture is desirable at the beginning of the freezing period until the temperature of the freezing mixture is lowered below the critical churning temperature. At 5°C (40°F) or above, agitation tends to cause the formation of clumps of butterfat, resulting in a buttery ice cream or in actual butter.

Rapid agitation after the mixture is chilled not only incorporates much air but also favors the formation of many nuclei and fine ice crystals. It is difficult to produce fine crystals in ice creams that are frozen without stirring, because relatively few nuclei for ice crystal formation are present and thus large crystal growth can occur.

In quick-freezing procedures that are practiced commercially, many nuclei and small crystals are formed because of the extremely low temperatures used [1]. The shortness of the time of freezing prevents the growth of crystals.

Packing the Freezer. The mixture to be frozen should occupy only about two-thirds of the capacity of the inner metal can to allow for overrun or swell during freezing. After the paddle or dasher is adjusted, the space between the inner can and the outer container is best filled about half-full with crushed ice before any salt is added. This tends to prevent the salt from collecting in the bottom of the freezer. The remainder of the ice and salt needed to fill the freezer may be added alternately. It is also possible to mix the crushed ice and salt together before adding it to the freezer, but the first cooling effect obtained when the salt is added to the ice is lost.

The brine that forms as the ice begins to melt is not drained off. When the mixture is frozen, the crank turns with difficulty. The lid may be removed, the dasher taken out, and the ice cream pressed down solidly in the can. The hole in the inner metal can top is corked to prevent the salty freezing mixture from getting into the can, and the excess brine is drained off.

If the frozen dessert is to be used soon, the freezer may be packed with a freezing mixture containing a percentage of salt higher than that used for freezing. The hardening of the dessert to a consistency desirable for serving is thus accomplished more rapidly. If the ice cream is to stand for a longer time before serving, the same mixture used for freezing may also be used for packing the frozen dessert.

Freezing Without Stirring

The freezing compartment of a refrigerator provides a temperature low enough for freezing as well as for holding frozen mixtures. Equipment is available for stirring the mixture as it freezes inside the freezing compartment. Without stirring, the rate of freezing is retarded and ice crystals tend to be larger than they are when stirring occurs.

Mixtures that can be frozen most successfully without stirring are those rich in fat, such as whipped cream products, or mixtures containing gelatin, cooked egg custard, evaporated milk, or a cooked starch base. These substances interfere with the formation of large ice crystals. Because these mixtures are not stirred to incorporate air, air must be beaten into cream or evaporated milk prior to freezing. Partially frozen mixtures may be removed from the freezing trays and beaten once or twice during the freezing period. Air cells tend to interfere with coarse-crystal formation.

Egg Custard. Custards thickened with egg yolk or whole egg are sometimes used in ice creams. (Raw eggs should not be used in frozen desserts because of the possible presence of *Salmonella* in unbroken eggs.) The cooked custard must be well chilled before it is combined with whipped cream. Three-fourths cup of custard is the maximum amount that will combine with a cup of whipping cream to give a smooth ice cream.

Time Required for Freezing. The time required for freezing refrigerator desserts depends on the quantity being frozen, the composition of the mixture, and the temperature. About 4 to 6 hours may be needed, and the cold control is best set on the lowest temperature. When the mixture is frozen without stirring, freezing as quickly as possible aids in the production of many small ice crystals. Faster freezing occurs if the mixture is stirred occasionally in the tray to permit unfrozen portions to come in contact with the tray.

STUDY QUESTIONS

1. Describe the major characteristics of a well-prepared frozen dessert such as ice cream or sherbet.
2. Describe identifying characteristics of each of the following.
   a. Sherbet   f. Sorbet
   b. Water ice   g. Tofutti
   c. Ice cream   h. Frozen yogurt
   d. Ice milk   i. Mellorine
   e. Mousse   j. Parevine
3. What is the effect of each of the following on the flavor, texture, and/or body of a frozen ice cream?
   a. Milkfat
   b. Nonfat milk solids
   c. Sweeteners
   d. Stabilizers
   e. Overrun
4. Discuss some of the problems often involved in the formulation of acceptable "light" frozen desserts. What are some possible solutions to these problems?
5. Explain how a mixture of ice and salt is able to act as a freezing mixture to freeze frozen desserts.
6. Describe an appropriate procedure for preparing homemade ice cream in an ice cream freezer. Explain what happens at each step.
7. What procedures should be used when freezing a frozen dessert without stirring and why?

REFERENCES

1. Arbuckle, W. S. *Ice Cream*, 4th ed. Westport, CT: Avi Publishing Company, Inc., 1986.
2. Buck, J. S., C. E. Walker, and M. M. Pierce. 1986. Evaluation of sucrose esters in ice cream. *Journal of Food Science 51*, 489.
3. Chan, A. S. M., R. R. Pereira, H. M. Henderson, and G. Blank. 1992. A nondairy frozen dessert utilizing pea protein isolate and hydrogenated canola oil. *Food Technology 46*, 88 (No. 1).

4. Code of Federal Regulations. Definitions and Standards under the Federal Food, Drug, and Cosmetic Act: Frozen Desserts. Title 21, Part 20.

5. Dziezak, J. D. 1989. Fats, oils, and fat substitutes. *Food Technology 43*, 66 (No. 7).

6. Keller, S. E., J. W. Fellows, T. C. Nash, and W. H. Shazer. 1991. Application of bulk-free process in aspartame-sweetened frozen dessert. *Food Technology 45*, 100 (No. 6).

7. Keller, S. E., J. W. Fellows, T. C. Nash, and W. H. Shazer. 1991. Formulation of aspartame-sweetened frozen dairy dessert without bulking agents. *Food Technology 45*, 102 (No. 2).

8. Pangborn, R. M., M. Simone, and T. A. Nickerson. 1957. The influence of sugar in ice cream: Consumer preferences for vanilla ice cream. *Food Technology 11*, 679.

9. Schmidt, K., A. Lundy, J. Reynolds, and L. N. Yee. 1993. Carbohydrate or protein-based fat mimicker effects on ice milk properties. *Journal of Food Science 58*, 761.

10. Tharp, B. W., and T. V. Gottemoller. 1990. Light frozen dairy desserts: Effect of compositional changes on processing and sensory characteristics. *Food Technology 44*, 86 (No. 10).

11. Thomas, E. L. 1981. Structure and properties of ice cream emulsions. *Food Technology 35*, 41 (No. 1).

12. Thompson, M. S. 1990. Light dairy products: Issues and objectives. *Food Technology 44*, 78 (No. 10).

13. Wittinger, S. A., and D. E. Smith. 1986. Effect of sweeteners and stabilizers on selected sensory attributes and shelf life of ice cream. *Journal of Food Science 51*, 1463.

Starch

13

Starch is one of the most abundant substances in nature. A storage form of carbohydrate in plants, starch is located in roots, seeds, fruits, and stems. During germination of a seed, the stored starch undergoes enzymatic **hydrolysis** to yield glucose, which then supplies energy for the **germination** and early stages of plant growth.

The human digestive system also produces enzymes, called **amylases**, that break down or hydrolyze this nutritive polysaccharide, yielding the disaccharide **maltose**. Maltose is then hydrolyzed to **glucose**, which is absorbed and metabolized by body cells, providing energy.

Starch is available to the food industry, and also to the consumer, as a purified material. In this form, it belongs to a group of substances called **hydrocolloids,** a group that also includes **pectin** and a number of vegetable gums. Hydrocolloids are **colloidal** substances: they are water loving and absorb relatively large amounts of water. They are often used as stabilizers, texturizers, thickeners, and binders in manufactured foods.

•SOURCES OF STARCH

The parts of plants that serve most prominently for the storage of starch are seeds, roots, and **tubers**. Thus, the most common sources of food starch are cereal grains, including corn, wheat, rice, grain sorghum, and oats; legumes; and roots or tubers, including potato, sweet potato, arrowroot, and the tropical cassava plant (marketed as tapioca). Sago comes from the pith or core of the tropical sago palm.

Corn is grown in temperate to warm climates with half of the world's production in the United States. Wheat is grown primarily in North America, Europe, and Russia. Approximately 90 percent of the world's rice supply is produced in southern and southeastern Asia, whereas about 70 percent of the world's potato supply is grown in the cool, moist climate of Europe and Russia.

Purified starch is generally separated from grains and tubers by a process called *wet milling*. This process employs various techniques of grinding, screen-

CHAPTER OUTLINE

SOURCES OF STARCH
COMPOSITION AND STRUCTURE
HYDROLYSIS OF STARCH
EFFECT OF HEAT ON STARCH
GEL FORMATION AND
 RETROGRADATION
STARCH COOKERY

Hydrolysis   a chemical reaction in which a molecular linkage is broken and a molecule of water is utilized

Germination   the sprouting of a seed

Amylase   an enzyme that hydrolyzes starch to produce dextrins, maltose, and glucose

Maltose   a double sugar or disaccharide made up of two glucose units

Glucose   a monosaccharide or simple sugar that is the basic building unit for starch

Hydrocolloid   a substance with particles of colloidal size that is greatly attracted to water and absorbs it readily

Pectin   a gel-forming polysaccharide found in plant tissues

Colloidal   a state of subdivision of dispersed particles; intermediate between very small particles in true solution and large particles in suspension

Tuber   an enlarged underground stem, for example, the potato

Modified starches   natural starches that have been treated chemically to create some specific change in chemical structure, such as linking parts of the molecules together or adding some new chemical groups to the molecules; the chemical changes create new physical properties that improve the performance of the starches in food preparation

Polysaccharide   a complex carbohydrate made up of many simple sugar (monosaccharide) units linked together; in the case of starch, the simple sugars are all glucose

Gel   a colloidal dispersion that shows some rigidity and will, when unmolded, keep the shape of the container in which it had been placed

ing, and centrifuging to separate the starch from fiber, oil, and protein. Natural starches are often chemically modified (**modified starches**) to enhance those properties that are desirable for specific applications in food manufacturing.

•COMPOSITION AND STRUCTURE

The Starch Molecule

Starch is a **polysaccharide** made up of hundreds or even thousands of glucose molecules joined together. Molecules of starch are of two types, called *fractions*: amylose and amylopectin.

Amylose is a long chainlike molecule, sometimes called the *linear fraction*, and is produced by linking together 500 to 2000 glucose molecules. A representation of the amylose molecule is shown in Figure 13.1. The amylose fraction of starch contributes gelling characteristics to cooked and cooled starch mixtures. A **gel** is rigid to a certain degree and holds a shape when molded.

The chemical structure of amylopectin differs from that of amylose in that it is a highly branched, bushy kind of molecule. In both amylose and amylopectin, however, the basic building unit is glucose. Figure 13.2 represents the chemical nature of amylopectin, with many short chains of glucose units branching from each other, much like the trunk and branches of a tree. Cohesion or thickening properties are contributed by amylopectin when a starch mixture is cooked in the presence of water, but this fraction does not produce a gel.

Most natural starches are mixtures of the two fractions. Corn, wheat, rice, potato, and tapioca starches contain 24 to 16 percent amylose, with the remainder being amylopectin. The root starches of tapioca and potato are lower in amylose content than are the cereal starches of corn, wheat, and rice. Certain strains of corn, rice, grain sorghum, and barley have been developed that are practically devoid of amylose. These are called *waxy* varieties because of the waxy appearance of the kernel when it is cut. They contain only the amylopectin fraction of starch and are nongelling because of the lack of amylose. Through genetic manipulation, high-amylose starches have also been produced. For example, a high-amylose corn, called *amylomaize*, has starch that contains approximately 70 percent amylose. High-amylose starches have a unique ability to form films and to bind other ingredients.

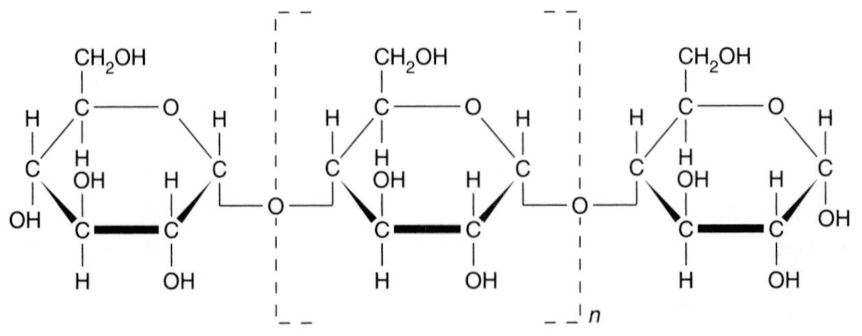

FIGURE 13.1

Amylose is a linear molecule with hundreds of glucose units linked together. A portion of the molecule is represented here. The glucose units are joined between the No. 1 carbon atom of one glucose molecule and the No. 4 carbon atom of the next one. The *n* may represent hundreds of similarly linked glucose molecules. See also Figure 5.6.

The Starch Granule

In the storage areas of plants, notably the seeds and roots, molecules of starch are deposited as tiny, organized units called *granules*. Amylose and amylopectin molecules are placed in tightly packed successive layers around a central spot in the granule called the *hilum*. The sizes and shapes of granules differ among starches from various sources, but all starch granules are microscopic. Figure 13.3 and 13.4 are photomicrographs of starch granules from several sources. Potato starch is also shown as viewed under polarized light. Because of the highly oriented and crystalline areas in a starch granule, the plane of **polarized light** is rotated to produce the appearance of a cross, as seen in Figure 13.3 (first photo on left). This phenomenon is called **birefringence**. The cross disappears when the highly organized structure of the granule is disrupted during cooking.

Polarized light   light that vibrates in one plane

Birefringence   the ability of a substance to refract light in two directions; this produces a dark cross on each starch granule when viewed with a polarizing microscope

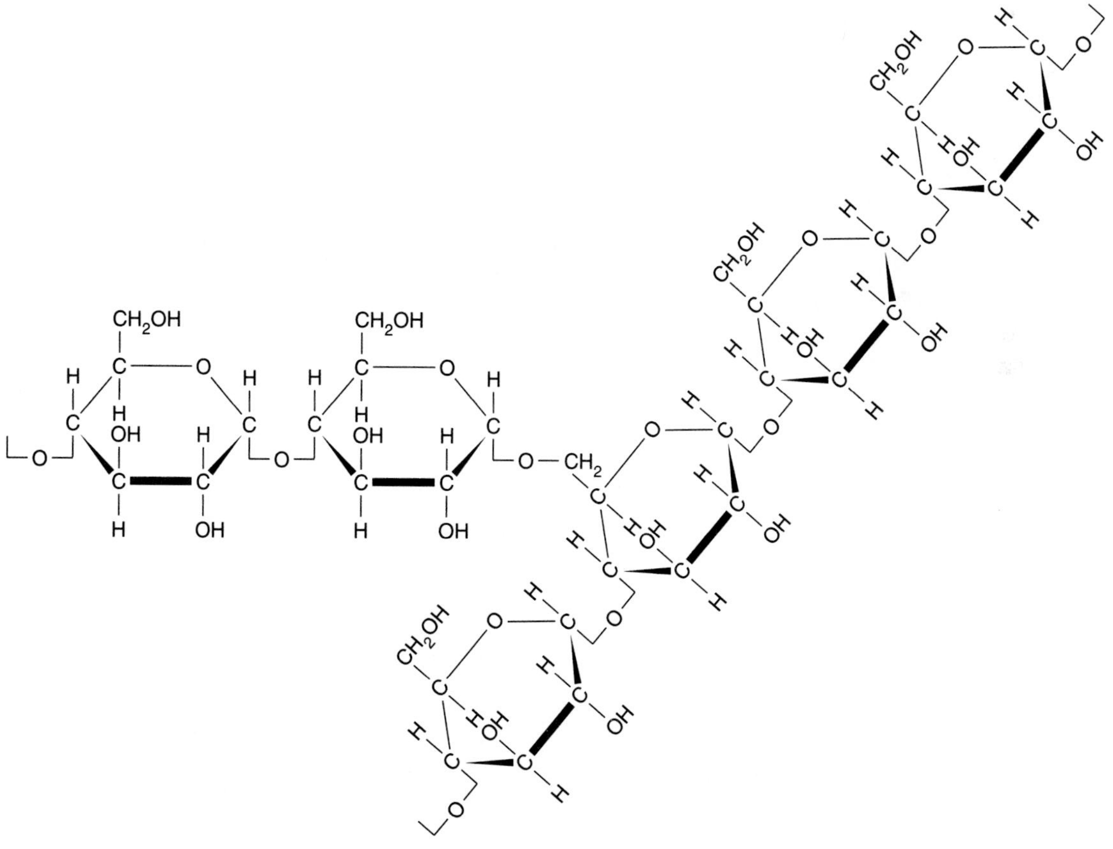

FIGURE 13.2

Amylopectin is a bushy, treelike molecule with many short branches of glucose units linked together. A portion of the molecule is represented here. The glucose units in the chains are joined between the No. 1 and the No. 4 carbon atoms. However, at the points of branching, the linkage is between the No. 1 carbon atom of one glucose unit and the No. 6 carbon atom of the other. See also Figure 5.6.

Modified Starches

Starches from different sources behave differently in food preparation because of their varying compositions and molecular structures. These differences should be considered when choosing a starch for a particular use, such as thickening a fruit pie filling or preparing a cream sauce. However, the natural starches still have limitations when they are employed in food processing. Some deliberate chemical modifications of natural starches are made by starch chemists to enhance the properties of many processed foods. The U.S. Food and Drug Administration (FDA) has published regulations governing the modification of natural food starches, providing guidelines concerning the types and amounts of modifiers allowed, the residuals permitted, if any, and the combina-

Potato starch seen under polarized light shows birefringent crosses resulting from the highly organized nature of the granules.

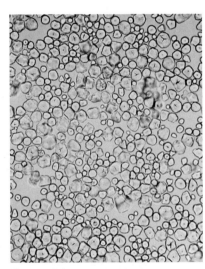

Cornstarch

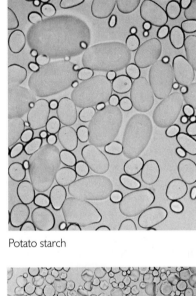

Potato starch

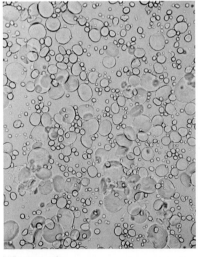

Wheat starch

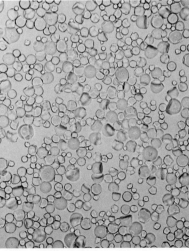

Tapioca starch

FIGURE 13.3

Photomicrographs of starch granules from four different plant sources (magnified 700x). (Courtesy of Eileen Maywald, Corn Products Company)

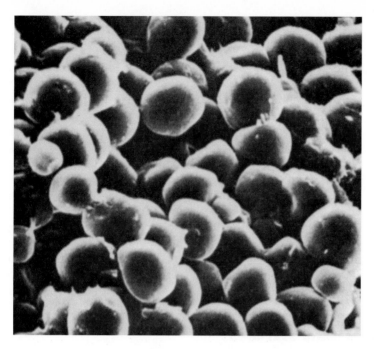

FIGURE 13.4
A scanning electron micrograph of the fractured surface of the endosperm of corn showing the cornstarch granules. (Courtesy of the Northern Regional Research Center, U.S. Department of Agriculture)

tions that are acceptable [7]. Within these guidelines, starch manufacturers work to develop new and innovative starch derivatives. The most common modifications of starch utilized by the food industry involve hydrolysis, crosslinking, and substitution [3]. Combinations of these treatments may also be applied in modifying natural starches.

Hydrolysis of starch may be accomplished by mixing starch with water and an acid to produce a random breaking of linkage points along the molecular chain. Most of the starch still remains in the form of granules and is dried after the acid treatment. This modified starch is known as *thin-boiling* or *acid-thinned starch*. It produces a less viscous paste when it is boiled and hydrates at a lower temperature than the unmodified starch, but it still retains its gelling properties. Acid-thinned starch is often used in the confectionary industry [7].

Crosslinking is produced by the use of reagents that have two or more reactive groups. These groups react with starch molecules at selected points and create a cross bond between two of the chains of the starch molecule. Reagents include phosphorus oxychloride and adipic acid. Pronounced changes in starch characteristics result from crosslinking, including lower viscosity, increased temperature for hydration, increased stability in acid conditions, increased resistance to shear or stirring, and increased tolerance to heat. Food processors, therefore, have increased flexibility and control when they use crosslinked modified starches in manufactured foods [7]. Crosslinking may be thought of as welding molecular starch chains together at various spots or locations, thus limiting the swelling of the granules. Starches modified by crosslinking are valuable for foods that are heated for extended periods of time or are subjected to exceptionally high shear, for example, spaghetti sauces and certain pie fillings.

Starches may be modified by substituting certain monofunctional chemicals (those having only one reactive group, such as acetate) on the hydroxyl groups (-OH) of the starch molecule at random points. This decreases the tendency of bonding between molecular chains of the starch and increases the stability of the starch-thickened product as it is frozen and then thawed. Substitution also improves the clarity and reduces *syneresis*, which is a weeping of liquid from the cooked starch mixture upon standing [7].

An example of the improved properties that result from modification of starches is found in lightly modified waxy maize starch. The natural starch is nongelling because it contains no amylose fraction, only amylopectin. In this regard, it should make a good thickening agent for fruit pies, providing a soft, thickened but not rigid mixture; however, it is very stringy in texture, which is an undesirable characteristic for fruit pies. When it is chemically treated to produce crosslinking, the resulting starch retains its nongelling properties but loses the stringy characteristic. It is also much more stable to heating and freezing and makes an ideal thickening agent for many of the frozen fruit pies that are marketed. Modified starches are tailor-made for specific uses in many convenience foods.

Instant Starches

Starch processors produce, for use by the food industry, starches that hydrate or absorb water in cold liquid systems. There are two types of these instant starches: precooked or pregelatinized starch, and so-called cold water-swelling starch. The pregelatinized starch is cooked and dried, and in the process is degraded into granule fragments. In the preparation of cold water-swelling starch, the starch granules remain intact. Because of this, foods prepared with cold water-swelling starch generally have better stability, appearance, and clarity, as well as a smoother texture, than foods prepared with pregelatinized starch [7, 10]. In both cases, however, the starches hydrate and produce thickened mixtures when cold liquid is added.

Instant starches are utilized in instant dry-mix puddings, gravies, and sauces. They are also useful in the preparation of many microwavable prepared foods. Newly improved instant starches are important tools for food technologists to use in meeting the demands of today's rapidly changing marketplace [10].

•HYDROLYSIS OF STARCH

Since glucose is the basic building block for starch molecules, complete hydrolysis of starch produces glucose. Intermediate steps in the breakdown first yield large chunks of starch molecules called **dextrins**, which are still large enough to be classified as polysaccharides; then sugars called **oligosaccharides**, which contain several glucose units; and finally maltose, a **disaccharide** with two **monosaccharide** units, which yields only glucose. Starch hydrolysis may be brought about or catalyzed by the action of enzymes called *amylases*. Acid may also act as a **catalyst** in the breakdown.

Dextrins   polysaccharides composed of many glucose units, produced at the beginning stages of starch hydrolysis; they are somewhat smaller than starch molecules

Oligosaccharide   the general term for sugars composed of a few—often between three and ten—simple sugars or monosaccharides

Disaccharide   a sugar composed of two simple sugars or monosaccharides

Monosaccharide   a simple sugar unit, such as glucose

Catalyst   a substance that changes the rate of a chemical reaction without being used up in the reaction; enzymes are catalysts

•EFFECT OF HEAT ON STARCH

Dry Heat

When dry heat is applied to starch or starchy foods, the starch becomes more soluble in comparison with unheated starch and has reduced thickening power when it is made into a cooked paste. Some of the starch molecules are broken down to dextrins in a process that is sometimes called *dextrinization*. Color and flavor changes also take place when starch-containing foods are subjected to high temperatures with dry heat. A nonenzymatic browning occurs, and a toasted flavor, which may turn to a burned flavor if the process is continued, develops. Brown gravy is usually relatively thin in consistency if the flour is browned in the process of making the gravy. Use of some white flour with the browned flour is necessary to obtain a thick gravy. Dry-heat dextrins, known as *pyrodextrins*, are formed in the crust of baked flour mixtures, on toast, on fried starchy or starch-coated foods, and on various ready-to-eat cereals.

Moist Heat

The starch granule is insoluble in cold water. A nonviscous suspension of starch is formed when raw starch is mixed with cold water and, on standing, the granules gradually settle to the bottom of the container. After this starch and water suspension is heated, a colloidal dispersion of starch in water is produced. The resulting thickened mixture is called a *starch paste*.

When starch is heated in water, a number of changes gradually occur over a temperature range that is characteristic for a particular starch. The starch granules absorb water and swell and the dispersion increases in **viscosity** or thickness until a peak thickness is reached. The dispersion also increases in **translucency** to a maximum as heating continues [5]. The granules of all starches vary in size and do not swell at the same rates. Large granules swell first. Potato starch, with its generally larger granules, begins to swell at a lower temperature than cornstarch. In any case, swelling is usually complete at a temperature of 88° to 92°C (190° to 194°F).

As starch is heated in water, the molecular order within each starch granule is disrupted as water is absorbed. This gradual process is called **gelatinization**. Irreversible changes that occur during this process include the swelling of granules, the melting of small crystallite areas within the granule, the loss of birefringence (the crosses seen when granules are viewed under polarized light), and the solubilization of some of the starch molecules [1]. Figure 13.5 shows some of the stages in the heating of starch in water.

When the heating of the starch-water mixture is continued after gelatinization, there is some further granular swelling, as well as movement of more molecular components from the granule into the surrounding medium, and eventually total disruption of the granules. This process is called *pasting*. Gelatinization and pasting are generally described as sequential processes [1].

Continued heating under controlled conditions after gelatinization is complete results in decreased thickness. Boiling or cooking starchy sauces and puddings in the home for longer periods usually does not produce thinner mixtures, however, because the loss of moisture by evaporation is usually not

Viscosity   resistance to flow; increase in thickness or consistency

Translucency   partial transparency

Gelatinization   the sum of changes that occur in the first stages of heating starch granules in a moist environment; includes swelling of granules as water is absorbed and disruption of the organized granule structure

controlled. The loss of moisture, which increases concentration of the starch, results in increased thickness and counterbalances the first process.

Most starch-based products prepared by the food industry are subjected to additional treatments after cooking is completed. These may include pumping, stirring, cooling, aging, drying, and packaging, all of which may cause additional changes that break up the swollen starch granules into fragments [12].

Some cooked starch pastes are opaque or cloudy and some are more clear in appearance. In general, the pastes made with cereal starches, such as those of corn and wheat, are cloudy in appearance, whereas those made from root starches, such as potato and tapioca, are more clear.

To obtain uniformity in the cooking of starch pastes, certain conditions must be standardized and controlled. These include temperature of heating,

Uncooked cornstarch

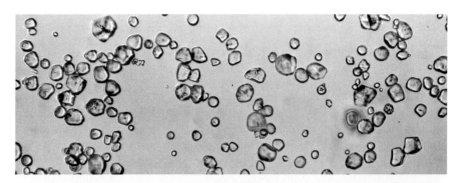

Cornstarch cooked to 72°C (162°F). Note that the granules are swollen but not ruptured.

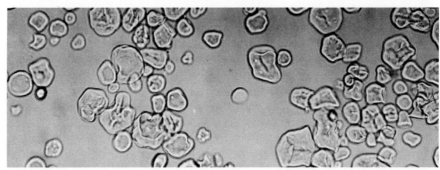

Cornstarch cooked at 90°C (192°F). Note that some of the granules appear to be rupturing. Continued cooking with extensive disintegration of the granule structure is accompanied by a loss of viscosity in the cooked mixture.

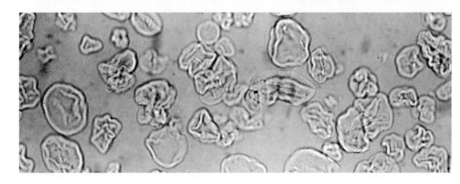

FIGURE 13.5

Photomicrographs showing the change in cornstarch granules (magnified 575x) as heating proceeds. (Courtesy of Corn Products Company)

time of heating, intensity of agitation or stirring (shear), acidity (pH) of the mixture, and addition of other ingredients.

Temperature and Time of Heating

Starch pastes may be prepared most quickly by bringing them to a boiling temperature over direct heat, constantly stirring as they thicken, and simmering them for approximately one minute. Longer cooking to improve the flavor is not necessary. Under carefully controlled conditions, starch pastes that are heated rapidly are somewhat thicker than similar pastes heated slowly [6]. More concentrated dispersions of starch show higher viscosity at lower temperatures than do less concentrated mixtures because of the larger number of granules that can swell in the early stages of gelatinization. Each type of starch gelatinizes over a characteristic temperature range, although this range may be affected by starch concentration.

pH a scale of 1 to 14 indicating the degree of acidity or alkalinity, 1 being most acid, 7 neutral, and 14 most alkaline

Agitation or Stirring

Stirring while cooking starch mixtures is desirable in the early stages to obtain a smooth product of uniform consistency. However, if agitation is too intense or is continued too long, it accelerates the rupturing of the starch granules, decreases viscosity, and may give a slick, pasty mouth-feel. Stirring should, therefore, be minimized.

Acidity (pH)

A high degree of acidity appears to cause some fragmentation of starch granules and hydrolysis of some of the starch molecules, thus decreasing the thickening power of the starch granules [4]. In cooked starch mixtures containing fruit juices or vinegar, such as fruit pie fillings and salad dressings, the acidity may be high enough (pH below 4) to cause some thinning. Specially prepared modified starches that are resistant to acid breakdown are used in commercial food processing when this may be a problem. When a high concentration of sugar is also present in a starch paste, the sugar may help to decrease the effect of acid, because sugar limits the swelling of starch granules, and the starch molecules are therefore not as available for hydrolysis by acid. Proportions of ingredients in recipes for acid-starch products, such as lemon pie filling, have been adjusted to compensate for the usual effects of acid and sugar so that a desirable consistency results. Acid juices, such as lemon juice, can also be added after the starchy paste has been cooked. This limits the acid's contact with starch molecules.

Addition of Other Ingredients

Various ingredients are used with starch in the preparation of food. Some of these ingredients have a pronounced effect on gelatinization and on the gel strength of the cooled starch mixture. Sugar raises the temperature at which a starch mixture gelatinizes [2, 10]. The use of a relatively large amount of sugar delays the swelling of the starch granules and thus decreases the thickness of the paste. It does this, at least partially, by competing with the starch for water. If not enough water is available for the starch granules, they cannot swell sufficiently. In a recipe calling for a large amount of sugar, only part of the sugar need be added before cooking. After the starch mixture has been cooked, the remainder of the sugar can be added with much less effect on viscosity.

High concentrations of sucrose (table sugar) are more effective in delaying swelling or gelatinization than are equal concentrations of monosaccharides such as glucose and fructose. At a concentration of 20 percent or more, all sugars and syrups cause a decided decrease in the gel strength of starch pastes. The presence of fats and proteins, which tend to coat starch granules and thereby delay hydration, also lowers the rate of viscosity development.

•GEL FORMATION AND RETROGRADATION

As a starch-thickened mixture is cooled without stirring after gelatinization is complete, additional changes ensue. These changes may include gel formation and also a process called **retrogradation**. Gel formation generally occurs first, followed by retrogradation.

Retrogradation the process in which starch molecules, particularly the amylose fraction, reassociate or bond together in an ordered structure after disruption by gelatinization; ultimately a crystalline order appears

Many starch molecules are disrupted during the process of gelatinization as the starch granules swell. Some of the molecules of amylose, the linear starch fraction, leach out from the granule. Two or more of these chains may form a juncture point, creating a new bond, which gradually leads to more bonds and more extensively ordered regions. Bonding with the amylose molecules begins immediately after cooking. Amylopectin, the branched fraction, usually remains inside the swollen granule where it more slowly forms new bonds between branches in a process of recrystallization [12]. Bonds formed between the branches of the bushy amylopectin molecules are weak and have little practical effect on the rigidity of the starch paste; however, bonds between the long-chain amylose molecules are relatively strong and form readily. This bonding produces a three-dimensional structure that results in the development of a gel, with the amylose molecules forming a network that holds water in its meshes. The rigidity of the starch mixture is increased.

Gel formation or *gelation* is different from gelatinization. Gelation takes place on cooling of the starch paste after the starch granules have been gelatinized. Gel formation in cooked starch pastes is a gradual process that continues over a several-hour period as the paste cools. Waxy varieties of starch without amylose do not form gels. Starches containing relatively large amounts of amylose, such as cornstarch, form firmer gels than starches with a somewhat lower concentration of amylose, such as tapioca.

As starch-thickened mixtures continue to stand after gel formation is complete, the process of retrogradation may continue to produce changes as additional bonds are formed between the straight-chain amylose molecules. The amylose molecules associate more closely together. Some of these molecules aggregate in a particular area in an organized, crystalline manner. As the amylose molecules pull together more tightly, the gel network shrinks, and water is pushed out of the gel. This process of weeping, called *syneresis*, results from the increased molecular association as the starch mixture ages. Ultimately an ordered crystalline structure develops [1]. Gel formation and retrogradation are illustrated in Figure 13.6.

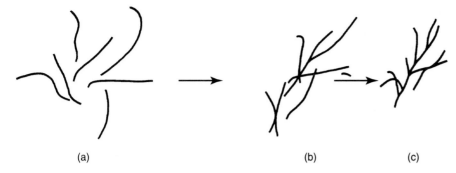

FIGURE 13.6
A diagram representing gel formation and further retrogradation of a starch dispersion: (a) solution, (b) gel, (c) retrograded. (From Elizabeth Osman, "Starch and Other Polysaccharides." In *Food Theory and Applications*. Pauline C. Paul and Helen H. Palmer, editors. Copyright © 1972, John Wiley & Sons, Inc. Reprinted by permission of John Wiley & Sons, Inc.)

•STARCH COOKERY

Combining Starch with Hot Liquids

A potential problem in starch cookery results from the tendency of dry starch particles to clump or form lumps. Before hot liquids are combined with starch, the particles of starch must be separated to bring about a uniform dispersion of well-hydrated starch granules. This can be accomplished by dispersing the particles with melted fat, by blending the starch with sugar, or by mixing starch with cold water to form a **slurry** before adding it to hot liquid.

Slurry a thin mixture of water and a fine insoluble material such as flour

White Sauces

A white sauce is a starch-thickened sauce made from fat, flour, liquid, and seasonings. When the liquid is milk, the basic sauce is called *béchamel (bay´ sha mel or besh´ a mel)*. When the liquid is a light stock of veal, chicken, or fish, the sauce is called a *vélouté (vel´ -oo-tay´)* [8]. White sauces are used in the preparation of a variety of dishes, including creamed eggs, fish, and vegetables; cheese sauce; cream soups; soufflés; croquettes; and certain casserole mixtures. The finished sauce should be smooth and satiny and free of lumps. The consistency depends on the amount of starchy agent used. Table 13.1 gives proportions for white sauces of various consistencies along with suggested uses.

TABLE 13.1
Proportions of Ingredients and Uses for White Sauce

Sauce	Fat*	Flour	Liquid	Salt	Pepper	Uses
Thin	1 Tbsp (14 g)	1 Tbsp (7 g)	1 c (237 ml)	¼ tsp (1.5 g)	fg	Cream soups
Medium	2 Tbsp (28 g)	2 Tbsp (14 g)	1 c	¼ tsp	fg	Creamed vegetables and meats; casseroles
Thick	3 Tbsp (42 g)	3 Tbsp (21 g)	1 c	¼ tsp	fg	Soufflés
Very Thick	4 Tbsp (56 g)	4 Tbsp (28 g)	1 c	¼ tsp	fg	Croquettes

* Amounts may be decreased, if desired.

Roux   a thickening agent made by heating a blend of fat and flour

Instantized flour   wheat flour that has been moistened and redried in such a way that many tiny particles of flour agglomerate to form larger, more uniform particles; does not pack down easily and pours more like salt

Oxidation   a chemical reaction that involves the addition of oxygen

With the current emphasis on reducing our fat intake, we Americans may well look for ways to modify recipes toward this end. An opportunity for fat reduction is present in the making of white sauces. Only enough fat to separate the starch granules is actually needed. Thus for the thicker white sauces, particularly, the amount of fat that has traditionally been recommended may be reduced substantially without affecting the quality of the finished sauce.

Ingredients for a white sauce may be mixed in different ways as long as a smooth, creamy product results. Most commonly, the fat is melted and the flour and salt are then stirred into it. This separates the starch granules so that lumping is less likely when the hot liquid is added. The fat-flour mixture, called a *roux*, is cooked until bubbly. Milk or other liquid is then added with constant stirring, and the sauce is brought to boiling over direct heat. A double boiler may also be used, but cooking is then slower.

In an alternative method for preparing white sauce, the flour is mixed with some of the cold liquid to form a paste. The remainder of the liquid is then added, and the mixture is cooked over direct heat until it boils. At this time the fat and seasonings are added (if butter is the fat, the volatile flavor may be better retained with this method). Since **instantized flour** has less of a tendency to form lumps when mixed with liquid than does noninstantized flour, it may be successfully used in the making of white sauce.

Cream Soups

Cream soups may vary in consistency, but their usual thickness corresponds to that of thin white sauce. One tablespoon of flour is used for each cup of liquid, which may be part milk and part vegetable cooking water or meat broth and vegetable pulp. Combined vegetable waters sometimes produce a soup of better flavor than the water from a single vegetable. If starchy vegetables are used for pulp, the flour must be reduced to about one-half the usual amount. The fat must then also be reduced, or, lacking enough flour to hold it in suspension, it will float on top of the soup. Some flour is desirable for starchy soups, such as potato or dried bean soup, to hold the pulp in suspension. In preparing a cream soup, a medium white sauce can be made from milk, fat, flour, and seasonings. An amount of vegetable juice and pulp equal to the milk used is then heated and added to the sauce, thus diluting the mixture to the consistency of thin white sauce.

If acid juices, such as tomato, are used, the acid is added gradually to the white sauce at serving time to minimize the tendency to curdle. Baking soda is not a necessary ingredient in cream of tomato soup, and its use is not recommended because it may increase the alkalinity of the soup so much that vitamin C and some of the B vitamins are essentially destroyed by **oxidation**. The use of soda may also seriously mar flavor if an excess is used. Making a tomato sauce from the tomato juice, fat, and flour instead of making a white sauce is preferred by some cooks and is a common practice in the production of canned tomato soup. The hot tomato sauce should be added to the hot milk just at serving time to minimize curdling.

Starch-Thickened Desserts

Cornstarch pudding is probably the most common starch-thickened dessert, although similar desserts are made from other cereal starches, including wheat flour combined with tapioca or sago as the main thickening agents. The consistency of starchy puddings varies according to personal preference. If a pudding stiff enough to form a mold is desired, it will have better flavor and texture if it is made as soft as possible while still holding its form when unmolded. Many prefer pudding to have a relatively soft consistency, in which case it must be spooned into individual dishes. Tapioca and sago puddings, particularly, are usually of a more desirable eating quality when they are relatively soft.

The preparation of puddings and pie fillings often combines starch and egg cookery to produce a creamy mixture. The product is thickened with starch before the egg is added, because starch tolerates higher temperatures than does egg. The pudding is first prepared in the same manner as a corn-starch pudding containing no egg. After starch gelatinization is complete, a small amount of the hot starchy mixture may be added to the egg. This dilutes the egg so that it does not coagulate in lumps when it is added to the bulk of the hot mixture. Alternatively, a small amount of cold milk may be withheld in the beginning of the preparation and mixed with the egg to dilute it. This milk-egg mixture is then added all at once to the hot starchy pudding mixture, producing a smooth, creamy product.

Starchy puddings containing egg should be cooked sufficiently after the addition of the egg to coagulate the egg proteins. If this is not done, the pudding may become thin on standing. If a fairly large amount of egg is used the temperature of the pudding after the egg is added should not reach boiling, since this may result in curdling of the egg with a consequent grainy texture of the pudding.

Numerous additions or substitutions may be made to the basic formula for corn starch pudding to change the flavor. These include the addition of chocolate or cocoa, caramelized sugar, shredded coconut, nuts, maple syrup, or diced fruits. Recipe books should be consulted for specific directions in preparing the variations.

BASIC FORMULA FOR CORNSTARCH PUDDING

2 to 3 Tbsp (16 to 24 g) cornstarch	2 c (474 ml) milk
1/4 c (50 g) sugar	1 tsp vanilla
1/8 tsp salt	1 egg or 2 egg yolks (optional)

Mix sugar, salt, and starch. Add one-half cup of cold milk gradually to form a smooth mixture. Heat remaining milk in a saucepan and add the starch-sugar mixture (in which the starch particles have been separated by the sugar and then the cold milk) to the hot milk with constant stirring. Cook the mixture over direct heat, stirring constantly, until the mixture boils; continue simmering for 1 minute. Remove from heat and add vanilla. Chill. If egg is used in the pudding, add a small amount of the hot boiled mixture to the slightly beaten egg; then add this to the hot mixture in the saucepan. Cook over moderate heat for 3 or 4 minutes. After cooking is completed, add vanilla. Chill.

Microwave Cooking of Starch Mixtures

The microwave oven is a quick and convenient tool in the preparation of relatively small quantities of starch-thickened sauces and puddings. For example, a smooth, creamy chocolate pudding to serve only one or two persons may be prepared in just a few minutes. First, semisweet baking chocolate is heated in milk in a 2-cup measure with the microwave oven on high for 1 to 2 minutes until the mixture is hot. A blend of dry cornstarch and sugar is then added to the hot chocolate milk, and the mixture is heated on high for 1/2 to 1 minute, stirring after each 30 seconds. Vanilla, butterscotch, and other types of cornstarch- or flour-thickened puddings are prepared in a similar manner. Microwaved sauces and puddings need less stirring than conventionally cooked sauces and puddings, since there is no tendency for the material on the bottom of the container to scorch as in range-top cooking [8].

It is just as easy to prepare a basic white sauce in the microwave oven. First, butter or margarine is melted by heating on high for 1/2 to 1 minute to make approximately 1 cup of sauce. The flour and seasonings are then added, and milk is blended into the fat-flour mixture. Microwaving 6 to 8 minutes then produces a smooth, creamy white sauce. The mixture is stirred at approximately 1-minute intervals during the cooking.

Gravies can be prepared in the microwave oven by first blending broth with flour and meat drippings. Then this mixture is heated in the microwave oven on high, with occasional stirring, until thickened.

Microwave cooking is not always efficient for large amounts of starch-thickened foods. If more than 3–4 cups of white sauce are to be prepared, for example, the microwave oven is not necessarily a timesaver. When large amounts of raw cereal are to be cooked, little time will be saved by using the microwave oven since larger volumes of water must be heated and there must be sufficient time for gelatinization of the starch. An individual serving of cereal such as oatmeal, however, can be cooked in a few minutes in the microwave oven. One type of starch-based food that is not cooked properly in any amount by microwaves is conventional pastas.

Manufacturers of foods designed specifically for reheating or cooking in the microwave oven need to choose carefully the type of starch they use. Since the rate of heating in the microwave oven is accelerated compared with that achieved by conventional methods, and the heat distribution throughout the food is generally more variable, traditional starches are not always appropriate. There may be insufficient time for proper hydration of the starch granules. Specially modified starches can, however, be designed to hydrate at a lower temperature. Instant starches of the cold water-swelling type may also be effectively used in the production of microwavable foods.

STUDY QUESTIONS

1. Starch is a storage form of carbohydrate deposited as granules in plant cells.
   a. Describe the appearance of starch granules when viewed under a microscope; how do the size and shape of starch granules differ from one plant source to another?
   b. Name the two fractions of starch and explain how they differ in structure.
   c. Explain why some natural starches are chemically modified and give examples of the types of chemical modification most commonly used.
   d. What products are produced as starch is hydrolyzed and what may catalyze this process?

2. a. Describe what happens when dry starches are heated. What is this process called?
   b. Why is gravy made from browned flour usually thinner than gravy made from the same amount of unbrowned flour? Explain.
   c. Describe what happens when starch granules are heated in water. What is this process called?
   d. Distinguish between the process described in question c. and *pasting* of starch.
   e. Describe the general effect of each of the following on the thickness of a cooked starch mixture: (1) rate of heating, (2) excessive stirring, and (3) addition of sugar.
3. Many starch-thickened mixtures become stiff or rigid on cooling.
   a. What is this process called and what happens in the starch mixture to bring it about?
   b. How does the amount of amylose in the starch affect the rigidity and why?
   c. What is meant by *retrogradation* of a starch paste?
   d. What is *syneresis* and why may it occur in cooked starch mixtures?
   e. Which of the common starches forms the stiffest and which the softest pudding when used in equal amounts? Explain.
4. Distinguish between *gelatinization* and *gelation* of starch mixtures.
5. Describe three ways to keep powdery starches from lumping when they are added to hot liquid. Explain what is happening in each case.
6. Describe appropriate methods for preparing each of the following items and explain why these methods should be successful.
   a. White sauce
   b. Cream of vegetable soup
   c. Cream of tomato soup
   d. Cornstarch pudding
   e. Cornstarch pudding with egg
7. What two types of instant starch are available to the food processor and how do these differ from each other? Give examples of products in which the consumer may expect to find instant starches used.
8. Suggest appropriate procedures for preparing puddings and white sauces in the microwave oven.

REFERENCES

1. Atwell, W. A., L. F. Hood, D. R. Lineback, E. Varriano-Marston, and H. F. Zobel. 1988. The terminology and methodology associated with basic starch phenomena. *Cereal Foods World 33*, 306.
2. Bean, M. M., and W. T. Yamazaki. 1978. Wheat starch gelatinization in sugar solutions. I. Sucrose: Microscopy and viscosity effects. *Cereal Chemistry 55*, 936.
3. Filer, L. J. 1988. Modified food starch: An update. *Journal of the American Dietetic Association 88*, 342.
4. Hansuld, M. K., and A. M. Briant. 1954. The effect of citric acid on selected edible starches and flours. *Food Research 19*, 581.
5. Holmes, Z. A., and A. Soeldner. 1981. Macrostructure of selected raw starches and selected heated starch dispersions. *Journal of the American Dietetic Association 78*, 153.
6. Holmes, Z. A., and A. Soeldner. 1981. Effect of heating rate and freezing and reheating of corn and wheat starch—water dispersions. *Journal of the American Dietetic Association 78*, 352.
7. Luallen, T. E. 1985. Starch as a functional ingredient. *Food Technology 39*, 59 (No. 1).
8. Methven, B. 1978. *Basic Microwaving*. Minnetonka, MN: Cy DeCosse Inc.

9. Mizer, D. A., and M. Porter. 1978. *Food Preparation for the Professional*. New York: Harper & Row.

10. Spies, R. D., and R. C. Hoseney. 1982. Effect of sugars on starch gelatinization. *Cereal Chemistry 59*, 128.

11. Staff. 1988. Introducing new line of cold water-swelling starches. *Food Technology 42*, 160 (No. 6).

12. Waniska, R. D., and M. H. Gomez. 1992. Dispersion behavior of starch. *Food Technology 46*, 110 (No. 6).

Cereals

•DEFINITION AND USES

Cereal grains are seeds of the grass family. The word *cereal* is derived from *Ceres*, the Roman goddess of grain. Wheat, corn (maize), rice, oats, rye, barley, and millet are the most important cereals used for human food. Grain sorghum is used chiefly for animal feed, but starch is extracted from it for commercial food use. Triticale is a grain produced by cross-breeding wheat and rye. Although it is not a seed of the grass family, buckwheat is often classified with the cereal grains because buckwheat flour has properties and uses similar to those of cereal flours. A rediscovered cereal-like plant is amaranth, which produces an abundance of tiny seeds (Figure 14.1). About 1,000 of these seeds weigh approximately 1 gram. Amaranth is one of those rare plants whose leaves are eaten as a vegetable, while the seeds are used as cereals [17, 19].

The term *cereal* is not limited to breakfast foods but applies to a large group of foods made from grains. These include flours, meals, breads, and alimentary pastes or pasta. The ease with which grains can be produced and stored, together with the relatively low cost and nutritional contribution of many cereal foods, particularly whole grain products, has resulted in the widespread use of grain commodities throughout the world. Actually, cereal grains are the principal crops that have made the continuation of humankind possible [10]. They are the staple in the diets of most population groups.

The consumption of many plant-based foods has risen steadily over the past 20 years in the United States [16]. These include grain products as well as fresh fruits, fruit juices, and both fresh and frozen vegetables. On the basis of **disappearance data** published by the U.S. Department of Agriculture (USDA), the annual per capita grain consumption, after falling dramatically from the levels of the first half of this century, has been increasing in recent years [13], as illustrated by Table 14.1.

In 1990, Americans consumed more wheat than all other grains combined, with the average per capita consumption of wheat flour reaching 138 pounds. Although total bread consumption has not changed dramatically, more whole-wheat bread is being eaten. We have also increased our consumption of

Disappearance data data about food that "disappears" into the nation's food distribution system; quantities calculated from inventories and from food produced and imported minus food exports

FIGURE 14.1

Amaranth seeds are very tiny, which is emphasized by showing them alongside the small wheat kernels (*on the left*). The dime in the picture helps you to judge sizes by comparison. (Photograph by Chris Meister)

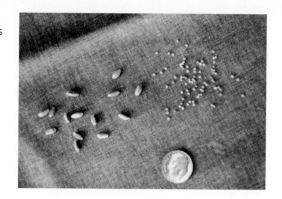

pizza, pasta, pitas, and fajitas—all of which are made from wheat flour [11, 13]. At the same time, rice, corn, and oat products have increased enough to capture some of wheat's market share.

•STRUCTURE AND COMPOSITION

All whole grains have a similar structure: outer bran coats, a germ, and a starchy endosperm portion, as shown in Figure 14.2. Cereal products vary in composition depending on what part or parts of the grain are used.

Bran

The chaffy coat that covers the kernel during growth is eliminated when grains are harvested. The outer layers of the kernel proper, which are called the *bran*, constitute about 5 percent of the kernel. The bran has a high content of fiber and mineral ash. Milled bran may also contain some germ. The *aleurone* layer comprises the square cells located just under the bran layers of the kernel (see Figure 23.1). These cells are rich in protein, phosphorus, and thiamin, and also contain some fat. The aleurone layer makes up about 8 percent of the whole kernel. In the milling of white flour, the aleurone layer is removed with the bran.

Endosperm

The *endosperm* is the large central portion of the kernel and constitutes about 83 percent of the grain. It contains most of the starch and most of the protein of the kernel, but very little mineral matter or fiber and only a trace of fat. The

TABLE 14.1

Annual Per Capita Grain Consumption in the United States

Years	Flour and Cereal Products (lbs)
1910–15	287
1945–49	204
1970–74	135
1980–84	148
1989	175
1990	185

Source: Reference 13.

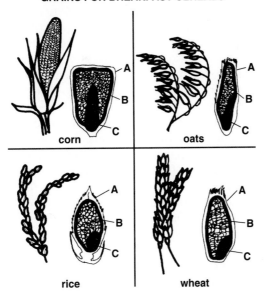

GRAINS FOR BREAKFAST CEREALS

corn

oats

rice

wheat

A BRAN consists of several thin outer layers of the grain kernel and is its protective coat.

B ENDOSPERM is the stored food supply for the new plant which develops as the kernel germinates. It comprises about 85% of the kernel.

C EMBRYO or GERM is the miniature plant which enlarges and develops after the kernel germinates.

FIGURE 14.2
Several common grains have similar structures. The are used to make a variety of breakfast cereals. (Courtesy of Cereal Institute, Inc.)

vitamin content of the endosperm is generally low. Milled white flour comes entirely from the endosperm.

Germ or Embryo

The *germ* is a small structure at the lower end of the kernel from which sprouting begins and the new plant grows. It usually makes up only 2 to 3 percent of the whole kernel. It is rich in fat, protein, ash, and vitamins. When the kernel is broken, as it is in certain processing procedures, the fat is exposed to oxygen in the air. This greatly reduces the storage life of the grain because the fat may become rancid. The broken or milled grain is also more susceptible to infestation by insects.

•NUTRITIVE VALUE AND ENRICHMENT

Cereal grains are important dietary components for a number of nutritional reasons. They provide the world population with a majority of its food calories and about half of its protein [10]. With the recent emphasis on the importance of dietary fat reduction and increased complex carbohydrate intake (starch and fiber), cereals grains are "made to order." They are excellent sources of starch, the nutritive polysaccharide, as well as indigestible fiber. They are low in fat and supply a number of valuable vitamins and minerals.

The proteins of cereal grains are generally of relatively low biological value; however, when cereals are used with other protein-containing foods that supply the amino acids lacking in cereals, the nutritive value of the cereal protein is greatly improved. Various cereals and legumes supplement each other with respect to essential amino acid content so that the quality of the protein actually eaten is considerably increased. In a vegetarian diet, the lack of the essential amino acid lysine in cereal grains is complemented by the sufficiency of lysine in legumes, including soybeans. The presence of the amino acid methionine in cereal grains makes up for its lack in legumes.

The nutritive value of cereal products varies with the part of the grain that is used and the method of processing [1, 10]. The endosperm, which is the part used in refined flours and cereals such as farina, contains chiefly starch and protein. Therefore, refined cereals and flours furnish little more than these two nutrients unless they are enriched with some of the vitamins and minerals lost in milling. It is to our benefit, therefore, to use whole-grain products.

Enriched flour, according to a legal definition, is white flour to which specified B vitamins (thiamin, riboflavin, and niacin) and iron have been added. Optional added ingredients include calcium and vitamin D. Enriched bread may be made from enriched flour, or the bread may be enriched by the addition of an enrichment wafer during mixing. The standards for enriched white flour published by the U.S. Food and Drug Administration (FDA) are listed in Table 14.2. Enrichment is required for refined cereal products that enter interstate commerce. Many states have also passed laws requiring that various refined cereal products and flours sold within their boundaries be enriched.

Enrichment of white flour does not make it nutritionally equivalent to whole-grain flour. Only a few of the nutrients lost in milling are replaced by the enrichment process. Whole-grain products are particularly valuable as dietary sources of iron, phosphorus, thiamin, and vitamin B_6, as well as fiber. Many breakfast cereals are highly fortified with vitamins and minerals, well beyond the usual enrichment standards.

•COMMON CEREAL GRAINS

Wheat

Wheat is one of the most widely cultivated plants on earth. Every month of the year, a crop of wheat is maturing at some place in the world. Wheat has been cultivated since early times. There are several thousand different varieties of

TABLE 14.2

Enrichment Standards Compared with Whole-Wheat Flour (milligrams per pound)*

	Thiamin	Riboflavin	Niacin	Iron
Whole-wheat flour	2.49	0.54	19.7	15.0
Enriched white flour	2.0–2.5	1.2–1.5	16–20	13.0–16.5
Enriched bread, rolls, or buns	1.1–1.8	0.7–1.6	10–15	8.0–12.5

* One pound of flour is usually equivalent to 1½ pounds of bread.

wheat. Plant breeders have created new wheat varieties with high yields and strong disease resistance that have contributed to the so-called green revolution in many parts of the world [17].

Wheats are commonly milled into flour. Wheats used for flour are often classified in terms of their "hardness" or "softness." Hard wheat varieties are higher in protein content than are soft wheats and usually have greater baking strength in that they result in a loaf of bread of large volume and fine texture. Wheat flour is uniquely suitable for bread making because it contains proteins that develop strong, elastic properties in a dough. No other cereal grain equals wheat in bread-making qualities. Classes of wheat, milling, and flour are discussed in more detail in Chapter 23.

Durum wheat is a very hard, non-bread-making wheat of high protein content. It is grown chiefly for use in making macaroni and other pasta.

Bulgur is wheat that is first boiled and then dried. A small amount of the outer bran layers is removed, and the wheat is then usually cracked. It is an ancient form of processing wheat, used in biblical times. Bulgur is often found in the gourmet food sections of supermarkets. Armenian restaurants commonly serve cooked bulgur in the form of pilaf.

Wheat is also used for the production of wheat starch and, in large quantity, for the making of various types of breakfast cereals. A comparison of composition and nutritive value for various cereals is given in Appendix C.

Corn

Corn is a native American plant. Early settlers in the New World were introduced to the uses of corn by Native Americans. The United States now produces almost half of the world's corn crop. Corn is a major food for the peoples of Mexico and Central America and is very popular in the southern United States.

The corn kernel has a great variety of uses in food products. It is made into hominy, which is the corn kernel endosperm freed of the bran and germ (see Figure 14.3). The whole endosperm of hominy is broken into fairly small pieces to make hominy grits. Corn is also milled into cornmeal, a ground granular product made either without the germ and most of the bran, or with all of the kernel except the larger bran particles. Both white and yellow corn are used to make cornmeal. Refined cornmeal and hominy grits may be enriched. In the southern part of the United States, hominy grits are often served as a breakfast cereal.

Mexican food is increasing in popularity in many parts of the United States. The corn tortilla plays an important role in Mexican cuisine. Tortillas are traditionally made from corn that is **steeped** and cooked in alkali solution, washed to remove excess alkali, and ground on a stone mill into a dough called *masa*. Masa is pressed into flat, circular shapes, which are then cooked on a hot griddle [9]. This traditional procedure for making tortillas, however, is now being replaced by large-scale commercial operations in which corn is cooked and ground immediately with little or no steeping, and the tortillas are cooked in large, automated cookers.

Corn is also an important component of many breakfast cereals. Corn flour is used in a number of commercial flour mixes. Corn oil, which contains a

Steep to soak

FIGURE 14.3

Hominy is the endosperm of the corn kernel, freed from bran and germ. (Photograph by Chris Meister)

high proportion of polyunsaturated fatty acids, is extracted from the germ of the corn kernel. Corn syrups and glucose are produced by the hydrolysis of corn starch, which is the principal starch used in the United States for culinary purposes.

Corn is clearly very versatile, which is why American farmers annually devote about 76 million acres to its growth. It has thousands of uses, not only in foods, but in all kinds of consumer and industrial products. For example, corn is the source of the ethanol that is blended with gasoline for cleaner-burning fuel, and corn starch is used as a clay binder in ceramics, an adhesive in glues, and a bodying agent in dyes.

Rice

Considered as a world crop, rice is one of the most used of all cereal grains. It is the major food in the diets of many people living in Asia. Although rice is still the staple food in Japan, it is being consumed in lesser quantities as the Japanese consume more red meats, poultry, milk, eggs, fruits, vegetables, and processed foods. The average annual per capita consumption of rice in Japan has declined from 244 pounds in 1955 to 154 pounds in 1990 [19]. Conversely, in the United States, rice consumption has increased from about 7 pounds per person per year in 1974 to 17 pounds in 1990 [13]. Six states now produce more than 90 percent of the rice consumed in America: Arkansas, California, Louisiana, Mississippi, Missouri, and Texas [6].

Cultivated rice is available as white polished rice. White rice is basically the starchy endosperm of the rice grain, the bran coats and germ having been rubbed off by an abrasive process. The polishing process also removes more than half of the minerals and most of the vitamins from the kernel. White rice may be enriched; often, a powdery material is applied to the surface of the grain. In this case, it is particularly important that the rice not be washed before cooking or rinsed after cooking to avoid loss of the enrichment nutrients. For brown rice, only the outer husk or chaffy coat is removed from the kernel. This is the least processed form, retaining the germ and most of the bran, which are rich in vitamins and minerals.

Grains of rice may be parboiled before milling in a special steam-pressure process, which gelatinizes the starch and changes the cooking characteristics of the rice. Parboiled rice, also called *converted* rice, requires longer cooking than regular white rice. Parboiling improves the nutritive value of milled white rice because the heating process causes migration of vitamins and minerals from the outer coats to the interior of the kernel and they are retained after milling. The keeping quality of parboiled rice is improved over that of the untreated grain.

Precooked or instant rice is a long-grain rice that has been cooked, rinsed, and dried by a special process. It requires very little preparation. Rice flour and rice starch are also manufactured. They have limited culinary uses in the United States, but they are useful to people with wheat allergies.

Although more than 40,000 varieties of rice have been identified, only about twenty are grown commercially in the United States. Rice is classified by long-, medium-, and short-grain varieties (Figure 14.4). The food industry also recognizes a fourth category called *specialty rices*. These are distinguished by characteristics other than shape and size and include varieties such as jasmine, basmati, arborio, and sweet glutinous or waxy rice [6]. Some of these have fragrant aromas. Specialty rices are found in gourmet shops and ethnic markets.

Long-grain varieties of rice have comparatively high **amylose** content and are light and fluffy when cooked. The cooked kernels tend to separate. The medium- and short-grain varieties contain less amylose, absorb less water in cooking, and the kernels are more clingy or sticky when cooked. Preference for fluffy versus sticky rice depends on the culture of the consumer. One cup of polished rice generally yields about three cups of cooked rice.

Rice bran is the outer brown layer that is removed during the milling of white rice. It deteriorates rapidly once it is removed from the rice kernel because a **lipase** enzyme is exposed to the oil in the bran. The fat breaks down

Amylose   the long-chain or linear fraction of starch

Lipase   an enzyme that catalyzes the hydrolysis of triglycerides to yield glycerol and fatty acids

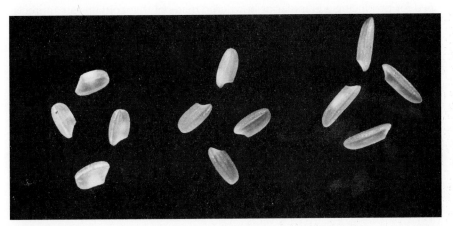

FIGURE 14.4
Short-, medium-, and long-grain varieties of rice. (Courtesy of The Rice Council)

and an unacceptable musty taste rapidly develops. The bran may be treated, using dry-heat extrusion equipment, so that the enzyme is deactivated and the bran is stabilized [3]. Stabilized rice bran is currently being promoted as a major source of fiber for use in various manufactured foods.

Wild rice is not true rice but the hulled and unmilled grain of a reedlike water plant. It is available only in limited quantity and is therefore usually relatively expensive. During the 1980s, methods were developed for cultivating wild rice. It is now grown in California, as well as in the Great Lakes region, where it was first discovered growing wild [6]. It is prized for its unusual nut-like flavor and uniquely long brown grains. Like many whole grain cereals, it has relatively poor keeping quality, especially at warm temperatures.

Oats

Oats are utilized in a rolled form as both old-fashioned and quick-cooking products. The husk clings very tightly to the oat kernel. When the grain is processed, the outer hull is removed, but most of the germ and bran remain with the endosperm. Rolled oats sold commercially, therefore, contain nearly the whole oat kernel. Because of the retention of most of the germ, rolled oats are higher in fat than most other cereals. They are also a good source of thiamin and other B vitamins and iron. Oat kernels with the outer hulls removed are called *groats*. Rolled oats are made by passing groats through rollers to form flakes. For quick-cooking rolled oats, the groats are cut into tiny particles that are then rolled into thin, small flakes. Regular or old-fashioned rolled oats are rolled without cutting.

Oatmeal is a common breakfast cereal and has become more popular in recent years with the publication of research indicating that oat bran is particularly effective in diets designed to lower elevated blood cholesterol levels. The use of oat fiber by the food industry has increased greatly, as evidenced by a dramatic rise in the sale of oat bran by the Quaker Oats Company from 1 million pounds per year in 1986 to 2 million pounds per *month* by 1989 [14]. The benefit appears to come from oat bran's content of beta-glucan, a glucose polymer. Still, there are other cereal sources of beta-glucan, including barley, which is the subject of continuing nutrition research.

At the USDA Northern Regional Research Center, a process was developed for producing a granular or powdered material that contains an appreciable amount of beta-glucan from enzyme-treated oat bran or oat flour. This product is called *oatrim* and is being marketed commercially as a fat replacer.

Many prepared breakfast cereals contain oats. In addition, oats are used in the making of cookies, granola bars, baby foods, variety breads, candy, and snack items.

Rye

Rye is grown and used in the United States chiefly as a flour-making grain. It is used much less than wheat, but it more nearly approaches wheat in baking quality than do other grains. Rye flour is available in three grades: white, medium, and dark. Rye is seldom used as a breakfast food.

Barley

Pearled barley is the chief form in which this grain is used at the present time in the United States. Pearling is a process that removes the outer hull of barley, leaving a small, round, white pearl of grain, the kind seen in some soups. Barley may become a valuable source of beta-glucan for the food industry. Some barley flour is available and may be used in breakfast cereals and baby foods. Sprouted barley is a source of malt, which is rich in the enzyme **amylase**. A commercially available source of barley for baking and cooking may be malted barley, which is a by-product of the beer-brewing industry. Although most of the beta-glucan is removed in the malting process, a concentrated oily substance called *tocotrienol* remains, and it appears to have blood cholesterol-lowering capabilities [14].

Triticale

Triticale is a hybrid plant produced by crossing wheat and rye. It combines desirable characteristics of each of the parent species. Generally, triticale has a higher protein content and better amino acid balance than does wheat. It could be a valuable source of nutrients for many peoples of the world. Certain varieties of triticale have been shown to produce acceptable breads, snack crackers, and noodles [8, 12, 15].

Buckwheat

Buckwheat is not a seed of the grass family; it is the seed of a herbaceous plant. Because it contains a glutenous substance and is made into flour, it is commonly considered a grain product. Fine buckwheat flour has little of its thick fiber coating included. In that respect, it is similar to refined white flour. It is prized for its distinctive flavor and is commonly used in the making of griddle cakes. The volume of buckwheat flour sold in the United States is relatively small.

•BREAKFAST CEREALS

Breakfast foods made from cereal grains vary widely in composition, depending on the kind of grain, the part of the grain used, the method of milling, and the method of processing. They may be uncooked, partially cooked, or completely cooked. Considerable amounts of sugars, syrups, molasses, or honey are added to some cereals. In some products, heating dextrinizes part of the starch and produces toasted flavors.

Ready-to-Cook and Instant Cereals

Raw cereals that are cooked in both home and industrial kitchens include whole grains, cracked or crushed grains, granular products made from either the whole grain or the endosperm section of the kernel, and rolled or flaked whole grains. The finely cut flaked grains cook in a shorter period and hence are described as being *quick cooking*. Disodium phosphate is sometimes

Amylase   an enzyme that catalyzes the hydrolysis of starch to yield dextrins and maltose

added to farina for quick cooking. It changes the pH of the cereal, making it more alkaline, and causes it to swell faster and cook in a shorter time.

The starch in instant cereals, including farina and rolled oats, has been pregelatinized by prior cooking. Therefore, when boiling water is added and the mixture is simply stirred, the cereal is ready for consumption.

Ready-to-Eat Cereals

Basic processes used in the production of prepared cereals include shredding, puffing, granulating, flaking, and extruding (see Figure 14.5). Mixtures of cereals or cereal flours are often used. Ingredients commonly added to ready-to-eat cereals include sweetening agents, salt, flavorings, coloring agents, and antioxi-

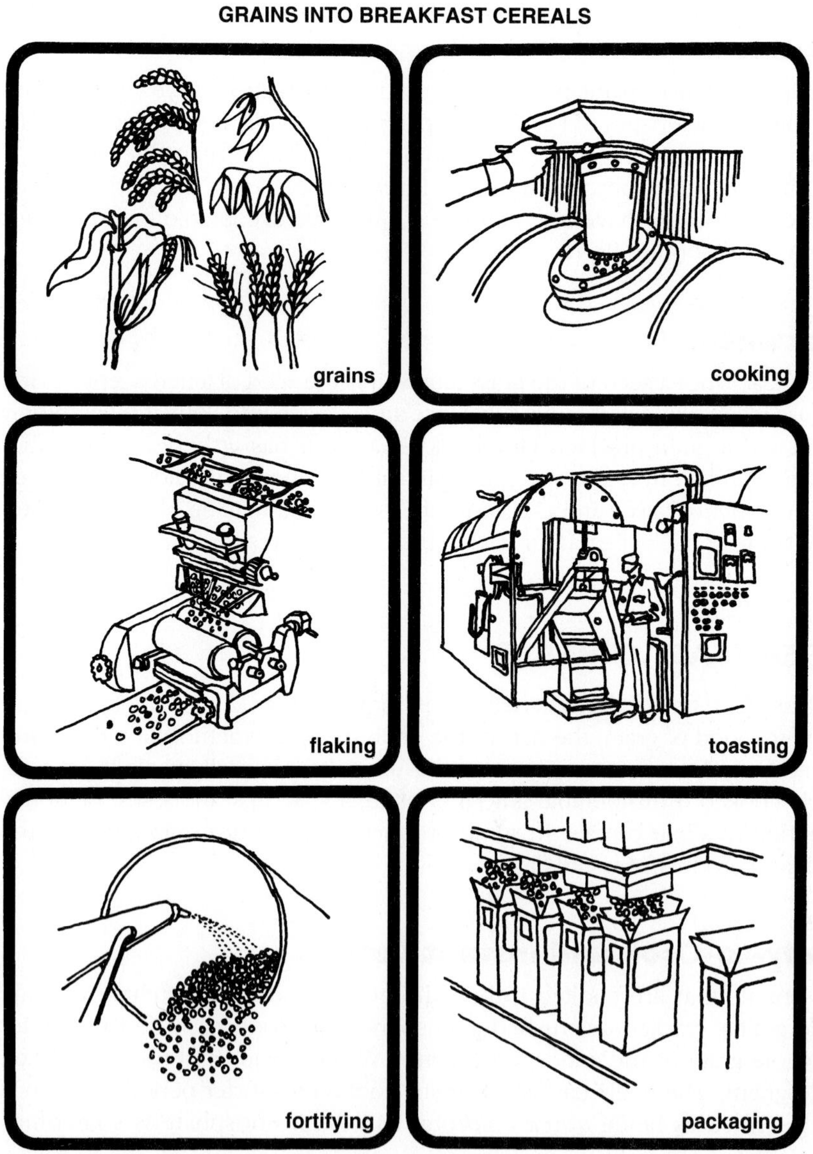

FIGURE 14.5

Major steps in the processing of grains into flaked cereals and types of prepared cereals. (Courtesy of Cereal Institute, Inc.)

GRAINS INTO BREAKFAST CEREALS

dants as preservatives. In most cases, the cereals are fortified to a comparatively high degree with minerals and vitamins, which are added at stages in the processing beyond which they are not subject to destruction by heat.

In the production of puffed cereals, the whole grain is cleaned and conditioned and put into a pressure chamber. The pressure in the chamber is raised to a high level and then suddenly released. The expansion of water vapor on release of the pressure puffs up the grains to several times their original size. The puffed product is dried by toasting, then cooled and packaged.

Flaked cereals are made by lightly rolling the grain between smooth rolls to fracture the outer layers of the cleaned and conditioned whole grain. This grain is then cooked, and various flavoring or sweetening substances are added so that they penetrate the rolled grain. The cooked product is dried, conditioned, flaked on heavy flaking rolls, toasted, cooled, and packaged.

In the preparation of granular breakfast cereals, a yeast-containing dough is made from a blend of flours. The dough is fermented and made into large loaves that are baked. The baked loaves are then broken up, dried, and ground to a standard fineness.

A white, starchy wheat is used for shredded cereals. The whole grain is cleaned and cooked with water so that it is soft and rubbery. The cooked grain is cooled, conditioned, and fed to shredders, which consist of a pair of metal rolls, one smooth and the other having circular grooves. The cereal emerges between the grooves as long parallel shreds. These shreds can be layered to form a thick mat. The mat is cut into the desired size, baked, dried, cooled, and packaged.

A number of fabricated products—snack foods as well as breakfast cereals—are extruded. In this process, the cereal-based material is made into a dough, which is fed into the extruder. Moisture content, time, temperature, and pressure are carefully controlled to achieve the desired result. A high-temperature, short-duration cooking period is used in many cases to produce expanded ready-to-eat cereals. Starch is gelatinized in the material as it moves through the extruder, and a colloidal gel is formed. When the product emerges from the nozzle of the extruder, the sudden drop in pressure permits the superheated water to form water vapor or steam. The mass then inflates with numerous tiny cells and is fixed in its expanded state [4].

Economics in Purchasing Cereals

Although the number and variety of cereals on the market in the United States have increased tremendously in recent years, no federal standard of identity has been developed for breakfast cereals other than farina. The great variety of available cereal products may cause confusion in the buying and use of cereals, particularly since a great deal of advertising of these cereal products is done in the mass media, much of it aimed at young children.

Information on nutritive value and cost are essential aids to making wise purchases. Too much food money is sometimes spent for products that are no better nutritionally than many others that are available at a fraction of the cost. A large amount of sugar, up to 35 percent of the product by weight, is used in the production of some prepared cereals.

In general, the more processing done to a breakfast cereal and the more ingredients added, the higher the retail price. Packaging costs may also be high. Cereals cooked in the kitchen are usually much less costly than ready-to-eat cereals; however, ready-to-eat cereals are often popular with children and they are convenient. Presweetened ready-to-eat cereals are generally more expensive than unsweetened products. Those concerned about the highest nutritional return for their food dollar as well as those who are interested in high-fiber, low-sugar products would do well to choose the less processed cereals over the more convenient ready-to-eat cereals. Whole-grain cereals should be given preference because of their fiber content and generally higher nutrient density.

Cooking of Breakfast Cereals

The main purposes of cereal cookery are to improve palatability and digestibility. Historically, cereals may have first been consumed as whole grains with no preliminary preparation. Later, heat was applied in the parching of grains. Still later came the addition of water before the application of heat.

Cereal cookery is fundamentally starch cookery because starch is the predominant nutrient of cereals. Other factors involved are fiber, which is chiefly exterior bran layers, and protein, which is also a prominent constituent of cereals. Until softened, or unless disintegrated mechanically, bran may interfere with the passage of water into the interior of the kernel and presumably may retard the swelling of starch. If cellulose is finely divided, its affinity for water is greatly increased. The temperatures necessary to cook starch are more than adequate for cooking the protein in the cereal.

Techniques for Combining Cereal and Water

If the cereal is in a finely divided form, as farina and cornmeal are, it should be added to water in a way that avoids lumping so that a uniform gelatinous mass is formed on heating. All of the cereal particles should be equally exposed to water and heat. If lumps form, dry material remains inside a gelatinous external coating. The following two methods are commonly used to combine cereal with water. (Salt is usually added to the boiling water before the cereal is combined with it.)

1. Gradually pour the dry cereal into boiling water. Slight stirring may be required, but if the water does not cease boiling, stirring may be unnecessary.
2. Mix the cereal with cold water before adding it to the boiling water. The cold water tends to hold the particles apart.

Excessive stirring breaks up cereal particles so that they lose their identity. Even granulated cereals may be broken up to form a more gummy mass than would result from heating with the minimum amount of stirring.

Temperatures and Time Periods

Cereals may be cooked entirely over direct heat using low to moderate temperatures, or they may be placed in a double boiler after the cereal has been added to the boiling water. Cooking times are somewhat less over direct heat than in a double boiler.

The principal factors that affect the time required for the cooking of cereals are the size of the particle, the amount of water used, the presence or absence of the bran, the temperature, and the method used. Finely granulated endosperm cereals, such as farina, quick-cooking, and precooked cereals, cook in less time than whole or cracked and completely raw cereals.

Whole wheat is available in some areas and may be used as a breakfast cereal. If it is soaked before cooking, it cooks in less time than when it is cooked without soaking. In any case, 1 to 2 hours of cooking is needed to soften the bran and completely gelatinize the starch granules. Soaking is best started in two cups of boiling water per cup of wheat. If the mixture is heated just to the boiling point after the grain is combined with the water, in a hot-soak method, undesirable fermentation is less likely to occur during a soaking period of several hours. The grain is cooked in the water in which it is soaked, more water being added as needed.

When relatively small quantities are prepared, the microwave oven cooks cereals rapidly and satisfactorily with little or no stirring. The water may be first brought to boiling, the cereal added, and cooking completed on high power. Whole wheat may be cooked in the microwave oven without presoaking. In the initial stage, the wheat is covered with water in a tightly closed dish and microwaved on high power for about 3 minutes. Additional water is added and cooking continued for another 3 minutes. This process may be repeated, with water being added to replace that absorbed by the wheat, until the kernels are swelled and soft. The cooked whole wheat may be stored in the refrigerator and reheated for cereal as desired. It may also be used in casseroles and salads.

Proportions of Water to Cereal

Proportions of water to cereal vary according to the type of cereal, the quantity cooked, the method of cooking, the length of cooking, and the consistency desired in the finished cereal. The majority of people appear to prefer a consistency that is fairly thick but not too thick to pour. The amount of water must be adequate to permit swelling of the starch granules. If the consistency is then too thin, further cooking may be necessary to evaporate the excess water.

Table 14.3 provides the common proportions used for various types of cereals. The amount of salt will vary according to taste.

•COOKING OF RICE

White Rice

The challenge of rice cookery is to retain the form of the kernel while at the same time cooking the kernel until it is completely tender. It is usually suggested that rice be cooked with amounts of water that will be fully absorbed during cooking. Rice needs no more than about twice its volume of water. Regular rice increases to about three times its volume in cooking. One-half tea-

Type of Cereal	Water (c)	Cereal (c)
Rolled or flaked	2 or 2½	1
Granular	4 or 5	1
Cracked grain	About 4	1
Whole grain	About 4 unless grain was soaked for several hours	1

TABLE 14.3
Approximate Proportions of Water to Cereal for Cooked Breakfast Foods

spoon of salt per cup of uncooked rice is usually used for seasoning. Enriched rice should not be rinsed before cooking because the enrichment mixture will be washed off.

When cooked by the boiling method, rice is added to two to two and one-fourth times its volume of boiling water, brought back to a boil, and then covered and finished over reduced heat. Fifteen to twenty minutes is usually required, although converted rice takes a little longer. If rice is cooked in a double boiler, the volume of water may be reduced to 1¾ cups per cup of rice. After the water is brought back to a boil over direct heat, the top of the double boiler is placed over boiling water and the covered rice is cooked for about 45 minutes or until tender.

For oven cooking, about the same amount of boiling water is needed as for the boiling method, because a longer time is required for cooking in a closed baking dish at 350°F—about 35 minutes. Rice can be cooked in milk with the use of the double-boiler method. Cooking rice in chicken or beef broth can also give it a desirable flavor. Rice can be used in a variety of hot and cold dishes (see Figure 14.6).

FIGURE 14.6

A molded salad can be made by pressing hot cooked rice into a mold and then cooling. With hard-cooked eggs and vegetables, this Golden Rice Salad Royale can be served as a main dish. (Courtesy of the American Egg Board)

Minerals in hard water in some sections of the country produce a grayish green or yellowish cooked rice. The addition of 1/4 teaspoon of cream of tartar or 1 teaspoon of lemon juice to 2 quarts of water will maintain the white color of cooked rice.

Brown Rice

Brown rice can be cooked by the same methods used to cook white rice, but it must be cooked about twice as long. Because of the longer cooking time, somewhat more water is needed to allow for evaporation—up to two and one-half times the volume of the rice. Brown rice can be soaked for an hour in water to soften the bran and to shorten the cooking period. It does not tend to become sticky with cooking. Precooked brown rice is also available. Wild rice is usually cooked in salted water for about 20 to 25 minutes until tender.

Precooked Rice

Precooked rice can be prepared very quickly. Boiling water is added to the rice, the mixture is brought back to a boil, removed from the source of heat, and allowed to stand closely covered until the rice swells.

Rice Pilaf

Browning rice in a small amount of hot fat before cooking it in water converts part of the starch to dextrins. Swelling will also be somewhat decreased. The rice develops an interesting color and flavor that make the method desirable to use as a basis for Spanish rice, as rice pilaf, or as a side dish. Chicken or beef broth rather than water is used as the cooking liquid for pilaf.

•PASTA

Definition and History

The term *pasta* or *alimentary paste* is applied to macaroni products, which include spaghetti, vermicelli, noodles, shells, linguine, rotini, and other shapes. Spaghetti is a long, solid, round rod. Capellini, vermicelli, spaghettini, and fettuccini are variations of spaghetti, ranging from very fine to oversize in diameter. Linguine is flat. Rotini is spiral-shaped. Shells come in many sizes, from large for stuffing to tiny for soup. Rigatoni are large, ridged, hollow tubes. The more than 150 different shapes and sizes of pasta add great variety to meals (see Figure 14.7).

The principal ingredient in the making of pasta is a flour coarsely ground from durum wheat called *semolina*. Durum wheat is a high-protein grain containing carotenoid pigments in higher concentration than is found in bread wheats, giving pasta its characteristic yellow or amber color. Macaroni products originated in the Orient many years ago and were brought to Italy by Venetian traders and explorers in the Middle Ages. The Italians adopted pasta as their national dish. From Italy, the popularity of pasta spread throughout Europe. European immigrants to the United States introduced the process of making macaroni, spaghetti, and egg noodles to this country before the Civil War. For many years these products were made in the home, although industrial production of pasta had developed in America by 1900. To supply durum wheat for pasta manufacture, the growing of this variety of wheat was introduced in the early 1900s to the farmers of the Dakotas and nearby states, where climatic conditions are well suited to its cultivation. This ensured an ample supply of durum wheat for American macaroni production.

Manufacture

In the commercial manufacture of pasta, measured amounts of flour and water are automatically fed into a mixer, which, under vacuum, thoroughly blends the ingredients into a dough. The dough then goes automatically into a single-

FIGURE 14.7
Pasta comes in many shapes and sizes. (Courtesy of the Wheat Flour Institute)

screw continuous extruder and is extruded through a thick disk or *die* with openings that produce the desired size and shape of pasta. As the dough is forced through the openings by tremendous pressure, these various shapes are formed. Cutting blades cut the strands to desired lengths [7]. The pasta is then automatically placed on drying trays. The drying process is carefully controlled to maintain the optimum temperature and humidity necessary to prevent the development of chips and cracks in the pasta. In recent years, high temperature drying has speeded up this process and improved the pasta products. The conventional drying process takes place at temperatures around 60°C (140°F), but the high-temperature process uses temperatures above 100°C (212°F) [7].

Optional ingredients in macaroni products, according to the federal standards of identity, include eggs and various seasonings.

In egg noodle products, whole eggs or egg yolks are added to the flour and water mixture to form a soft dough. The dough is run between rollers until it is of the desired thickness. The sheet of dough is automatically cut into ribbons of the desired width or into other shapes. The cut dough is then carefully dried.

Precooked pasta and quick-cooking noodles can now be manufactured using twin-screw extruders [5]. The process involves a high-temperature–short-time extrusion following a preconditioning period that utilizes steam. The starch in the pasta is gelatinized before drying. The precooked pasta can therefore be reconstituted with boiling water in a very short time. Pregelatinized lasagna noodles, for example, are produced. During consumer preparation, the dry lasagna product can be layered directly with the sauce, cheese, and other ingredients, and then baked in less than half the time required in traditional preparation. The pasta will absorb about twice its weight in water. This precooked product can also be conveniently used in cooked prepared foods for both industrial and foodservice applications [7].

Durum flour is available in some areas for use in the home production of pasta. Pasta machines or pasta attachments to food processors are used to make the pasta.

High-protein macaroni products have been developed that contain 20 to 25 percent protein on a dry-weight basis. Soy and corn flour are often combined with wheat flour in the production of these protein-fortified, enriched macaroni-type products. Nonfat dry milk may also be used. The USDA has issued specifications for the use of these products as alternatives to meat in school foodservice.

Preparation of Pasta

Macaroni, spaghetti, and other pastas are cooked by adding the pasta to boiling water, which is usually salted. Approximately 2 to 3 quarts of boiling water are used for 8 ounces of pasta product. The more water used, the less likely it is that the pasta will stick together. Addition of a small amount of oil to the cooking water also helps keep the pasta pieces separate. The pasta should be added gradually so that the water continues to boil rapidly.

Pasta generally increases two to two and one half times its original volume on cooking. Pasta that is to be served without further preparation is cooked, uncovered, and occasionally stirred, until it is tender yet still firm to the bite. The standard for final cooking is called *al denté* (to the tooth). Because of the very high protein content of the flour used in the manufacture of pastas of good quality, their form is almost always retained on cooking.

If the pasta is to be further baked or simmered with other ingredients, it should be cooked until almost tender. Cooking is completed after the pasta is combined with the other ingredients.

When the boiling process is complete, the pasta should be drained thoroughly in a colander or strainer. It is usually suggested that enriched pasta not be rinsed in water after cooking because this process increases the loss of vitamins and minerals. If cooked pasta must be held a while before serving, it may be placed over hot water in a strainer. Steam will keep the product hot and moist without further cooking. Stickiness is reduced by this procedure as compared with overcooking.

If pasta needs to be held for a length of time in a foodservice setting, several problems may be encountered. Spaghetti combined with meat sauce, for example, becomes soft and sticky when held hot for an extended time. Refrigerating the spaghetti before it is combined with the meat sauce, then reheating it by pouring boiling water over it shortly before serving, has been suggested as an alternative procedure [2].

Pasta can be designed especially for use in microwave ovens. Since most conventional pastas are too thick to be cooked properly and uniformly by microwaves and will not achieve the desired firm texture, special pasta can be produced with thinner walls and selected additional ingredients such as egg albumen. The additional protein helps to form an insoluble network that traps starch granules and controls gelatinization more effectively [6].

Fresh or high-moisture pasta packaged in barrier trays under a modified atmosphere is being marketed successfully as a convenience food, along with companion sauces [6]. Since microbial safety is not assured by the modified atmosphere packaging alone, care must be taken to keep the product refrigerated after it has been processed and packaged under carefully controlled conditions.

The variety of dishes that can be prepared with macaroni products is almost endless. They include soups, salads, main dishes, and meat accompaniments.

STUDY QUESTIONS

1. Name the most important cereal grains used for food.
2. The structures of all grains are somewhat similar.
   a. Name three major parts of a grain and describe the general chemical composition of each part.
   b. What is the *aleurone* of a cereal grain? Describe its general composition and indicate where it usually goes during the milling of grain.
3. a. What is meant by *enrichment* of cereals and flours? What nutrients must be added to meet the standards of the federal government?
   b. Compare the general nutritional value of refined unenriched, enriched, and whole-grain cereal products.
4. Cereal grains are often processed in preparation for use. Indicate which grains are commonly used to make the following products and briefly describe the processes involved in preparing the grain.

a. Uncooked breakfast cereals

b. Prepared breakfast cereals

c. Flour

d. Meal

e. Hominy

f. Grits

g. Pasta

5. What are the main purposes for cooking cereals?

6. Suggest appropriate methods for cooking each of the following cereal products and explain why these methods are appropriate.

a. Granular cereals such as farina and cornmeal

b. Rolled oats

c. Rice

d. Macaroni or spaghetti

7. Describe the general processes involved in the production of each of the following types of ready-to-eat cereal.

a. Puffed

b. Flaked

c. Granulated

d. Shredded

e. Extruded

8. Discuss several factors to consider when purchasing cereals.

REFERENCES

1. Anderson, R. H., D. L. Maxwell, A. E. Mulley, and C. W. Fritsch. 1976. Effects of processing and storage on micronutrients in breakfast cereals. *Food Technology 30*, 110 (No. 5).

2. Brown, N. E., and A. I. Bernard. 1988. Sensory and instrumental assessments of spaghetti and meat sauce subjected to three holding treatments. *Journal of the American Dietetic Association 88*, 1587.

3. Carroll, L. E. 1990. Functional properties and applications of stabilized rice bran in bakery products. *Food Technology 44*, 74 (No. 4).

4. Chinnaswamy, R., and M. A. Hanna. 1987. Nozzle dimension effects on the expansion of extrusion cooked corn starch. *Journal of Food Science 52*, 1746.

5. Cole, M. E., D. E. Johnson, R. W. Cole, and M. B. Stone. 1991. Color of pregelatinized pasta as influenced by wheat type and selected additives. *Journal of Food Science 56*, 488.

6. Dziezak, J. D. 1991. Romancing the kernel: A salute to rice varieties. *Food Technology 45*, 74 (No. 6).

7. Giese, J. H. 1992. Pasta: New twists on an old product. *Food Technology 46*, 118 (No. 2).

8. Kahn, C. B., and M. P. Penfield. 1983. Snack crackers containing whole-grain triticale flour: Crispness, taste, and acceptability. *Journal of Food Science 48*, 266.

9. Khan, M. N., M. C. Des Rosiers, L. W. Rooney, R. G. Morgan, and V. E. Sweat. 1982. Corn tortillas: Evaluation of corn cooking procedures. *Cereal Chemistry 59*, 279.

10. Lachance, P. A. 1981. The role of cereal grain products in the U.S. diet. *Food Technology 35*, 49 (No. 3).

11. Leveille, G. A. 1988. Current attitude and behavior trends regarding consumption of grains. *Food Technology 42*, 110 (No. 1).

12. Lorenz, K. 1972. Food uses of triticale. *Food Technology 26*, 68 (No. 11).

13. Putnam, J. J. 1991. Food consumption, 1970–90. *Food Review 14*, 2 (No. 3).

14. Raloff, J. 1991. Beyond oat bran. *Food Technology 45*, 62 (No. 8).

15. Rao, D. R., G. Patel, and J. F. Nishimuta. 1980. Comparison of protein quality of corn, triticale, and wheat. *Nutrition Reports International 21*, 923.

16. Raper, N. 1991. Nutrient content of the U.S. food supply. *Food Review 14*, 13 (No. 3).

17. Reitz, L. P. 1970. New wheats and social progress. *Science 169*, 952.

18. Saunders, R. M., and R. Becker. 1984. Amaranthus: A potential food and feed resource. In Pomeranz, Y., Ed.: *Advances in Cereal Science and Technology*, Vol. VI. St. Paul, MN: American Association of Cereal Chemists, Inc.

19. Taha, F. A. 1993. Japan adds western flavor to its traditional diet. *Food Review 16*, 30 (No. 1).

20. Teutonico, R. A., and D. Knorr. 1985. Amaranth: Composition, properties, and applications of a rediscovered food crop. *Food Technology 39*, 49 (No. 4).

Vegetables and Vegetable Preparation

15

What exactly is a vegetable? We can define vegetables broadly as plants or parts of plants that are used as food. However, so broad a definition includes fruits, nuts, and cereals, which, although of vegetable origin, are not *commonly* classified as vegetables. The term *vegetable* has through usage come to apply in a more narrow sense to those plants or parts of plants that are served either raw or cooked as part of the main course of a meal. Sweet corn and rice are two examples of cereals that, through usage, are sometimes given the place of vegetables on the table.

Various parts of plants are used as vegetables. A grouping of vegetables by plant part is shown in Table 15.1. Some vegetables could technically be placed under more than one heading.

•COMPOSITION AND NUTRITIVE VALUE

The functions of the various parts of a plant influence their composition and nutritional value. For example, the leaf is an actively working or metabolizing part of a plant and does not generally store energy nutrients. It is low in energy value but high in many vitamins that function in metabolism. The root and seed act more as storage depots for starch and protein.

Vegetables as a group may be depended on to contribute indigestible fiber, minerals, and vitamins to the diet. Potatoes and sweet potatoes supply starch and sugars, and many dried legumes are high in both starch and protein. The protein of most vegetables, with the exception of soybeans, is of lower biological value than that of most animal foods such as meat and milk.

Vegetables are low in fat. Encouraging vegetable and fruit consumption is a major emphasis of the Dietary Guidelines for Americans, which recommend that we choose a diet with *plenty* of vegetables, fruits, and grain products. This means *at least* three servings of vegetables and two servings of fruits daily for adults. Americans now appear to be generally more concerned about health than they were a few years ago and are learning to appreciate the important relationship of nutrition to the prevention of disease. Although consumption of vegetables and fruits in the United States, on a per capita basis, has

TABLE 15.1

Parts of Plants Commonly Used as Vegetables

Leaves	Seeds	Roots	Tubers	Bulbs	Flowers	Fruits	Stems and Shoots
Beet greens	Beans, dry	Beet	Ginger root	Chives	Artichoke	Cucumber	Anise (fennel)
Bok choy	Corn (a seed	Carrot	Potato (Irish)	Garlic	(French	Eggplant	Asparagus
(Chinese	of the grass	Celeriac	Sunchoke	Leek	or Globe)	Okra	Celery (a leaf
chard)	family fre-	(Celery	(Jerusalem	Onion	Broccoli	Pepper	stem)
Brussels	quently	root)	artichoke)	Shallot	Cauliflower	Pumpkin	Kohlrabi
sprouts	served as a	Jicama				Snap beans	
Cabbage	vegetable)	Parsnip				Squash	
Chard	Lentils	Radish				Sweet corn	
Chinese	Peas	Rutabaga				(on the	
cabbage		Salsify				cob)	
Collards		Sweet				Tomato	
Dandelion		potato					
greens		Turnip					
Endive							
Escarole							
Kale							
Lettuce							
Mustard							
greens							
Parsley							
Romaine							
Spinach							
Turnip greens							
Watercress							

increased in the past two decades, consumption still remains below recommended amounts [19, 30]. Both public and private organizations are instituting programs aimed at consumers to make them more aware of the importance, as well as the enjoyment, of including more fruits and vegetables in their diets. Results of supermarket promotions that featured point-of-purchase nutrition information on fresh produce indicated that labeling can encourage purchases of vegetables and fruits, especially when accompanied by tips on preparation and menu planning [19].

Most fresh vegetables furnish about 25 kilocalories for an average serving, but some leaves and stems, such as lettuce and celery, are even lower in caloric value, and some roots, such as carrots and beets, and seeds, such as peas, furnish 35 to 50 kilocalories per average serving. These differences in caloric value are due basically to differences in composition. The leaves are high in water content and low in carbohydrate and protein, and, therefore, low in calories. The roots contain a little less water and a little more sugar, whereas the seeds store starch and are therefore higher in carbohydrate and lower in water, particularly as they mature.

Vegetables and fruits probably do more than any other group of foods to add appetizing texture, color, and flavor to daily meals. The composition and nutritive value of selected vegetables are given in Appendix C.

Fiber Components

Cellulose, a long chain **polymer** of glucose, is the main structural component of plant cell walls. Other structural compounds include hemicelluloses and pectins. All of these substances are complex carbohydrates called **polysaccharides** and, since they are not broken down or hydrolyzed by enzymes in the human digestive tract, make up a major part of dietary fiber [29]. Pectins are found not only in the cell walls but between the cells as well, where they act as a cementing substance to bind cells together. Pectic substances include protopectin, the insoluble "parent" molecule, pectinic acid or pectin, and pectic acid. Beta-glucans are also fiber components. These are glucose polymers with linkages somewhat different from cellulose that make them more soluble in water. A complex noncarbohydrate molecule, lignin, is present in woody parts of plants. Various gums and mucilages are also found in plants as fiber components, but they are nonstructural polysaccharides.

Heating can cause pectic substances to be broken down. This is one factor that affects the ease with which cooked plant tissues disintegrate. Acids and alkalies affect the structure of fruits and vegetables when they are boiled. Acids make the structure more firm, whereas alkalies tend to disintegrate the fibrous components, particularly the hemicelluloses.

Some fresh vegetables, depending partly on the way they are trimmed for marketing, may have a relatively high percentage of refuse or waste parts that are thrown away. Table 15.2 shows the percentage of refuse from some vegetables.

The Leaf Vegetables

Leaf vegetables may be generally characterized as being high in water and low in carbohydrate and calories, with only small amounts of protein and little or no fat (Figure 15.1 and Plate III). These vegetables' chief nutritive contribution is providing vitamins and minerals, and they are particularly important sources of iron, vitamin A value, riboflavin, and vitamin C. The greener the leaf, the higher its vitamin A value. The bleached inner leaves of plants that form compact heads and bleached celery leaves contribute little vitamin A value. Green leaves are also one of the better vegetable sources of calcium, but most of the calcium in spinach, chard, and beet greens is combined with **oxalic acid** in the plant and is not available for absorption from the digestive tract.

Vegetable–Fruits

Most of the commonly eaten **vegetable–fruits** (Figure 15.2) are relatively high in water content (92 to 94 percent), with small amounts of carbohydrate. Because they do not taste sweet and are generally prepared in combination with other vegetables, many people do not think of them as fruits. Botanically, however, they are fruits since they each develop from a flower. Winter squash is an exception to the usually high water content of this group; it contains only about 85 percent water and 12 percent carbohydrate in the raw state, comparable in carbohydrate content to many of the sweet, fleshy fruits. Cucumbers are particularly low in carbohydrate content and high in water content—about 97 percent.

Polymer a large molecule formed by linking together many smaller molecules of a similar kind

Polysaccharides complex carbohydrates containing many simple sugar units linked together

Oxalic acid an organic acid that forms an insoluble salt with calcium

Vegetable–fruit botanically, a fruit is the ovary and surrounding tissues, including the seeds, of a plant; a vegetable–fruit is the fruit part of a plant that is not sweet and is usually served with the main course of a meal, for example, squash, cucumbers, and tomatoes

TABLE 15.2
Refuse from Vegetables

Vegetable	Source of Refuse	Refuse (%)
Asparagus	Butt ends	44
Beans, snap	Ends, strings, trimmings	12
Beets, without tops	Parings	30
Broccoli	Tough stalks, trimmings	25
Brussels sprouts, fair quality	Trimmings, outer leaves	26
Cabbage	Outer leaves, core	21
Carrots, without tops*	Scrapings	18
Cauliflower, untrimmed	Jacket leaves, inner leaves, stalk, base, core	60
Celery	Leaves, root ends, trimmings	25
Chard, Swiss, good quality	Tough stem ends, damaged leaves	8
Corn, sweet		
with husk	Husk, silk, cob, trimmings	64
without husk	Cob	45
Cucumber, pared*	Parings, ends	27
Lettuce, crisphead,		
good quality	Core	5
fair quality	Coarse leaves, core	26
Onions	Skins, ends	9
Peas, green	Pods	62
Potatoes*	Parings, trimmings	19
Spinach, trimmed, (packaged)		
good quality	No refuse	0
fair quality	Damaged leaves, trimmings	8
Squash, winter	Cavity contents, rind, stem ends, trimmings	29
Tomato, peeled	Skins, hard cores, stem ends	12

* Refuse will be less when the vegetable is not pared or scraped.

Source: Reference 10.

Carotenoids yellow-orange, fat-soluble pigments

Precursor a substance that "comes before"; a precursor of vitamin A is a substance out of which the body cells can make vitamin A

Tomatoes and green peppers are vegetable–fruits that are important sources of vitamin C. Pumpkin and yellow squash as well as tomatoes and green peppers contain **carotenoid** pigments, some of which are **precursors** of vitamin A. While green and red peppers, string beans, and okra can be classified as vegetable–fruits, they are also seed pods.

Flowers and Stems

Flowers and stems (Figure 15.3) are, in general, high in water and low in carbohydrates. Broccoli has been shown to be a particularly nutritious green vegetable in terms of its vitamin and mineral content. It is one of the richest vegetable sources of vitamin C; even the stems contain enough vitamin C so that, whenever possible, the stems should be pared and used. Broccoli is also a good source of vitamin A value and contributes some riboflavin, calcium, and iron. Cauliflower and kohlrabi are good sources of vitamin C, and green asparagus has vitamin A value.

Swiss chard

Chinese cabbage

Spinach

Brussels sprouts

Cabbage

FIGURE 15.1

Leaf vegetables. (Courtesy of Burpee Seeds)

Hubbard squash

Eggplant

Okra

Summer squash

Zucchini squash

FIGURE 15.2

Vegetable–fruits. To aid in identifying squash, three types are shown. (Courtesy of Burpee Seeds; eggplant, courtesy of Western Growers Association)

Kohlrabi

Celery

Cauliflower

Broccoli

FIGURE 15.3
Flowers and stems used as vegetables. (Courtesy of Burpee Seeds)

FIGURE 15.4
Roots and bulbs used as vegetables.
(Courtesy of Burpee Seeds; beets,
carrots, and turnips courtesy of the
U.S. Department of Agriculture)

Beets, carrots, and turnips

Roots, Bulbs, and Tubers

Root vegetables include beets, carrots, turnips, rutabagas, and parsnips. Examples of bulbs, which are enlargements above the roots, are onions, leeks, and shallots (Figure 15.4). The shallot is composed of several cloves covered by a thin skin, as is garlic, which is also a bulb vegetable. The potato is an example of a **tuber**, which is an enlarged underground stem. Bulb, root, and tuber vegetables are, in general, higher in carbohydrate and lower in water content than leaves, stems, and flowers. Most of the carbohydrate in potatoes is in the form of starch. Sweet potatoes also contain a fairly large amount of starch but have more sugar than white potatoes. Potatoes (Plate II) are significant sources of vitamin C, whereas the yellow carotenoids in sweet potatoes contribute vitamin A value.

There are two basic types of sweet potatoes. One has a somewhat dry, mealy, pale-colored flesh; the other has a soft, moist, orange-colored flesh. The moist type is known as the *yam*; however, the true yam is the root of a tropical vine that is not grown in the United States.

Tuber a short, thickened, fleshy part of an underground stem, such as a potato; new plants develop from the buds or eyes

Seeds

Legumes are seeds of the Leguminosae family and include many varieties of beans, peas, soybeans, and lentils (Figure 15.5). They are used in both the green or fresh state and in the mature or dried state, in which the water content is very low and the starch content high. There is more protein in dried legumes than in any other vegetable group. Although the biological quality of

Legume any of a large family of plants characterized by true pods enclosing seeds; dried beans and peas

Purple-top yellow rutabaga

Parsnips

Leeks

the protein in most of the legumes, with the exception of soybeans, is substantially less than that of meat, fish, and poultry, legumes can make a valuable contribution to the body's protein requirement. Legumes can be used as alternates for meat in meal planning and play an important role in vegetarian diets.

Although it is a cereal product, corn is commonly used as a vegetable in the United States. It is relatively high in carbohydrate, chiefly in the form of starch.

The technique of sprouting soybean and mung bean seeds was developed by the Chinese centuries ago. Sprouts from many different seeds have become popular as vegetables and are particular favorites at fresh salad bars. The sprouts of some seeds provide significant sources of vitamin C, thiamin, riboflavin, and several minerals [15].

•SELECTION

Vegetables selected for purchase should be firm, crisp, and bright in color. In surveys of consumers, a high percentage of respondents have indicated that freshness, appearance, condition, and also taste are important selection criteria [30]. Appearance factors include size, shape, gloss, color, and absence of defects. Usually, vegetables are highest in quality and lowest in price when they are in season in nearby production areas. Because of efficient transportation and marketing procedures, however, many vegetables are now available in local markets throughout the year and maintain generally good quality. Prices vary, of course, depending on growing conditions, supply, demand, and the distance

FIGURE 15.5
Seed vegetables. (Courtesy of Burpee
Seeds; lima beans, courtesy of the
U.S. Department of Agriculture; pinto
beans, soybeans, and lentils, photo-
graph by Chris Meister)

Sweet corn

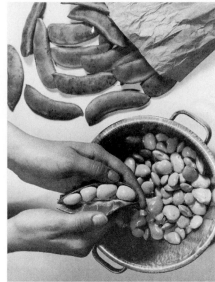

Lima beans

Green peas

Pinto beans (*far right*), soybeans (*bottom*), and
lentils (*left*)

the produce must be shipped. (The availability in the United States of fresh
fruits and vegetables on a monthly basis is detailed in Reference 57.)

It is unwise to purchase greater quantities of fresh vegetables than you
can properly store and utilize without waste. In making selections, you should
distinguish between defects that affect appearance only and those that affect
edible quality. Fruits and vegetables should not be handled unnecessarily while
selections are being made. Some quality characteristics to look for in specific
vegetables are provided in Table 15.3.

TABLE 15.3
Selection of Fresh Vegetables

Vegetable	Quality Characteristics to Look For
Artichoke, globe	Plump and compact; heavy in relation to size; green, fresh-looking scales
Asparagus	Closed, compact tips; smooth, round spears, mostly green; stalks tender almost as far down as the green extends
Bean, snap	Young, tender beans; pods firm and crisp
Beet	Firm, round, deep red color, smooth surface
Broccoli	Firm, compact clusters of small flower buds with none opened to show yellow flower; dark green; stems not too thick or tough
Brussels sprouts	Tight outer leaves; bright green color and firm body
Cabbage	Firm heads, heavy for size; outer leaves good color for variety, fresh, and free from serious blemishes
Carrot	Well formed, smooth, firm, and bright colored
Cauliflower	White to creamy, compact, solid, and clean curd; good green color in jacket leaves
Celery	Crisp, stalk with solid, rigid feel and fresh leaflets
Cucumber	Good green color; firm over entire length; well shaped but not too large
Eggplant	Firm, heavy, smooth, uniformly dark purple
Greens (chard, spinach, kale)	Fresh, young, tender leaves that are free from blemishes; good green color
Lettuce,	
iceberg	Large, round, solid heads with crisp medium green outer leaves
leaf	Fresh, unwilted leaves; bright color; somewhat soft texture in many varieties
Okra	Tender pods under 4½ inches long; bright green
Onion,	
globe	Firm, dry, with small necks; papery outer scales
green	Fresh, crisp, green tops; white portions 2–3 inches up from root
Pepper	Glossy sheen, firm and crisp; dark green
Potato	Well shaped, reasonably smooth, firm; free from blemishes, sun burn, and decay; no signs of sprouting
Radish	Medium size, plump, round, firm, good red color
Squash,	
summer	Firm, fresh-appearing, well formed, glossy skin
winter	Hard, tough rind; heavy for its size; free from cuts, sunken spots, or mold
Sweet potato	Well shaped, firm, smooth skins uniformly colored; free from signs of decay
Tomato	Well formed, smooth, well ripened; reasonably free from blemishes

Source: Reference 26.

USDA Grades

In the wholesale market, most fresh vegetables and fruits are sold on the basis of U.S. Department of Agriculture (USDA) grades. These grades specify such characteristics as size, shape, color, texture, general appearance, uniformity, maturity, and freedom from defects. A common language is thus provided for wholesale trading and aids in establishing prices based on quality.

Grading is provided by the USDA upon request and a fee is charged to the producer or distributor. Grade labeling is not required by law, however, and there is not a large quantity of grade-marked produce available in most retail stores. Generally, potatoes, carrots, and onions are the only fresh vegetables labeled for the consumer with a grade name. Sometimes, consumer fruit packages are marked with a grade; however, this is usually limited to citrus fruits and apples.

Four uniform grade terms for all fresh fruits and vegetables are being phased in by the USDA as existing grades are revised: U.S. Fancy, U.S. No. 1, U.S. No. 2, and U.S. No. 3. U.S. Fancy is premium quality and only a few vegetables or fruits are packed in this grade. Some packers use their own grades. Because fresh vegetables are perishable, the quality may change between the time of grading and the time of purchase. This severely limits the usefulness of consumer grades on fresh fruits and vegetables. Extensive use of prepackaging may help to overcome this problem and make the use of consumer grades for fresh produce more practical. (See pages 76–79 for a general discussion of grading.)

USDA grades of quality have been established for many canned and frozen vegetables and fruits, based on color, uniformity of size, shape, tenderness or degree of ripeness, and freedom from blemishes (Figure 15.6 and Plate IV). The label may designate U.S. Grade A or Fancy, U.S. Grade B or Choice, and U.S. Grade C or Standard.

Availability of graded products allows the buyer to select the quality that will be most satisfactory for the intended use. Lower grades of fruits and vegetables are still good and wholesome although they are less perfect than Grade A in color, uniformity, and texture. When a product has been officially graded under continuous inspection by a USDA inspector, it may carry the official grade name and the statement "Packed under continuous inspection of the U.S. Department of Agriculture." The grade name and the statement may also appear within a shield-shaped outline.

Most canned and frozen vegetables and fruits are packed according to grade, whether or not it is indicated on the label, and are generally priced according to their quality. Most products marketed are at least Grade B quality, which is quite good. As with fresh produce, the use of the USDA grades is voluntary and is paid for by the packer. The specific brand name of a frozen or canned vegetable or fruit may be an indication of quality, since the packers set their own standards.

Federal regulations require that certain information appear on the label of canned and frozen fruits and vegetables:

1. Common or usual name
2. Form or style, such as whole, slices, or halves, unless the product is visible through the package
3. Variety or color for some products
4. List of syrups, sugar, or liquid in which the product is packed
5. Total contents (net weight)
6. Additional ingredients, if used
7. Any special type of treatment
8. Packer's or distributor's name and place of business
9. Nutrition labeling

Labels may give other useful information about canned and frozen vegetables and fruits such as size and maturity, cooking directions, and recipes or serving ideas.

FIGURE 15.6
USDA graded canned and frozen fruits and vegetables let the buyers choose the quality they want. (Courtesy of the U.S. Department of Agriculture)

Variety in Vegetables

In selecting vegetables, it is wise to remember that a liking for vegetables, as for other foods, is largely a matter of cultivation of habits and attitudes. A wider selection and variety in the preparation of vegetables can brighten up menus and, at the same time, bring nutritional dividends. New and sometimes strangely unfamiliar vegetables as well as fruits are constantly appearing on grocers' shelves. Mostly tropical and often native to Asia, Latin America, and the Caribbean, these exotic products include winged beans from the Philippines, tamarillos (tart, egg-shaped tree tomatoes) from New Zealand, chayote (a green, soft, watery, squashlike vegetable known in Louisiana as *mirliton*), plantains (something like green bananas) from Central America, and jicama (knobby, earth-colored root) from Mexico (Plates IV and V). Some of these vegetables will probably become common in the United States in just a few years, as did ginger root, bean sprouts, shallots, tomatillos, and cilantro not so long ago. (More information about purchasing vegetables and fruits can be found in References 57 and 60.)

•STORAGE

Fresh vegetables and fruits are perishable, having limited shelf life. They are composed of living, respiring tissue that is also **senescing** and dying [30]. Although tomatoes will ripen after harvest, developing desirable color and flavor, most other vegetables show little or no improvement in quality upon holding. However, most packing and handling systems move fresh produce from farm to consumer expeditiously with minimum deterioration of quality.

Most fresh immature vegetables retain their top quality for only a few days, even under ideal conditions of temperature and humidity for storage. Leafy vegetables are particularly perishable. All fresh vegetables of high water content, if they are allowed to stand long after harvesting without low-temperature and high-humidity controls, wilt and toughen through loss of moisture, called *loss of turgor* [33]. The flavor is also impaired, mainly because of enzyme actions in the tissues. Mature vegetables, particularly roots, tubers, and bulbs, deteriorate less in storage than do immature ones.

The short storage life of many vegetables is due to their rapid respiration or metabolism. A thin coating of a vegetable-oil **emulsion** on snap beans and other fresh vegetables has been found to decrease the **respiration** process [49]. When stored at 4°C (40°F), the waxed beans were generally in better condition than the unwaxed beans. Using this procedure to extend storage life and maintain product quality is common in the marketing of fresh vegetables such as cucumbers and tomatoes, as well as many fruits. In practice, the vegetable or fruit is first washed thoroughly and rinsed, which removes the natural protective wax coating along with dust and dirt. The manmade edible wax is then applied to restore nature's own coating and extend the shelf life of the product [57].

Lettuce may be stored in a controlled atmosphere to extend its shelf life [48]. In an atmosphere containing 2.5 percent carbon dioxide and 2.5 percent oxygen, lettuce heads can be stored up to 75 days. The controlled atmosphere combined with polyethylene packaging reduces the rate of respiration in the

Senescence   the state of growing old or aging

Emulsion   the dispersion of one liquid in another with which it is usually immiscible, for example, oil in water

Respiration   a metabolic process by which cells consume oxygen and give off carbon dioxide; continues after harvest

Controlled atmosphere storage the monitoring and control of content of gases in the storage warehouse atmosphere; a low oxygen content slows down plant respiration and delays senescence (aging)

lettuce tissues (see page 325 for a discussion of **controlled atmosphere storage** of fruits).

The superior quality of vegetables stored under refrigeration is well known. It is interesting to note that such treatment usually is useful in conserving vitamin content as well. Vegetables do vary, however, in the extent of change in vitamin C content, even when they are kept under refrigeration. In one study [13], fresh broccoli did not lose vitamin C when stored up to 7 days, whereas green beans lost as much as 88 percent when stored for 6 days at 2°C (36°F) and 95 to 100 percent relative humidity. A decrease in vitamin C content during 240 days of storage at 7°C (45°F) was observed in potatoes [1].

Most fresh green vegetables, such as lettuce and celery, can be kept fresh and crisp in kitchen storage by placing them in covered containers or plastic bags in the refrigerator. If they are washed before storing, they should be drained thoroughly because too much moisture can increase the possibility of spoilage or decay. Seeds, such as peas and limas, remain fresh longer when left in the pods. Tubers and bulbs that are to be held temporarily may be stored in a cool place without refrigeration.

If tomatoes are picked before being fully ripened, the quality and vitamin value will be better if the tomatoes are ripened at room temperature or a little below, that is, 15° to 24°C (59° to 75°F) and are kept in a lighted place unwrapped. Ripe tomatoes should be stored uncovered in the refrigerator.

•BIOTECHNOLOGY AND VEGETABLE PRODUCTION

For centuries man has exploited the genetic diversity of living systems for improvement of the food supply [20]. Conventional plant and animal breeding and selection techniques have contributed to the development of food products that fit the demands of modern living. Now there are more opportunities for developing new and improved food supplies with the use of biotechnology. Specifically, genetic engineering provides a new set of tools for improving the variety and efficiency of food production in less time and with more precision and control than with traditional methods. Small-scale field trials of genetically engineered tomatoes, potatoes, cucumbers, and corn have been conducted in several different growing locations [21].

How does genetic engineering work for vegetable crops? It allows genetic information, even a single genetic trait, to be taken from one living organism and transferred to another. A gene may be taken from a bacterium and transferred to a plant. For example, some bacteria make insecticidal proteins; this capability can be given to plants to confer natural resistance to pests and thus decrease dependence on insecticides. Of course, there is concern that the "natural" insecticide in the plant may be toxic to humans. This possibility must be considered in the development of the product, and adequate testing must be done to assure safety [44].

Genetic engineering is being used to develop temperature-tolerant plants that can survive in warmer or cooler climates than those that they can naturally tolerate. One major advantage thereby produced is the ability to control frost damage, which presently causes billions of dollars annually in crop losses worldwide. Varieties of potato and strawberry with greater resistance to frost have been produced. Genetic engineering can also be used to improve flavor, texture, color, and shelf life of vegetables such as tomatoes, thus enticing people to increase their consumption of vegetables and fruits [20]. A tomato that does not soften as rapidly as other tomatoes, thereby enabling it to be left on the vine until its natural flavor is fully developed, has also been produced.

The general public is interested in plants that may be developed through biotechnology. This interest is certain to increase as genetically improved plants get nearer to grocery store shelves. It is important for scientists to communicate effectively with the public about the processes involved in and the safety of agricultural crops produced by genetic engineering in order to help dismiss unsupported claims of critics and gain acceptance of these means of crop improvement [31].

Research studies have suggested that a number of vegetables, including garlic, cabbage, and carrots, may possess cancer-preventive properties. The next logical step is to determine more precisely the exact nature of the cancer-preventive substances in the vegetables, or other foods, and then actually design foods, through genetic engineering, with enhanced levels of those substances [5]. Exciting possibilities lie ahead in the field of biotechnology.

•VEGETABLE PREPARATION

Emphasis on the important nutritional contributions of vegetables, along with the greater availability of vegetables year-round and the introduction into the U.S. market of new and interesting vegetables, has given impetus to the study of vegetable preparation. The nutrients that vegetables contain should be conserved as completely as possible. Also, such factors as changes in color, flavor, texture, and general appearance during preparation require careful consideration to assure that both raw and cooked vegetables retain their attractive and appetizing characteristics until they are served.

The vegetables that are generally eaten raw are those of high water and low starch content. Many such vegetables are tender and crisp and have distinctive pleasant flavors.

Color

Much of the appeal of vegetables and fruits is due to their bright colors, which result from the presence of various pigments in the plant tissues. Under appropriate temperatures for postharvest storage, green vegetables have been reported to undergo little change in color over a 12 day period [17]. Other vegetables also retain color well when they are stored properly. One of the challenges of cooking vegetables is to retain these bright colors, since heat and the various conditions of preparation may produce pigment changes that make them dull and less attractive.

Depending on the predominant colors, vegetables and fruits can be classified into four groups: green, yellow-orange, red-blue, and white. The yellow-orange and red-blue pigments predominate in fruits. Specific groups of plant pigments are responsible for these colors. The chlorophylls are green pigments; the carotenoids are yellow and orange (and some are pink or red); the anthocyanins are red, purple, and blue; the betalains are purplish red (although some are yellow); and the anthoxanthins are creamy white to colorless. Anthocyanins and anthoxanthins have many similarities in chemical structure. They are called **flavonoid pigments**.

Chlorophyll

Chlorophyll plays an important role in photosynthesis, in which the plant uses the energy of the sun's rays along with gases from the air to synthesize carbohydrates. Chlorophyll is concentrated in the green leaves, where it is present in tiny bodies called *chloroplasts*. It is mostly insoluble in water. When chlorophyll comes in contact with acids, which may be liberated during the cooking of vegetables, it chemically changes to a compound called *pheophytin*, which is a dull olive green. In canned green vegetables, which have been subjected to prolonged periods of heating at high temperatures, essentially all of the chlorophyll is degraded to pheophytin and pyropheophytin, which appear to be responsible for the olive green to olive brown color that is characteristic of many canned green vegetables. Pyropheophytin is apparently the major degradation product of chlorophyll in canned vegetables [47]. The bright green to dull color change is obvious when you compare a newly cooked fresh vegetable such as garden peas with canned peas. Removing the cover from the pan during the first few minutes of boiling should allow some volatile acids to escape, decreasing the likelihood of their affecting the chlorophyll adversely. However, heating is not as even or as complete in an uncovered pan and the total cooking time may be slightly extended.

The hues of green vegetables progress from green-yellow toward yellow as cooking time increases beyond the just tender stage [41]. Green beans, broccoli, brussels sprouts, cabbage, and other green vegetables show considerable change in color with 5 minutes of overcooking in boiling water and with even 1 minute of overcooking in a pressure saucepan. It is important, therefore, to cook vegetables for the *minimum* amount of time necessary to tenderize. The length of holding time for vegetables should be minimized as well. Green vegetables that are held on a steam table before serving often show pronounced loss of chlorophyll and color [54]. The cooking of frozen broccoli has also been reported to produce large losses of total chlorophyll [8].

When a small amount of baking soda (an alkaline substance) is added to green vegetables during cooking, it changes the chlorophyll to a bright green, more water-soluble pigment called *chlorophyllin*. However, the use of baking soda in cooking vegetables is *not* recommended, because it is difficult to avoid adding too much and the flavor, texture, and vitamin content of the vegetables may be adversely affected. The vitamins thiamin and vitamin C are particularly susceptible to destruction when baking soda is added during cooking. Texture may be undesirably soft because soda has a disintegrating effect on the hemicelluloses. When proper methods for cooking green vegetables are employed, the addition of soda serves no purpose.

An intensified green color that occurs at the beginning of cooking is explained in part by the removal of air from the tissues when the green vegetable is dropped into boiling water. This removal of air permits greater visibility of the underlying chlorophyll. The bright green color of frozen green vegetables results from brief blanching in boiling water or steam.

Carotenoids

Carotenoids, like chlorophyll, are insoluble in water. They are present, along with chlorophyll, in the chloroplasts of green leaves. In the autumn, when the chlorophyll disappears, the yellow color can usually be seen. Carotenoids constitute a group of similar pigments, some of which are called *carotenes*. Three of the carotene pigments, α, β, and γ-carotene, are found in relatively large amounts in carrots. Other carotenoids, which contain some oxygen in addition to carbon and hydrogen, are called *xanthophylls*. Cryptoxanthin is a xanthophyll that is found in many yellow vegetables. The red pigment of tomatoes, named *lycopene*, is a carotenoid.

Some of the carotenoid pigments, including α, β, and γ-carotene and cryptoxanthin, may be changed into vitamin A in the body and, therefore, contribute substantially to the vitamin A value of the diet. Carotenoid pigments may lose some of their yellow color when exposed to air because they are susceptible to **oxidation**. This may occur in vegetables such as carrots when they are dehydrated.

The carotenoid pigments are quite stable during ordinary cooking procedures. The presence of alkali has little effect on the color. However, with prolonged heating, the pigments may be susceptible to some chemical change by a process called **isomerization** in the presence of acid and heat, so that the orange color becomes somewhat more yellow.

Anthocyanins

The flavonoid pigments are water soluble and are found in the cell sap. The pigments in the anthocyanin group of flavonoids are usually red in an acid medium and change to blues and purples as the pH becomes more alkaline.

Not all anthocyanins as they occur in the plant behave in the same way with changes of acidity and alkalinity. This may be the result of the admixture of other pigments or of substances that modify the reactions. Red cabbage is very easily changed in color, and it is difficult to retain its typical color while cooking it. The German custom of cooking red cabbage with an apple and adding a small amount of vinegar when it is ready to be served aids in retaining the desirable red color.

When it is cut with a nonstainless-steel knife, red cabbage reveals another property of anthocyanins—their ability to combine with metals to form salts of various colors. The use of **lacquered tin** for canning red fruits and vegetables prevents the bluish red or violet that results from the combination of anthocyanin pigment with tin or iron. The salts of iron combined with anthocyanins are more blue than those formed with tin.

Betalains

The pigments in the root tissue of red beets have some properties similar to those of anthocyanins, but they contain nitrogen and are called *betalains* [62]. Some of these pigments are purplish red, whereas others are yellow and somewhat resemble the anthoxanthins. Beets lose much pigment and become pale when they are pared and sliced before cooking, because the pigments are very soluble in water and leach from the tissues.

Oxidation   a chemical reaction in which oxygen is added; addition of oxygen to carotenoid pigments lightens the color

Isomerization   a molecular change resulting in a molecule containing the same elements in the same proportions but having a slightly different structure and, hence, different properties; in carotenoids, heat causes a change in the position of the double bonds between carbon atoms

Lacquered tin   an enamel coating on the inside of tin cans

pH   a scale of 1 to 14, with 1 most acid, 14 most alkaline, and 7 neutral

Phenolic compounds   organic compounds that include in their chemical structure an unsaturated ring with —OH groups on it; these compounds are easily oxidized, producing a brownish discoloration

Oxidase   an enzyme that catalyzes an oxidation reaction

Anthoxanthins

The anthoxanthin pigments change from white or colorless to yellowish as the pH increases from acidic to alkaline ranges. These pigments are widely distributed in plants and often occur with anthocyanins. They may combine with some metals, such as iron, to form a dark-colored complex. Some combinations with aluminum produce a bright yellow. The anthoxanthin pigments are generally quite stable to heating. However, if the cooking water is alkaline, the pigments may appear yellow. Also, if heating is excessive or prolonged, the pigments darken. Table 15.4 summarizes the effect of various factors on the color of plant pigments.

Enzymatic Oxidative Browning

Some raw fruits, such as bananas, apples, and peaches, and some pared vegetables, including potatoes and sweet potatoes, darken or discolor on exposure to air. The darkening results from the oxidation of **phenolic compounds** in the fruit when oxygen from the air is available; the reaction is catalyzed by oxidizing enzymes, called **oxidases**, present in the plant tissue (see pages 107–109 for a discussion of enzymes). Unattractive, brown-colored pigments are the end products of this enzymatic oxidative reaction.

It is, of course, desirable to prevent or control enzymatic darkening because it is aesthetically unappealing both in food freshly prepared for con-

TABLE 15.4
Solubility in Water and Effect of Various Factors on the Color of Plant Pigments

Name of Pigment	Color	Solubility in Water	Effect of Acid	Effect of Alkali	Effect of Prolonged Heating	Effect of Metal Ions
Chlorophylls	Green	Slightly	Changes to olive green (pheophytin)	Intensifies green (chlorophyllin)	Olive green (pheophytin and pyro-pheophytin)	
Carotenoids	Yellow and orange; some red or pink	Slightly	Less intense color	Little effect	Color may be less intense*	
Anthocyanins	Red, purple, and blue	Very soluble	Red	Purple or blue	Little effect	Violet or blue with tin or iron
Betalains	Purplish red; some yellow	Very soluble	Little effect	Little effect	Pale if pigment bleeds from tissues	
Anthoxanthins	White or colorless	Very soluble	White	Yellow	Darkens if excessive	Dark with iron; bright yellow with aluminum

* Heating *usually* produces little effect.

sumption and in susceptible products held prior to freezing, drying, or canning. Lemon juice, which is high in acid and evidently interferes with enzyme activity, can be used to coat fruit surfaces to reduce discoloration. Pineapple juice accomplishes the same purpose, although it is less acid than lemon juice. Pineapple juice contains a **sulfhydryl compound** that seems to act as an **antioxidant** in retarding browning. Added vitamin C, either alone or as part of several available commercial products, also aids in reducing discoloration because of its ability to act as an antioxidant. Commercially, sulfur dioxide is sometimes used to inhibit enzyme activity before fruits are dehydrated.

Sulfites are also able to control browning on processed raw potatoes and other fresh fruits and vegetables. However, the U.S. Food and Drug Administration (FDA) has prohibited their use on fresh potatoes that are intended to be served or sold unpackaged and unlabeled and also on salad-bar produce because of the possible danger to individuals who are sensitive to sulfites, especially asthmatics. Frozen, canned, or dehydrated potatoes must state on the label that sulfites are present. Vitamin C derivatives and citric acid are more commonly used than are sulfites to retard undesirable enzymatic browning in fresh fruits and vegetables.

Flavor

Wide variation occurs in the flavor of vegetables; some are very mild, whereas others, such as asparagus and parsnips, have relatively strong distinctive flavors. The sugar content is high enough to produce a definite sweet taste in carrots and sweet potatoes. The flavor of spinach includes a slightly bitter component, whereas anise or fennel, a vegetable similar in appearance to celery, has a spicy, licoricelike flavor.

The natural flavors that make each vegetable distinctive probably result from mixtures of many compounds, most of them present in very small amounts. These compounds include **aldehydes**, **alcohols**, **ketones**, **organic acids**, **esters**, and sulfur compounds. The flavoring compounds in a number of vegetables and fruits have been and are being studied extensively with the use of modern analytical equipment to find out more about the complex mixtures of substances that contribute to their individual flavors. Vegetables, with some exceptions, are relatively bland in flavor, different from the tart, fragrant flavor of fruits.

Vegetables of the cabbage and onion families contain several sulfur compounds. They are sometimes described as strong flavored, but they are not all strong flavored in the raw state.

Cabbage Flavors

Vegetables of the cabbage or Cruciferae family include cabbage, cauliflower, broccoli, brussels sprouts, kale, kohlrabi, mustard, rutabaga, and turnips. These vegetables are relatively mild when raw, but may develop strong flavors or odors when improperly cooked because of extensive decomposition of certain sulfur compounds.

Some vegetables of the cabbage family contain a sulfur compound called *sinigrin*. When tissues are damaged by cutting or shredding, an enzyme (myrosinase) breaks down the sinigrin to produce a mustard oil, chemically

Sulfhydryl compound a chemical substance that contains an -SH group

Antioxidant a substance that stops unwanted oxidations

Aldehydes chemical compounds characterized by a ($-\overset{\overset{\displaystyle O}{\|}}{C}-H$) group

Alcohols chemical compounds characterized by a -OH group

Ketones chemical compounds characterized by a ($-\overset{\overset{\displaystyle O}{\|}}{C}-$) group

Organic acids generally weak acids characterized by a carboxyl ($-\overset{\overset{\displaystyle O}{\|}}{C}-OH$) group

Ester a chemical linkage joining an organic acid and an alcohol group, with the removal of one molecule of water

called *allyl isothiocyanate*, that gives a sharp, pungent flavor. This flavor is typical of shredded raw cabbage. An amino acid, *S*-methyl-L-cysteine sulfoxide, is also present in raw cabbage and several other members of the cabbage family. From this compound, on cooking, comes dimethyl disulfide, which contributes to the characteristic and desirable flavor of the cooked vegetable, along with a number of other volatile compounds [36].

In overcooked vegetables of the cabbage family, hydrogen sulfide and other volatile sulfur compounds may produce a strong, pungent, sulfurous flavor and odor. Vegetable acids may aid in the decomposition. Leaving the lid off for the first part of cooking, to allow some volatile acids to escape, may help to control these changes; however, it is more important to cook the vegetables for the shortest time possible, until just tender to a fork, before substantial decomposition of sulfur compounds occurs.

Vegetables of the cabbage family have a milder flavor when they are cooked in an open pan with enough water to cover them than when they are cooked in a tightly covered pan, a steamer, or a pressure saucepan. A large amount of water dilutes the natural flavors of the vegetables, usually to a very substantial degree. The desirability of a milder flavor or stronger natural flavor is a matter of personal preference. The absence of many volatile flavor substances from dehydrated cabbage has been reported [35], and this has been suggested as an explanation for the dehydrated product's being a poor substitute for freshly cooked cabbage in terms of eating quality.

Onion Flavors

The onion family includes onions, leeks, garlic, and chives. These vegetables are usually strong flavored in the raw state, but tend to lose some of their strong flavors when they are cooked in water. Raw onions contain sulfur compounds that are acted on by enzymes in the tissues when the vegetable is peeled or cut to produce the volatile sulfur compounds that irritate the eyes and produce powerful sensations on the tongue.

The sharp flavor of onions is reduced on cooking. The flavor of onions can also be very mild when they are cooked in a large amount of water with the lid of the pan loose or off, or the flavor can be sweeter and more concentrated when they are cooked in a small amount of water with the lid on.

Preliminary Preparation

Most vegetables grow near or in the ground. They are contaminated by dirt, sand, and various microorganisms, some of which are acquired from the soil and some from the many contacts incident to marketing. They may also be contaminated with pesticide residues unless they are organically grown. In organically grown produce, insects and rodents can inoculate plants in the field with microorganisms that can present a health hazard. In addition, molds can infect vegetables and fruits and produce mycotoxins [30]. Thorough washing in water that is safe for drinking is therefore essential. The use of a stiff vegetable brush is often necessary to aid in the removal of dirt. If vegetables are to be consumed raw, extra care is needed in cleansing them. All spoiled and discolored portions should be trimmed off. If pods, such as lima bean and pea pods, are dirty, they should be washed before being shelled. Leafy vegetables should have all undesirable leaves and coarse stems removed. The usable leaves require several washings to remove all grit. In washing, the vegetables should be lifted out of the wash water so that the heavier particles of dirt remain in the water. Alternatively, they may be washed under running water.

Roots and tubers that are covered with skins may or may not have their skins removed, depending on the method to be used in cooking them and depending in part on the vegetable itself. Beets, for example, should not be peeled unless they are to be diced or sliced and cooked in a closely covered container with little or no water. The red coloring matter of beets is very soluble in water and is best protected from loss by cooking the beets in the skin, with the roots and two or more inches of the tops left on.

When properly scrubbed with a brush, carrots can be cooked without paring or scraping. In some cases, however, the skins tend to make the vegetable appear darker. Carrots are delicious when they are cooked in their skins and scraped after cooking. When plunged into cold water after boiling, they are easily skinned and retain their sweetness and nutrients better than when they are scraped before cooking. If the method of preparation requires that carrots have the skin removed before cooking, they should be scraped or pared so as to remove as little tissue as possible with the peel, to retain more of the vitamins and minerals. Vegetables usually have a valuable layer of nutrients lying directly underneath the skin. Some roots and tubers, such as potatoes, have skins that are too thick to be removed by scraping. These also can be cooked in their skins and peeled after cooking. If they must be pared before cooking, parings should be as thin as possible. The floating-blade type of peeler removes very thin layers.

Only the tips and tender stems of asparagus should be used. The woodiest parts of asparagus can be easily removed if the lower stems are snapped off with the fingers (Figure 15.7). The stems should break where the stalk is tender.

If the twigs and leaves of broccoli are tender, they may be used in addition to the flower buds. Woody stems are not easily softened by cooking and are usually inedible; however, large broccoli stems may be peeled and the tender center cores cooked. The outer leaves and heavy stalks of cauliflower and cabbage are usually discarded, although the process of prepackaging fresh vegetables often includes removal of the outer, less edible portions before the vegetables are placed in the retail market. When cooking heavier stalks with more tender portions of a vegetable, it is best to add the more tender parts to the stalks after a few minutes of cooking, so that the tender portions are not overcooked by the time the stalks are tender. Parsnips may have a woody core, which should be removed. See Figure 15.8 for the preparation of globe artichokes.

Some vegetables that are prepared in advance of being used or cooked discolor unless they are covered with water. As a general precaution against the loss of water-soluble nutrients, the soaking time should be kept to a minimum. Also, cabbage shredded with a *sharp* knife in advance of its use loses a negligible amount of vitamin C when it stands at room temperature for one hour in air or three hours in water. By use of a sharp knife, bruising is avoided, thereby decreasing loss of the vitamin. These results with cabbage, however, do not justify indiscriminate and unnecessary cutting, shredding, and exposure of vegetables to air or soaking in water. In some vegetables, certain nutrients may occur

Asparagus can be washed under running water with the use of a small brush to remove soil.

Lower stems can be snapped off with the fingers to leave the tips and tender stems for cooking.

FIGURE 15.7
Preparation of asparagus for cooking. (Courtesy of Western Growers Association)

in a form that is more stable or better protected against destruction than in other vegetables.

National media attention has heightened concern among some members of the public about chemical residues on vegetables and fruits as marketed. Government studies that have monitored actual pesticide residue levels in foods as prepared and consumed have shown no pesticide residues in more than half of the samples tested, and levels below the Environmental Protection Agency tolerances in more than 99 percent of the samples tested [30]. The government continues to monitor and evaluate the use of pesticides on vegetable crops. It has been suggested that researchers reevaluate pesticide tolerances on food in relation to the usual intake of agricultural products, particularly by children.

Why Cook Vegetables?

Many vegetables are improved in palatability and are more easily and completely digested when they are cooked. Some valuable vegetables, such as dried legumes, could not be masticated or digested in the raw state. The fla-

FIGURE 15.8

To prepare globe artichokes, (1) cut off the stem about 1 inch from the base, leaving a stub; (2) cut off about 1 inch of the top, cutting straight across with a knife; (3) pull off any heavy loose leaves around the bottom; (4) with scissors, clip off the thorny tip of each leaf; (5) drop into boiling, salted water. Season by adding a small clove of garlic, a thick slice of lemon, and 1 tablespoon of olive or other salad oil for each artichoke. Cover and boil until a leaf can be pulled easily from the stalk or until the stub can be easily pierced with a fork (20 to 45 minutes). Remove carefully from the water. Cut off the stub. (Courtesy of Western Growers Association)

vors of cooked vegetables are different from those of raw vegetables, adding variety to their use.

Heating improves the utilization of protein from dried legumes, and some of the minerals and vitamins, particularly of soybeans, are more available after the beans are heated [34]. Cooking also **gelatinizes starch** and increases its digestibility. Microorganisms are destroyed by the heating process. Moreover, the bulk of leafy vegetables is greatly decreased as they wilt during cooking.

Gelatinization of starch the swelling of starch granules when heated in the presence of water

How Cooking Losses Occur

Cooking losses can occur (1) through the dissolving action of water or dilute salt solutions; (2) by chemical decomposition, which may be influenced by the alkalinity or acidity of the cooking medium; (3) by oxidation of specific molecules such as vitamins; (4) by the mechanical loss of solids into the cooking water; and (5) by volatilization. Mechanical losses of nutrients in vegetable cookery are the result of paring, rapid boiling (agitation), and overcooking. There is loss of starch cells, as well as other nutrients, from cut surfaces. Losses are greater when parings are thick and when overcooking results in marked disintegration. The chief volatile loss is water, although volatilization of other substances may cause loss of flavor.

Changes During Cooking

Changes in Fiber Components

Fiber indigestible substances including cellulose, hemicelluloses, and pectin (all polysaccharides), and also lignin, which is a noncarbohydrate material found particularly in woody parts of a vegetable

There appears to be no great loss of **fiber** when vegetables are prepared by typical kitchen methods or commercial processing [64]. Cellulose is somewhat softened by cooking but appears to be mostly indigestible for humans. When calculated on a dry-weight basis, cellulose content seems to increase somewhat when vegetables are boiled. This has been suggested to result from the liberation of cellulose from the cell walls, making it more available for analysis [22, 23, 38].

Sodium bicarbonate (baking soda) added to cooking water tends to cause the hemicelluloses to disintegrate, producing a soft texture in a short cooking period. Acid, on the other hand, prevents softening of vegetables. Neither of these substances should be added in the cooking of vegetables.

Hydrolyze to break chemical linkages, by the addition of water, to yield smaller molecules

The pectic substances in the intercellular cementing material may be **hydrolyzed** to a certain extent during cooking so that there is some cell separation; however, the total pectin content appears to be well retained [64]. In the canning of many vegetables, the solubilization and hydrolysis of pectin apparently contribute to excessive softening. During prolonged cooking at approximately neutral pH, **de-esterification** as well as depolymerization (hydrolysis) occur [59].

De-esterification the removal of the methyl ester groups from the galacturonic acid building blocks of the pectin molecule

Calcium salts, as calcium chloride, make vegetable tissues more firm, probably by forming insoluble calcium salts with pectic substances in the plant tissue. Commercially, traces of calcium are added during canning to help preserve the shape and firmness of tomatoes. The FDA allows calcium chloride to be added up to 0.07 percent. It can also be used to make melon rinds firm and brittle for pickling.

Other Changes

The water content of vegetables is altered during cooking. Water may be absorbed if the vegetable is cooked submerged in water or, to a lesser extent, in steam. Removal of water occurs during baking.

More flavor substances are extracted, and thereby lost, by cooking in a large amount of water than in a small amount. Sugars, acids, and some minerals that contribute to flavor are water soluble and easily extracted from the tissues.

The gelatinization of starch, described as the swelling of starch granules in the presence of moisture, occurs during the cooking of vegetables. This gelatinization may be partial or complete.

Vitamin Losses

There are two ways in which vitamins may be lost during cooking. Some of the vitamins may actually be destroyed by oxidation and some may be dissolved in the cooking water, although the latter applies only to the water-soluble vitamins (the B vitamins and vitamin C). Vitamin C is particularly easily oxidized and hence tends to be better retained if conditions favoring oxidation can be eliminated.

Some of the undesirable effects of covering the pan have been mentioned, but a covered pan hastens cooking and thus gives less time for either solution losses or inactivation of vitamins. A covered pan does not completely exclude air but reduces the exposure to air.

The vitamin A value of vegetables is usually well retained during cooking. Thiamin is more unstable to heat than are riboflavin and niacin, and it appears to be less stable when heated in a water medium than when heated in the dry state. The extent of destruction increases with increase in temperature. Riboflavin and niacin are very stable to heat even at temperatures above 100°C (212°F). The more alkaline the cooking water, the faster the rate of oxidation of several vitamins, particularly thiamin and vitamin C.

Losses of vitamin C during the cooking of broccoli have been studied with the conclusion that some loss occurs regardless of the method used. Leaching of the vitamin into the cooking water rather than destruction by heat is the chief factor responsible for the loss. Except when excessive cooking liquid is used, broccoli cooked to satisfactory doneness retains 60 to 85 percent of the original vitamin C [55, 56].

Cooked vegetables lose significant amounts of vitamin C during even 1 day of refrigerator storage, and reheating causes additional loss [8]. Holding vegetables at a warm temperature after cooking causes loss of both flavor and nutritive value. It is probably better if vegetables are cooled and quickly reheated when they are to be served.

Increasing emphasis is being placed by the foodservice industry on the nutritional quality of meals served. For cooking vegetables in a foodservice operation, convection steaming has been found to retain vitamin C well. However, when broccoli and cauliflower were held an additional 30 minutes at 63°C (145°F) after cooking, considerable additional loss occurred. Although convection steaming of the fresh vegetables resulted in losses of only 6 to 12 percent of the vitamin C, the total loss after a 30-minute holding period was 36 to 45 percent [6]. Preservice holding of whipped potatoes in a simulated conventional foodservice system resulted in loss of 36.2 percent of the vitamin C present [57]. Care needs to be exercised during the entire foodservice cycle to ensure retention of nutritional value.

Specific Methods of Cooking Vegetables

Baking, frying, stir-frying or panning, steaming, cooking in steam under pressure, and microwave cooking are common methods of cooking vegetables. Broiling can also be utilized, for example, as with the broiling of fresh tomatoes.

The desire for variety is one factor that influences the choice of cooking method, as is the suitability of the method for the type of vegetable being cooked. A third and important factor is the influence of the method on the retention of nutrients.

Some loss of food value probably occurs in most methods employed in vegetable cookery. For this reason it is important to serve some vegetables in the raw state. Baking, steaming, panning, and cooking in the skins have been called *conservation methods* of cooking vegetables because they may retain food value more completely than do some other methods.

Baking

Baking can be accomplished by the direct heat of the oven, or the vegetable can be pared, sliced, or diced and placed in a covered casserole. In the casserole, however, a moist atmosphere surrounds the vegetable as it cooks. All vegetables that contain a high enough water content to prevent drying out and that have little surface exposed to the heat lend themselves well to baking. These include potatoes, sweet potatoes, winter squash, and onions. Vegetables are commonly baked in the skin. Figure 15.9 shows several ideas for stuffing and serving baked vegetables.

The overbaking of starchy vegetables and failure to open the skin of the vegetable when baking is finished result in sogginess. Because the time required for baking is greater than for boiling, time and fuel must be considered in the use of this method. Moderately hot oven temperatures, which form steam quickly within the vegetable, give better texture to starchy vegetables than is obtainable at low temperatures. Prompt serving of baked vegetables as soon as they are done is recommended to maintain quality and lessen vitamin losses.

Frying

Panfrying (cooking to doneness in a small amount of hot fat) and deep-fat frying (cooking submerged in hot fat) are both methods of frying. Potatoes,

FIGURE 15.9
Baked stuffed onions, cabbage, artichokes, or tomatoes make delicious and nourishing entrees or meat accompaniments. They may be stuffed with ground beef, diced ham, or seasoned celery and bread crumbs (*left*). Eggs can be baked in tomato halves as a luncheon dish (*right*). (Courtesy of Western Growers Association)

onions, eggplant, and parsnips are probably more commonly cooked by this method than are other vegetables; however, many others could be satisfactory fried.

Onion rings, eggplant, and zucchini are often dipped in a batter before being fried in deep fat. Carrots, green peppers, parsnips, and mushrooms should be parboiled before being covered with batter and fried in deep fat. There appears to be little loss of vitamins and minerals in the frying of vegetables. Table 15.5 gives approximate temperatures and time periods for the deep-fat frying of some vegetables and vegetable mixtures. Frying is discussed in more detail in Chapter 18.

Stir-Frying or Panning

In panning, the vegetable is stirred briefly in a small amount of melted fat before the pan is covered. The pieces of vegetable should be thin, so that the heat will penetrate rapidly and the cooking time can be short. Overcooking should be avoided. When done, the vegetables should still be slightly firm or crisp. The short cooking time and the small amount of water used (usually only that which clings to the vegetable) aid in conserving vitamins and minerals.

This method could be considered a modification of frying, since a small amount of fat is used in the pan. However, the vegetable is cooked mainly by steam produced from the vegetable's own moisture and held in with a tight-fitting cover. Finely shredded or diced roots, celery, sweet corn, french-cut green beans, and finely shredded cabbage are very satisfactorily cooked by this method. We often associate stir-frying with Chinese cooking because many vegetables and mixtures are so prepared in that cuisine.

Boiling

When vegetables are boiled, they are either partially or fully submerged in water, which means that soluble constituents are likely to be lost in the cooking water. Soluble substances in vegetables include water-soluble vitamins, relatively soluble mineral salts, organic acids, flavor substances, and sugars. Much less loss of soluble material occurs if vegetables are boiled in their skins. For example, pared potatoes may lose up to nine times as many minerals and up to four times as much total dry matter as potatoes cooked in their skins.

Losses of water-soluble constituents vary with the time of cooking and the amount of surface exposed to the water. In general, the more surface exposed and the longer the cooking time, the greater is the loss. Losses are also influenced by the amount of cooking water, more losses occurring as the quantity of cooking water increases. If the vegetables are such that cooking can

Food	Temperature of Fat		Time (min)
	°C	°F	
Croquettes (cooked mixtures)	190–199	375–390	2–5
French-fried onions, potatoes, and cauliflower	196–202	385–395	6–8
Fritters	182–190	360–375	3–5

TABLE 15.5

Approximate Temperatures and Times for Frying Vegetables

be done in little or no water, or if the cooking water is evaporated by the time the vegetable is done, little or no loss of soluble material may occur. Also, cooking waters should be utilized for soups, sauces, and gravies to save valuable nutrients that would otherwise be thrown away. Of all these factors affecting loss, probably the most important is the length of cooking time. It is very important to avoid overcooking; cook vegetables only to the just-tender stage, as tested with a fork.

Several studies [9, 18] have compared the losses of vitamin C incurred by cooking vegetables in various amounts of water and by "waterless" methods using only the water that clings to the vegetables after washing. The percentage of retention in the cooked vegetable varies with the vegetable, but seems to be higher when cooking is done by the "waterless" method or in a small amount of water.

To cover or not to cover boiling vegetables is a somewhat controversial matter. It is probably desirable to cover all vegetables whose flavor and/or color are not impaired by covering because cooking occurs more rapidly and uniformly in a covered pan. The continuous exposure to air is avoided, although air is not totally excluded, and thus vitamins may be better conserved. The cover makes possible the use of a smaller volume of water. Some heavy, tightly covered saucepans may develop a small amount of pressure, also hastening cooking.

In general, it is the chlorophyll-containing vegetables and high-sulfur vegetables whose color and flavor may be most adversely affected by covering, although there are exceptions. In an uncovered pan, some of the less desirable volatile sulfur compounds from high-sulfur vegetables can escape. However, enough water to cover the vegetable is necessary for more uniform heating in an uncovered pan, with a greater loss of soluble nutrients and other flavor compounds. Young, tender green peas may be sweeter and have more marked flavor when they are cooked covered; however, when compared with a like sample cooked in an open pan, particularly if more water is used, the color is likely to be superior in the latter. Thus, the choice to cover or not to cover may be made for different reasons.

From the standpoint of flavor, it is usually best to add salt to vegetables when they are put on to cook. The loss, if any, of nutrients as a result of the added salt is probably very small. The Dietary Guidelines for Americans recommend that salt be used in moderation. Cooking fresh or frozen vegetables without salt and seasoning them with a variety of herbs is an excellent way to help achieve this goal.

In general terms, placing vegetables in just enough boiling water to prevent scorching, covering with a tight-fitting lid, and cooking until just tender constitute an appropriate method for boiling most vegetables to retain maximum flavor, sweetness and aromatic characteristics, and nutritive value (Figure 15.10).

Steaming and Pressure Cooking

Steaming consists of cooking in steam, with the vegetable suspended in a perforated container over boiling water. Although some tender young vegetables may cook quickly in steam, most vegetables cooked in an ordinary steamer take somewhat longer to cook than those that are boiled. The fact that the veg-

FIGURE 15.10
A vegetable platter can be a meal in itself, or it may include meat or meat substitutes, such as shrimp and egg slices. (Courtesy of United Fresh Fruit and Vegetable Association)

etable is not actually in water favors the retention of water-soluble constituents, but the longer time required to cook most vegetables tends toward a loss of color in many green vegetables.

Cooking in a pressure saucepan is cooking in steam, but the steam is confined in the tightly closed pan and a high pressure is created. The cooking temperature rises as the steam pressure rises. At 15 pounds of pressure the temperature is 121°C (250°F). Small, lightweight pressure saucepans can conveniently be used to cook a variety of foods (Figure 15.11) and may be especially well used to cook roots, tubers, and legumes. With young tender vegetables such as spinach, the pressure saucepan may easily result in overcooking, with accompanying loss of color and flavor. The fact that acids released from the vegetable are trapped in the pressure saucepan also contributes to a loss of green color.

Many models of pressure saucepans are adjustable for 5, 10, and 15 pounds of pressure, and the temperature may be quickly reduced by placing the pan in cold water as soon as the cooking period is ended. These features are an aid in obtaining desirable results for various types of vegetables. One disadvantage is the difficulty of testing for doneness during the cooking period if one happens to be using a variety of vegetable that requires a shorter or longer cooking time than the average periods recommended.

Flavor, color, and vitamin C retention in vegetables cooked in a pressure saucepan, in sufficient boiling water to cover, and by "waterless" methods have been compared [18]. Vegetables cooked in boiling water were generally more mild and green than those cooked by the other methods. Percentage retention of vitamin C was greatest in the pressure saucepan for the majority of vegetables. In cabbage, cauliflower, rutabagas, and turnips, vitamin C retention was somewhat greater with "waterless" cookery than with boiling water, but the reverse was true for broccoli and brussels sprouts. The investigators concluded

FIGURE 15.11

A pressure saucepan that can be adjusted for 5, 10, and 15 pounds of pressure. (Courtesy of Aluminum Goods Manufacturing Company)

that if the acceptability of cooking methods is based on a cooked vegetable that is mild, has good color, and retains vitamin C well, no one method is completely satisfactory for all vegetables.

In Table 15.6, the approximate times for cooking vegetables by several methods are given. It should be emphasized that all timetables used in cookery are approximate and are to be used merely as guides. In using a timetable, it is best to cook for the minimum time suggested and then test for doneness with a fork before continuing to cook. Variations in the maturity of samples of vegetables, the sizes of whole vegetables or cut pieces, the variety, the temperature of the vegetable when placed in the water as well as the temperature of the water itself, and the amount of water are known factors affecting the time required to cook the vegetable until tender. Some varieties cook in half the time required by other varieties of the same vegetable.

Microwave Cooking

Both fresh and frozen vegetables generally can be satisfactorily cooked in a microwave oven. Some vegetables have better color and/or flavor when cooked by microwaves, whereas other vegetables have higher quality characteristics when boiled in a saucepan or cooked by other conventional methods [2, 53].

A comparison of several varieties of potatoes cooked by microwaves and conventional baking resulted in somewhat higher taste panel scores for the conventionally baked vegetables in all cases [37]. Cooking potatoes in the microwave oven for a shorter period, removing them, and immediately wrapping them in aluminum foil for a standing time of 10 to 15 minutes allow cooking to be completed with improvement in texture and aroma. Potatoes hold their heat for up to 45 minutes when wrapped in foil.

Greater retention of vitamin C has been reported in broccoli cooked by microwaves than in broccoli cooked by various conventional methods [4, 7]. In a comparison of steaming, microwave cooking, and boiling fresh and frozen broccoli, steaming generally produced the least loss of vitamins while boiling caused the greatest. However, frozen broccoli samples retained similar amounts of vitamin C and thiamin when steamed or cooked by microwaves [27].

Fresh spinach cooked by microwaves retained 47 percent of its vitamin C, whereas spinach boiled in a small amount of water retained 52 percent [32]. In many cases, vegetables may be cooked in a microwave oven without the addition of water, thus decreasing the nutrient loss through leaching.

Whole vegetables or pieces should be of uniform size for the microwave oven so that they cook evenly. Large pieces take longer to cook than small pieces, and microwaving time increases with the amount of food being cooked. Vegetables cooked in their skins should be pricked or cut to allow excess steam to escape. Tender portions of vegetables, such as the buds of asparagus and the flowerets of broccoli, should be arranged toward the center of the dish (Figure 15.12). Standing time outside the microwave oven should be considered in the cooking of large vegetables. If these vegetables are cooked until the center is tender, the outer portions become mushy. Microwaving is a good method for cooking corn on the cob. General principles of microwave cookery are discussed in Chapter 8.

Frozen Vegetables

Essentially, the cooking of frozen vegetables is no different from the cooking of fresh vegetables. With the exception of frozen green soybeans, which require about as long to cook as do fresh ones, the cooking time of frozen vegetables is about half that required for fresh vegetables because they have been blanched before freezing. Vegetables may be defrosted before cooking, or the frozen vegetable may be placed in boiling water. The vegetable cooks more uniformly and in slightly shorter time when defrosted, at least partially, before being cooked. It has been suggested that vegetables defrosted prior to cooking may rate higher in texture and flavor because more water is taken up by the tissues when vegetables thaw slowly. Because some vegetables lose vitamin C more rapidly after defrosting and because many users of frozen foods are poorly informed regarding the changes that occur in vegetables after defrosting, the

Asparagus Spears

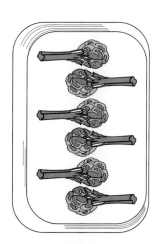

Broccoli

FIGURE 15.12
Arrange tender portions of a vegetable toward the center of the dish when cooking in the microwave oven.

TABLE 15.6
Approximate Cooking Time for Vegetables

Vegetable	Approximate Amount for 4 Servings	Preparation for Cooking	Approximate Amount of Water for Boiling	Amount of Water for Pressure Saucepan	Time (min)			
					Boiling	Steaming	Baking	Pressure Saucepan (15 lb. of pressure)
Artichokes, French	2 lb	Whole	To cover	1 c	25–40	35		10
Jerusalem	1 lb	Whole, pared	Partially cover	1 c	20–30		30–60	15
Asparagus	1 lb	Woody ends broken off, scales removed	To cover butts	⅓ c	Tips, 5–10 Butts, 10–15	10–15		Tips, 1–½ Large tips, 2
Beans, young green or wax	¾ lb	Whole or broken, strings removed	About half the volume of beans	⅓ c	20–25	25–30		1½–3
Beans, fresh lima	2 lb in pod (2 c shelled)	Shelled	About 2 c	⅓ c	25–35	25–40		2–3 (5 lb pressure)
Beets, young	6 medium or 1½ lb	Whole, skin, root, and 2 in. of stem left on	To cover	¾ c	30–45	60–75		12, small 18, large
Beet greens	1–1½ lb	Whole leaf with tender stem and midrib	Partially cover	½ c	5–15			2
Broccoli	1 medium bunch (1½–2 lb)	Woody stems removed, coarse leaves removed, smaller stems pared and split to hasten cooking	To cover stems	⅓ c	Flowerets, 5–10 Stems, 10–15			1½–2
Brussels sprouts	¾–1 qt	Whole, outer leaves removed; larger compact heads may be partially split	Partially cover	½ c	10–15			1–2
Cabbage, new green	1 lb	Outer leaves and stalk removed; shredded.	Partially cover	½ c	6–9	9–10		1–1½
Mature, white	1 lb	Outer leaves and stalk removed; shredded.	Partially cover	½ c	8–10	10–12		2–3
Red	1 lb	Outer leaves and stalk removed; shredded; cook with tart apple or add 2–3 Tbs vinegar after cooking	Partially cover	½ c	15–20	25–30		3–4

Vegetable	Amount	Preparation	How to cover	Water	Boiling (min)	Steaming (min)	Baking (min)	Pressure cooking (min)
Carrots, young	1 lb	Whole, skins on or scraped	Partially cover	⅓ c	20-25	25-30	35-45	4
		Scraped, cut into halves or quarters lengthwise or diced			10-15			2-3
Cauliflower	1½-2 lb	Outer leaves and stalks removed; separated into flowerets / Whole flower	Partially cover	½ c	8-10	10-15		1½
Celery	1 medium bunch	Cut into ½-to-¾-in. pieces	Partially cover	½ c	20-25	25-30		3-4
			½-in. depth in pan; add water if needed	⅓ c	15-20	25-30		2-3
Corn, young green	4 ears	On cob or cut off	Cover ears; partially cover cut corn	½ c on cob / ⅓ c off cob	5-10	10-15		1-2
					5			2
Okra	1 lb	Sliced or whole	Partially cover	⅓ c	10-20	20-25		3 (sliced)
Onions	1 lb	Two outer layers removed / Whole, cut into halves or quarters or slices	Cover or partially cover	½ c	Whole, 25-35 / Quarters, 15-20	45-60		6-7
								3
Parsnips	1 lb	Scraped or pared; cooked whole or cut in half lengthwise; woody core removed	Partially cover	½ c	15-25	30-35		2 (sliced)
								7 (whole)
Peas, green	2 lb in pod	Shelled	½- to 1-in. depth in pan; add as needed	⅓ c	10-15	15-20		2-2½ (5 lb pressure)
Potatoes, Irish	1-1½ lb	Whole, with or without skins	Barely cover	1 c	30-35	40-60		15
		Pared, cut lengthwise into halves or quarters	Partially cover	¾ c	20-30	30-35		8
Potatoes, sweet	1-1½ lb	Whole, with or without skins	Barely cover	1 c	30-35	35-40		8-10
Rutabaga	1¼ lb	Pared, halved	Partially cover	½ c	20-30	30-35		6-8
		Pared and diced	Partially cover	½ c	20-30			4
Spinach	1 lb	Coarse stems and roots removed	1 c per lb or none	½ c	3-6	5-10		1-1½
		Stems not removed			8-10	6-12		1-1½

TABLE 15.6, *continued*

Vegetable	Approximate Amount for 4 Servings	Preparation for Cooking	Approximate Amount of Water for Boiling	Amount of Water for Pressure Saucepan	Time (min)			
					Boiling	Steaming	Baking	Pressure Saucepan (*15 lb. of pressure*)
Squash								
Hubbard	1½–2 lb	Pared; cut into 2 × 3-in. pieces	½- to 1-in. depth in pan	¾ c	20–25	30–35		6–8
		Cut into one-portion pieces; rind on					45–60	
Summer	1½–2 lb	Pared and sliced	½- to 1-in. depth in pan	⅓ c	5–15	10–20	15–20	2
Tomatoes	1 lb	Whole	Little or none	¼ c	5–10	10	20–30 (whole stuffed)	1–2
Turnips	1 lb	Pared, sliced or diced	Partially cover 1–2 c	½ c	15–20	20–25		1½–4
Turnip Greens	1–1½ lb				15–25			1–1½

producer generally recommends that all vegetables remain frozen until cooking is started.

Corn on the cob should be defrosted before cooking because the time required for cooking the corn is not sufficient to defrost the cob. In preparation for freezing, corn on the cob requires a longer blanching time to destroy enzymes than does cut corn. This longer blanching time cooks the corn more completely; thus, a short heating period is desirable in the final preparation after freezer storage.

Spinach and other leafy vegetables are better when they are partially defrosted before cooking to avoid overcooking the outer leaves before the block is defrosted. Using a fork to break solid blocks of frozen vegetables is an aid in shortening cooking time.

Frozen vegetables may be easily defrosted in a microwave oven. This is also a satisfactory method for completing the cooking process. If frozen vegetables are in compact blocks before cooking in a microwave oven, cooking should be interrupted midway during the process to separate the unthawed portion in the center and distribute it toward the edges of the container.

Canned Vegetables

Canned vegetables are already overcooked in the processing; hence, a relatively short reheating time is preferable to avoid further softening of the vegetables. A short heating period is safe for commercially canned foods; however, it is recommended that, if home-canned vegetables have not been processed using USDA-recommended procedures, they should be boiled for at least 10 minutes before tasting them in case **botulinum toxin** is present. Canned vegetables may be easily heated in the microwave oven as well as by conventional methods.

Retention of vitamins has been measured when canned vegetables were reheated in two ways: (1) concentrating the drained liquid, then heating the vegetable in the liquid and serving the small amount of concentrated liquid with the vegetable; (2) reheating vegetable and liquid together and discarding the liquid [24]. Vitamin C loss varied from 20 to 60 percent when the liquid was concentrated first; however, the loss was distinctly greater for the method in which the liquid was discarded. No thiamin or riboflavin was lost by oxidation in either method, but approximately 30 to 40 percent of these two vitamins was lost when the liquids were discarded. Obviously, other soluble nutrients are also lost when liquids are discarded. The flavor of many canned vegetables may be improved by concentrating and using the liquid in the can.

•PARTIALLY PROCESSED VEGETABLES AND FRUITS

Fresh vegetables and fruits can be trimmed, peeled, cut, sliced, and so on for direct use by restaurants and other foodservice establishments without additional preparation. They offer freshlike quality along with convenience. These minimally processed vegetables and fruits are very perishable. In most cases they are more perishable than the unprocessed raw materials because the degradative changes related to senescence in the mature product are

Botulinum toxin   a very potent toxin produced by *Clostridium botulinum* bacteria; in a low-acid environment, the high temperatures achieved in a pressure canner are required for complete destruction of the spores of this microbe

enhanced by the physical actions of cutting and slicing. Respiration by the cells increases in response to the injuries [63].

Food manufacturers are using a variety of technologies to produce minimally processed vegetables and fruits [46]. These include refrigeration, **modified-atmosphere packaging** in combination with refrigeration, and heat treatment in combination with **hermetic packaging** and refrigeration. The addition of vitamin C and calcium can help to maintain quality in some products while also enhancing nutritive value.

•POTATOES

Potatoes are among the most important and economical of vegetables. The white potato is a tuber of American origin, having been grown in northern Chile and Peru before the arrival of the Europeans.

Characteristics of Varieties

Many varieties of potatoes are presently marketed. In the industry, potatoes are generally classified into five basic types: (1) round white, (2) russet Burbank (long russet group), (3) russet rural or round russet, (4) round red group, and (5) long white group. The skin of russet potatoes has a reddish brown, slightly mottled appearance. Several varieties of potatoes are pictured in Plate II. The Cobbler and Cherokee varieties are examples of the round white type; the Pontiac is a round red type; and White Rose is a long white type. A russet Burbank is also shown.

Mealiness and waxiness are qualities ascribed to cooked potatoes. A mealy potato separates easily into fluffy particles that feel dry. A variety of potato exhibiting this quality to a marked degree is the russet Burbank, which is excellent for baking. On the other hand, a waxy potato is more compact and moist, or almost soggy, and does not separate easily into fluffy particles. Potato varieties that possess this characteristic are especially good for boiling and for salads and include Chippewa, Cobbler, Katahdin, Red Pontiac, and White Rose. Some varieties, such as Kennebec and Cherokee, are good all-purpose potatoes and function quite well in both boiling and baking.

Why some potatoes are mealy and others are waxy has not been completely clarified. The variety is an important influence on these cooking characteristics, but the soil in which they are grown, fertilizers, and climate also have an effect. The content of starch in the potato may be related to its mealy or waxy tendencies. The starch granules swell markedly when potatoes are cooked, and water tends to be absorbed when they are boiled. It has been suggested that the swelling of starch causes the separation of plant cells that occurs in mealy potatoes.

Even though the basic causes of mealiness and waxiness are not clarified, it has been shown that potatoes with higher starch content are more dense, and that potatoes with a higher **density** tend to be more mealy. It is possible to test this characteristic by placing a potato in a brine solution of 1 cup salt to 11 cups water. If the potato floats, indicating a low solids content, it is probably best for boiling; if it sinks, it is a baker. Mealy potatoes that are high in starch content tend to slough off their outer layers when they are boiled. Storage at temperatures between 10° and 21°C (50° and 70°F) seems to decrease the tendency of the potato to slough during cooking. Also, if the cooking water contains enough calcium salt to maintain or slightly increase the calcium content of the potato, sloughing can be partially controlled.

Grading

The U.S. quality standards for potatoes are revised as needed to keep up with changes in production and marketing. The top grade for potatoes is U.S. Extra No. 1, and the second grade is U.S. No. 1. Tolerances are set for defects, such as cuts, bruises, and sprouts, within each grade. Optional size designations may also be used by packers. The wholesale grade, usually U.S. No. 1, often appears on the bags of potatoes sold in retail stores.

Processing

Large quantities of potatoes are processed in the United States into frozen, dehydrated, and canned potato products that are partially prepared for serving before they are brought into the kitchen. These products are part of the group of convenience foods discussed in Chapter 2. Frozen french-fried potatoes are a popular convenience item for consumers when they can be baked in the oven rather than finish-fried in the home. A surface-texturizing process that improves the quality of baked french-fried potatoes has been developed at the USDA's Western Regional Research Laboratory [43]. Fabricated french-fried potatoes prepared from mashed potatoes are competing with fries made directly from raw potatoes [42].

Potatoes stored at refrigerator temperatures (below 5°C or 41°F) increase in sugar content because of changes in the metabolism of the plant tissue. Holding at room temperature for several days after refrigeration brings down the elevated sugar content. For the potato-chip processing industry, the sugar level is critical for the control of browning during frying.

A number of years ago, the prepeeled potato processors recognized the need for a raw but more convenient potato in the restaurant and institutional foodservice market. After first offering only peeled and trimmed raw potatoes, they went on to provide many other convenient forms including diced, sliced, and french-fry strips. Some were preblanched or parfried. These products are primarily preserved by refrigeration or chilling [28].

Preparation

When harvested potatoes are exposed to light, a green pigmentation may develop on the surface. This greening has occurred even in retail stores, where the potatoes are exposed to artificial light. Unfortunately, greening is accompanied by the formation of solanine, a bitter alkaloid substance that is toxic if consumed in relatively large amounts. Controlled atmosphere storage of potatoes may help to control greening [16]. Green potatoes should be avoided. If potatoes start to turn green before they are used, the green-colored portions should be cut away during preliminary preparation.

Popular methods of preparing fresh potatoes include boiling and baking. Potatoes that are wrapped in aluminum foil before being baked compare favorably in mealiness and flavor with those baked unwrapped [11], but baking time is somewhat increased for the foil-wrapped potatoes and the outside skin is softer.

Potatoes may be cooked very rapidly in the microwave oven, making it a convenient preparation method. Even though trained taste panels have rated microwave-cooked potatoes lower in eating quality than conventionally baked ones, a group of 120 consumers tasting both products in a supermarket found no significant differences in their acceptability [3].

Some potatoes darken after cooking, the degree varying with the variety, the locality and/or soil where grown, the season, and differences in chemical composition. Discoloration apparently results from the formation of a dark-colored complex of **ferric iron** and a polyphenol, probably chlorogenic acid. Addition of a small amount of cream of tartar (about 1 teaspoon per quart of water) to make the cooking environment more acidic appears to retard the development of after-cooking darkening in susceptible varieties.

Ferric iron   iron with a valence of $3+$ (Fe^{3+})

•DRIED LEGUMES

Legumes have been the heart of many traditional cuisines for thousands of years [39]. Although consumption in the United States has been modest (5–7 pounds per capita per year), it appears to be increasing. Many people are now recognizing the healthful benefits of a product that is rich in complex carbohydrate, dietary fiber, and protein, and is low in fat. Legumes are also relatively inexpensive as meat substitutes. They include dried beans, peas, and lentils in many different varieties, varying in color, shape, and size (see Figure 15.5). Table 15.7 lists some types of legumes. In the Northeastern United States, white beans for baking are the most popular. In the West, especially where there are Hispanic populations, pinto beans are preferred. Black-eyed peas, also known as cowpeas, are favored in the South.

Cooking

Legumes require cooking before eating. When they are cooked, proteins are made more available, starch is at least partially gelatinized [14], flavor is improved, and some potentially toxic substances are destroyed. A special problem in cooking is offered by the dry seeds. Water lost in ripening and drying must be replaced by soaking in water and by heating. Because legumes are hard and the cellulose and other fiber components well developed, the legumes must also be softened during the cooking process. The ease of softening depends somewhat on how readily the legumes absorb water.

Alkali in the form of baking soda has been used to hasten the softening of dried beans during cooking. Alkali increases water absorption, but there has been some question concerning the use of baking soda because of its destructive effect on the thiamin content of legumes. Another point of objection to the use of baking soda has been the possibility that the bean texture will become too soft.

TABLE 15.7

Some Varieties of Legumes

Type	Description and Use
Black beans	Sometimes called *black turtle-soup beans;* used in thick soups and in Oriental and Mediterranean dishes
Black-eyed peas	Also called *black-eyed beans* or *cowpeas;* small, oval-shaped, and creamy white with a black spot on one side; used primarily as a main-dish vegetable
Garbanzo beans	Also known as *chick peas;* nut-flavored and commonly pickled in vinegar and oil for salads; may also be used as a main-dish vegetable
Great Northern beans	Larger than but similar to pea beans; used in soups, salads, casserole dishes, and baked beans
Kidney beans	Large, red, and kidney-shaped; popular for chili con carne; used also in salads and many Mexican dishes
Lima beans	Broad, flat, and in different sizes; used as main-dish vegetable and in casseroles
Navy beans	Broad term that includes Great Northern, pea, flat small white, and small white beans
Pea beans	Small, oval, and white; hold shape even when cooked tender; used in baked beans, soups, and casseroles
Pinto beans	Beige-colored and speckled; of the same species as kidney beans and red beans; used in salads, chili, and many Mexican dishes
Red and pink beans	Pink beans more delicate in flavor than red beans; both used in many Mexican dishes and chili
Dry split peas	Specially grown whole peas from which skin is removed and then pea broken in half; used mainly for split pea soup but combine well with many different foods
Lentils	Disk-shaped and about the size of a pea; short cooking time (about thirty minutes); combine well with many different foods

Source: Reference 25.

It is generally not necessary to use baking soda. If it is used, however, the amount of soda needs to be carefully regulated (1/8 teaspoon per pint of water) to prevent deleterious effects insofar as the flavor and appearance of cooked beans are concerned. In these amounts, baking soda can serve as an aid in softening the seed coats if it is necessary to use hard water to cook the beans. Soft water is preferable for both soaking and cooking dry beans, because the calcium and magnesium salts in hard water may form insoluble salts with pectic substances in the cell walls and between cells in the bean tissue and inhibit proper hydration. There is more water absorbed and fewer hard beans remaining at the end of cooking when soft water rather than hard water is used.

The rate of hydration is faster in hot water than at room temperature or by the method of soaking all night in cold water [12]. Dry beans absorb as much water in 1 hour, when soaking is started by first boiling the beans for 2 minutes, as they do in 15 hours of soaking in cold water. If they are hot soaked, as generally recommended, the beans are cooked in the water used for soaking. Additional water is absorbed during the cooking process, making a gain in weight of 150 to 160 percent (about 4 cups of water per cup of dry beans for both soaking and cooking).

Legumes contain appreciable amounts of the oligosaccharides raffinose and stachyose, which are not digested by enzymes in the intestinal tract. It is assumed that the flatulence resulting from the ingestion of legumes results from the degradation of these carbohydrates by intestinal microorganisms. It has been suggested, as a result of one study on the carbohydrate content of various legumes after soaking and cooking, that the soaking and cooking water be discarded to maximize the removal of these gas-forming carbohydrates [61]. Flavor substances would then also be discarded, however.

One constraint limiting the utilization of dried beans is the length of preparation time required. The use of canned beans is convenient and saves time in preparation. A process involving a vacuum treatment in salt solutions before rinsing and drying has been developed to produce quick-cooking beans [45]. The resulting product cooks in less than 15 minutes. This process has not gained broad commercial application, however, partly because of the high energy cost [58]. A number of precooked frozen and dehydrated bean products are available for the institutional market.

•PLANT PROTEINS AND VEGETARIAN DIETS

There are currently an estimated 7 million vegetarians in the United States, and interest in vegetarian diets is growing. Adoption of a vegetarian diet may be motivated by various factors including religious beliefs, ecological concerns, and ethical concerns. The following general classifications of vegetarians have been outlined by the Institute of Food Technologists.

> *Semi-vegetarian*: eats dairy products, eggs, chicken, and fish but no other animal flesh.
> *Pesco-vegetarian*: eats dairy products, eggs, and fish but no other animal flesh.
> *Lacto-ovo-vegetarian*: eats dairy products and eggs but no animal flesh.
> *Lacto-vegetarian*: eats dairy products but no animal flesh or eggs.
> *Ovo-vegetarian*: eats eggs but no dairy products or animal flesh.
> *Vegan*: eats no animal products of any type.

Vegetarian diets are nutritionally adequate when they are appropriately planned. The lesser biological value of most plant proteins in comparison with animal products must be considered in choosing plant foods that will complement each other in essential amino acid content. For example, combining cereal grains that are low in the essential amino acid lysine but supply sufficient methionine with legumes that are lacking in methionine but supply adequate amounts of lysine yields a balanced protein. Vegetarian diets are generally high in dietary fiber and complex carbohydrate and low in fat, resulting in potential health benefits as recommended in the Dietary Guidelines for Americans.

The food industry has responded to the interests of vegetarians in various ways. Meat analogs made from plant proteins are available as canned or frozen entrees; plant protein concentrates are produced from soy, wheat, peanut, glandless cottonseed, and other sources; tofu and wheat gluten are available; and more manufactured foods free of animal fats and milk proteins are being made.

Soybeans

Soybeans are a good source of protein of high biological value and have been used for centuries in various forms as a food staple by millions of people in China and Japan. Soybean products can play an important role in vegetarian diets. Soybeans were first grown in the United States in the 1920s, primarily because of their oil content. They still supply a large share of the vegetable oil used in this country. In the 1950s, processors began making protein products from soy: soy flour, soy protein concentrate, and isolated soy protein. More recently, soy fiber has been produced. Many uses are made of these products in food manufacturing [50]; for example, a number of soy products, such as soy lecithin, are used in emulsifier systems for various processed foods.

In past years, the use of soybeans in the United States has been limited by their objectionable flavor and odor, sometimes characterized as being "painty" or "beany." Much research has gone into the study of this flavor problem, and a number of processes have been developed to control it. The off-flavor appears to be caused by the enzyme **lipoxygenase**, and it is now possible to inactivate the enzyme before it can catalyze any off-flavor.

Soy Protein Products

Soy flour may be made from dehulled soybeans that contain the oil normally present in this product (about 18 percent). However, soy flour is more commonly prepared by grinding soy flakes from which soybean oil has been pressed. When soluble carbohydrates are extracted from defatted soy flour, *soy protein concentrate* is produced. It contains 70 percent or more protein. On further removal of nonprotein substances, *isolated soy proteins* remain. These products contain 90 percent or more protein. The soy products are used for various purposes in food processing.

Texture is given to soy and other high-protein products by special treatments. In one method, the protein isolate is spun into long fibers (shown in Figure 15.13) by a process similar to the spinning of textile fibers. The wet protein mixture is forced through spinnerettes into a coagulating bath. The resulting fibers are gathered into bundles. Spun protein fibrils may be blended with other ingredients, often using egg albumen as a binding agent, and fabricated

Lipoxygenase   an enzyme that catalyzes the oxidation of unsaturated fatty acids

FIGURE 15.13
Meatlike spun protein fiber can be produced from soybean protein and used to fabricate various food products (see also Figure 21.21). (Courtesy of Worthington Foods)

into many different food products. Some of these simulate slices of beef or bacon.

A second method for producing textured vegetable protein involves a process called *extrusion*. In this process, soy flour or protein concentrate is blended with water, flavors, colors, and possibly other additives. The mixture is then fed into a cooking extruder that works the material into a dough. As the dough flows within the channels of an extrusion screw and moves through the small openings of a die, the large protein molecules lose their original structure and form layered masses that crosslink with each other. These masses resist disruption on further heating or processing. The release of pressure as the protein mixture is extruded causes expansion, with tiny air pockets being uniformly dispersed throughout the mass.

Textured soy protein is available to the consumer and can be combined with other foods, such as ground beef. However, consumer demand for the product has not been great. Extruded soy protein is used by food processors in such products as meat patties, tacos, chili, pizza, lasagna, stews, omelets, and stuffed peppers.

Before textured soy products are combined with other foods, they are generally hydrated. Both seasoned and unseasoned forms are available. The USDA has written specifications for textured vegetable protein products that permit their use, on a voluntary basis, in school foodservice and other child-feeding programs. The vegetable protein mixtures are blended in specified amounts up to 30 percent with ground or diced meats in various menu items.

Many acceptable soybean products can be prepared, including canned soybeans with chicken or pork, vegetarian-style soybeans, and soybean soup [40]. A USDA pamphlet [52] gives suggestions for the use of soybeans in family meals.

Tofu, also known as soy cheese or bean curd, has a 2,000-year-old tradition as the protein staple for millions of people throughout the Orient. Now it is rising in popularity with Americans. Made by coagulating **soy milk** with a calcium or magnesium salt and then squeezing out the whey from the curd, tofu is a smooth-textured, bland-flavored, high-moisture product. It is available in different consistencies—silken, soft, firm, and extra firm. The soft, creamy textures blend well with other ingredients, whereas the firmer types can be cubed, sliced, deep fried, and baked. Many interesting dishes can be created with tofu. It can be **marinated** in a soy sauce and spice mixture to give it flavor; used to extend fish and chicken dishes; crumbled in salads; or blended with other ingredients in making salad dressing, dips, and puddings.

Soy milk   the liquid produced by cooking, mashing, and straining soybeans

Marinate   to soak in a prepared liquid for a time, in this case for seasoning purposes

STUDY QUESTIONS

1. What are *vegetables*? (Define them.)
2. List eight classification groups of vegetables based on the parts of the plant that are used as food and give examples of vegetables in each category.
3. The composition and nutritive value of vegetables differ depending on the part of the plant used. Indicate which types of vegetables are generally
   a. high in water content
   b. high in starch
   c. high in protein

d. high in fiber

e. good sources of vitamins A and C

f. low in kilocalories

4. a. List at least three plant polysaccharides that are components of dietary (indigestible) fiber.

    b. Name three pectic substances. What roles do these play in plant structure? Which pectic substance is important in making fruit jellies and jams?

5. The color of fruits and vegetables is due to their content of certain pigments.

    a. List five groups of plant pigments and describe the color for each group.

    b. How do the pigments and/or colors change in the presence of acid and alkali and with prolonged heating?

    c. Explain why it is important to preserve the natural colors of vegetables and fruits during cooking.

6. Flavor varies from one vegetable to another and many substances contribute to the characteristic flavors.

    a. List two different families of vegetables that are considered to be strong flavored and indicate what types of compounds are responsible for these flavors.

    b. Explain how cooking procedures may change these flavors.

7. a. Describe the usual characteristic of fresh vegetables of good quality.

    b. Suggest important factors to consider in purchasing fresh vegetables.

8. Both fresh and processed vegetables and fruits may be graded.

    a. What advantages result from the use of grades on fresh fruits and vegetables?

    b. What factor most limits the use of consumer grades for fresh fruits and vegetables?

    c. List three USDA grades that may be used on canned and frozen vegetables and fruits and discuss the value to the consumer of grading these products.

9. Suggest appropriate methods for the storage of various types of fresh vegetables so that their quality is retained.

10. Describe some advances in biotechnology that can be used to improve vegetable and fruit crops. Give examples.

11. Why is it important to thoroughly cleanse fresh vegetables as a first step in their preparation?

12. Describe several ways in which losses may occur during the cooking of vegetables.

13. In the following list, check the items that describe what may happen when vegetables are cooked and correct any incorrect statements.

    a. Starch swells and gelatinizes.

    b. Cellulose fibers harden.

    c. Volatile flavors are trapped inside the cells.

    d. Leafy vegetables become limp.

    e. Cellulose fibers soften slightly.

    f. Intercellular cement is hardened.

    g. Vitamins go off in the steam.

    h. Some vitamins and minerals dissolve in the cooking water.

    i. Texture becomes softer.

    j. Some vitamins are lost by oxidation.

    k. Some volatile flavors are lost.

    l. Chlorophyll may be changed to anthocyanins.

    m. Carotenes may become white.

    n. Some volatile acids are released.

    o. Pheophytin, an olive green pigment, may be produced from chlorophyll.

    p. Proteins are coagulated.

    q. Pectic substances are hydrolyzed or broken down.

14. Outline an appropriate procedure for boiling each of the following vegetables and explain why you would use the procedure in each case.

a. A green vegetable such as broccoli
b. Cabbage
c. Onions
d. Beets

15. Describe five appropriate methods for cooking vegetables in addition to boiling.

16. Describe an appropriate method for preparing frozen vegetables and canned vegetables.

17. Explain why frozen vegetables require less time for cooking than similar fresh vegetables.

18. a. Describe characteristics of mealy potatoes and waxy potatoes.
    b. For what uses is each type of potato best suited and why?
    c. Compare the probable characteristics of potatoes baked after wrapping in foil, those baked unwrapped, and those baked in a microwave oven.

19. Explain why the green pigmentation that sometimes develops on potatoes exposed to light should not be eaten.

20. a. Outline a satisfactory method for cooking dried beans and explain why this procedure would be appropriate.
    b. List and describe several different legumes.

21. Describe various types of vegetarian diets.

22. a. What flavor problem has limited the use of soybeans in the United States in past years? How has it been solved?
    b. Describe several soy products that are available for use in manufactured foods.
    c. Describe two methods by which plant proteins may be texturized. Give examples of the use of these products in food processing and preparation.
    d. What is *tofu* and how might it be used in food preparation?

REFERENCES

1. Augustin, J., R. E. McDole, G. M. McMaster, C. G. Painter, and W. C. Sparks. 1975. Ascorbic acid content in russet Burbank potatoes. *Journal of Food Science 40*, 415.

2. Bowman, F., E. Page, E. E. Remmenga, and D. Trump. 1971. Microwave vs. conventional cooking of vegetables at high altitude. *Journal of the American Dietetic Association 58*, 427.

3. Brittin, H. C., and J. E. Trevino. 1980. Acceptability of microwave and conventionally baked potatoes. *Journal of Food Science 45*, 1425.

4. Campbell, C. L., T. Y. Lin, and B. E. Proctor. 1958. Microwave vs. conventional cooking. I. Reduced and total ascorbic acid in vegetables. *Journal of the American Dietetic Association 34*, 365.

5. Caragay, A. B. 1992. Cancer-preventive foods and ingredients. *Food Technology 46*, 65 (No. 4).

6. Carlson, B. L., and M. H. Tabacchi. 1988. Loss of vitamin C in vegetables during the foodservice cycle. *Journal of the American Dietetic Association 88*, 65.

7. Chapman, V. J., J. O. Putz, G. L. Gilpin, J. P. Sweeney, and J. N. Eisen. 1960. Electronic cooking of fresh and frozen broccoli. *Journal of Home Economics 52*, 161.

8. Charles, V. R., and F. O. van Duyne. 1958. Effect of holding and reheating on the ascorbic acid content of cooked vegetables. *Journal of Home Economics 50*, 159.

9. Charles, V. R., and F. O. van Duyne. 1954. Palatability and retention of ascorbic acid of vegetables cooked in a tightly covered saucepan and in a "waterless" cooker. *Journal of Home Economics 46*, 659.

10. *Composition of Foods*, rev. 1963. Agriculture Handbook No. 8, Washington, DC: Agricultural Research Service, U.S. Department of Agriculture.

11. Cunningham, H. H., and M. V. Zaehringer. 1972. Quality of baked potatoes as influenced by baking and holding methods. *American Potato Journal 49*, 271.

12. Dawson, E. H., J. C. Lamb, E. W. Toepfer, and H. W. Warren. 1952. *Development of Rapid Methods of Soaking and Cooking Dry Beans*. Technical Bulletin No. 1051. Washington, DC: U.S. Department of Agriculture.

13. Eheart, M. S., and D. Odland. 1972. Storage of fresh broccoli and green beans. *Journal of the American Dietetic Association 60*, 402.

14. Elbert, E. M., and R. L. Witt. 1968. Gelatinization of starch in the common dry bean, *Phaseolus vulgaris. Journal of Home Economics 60*, 186.

15. Fordham, J. R., C. E. Wells, and L. H. Chen. 1975. Sprouting of seeds and nutrient composition of seeds and sprouts. *Journal of Food Science 40*, 552.

16. Forsyth, F. R., and C. A. Eaves. 1968. Greening of potatoes: CA cure. *Food Technology 22*, 48.

17. Gnanasekharan, V., R. L. Shewfelt, and M. S. Chinnan. 1992. Detection of color changes in green vegetables. *Journal of Food Science 57*, 149.

18. Gordon, J., and I. Noble. 1964. "Waterless" vs. boiling water cooking of vegetables. *Journal of the American Dietetic Association 44*, 378.

19. Guthrie, J. F., C. Zizza, and N. Raper. 1992. Fruit and vegetables: Their importance in the American diet. *Food Review 15*, 35 (No. 1).

20. Harlander, S. K. 1991. Biotechnology: A means for improving our food supply. *Food Technology 45*, 84 (No. 4).

21. Harlander, S. K. 1991. Social, moral, and ethical issues in food biotechnology. *Food Technology 45*, 152 (No. 5).

22. Herranz, J., C. Vidal-Valverde, and E. Rojas-Hidalgo. 1983. Cellulose, hemicellulose and lignin content of raw and cooked processed vegetables. *Journal of Food Science 48*, 274.

23. Herranz, J., C. Vidal-Valverde, and E. Rojas-Hidalgo. 1981. Cellulose, hemicellulose and lignin content of raw and cooked Spanish vegetables. *Journal of Food Science 46*, 1927.

24. Hinman, W. F., M. K. Brush, and E. G. Halliday. 1945. The nutritive value of canned foods. VII. Effect of small-scale preparation on the ascorbic acid, thiamine, and riboflavin content of commercially canned vegetables. *Journal of the American Dietetic Association 21*, 7.

25. *How to Buy Dry Beans, Peas, and Lentils*. 1970. Home and Garden Bulletin No. 177. Washington, DC: Consumer and Marketing Service, U.S. Department of Agriculture.

26. *How to Buy Fresh Vegetables*. 1980. Home and Garden Bulletin No. 143. Washington, DC: Consumer and Marketing Service, U.S. Department of Agriculture.

27. Hudson, D. E., A. A. Dalal, and P. A. Lachance. 1985. Retention of vitamins in fresh and frozen broccoli prepared by different cooking methods. *Journal of Food Quality 8*, 45.

28. Huxsoll, C. C., and H. R. Bolin. 1989. Processing and distribution alternatives for minimally processed fruits and vegetables. *Food Technology 43*, 124 (No. 2).

29. Institute of Food Technologists' Expert Panel on Food Safety and Nutrition. 1989. Dietary fiber. *Food Technology 43*, 133 (No. 10).

30. Institute of Food Technologists' Expert Panel on Food Safety and Nutrition. 1990. Quality of fruits and vegetables. *Food Technology 44*, 99 (No. 6).

31. Ingenthron, G. D. 1991. Genetically improved food crops. *Food Technology 45*, 110 (No. 4).

32. Klein, B. P., C. H. Y. Kuo, and G. Boyd. 1981. Folacin and ascorbic acid retention in fresh raw, microwave, and conventionally cooked spinach. *Journal of Food Science 46*, 640.

33. Lazan, H., Z. M. Ali, A. Mohd, and F. Nahar. 1987. Water stress and quality during storage of tropical leafy vegetables. *Journal of Food Science 52*, 1286.

34. Liener, I. 1979. Significance for humans of biologically active factors in soybeans and other food legumes. *Journal of the American Oil Chemists' Society 56*, 121.

35. MacLeod, A. J., and G. MacLeod. 1970. The flavor volatiles of dehydrated cabbage. *Journal of Food Science 35*, 739.

36. MacLeod, A. J., and G. MacLeod. 1970. Effects of variations in cooking methods on the flavor volatiles of cabbage. *Journal of Food Science 35*, 744.

37. Maga, J. A., and J. A. Twomey. 1977. Sensory comparison of four potato varieties baked conventionally and by microwaves. *Journal of Food Science 42*, 541.

38. Matthee, V., and H. Appledorf. 1978. Effect of cooking on vegetable fiber. *Journal of Food Science 43*, 1344.

39. Morrow, B. 1991. The rebirth of legumes. *Food Technology 45*, 96 (No. 9).

40. Nelson, A. I., L. S. Wei, and M. P. Steinberg. 1971. Food products from whole soybeans. *Soybean Digest* (January).

41. Noble I. 1967. Ascorbic acid and color of vegetables. *Journal of the American Dietetic Association 50*, 304.

42. Nonaka, M., R. N. Sayre, and K. C. Ng. 1978. Surface texturization of extruded and preformed potato products by a three-step, dry-steam-dry process. *Journal of Food Science 43*, 904.

43. Nonaka, M., and M. L. Weaver. 1973. Texturizing process improves quality of baked French fried potatoes. *Food Technology 27*, 50 (No. 3).

44. Pariza, M. W. 1992. Foods of new biotechnology vs traditional products: Microbiological aspects. *Food Technology 46*, 100 (No. 3).

45. Rockland, L. B., and E. A. Metzler. 1967. Quick-cooking lima and other dry beans. *Food Technology 21*, 334.

46. Ronk, R. J., K. L. Carson, and P. Thompson. 1989. Processing, packaging, and regulation of minimally processed fruits and vegetables. *Food Technology 43*, 136 (No. 2).

47. Schwartz, S. J., and J. H. Von Elbe. 1983. Kinetics of chlorophyll degradation to pyropheophytin in vegetables. *Journal of Food Science 48*, 1303.

48. Singh, B., C. C. Yang, D. K. Salunkhe, and A. R. Rahman. 1972. Controlled atmosphere storage of lettuce. 1. Effects on quality and the respiration rate of lettuce heads. *Journal of Food Science 37*, 48.

49. Singh, R. P., R. H. Buelow, and D. B. Lund. 1973. Storage behavior of artificially waxed green snap beans. *Journal of Food Science 38*, 542.

50. Slavin, J. 1991. Nutritional benefits of soy protein and soy fiber. *Journal of the American Dietetic Association 91*, 816.

51. Snyder, P. O., and M. E. Matthews. 1983. Percent retention of vitamin C in whipped potatoes after pre-service holding. *Journal of the American Dietetic Association 83*, 454.

52. *Soybeans in Family Meals*. 1982. Home and Garden Bulletin No. 208. Washington, DC: U.S. Department of Agriculture.

53. Stone, M. B., and C. M. Young. 1985. Effects of cultivars, blanching techniques, and cooking methods on quality of frozen green beans as measured by physical and sensory attributes. *Journal of Food Quality 7*, 255.

54. Sweeney, J. P. 1970. Improved chlorophyll retention in green beans held on a steam table. *Food Technology 24*, 490.

55. Sweeney, J. P., G. L. Gilpin, M. E. Martin, and E. H. Dawson. 1960. Palatability and nutritive value of frozen broccoli. *Journal of the American Dietetic Association 36*, 122.

56. Sweeney, J. P., G. L. Gilpin, M. G. Staley, and M. E. Martin. 1959. Effect of cooking methods on broccoli. I. Ascorbic acid and carotene. *Journal of the American Dietetic Association 35*, 354.

57. *The Buying Guide for Fresh Fruits, Vegetables, Herbs, and Nuts*, 8th rev. ed. 1986. Shepherdstown, WV: Blue Goose Growers, Inc.

58. Uebersax, M. A., S. Ruengsakulrach, and L. G. Occena. 1991. Strategies and procedures for processing dry beans. *Food Technology 45*, 104 (No. 9).

59. Van Buren, J. P., and L. A. Pitifer. 1992. Retarding vegetable softening by cold alkaline pectin deesterification before cooking. *Journal of Food Science 57*, 1022.

60. *Vegetables in Family Meals*. 1980. Home and Garden Bulletin No. 105. Washington, DC: U.S. Department of Agriculture.

61. Vidal-Valverde, C., J. Frias, and S. Valverde. 1993. Changes in the carbohydrate composition of legumes after soaking and cooking. *Journal of the American Dietetic Association 93*, 547.

62. Von Elbe, J. H., I. Maing, and C. H. Amundson. 1974. Color stability of betanin. *Journal of Food Science 39*, 334.

63. Watada, A. E., K. Abe, and N. Yamuchi. 1990. Physiological activities of partially processed fruits and vegetables. *Food Technology 44*, 116 (No. 5).

64. Zyren, J., E. R. Elkins, J. A. Dudek, and R. E. Hagen. 1983. Fiber contents of selected raw and processed vegetables, fruits and fruit juices as served. *Journal of Food Science 48*, 600.

Fruits and Fruit Preparation

16

•DEFINITION AND CLASSIFICATION

What are fruits? To answer this question, we might begin by saying that all fruits are produced from flowers and are the ripened **ovaries** and adjacent tissues of plants. In this respect, from a botanical point of view, some foods used as vegetables, nuts, or grains are fruits of the plants from which they were harvested. However, the foods usually designated and used as fruits in food preparation have some common characteristics in addition to the botanical similarity—they are fleshy or pulpy, often juicy, and usually sweet, with fragrant, aromatic flavors.

Thus, the definition of fruits according to botanical characteristics does not always agree with the classification of common usage. Several fleshy botanical fruits, including tomatoes and squash, are not sweet and are used as vegetables. Cereal grains, nuts, and legumes are dry (not fleshy) fruits and have been classified into separate groups for practical use. Rhubarb, which is not a fruit in the botanical sense, is often used as a fruit in meal preparation.

Fleshy fruits may be classified as simple, aggregate, or multiple, depending on the number of ovaries and flowers from which the fruit develops. Examples of simple fleshy fruits, which develop from a single ovary in one flower, are citrus fruits, such as oranges (Figure 16.1), grapefruit, lemons, and limes; drupes, such as apricots, cherries, peaches, and plums, in which a stone or pit encloses the seed; and pomes, such as apples and pears, which have a core. Examples of aggregate fruits, which develop from several ovaries in one flower, are raspberries, strawberries, and blackberries. Pineapple is an example of a multiple fruit that has developed from a cluster of several flowers.

•COMPOSITION AND NUTRITIVE VALUE

Most fruits comprise an edible portion combined with some refuse. The refuse or waste may be as high as 33 to 39 percent in certain fruits, such as banana and pineapple. The chief energy nutrient present is carbohydrate, which occurs mainly as sugars. Most fruits have only a trace of fat; two exceptions are coconut (35 percent) and avocado (17 percent). Only a very small amount of protein is

Ovary   part of the seed-bearing organ of a flower; an enlarged hollow part containing ovules that develop into seeds

FIGURE 16.1

A cross section of an orange shows the various parts of the fruit. (Reprinted from Matthews, R. F. and R. J. Braddock. Recovery and applications of essential oils from oranges. *Food Technology*, Vol. 41, No. 1, p. 57. 1987. Copyright© by Institute of Food Technologists.)

Schematic cross-section of an orange

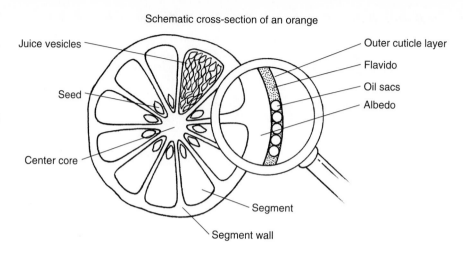

found in fruits, and their water content averages about 85 percent. From a nutritional standpoint, fruits, as well as vegetables, are valuable chiefly for their vitamin and mineral content and for their indigestible dietary fiber or bulk.

Whole fresh fruits provide the most fiber. For example, a whole apple, with peel, has two grams of fiber. One-half cup of applesauce provides 0.65 gram of fiber, and three-fourths cup of apple juice supplies only 0.25 gram of fiber [21]. The caloric value of fruits, as served, is usually higher than that of **succulent** vegetables because of fruits' higher sugar content [24].

Succulent having juicy tissues; not dry

Certain fruits are especially valuable sources of vitamin C (Figure 16.2), whereas others contain only small amounts of this vitamin. The most dependable year-round source of vitamin C is probably citrus fruits. Tomatoes, although they contain only about half as much, are a significant source of vita-

FIGURE 16.2

Excellent sources of vitamin C include fresh strawberries, citrus fruits, and cantaloupe. Fresh blackberries also contain appreciable amounts of vitamin C. Combined with cottage cheese, fresh fruits make an appetizing fruit salad. (Courtesy of Sunkist Growers, Inc.)

min C because of their wide use. In season, strawberries and cantaloupe make significant contributions. A generous serving of strawberries may easily provide the recommended daily allowance of vitamin C for an adult. So long as strawberries are not bruised or hulled, they retain vitamin C well. Slicing strawberries rather than crushing them in preparation for certain uses decreases loss of vitamin C.

When cantaloupe are at their optimum ripeness for fine flavor they have the greatest concentration of vitamin C, and the soft center flesh is richer in the vitamin than the harder, firmer flesh near the rind. Honeydew melons rate lower than cantaloupes, and watermelon is a comparatively poor source of vitamin C. The guava is extremely rich in vitamin C, containing an average of 242 milligrams per 100-gram portion of edible fruit.

Yellow fruits contain carotenoid pigments that are precursors of vitamin A. Pink varieties of grapefruit have higher vitamin A value than white varieties. The B vitamins occur in relatively low concentration in fruits. Fruits vary widely in their vitamin content. Variety, growing climate and sunlight, and stage of maturity have been shown to be significant factors. In addition, handling practices, methods of processing, storage temperatures, and length of storage of fruits may produce a decrease of as much as 50 percent in some vitamin values. The composition and vitamin content of some selected fruits and fruit juices are given in Appendix C.

Plants tend to concentrate calcium and iron in leaves and phosphorus in seeds. Fruits are therefore not generally considered excellent sources of these minerals. However, blackberries, raspberries, strawberries, dried apricots, prunes, dates, and figs may contribute appreciable amounts of iron to the diet. Of the fruits available year-round, only oranges, grapefruit, and figs are fair sources of calcium.

As with vegetables, fruit consumption is increasing, partly because many people eat fresh fruits as snacks. Survey data have indicated that 43 percent of those surveyed ate fresh fruit most often as a snack. The most popular snack fruits were bananas, apples, and seedless grapes [21]. Other factors responsible for increased consumption include the availability of high-quality products, higher disposable personal income, the desire of many health-conscious Americans to improve their diets, and improved food distribution systems [18].

•COLOR

The pigments that give fruits their characteristic colors are the same as those in vegetables. In fruits, the predominant pigments are the yellow-orange carotenoids and the red-blue anthocyanins. Enzymatic oxidative discoloration is also similar for fruits and vegetables. Chapter 15 provides a discussion of these topics.

Mixing various colored fruit juices may sometimes produce surprising, often unattractive results. The tin or iron salts present in canned juices can explain some of the reactions that occur: the metals combine with the anthocyanin pigments to produce violet or blue-green colors. Pineapple juice contains a small amount of iron from the equipment used in its processing and, when added to red or purple fruit juices, changes their color to blue or intensifies the original blue color. Usually, acid in the form of lemon juice intensifies the red color of red or blue fruit juice mixtures. Orange juice is best omitted from combinations of red or blue fruit juices since it often produces a brownish color when it is present in a fairly large quantity.

The color of canned fruits containing anthocyanin pigments tends to deteriorate on storage whether the container is tin or glass. This deterioration is greater in the presence of light and warm temperatures.

•FLAVOR

The flavor of each fruit is characteristic of that fruit. For example, a raw ripe banana is readily identified by its odor and taste, which result from a specific combination of flavor components. The flavor of fruits, in general, may be described as tart, fragrant, and sweet, these characteristics blending together in a pleasant and refreshing flavor bouquet.

Aspartame, a high-intensity sweetener gaining widespread use, appears to enhance the fruitiness of natural fruit-flavored systems such as orange and strawberry. The addition of sucrose or table sugar does not produce a similar enhancement of fruit flavor [25].

Aromatic Compounds

Aromatic compounds   compounds that have an aroma or odor

Ester   a type of chemical compound that results from combination of an organic acid (-COOH) with an alcohol (-OH)

Fruits owe their characteristic flavors largely to certain **aromatic compounds** that are present. Many of these compounds are **esters**, such as methyl butyrate, which is responsible for the typical odor and flavor of pineapple. Other compounds include aldehydes, such as benzaldehyde derivatives, and various alcohols, which have been found to be responsible for the floral and fruity part of the aroma of apricots [5]. Many different compounds contribute to flavor; at least 32 flavor substances have been identified in the aroma of apricots and 37 components in extracted orange essence [15]. In loquat fruit, a tropical or subtropical fruit with a flavor described as being mild, subacid, and applelike, researchers have identified 80 aroma substances. Benzaldehyde was a major aroma compound [10]. Some of the fruit flavor compounds can be synthesized in the laboratory, thus aiding in the development of better artificial flavorings.

Acids

Organic acid   an acid containing carbon atoms, for example, citric acid and acetic acid

Salt   a chemical compound derived from an acid by replacement of the hydrogen (H+), wholly or in part, with a metal or an electrically positive ion, for example, sodium citrate

Organic acids, occurring in fruits in the free form or combined as **salts** or esters, also contribute to flavor. Malic and critic acids are most commonly present, but tartaric acid is a prominent constituent of grapes. Although mixtures of acids may occur, one component usually predominates in each fruit. Fruits of the plum family and cranberries contain some benzoic acid that cannot be used by the body but is excreted as hippuric acid. Rhubarb contains variable amounts of oxalic acid, depending on the maturity of the plant. Oxalic acid usually combines with calcium in the plant to form insoluble calcium oxalate, which is not absorbed from the digestive tract. Fruits vary in acidity, and some of this variation depends on variety and growing conditions. Scores for flavor have been positively correlated with pH in fruits such as peaches and raspberries [22].

Essential Oils

Some fruits, as well as other plants, contain essential oils. Oil of lemon and oil of orange, well-known examples of such oils, occur in the leathery skin of the fruit (see Figure 16.1). They may be expressed and used as flavoring or as the basis of extracts, which are made by combining the oil with alcohol.

Other Components

Sugars, some mineral salts, and a group of **phenolic compounds** (at one time called *tannins*) contribute to fruit flavor. Fruits cooked in metal containers may form some acid salts with the metals. Tin or iron salts in canned fruits may sometimes produce a metallic flavor, but these salts are not harmful. Phenolic compounds impart a bitter taste and produce an astringent or puckery feeling in the mouth. They appear to be present in the largest amount in immature fruits.

•CHANGES DURING RIPENING

Distinct changes occur in fruits during ripening: (1) a decrease in green color and development of yellow-orange or red-blue colors, (2) a softening of the flesh, (3) the development of characteristic pleasant flavors, and (4) changes in soluble solids such as sugars and organic acids. The change in color is associated with both synthesis of new pigments and breakdown of the green pigment chlorophyll. Chlorophyll may mask yellow carotenoid pigments in the immature fruit. Anthocyanins are probably synthesized as ripening proceeds.

Involved in the softening of fruits are the pectic substances, the complex insoluble protopectin being degraded to pectin, which is also called *pectinic acid*. Gel-forming properties are characteristic of pectin, making it important in the preparation of jams and jellies. Further softening in ripening fruit produces pectic acid from pectin, with a consequent loss of gelling ability. The breakdown of pectic substances found between plant cells may cause separation of cells as part of the softening process. Many fruits soften faster when the temperature of the surrounding air is increased [4].

The development of a characteristic pleasant flavor in ripened fruit involves a decrease in acidity and an increase in sugar, along with the production of a complex mixture of volatile substances and essential oils. In some fruits, such as bananas, the increase in sugar is accompanied by a decrease in starch; however, sugar content increases even in such fruits as peaches, which contain no appreciable amount of starch at any time. Some cell wall polysaccharides may decrease as the sugar content increases. In addition, the phenolic compounds, with their astringent properties, seem to decrease.

Ethylene gas is usually produced in small amounts in the fruit during maturation and causes some physiological changes associated with the ripening process. Fruits that have been harvested well before ripening has started may be stored in an atmosphere that contains ethylene gas to speed up the ripening process. In general, there is no material difference in the gross composition (protein, fat, and carbohydrate) of fruits that ripen naturally and those that ripen by ethylene gas.

Phenolic compound an organic compound that includes in its chemical structure an unsaturated ring with -OH groups on it; polyphenols have more than one -OH group

Ethylene a small gaseous molecule (C_2H_4) produced by fruits and vegetables as an initiator of the ripening process

Ethylene production is stimulated when plant tissues are injured. Preparation of lightly processed fruits and vegetables for institutional use involves peeling, slicing, and cutting, which injure tissues and induce ethylene production. When these products are placed in sealed containers, the ethylene accumulates and accelerates undesirable changes in quality such as a decrease in firmness and loss of the pigment chlorophyll. It has been reported that when an absorbent for the ethylene gas (charcoal with palladium chloride) was placed in a small paper packet and enclosed in the package containing the processed fruit, the accumulation of ethylene was deterred, thereby preventing the softening of fruits such as kiwifruits and bananas [1].

Ripeness and the method of ripening may influence the vitamin content of fruits. For example, the vitamin C content of bananas is greatest in fully ripe fruits, although the total amount present is relatively small. Also, vine-ripened tomatoes have a higher vitamin C value than tomatoes picked green and ripened off the vine.

•SELECTION OF FRESH FRUITS

An abundance of fresh fruits is available in U.S. markets year-round. In making selections from a wide variety, the consumer should look for signs of good quality, which are generally evident from the external appearance of the product. These signs include the proper stage of ripeness, good color, freedom from insect damage, and the absence of bruises, skin punctures, and decay. The grading of fruits, which may be useful to the consumer in making selections, is discussed along with the grading of vegetables in Chapter 15. Generally, quality is usually best and prices lowest when fruit is in season in nearby areas. Table 16.1 summarizes some points to consider in selecting various fruits.

Apples

Apples are among the most widely used fruits. They rank third in world fruit production, behind grapes and bananas [21]. Apples are found locally in most parts of the United States in many varieties that differ in characteristics and seasonal availability. Controlled atmosphere storage (discussed later in this chapter) has lengthened their seasons of availability. Of the 2,000 or more different varieties of apples grown in the United States, only about 20 are commonly marketed.

Apples have many culinary uses. They may be served fresh in salads or as desserts and cooked in sauces, pies, and cobblers. Varieties differ in their suitability for being cooked or eaten fresh. Table 16.2 gives some suggestions for use, and Plate I pictures several different varieties of apples.

Avocados

The bland flavor and smooth texture of avocados blend well with many food combinations. Avocados are unique fruits in that they contain about 17 percent fat. Many varieties are grown in both California and Florida, and avocados are available all year. They may be purchased slightly underripe and ripened at

TABLE 16.1
Selection of Fresh Fruits

	Quality Characteristics to Look For
Fruit	
Apple	Firm, crisp, well colored; mature when picked; varieties vary widely in eating and cooking characteristics (see Table 16.2)
Apricot	Plump, firm, golden yellow; yield to gentle skin pressure when ripe
Avocado	Shape and size vary with variety; may have rough or smooth skin but no dark, sunken spots; yield to gentle skin pressure when ripened and ready for use
Banana	Shipped green and ripened as needed at 16° to 20°C (60° to 68°F); refrigerate only after ripened; firm, yellow, free from bruises
Blueberry	Dark blue, silvery bloom, plump, firm, uniform size
Cherry	Very delicate; handle carefully; fresh, firm, juicy, well matured, well colored
Citrus	Firm, well shaped, heavy for size, reasonably smooth-textured skin
Cranberry	Plump, firm, lustrous color
Grape	Well colored, plump, firmly attached to stem
Guava	Skin color green to yellow, depending on variety; flesh white to deep pink; round, firm but yielding to slight pressure when ripe
Kiwifruit	Chinese gooseberry renamed kiwifruit; light brown, furry, tender soft skin
Mango	Vary in size and shape; yellowish; firm, smooth skin; ripen at room temperature until yields to slight pressure; soft, aromatic flesh
Nectarine	Plump, rich color, slight softening along "seam," well matured
Papaya	Well shaped; well colored, at least half yellow and not green; smooth, unbruised
Peach	Fairly firm, yellow between red areas, plump, well shaped, "peachy" fragrance
Pear	Firm, well shaped, color appropriate for variety
Pineapple	Well shaped, heavy in relation to size; bright color, fragrant odor, slight separation of eyes
Plum	Fairly firm to slightly soft; good color for variety; smooth skin
Pomegranates	Unbroken, hard rind covering many seeds; varies in color from yellow to deep red; heavy for size; large sizes juicier; only seeds are edible
Strawberry	Full red color, bright luster, firm flesh, cap stem attached, dry, clean
Variety Fruits	
Atemoya	Small, green, rough skinned; creamy, soft, sweet pulp; large black seeds
Breadfruit	Oval or round, 2–15 pounds; yellowish-green rind with rough surface; white to yellow fibrous pulp; important food in South Sea Islands
Carambola (star fruit)	Waxy, yellow; five fluted sides; tart, sweet-sour flavor
Cherimoya (custard apple)	Almost heart-shaped; uniform green when ripe; no mold or cracks at stem end; fresh pineapple–strawberry–banana flavor
Passion fruit (granadilla)	Size and shape of an egg; tough, purple skin; yellowish meat with many black seeds
Kumquat	Small, football-shaped, yellow, firm; sweet skin and tart flesh
Loquat	Small, round or oval; pale yellow or orange; somewhat downy surface; thin skin; firm, mealy flesh
Persimmon	Bright orange; Hachiya variety slightly pointed and soft when ripe; Fuyu variety more firm when eaten (like an apple); smooth, rich taste
Plantain	Greenish looking bananas with rough skins and blemishes; frequently used as a vegetable; never eaten raw
Ugli fruit	About the size of a grapefruit; spherical; extremely rough peel, badly disfigured, with light green blemishes that turn orange when fruit is mature; very juicy with orangelike flavor

Source: Reference 23.

TABLE 16.2

Desirability of Apple Varieties for Different Uses

Variety	Flavor and Texture	Fresh and in Salads	Pies	Sauces	Baking	Freezing (Slices)	Main Season
Cortland	Mild, tender	Excellent	Excellent	Very good	Good	Very good	Oct. to Jan.
Red Delicious	Sweet, mellow	Excellent	Poor	Fair	Poor	Fair	Sept. to May
Golden Delicious	Sweet, semifirm	Excellent	Very good	Good	Very good	Very good	Sept. to Apr.
Gravenstein	Tart, crisp	Good	Good	Good	Good	Good	July to Sept.
R. I. Greening	Slightly tart, firm	Poor	Excellent	Excellent	Very good	Excellent	Oct. to Mar.
Jonathan	Tart, tender	Very good	Very good	Very good	Poor	Very good	Sept. to Jan.
McIntosh	Slightly tart, tender	Excellent	Excellent	Good	Fair	Good	Sept. to Apr.
Rome Beauty	Slightly tart, firm	Good	Very good	Very good	Excellent	Very good	Oct. to Apr.
Stayman	Tart, semifirm	Excellent	Good	Good	Good	Good	Oct. to Mar.
Winesap	Slightly tart, firm	Excellent	Good	Good	Good	Very good	Oct. to June
Yellow Transparent	Tart, soft	Poor	Excellent	Good	Poor	Poor	July to Aug.
York Imperial	Tart, firm	Fair	Good	Very good	Good	Good	Oct. to May

Source: Reference 23.

room temperature, preferably in a dark place. When ready for use they should yield to gentle pressure on the skin. Avocados should be refrigerated only after ripening. Figure 16.3 provides suggestions for avocado preparation.

Bananas

Banana plants grow in tropical areas and bananas of many different varieties are produced. As the plant blooms, a cluster of tiny blossoms emerges, each blossom producing one banana. The fruits grow together on a stem of about 300 bananas. After harvest, the stem is divided into hands, each of which contains 10 to 12 individual bananas. Bananas are picked green and ripen best after harvesting. As they ripen, the skin gradually turns yellow.

Bananas rank second in world fruit production but are first in fruit sales in the United States. They are generally available year-round. Until they are fully ripe, they should be kept at room temperature. When the skin is green-tipped, bananas are best for cooking—baking or broiling. Fully yellow bananas are good for eating or using in salads and desserts. Brown-speckled skins indicate very ripe fruit that is excellent for mashing and use in baked products.

Citrus Fruits

Oranges, lemons, grapefruit, limes, tangerines, kumquats, and tangelos, which are a cross between a tangerine and a grapefruit, are included in the citrus fruit classification. The chief producing areas of these fruits in the United States are Florida, California, Texas, and Arizona. Citrus fruits are a most valuable and reli-

Halve the avocado.

Twist the halves apart.

Remove the seed by striking it with a knife.

Peel off the skin and cut balls, crescents, cubes, or slices.

FIGURE 16.3
Preparation of avocados. (Courtesy of Calavo)

able source of vitamin C in the diet and are also noted for the tart and appetizing flavor they contribute to fruit desserts and salads.

In addition to being graded, citrus fruits can be classified on the basis of size, depending on the quantity of fruit required to fill certain standard-sized containers. Cartons holding 35 to 38 pounds are often used. Large oranges may be 56 count (56 oranges per carton); medium oranges may be 88 count; and small oranges may be 113 or even 138 count. Large oranges are usually about 4⅜ inches in diameter, medium ones about 3½ inches, and small ones about 2½ inches.

Except for making juice, large oranges are generally preferred by consumers over small ones. The most common criticisms of large oranges are excessive waste from thick skins and excessive expense. Large fruit is often classed as fancy fruit and its price may increase at a faster rate than does the edible portion. For juice extraction, small sizes or ungraded stock may be most economical. Generally, the juice from small oranges is higher in total solids, acid, and vitamin C than that of medium-sized fruit and higher still than that of large fruit. In the purchase of citrus fruits, it should be noted that fruits that are relatively thin skinned, firm, and heavy in relation to size usually contain more juice than thicker-skinned and lighter-weight products. Russeting, which is a tan, brown, or blackish mottling or speckling on the skin of some Florida and Texas oranges and grapefruit, has no effect on eating quality.

Two principal market varieties of oranges are the Valencia and the navel. For juice extraction, the Valencia orange is often preferable, whereas for slicing or sectioning, the navel orange may be more satisfactory. The navel orange is distinguished by the formation of a navel at the apex or blossom end of the fruit. This formation appears to be a tiny orange within a larger one. The navel orange is available from California and Arizona from November until early May and has no seeds, less juice and a thicker, somewhat more pebbled skin than the Valencia, a skin that is easily removed by hand, and segments that separate easily. The western Valencia is available from late April through October. Florida and Texas oranges are marketed from early October until late June and include several varieties, with the Valencias being marketed from late March through June. All Valencias have seeds, but the California Valencia has only a few. Most of the Florida Valencias have yellow skins, much juice, and light-colored juice and pulp. Valencia oranges have a tendency late in the season to turn from a bright orange to greenish tinged, particularly around the stem end. This change in color affects only the outer skin. The oranges are matured and fully ripe inside. Some oranges are artificially colored to improve their external appearance.

Some varieties of grapefruit are classed as seedless, though they often contain a few seeds, and some as seeded. Some grapefruit varieties have white flesh, whereas others have pink or red flesh. Although Florida is the main producer of grapefruit, it is also supplied by Texas, California, and Arizona. Grapefruit is available all year but is most abundant from January through May.

Grapes

Grapes are the leading fruit crop in the world and the number-two crop in the United States. However, over half of the grapes grown in the U.S. are used to make wine [21]. European types of grapes, which are firm fleshed and very sweet, include the Thompson seedless (an early green grape), the Tokay and Cardinal (early, bright red grapes), and the Emperor (late, deep red grape). American types of grapes have softer flesh and are very juicy. The blue-black Concord variety is one commonly marketed and is unexcelled for juice and jelly making.

Melons

Melons (Figure 16.4) are among the most difficult of fruits to select. No absolute guide for selection is available, but desirability is indicated by such qualities as ripeness, heaviness in relation to size, usually a characteristic aroma, characteristic color, and freedom from abnormal shape, decay, and disease. The ripeness of some melons, such as honeydew, crenshaw, casaba, and cantaloupe, is indicated by color and by a slight yielding to thumb pressure on the bud end or on the surface. If the melon was mature when picked, it usually shows a round dent where the stem broke away from the melon.

Most cantaloupes are firm and not completely ripe when first displayed in markets. Holding them a few days at room temperature allows the completion of ripening. The color of uncut watermelons is probably the best key to ripeness. A yellowish underside, regardless of the green color of the rest of the melon, is a good sign. Other guides in selection might be a relatively smooth surface, a slight dullness to the rind, and ends of the melon that are filled out and rounded. In cut melons, desirable characteristics include firm, juicy flesh with a good red color, dark brown or black seeds, and no white streaks.

Peaches

The peach is the third most purchased fruit in the United States, behind bananas and apples. Although peaches and nectarines are similar, they each are distinct fruits. Nectarines do not have the fuzzy coat of peaches. Both fruits originated in Asia thousands of years ago.

An important factor in peach quality is the stage of maturity at harvest. Peaches will ripen off the tree. Once picked, they are immediately dipped in ice water to remove the field heat and stop the ripening process. Then they are stored at 1° to 5°C (34° to 40°F) to keep ripening at a minimum and retard decay. If peaches are picked too soon, they will never ripen after cold storage and they lack flavor [20].

The best quality peaches have a good yellow undercover and yield slightly to finger pressure. The appearance of a peach does not always indicate the flavor, however, although our marketing system is such that appearance is of prime importance [20]. Peaches should be eaten at optimum ripeness. It may be necessary to keep them at room temperature in a paper bag until this stage is reached.

Pineapple

The pineapple plant bears its first fruit 18 to 22 months after planting. Each plant produces a single four-to-five-pound fruit. The fruit is harvested when the appropriate stage of sweetness is reached. The optimum flavor is a balance

FIGURE 16.4

A Persian melon half is filled with grapes and is larger than the cantaloupe just behind it. The casaba, directly to the left of the cantaloupe, has a globular shape with a pointed stem. The gold-with-a-green-flecked rind and oblong shape of the Santa Claus or Christmas melon can be seen directly behind the cantaloupe. Honeydew melon, a sweet, mildly scented fruit, is pictured on the elevated plate, and a crisp quarter of a watermelon is shown at the back of the group. (Courtesy of Western Growers Association)

between sweet and tart. The sweetest flavor and brightest yellow color are found at the base of the pineapple fruit.

A ripe pineapple has a rich fragrance. It springs back slightly when touched. Color may vary from green through brown to gold and is not an indication of ripeness. A hard pineapple should be kept at room temperature until it becomes fragrant and springy. Once ripe, it can be refrigerated.

Variety Fruits

Many uncommon fruits have been appearing on the market throughout the United States. As consumers become more familiar with these fruits and learn to use them, their market share increases. Kiwifruit, grown in New Zealand, for example, has become a widely accepted fruit in a relatively short period of time. Some of the exotic fruits are cherimoya, which can be chilled, cut in half, and served with a spoon; passion fruit, which has an intense and tart flavor that goes well with fruit punches, juices, and sherbets; and prickly pear, which can be chilled, the spines and peel cut away, sliced, and served raw. Other variety fruits are listed in Table 16.1 and pictured in Plate V.

•STORAGE OF FRESH FRUITS

Fruits are actively metabolizing tissues and, even after harvesting, continue to respire, that is, to take in oxygen and give off carbon dioxide. Cold temperatures reduce the rate of metabolism and retard ripening but do not completely stop these processes. An additional aid in controlling metabolic changes and thus lengthening the possible storage period for certain fruits is an industrial process called *controlled atmosphere storage* [14].

In controlled atmosphere storage, the oxygen in the atmosphere is reduced below the usual 21 percent level to as low as 2 to 3 percent. This markedly lowers the rate of cell metabolism and aging in the fruit, delaying the changes that would normally occur and prolonging the storage life. For example, changes in pigments, decrease in acid, loss of sugars, and breakdown of pectic substances are retarded in apples stored at 4°C (38°F) in an atmosphere containing 5 percent carbon dioxide and 3 percent oxygen [12].

There is a critical oxygen level for each stored fruit, below which injury to the tissues occurs. Relatively high carbon dioxide levels are sometimes used with the low-oxygen atmosphere; however, the atmosphere is carefully monitored and excess carbon dioxide, produced by the fruit during respiration, is removed so that a desirable level of carbon dioxide is constantly maintained. Temperature and humidity are also carefully controlled.

Commercial generators and sensitive monitoring equipment make it possible to control the atmosphere not only in airtight storage warehouses but also in transportation vehicles. This process allows a higher quality to be maintained in fresh fruits and vegetables shipped over long distances. Not all products respond equally well to controlled atmosphere storage, and some may not be at all suited to this kind of treatment.

Most fresh fruits are very perishable and require refrigeration. Soft fruits such as berries keep better when they are spread out on a flat surface. Citrus fruits, except lemons, which keep best at a temperature of 13° to 15°C (55° to 58°F), should be refrigerated and can be kept from drying out by covering. Avocados and bananas are so injured by chilling that they discolor and lose the power of ripening even if they are later held at warmer temperatures. In fact, bananas are injured when they are held at temperatures lower than 13°C (55°F) *before* ripening. If these and other tropical fruits must be held for a while, they should be ripened before being stored at colder temperatures. After ripening, avocados hold best at about 4°C (40°F).

•FRUIT JUICES

Fruit juices are a very important means of utilizing fresh fruits. The commercial fruit juice industry in the United States has had a spectacular rise since 1925, with fruit juice consumption in this country surpassing that of fruit processed in all other forms. Much of the increase in fruit juice production has been with citrus fruits. Since the commercial introduction of frozen orange concentrate in 1945 and 1946, this product has become the leader among processed fruits in terms of fresh-weight-equivalent consumed. More than 80 percent of the Florida orange crop is used to produce juice [7]. Recently, the retail market for frozen concentrated juices has been declining in favor of chilled, single-strength, ready-to-serve juices, which are more convenient.

Sources of Vitamin C

Some edible material is lost when juices are extracted and the juice is strained, with the result that the total nutritive value of the whole fruit is somewhat higher than the juice coming from it. There is little loss of vitamin C during preparation and processing of citrus juices, however. The freezing and subsequent storage of orange juice at −18°C (0°F) or below does not cause a significant loss of vitamin C, especially if aeration before freezing is avoided. Possibly because of their high acidity, citrus juices tend to retain vitamin C well. Even after eight days of storage at 3°C (37°F), 80 to 85 percent of the original vitamin C has been reported to be retained in reconstituted frozen orange juice [2].

Apple, cranberry, grape, pineapple, and prune juices and apricot nectar contain little or no vitamin C unless they are fortified with the added vitamin. Vitamin C is added to some juices, partly to increase the nutritive value and partly to improve their appearance, flavor, and stability during storage. The added vitamin C in noncitrus juices may be less stable than the vitamin naturally present in citrus juices. In opened containers stored in a refrigerator, the vitamin C in canned orange juice has been found to be much more stable, up to 16 days, than that in vitamin C-fortified canned apple juice [16].

Juice Processing

In the preparation of orange juice concentrate, the fruit is usually graded, washed, and sanitized before it enters the juice extractors. After leaving the extractors, the juice may go through a series of finishers to remove the seeds and pulp. It is then concentrated [6]. Several different processes can be used to remove water from the juice, including evaporation under vacuum, use of osmosis or **reverse osmosis** through selective membranes, and partial freezing with separation of the resulting ice crystals. Evaporation is the most commonly used procedure, with thermally accelerated short-time evaporators being widely used in the juice processing industry. With this equipment, evaporation can be accomplished in 6 to 8 minutes [6].

The concentrated juices are blended to produce the highest uniform quality. Concentrated orange aroma or essence solutions that are lost in the evaporation process are commonly recovered and returned to the concentrated juice to maintain fresh flavor [11]. The chilled concentrate is then quick-frozen. Frozen concentrated juices should be kept at −18°C (0°F) or below, both in market channels and in the kitchen, to retard losses of nutritive value, flavor, and other quality characteristics.

Membrane technology has made it possible to process fruit juices with fewer stages, less energy cost, and greater retention of flavor and aroma com-

Reverse osmosis   a process of "dewatering" whereby ions and small molecules do not pass through a membrane but water does pass through

ponents [13]. This technology includes **microfiltration** and **ultrafiltration**, as well as reverse osmosis [8].

Noncitrus juices are also sold as concentrates. One of the major advantages of fruit juice concentrates is that the volume is greatly reduced and shipping and handling costs are less. Concentrated juices and fruit purees may be dehydrated by roller or drum drying, spray drying, or foam mat drying. Although some flavor loss occurs in drying, the final product is acceptable.

Pectic substances in citrus juices are partly responsible for the desirable haze or cloudy appearance; they also contribute a characteristic body or consistency. Present in cell walls and between cells, pectic substances are released into the juice when it is extracted. In citrus juices this cloud may be stabilized by flash heating to a temperature higher than usual pasteurization temperatures to destroy **pectin esterase** enzymes that destabilize the cloud; however, apple and grape juices are preferred when they are clear. Pectin-degrading enzymes (**pectinases**) may be added to these juices to aid in the processing. The treated juice is less viscous and can be easily filtered. This process is called *clarification*. The color and flavor of the clarified juices are also stabilized.

Liquid fruit juices are sometimes transported in bulk. Tanks for this purpose are installed on trucks, on railway cars, and in ships. However, when stabilized orange juice, after pasteurization, is quickly cooled and packaged, it has several times the shelf life of fresh untreated juice.

To eliminate some of the problems associated with the marketing of fresh or stabilized single-strength fruit juice, a concentrate can be prepared at the point of production. It varies from 42 to 60 percent of its original volume. The concentrate is bulk-packaged, quickly frozen at $-24°C$ ($-10°F$), and held until needed for reconstitution to its original volume. It may be shipped as a concentrate in refrigerated trucks and reconstituted at the point of sales. This is a great saving in the cost of transportation. If facilities permit, the concentrate can be held frozen and reconstituted and packaged as needed.

Until recently, single-strength, ready-to-serve citrus juices on the market were generally reconstituted from frozen concentrate. Now, several citrus processors have begun using **aseptic** bulk storage of chilled, pasteurized, single-strength orange and grapefruit juices to market not-from-concentrate single-strength juices. Many consumers perceive them to be more wholesome, with better flavor than reconstituted juices. These juices require careful handling and storage to prevent microbial spoilage since they rely primarily on cold temperatures and asepsis, or keeping out harmful microorganisms, for preventing spoilage [17].

Fruit drinks are also aseptically packaged, but in individual paperboard containers. This convenience has led to growth in fruit drink consumption [18].

Orange juice is often sold in foodservice establishments from dispensers in which it is kept chilled and aerated. The Florida Citrus Commission has reported that, in a study on eight juice dispensers, the retention of vitamin C in the juice was 94 to 97 percent after 4 days of holding [3].

A wide variety of dry orange-beverage mixtures are now being marketed, some of them synthetic in nature. In one preference study of 630 consumers, dry orange drink formulations were found to compare favorably with frozen juices and sweetened canned juices and were rated higher than unsweetened canned juices [9].

Microfiltration   a membrane process that filters out or separates particles of very small size (0.02-2.0 microns), including starch, emulsified oils, and bacteria

Ultrafiltration   a membrane process that filters out or separates particles of extremely small size (0.02-0.2 microns), including proteins, gums, glucose, and pigments

Pectin esterase   an enzyme that catalyzes the hydrolysis of a methyl ester group from the large pectin molecule, producing pectic acid; pectic acid tends to form insoluble salts with such ions as calcium (Ca^{2+}); these insoluble salts cause the cloud in orange juice to become destabilized and settle

Pectinase   an enzyme that hydrolyzes the linkages that hold the small building blocks of galacturonic acid together in the pectic substances, producing smaller molecules

Aseptic   free from disease-producing microorganisms

•DRIED FRUITS

When fruits are preserved by drying, the water content is reduced to less than 30 percent. In some fruits, such as dates, figs, raisins, pears, and peaches, the water content may be only 15 to 18 percent when fruits come from the drying yards and dehydrators. As marketed, these fruits usually contain 28 percent or more moisture. Therefore, they may be partially rehydrated before being packaged for the consumer. Dried fruits with 28 to 30 percent water are examples of intermediate-moisture foods that are plastic, easily chewed, and do not produce a sensation of dryness in the mouth, but are microbiologically stable.

In **vacuum-drying**, the water content is reduced to very low levels, about 2.5 to 5 percent. Fruits dried by this method are usually stored in sealed containers to retain the low moisture levels.

Carbohydrate, caloric, and mineral values of dried fruits are higher by weight than those of the corresponding fresh fruits because of the removal of water. Also, the flavor is more concentrated than that of fresh fruit.

The vitamin content of fruits is changed in drying depending on the methods of drying and sulfuring. Some fruits, such as apricots and peaches, are subjected to the fumes of sulfur dioxide gas or are dipped in a sulfite solution to prevent darkening of color and to kill insects. Sulfuring aids in the preservation of vitamin A and vitamin C but adversely affects thiamin. A fruit-drying process involving osmotic dehydration has been developed, in which the fruit is partially dehydrated in the first stages by being placed in a concentrated sugar solution. This protects the color and flavor with little or no use of sulfur dioxide [19]. Although peaches and apricots dried by methods involving artificial sources of heat seem to retain vitamins A and C better than do sun-dried fruits, many of these fruits still are sun-dried.

Methods and Storage

The term *dried* is commonly applied to all fruits in which the water content has been reduced to a low level. Sun-drying methods use the sun as a source of heat. Dehydration can also be accomplished by artificial heat under well-controlled conditions of humidity, temperature, and circulation of air. The sanitary practices involved in dehydration with artificial heat and the preservation of such physical properties as color, texture, and flavor in cooked dehydrated fruits as compared with cooked sun-dried fruits may represent possible advantages for this method.

Vacuum-drying results in fruit with very low moisture levels, although relatively low temperatures are used in the process. Under vacuum, water evaporates at a lower temperature. These fruits usually have excellent eating quality and they rehydrate quickly and easily. Fruits may also be **freeze-dried**.

Since dried fruits are greatly reduced in water content and consequently have increased sugar content, they are resistant to microbial spoilage. Light-colored fruits that have been exposed to sulfur dioxide to prevent darkening also become more insect-resistant as a result of the sulfur treatment. Dried fruits should be stored in tightly closed plastic, glass, or metal containers to protect them against insect infestation.

Vacuum-drying drying a product in a vacuum chamber in which water vaporizes at a lower temperature than at atmospheric pressure

Freeze-drying a drying process that involves first freezing the product and then placing it in a vacuum chamber; the ice sublimes (goes from solid to vapor phase without going through the liquid phase); the dried food is more flavorful and fresher in appearance because it does not become hot in the drying process

Prunes

Prunes are varieties of plums that can be dried without fermenting while still containing the pits. Two main varieties are the French plum, grown chiefly in California and France, and the Italian plum, grown chiefly in Oregon. These fruits are blue or purple on the outside, with greenish yellow to amber flesh. They have a high sugar content, so they produce a sweet-flavored prune when dried.

Before drying, plums are dipped in lye to puncture the skin and make it thinner, thus permitting rapid drying and improving the texture of the skin. Careful washing removes the lye before further processing. Some packaged prunes have been sterilized and packed hot in a package lined with aluminum foil. The residual heat in the pits seems to be sufficient to sterilize the package and also to tenderize the prune fiber to some extent, thus giving the prune its quick-cooking quality.

Prunes are classified according to size, that is, the approximate number to the pound. It is generally conceded that large prunes of the same variety and quality as small prunes have no better flavor than the small fruit. Large fruit may be preferred for dessert purposes, but it must be remembered that price usually increases with size at a faster rate than does the amount of the edible portion. For the making of pulp, small and medium sizes are more economical.

The laxative value of prunes is the result, in part, of their fiber content and, in part, of a water-soluble extractive that stimulates intestinal activity. This substance is called *diphenylisatin*. Prune juice also contains the active laxative agent.

•CANNED FRUITS

Canned fruit is essentially cooked fruit that has been sealed and processed for keeping and, as such, represents a widely used convenience food. Flavors and textures are somewhat altered by cooking or canning and vitamin values may be slightly reduced. The vitamins and minerals that go into solution are conserved because juices are usually eaten with the fruit.

Canned fruits lose nutrients and flavor less readily when stored at relatively low temperatures. If they are stored for prolonged periods above 22°C (72°F), they deteriorate in quality at a relatively rapid rate.

In recent years, more "light" canned fruit products have been marketed in response to increasing concerns about health and nutrition. These fruits contain less sugar than the traditional canned products, often because they are packed in their juice with no sugar added.

•FROZEN FRUITS

The fruits that are most commonly frozen are cherries (both sour and sweet), strawberries (both sliced in sugar and whole), boysenberries, loganberries, red and black raspberries, blueberries, and sliced peaches. Frozen mixed fruits, rhubarb, plums, black mission figs, cranberries, pineapple, apple slices, and some varieties of melon are also available in some markets. Most frozen fruits

To section citrus fruits, pare deeply enough to remove the membrane that covers the pulp.

Cut toward the center along the membrane and remove the section.

FIGURE 16.5
Methods of preparing citrus for serving. (Courtesy of Sunkist Growers, Inc.)

are not heated during processing but are often frozen in a sugar syrup. Commercially, small whole fruits may be frozen quickly in liquid nitrogen. No sugar or syrup need be added in this process.

Frozen apples, cherries, and some other fruits used for pies should be partially defrosted to facilitate their use and to drain some of the juice. Otherwise, they are used in the same manner as fresh fruit. If the fruit has been frozen with some sugar or syrup, allowance must be made in adding sugar to prepared products. Rhubarb should be cooked without defrosting. Blueberries and other fruits frozen dry can be used either frozen or thawed in cooked dishes.

Frozen fruits should be moved quickly in market channels with proper precautions for maintaining cold temperatures. They should also be moved quickly from the market to the kitchen freezer to avoid partial thawing and consequent loss of quality on refreezing. For best quality retention, frozen fruits need to be stored at a temperature of −18°C (0°F) or lower.

All frozen fruits to be used raw should be barely defrosted. If all of the crystals have thawed, the fruit tends to become flabby. This is particularly true in using berries or peaches in shortcake, which is often warm when served.

PLATE I

Eight varieties of apples. (Courtesy of Blue Goose, Inc.)

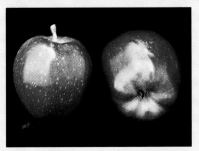
Red Delicious

Golden Delicious

McIntosh

Winesap

Rome Beauty

White Astrachan

Newtown

Jonathan

PLATE II

Eight varieties of potatoes. (Courtesy of Blue Goose, Inc.)

Irish Cobbler

Long White

Russet Burbank

Katahdin

Cherokee

Chippewa

Red Pontiac

Kennebec

PLATE III

Several types of salad greens. (Courtesy of Blue Goose, Inc., and Elisabeth Belfer)

Head lettuce

Butter leaf lettuce

Romaine lettuce

Red leaf lettuce

Escarole

French and Italian (flat leaf) parsley

Watercress

Chicory endive

French endive

PLATE IV

Typical samples of graded frozen green beans and canned peaches. (Courtesy of the U.S. Department of Agriculture)

FROZEN GREEN BEANS

U.S. Grade A

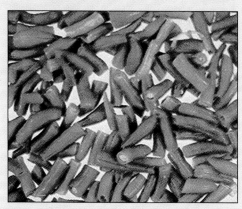

U.S. Grade B

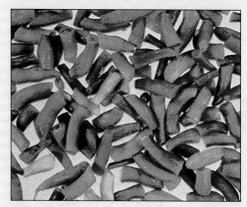

U.S. Grade C

As the quality increases, the pods are smaller and less mature, the color more uniform, and the defects fewer.

CANNED PEACHES

U.S. Grade A halves

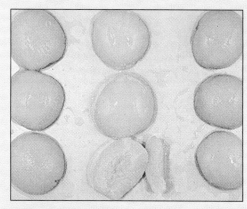

U.S. Grade B halves

U.S. Grade C mixed pieces

PLATE V

Specialty fruits and vegetables. (Courtesy of the United Fresh Fruit and Vegetable Association)

(Lower left) tomatillos, chayote (cut); (Upper right to lower right) cilantro, radicchio, arugala; (Upper left to lower right) enoki mushrooms, shiitake mushrooms, oyster mushrooms

(Lower left) Asian pear, prickly pears, feijoas, figs (in front); (Right) passion fruit, tamarinds, tamarillos, carumbola (star fruit); (Upper left) atemoya (black seeds), cherimoya

PLATE VI

Some produce exotics. (Courtesy of the United Fresh Fruit and Vegetable Association)

Fresh fruit combo with molded salad dressing combines a variety of colorful fruits with a bleu cheese-flavored gelatin salad dressing mold containing either mayonnaise or sour cream. This tempting plate may be served as a buffet salad or as a dessert. (Courtesy of Sunkist Growers, Inc.)

PLATE VII

A variety of fruits and vegetables may be attractively served as salads to accompany the main course of a meal or as a separate course. (Courtesy of The Betty Crocker Kitchens, General Mills, Inc.)

(Upper row, left to right) Orange-Bermuda Onion Salad, Apple and Grapefruit Salad, Festival Peach Salad (peaches filled with a mixture of cottage cheese, slivered almonds, chopped maraschino cherries, and flaked coconut)

(Lower row, left to right) tossed salad, tomatoes vinaigrette (tomato slices marinated in a tart dressing), asparagus tips with mayonnaise

A chef's salad containing strips of cold cooked meat, poultry, and cheese, along with a variety of fresh, crisp greens, and topped with a tangy dressing, makes an attractive and nutritious main dish. (Courtesy of the Betty Crocker Kitchens, General Mills, Inc.)

PLATE VIII

Cuts of beefsteak. (Courtesy of the National Live Stock and Meat Board)

Beef rib steak

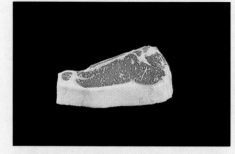

Beef loin, top loin steak

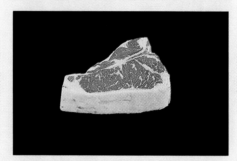

Beef loin, T-bone steak

Beef loin, Porterhouse steak

Beef loin, flat-bone sirloin steak

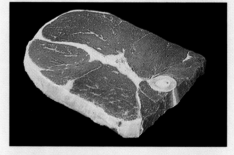

Beef round steak

Beef chuck, arm steak

Beef chuck, blade steak

PLATE IX

Cuts of beef. (Courtesy of the National Live Stock and Meat Board)

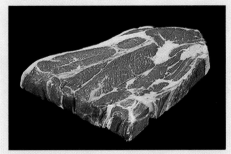

Beef chuck, seven-bone steak

Beef plate, skirt steak boneless (inner diaphragm muscle)

Beef flank steak

Beef loin, tenderloin steak

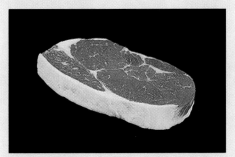

Beef loin, top sirloin steak boneless

Beef round, top round steak

Beef shank, cross cuts

Beef round, eye round roast

PLATE X

Cuts of beef. (Courtesy of the National Live Stock and Meat Board)

Beef chuck, top blade
pot roast

Beef chuck, shoulder
pot roast boneless

Beef chuck, under-blade
pot roast (bottom portion
of blade)

Beef chuck, short ribs

Beef brisket boneless

Beef for stew

Beef rib roast, small end

Beef rib eye roast

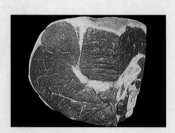

Beef round, rump roast

Beef round, rump roast
boneless

Beef round, tip roast

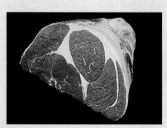

Beef round, heel of round

PLATE XI

Cuts of pork. (Courtesy of the National Live Stock and Meat Board)

Pork shoulder, blade steak

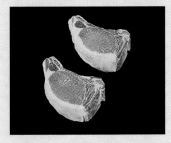
Pork loin, rib chops

Pork loin chops

Pork loin, tenderloin whole

Pork spare ribs

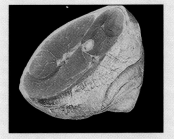
Smoked ham, shank portion

Smoked ham, rump portion

Pork loin, sirloin roast

Pork shoulder, arm roast

Pork shoulder, arm picnic

PLATE XII

Cuts of lamb and veal. (Courtesy of the National Live Stock and Meat Board)

Lamb shoulder, arm chops

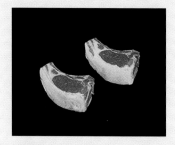

Lamb rib chops

Lamb loin chops

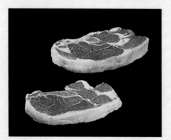

Lamb leg, sirloin chops

Lamb leg, French-style roast

Lamb leg, American-style roast

Veal shoulder, arm steak

Veal loin chops

Veal leg, round steak

Veal cutlets (thin, boneless leg slices)

PLATE XIII

Variety meats. (Courtesy of the National Live Stock and Meat Board)

Livers (top, beef; middle left, veal; middle right, lamb; bottom, pork)

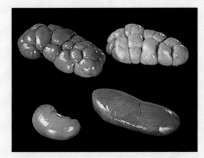

Kidneys (top left, beef; top right, veal; lower left, lamb; lower right, pork)

Hearts (in order of size: beef, veal, pork, and lamb)

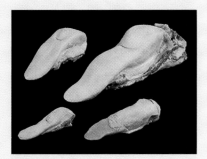

Tongues (in order of size: beef, veal, pork, and lamb)

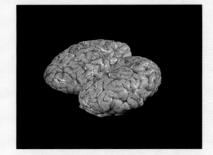

Brains

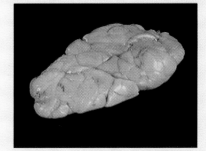

Sweetbreads

Large heavy muscles contribute to minimal waste in a pork carcass. (Courtesy of R.E. Hunsley, Purdue University)

PLATE XIV

Meat may be cooked and presented in many different forms that add variety to menus. (Courtesy of the National Live Stock and Meat Board)

Braised beef chuck arm pot roast is served with steamed baby carrots, Brussels sprouts, and cauliflower flowerets.

Swiss steak piperade uses beef round steak with tomatoes, bell peppers, and seasonings and is served on a bed of cooked farfalle (bowtie) pasta.

Tropical grilled flank steak is served with fresh fruit salsa which contains green apple, mango, papaya, pineapple, green and red bell peppers, and cilantro.

Beef, pepper, and mushroom kabobs use beef top sirloin steak. A mixture of oil, lemon juice, mustard, honey, oregano, and pepper coats each kabob before broiling.

Fruit 'n pecan stuffed veal crown roast is an eye-catching entree. The ribs are stuffed with dried apricots and prunes, celery, onion, toasted pecans, and cooked brown rice.

Spicy grilled short ribs are marinated in barbecue sauce, lemon juice, minced jalapeno peppers and green onion for several hours before cooking.

Sizzling beef fajitas add a Mexican flavor.

Savory mushroom-stuffed steak uses boneless beef top sirloin steak, fresh mushrooms, shallots, and seasonings.

PLATE XV

Cheese comes in many varieties, shapes, and sizes. Shown here are (right to left) brick, Colby, Swiss, cheddar, Monterey Jack, and pasteurized processed cheese slices. (Courtesy of the National Dairy Council)

A prototype tray containing a typical evening meal from space station Freedom's 28-day menu. The utensils are anchored to the tray. (Courtesy of the National Aeronautics and Space Administration (NASA) Johnson Space Center)

PLATE XVI

Baking yeast breads can be a rewarding creative experience. (Courtesy of Fleischmann's Yeast)

A handsome loaf, called Hearth Braid, is made by braiding three pieces of dough, each rolled into 16-inch ropes.

The classic dinner roll is tender and light. The dough may be shaped as lucky clovers, rosettes, bow ties, or made into balls that are placed close together to make pan rolls.

Multigrain bread makes an attractive loaf with rolled oats on top.

Citrus sections without membranes can be served in many attractive ways.

For a basketball method of peeling, first slice off the stem end of the orange. Without cutting into the meat, score the peel with a knife. Pull the peel away with the fingers, leaving the white inner skin that clings to the fruit.

The warm shortcake may complete the defrosting. Some frozen fruits, such as peaches and apples, tend to turn brown during frozen storage and after thawing. Use of vitamin C in the syrup aids in the retention of natural color by preventing oxidation. Fruits may be defrosted by leaving them in the refrigerator or at room temperature for shorter periods.

•PREPARATION

Most fresh fruits are generally considered to be at their best in the raw, ripened state and are thus served without cooking whenever possible (Figures 16.5 and 16.6). Fresh fruits should always be washed to remove dust, soil, some spray residues, and some microorganisms. If fruits that brown easily, such as bananas and apples, are to be peeled and cut, they should be dipped in or covered with lemon juice, pineapple juice, or solutions of vitamin C mixtures so that discoloration does not readily occur. The acids and/or antioxidants in these solutions retard the enzyme activity and/or tie up oxygen so that the brown-colored compounds do not form. Placing the fruit in a sugar syrup or even immersing it

FIGURE 16.6

A sliced orange filled with grapes makes an attractive addition to breakfast. For lunch or supper, various fruit combinations create interest and contribute essential nutrients to the diet. Orange slices, melon balls, sliced bananas, and fresh berries make an attractive combination. Pieces of banana, orange, melon, and pineapple combine well with strawberries and may be served on picks. Slice 'N Serve Blue Cheese Dressing goes especially well with an attractive platter of fresh fruits. (Courtesy of Sunkist Growers, Inc.)

in water retards browning to some degree by excluding air. Enzymatic oxidative browning is discussed in Chapter 15.

For some fruits, including green apples and rhubarb, cooking is sometimes desirable or necessary because they are more palatable and digestible when cooked. Cooking is also one way to add variety as fruits are included in daily menus. Overripe fruits may be further preserved by cooking.

Cooking in Syrup and Water

Whether or not pieces of fruit or vegetable become soft and break up during cooking is influenced by the cooking medium. If it is desirable to have fruits retain their shape, they may be cooked in a sugar syrup. If sauce is the expected end product, cooking in water hastens disintegration of the tissues.

The reason for these differences lies with the imbalance between sugar concentrations inside the fruit and in the cooking liquid. In uncooked fruit tissue, the cell walls act as *semipermeable membranes*, allowing passage only of water. If there is a difference in sugar concentration within and without the cells, as is the case when sugar is sprinkled on fresh strawberries, for example, water exits the cells in an attempt to dilute the concentrated sugar solution that has formed on the surface of the fruit: thus, the formation of juice when strawberries are left to stand with sugar. The reverse occurs, that is, water enters fruit cells, when fruit is placed in plain water, because the concentration of sugar within the cells is greater than in the water outside. This movement of water through a semipermeable membrane is called *osmosis*.

As fruit is heated, however, the permeability of the cell walls changes to allow not only the passage of water but the movement of sugar and other small molecules as well. Simple **diffusion** then occurs as sugar and water move into or out of tissues. Therefore, in fruit slices cooked in a sugar syrup more concentrated than the 12 to 15 percent sugar solution found naturally in most fruits, sugar moves into the cells and water moves out into the cooking liquid in an attempt to equalize the sugar concentration throughout (Figure 16.7).

Diffusion   the movement of a substance from an area of higher concentration to an area of lower concentration

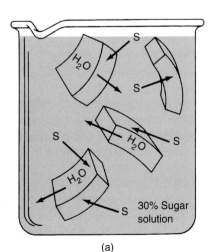 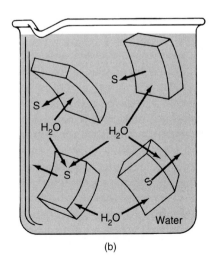

(a)   (b)

FIGURE 16.7
Cooking of fruit. Apple slices cooked in a sugar solution will retain their shape. (a) Sugar (S) moves into the fruit cells, and some water (H_2O) comes out into the surrounding sugar solution in an attempt to dilute it. (b) Apple slices cooked in plain water tend to break up more as water moves into the cells, expanding them.

Because fruits shrink slightly, they appear shiny and translucent and the tissue is firm. A desirable proportion of water to sugar for most fruits is about two to one by measure. When the shape of the fruit pieces is to be retained, the fruit should not be stirred during cooking.

On the other hand, when fruit is cooked in water alone, sugar moves from the more concentrated solution within the cells to the plain surrounding water and some water moves back into the tissues (Figure 16.7). Fruits that are to be cooked to a smooth pulp are stewed in water until they attain the desired softness, after which sugar is added. These fruits may be stirred during cooking. The same principles described earlier apply to vegetables cooked in water containing sugar versus plain water. The sugar content of most vegetables, however, is low, and they are usually enjoyed without sweetening.

Contrary to these general principles, some varieties of fruits do not cook to a smooth pulp in any circumstances, and not every variety holds its shape well when cooked in syrup. The final product obtained is, therefore, partly a matter of choice of variety.

Cooking proceeds most evenly when the pan is covered during cooking. The heat source should be regulated so that the liquid in the pan simmers or boils slowly.

Rhubarb is easily overcooked. The use of a very small amount of water and careful, slow cooking, only until the pieces are tender and partially broken up, produces a desirable sauce from rhubarb. Apples sliced for cooking may sometimes include the skin, for added color, flavor, and nutritive value. After cooking, the fruit may be quickly run through a strainer or food mill to increase the smoothness of the pulp if applesauce is being prepared.

Excess sugar in fruit sauces mars the delicate flavor of many fruits. The desirable amount is often difficult to determine, especially when fruits are made into pies and other products, in which the amount of sugar may not be added gradually until the desired amount is determined. The same variety of apple or other fruits varies in acidity from season to season and at different times during the storage period.

Cooking Dried Fruits

Some of the water that has been removed from fruit in the drying process is returned by soaking. Cooking after soaking softens the tissues. Soaking in hot water for a short time results in good water absorption. The dried fruit, covered with water, may be brought to a boil, immediately covered and removed from the heat source, and then left to stand for 20 to 30 minutes (no longer than one hour). After soaking, the fruit is simmered until the desired degree of softness is achieved. Some commercially available dried fruits are tenderized and have a higher moisture content. They require little or no soaking and a short cooking period.

The higher sugar content of dried fruits makes the use of much sugar for sweetening undesirable. The small amount of sugar that is sometimes used is added at the end of the cooking period. The degree of acidity of the fruit determines the amount of sugar to be used: dried apricots, being much more tart, require more sugar than prunes.

Baking

Some fruits lend themselves well to baking. The aim is to have the fruit hold its form but be cooked until tender throughout. Apples and pears are often baked in their skins (cores removed) to hold in the steam that forms within the fruit and cooks the interior. Pared slices or sections may be baked in a covered casserole (350° to 400°F oven temperature). Bananas are sometimes baked, although in general they are preferred raw. Rhubarb can also be baked and will keep its shape.

Glazing

A top-of-the-range method known as *glazing* can be satisfactorily used to cook apples. The apples are cored as for baking, and a slit is cut in the skin all around the apple at right angles to or parallel to the core. The apples are then placed in a saucepan with 1/4 cup of water and 1/8 cup of sugar for each apple in the pan. They are covered and cooked over low heat. The apples are turned once while cooking and are cooked until tender. The cover is removed for the last minute before the apples are done.

Broiling

Bananas, grapefruit halves, and pineapple slices are some of the fruits that can be satisfactorily broiled. To modify the bland flavor of cooked bananas, lemon juice or broiled bacon may be combined with the fruit.

Sautéing

Apples, bananas, and pineapple slices may be prepared by sautéing, or cooking quickly in a small amount of fat. The fat is usually a flavorful fat such as butter.

STUDY QUESTIONS

1. What is a *fruit*? Also define a *pome* and a *drupe*. Give examples of each.
2. a. What is the usual percentage of water found in fruits? What is the usual percentage of carbohydrate? What type of carbohydrate usually predominates in ripe fruits?
   b. List and be able to recognize fruits that are good sources of vitamin C.
3. Describe common characteristics of fruit flavor. List four types of chemical substances that contribute to the flavor of fruits.
4. a. What pigments are often present in fruits?
   b. Explain why pigment content should be considered when mixing various fruit juices to make a fruit drink.
5. Describe the major changes that occur during the ripening of fruit.
6. a. Describe the usual characteristics of fruits of good quality and suggest appropriate storage conditions to maintain quality.
   b. What factors are generally monitored during *controlled atmosphere storage* of fruits and vegetables? Why is this type of storage effective for some fruits?
7. a. Describe major steps involved in the production of orange juice concentrate.
   b. What contributes to the stability of the hazy cloud characteristic of orange juice? To what treatment may the juice be subjected during processing to maintain cloud formation? Explain why this treatment is effective.

c. What special processing involving enzyme action may be used to produce a sparkling clear fruit juice? Describe and explain.

8. Why are some fruits treated with sulfur before drying? Describe some effects of this process on nutritive value.

9. a. Compare the general effects of cooking fruits in water and in sugar syrups. Explain what is happening in each case.

   b. Suggest an appropriate procedure for cooking dried fruits and explain why you would recommend this procedure.

REFERENCES

1. Abe, K., and A. E. Watada. 1991. Ethylene absorbent to maintain quality of lightly processed fruits and vegetables. *Journal of Food Science 56*, 1589.

2. Andrews, F. E., and P. J. Driscoll. 1977. Stability of ascorbic acid in orange juice exposed to light and air during storage. *Journal of the American Dietetic Association 71*, 140.

3. Attaway, J. A. 1973. Florida Citrus Commission adds information on vitamin C retention. Letter. *Food Technology 27*, 14 (No. 4).

4. Bourne, M. C. 1982. Effect of temperature on firmness of raw fruits and vegetables. *Journal of Food Science 47*, 440.

5. Chairote, G., F. Rodriguez, and J. Crouzet. 1981. Characterization of additional volatile flavor components of apricot. *Journal of Food Science 46*, 1898.

6. Cook, R. 1983. Quality of citrus juices as related to composition and processing practices. *Food Technology 37*, 68 (No. 6).

7. Deshpande, S. S., H. R. Bolin, and D. K. Salunkhe. 1982. Freeze concentration of fruit juices. *Food Technology 36*, 68 (No. 5).

8. Dziezak, J. D. 1990. Membrane separation technology offers processors unlimited potential. *Food Technology 44*, 108 (No. 9).

9. Ennis, D. M., L. Keeping, J. Chin-ting, and N. Ross. 1979. Consumer evaluation of the inter-relationships between the sensory components of commercial orange juices and drinks. *Journal of Food Science 44*, 1011.

10. Frohlich, O., and P. Schreier. 1990. Volatile constituents of loquat (Eriobotrya japonica Lindl.) fruit. *Journal of Food Science 55*, 176.

11. Guadagni, D. G., J. L. Bomben, and H. C. Mannheim. 1970. Storage stability of frozen orange juice concentrate made with aroma solution of cutback juice. *Food Technology 24*, 1012.

12. Knee, M. 1971. Ripening of apples during storage. III. Changes in chemical composition of Golden Delicious apples during the climacteric and under conditions simulating commercial storage practice. *Journal of the Science of Food and Agriculture 22*, 371.

13. Koseoglu, S. S., J. T. Lawhon, and E. W. Lusas. 1990. Use of membranes in citrus juice processing. *Food Technology 44*, 90 (No. 12).

14. Lidster, P. D., H. J. Lightfoot, and K. B. McRae. 1983. Production and regeneration of principal volatiles in apples stored in modified atmospheres and air. *Journal of Food Science 48*, 400.

15. Moshonas, M. G., and P. E. Shaw. 1973. Some newly found orange essence components including trans-2-pentenal. *Journal of Food Science 38*, 360.

16. Noel, G. L., and M. T. Robberstad. 1963. Stability of vitamin C in canned apple juice and orange juice under refrigerated conditions. *Food Technology 17*, 947.

17. Parish, M. E. 1991. Microbiological concerns in citrus juice processing. *Food Technology 45*, 128 (No. 4).

18. Pearl, R. C. 1990. Trends in consumption and processing of fruits and vegetables in the United States. *Food Technology 44*, 102 (No. 2).

19. Ponting, J. D., G. G. Watters, R. R. Forrey, R. Jackson, and W. L. Stanley. 1966. Osmotic dehydration of fruits. *Food Technology 20*, 1365.

20. Pratt, S. 1992. The 'peachfuzz' plot. *Food Technology 46*, 46 (No. 8).

21. Segal, M. 1988. Fruit. U.S. Department of Health and Human Services Pub. No. (FDA) 88-2226. Rockville, Md.

22. Sweeney, J. P., V. J. Chapman, and P. A. Hepner, 1970. Sugar, acid, and flavor in fresh fruits. *Journal of the American Dietetic Association 57*, 432.

23. *The Buying Guide for Fresh Fruits, Vegetables, Herbs, and Nuts*, 8th rev. ed. 1986. Shepherdstown, WV: Blue Goose Growers, Inc.

24. White, P. L., and N. Selvey, eds. 1974. *Nutritional Qualities of Fresh Fruits and Vegetables*. Mount Kisco, NY: Futura Publishing.

25. Wiseman, J. J., and M. R. McDaniel. 1991. Modification of fruit flavors by aspartame and sucrose. *Journal of Food Science 56*, 1668.

Salads and Gelatin

•SALADS

At one time the term *salad* may have applied only to green leaves or to stalks that were eaten raw. Although today we often refer to green leafy vegetables, such as lettuce, endive, and romaine, as *salad greens*, the term *salad* has a much broader meaning. It now includes mixtures of meat, fish, poultry, cheese, nuts, seeds, and eggs, as well as all kinds of vegetables and fruits. Often, salads are made with raw or uncooked foods, but they are certainly not limited to these items. A salad may be composed entirely of cooked or canned products, or mixtures of raw and cooked items may be used. Congealed salads containing a variety of ingredients are popular menu items. A dressing is usually served either mixed with or accompanying the salad. The dressing may be rich and elaborate, or it may be as simple as lemon juice.

The salad is not a modern preparation. Green leaves were used by the ancient Romans. Other nationalities from the fifteenth century onward favored the use of flavorful herbs and raw vegetables. The introduction of salads into England was apparently made by Catherine of Aragon, one of the wives of Henry VIII and a daughter of Ferdinand and Isabella of Spain. The origin of present-day meat and fish salads was probably the salmagundi of England, used for many years as a supper dish. This meat dish made use of numerous garnishes that are used today, such as hard-cooked eggs, pickles, beets, and anchovies.

The influence of southern France is apparent in the use of french dressing for salads. The original dressing was made of olive oil and was seasoned to perfection. Spain has made the pepper a popular salad vegetable, and the Mediterranean countries introduced garlic flavor. The original german potato salad has many present-day variations.

The salad is an appetizing form in which to use fresh fruits and vegetables. The element of crispness, which most salads introduce, improves the texture in many menus. Tartness and delicious, fresh flavors are also easily added to the meal in the form of salads.

Uses of Salads

The salad may be served at a number of different points in a meal. Often, it accompanies the roast or the main course, but it is sometimes served as a separate course, either between the main course and the dessert or before the main course. Some salads, especially those with fruit and nuts that are dressed with a rich or somewhat sweet dressing, are appropriately served for dessert. For luncheon or supper, the salad may be the main course, with the remainder of the menu being built around it.

The type of salad served depends on its use in the meal. The dinner salad is usually a light, crisp, tart accompaniment to the meat. Heavy, high-calorie salads, such as macaroni and tuna fish or meat and potato, are not appropriately used in a meal already composed of filling, high-protein foods. Instead, meat, poultry, fish, egg, cheese, and potato salads that are combined with some crisp vegetables and relishes are suitable for use as a main course. Some small fish salads of high flavor, such as crab, shrimp, lobster, and anchovy, may serve as an appetizer, just as cocktails and canapés made of these fish do. Usually, the amount of fish used is not large, and it is combined with crisp, flavorful foods.

Potato salad may be an accompaniment to cold meats on a supper platter. Used in this way, the starchy potato functions as it does in the dinner menu. Potato salad is sometimes served hot, as was the original german potato salad.

The fruit salad is particularly suitable as an appetizer or dessert. If kept tart and not too large, it may also be appropriately used as an accompaniment in the dinner menu. A fruit salad can be a popular choice for refreshments at an afternoon or evening party. When a fruit salad is used as dessert, it may be served with a cheese plate and crisp crackers.

Nutritive Value

Nutritive value varies with the salad. Starchy salads, such as potato, are higher in kilocalories than are salads made from many fruits and from succulent vegetables. Meat, fish, egg, and cheese salads furnish chiefly protein, although some crisp vegetables usually form a part of such mixtures.

The majority of salads prepared from fresh fruits and vegetables are comparatively low in kilocalories (not including the dressing) but are important sources of minerals, vitamins, and fiber. The green-leaf vegetable salads are especially valuable for iron, vitamin A, vitamin C, and beta carotene.

The final caloric value of salads, as consumed, is greatly influenced by the type and quantity of dressing used. The amount of fat, usually contained in the salad oil or cream, is the major factor influencing the caloric content of dressings. Cooked dressings, particularly those made with water or milk, have a lower caloric value than do mayonnaise and french dressings. French and a variety of commercial salad dressings average 60 to 80 kilocalories per tablespoon. Mayonnaise contains about 100 kilocalories per tablespoon. There are, however, many reduced-fat dressings on the market. Special fat-free dressings may furnish as little as 6 kilocalories per tablespoon.

Salad Ingredients and Their Preparation

Salad Plants

The best-known salad plant is lettuce, of which there are several types. Iceberg lettuce is a crisphead type and is the most popular of the salad greens. Butterhead types have soft, pliable leaves and a delicate, buttery flavor. They include the Bibb and Big Boston or butterhead varieties. Another type of lettuce, romaine, or Cos, is characterized by leaves that appear coarse yet are actually tender, sweet, and tasty. They have a somewhat stronger flavor than iceberg lettuce. Leaf lettuce, including both green and red varieties, is a still different type, with leaves loosely branching from the stalk.

Endive, escarole, and chicory are often used as salad greens; however, there is some confusion concerning the use of these three terms in various parts of the country. Curly endive grows in a head with narrow, ragged-edged leaves that curl at the ends. A broader leaf variety of endive that does not curl at the tips is usually marketed as escarole. Witloof chicory, commonly known as French endive, is a tightly folded plant that grows upright in a thin, elongated stalk. It is usually white. Watercress and Chinese cabbage or celery cabbage are also highly acceptable as salad plants. Plate III shows some of the common salad greens.

Any crisp, tender, young leaves, such as spinach, sorrel, mustard, and dandelion, may be used as salad plants. Shredded cabbage may make up the entire salad, as in cole slaw, it may serve as a foundation or bed for other salad ingredients, or it may be part of a vegetable salad mixture. Other, very flavorful ingredients include tomatoes, cucumbers, radishes, red and green peppers, green onions, and celery. Many of these vegetables are particularly valuable for their crisp textures. Foods with very pronounced flavor, such as pineapple, should be used sparingly in mixtures to avoid masking more delicate flavors.

Cooked beets have a desirable texture and flavor for some types of salads; however, because of the soluble red pigment present, they may mar the color of other salad ingredients. If used carefully and kept separate from other ingredients, beets are valuable additions.

Raw turnip is another interesting ingredient for salads. It can be used in thin slices (often allowed to curl in cold water), sticks, or fine shreds. Raw carrots can be used similarly. Small pieces of raw cauliflower and broccoli flowerets are also desirable salad components.

Edible flowers may also be used as salad ingredients or as garnishes. For example, nasturtium blossoms can be filled with a seafood stuffing and served on a bed of dark green nasturtium leaves.

Preparation of Salad Ingredients

Many salad ingredients should be prepared shortly before the salad is to be made and served, for maximum retention of nutrients and freshness. However, green leaves and celery will be crisp and fresh if they are washed, closely wrapped, and chilled in the refrigerator for several hours. Certain other ingredients that go into a salad, for example, sections of citrus fruits, can be prepared well in advance. If salad materials are kept ready in the refrigerator, salad preparation becomes a simple, easy procedure. Unless salads are purposely served hot, as are german potato salad and wilted lettuce, all materials should be cold.

In the preparation of salad plants, all inedible portions should be removed. Thorough cleansing is essential when the plants are used raw (Figure 17.1). Although some soluble nutrients are dissolved when the vegetables are allowed to stand too long in water, they need to take in some water through cut stems or cores to become crisp. The water that clings to leaves and stems after washing helps to develop crispness, provided that enough time is allowed for chilling in the refrigerator.

FIGURE 17.1

A head of lettuce that is not to be used for 2 or 3 days can be washed in cool water, drained thoroughly, and wrapped in plastic film or put in a plastic bag before refrigerating. Lettuce to be used sooner can be trimmed, the core removed, cold water run into the center to loosen the leaves, and the head then turned upside down and drained thoroughly before storage in a plastic bag or film wrap. (Courtesy of Western Growers Association)

Salad plants can be wrapped in plastic material or in a wet cloth or stored in a tightly closed hydrator. All excess water should be removed from the vegetables before use to avoid a watery salad. Careful drying prevents the bruising of leaves. Although the butterhead types of lettuce do not become crisp, their tender leaves and delicate flavors make them valuable salad ingredients. The softer texture of this type of lettuce provides an attractive contrast when combined with crisp salad plants.

Cutting out the core or stem from a head of iceberg lettuce speeds up the absorption of water and simplifies separation of the leaves from the head. Firmly striking the core of a head of lettuce on a hard surface loosens the core for easy removal.

Sections of citrus fruits used in salads are usually left whole, but many fruits are cut into bite-sized pieces. Canned pineapple, peach, and pear can be cut easily with a fork and may be left whole.

Vegetables are left whole or are diced, shredded, sliced, or sectioned, depending on the type of vegetable (Figure 17.2). Potatoes used for salad should be of a variety that holds its form when diced. Mealy potatoes tend to form a starchy mass when made into salad. Tiny beets can be left whole; cauliflower and broccoli can be used in separate flowerets. Tomatoes are often peeled and left whole or cut into wedges or slices. Cucumbers are sliced or diced depending on the type of salad. Celery is usually diced but may be cut into sections that are prepared to form celery curls or cut into shreds. Although green beans in a combination salad are usually cut into short lengths, they may be left whole. Asparagus tips can also be used. As carrots are very firm, they are best used as tiny sticks, thin slices, or shredded. Peppers are often cut into rings, but may be coarsely chopped or slivered for some purposes. It is important in most cases that salad ingredients not be finely minced, as soft foods that are too finely cut tend to form a paste when they are mixed with salad dressings.

FIGURE 17.2

Fresh vegetables, cut in various forms and served with cheeses or tangy dips, may constitute the salad dish itself. They may also be used as accompaniments to a tossed green salad. Vegetables include radish roses, rings of green pepper, celery curls or sticks, carrot curls, thin cucumber slices, cherry tomatoes, cauliflower sections, slices of mushroom, jade trees from green onion stems, marinated artichokes, red onion rings, and water chestnuts. (Courtesy of Western Growers Association)

FIGURE 17.3

Heads of lettuce cut into wedges make simple, yet attractive salads. (Courtesy of Western Growers Association)

Vegetables are often cut finer for molded gelatin salads than for salads that are not molded. Cabbage, regardless of how it is used, is more attractive and becomes better seasoned if it is finely shredded. Coarse shreds of cabbage are difficult to chew, particularly if the variety of cabbage is one that does not become crisp easily.

Meats and chicken used in salads are usually diced, but fish is most often coarsely flaked with a fork. Small shellfish, such as shrimp, may be left whole or diced. Canned salmon and tuna fish are difficult to prepare in a way that retains the form of pieces, although tuna is more firm than salmon. Fish canned with a considerable amount of oil can be washed off with hot water before being chilled. Alternately, the oil may become part of the dressing.

Salad bars have become a popular self-service feature in many restaurants. A wide variety of salad ingredients are presented separately, and the client chooses from the assortment, according to his or her personal taste. Various dressings are also offered separately.

Marinating

Meat, fish, starchy vegetables, and whole firm pieces of more succulent vegetables may be improved by *marinating*, which is the process of coating foods lightly with a dressing or oil (in this case called a *marinade*) and letting the mixture stand in the refrigerator for an hour or more before being made into a salad. The major purpose of marinating is to improve the flavor. Leafy vegetables generally cannot be so treated, because they wilt. Excess marinade is drained off when the salad is prepared.

Preparing the Salad

Arrangement and Garnishing

Salads should be attractively arranged, whether they are elaborate or very simple. Whole stuffed tomatoes, halves of peaches or pears, slices of pineapple,

A shimmering gelatin mold containing green peppers, celery, radishes, and cucumber slices.

An elegant gelatin salad ring including carrots, pimiento cheese, and minted pineapple is garnished with deep red grapes.

FIGURE 17.4
Gelatin molds take on a more fixed, formal appearance than do many other salads. (Courtesy of United Fresh Fruit and Vegetable Association and Western Growers Association)

and gelatin molds necessarily take on a more fixed appearance than do combination salads made from cut pieces (Figures 17.3 and 17.4). Color can be added by mixing a colorful ingredient in the main body of the salad or by placing it in a fixed form on top (Figure 17.5). The use of contrasting colors is especially effective. Some colors may not combine attractively, for example, the clear red **lycopene** pigment of tomato and the purplish red pigment of beets.

Garnishes are not used solely as decorations, but are also edible constituents that form part of the salad. Ripe or stuffed green olives, radishes, and small cheese-stuffed celery stalks often have the effect of garnishes when placed on lettuce beside the salad proper. Sprigs of watercress or parsley, which introduce a darker green color and an interesting leaf design, add appeal to many vegetable salads. Strips of pimiento or a bit of paprika adds a touch of color, but too much paprika may be unattractive. Overgarnishing should be avoided. Plates VI and VII illustrate several different types of salads and their arrangements.

Dressing the Salad

A wide variety of salad dressings are available. Most salad dressings are examples of **emulsions**, either temporary or permanent, and are discussed in Chapter 18.

Lycopene   a reddish, fat-soluble pigment of the carotenoid type

Emulsion   the dispersion of one liquid within another with which it is immiscible, such as oil and water

FIGURE 17.5

Salads contribute valuable nutrients to the diet and may also provide the main attraction for a luncheon or supper menu. A chef salad with marinated cooked vegetables and hard-cooked eggs is an example of a salad dish contributing valuable protein. (Also see Plate VI.) Bright green cabbage, a good source of vitamin C, may be attractively combined with red cabbage, coconut, and pineapple in a slaw. Individual salads, displayed all on one platter, combine orange, banana, and pineapple slices with whole apricots on a bed of lettuce. Whole blueberry-sour cream dressing adds zest and color. (Courtesy of Western Growers Association; individual salads, courtesy of Sunkist Growers, Inc.)

Certain types of salad, including potato, macaroni, meat, chicken, and fish, and some fruit salads as well, are improved by being left to stand for a time with the dressing. These salads are often mixed with the dressing and chilled for several hours before serving.

The hot summer months and the popularity of picnics combine to encourage the holding of meat and starchy salads with mayonnaise or creamy salad dressings for extended periods without chilling. These types of salads have caused outbreaks of food poisoning when they were held too long without adequate refrigeration, which is why it is particularly important that they be refrigerated during the standing time to prevent the growth of any undesirable microorganisms. Shredded cabbage may be improved by brief contact with the dressing. For most other leafy salads, however, the texture, appearance, and flavor are better if the dressing is added when the salad is served. The dressing may coat all the salad ingredients, as when the dressing is applied to a large amount of salad in a bowl either at the table or immediately before serving. The ingredients are tossed with a serving spoon and fork until they are well coated with dressing. Light mixing is necessary to retain the characteristic form of each of the salad plants in the mixture. Alternatively, a small amount of dressing may be applied to individual servings before the salad is placed on the table, or the dressing may be passed for individuals to serve themselves.

•GELATIN AND GELS

A gel is a special kind of structure that might be described as somewhere between a solid and a liquid. Gels occur in a number of different food products, including most starch-thickened puddings and pie fillings, egg custards, fruit jellies, and gelatin molds used either as salads or as desserts. Starch-thickened mixtures and egg custards are treated in other chapters; gelatin is discussed in this chapter. First, however, let us discuss certain characteristics common to all gels.

Gel Structure and Characteristics

Gels are composed mainly of fluid but they behave much like rigid solids. These interesting characteristics appear to be the result of their special type of structure. Gels contain long, thin chainlike molecules, called **polymers**, that are joined together or crosslinked at random spots to produce a three-dimensional structure something like a pile of dry brush (Figure 17.6).

Examples of polymers that form gels are (1) the **amylose** fraction of starch with its long chain of glucose molecules linked together; (2) the large protein molecules of egg, which are composed of long chains of **amino acids**; (3) the linear protein molecules of gelatin; and (4) the **pectin** molecules, which are long chains of **galacturonic acid** and its **methyl esters**. Pectin is responsible for the setting of fruit jellies and jams.

The polymer network that is responsible for gel formation is immersed in a liquid medium to which it is attracted. In a sense, it traps the liquid in its chainlike network. But the liquid and the polymer network work together— the liquid keeps the polymer network from collapsing into a compact mass, and the network keeps the liquid from flowing away.

Polymers   molecules of relatively high molecular weight that are composed of many small molecules acting as building blocks

Amylose   a straight-chain fraction of starch

Amino acids   small organic molecules, containing both an amino group and an acid group, that constitute the basic building blocks of proteins

Pectin   a complex carbohydrate (polysaccharide) composed of galacturonic acid subunits, partially esterified with methyl alcohol and capable of forming a gel

Galacturonic acid   a derivative of the sugar galactose, with an organic acid group

Methyl ester   the chemical combination of methyl alcohol with an organic acid, such as galacturonic acid

FIGURE 17.6
When a gel is formed, a network of long, thin molecules traps liquid in its meshes.

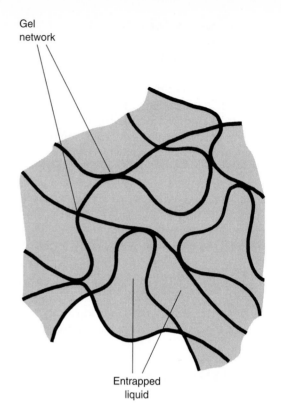

Gel network

Entrapped liquid

Gels are sometimes described as mixtures that hold the shape of the container after they are removed from it; however, gels vary from being soft to fairly rigid [2]. Most food gels are relatively soft but are resilient or elastic.

Environmental conditions affect the characteristics of many gels. Some gels shrink or swell with changes in temperature. Many food gels liquefy or melt over a relatively narrow temperature range. The melting and solidifying constitute a reversible process in such gels as gelatin mixtures. Gels may also be affected by pH, becoming softer with greater acidity. Some gels exhibit **syneresis**. This may occur in overcooked egg mixtures and in some starch and gelatin gels stored in the refrigerator for a few days.

Syneresis the oozing of liquid from a rigid gel; sometimes called *weeping*

Manufacture of Gelatin

Collagen a fibrous type of protein molecule found in the connective tissue of animals; produces gelatin when it is partially hydrolyzed

Gelatin is obtained by the hydrolysis of **collagen**, which is found in the connective tissues of animals. The chief sources of commercial gelatin are animal hides, skins, and bones [1]. The conversion of collagen to gelatin is, in fact, a fundamental part of the cookery of less tender cuts of meat. As cooked meat cools, the formation of a gel from the gelatin produced in the meat juices is often visible.

The industrial manufacture of gelatin comprises three basic stages: (1) the raw material is treated so as to separate the collagen from the other components present; (2) the purified collagen is converted into gelatin; and (3) the gelatin is purified, refined, and recovered in dry form [3]. The conditions of manufacture for edible gelatin ensure a product of high sanitary quality. The dry form in which gelatin is marketed also favors a low bacterial count. When gelatin is hydrated, however, and used to make a gel, the moist product is favorable medium for bacterial growth and should be refrigerated as are other perishable foods.

Gelatin is marketed in both granular and pulverized forms. Fine division of the gelatin allows it to be dispersed more easily in hot water. Gelatin mixes, which include sugar, acid, coloring, and flavoring substances, usually contain pulverized gelatin. A good quality of plain gelatin should be as nearly flavorless and odorless as possible.

Uses of Gelatin

Edible gelatin, which has met specified standards of quality, is used to form a basic gel structure. This structure may carry fruits, vegetables, cheese, meats, whipped cream, nuts, and other appropriate foods as various salads and desserts are prepared. It may also act as a foam stabilizer in whipped products and as a thickener in some puddings and pies. It is used in the making of certain candies, such as marshmallows, and in some frozen desserts in which it acts to control crystal size.

Gelatin is a very efficient gelling agent. As little as 1 to 3 parts of gelatin in 97 to 99 parts of water produces a moldable gel.

Nutritive Value of Gelatin

Gelatin is a protein food derived from animal sources, yet it is a protein of low biologic value. It lacks several essential amino acids, particularly tryptophan. Regardless of the quality of protein, the amount of gelatin required to form a gel is so small (1 tablespoon per pint of liquid) that its nutritive contribution is insignificant. One tablespoon of granulated gelatin furnishes about 30 kilocalories and 9 grams of protein.

Some gelatin desserts and salads may provide the means by which significant amounts of fresh fruits and vegetables are incorporated into the diet, but it is the added foods rather than the gelatin that are nutritionally valuable.

Hydration and Swelling of Gelatin

Dry gelatin hydrates and swells when it is soaked in cold water. The water molecules are attracted to the gelatin molecules and form a water shell around them. This aids in later dispersion of the gelatin in hot water.

The ease, rapidity, and extent of swelling depend on several factors. If the gelatin is finely granulated or pulverized, more surface is exposed to the water. Consequently, the rate of swelling is increased. Directions on packages of most gelatin mixes suggest omission of the soaking in cold water and addition of boiling water directly to the pulverized gelatin, which has previously been mixed with sugar or nonnutritive sweeteners and flavorings.

The degree of acidity or alkalinity, the kinds of salts present, and the presence of sugar all influence the swelling of gelatin. Sugar and certain salts inhibit swelling, whereas other salts accelerate it. Because the fruit acids and sugar used for flavor are usually not added until the unflavored gelatin has swelled and been dispersed, they do not affect these processes.

Dispersion of Gelatin

When the temperature of soaked gelatin is elevated to 35°C (95°F) or higher, the gelatin molecules separate or disperse. Some hot liquid can be added to the hydrated gelatin to disperse it, after which the remaining liquid can be added cold; or the hydrated gelatin can be suspended over hot water until dispersion takes place, after which all remaining liquid can be added cold. Boiling all the remaining liquid before adding it is unnecessary and undesirable for two reasons: more time is required to cool the mixture, and some volatile flavor substances are lost with high temperatures.

Gelation

Gelation means gel formation or the stiffening of a gelatin dispersion. Gelation does not occur at a fixed or clearly defined point but rather is a gradual process. It evidently involves the joining or linking together of gelatin molecules in various places to form the three-dimensional "brush-heap" structure that is typical of gels (see Figure 17.6).

Effect of Temperature

Different samples of gelatin set at different temperatures, but all require cooling below the temperature of dispersion, 35°C (95°F). Gelatins that require a low temperature to solidify tend to liquefy readily when brought back to room temperature. Also, gelatin dispersions that have set quickly because they were subjected immediately to very low temperatures melt more readily at room temperature than similar gelatin mixtures that set at somewhat higher temperatures.

It is possible, because of rapid cooling, for a gelatin dispersion to remain liquid at temperatures that would ordinarily be low enough for gelation. Because of time schedules, it is sometimes necessary to chill gelatin dispersions rapidly and to hold them at low temperatures for quick setting. Sometimes, ice cubes are added as part of the cold water to speed up the setting process. If more time is allowed, however, gelation occurs at a higher temperature. It also occurs more quickly at a cold temperature if the gelatin dispersion stands at room temperature for a time before being chilled. Temperatures required for the solidification of a gelatin dispersion vary from less than 10°C (50°F) to around 14° to 16°C (57° to 61°F).

Concentration

The concentration of gelatin affects not only the firmness of the gel but also the rate of setting. The higher the concentration, the firmer the gel and the faster the rate of setting.

The usual percentage of gelatin in a gelatin mold of good texture is about 1.5 or 2 percent, depending on the ingredients used in the mixture. One tablespoon (7 grams) of unflavored gelatin per 2 cups of liquid gives a gelatin concentration of about 1.5 percent. Beating the gelatin dispersion to a **foam** or

Foam   the dispersion of a gas in a liquid

sponge increases the volume sufficiently to decrease the firmness of the gel. A higher concentration of gelatin is thus required to produce a firm texture in whipped products. Very weak dispersions of gelatin, such as those used in ice creams, eventually set if given a long time and a low temperature. If excess gelatin is used in ice cream, gumminess increases with longer storage.

Gels become stiffer with longer standing. Unless a relatively high concentration of gelatin is used, it is usually desirable to allow gelatin mixtures to stand several hours or overnight at a low temperature to develop optimum stiffness.

Degree of Acidity

The fruit juices and vinegar that are frequently added to the gelatin mixtures used for desserts and salads increase the acidity of the dispersions. Too high a concentration of acid can prevent gelation or cause the formation of a soft gel, even when a fairly high concentration of gelatin is present.

Lemon juice and vinegar have a more pronounced effect on gelation than do tomato juice and some other fruit juices of lower acidity. Two tablespoons of lemon juice as part of 1 cup of liquid is usually enough for good flavor unless the dispersion is to be beaten to a foam. In this case, the flavor is diluted. This dispersion forms a more tender gel than one made without acid and yet is usually satisfactorily stiff even when no extra gelatin is added.

Chopped vegetables or diced fruits added to a gelatin mixture mechanically break up the gel and may prevent its setting into a sufficiently firm mass. If, in addition, enough acid is added to give good flavor, the resulting gel may be too weak to be molded. Use of a somewhat higher concentration of gelatin may be necessary in such circumstances. The time required for acid gelatin dispersions to set is greater than that required for neutral ones.

Effect of Salts

Gel strength is increased when milk is used as a liquid in gelatin mixtures, probably as a result of the salts present in milk. Even hard water that contains minerals produces a firmer gel than does distilled water.

Addition of Sugar

Sugar weakens a gelatin gel and retards the rate of setting. Usual recipes for gelatin mixtures have been adjusted so that the weakening effect of sugar is counterbalanced by the firming effect of increased gelatin concentration.

Effect of Enzymes

The bromelain enzyme in fresh pineapple is a **proteinase** that hydrolyzes protein. Some other tropical fruits, including kiwifruit and papaya, also contain proteinases. If these enzymes are not destroyed by heat before the fruit is added to a gelatin dispersion, they will break down gelatin molecules so that they cannot form a gel. Because the heat of processing has destroyed the enzyme in canned pineapple pieces or juice, these products can be satisfactorily used in gelatin mixtures. Freezing does not affect the activity of the enzyme, however, and thus frozen pineapple cannot be used in a gelatin gel.

Proteinase an enzyme that hydrolyzes protein to smaller fragments, eventually producing amino acids

Gelatin Salads and Desserts

Fruit, Vegetable, Meat, and Fish Gelatin Mixtures

Before fruits, vegetables, or other solid food materials are added to a gelatin mixture, they should be thoroughly drained of juices. The juices of fruits and some vegetables may be added as part of the liquid required to disperse the gelatin. Gelatin mixtures should stand until they are thickened and just ready to form a gel before solid food materials are added to them. If the gelatin mixture is too liquid, the added pieces will float. Waiting until the mixture is thickened allows the added materials to be dispersed more evenly throughout.

Aspics

Aspic is usually a beef-flavored gelatin mixture, although fish and poultry flavors may also be used. Tomato aspic salad is made with unflavored gelatin and seasoned tomato juice. Chopped celery is usually added to a tomato aspic salad. As a variation of this salad, avocado slices can be placed in the salad mold before the tomato aspic mixture is added, or the aspic can be layered with a cottage cheese and sour cream mixture to which unflavored gelatin has been added. Aspic is often used to make fancy canapés that may be part of buffet platters.

Unmolding the Gel

To unmold a gelatin gel, the mold containing the gel should be dipped for a few moments in lukewarm (not hot) water. One side of the gel should then be carefully loosened with a knife to allow air to come between the gel and the mold. The gel should then slide easily from the mold. The mold can be very lightly oiled before the gelatin mixture is placed in it to facilitate removal of the gel.

Foams and Sponges

A gelatin dispersion can be beaten to form a foam. It increases two or three times its original volume, depending largely on the stage at which the dispersion is beaten. If beating is not started until the gelatin begins to set, the volume obtained is small, and finely broken bits of solidified gelatin are evident throughout the mass. The best stage for beating is when the dispersion is about the consistency of whipping cream or thin egg whites. The gelatin mixture is elastic and stretches to surround the air bubbles. Beating is continued until the mass is very stiff, to avoid the formation of a clear layer in the bottom of the mold. However, it may be necessary to stop and chill the beaten mixture again in the middle of beating. Just the friction of continued beating can warm the mixture enough to thin it. On standing, the gelatin sets and stabilizes the foam. An increase in gelatin, sugar, and flavoring is required if the gelatin dispersion is to be beaten to a foam because the increased volume of a foam dilutes these ingredients.

Fillings for chiffon pies have gelatin as a basic foam stabilizer. In the preparation of most chiffon fillings, a custard mixture containing egg yolk and sugar is thickened with gelatin. Whipped egg whites and possibly whipped cream are folded into the mixture. The gelatin sets and stabilizes the egg and/or cream foam.

To form a sponge, whipped egg white is beaten into the mixture after the syrupy gelatin mixture is beaten until it is thick and foamy. The sponge can be poured into molds and should be refrigerated until it solidifies.

Bavarian and Spanish Creams

Gelatin mixtures that have stood long enough to be thickened and syrupy may have fruit pulp added and whipped cream folded into them to make bavarian creams. Charlottes are similar to bavarian creams but may contain a large proportion of whipped cream and are usually molded with lady fingers. Whipped evaporated or dried milks are sometimes substituted for whipped cream in gelatin desserts.

Spanish cream is a soft custard made with egg yolks that is set with gelatin. The egg whites are beaten to a stiff foam and folded into the mixture after it is partially set.

STUDY QUESTIONS

1. a. Describe four or five ways in which salads may be used in a meal.
   b. Describe ten or twelve different salads and suggest appropriate uses for them in a menu.
2. a. Describe and be able to identify several leafy plants that can be appropriately used as salad greens.
   b. Suggest a satisfactory way to prepare these greens for use in salads and explain why this procedure is effective.
3. Marinating may be appropriate for what types of salads? Explain why.
4. Give several appropriate suggestions for arranging salads as they are served.
5. Gels of various types have common characteristics.
   a. Give several examples of food products that are gels.
   b. Describe the theoretical structure of a gel.
   c. What is *syneresis*?
6. What is *gelatin*? What is its source commercially?
7. In what forms is gelatin usually sold on the market?
8. How should unflavored gelatin be treated—and why—as it is used in the preparation of gelatin gels?
9. Describe what probably happens as gelatin forms a gel.
10. What is the effect of each of the following on the gelation of gelatin gels?
    a. Temperature
    b. Concentration of gelatin
    c. Addition of acid
    d. Addition of sugar
    e. Addition of raw pineapple
11. Describe major characteristics of each of the following gelatin mixtures.
    a. Aspics
    b. Foams
    c. Sponges
    d. Bavarian creams
    e. Spanish creams

REFERENCES

1. Gross, J. 1961. Collagen. *Scientific American 204*, 121 (No. 5).
2. Tanaka, T. 1981. Gels. *Scientific American 244*, 124 (No. 1).
3. Ward, A. G., and A. Courts, Eds. 1977. *The Science and Technology of Gelatin*. New York: Academic Press.

Fats, Frying, and Emulsions

18

Fat is present naturally in many of our foods. This fat is often referred to as **invisible fat**. Examples of foods containing appreciable quantities of invisible fat include meat, poultry, fish, dairy products, eggs, nuts, and seeds. Sometimes labeled as **visible fats** are shortening, lard, salad and cooking oils, margarine, and butter. These fats are incorporated by the food-processing or foodservice industries into baked products, such as cakes and cookies, and into fried foods, such as french-fried potatoes and doughnuts. If one does not have a clear understanding of food composition, the fat in these prepared foods may also be "invisible."

Classification of **lipids**, including **triglycerides** (triacylglycerols), **fatty acids, phospholipids**, and **sterols**, is discussed on pages 98–102. In food preparation, we are concerned mostly with only one of these groups, the triglycerides, as these make up the major part of the fat naturally found in foods as well as the more purified fats.

Fats play a variety of roles in both food preparation and nutrition. They give flavor and a mouth-feel that is associated with moistness, thus contributing greatly to the palatability of foods. As an ingredient in baked products, they "shorten" strands of the protein **gluten** and thereby tenderize it. Some fats also contribute to the aeration of batters and doughs. Their capacity to be heated to high temperatures makes them an excellent medium for the transfer of heat to foods in the process of frying. They are major components of salad dressings, in which they usually constitute one phase of an **emulsion**. Some fats, such as butter and bacon fat, are used specifically to add flavor. In addition, fats are a concentrated source of energy for the body.

•FAT CONSUMPTION AND NUTRITIVE VALUE

There is considerable public interest in the amounts and types of fat present in foods because of certain relationships between fat consumption and health that have been identified in recent years. Research is continuing to clarify these relationships, which often appear to be complex. Many people are now paying more attention to the kinds and amounts of fat they eat, partly because the

Invisible fat   fat that occurs naturally in food products such as meats, dairy products, nuts, and seeds

Visible fat   refined fats and oils used in food preparation, including edible oils, margarine, butter, lard, and shortenings

Lipids   a broad group of fatlike substances with similar properties

Triglycerides   a type of lipid consisting chemically of one molecule of glycerol combined with three fatty acids

Fatty acid   a chemical molecule consisting of carbon and hydrogen atoms bonded in a chainlike structure; combined through its acid group (—COOH) with the alcohol glycerol to form triglycerides

Phospholipid   a type of lipid characterized chemically by glycerol combined with two fatty acids, phosphoric acid, and a nitrogen-containing base, for example, lecithin

Sterol   a type of lipid with a complex chemical structure, for example, cholesterol

Gluten   a protein found in wheat that gives structure to baked products

Emulsion   the dispersion of one liquid within another with which it usually is immiscible (does not mix)

Linoleic acid   a polyunsaturated fatty acid with 18 carbon atoms and 2 double bonds

ω-6 fatty acids   polyunsaturated fatty acids that have the first double bond on the sixth carbon atom from the methyl (—CH₃) end of the carbon chain

ω-3 fatty acids   polyunsaturated fatty acids that have the first double bond on the third carbon atom from the methyl (—CH₃) end of the carbon chain

Dietary Guidelines for Americans recommend that we choose a diet low in fat, saturated fat, and cholesterol (see p. 4).

A measure of the quantities of fats and oils present in the food supply can be obtained by analyzing data about the manufacture of visible-fat products such as shortening, margarine, and salad and cooking oils [22]. This information indicates that, between 1970 and 1986, the estimated per capita consumption of manufactured fats and oils increased 22 percent, from 52.6 pounds in 1970 to 64.4 pounds in 1986, at which time the figure peaked and began to decrease. The share of total manufactured fat coming from animal sources decreased from 27 percent in 1970 to 17 percent in 1989. Apparent per capita consumption of fats and oils in 1989 was 60.9 pounds.

When we look at the total amount of fat in the U.S. food supply, including those foods containing invisible fat, we find an increase from 158 grams per person per day in 1968 to 168 grams in 1988 [23]. This is equivalent to approximately 135 pounds of total fat per person per year. Between 1968 and 1988, animal sources of total fat in the food supply declined relative to plant sources (Figure 18.1), with apparent consumption of butter and lard having decreased since 1965 (Figure 18.2). Data on fats and oils available for consumption likely *overestimate* trends in actual consumption, in part because they may not take into account the increase in eating at restaurants and other foodservice establishments that discard significant amounts of fats used to fry foods.

Fats are valuable in the diet as concentrated energy sources. On a weight basis, pure fat supplies more than two times the kilocalories of pure carbohydrate or protein. Table 18.1 gives the approximate weight and measure of various fats and fat-rich foods required to furnish 100 kilocalories. The percent of fat in each food is also indicated.

Fats provide essential fatty acids. **Linoleic acid**, an **ω-6 polyunsaturated fatty acid** (PUFA), is an essential nutrient. The role of the more highly unsaturated **ω-3 fatty acids** in body metabolism continues to be investigated. Research studies have linked the dietary intake of ω-3 PUFAs in Eskimos to their low incidence of coronary heart disease [9]. It has been suggested that an increased intake of ω-3 PUFAs may be beneficial for other Americans in decreasing their risk of developing coronary heart disease. The most important of these fatty

FIGURE 18.1

Animal sources of fat in the U.S. have declined relative to plant sources. (Courtesy of the U.S. Department of Agriculture. From Raper, N. Nutrient content of the U.S. Food Supply. *Food Review* Vol. 14, No. 3, p. 14, 1991.)

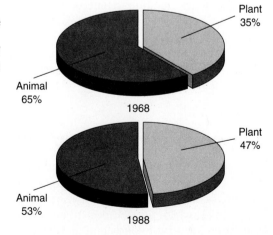

Plant 35%

Animal 65%

1968

Plant 47%

Animal 53%

1988

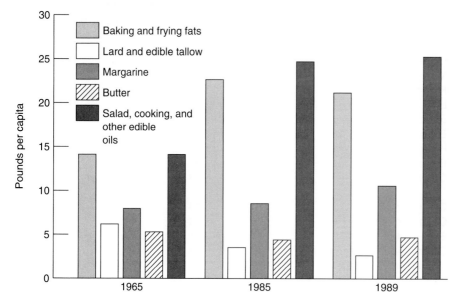

FIGURE 18.2

Salad, cooking, and other edible oils are now our largest source of visible fat. These oils accounted for 39 percent of visible fat (in pounds per capita) in 1989, compared with only 30 percent in 1965. (Courtesy of the U.S. Department of Agriculture. From Bailey, L., et al. Food consumption. *National Food Review*, Vol. 11, No. 2, p. 1, 1988. Also from Putnam, J. J. Food consumption, 1970–90. *Food Review*, Vol. 14, No. 3, p. 14, 1991.)

acids would appear to be *eicosapentaenoic acid (EPA)*. Fish is an excellent source of this lipid, from which the body can make a hormonelike compound called a *prostaglandin* [14]. This particular prostaglandin reduces the blood clotting rate and thus the likelihood of a clot blocking the coronary arteries.

Fats carry the fat-soluble vitamins. The average vitamin A content of butter is around 15,000 International Units (IU) or 3,000 Retinol Equivalents (RE) per pound, and margarines are fortified with a similar amount of this vitamin. Refined vegetable oils and hydrogenated shortenings contain little or no vitamin A, but vegetable oils are good sources of vitamin E.

With current recommendations from public health groups that Americans should decrease their usual consumption of total fat from about 38 to no more than 30 percent of kilocalories, many food processors are attempting to develop food products that are lower in fat yet are still palatable and acceptable. As a result, the number of low-fat foods on the market has grown dramatically during the past few years.

Nutrition labeling requirements for packaged foods include the number of calories from fat, and grams of total fat, saturated fat, and cholesterol. Food products labeled *low fat* must contain less than 3 grams per serving, while those labeled *low in saturated fat* must have less than 1 gram per serving and less than 15 percent of total calories from saturated fat. This label information should be useful to anyone seriously attempting to follow recommendations for a low-fat intake.

•PROPERTIES OF FATS

The chemical structure of triglycerides and their component fatty acids is discussed on pages 98–101.

TABLE 18.1

Approximate Amounts of Various Fat and Fat-Rich Foods Required to Furnish 100 Kilocalories

Food	Fat Content (%)	Weight (g)	Approximate Measure (Tbsp)
Butter	80	13	1
Margarine	80	13	1
Hydrogenated fat	100	11	1
Lard	100	11	1
Salad oil	100	11	1
Bacon fat	100	11	1
Peanut butter	46	16	1
Cream, light	20	50	3
Cream, whipping	35	33	2, or about double the volume if whipped
Cream, sour	25	48	4
Cheese, cheddar	32	24	1" cube
Egg, scrambled	11	61	1 egg
Ground beef, regular, broiled	21	35	1 ounce
Doughnut, yeast	21	26	½ doughnut

Solubility

Fats are insoluble in water and therefore do not mix readily with water-based food systems. They also have a greasy feel. In the laboratory they are soluble in a group of organic solvents that include chloroform, ether, and petroleum ether.

Melting Point

Melting point the temperature at which a solid fat becomes a liquid oil

Saturated fatty acid a fatty acid with no double bonds between carbon atoms; it holds all of the hydrogen that can be attached to the carbon atoms

Unsaturated fatty acid a general term used to refer to any fatty acid with one or more double bonds between carbon atoms; capable of binding more hydrogen at these points of unsaturation

Polyunsaturated fatty acid a fatty acid with two or more double bonds between carbon atoms, for example, linoleic acid with two double bonds

P/S ratio the ratio of polyunsaturated to saturated fatty acids in a food, also sometimes calculated for a total diet; for example, a diet sometimes prescribed for certain individuals with high blood lipids may have a P/S ratio of 3/1 or 3

In common usage, fats that have a relatively high **melting point** and are solid at room temperature are called *fats*, whereas those that have lower melting points and are liquid at room temperature are called *oils*.

The melting point of a fat is greatly influenced by the types of fatty acids it contains. The chemical structures of some common fatty acids, both **saturated** and **unsaturated**, are described on pages 99–100. When fats contain a relatively high proportion of saturated fatty acids, such as palmitic and stearic acids, they have relatively high melting points and are usually solid at room temperature. However, when fats contain a relatively high proportion of unsaturated fatty acids, such as the monounsaturated oleic acid and the **polyunsaturated** linoleic acid, they have relatively low melting points and are oils at room temperature. Fatty substances that have a relatively high content of polyunsaturated fatty acids, or a high ratio of polyunsaturated fatty acids to saturated fatty acids (**P/S ratio**), are commonly called *polyunsaturated oils* or *fats*. Examples of such products are corn, soybean, cottonseed, and safflower oils, and special soft margarines.

In addition to the degree of unsaturation, another effect on melting point results from the structure of the fatty acids that make up the triglycerides. As the number of carbon atoms in the fatty acids increases, thus making longer-chain fatty acids, the melting point also increases. For example, butyric acid with four carbon atoms melts at a lower temperature than does stearic acid with eighteen carbon atoms. Both of these fatty acids are saturated. Butter contains a relatively large proportion of short-chain fatty acids, many of them saturated, and melts at a lower temperature than does beef fat or hydrogenated shortenings, which contain more long-chain fatty acids.

All food fats are mixtures of triglycerides, although each contains different kinds of triglyceride molecules. Because of this, fats usually do not have a sharp melting point, but rather melt over a range of temperatures. An exception is the fat in chocolate. Since many of its triglyceride molecules are alike in chemical structure, having similar component fatty acids, chocolate melts over a fairly narrow temperature range that is close to body temperature, thus releasing in the mouth, as it is eaten, its delightful flavor bouquet and smooth mouth-feel.

Plasticity

Most fats that appear to be solid at room temperature actually contain both solid fat crystals and liquid oil. The liquid part is held in a network of small crystals. Because of this unique combination of liquid and solid, the fat can be molded or pressed into various shapes without breaking, as would a brittle substance. The fat is said to exhibit **plasticity**. The type and size of the crystals in a plastic fat influence the performance of the fat in baked products and pastry. Plastic fats can be creamed, that is, mixed with the incorporation of air.

Plasticity   the ability to be molded or shaped; in plastic fats, both solid crystals and liquid oil are present

Flavor

Some fats that are used for seasoning, at the table, and in salad dressings possess distinctive and pleasing flavors. These include butter, bacon fat, olive oil, and margarines. Margarines have a certain amount of butterlike flavor because in their manufacture, the fat is churned with cultured milk or whey and additional flavoring substances are often added.

In choosing fats for flavor purposes, the cost may also have to be considered. Corn, soybean, and cottonseed oils are commonly used to make satisfactory salad dressings but lack the flavor of the more expensive olive oil. Similarly, butter may be an expensive fat for use in cakes. Other fats, such as hydrogenated shortenings, make cakes of excellent texture and volume but obviously lack the flavor of butter.

The ability of fats to take up or dissolve certain aromatic flavor substances is frequently used in food preparation. Onions, celery, peppers, and other flavorful foods are cooked in fat to produce a savory fat that can immediately be incorporated into other foods or stored for future use. Aromatic fruit and other flavors are also dissolved by fat.

•PROCESSING AND REFINING OF FATS

Fats and oils commonly used in food preparation are separated from various materials and refined. Many oils come from seeds or fruits, lard comes from pork tissue, and butter comes from cream. Further processing produces fats such as margarines and hydrogenated shortenings.

Rancidity the deterioration of fats, usually by an oxidation process, resulting in objectionable flavors and odors

Hydrogenation

The process of hydrogenation was developed to change liquid oils into more solid plastic shortenings and to increase the stability of the oils to prevent spoilage from oxidation, which results in undesirable **rancid** flavors and odors. Fluid shortenings that can be poured or pumped, and thereby meet certain requirements for use in food processing or foodservice operations, are also prepared by partial hydrogenation. The final crystallization process differs, however, from that used for regular shortenings.

Hydrogenation takes place in a reactor, where hydrogen gas is bubbled through the liquid oil in the presence of a nickel catalyst, which speeds up the reaction. In the process of hydrogenation, some of the double bonds between the carbon atoms of the fatty acid portion of the triglyceride molecule are broken and hydrogen is added. This chemical change makes the fatty acids more saturated. The melting point of the fat is thereby increased. With sufficient hydrogenation it becomes a solid at room temperature. Careful control of temperature and pressure in the hydrogenation process allows the food processor to achieve the desired end result, that is, the proper degree of plasticity. The fat can then be creamed and blended with other ingredients [17].

The hydrogenation process can be easily stopped at any point. A completely hydrogenated oil would be very hard and brittle. Plastic shortenings are hydrogenated only enough to obtain the desired consistency and stability. Often, products that have received different degrees of hydrogenation are blended together to produce the desired effect [17].

The major source of hydrogenated shortenings in the United States is soybean oil. Smaller amounts of cottonseed and palm oils are often included with soybean oil. Hydrogenation greatly improves the stability of soybean oil and therefore its resistance to the development of undesirable flavors, sometimes called *flavor reversion* (see page 366), to which soybean oil is particularly susceptible.

Cis hydrogen atoms are on the same side of the double bond

$$\begin{matrix} H & H \\ | & | \\ (-C & = & C-) \end{matrix}$$

Trans hydrogen atoms are on opposite sides of the double bond

$$\begin{matrix} H \\ | \\ (-C = C-) \\ | \\ H \end{matrix}$$

Normocholesterolemic having a normal blood cholesterol level

In a partially hydrogenated fat, changes take place in some of the remaining double bonds. For example, a bond may move along the fatty acid molecule to a different position not normally found in nature. The double bond may also change from the usual configuration, which is called **cis**, to one called **trans**. Although some trans fatty acids occur naturally in foods such as butter, the main source of trans fatty acids in the American diet is partially hydrogenated vegetable oil (margarines and shortenings). The exact percentage of trans fatty acids in margarines varies widely, depending on the method of hydrogenation and processing of the product. A typical range is perhaps 15 to 35 percent of the total fat. Trans fatty acids are not metabolized in the body as are cis fatty acids. Some research has suggested that trans fatty acids have a plasma cholesterol-elevating effect when they are substituted for linoleic acid in the diets of **normocholesterolemic** subjects [29]. Research is continuing in an attempt to clarify the role of trans fatty acids in the diet.

Winterization

Some cooking oils become cloudy when they are stored in the refrigerator. This occurs because some of the triglyceride molecules in the oil have higher melting points than other molecules in the mixture and crystallize or become solid at the low refrigerator temperature.

In manufacturing oils intended to be used primarily for the making of salad dressings, a winterizing process is applied. In this process, the temperature of the oil is lowered to a point at which the higher-melting triglycerides crystallize. Then the oil is filtered to remove these crystals. The remaining oil has a lower melting point and does not crystallize at refrigerator temperatures. It is referred to as a *salad oil* [17].

Churning Cream

Butter is the fat of cream that is separated more or less completely from the other milk constituents by agitation or churning. The mechanical rupture of the protein film that surrounds each of the fat globules in cream allows the globules to coalesce. Butter formation is an example of the breaking of an oil-in-water emulsion by agitation. The resulting emulsion that forms in butter itself is a water-in-oil emulsion, with about 18 percent water being dispersed in about 80 percent fat and a small amount of protein acting as the **emulsifier**. Buttermilk remains after butter is churned from cream.

Emulsifier or emulsifying agent a substance adsorbed at the interface between two immiscible liquids that aids in the formation and stabilization of an emulsion

Butter is made from either sweet or sour cream. Butter from sour cream has a more pronounced flavor. The cream may be allowed to sour naturally or a pure culture of lactic acid bacteria may be added to pasteurized sweet cream. The latter method yields butter of better flavor and keeping quality, as it excludes many undesirable types of microorganisms that may cause off-flavor. Pasteurization also destroys any pathogenic bacteria present. Ripening of the cream after pasteurization by the addition of acid-forming bacteria permits acid fermentation to occur.

After churning separates the butterfat from the other constituents, the mass is washed, salted, and worked to remove excess water or buttermilk and to distribute added salt. Some sweet-cream butter is marketed unsalted as sweet butter. Salted butter is preferred by most Americans; sweet butter is used extensively in Europe and by European-trained chefs.

If coloring matter is used, it is added to the cream before churning. The season of the year and the demands of various markets for butter of different degrees of color affect the use of coloring matter. Butter produced when cows are on green feed is naturally more highly pigmented than butter produced when green feed is not consumed. Carotene is the coloring agent commonly used.

The U.S. Department of Agriculture (USDA) has set grade standards for butter. They are U.S. Grade AA, U.S. Grade A, and U.S. Grade B. U.S. Grade AA butter must have a smooth, creamy texture and be made from high-quality fresh, sweet cream. U.S. Grade A butter rates close to the top grade. U.S. Grade B butter is made from selected sour cream and may have a slightly acid flavor.

Butter flavor is complex, resulting as it does from the combination of many flavor compounds. A substance called *diacetyl*, formed from bacterial action, is an important flavor component of butter. Butter is highly valued by many for its flavor.

Margarine

Oleomargarine was first developed in 1869 by a French chemist, Mege-Mouries, in response to the offer of a prize by Napolean III for a palatable, nutritious, and economical alternate for butter. Beef fat was the chief constituent of the

Standard of identity a standard set by the U.S. Food and Drug Administration to specifically describe a food; to be labeled as such, a food must meet these specifications

original margarine. Since that time, many changes have occurred in the composition and processing of margarine.

Over the years, the use of butter as a table spread has decreased, while margarine consumption has markedly increased. The lower cost of margarine has undoubtedly been a major factor in this shift. Other reasons for using margarines are its improved quality and uniformity, and a desire to decrease the cholesterol content of the diet.

Margarine is made from one or more optional fat ingredients churned with cultured pasteurized skim milk or whey. It is a water-in-fat emulsion and must contain not less than 80 percent fat according to the **standard of identity** for margarine established by the U.S. Food and Drug Administration (FDA). Most regular margarines contain about 80 percent fat.

Soybean and cottonseed oils, refined and partially hydrogenated to the desired consistency, are extensively used to produce margarines. Liquid oils may be blended with partially hydrogenated oils in such a way that the total polyunsaturated fatty acid content is higher than in ordinary margarines. If the first ingredient listed on the label is oil, rather than partially hydrogenated oil, the polyunsaturated fatty acid content of the margarine is likely to be relatively high. Soft margarines with particularly high percentages of polyunsaturated fatty acids are often sold in plastic tubs [7].

Other ingredients permitted in margarine by the federal standard of identity are vitamins A and D for nutritive purposes; diacetyl as a flavor constituent; lecithin, monoglycerides, and/or diglycerides of fat-forming fatty acids as emulsifying agents; artificial color; salt; citric acid or certain citrates; and sodium benzoate, benzoic acid, or sorbic acid as a preservative to the extent of 0.1 percent.

In addition to regular margarine and margarine with a particularly high content of polyunsaturated fat, a variety of other margarine products are available. For example, you can purchase sweet unsalted margarine that is made with no milk products if you are concerned about sodium and/or milk in your diet. A whipped margarine containing an inert gas to increase the volume and decrease the density is available, with six sticks to the pound instead of four. The caloric value of whipped margarine is similar to that of regular margarine, but less whipped margarine is likely to be used because of its fluffy nature. Blends of margarine and butter are also available.

Reduced-calorie margarines contain a lesser amount of fat, a greater amount of water, and a stronger emulsifying system than do regular margarines. Thus, they do not meet the standard of identity established for margarine. Many such products have appeared on the market in recent years, often labeled *vegetable oil spread* or *corn oil spread*. The amount of oil and/or hydrogenated oil contained in these products varies between roughly 45 and 75 percent. The modified margarines are labeled in accordance with the rules established by the 1990 Nutrition Education and Labeling Act (see Chapter 2). If health claims are made for relationships between fat and cancer or between fat and cholesterol and coronary heart disease, the claims must meet the specifications outlined by the FDA.

Lard

Lard is one of the oldest culinary fats; however, the lack of uniformity in the production of lard, as well as its flavor and some of its physical properties, such as grainy texture, have resulted in a reduction in the use of lard by many Americans as other shortenings became available. In 1989, the per capita annual consumption of lard in the United States was less than 2 pounds [22]. Lard is still the preferred fat in Mexican cuisine for such dishes as refried beans.

Because lard is the fat rendered from the fatty tissues of the hog, the supply of lard depends on the number and size of hogs slaughtered. With the trend toward producing leaner pork meats, the supply of lard has decreased somewhat [17].

Rendering involves subdividing the fatty tissue into small particles and heating. The melted fat then separates from the connective tissue and other cell residues. The quality of lard depends on such factors as the part of the body from which the fat is obtained, the feed used for fattening the animal, and the rendering process. Leaf fat, which lines the abdominal cavity, is used to make the better qualities of lard.

Lard is susceptible to spoilage by the development of rancidity. **Antioxidants** are added to lard in processing to increase its shelf life. Some lard samples have relatively low smoking temperatures and have not been commonly used for frying; however, lards with high **smoke points** can be produced. One of the most desirable properties of lard is its excellent shortening power.

Technology has provided methods for improving the quality, uniformity, and functional properties of lard. Improved rendering methods have been developed; one involves the division of the fatty tissues into fine particles, after which flash heating is applied for 15 seconds. The product is then pulverized and centrifuged. This method gives a high yield and a bland and stable product at minimum cost.

A chemical modification, called *interesterification*, can be applied to lard to improve its plasticity and creaming qualities. Interesterification involves treating the fat with a catalyst at a controlled temperature, which produces a movement of some of the fatty acids to other triglyceride molecules in the mixture. This creates a more random distribution of fatty acids on the triglyceride molecules. The degree of unsaturation is not changed, but the way the fat crystallizes does affect its creaming properties and improves its performance in such baked products as shortened cakes. Some of this lard may be combined with hydrogenated vegetable fat in combination shortening or margarine. Antioxidants are added to shortenings containing lard to improve their keeping quality.

Hydrogenated Shortening

The process for hydrogenation of vegetable oils (described earlier in this chapter) was discovered more than 85 years ago and has since developed into one of the major chemical processes in the fat and oil industry. The fats produced are neutral in flavor, have a high enough smoke point to make them useful for frying, and have good shortening power.

In making hydrogenated shortenings, it is important to develop the best possible crystal structure in order to produce a shortening that is smooth in appearance and firm in consistency. To accomplish this, the chilling of the fat must be carefully controlled. The melted fat is chilled very rapidly in a large heat exchanger that vigorously agitates the fat while heat is removed from it. An inert gas is also whipped into the crystallizing fat. After packaging, the shortening is then *tempered*, that is, held for 24 to 72 hours at about 30°C

Antioxidant   a substance that slows down or interferes with the deterioration of fats through oxidation

Smoke point   the temperature at which smoke comes continuously from the surface of a fat heated under standardized conditions

Monoglyceride   glycerol combined with only one fatty acid

Diglyceride   glycerol combined with two fatty acids

(85°F) to further ensure proper crystal growth [17]. The desired crystals are small, long, and needlelike when examined under the microscope. In the production of fluid shortenings, the fat is agitated during tempering to form a larger crystal that contributes to its fluidity.

Hydrogenated shortenings often have emulsifiers, such as **monoglycerides** and **diglycerides**, added to them. The addition of emulsifiers to fats used in cakes makes possible the addition of higher proportions of sugar and liquid to fat, as is desired for some cake formulas. The presence of mono- and diglycerides in hydrogenated shortening, however, decreases the smoke point of the fat, thus making it somewhat less valuable for frying purposes. Special shortenings are used in commercial food-processing and foodservice establishments for frying and for cake making. General-purpose shortenings are also available. These are commonly sold on the retail market.

Refined Oils

In 1989, the estimated U.S. consumption of salad and cooking oils was 23.9 pounds per capita [22]. A variety of refined vegetable oils are marketed for consumption, including soybean, cottonseed, sunflower, peanut, olive, corn, canola, and safflower oils. Coconut, palm, and palm-kernel oils are also used by food processors in a number of foods.

Vegetable oils are removed from oil-containing seed fruits or nuts by various pressing processes, by solvent extraction, and by a combination of these. A seed cake that is relatively high in protein remains after fat extraction and is often used for animal feed.

After extraction, the crude oils are refined. The first step is usually to react the oil with an alkaline material to remove the free fatty acids that are not attached to a glycerol molecule. Free fatty acids in excess can detract from the oil's flavor and decrease its effectiveness when used for frying. The unwanted products of this reaction are then removed by centrifuging and washing, with a final drying process. This is followed by bleaching and deodorizing to remove color pigments and further purify the oil [17]. *RBD* refers to an oil that has been refined, bleached, and deodorized.

Soybean oil is the dominant edible oil in the United States, accounting for over 60 percent of the vegetable oil used. Until the early 1940s, it was not used in this country chiefly because of its susceptibility to oxidation and development of off-flavors described as being "grassy" and "painty." Partially hydrogenated soybean oil has improved stability and is the major component of vegetable shortenings and margarines [10].

Cottonseed oil was America's first vegetable oil, developed over a century ago as a by-product of the cotton industry. With lower cotton production, the supply of cottonseed oil has decreased. Approximately 70 percent of the cottonseed oil used today in the United States is consumed as a salad or cooking oil, while another 20 percent is formulated into shortenings that are used in baking and frying. Unhydrogenated and unwinterized cottonseed oil is used chiefly in restaurants and for food-processing frying applications for such products as potato chips, seafoods, and snack foods. It has a neutral flavor that does not mask the flavor of other products [10].

The most expensive of the edible oils is olive oil, also one of the most ancient oils. It has always been prized for its flavor, particularly by those who have lived in the Mediterranean area, where olive oil is the major cooking and salad oil. It is used in relatively small amounts in the United States, but its popularity is growing. Olive oil contains a high percentage (approximately 92 percent) of the monounsaturated fatty acid oleic. It is also more stable to oxidation than most oils because of its low content of linoleic acid, a polyunsaturated fatty acid. Good grades of olive oil are those that have not been refined, deodorized, or otherwise processed. The term *virgin olive oil* applies only to oil obtained from the first pressing of the olives without further processing. The term *pure* can be used for blends of virgin and refined oils. A top grade, with very low acidity, may be labeled *extra virgin* [10].

Canola is the name given to recently developed cultivars of rapeseed that are low in erucic acid, an unsaturated fatty acid suspected of being physiologically harmful. Canola oil is a very stable oil that is high in unsaturated fat (94 percent), over half of which is the monounsaturated fatty acid oleic. This oil is a newcomer to the market, but it is being used in some salad dressings, margarines, and shortenings [10].

Coconut oil is solid at room temperature because it contains a high proportion of saturated fatty acids, about 92 percent. Many of these are short-chain fatty acids, particularly lauric acid. Coconut oil has a sharp melting point, similar to the fat found in chocolate, and is therefore useful in confections and cookie fillings.

Palm-kernel oil is much like coconut oil. Palm oil, which is extracted from the fruit rather than the kernel of the palm tree, is different [2]. Although half of its fatty acids are saturated, it contains few short-chain fatty acids. It is semisolid at room temperature and has a long shelf life. Palm oil has been used in margarine and shortening but accounts for only a small percentage of all fats in the U.S. food supply [10]. The world supply of palm oil, however, has increased greatly in recent years. Palm oil now ranks as number two behind soybean oil in world edible oil production [28].

Sunflower oil has good flavor stability and is growing in popularity. The oil with the highest polyunsaturated fatty acid content is safflower oil, with 75 to 80 percent linoleic acid. Its use has been limited, however, because of short supply, high cost, and lack of flavor stability [17]. Peanut oil, on the other hand, has excellent oxidative stability. It is preferred by some snack food manufacturers because of its flavor [10]. Corn oil is used primarily in margarines.

•DETERIORATION OF FAT AND ITS CONTROL

A special type of chemical spoilage that commonly occurs in fats and fatty foods is rancidity. It may develop on storage, particularly if the fats are highly unsaturated and the environmental conditions are appropriate for initiating the reaction. The chemical changes that result in rancidity are chiefly of two types: hydrolytic and oxidative.

Hydrolytic Rancidity

Hydrolysis involves the breaking of chemical bonds and the addition, in the process, of the elements of water. When triglycerides are hydrolyzed, they yield free fatty acids and glycerol. This reaction may be catalyzed by an enzyme

Hydrolysis a chemical reaction in which a linkage between subunits of a large molecule is broken; a molecule of water enters the reaction and becomes part of the end products

Butyric acid   a saturated fatty acid with 4 carbon atoms that is found in relatively large amounts in butter

Caproic acid   a saturated fatty acid with 6 carbon atoms; as a free fatty acid, it has an unpleasant odor

called *lipase*. Release of free fatty acids does not produce undesirable odors and flavors in fats unless they are *short-chain* fatty acids, such as **butyric acid** and **caproic acid**. These fatty acids predominate in butter. They are volatile and are largely responsible for the very unpleasant odor and flavor of rancid butter. They may render butter inedible even when they are present in low concentrations. *Long-chain* free fatty acids, such as stearic, palmitic, and oleic acids, do not usually produce a disagreeable flavor unless other changes, such as oxidation, also occur.

Oxidative Rancidity

The characteristic unpleasant odor of fats in which oxidative rancidity has developed is difficult to describe but widely recognized. Oxidative rancidity may be caused by the action of an enzyme called *lipoxygenase*, which is present in some foods. However, it most often results from a strictly chemical reaction that is self-perpetuating, called a *chain reaction*. Primarily it is the unsaturated fatty acid portions of triglycerides that are susceptible to oxidative changes. Highly hydrogenated fats and natural fats composed largely of saturated fatty acids are relatively resistant to this type of chemical change.

The theory currently accepted as explaining the chemical oxidation of fat suggests that the addition of oxygen to carbon atoms next to a double bond in a fatty acid chain results in the formation of a product called a *hydroperoxide*.

hydroperoxide formed on portion of long-chain fatty acid

Hydroperoxides themselves do not appear to have unpleasant rancid odors and flavors, but these molecules readily break into pieces, producing smaller volatile substances that give the characteristic odors of rancid fat. Because the reaction is a chain reaction, once a fat develops a slight rancid odor, the production of more pronounced rancidity occurs very rapidly. This type of rancidity is responsible for most of the spoilage of fats and fatty foods. It may also be a problem in dry foods containing only small quantities of fat, such as prepared cereals. When rancidity develops in fatty foods, the fat-soluble vitamins A and E that are present may also be oxidized.

Flavor Reversion

A special type of oxidative deterioration, called *flavor reversion*, involves a change in edible fats characterized by the development, in the refined material, of an objectionable flavor prior to the onset of true rancidity. Reversion may develop during exposure of the fat to ultraviolet or visible light or heat. A small amount of oxygen seems to be necessary for the reaction, which is catalyzed by the presence of small amounts of metals such as iron and copper.

The kinds of off-flavors that develop during reversion vary with the particular fat and with the conditions that cause the change. Reverted soybean oil has been described as "painty," "beany," "haylike," and "grassy" and, in the final stages, "fishy."

No fat is entirely free from the tendency to develop flavor reversion, but some oils, such as corn and cottonseed oils, are quite resistant to this type of deterioration. Soybean oil is very susceptible to flavor reversion. This could cause problems in food processing because soybean oil is so widely used in the preparation of edible fats. Soybean oil is known to contain traces of iron and copper, which may act as **pro-oxidants**. The flavor of soybean oil is stabilized by the use of metal inactivators or sequestrants, which tie up the trace amounts of iron and copper that are present.

The chief precursors of the reversion flavor in oils are thought to be the triglycerides containing **linolenic acid**, although linoleic acid is probably also involved to some degree [25]. The fats that are most susceptible to reversion contain linolenic acid in larger amounts than do the fats that are relatively stable. Selective hydrogenation of soybean oil to decrease the amount of linolenic acid aids in preventing flavor reversion.

Pro-oxidant   a substance that encourages the development of oxidative rancidity

Linolenic acid   a polyunsaturated fatty acid with 18 carbon atoms and three double bonds between carbon atoms; ω-3 fatty acid

Antioxidants and the Prevention of Rancidity

Fats can be protected against the rapid development of rancidity by controlling the conditions of storage. Storage at refrigerator temperature along with the exclusion of light, moisture, and air aid in rancidity prevention. Because only certain rays of light catalyze the oxidation of fats, the use of colored glass containers that absorb the active rays protects fats against spoilage. Certain shades of green in bottles and wrappers and yellow transparent cellulose have been found to be effective in retarding rancidity in fats and fatty foods such as bacon. Vacuum packaging also helps to retard the development of rancidity by excluding oxygen. Since products such as peanut butter and hydrogenated shortening are used from a package or container, it is well to compact the material remaining in the container and smooth off the surfaces or repackage it in a smaller container to reduce the amount of air that comes in contact with the product.

Antioxidants have been used in the United States since 1947 to stabilize fats and control the development of rancidity [11]. Several compounds with antioxidant activity, including the nutrients vitamin C and beta carotene, are naturally present in certain foods. Vitamin E (tocopherols), present in seeds and in the oil extracted from seeds, is a very effective antioxidant that protects edible vegetable oils.

Antioxidants appear to act as oxygen interceptors in the oxidative process that produces rancidity, thereby breaking the chain reaction that perpetuates the process. Thus, they greatly increase the shelf life of fats and fatty food. Once the antioxidant itself is used up, however, the oxidative process may continue.

The addition of antioxidants to fats and fatty foods to retard the development of rancidity has become an important commercial practice. For example, lard, used as an ingredient in a number of food products, has no natural antioxidants of its own and must be protected from the development of rancidity by the use of antioxidants. Some of the substances approved as food additives for this purpose by the FDA include butylated hydroxyanisole (BHA), butylated hydroxytoluene (BHT), tertiary butyl hydroquinone (TBHQ), and propyl gallate. Some substances, such as citric acid, may be used along with antioxidants in foods as *synergists*. A synergist increases the effectiveness of an antioxidant, but is not as effective an agent when used alone. Metals such as iron and copper that may be present in trace amounts in foods act as pro-oxidants in encouraging the development of oxidative rancidity. Some synergists may be effective because of their ability to bind or chelate the metals and prevent them from catalyzing the oxidation process. Chelating agents are sometimes called *sequestering agents*.

The protection of fats against spoilage is important not only for more or less purified fats, but also for many other foods of high fat content, such as processed meats, whole-grain and dry-prepared cereal products, nuts, fat-rich biscuits and crackers, potato chips, and flour mixes.

•FRYING

There are two methods of frying: panfrying, in which a shallow layer of fat is used (Figure 18.3), and deep-fat frying, in which the food is submerged in heated fat.

Panfrying

Panfrying is used to cook such foods as hamburgers, chicken, fish fillets, bacon, potatoes, eggplant, and eggs. It is difficult in panfrying to know the exact temperature of heating because of the shallow depth of the fat, which is usually less than one-half inch; however, smoking of the fat is a definite indication that decomposition is occurring and should never be permitted. Moderate temperatures are generally used.

The frypan should be seasoned before its first use. To do this, a small amount of shortening is poured into the warm frypan. Then the pan surface is rubbed with a cloth until a mirrorlike finish is obtained. Once the pan is seasoned, it is best to wipe it clean after each use but not wash it [17].

Panfrying is often done using butter, margarine, or shortening. In foodservice operations, a specialty griddle shortening is generally used. For frying, the skillet should be merely coated with fat, not filled with an excessive amount.

Deep-Fat Frying

The deep-fat frying process is of interest to several different groups, including suppliers of oils, ingredients, and equipment, processors of deep-fat fried foods and their quality control laboratories, and foodservice outlets. In recent years, deep-fat frying has become common in many foodservice establishments (Figure 18.4). Nearly half of all lunch and dinner food orders in restaurants include deep-fried items [20]. People generally enjoy these foods, and having them prepared by restaurant employees eliminates some problems that are encountered when they prepare them in their own kitchens. These include handling hot frying fat with the dangers of spilling and burning, filtering the

FIGURE 18.3
Panfrying fish fillets. (Courtesy of Lever Brothers Company)

used fat, and storing the remaining fat when frying is done only infrequently. For foodservice operations, deep-fat frying is fast and economical in terms of energy and labor costs. Specialty frying fats and frying equipment developed in recent years make possible the production of quality fried foods [17]. The popularity of fried foods continues in spite of public concern about dietary fat and caloric intake [6].

In deep-fat frying, there is a direct transfer of heat from the hot fat to the cold food that continues until the food is cooked. Water present in the food to be fried plays some important roles in heat transfer and the frying process [3]. Water is lost from the exterior surfaces of the food as it is converted to steam. The steam carries off energy from the surface of the food and prevents charring or burning. While water is being evaporated, the temperature of the food is only about 100°C (212°F). Water then migrates from the central portion of the food outward to the edges to replace that lost by evaporation. Finally, the interior of the food is cooked. Sufficient heat must be transferred to gelatinize starch and coagulate proteins that may be present in the food.

When cold food is first placed in the fryer, the temperature of the frying fat decreases. A thermostatic control on the fryer then signals for the production of additional heat energy to bring the temperature back to the desired frying temperature. If an automatic fryer is not used, a thermometer should be employed to monitor the temperature and protect against overheating. A test for approximate temperatures that has some value, in case no thermometer is available, involves measuring the time required to brown a cube of bread in the hot fat. Fats of a suitable temperature for thoroughly frying some raw foods, as

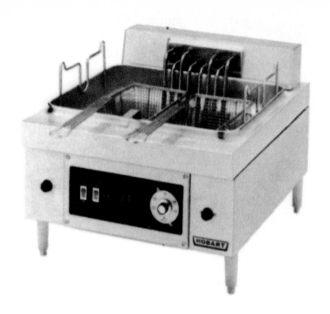

FIGURE 18.4

Deep-fat frying is common in many foodservice establishments. A small counter fryer holds 28 pounds of shortening, whereas a freestanding electric fryer has a capacity of 50 pounds of shortening and produces up to 110 pounds of french-fried potatoes per hour. (Courtesy of Hobart Corporation)

well as for browning, require about 60 seconds to brown a cube of bread. Fats that are hot enough to fry cooked foods brown or to cook some raw, watery foods will brown a cube of bread in about 40 seconds. Table 18.2 provides a range of temperatures that can be used for deep-fat frying.

Changes in Heated Fats and Interaction with Food

When fats are heated to very high temperatures, certain chemical and physical changes occur. For example, overheated fats begin to give off smoke. The *smoke point* of a fat is defined as the temperature at which smoke is continuously emitted from the surface of the fat, and this point is measured under standardized conditions as a specific temperature. Present in the smoke that comes from overheated fats is a substance called *acrolein*. Acrolein results from the dehydration of glycerol. It is highly irritating to the eyes and throat.

$$
\begin{array}{ccc}
\mathrm{CH_2OH} & & \mathrm{CH_2} \\
| & & || \\
\mathrm{CHOH} & \xrightarrow{\text{heat}} & \mathrm{CH} \qquad + 2\mathrm{H_2O} \\
| & & | \\
\mathrm{CH_2OH} & & \mathrm{C}=\mathrm{O} \\
& & | \\
& & \mathrm{H} \\
\text{glycerol} & & \text{acrolein \quad water}
\end{array}
$$

TABLE 18.2
Temperature Ranges for Deep-Fat Frying

Type of Product	Temperature of Fat	Approximate Time to Brown a 1-Inch Cube of Bread in Hot Fat (sec)
Doughnuts Fish Fritters Oysters, scallops, and soft-shelled crabs	350°–375°F (175°–190°C)	60
Croquettes Eggplant Onions Cauliflower	375°F (190°C)	40
French-fried potatoes	385°–395°F (195°–200°C)	20

Source: The American Home Economics Association, *Handbook of Food Preparation.*

The glycerol from which acrolein is produced comes from the hydrolysis of some of the triglyceride molecules of the fat to their component parts, free fatty acids and glycerol. The development of free fatty acids during frying contributes to a decrease in the smoke point. Frying large amounts of high-moisture foods tends to increase the rate of development of free fatty acids. Suspended matter, such as flour or batter particles, also lowers the smoke point. In addition, the greater the surface of the fat exposed to air, the more rapidly the smoke point is lowered.

Heated oils and their degradation products interact with the food being fried. Some materials are leached from the food into the frying fat and some of the fat itself is gradually broken down or degraded. Oxygen from the air may react with the fat in the fryer at the oil-air interface. This creates many different chemical compounds in the frying fat in addition to the basic triglyceride molecules that originally made up the fat. Some of the chemicals produced are surfactants, that is, molecules that interact at the air-oil or oil-food interfaces and lower the surface or interfacial tension. A surfactant theory of frying suggests that the lowered surface tension allows oxygen to be drawn in, producing some oxidized compounds that aid in heat transfer. Also, the contact time between the hot oil and the aqueous food surfaces is increased and more heat is transferred to cook the food. If surfactant levels become too high, however, degradation of the fat is enhanced, **polymers** are formed, increased viscosity results from the gum formation, and foaming is excessive. There is an optimum level of surfactants in the frying fat that results in a quality fried product that is golden-brown in color, crisp with rigid surfaces, and has delicious odors, fully cooked centers, and optimal oil absorption [3].

As frying fat is used, darkening occurs. As the fat darkens, the foods fried in it darken more rapidly and may be uneven in color. The ingredients in the product being fried influence the color changes of the frying fat. Potatoes form little color in the frying fat, whereas chicken causes considerably more darkening. The composition of the breading mixture also affects darkening. The presence of egg yolk in a batter or dough causes greatly increased darkening of the fat with continued use (Figure 18.5).

Polymers very large molecules produced by linking small molecules together; sometimes forming a gummy material

FIGURE 18.5

Ingredients in the product being fried will influence the darkening of the frying fat. The sample of corn oil at the top center has not been used for frying. All other samples in the picture have been used for 8½ hours of continous frying of fritter-type batters containing various combinations of egg and baking powder. The presence of egg yolk causes a marked darkening of the fat during frying. (BK PD, baking powder; WH EGG, whole egg; YOLK, egg yolk; WHITE, egg white.)

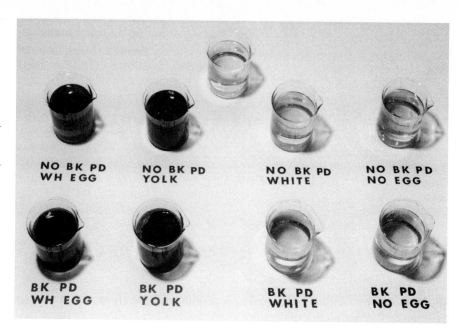

NO BK PD WH EGG   NO BK PD YOLK   NO BK PD WHITE   NO BK PD NO EGG

BK PD WH EGG   BK PD YOLK   BK PD WHITE   BK PD NO EGG

It is very important to control frying temperatures and to use proper procedures to avoid undesirable chemical changes in the fat. Scientific literature contains many studies concerned with the safety of heated fats and oils [6]. Some of these studies involved fats that were excessively abused and therefore did not simulate ordinary conditions of frying. Fats can apparently be seriously damaged when they are heated to very high temperatures over long periods, particularly when they are heated in the laboratory without frying. However, under reasonably well-controlled conditions of actual frying, adverse effects are generally not apparent [1], and the fried products become unacceptable from a sensory standpoint before the fat appears to be damaged excessively [6]. The fats in baked products appear to change very little under ordinary conditions of baking [21].

Fat Turnover

By *turnover* is meant the amount of fat in the frying kettle that is replaced by fresh fat in a given period. As fat is absorbed by the foods that are fried, the amount of fat in the kettle continuously decreases as frying proceeds unless fresh fat is added periodically. In the processing of such foods as potato chips, which is done on a continuous basis, the frying fat may be turned over completely (100 percent) in only one day of frying; however, in foodservice operations, frying is usually intermittent and the rate of fat turnover may average only about 20 to 35 percent each day. When turnover is slow, it is necessary to periodically discard all of the fat in the kettle and start again with fresh fat. To avoid the excessive costs resulting from the disposal of large amounts of used frying fat, it is best to use the smallest amount of fat possible in relation to the amount of food to be fried [17].

Fat Absorption

From the standpoint of both palatability and ease or rapidity of digestion, it is desirable to hold fat absorption by fried food to a minimum. Among the factors that affect the amount of fat absorbed are (1) the character and composition of the food, (2) the condition of the frying fat, including the level of surfactants present, (3) the amount of surface exposed to the fat, and (4) the length of time of heating. An optimum level of surfactants in the frying fat produces optimal fat absorption. With excessive amounts of surfactants, more oil is drawn into the food.

The temperature of the fat indirectly affects the amount of fat absorbed during frying, because foods cooked at a lower temperature must be cooked for a longer period to achieve the desired amount of brownness. In general, the longer the food remains in the fat, the greater the absorption. The greater the amount of surface area exposed to the fat, the greater the fat absorption.

The proportions and types of ingredients in doughnuts and fritters and various manipulative procedures affect fat absorption. Doughnuts containing a high percentage of sugar and fat absorb more fat while frying than do doughnuts containing lesser amounts of sugar and/or fat. Doughnuts containing more lecithin (a phospholipid) have been reported to absorb more fat than doughnuts with lesser amounts of lecithin [18]. The addition of egg to a fritter-type batter that contains no additional shortening significantly increases fat absorption. Egg yolk contains phospholipids.

Doughnuts made from soft wheat flours and from soft doughs absorb more fat than doughnuts made from strong flours and from stiff doughs. The development of gluten by the extensive manipulation of the dough decreases fat absorption as compared with doughs in which gluten has not been developed. Rough dough surfaces caused by cracks or undermanipulation, or by allowing the dough to stick to the board, increase the surface area and therefore increase fat absorption.

For most fried food, high fat temperatures of 196° to 199°C (385° to 390°F) tend to produce too brown a crust by the time the food is completely cooked, although fat absorption is relatively low. Doughnuts fried at high temperatures are usually of comparatively small volume because the crust hardens before expansion is complete. The decreased volume may explain, in part, the lower fat absorption, as a low volume would mean exposure of less surface area to the frying fat.

The type of fat does not appear to significantly affect the amount of fat absorbed during frying. Under identical conditions of time, temperature, and type of food being fried, various fats commonly used for frying appear to be absorbed in similar amounts.

Choosing the Frying Fat

A number of factors affect the choice of a frying medium. First, it should be a fat that, during use, develops flavor that enhances the quality and acceptability of the fried product. It has been reported, for example, that the volatile materials produced by hydrogenated soybean oils were less favorably judged on the basis of flavor and odor than were those from hydrogenated corn, cottonseed, or peanut oil [16]. The flavor should also be stable enough that it remains appetizing throughout the shelf life of the product. Antioxidants having effects that carry through after heating may be added to frying fats to lengthen the shelf life of the fried product. Minute amounts of methyl silicone are often added to fats during processing to help retard foaming and deterioration during frying.

A certain amount of hydrogenation of the frying oil is needed to provide good flavor stability and to increase the frying life of the fat before too much degradation occurs. Partially hydrogenated fluid shortening can be poured and is therefore easier to handle in foodservice operations than is solid shortening. Shortenings that are specially formulated for frying are available for foodservice use.

It is interesting to note that many in the fast-food industry are switching from the use of a mixture of animal tallow and vegetable fat for frying to the use of all-vegetable shortenings [13]. Some fast-food restaurants use a canola-based frying fat because of its superior heat stability [5]. Canola oil contains a relatively low proportion of saturated fatty acids and a high percentage of monounsaturates, particularly oleic acid, which appeals to some consumers from a nutritional standpoint.

The resistance of a fat to smoking at high temperatures is also important in choosing a frying medium. The smoke point of a fat is partly a result of its natural composition and partly a result of the processing it has received. Most oils on the market are highly refined and deodorized, and they have relatively high smoke points, usually above 228°C (442°F). They can be used for frying in the home kitchen but do not have the stability needed for most foodservice operations.

Hydrogenated shortenings without added emulsifiers may smoke within the range 220° to 232°C (430° to 450°F); however, most shortenings sold on the retail market are for general-purpose use and contain added mono- and diglycerides as emulsifiers. This makes them particularly suitable for making shortened cakes but less desirable for frying, because the addition of these emulsifiers lowers the smoke point. In this case, the first smoke given off is not from the breakdown of the fat itself but from the emulsifier. It is an interesting fact that on continued heating, as the emulsifier is decomposed, the smoke point may rise somewhat.

Other desirable factors to look for in choosing a fat are light color, resistance to foaming and gum formation, uniformity in quality, stability for long-term use, and ease of use, considering both form and packaging.

Care of Frying Fat

To maintain high quality in fried foods, it is important to regularly monitor the frying fat. A fat that is fabricated for frying may be used for a considerable period if the turnover with fresh fat is fairly high and if the fat is cared for properly. The maintenance of proper frying temperatures and avoidance of overheating are important considerations in caring for fat. The thermostats on fryers should be checked regularly.

In the beginning, efficient frying equipment should be selected. In foodservice operations, the frying fat should be filtered at least daily. It is necessary to remove charred batter and breading or other materials that have accumulated in the frying fat, since these can ruin the appearance of the fried product, contribute bitter flavor, lower the smoke point, and darken the fat as well [16]. These materials are sometimes referred to as *cracklings*. Various types of screens, cartridges, and paper filters with and without filter aids can be used to remove cracklings. Some filters are built into the frying equipment; portable filters are also available. In the use of pressure fryers, which were developed primarily for the frying of poultry, filtering of fat should be done more frequently. Frying under pressure when steam is retained places an extra burden on the frying shortening [17]. Frying equipment and hoods over the equipment should be kept clean and in proper working order.

After fat has been used for home frying, all foreign matter should be strained from the fat. The fat should then be stored in a cold place out of contact with light and air.

Commercial kits are available for the measurement of **polar materials** in the frying fat [16]. These materials reflect the total level of degradation products that have resulted from the frying process. This is considered by many to be a reasonable indicator of the overall quality of the fat and can be useful in any frying operation.

Polar materials   chemical molecules that have electric charges (positive or negative) and tend to be soluble in water

•BUYING FATS

It is important in purchasing fats to consider their specific uses in food preparation and to select fats in accordance with needs and budget. Fats are often tailored for specific uses in foodservice operations, such as deep-fat frying, panfrying or griddling, and cake making. Separate fats are generally purchased for each of the specific needs.

Most consumers probably do not need to keep more than three or four different household fats on hand. Butter, because of its flavor, is sometimes preferred for table use, as well as for use in some baked products and for the seasoning of certain foods. Margarine serves a similar purpose, usually at a somewhat lower cost, although the different brands of margarine vary widely in price. A blend of butter and margarine is also available. Margarines, particularly those types that are high in polyunsaturated fatty acids, may be chosen over butter for health reasons. However, margarines contain various levels of trans fatty acids, which may be a concern for some consumers. Some flavorful drippings, such as bacon fat, are also used for flavoring.

Most households require some shortening, but one general-purpose shortening can be used satisfactorily for both shortening and frying purposes. If no oil dressings are made in the home, there may be no need to purchase oil unless oil is preferred for frying or for shortening. Lard is preferred by some for use in pastry or biscuits; usually, modified methods of mixing are required to produce desirable results in shortened cakes. Lard is commonly added to refried beans in the preparation of Mexican food, primarily because of its flavor. The use of fats for shortening is considered in Chapter 23.

•FAT REPLACERS

The low-calorie and dietetic food market in the United States continues to grow, indicating that consumers are concerned about what they eat. Public health agencies have pointed out the relationship between fat intake and the development of chronic disease, and dietary guidelines recommend decreased fat intake. In response to these concerns, the food industry is researching new products and new ingredients that will replace part or all of the fat in foods.

Fat plays a number of roles in various food products. Although many of its functions are related to texture, it is very difficult, if not impossible, to find a fat substitute that will perform well in all food products [27]. Several substances, however, are presently being used as fat replacers in foods that are on the market. Others are still under review by the FDA. Fat replacers can be categorized, according to their chemical nature, as carbohydrate-based, protein-based, or fat-based [4]. Often a combination of substances is used as a fat replacer to achieve the desired effect.

Carbohydrate-Based Replacements

Most of the reduced-fat products introduced into the market in recent years have contained carbohydrate-based fat replacers. These include derivatives of cellulose, maltodextrins, gums, modified starches, and polydextrose. Ingredient developers have produced a number of products marketed under specific brand names, using, in many cases, a combination of ingredients [10].

Carbohydrates such as starches, cellulose, and gums have a long history of use in the food industry. They often function as thickeners and stabilizers. When used to replace fat, they add form and structure, hold water as hydrophilic agents, and act as emulsifiers when a small amount of fat is used. They may produce a mouth-feel that is similar to that created by fat, but they do not taste exactly like fat. Stickiness and other textural problems may result if large amounts are used [26]. A combination of gums, cellulose, and/or modified starches can be used to produce a fat replacement system.

Maltodextrins are nonsweet carbohydrates made from partially hydrolyzed starch. They can partly or totally replace fat in a variety of products, including margarine, frozen desserts, and salad dressings. They are classified as GRAS (generally regarded as safe) by the FDA and have the same caloric value as starch [10].

Sorbitol　a sugar alcohol similar to glucose in chemical structure

Humectant　a substance that can absorb moisture readily

Polydextrose is a "designed" ingredient, prepared from a mixture of dextrose (glucose), **sorbitol**, and citric acid. It has multiple functions, which include acting as a bulking agent, a texturizer, and a **humectant**, and it may be used to replace sugar or fat. Polydextrose contains only one kilocalorie per gram, in comparison with four kilocalories provided by sugars and starch. It is approved by the FDA for use in such products as frozen dairy desserts, baked goods, confections, puddings, and salad dressings [12].

Protein-Based Replacements

A fat substitute called Simplesse™ has received approval by the FDA as a GRAS substance. It is a microparticulated protein, which means that it is produced by reshaping, into tiny round particles, proteins from milk and egg. This process produces protein particles so small that they are perceived as fluid. Microparticulated protein has a caloric value of 1⅓ kcal/gram, compared with 9 kcal/gram for the fat it replaces. It is especially useful in frozen and refrigerated products but has potential for use in such foods as cream soups and baked goods [4, 15]. It cannot be used for frying.

Fat-Based Replacements

Most foods were not originally developed for the purpose of optimizing the fat content. Therefore, some reduction in fat is usually possible without changing product characteristics to an appreciable degree. The use of emulsifier systems that will "stretch" the function of the fat makes possible some fat reduction in many fat-containing products. For example, the addition of mono- and diglycerides as emulsifiers to cake shortenings allows a reduction in the fat content without sacrifice to quality. Emulsifier systems can be designed to function well in many low-fat products, but other ingredients must also be used in conjunction with the emulsifier system to help replace the fat that is lost.

Long-chain fatty acids can be combined as **esters** with sucrose to produce a compound called *sucrose polyester*. This product is neither digested nor absorbed from the human digestive tract and is therefore noncaloric. Yet it has characteristics similar to triglycerides when used in food preparation. One such compound, called Olestra™, is being evaluated by the FDA as a food additive for use in shortenings and oils. Sucrose polyester could be used interchangeably with other fats in a variety of foods or could be blended with oils. It is heat stable and could be used in frying [26].

Ester a chemical combination of an alcohol (—OH) with an organic acid (—COOH)

•EMULSIONS

The term *emulsion* is applied to a system consisting of one liquid dispersed in another liquid with which it is **immiscible**. A third substance, called an *emulsifying agent* or *emulsifier*, is necessary to stabilize the system and keep one liquid dispersed in the other on a permanent basis (see Figure 18.6).

Immiscible describing substances that cannot be mixed or blended

Emulsions in Foods

Emulsions are found naturally in many foods, for example, milk, cream, and egg yolk. In all such foods the fat is divided into small particles or globules and dispersed throughout the watery portion of the food. The **homogenization of whole milk** further divides the naturally emulsified fat into particles that are so fine they tend to remain in suspension and do not rise to the surface on standing, as does the fat in nonhomogenized milk.

Many food products are emulsions that have been formed during processing or preparation. The manufacture of emulsions is a highly energetic and dynamic process [8]. Work is necessary to divide the fat into tiny globules or

Homogenization of whole milk a process in which whole milk is forced, under pressure, through very small openings, dividing the fat globules into very tiny particles

Fats, Frying, and Emulsions

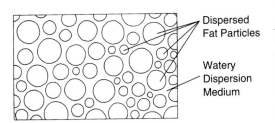

Dispersed Fat Particles

Watery Dispersion Medium

FIGURE 18.6
An emulsion consists of one substance dispersed in another substance with which it is immiscible. An emulsifying agent surrounds each dispersed particle. This diagram represents an oil-in-water emulsion; the oil droplets, surrounded by an emulsifying agent, are dispersed in water.

droplets. These newly formed globules must be rapidly protected against coalescence by the adsorption of an emulsifier at their surface. Shaking, beating, stirring, whipping, and high-pressure homogenization are some methods used to form an emulsion of one immiscible liquid dispersed in another.

Examples of food emulsions are mayonnaise and other salad dressings, sauces, gravies, puddings, cream soups, shortened cake batters, and other flour mixtures in which the fat is dispersed. Other emulsions are produced in the processing of foods such as peanut butter, confections, frozen desserts, sausages, and frankfurters. The dispersing medium may be water, milk, dilute vinegar, lemon or other fruit juice, or some similar liquid. The dispersed substance may be any of the commonly used food fats and oils. Some emulsions, such as margarine, have fat as the dispersing medium and water as the dispersed substance. Even though the fat is not always a liquid at ordinary temperatures of holding, the food system is still called an emulsion.

A variety of substances act as emulsifying agents and stabilizers in manufactured food systems, including the isolated milk protein casein, whey proteins and concentrated whey products, isolated soy proteins, oilseed protein concentrates, gelatin, lecithin, cellulose derivatives, fine dry powders such as ground spices, various vegetable gums, and starch pastes [19, 24]. Several emulsifiers are present in some batters. For example, shortened cake batter contains egg lipoproteins, casein from milk, gluten and starch from flour, and mono- and diglycerides.

Temporary Emulsions

If only oil and water are shaken together, an emulsion is formed, but on standing, the oil particles reunite and separate from the water. Emulsions of this kind are called *temporary emulsions*. They must be used immediately or, if they are made in quantity and stored, they must be reshaken or beaten each time they are used. Simple french and italian dressings are examples of this type of emulsion.

Permanent Emulsions

Permanent emulsions, which can be held or stored without separation of the two immiscible liquids, require an emulsifying agent or emulsifier to form a protecting or stabilizing film around the dispersed droplets and prevent them from reuniting. The term *stabilizer* is also used to describe the emulsifier or the substance that assists the emulsifier in some food products. Mayonnaise is an example of a permanent emulsion. Actually, any food containing fat that is distributed throughout and does not appear on the surface as a separate layer is a permanent emulsion.

Two general types of emulsions are possible: an oil-in-water emulsion and a water-in-oil emulsion. Oil-in-water emulsions are more common in foods, but butter and margarine are examples of water-in-oil emulsions. The type of emulsion formed depends on the nature of the emulsifier.

How does an emulsifier act to form an emulsion? Emulsifiers have a special type of chemical nature; they are **amphiphilic** molecules. Part of the emulsifier molecule is attracted to or soluble in water (hydrophilic), while another part of the same molecule is soluble in fat (lipophilic). Thus, the emulsifier

Amphiphilic   liking or being attracted to both water and fat

molecule may be oriented at the interface of the two immiscible liquids with its hydrophilic group in the watery phase and its lipophilic group in the fat or oil phase. One of these amphiphilic groups is a little stronger than the other and causes one phase to form droplets that are dispersed in the other continuous phase, with the emulsifier between them as it surrounds droplets of the dispersed phase. Figure 18.7 suggests how an emulsifier might orient itself at an oil-water interface to form an emulsion.

If the emulsifier is *more* attracted to the water, or more water soluble, it promotes the dispersion of oil in water. If the emulsifier is more attracted to the oil, or more oil soluble, it tends to produce a water-in-oil emulsion. A photomicrograph of the fat-in-water emulsion of milk, both before and after homogenization, is shown in Figure 20.1. Breaking of emulsions or separation of the two phases may occur under certain conditions. In some cases, the emulsion can re-form.

•SALAD DRESSINGS

Classification

Definitions and standards of identity for mayonnaise, french dressing, and salad dressing have been published by the FDA. If products are labeled and sold under these names they must meet the standards of identity. Mayonnaise must contain not less than 65 percent by weight of edible vegetable oil and an egg yolk-containing ingredient. French dressing must contain not less than 35 percent by weight of edible vegetable oil. Salad dressing must contain not less than 30 percent by weight of edible vegetable oil and also may contain a cooked starchy paste as well as an egg yolk-containing ingredient. All three of the dressings contain an acidifying ingredient. Many variations of these three basic dressings are created by the use of different optional ingredients. Thus, a wide variety of dressings are available commercially, for example, thousand island, blue cheese, bacon and tomato, creamy cucumber, italian, ranch, and taco dressings.

Dry salad dressing mixes contain a mixture of seasonings and emulsifiers or stabilizers. They are usually added to sour cream or to milk and mayonnaise to make a creamy dressing or to vinegar and oil to make a french-type dressing.

Dressings for salads made in home kitchens are not, of course, governed by standards of identity. Many of these dressings are very simple combinations of ingredients and are difficult to classify. In fruit dressings, fruit juices replace vinegar and other liquids. Sour cream, sometimes with added ingredients such as crumbled cheese, can be added to vegetable or fruit salads. Mixtures of vinegar or lemon juice and seasonings, with or without small amounts of fat-containing ingredients, are sometimes used as low- or reduced-calorie dressings. Dry salad-seasoning mixes can also be prepared in home kitchens. Cost as well as flavor comparisons might well be made between commercial dressings and those prepared from scratch.

Salad Dressing

Salad dressing is the emulsified semisolid food prepared from edible vegetable oil, an acidifying ingredient, egg yolk or whole egg, and a cooked or partly cooked starchy paste prepared with a food starch or flour. Water may be added in the preparation of the starchy paste. Optional seasonings and emulsifying agents may also be used. Salad dressing must contain not less than 30 percent by weight of edible vegetable oil and not less than 4 percent by weight of liquid egg yolks or their equivalent. All of this is specified in the standard of identity for salad dressing.

SECTION THROUGH OIL DROPLETS
DISPERSED IN WATER

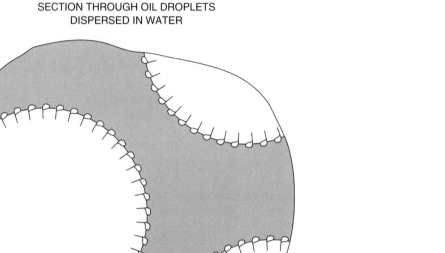

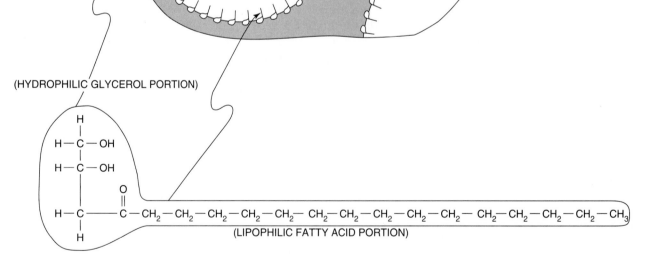

(HYDROPHILIC GLYCEROL PORTION)

(LIPOPHILIC FATTY ACID PORTION)

FIGURE 18.7

An emulsifier stabilizes an emulsion by virtue of its chemical structure. In a simplified presentation, this structure includes one part that is attracted to water and another part that is attracted to fat. The attraction of one of the groups is somewhat stronger than the other. For example, a mono-glyceride molecule is shown with the fatty acid portion being attracted to the oil and the glycerol portion attracted to the water, forming a filmlike layer around the oil droplets and keeping them dispersed in the continuous watery phase.

Many different dressings for salads can be made in both home and institutional kitchens. Some of these are cooked dressings and may be of the custard type, in which all thickening is accomplished with egg yolk or whole egg. More frequently, a starchy agent is used to aid in thickening because there is less tendency for curdling to occur when cream or milk is used as the liquid. Some cooked dressings made with milk or cream are of a consistency suitable for immediate use but the dressing may be made thicker than is desirable and highly seasoned to permit dilution without impairment of flavor.

French Dressing

According to its standard of identity, french dressing is the separable liquid food or the emulsified viscous fluid food prepared from edible vegetable oil (oil content not less than 35 percent by weight), specified acidifying agents, and optional seasonings. It may be emulsified, in which case certain gums, pectin, or other emulsifier, including egg or egg yolk, may be used to the extent of 0.75 percent by weight of the finished dressing. Large amounts of paprika and other powdered seasonings also help to keep the oil and acid emulsified. In unemulsified french dressing, a temporary emulsion is formed as the dressing is shaken or beaten. Oil and acid ingredients separate soon after mixing, but can be shaken or mixed each time the dressing is used.

The usual proportions for french dressing are 3/4 cup salad oil for each 1/3 cup vinegar or lemon juice. Various seasonings can be used.

Reduced-Fat Dressings

Reduced-fat salad dressings and mayonnaise are sold on the retail market and are prominently labeled as such. The caloric content of reduced-calorie dressings depends on how much oil is used. Those that contain essentially no fat in the finished dressing contain 6 to 14 kilocalories per tablespoon. Others, with up to 3 grams of fat per tablespoon of finished dressing, provide 30 to 40 kilocalories per tablespoon. A comparable full-fat salad dressing contains 60 to 80 kilocalories per tablespoon.

A mixture of emulsifying agents and stabilizers, including xanthan gum, alginate, cellulose gum, locust bean gum, and modified starch, is used to produce an emulsion and to substitute for the fat that is being eliminated. These stabilizers are hydrophilic and hold relatively large amounts of water, giving body or thickness to the product.

The 1990 Nutrition Education and Labeling Act requires that a product labeled *fat free* has less than 0.5 gram fat per serving and no added fat. One labeled *low fat* must contain less than 3 grams of fat per serving. A product labeled *light* must contain 33 percent fewer calories or 50 percent of the fat in a reference food. If 50 percent or more of the calories in the product come from fat, the reduction must be 50 percent of the fat.

No-oil low-calorie dry dressing mixes are also available. The dry mix is added to water and vinegar, producing a product with about 6 kilocalories per tablespoon. Some reduced-calorie dry mixes require the addition of milk and mayonnaise. These produce creamy dressings with about 35 kilocalories per tablespoon. The dry mixes contain stabilizers and emulsifiers along with various herbs and other flavoring materials.

Mayonnaise

According to its standard of identity, mayonnaise or mayonnaise dressing is the emulsified semisolid food prepared from edible vegetable oil, vinegar and/or lemon juice or citric acid, egg yolk or whole egg, and one or more optional ingredients, such as salt, mustard, paprika, a sweetening agent, and monosodium glutamate. The edible oil content of mayonnaise must be not less than 65 percent by weight and is emulsified or finely divided in the vinegar or lemon juice. Mayonnaise, therefore, is an emulsion, with one liquid (oil) dispersed in a second liquid (vinegar or lemon juice). These liquids do not usually mix, and it is a third agent, an emulsifier, that makes possible the mixing on a relatively permanent basis. Certain components of egg or egg yolk (apparently lipoproteins) act as the emulsifying agent, coating the dispersed particles of oil to keep them dispersed.

Mayonnaise can be made in the home kitchen. The factors that affect the formation of mayonnaise, its stability, and the ease of preparation are similar wherever the product is made.

Factors Affecting Mayonnaise Preparation

Cold oil is more difficult to break up into small globules than is warm, less viscous oil. Thus, the start of emulsification is delayed by chilling, but after the emulsion is formed, chilling thickens and stabilizes the product.

Egg yolk is the chief emulsifying ingredient in mayonnaise. Freezing egg yolks, particularly without an additive such as salt or sugar, changes their physical properties so that on thawing they are very viscous. A larger quantity of frozen yolk than of fresh yolk is required for making mayonnaise. Salt, mustard, paprika, and pepper are used mainly for flavor, but both the salt and the powdery seasoning ingredients help to stabilize the emulsion as well.

Mayonnaise usually contains about 3/4 to 1 cup of oil per egg yolk and 2 tablespoons of acid ingredient. Stable mayonnaise can be mixed by various methods:

1. All of the acid and seasonings can be added to the egg yolk before any additions of oil.
2. Acid can be added at various intervals during the mixing.
3. Acid can be added alternately with the oil.
4. Acid can be added after a large percentage of the oil is added to the egg yolk.

The first additions of oil must be small to allow a stable emulsion to form. After the first two or three additions of oil, the volume of oil that is added at one time may be increased to a variable extent, depending on the temperature of the ingredients, the rate of beating, and other factors, but in any case it should be less than the volume of emulsion that is already formed.

Breaking and Re-Forming an Emulsion

If oil particles coalesce, the emulsion breaks, and the oil separates from the watery portion of the dressing. When this occurs while the emulsion is forming, the cause is incomplete preliminary emulsification, too rapid an addition of oil, too high a ratio of oil to emulsifier (or another wrong proportion), or an inefficient method of agitation.

Prepared emulsified mayonnaise may separate during storage. Freezing may damage or rupture the film of emulsifying agents and allow the dispersed oil to coalesce, resulting in a broken emulsion. Mayonnaise stored at too high a temperature may separate because of differences in the rate of expansion of warm water and oil. Mayonnaise stored in an open container may lose sufficient moisture from the surface by evaporation to damage the emulsion. Excessive jarring or agitation, particularly during shipping and handling, can cause separation. This is, however, an uncommon occurrence.

A broken mayonnaise emulsion may be re-formed by starting with a new egg yolk, or with a tablespoon of water or vinegar, and adding the separated mayonnaise to it gradually. Thorough beating after each addition of separated mayonnaise is important. If separation occurs in the preparation of mayonnaise before all of the oil is added, the remainder of the original oil may be added only after re-emulsification has been achieved as described.

Variations

Additions can be made to mayonnaise to vary the flavor and consistency. Chopped foods, such as vegetables, olives, pickles, hard-cooked eggs, and nuts, may be added with discretion. Chili sauce, sour cream, and whipped cream can also enhance flavor and consistency for certain uses.

STUDY QUESTIONS

1. For what general purposes are fats used in food preparation? Name at least four uses.
2. Explain two chemical reasons why fats vary in their melting points so that some are liquid at room temperature, whereas others are solid.
3. Most fats used in food preparation are separated from other tissues and refined or processed. Briefly describe how each fat listed below is produced. Also indicate for which of the general uses listed in question 1 each fat may be appropriate.
   a. Butter
   b. Margarine
   c. Lard
   d. Hydrogenated shortening
   e. Oil
4. a. Explain what happens when oils are hydrogenated and when they are winterized.
   b. What purposes do these processes serve in the production of food fats?
   c. What is a *plastic* fat? Give examples.
5. a. What is *rancidity*?
   b. Distinguish between hydrolytic rancidity and oxidative rancidity.
   c. Explain what probably happens when a fat is oxidized and becomes rancid.
   d. List several factors that may contribute to the development of rancidity. How can these be controlled?
   e. How does an antioxidant retard the development of rancidity?
   f. Name several antioxidants that may be added to or are present in fatty foods.
6. a. What is *panfrying*? What is *deep-fat frying*?
   b. Explain the importance of using a proper temperature in frying foods. What do smoke point and acrolein have to do with a proper temperature for frying?
   c. Discuss factors to consider when choosing a frying fat.

    d. Give suggestions for the appropriate care of used frying fat.

    e. What is meant by fat *turnover*? Why is it important in frying?

    f. Discuss several factors that may influence the amount of fat absorbed during frying.

7. Discuss several factors to consider in deciding which fats to purchase.

8. a. What types of substances are being used or tested for use as fat replacers in food products? Discuss.

    b. Give examples of carbohydrate-based, protein-based, and fat-based fat replacers.

9. a. What is an *emulsion*? What is necessary to produce a permanent emulsion?

    b. Give several examples of emulsions in natural foods and of emulsions in prepared or processed foods.

    c. Describe the difference between an oil-in-water emulsion and a water-in-oil emulsion.

    d. How does an emulsifier act to stabilize an emulsion?

10. a. Standards of identity have been published for which three types of dressings for salads?

    b. What percentage of oil is specified for each type?

    c. Which governmental agency is responsible for these standards?

11. a. Describe mayonnaise and list its major ingredients.

    b. Discuss several factors that may affect the formation of a stable emulsion in the making of mayonnaise.

    c. Describe what happens when an emulsion breaks. How can a broken mayonnaise emulsion be reformed?

12. Describe french dressing and list its major ingredients.

13. Explain how salad dressing generally differs from mayonnaise.

REFERENCES

1. Alexander, J. C., B. E. Chanin, and E. T. Moran. 1983. Nutritional effects of fresh, laboratory heated, and pressure deep-fry fats. *Journal of Food Science 48*, 1289.

2. Berger, K. 1986. Palm oil products. *Food Technology 40*, 72 (No. 9).

3. Blumenthal, M. M. 1991. A new look at the chemistry and physics of deep-fat frying. *Food Technology 45*, 68 (No. 2).

4. Calorie Control Council. 1992. Fat Replacers. Calorie Control Council, Suite 500-G, 5775 Peachtree-Dunwoody Road, Atlanta, Georgia 30342.

5. Carr, R. A. 1991. Development of deep-frying fats. *Food Technology 45*, 95 (No. 2).

6. Clark, W. L. and G. W. Serbia. 1991. Safety aspects of frying fats and oils. *Food Technology 45*, 84 (No. 2).

7. Cochran, W. M. and R. J. Baeuerlen. 1981. Formulation innovations and other developments in shortenings, margarines and oils. *Baker's Digest 55*, 16 (October).

8. Dickinson, E. and G. Stainsby. 1987. Progress in the formulation of food emulsions and foams. *Food Technology 41*, 74 (No. 9).

9. Dyerberg, J., H. O. Bang, E. Sloffersen, S. Moncada, and J. R. Vane. 1978. Eicosapentaenoic acid and prevention of thrombosis and atherosclerosis. *Lancet 2*, 117.

10. Dziezak, J. D. 1989. Fats, oils, and fat substitutes. *Food Technology 43*, 66 (No. 7).

11. Dziezak, J. D. 1986. Preservatives: Antioxidants. *Food Technology 40*, 94 (No. 9).

12. Giese, J. H. 1993. Alternative sweeteners and bulking agents. *Food Technology 47*, 114 (No. 1).

13. Haumann, B. F. 1987. Fast food trends in frying fat usage. *Journal of the American Oil Chemists' Society 64*, 789.

14. Hearn, T. L., S. A. Sgoutas, J. A. Hearn, and D. S. Sgoutas. 1987. Polyunsaturated fatty acids and fat in fish flesh for selecting species for health benefits. *Journal of Food Science 52*, 1209.

15. Institute of Food Technologists' Expert Panel on Food Safety & Nutrition. 1989. Low-calorie foods. *Food Technology 43*, 113 (No. 4).

16. Jacobson, G. A. 1991. Quality control in deep-fat frying operations. *Food Technology 45*, 72 (No. 2).

17. Lawson, H. W. 1985. *Standards for Fats and Oils*. Westport, CT: Avi Publishing.

18. McComber, D. and E. M. Miller. 1976. Differences in total lipid and fatty acid composition of doughnuts as influenced by lecithin, leavening agent, and use of frying fat. *Cereal Chemistry 53*, 101.

19. Mittal, G. S. and W. R. Usborne. 1985. Meat emulsion extenders. *Food Technology 39*, 121 (No. 4).

20. Orthoefer, F. T. 1987. Oil use in the food service industry. *Journal of the American Oil Chemists' Society 64*, 795.

21. Phillips, J. A. and G. E. Vail. 1967. Effect of heat on fatty acids. *Journal of the American Dietetic Association 50*, 116.

22. Putnam, J. J. 1991. Food consumption, 1970–90. *Food Review 14*, 2 (No. 3).

23. Raper, N. 1991. Nutrient content of the U.S. food supply. *Food Review 14*, 13 (No. 3).

24. Sharma, S. C. 1981. Gums and hydrocolloids in oil-water emulsions. *Food Technology 35*, 59 (No. 1).

25. Smouse, T. H. 1979. Review of soybean oil reversion flavor. *Journal of the American Oil Chemists' Society 56*, 747A.

26. Stern, J. S. and M. G. Hermann-Zaidins. 1992. Fat replacements: A new strategy for dietary change. *Journal of the American Dietetic Association 92*, 91.

27. Szczesniak, A. S. 1990. Texture: Is it still an overlooked food attribute? *Food Technology 44*, 86 (No. 9).

28. Wood, R. 1992. Biological effects of palm oil in humans. In *Fatty Acids in Foods and Their Health Implications*, New York: Marcel Dekker, Inc.

29. Zock, P. L. and M. B. Katan. 1992. Hydrogenation alternatives: effects of trans fatty acids and stearic acid versus linoleic acid on serum lipids and lipoproteins in humans. *Journal of Lipid Research 33*, 399.

Eggs and Egg Cookery

19

Although the eggs of all birds may be eaten, the egg of the chicken is used more often than any other. This discussion, therefore, pertains to chicken eggs unless otherwise specified.

The natural function of the egg is to provide for the development of the chick. Its whole structure and composition are designed to fulfill this natural purpose. Partly because the egg is associated with the beginning of "life," much symbolism has been attached to it, taking a variety of forms in different cultures over the centuries. In Christian communities, for example, the egg has special significance at Easter time, to the particular delight of children as they enjoy this symbol in many different forms.

In the preparation of food, the egg functions in several different roles, apparently unrelated to its original purpose of providing for the chick. It is used to make **emulsions** because it contains emulsifying agents of proven effectiveness. It also contains foaming agents that allow it to be used to advantage in the production of food **foams**, including meringues and angel food cakes. The ability of the proteins of the egg to **coagulate** on heating allows it to perform a variety of functions, which include forming gels such as baked custards, coating breaded meats and fish, and **clarifying** some liquids such as broth and coffee. Egg yolk also provides color. And just plain eggs—soft cooked, hard cooked, scrambled, and fried—also provide eating enjoyment. The egg gives all this to food preparation besides providing a package of essential nutrients that enrich the diet.

• COMPOSITION AND NUTRITIVE VALUE

Whole egg contains about 75 percent water, 12 percent protein, 10 percent fat, 1 percent carbohydrate, and 1 percent minerals. The white and the yolk are very different from each other in composition, however, as can be seen by an examination of Table 19.1. Essentially all of the fat of the egg is found in the yolk; the white contains a larger percentage of water. Making up about 11 percent of the total weight of the egg is the shell, which is composed of approximately 95 percent calcium carbonate in crystal form [23].

CHAPTER OUTLINE

COMPOSITION AND NUTRITIVE VALUE
STRUCTURE
EGG QUALITY
PRESERVATION
EGGS IN FOOD PREPARATION
EGG SUBSTITUTES

Emulsion   the dispersion of one liquid within another with which it is usually immiscible

Foam   the dispersion of a gas in a liquid

Coagulate   to produce a firm mass or gel by denaturation of protein molecules followed by formation of new crosslinks

Clarify   to make clear a cloudy liquid such as heated soup stock by adding raw egg white and/or egg shell; as the proteins coagulate, they trap tiny particles from the liquid that can then be strained out

TABLE 19.1

Chemical Composition of Egg without Shell

	Amount	Weight (g)	Water (%)	Energy (kcal)	Protein (g)	Fat (g)	Iron (mg)	Vitamin A (RE)	Thiamin (mg)	Riboflavin (mg)
Whole egg, large	1	50	75	72	6	5	0.7	95	0.03	0.25
Egg white	1	33	88	15	4	0	trace	0	trace	0.15
Egg yolk	1	17	49	60	3	5	0.6	97	0.03	0.11

Source: *Nutritive Value of Foods*. Home and Garden Bulletin No. 72. Washington, DC: U.S. Department of Agriculture, 1991.

Although the ratio of white to yolk varies in individual eggs, the white is usually about two-thirds by weight of the total edible portion and the yolk is approximately one-third. In general, the yolk has higher nutrient density than does the white, containing more minerals and vitamins relative to its weight. Cooked egg white is somewhat more completely digested than raw white, especially if raw whites are ingested clear or unbeaten.

Proteins

Protein efficiency ratio a measure of protein quality assessed by determining the extent of weight gain in experimental animals when fed the test item

Egg proteins are of excellent nutritional quality, having the highest **protein efficiency ratio** (PER) of any of the common foods. The major protein in egg white is *ovalbumin*, a protein that is easily denatured by heat. Other egg white proteins are *ovotransferrin, ovomucoid, ovomucin*, and *lysozyme*. Ovomucin, although present in a comparatively small amount, has a large effect on the consistency of thick egg white. It is a very large molecule with a filamentous or fiberlike nature.

Lipoproteins proteins combined with lipid or fatty material such as phospholipids

The major proteins in egg yolk are **lipoproteins**, which include *lipovitellin* and *lipovitellinin*. The lipoproteins are responsible for the excellent emulsifying properties of egg yolk when it is used in such products as mayonnaise.

Lipids

Atherogenic capable of contributing to the development of atherosclerosis (fatty deposits in the walls of the arteries)

The fatty materials in egg yolk, making up about one-third of the weight of fresh yolk, include triglycerides, phospholipids, and cholesterol. One large egg yolk contains about 215 milligrams of cholesterol; there is no cholesterol in egg white. Because of the high level of cholesterol in the yolk, the egg is often considered to be an **atherogenic** food. A number of efforts have been made to produce an egg containing less cholesterol, but these have met with marginal results. However, the fatty acid composition of egg yolk may be altered by changing the diet of the hen. For example, an increased level of ω-3 fatty acids has been reported to result from the addition of small amounts of menhaden fish oil to the laying hen's diet [26].

Pigments

Because certain yellow carotenoid pigments can be converted into vitamin A in the body, the question has been raised as to whether more highly colored egg yolks are a better source of vitamin A than pale-colored yolks. The predominant yellow pigment of egg yolk is a xanthophyll, which is not changed to vitamin A in the body. Usually, however, deep-colored yolks are high in vitamin A content because the same rations that produce color in the yolks also contain more provitamin A, which the hen is able to convert into vitamin A and deposit in the yolk. Hens that do not have access to green or yellow feed and that produce pale yolks may be given vitamin A-supplemented rations. When this is done the pale yolks are high in vitamin A. The vitamin A content of egg yolk, therefore, cannot be predicted solely on the basis of the depth of the yellow color. In practice, egg producers usually feed chickens either sufficient green vegetation or xanthophyll pigments to yield a yolk of medium color intensity.

•STRUCTURE

The egg shell is porous and allows exchange of gases and loss of moisture from the egg. It is brown or white, depending on the breed of the hen. The color of the shell has no effect on the flavor or quality of the contents. An air cell formed at the large end of the egg is produced on cooling by the separation of two thin fibrous protein membranes that are present between the shell and the egg white (Figure 19.1).

In the past, it has been suggested that the protective dull waxy coat on the outside of the egg, referred to as the *cuticle* or the *bloom*, should not be washed off. When it is washed, the porous shell may then more easily permit bacteria, molds, and undesirable flavors or odors to enter the egg. There may also be a greater evaporation of moisture unless preventive measures are taken. However, dirt or soil on shells is probably the most prominent cause of the bacterial invasion of eggs. In commercial practice, therefore, dirty eggs are washed. The eggs are usually washed in automatic washers using alkaline cleaning compounds. After washing, the eggs may be rinsed with a sanitizing agent. If eggs are washed properly, the undesirable effects of washing are kept at a minimum [15].

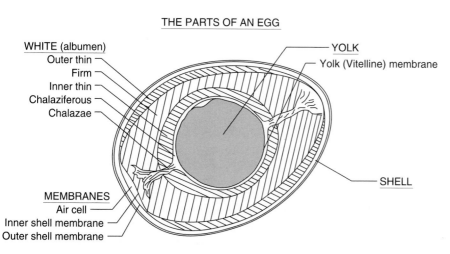

THE PARTS OF AN EGG

WHITE (albumen)
Outer thin
Firm
Inner thin
Chalaziferous
Chalazae

YOLK
Yolk (Vitelline) membrane

SHELL

MEMBRANES
Air cell
Inner shell membrane
Outer shell membrane

FIGURE 19.1
The parts of an egg.

Egg white is composed of thin and thick portions. The proportions of thin and thick white vary widely in different eggs and change during storage under varying conditions. It has been estimated that about 20 to 25 percent of the total white of fresh eggs (1 to 5 days old) is thin white. Thick white is characterized by a higher content of the protein ovomucin than is found in thin white.

Immediately adjacent to the *vitelline membrane*, the thin membrane that surrounds the egg yolk, is a *chalaziferous* or inner layer of firm white. This chalaziferous layer gives strength to the vitelline membrane and extends into the *chalazae*. The chalazae appear as two small bits of thickened white, one on each end of the yolk, and anchor the yolk in the center of the egg. Chalazae appear to have almost the same molecular structure as ovomucin [17].

The yolk is actually composed of concentric layers of light and dark material. Marketed eggs are usually infertile and the germinal disc on the surface of the yolk does not develop. No difference in nutritive value is noted between infertile and fertilized eggs, but fertile eggs may tend to deteriorate more rapidly.

•EGG QUALITY

Characteristics of Fresh and Deteriorated Eggs

A very fresh egg, when broken onto a flat plate, stands up in rounded form. This is due, to a considerable extent, to the viscosity of the thick portion of the egg white. As eggs deteriorate, the proportion of thin white increases, whereas that of thick white decreases. The exact cause of this thinning of the thick white has not been clarified, but it would appear to involve some change in the filamentous protein ovomucin.

The yolk takes up water from the white, and the yolk membrane stretches. When broken out, the deteriorated egg flattens and tends to spread over a level surface. If stretched excessively by movement of water into the yolk, the yolk membrane is weakened and may break when the egg is removed from the shell. Separation of the yolk from the white is thus rendered difficult or impossible. The chalazae start to disintegrate and no longer hold the yolk in the center of the egg, and the yolk moves freely. As an egg ages, especially in a warm, dry atmosphere, there is loss of moisture through the shell. The air cell, which is very small in a fresh egg, increases in size.

The yolks of fresh eggs are slightly acid (usual pH 6.0 to 6.2), whereas the whites are alkaline (usual pH 7.6 to 7.9). A loss of carbon dioxide from the egg on storage results in increased alkalinity of both white and yolk. The white may eventually reach a pH of 9.0 to 9.7. This increase in pH or alkalinity of eggs during storage may be slowed to an appreciable degree by coating the egg shells with a thin layer of oil on the day the eggs are laid. It has been suggested that damage to some egg white proteins by a very alkaline pH results in angel food cakes of decreased volume [22].

The flavor and odor of fresh eggs are affected by the feed of the hen and by the individuality of the hen. During storage, off-flavors may be produced in eggs by the invasion of microorganisms or by the absorption of flavors from the environment. Egg storage is discussed later in this chapter.

Studies of cooked egg flavor have been important in developing acceptable low-cholesterol egg substitutes and convenience egg products, a number of which are appearing on the market. One study of the **headspace** over scrambled eggs reported the presence of 38 volatile substances, including alcohols, aldehydes, ketones, esters, benzene derivatives, and sulfur-containing compounds [21]. A comparison with the volatile compounds of polystyrene packaging materials, commonly used in egg cartons, suggested that some migration of volatile compounds from the packaging into the eggs may have occurred during storage. Further studies of cooked egg flavors would be interesting and useful.

Headspace the volume above a liquid or solid in a container

Measuring Quality

Candling is the method used to determine the interior quality of eggs that go into trade channels. Hand candling, shown in Figure 19.2, is used very little in present commercial grading operations, having been replaced by automated equipment and mass scanning devices. However, it is still used for spot checking and is useful for teaching and demonstrating quality determination. In candling by hand, the egg is held up to an opening behind which is a source of strong light. As the light passes through the egg, it shows the quality of the shell, the size of the air cell, the position and mobility of the yolk, blood spots, molds, and a developing embryo, if one is present. As eggs deteriorate and the chalazae weaken, the yolk tends to settle toward the shell rather than remain suspended in the firm white. In such circumstances the yolk is more fully visible when the egg is candled. Dark yolks also cast a more distinct shadow than light-colored yolks. U.S. Department of Agriculture (USDA) grades for eggs are based on their candled appearance.

Although candling is the best method available for rating unbroken eggs, it may not always be reliable in indicating the quality of the egg when it is opened. Some tests done on the broken-out egg include the measurement of the height of the thick white in relation to the weight of the egg (Haugh unit)

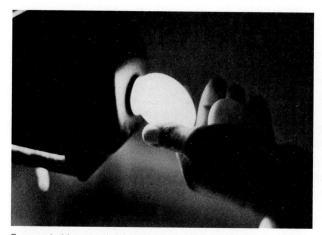

Eggs are held up to a bright light during hand candling.

Mass scanning devices speed up the candling process.

FIGURE 19.2
Candling is used to determine the interior quality of eggs. (Courtesy of the U.S. Department of Agriculture)

FIGURE 19.3

A micrometer is used to evaluate the quality of an egg that has been removed from the shell. This is done by measuring the height of the thick white. This instrument gives a direct reading in Haugh units. (Courtesy of the U.S. Department of Agriculture)

TABLE 19.2

Summary of U.S. Standards for Quality of Individual Shell Eggs

Quality Factor	Specifications for Each Quality Factor		
	AA Quality	**A Quality**	**B Quality**
Shell	Clean Unbroken Practically normal	Clean Unbroken Practically normal	Clean to slightly stained Unbroken Somewhat abnormal
Air Cell	⅛ in. or less in depth Unlimited movement and free or bubbly	3/16 in. or less in depth Unlimited movement and free or bubbly	Over 3/16 in. in depth Unlimited movement and free or bubbly
White	Clear Firm	Clear Reasonably firm	Clear Somewhat watery Small blood and meat spots may be present
Yolk	Outline slightly defined Practically free from defects	Outline fairly well defined Practically free from defects	Outline plainly visible Enlarged and flattened Clearly visible germ develop- ment but no blood

Source: Reference 4.

and the measurement of the height of the yolk in relation to the width of the yolk (yolk index). Figure 19.3 shows the operation of an instrument for measuring Haugh units in a broken-out egg.

Grading

The classification of individual eggs according to established standards constitutes grading for quality. The egg grade standards widely used throughout the United States have been formulated by the U.S. Department of Agriculture; these are summarized in Table 19.2.

In grading, the candled appearance of the egg shell, air cell, white, and yolk are considered. According to the results of the candling inspection, the eggs are assigned one of three consumer grades: U.S. Grade AA, U.S. Grade A, or U.S. Grade B. These grades are illustrated by photographs of broken-out eggs in Figure 19.4, and the grade marks are shown in Figure 19.5.

U.S. Grade AA   U.S. Grade A   U.S. Grade B

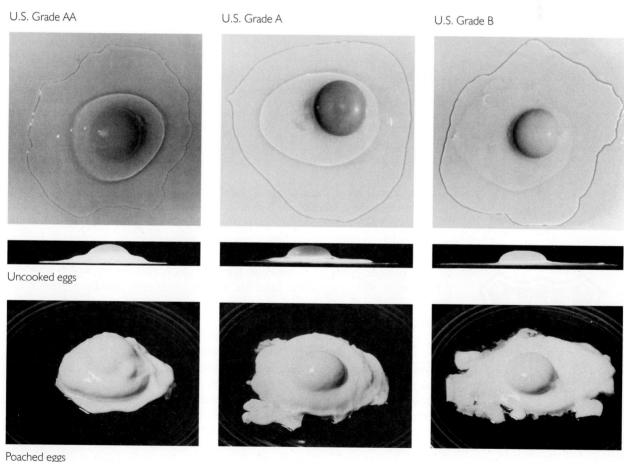

Uncooked eggs

Poached eggs

FIGURE 19.4
Characteristics of egg quality, with the yolk standing highest on the thick white of the U.S. Grade AA eggs, are evident in broken-out eggs and in poached eggs. (Courtesy of the U.S. Department of Agriculture)

FIGURE 19.5

Three grade marks for eggs graded under federal and state supervision. The marks show both grade and size. (Courtesy of the U.S. Department of Agriculture)

AA

A

B

Grades AA and A have a large proportion of thick white that stands up around a firm high yolk. These eggs are especially good for frying and poaching, when appearance is important. Grade B eggs, which have thinner whites and spread out more, are good for general baking and cooking. Grade B eggs are generally not found in retail stores. The nutritional value for all grades is similar.

Eggs must be properly handled at all times, because egg quality is relatively unstable. The interior quality of the egg deteriorates from the time it is laid until it is consumed. Figure 19.6 indicates how egg quality decreases with the time of holding. With proper care, however, this decline in quality can be minimized.

USDA grading services are available for individuals, firms, and agencies that request them on a fee-for-service basis. Cooperative agreements may be made between the USDA and parties within each state to supply official graders and services. The Egg Products Inspection Act of 1970 assures the consumer that only wholesome, unadulterated, and truthfully labeled egg products are marketed. Among the provisions of this act is the requirement that frozen and dried egg products be treated so that they are free from any contamination by *Salmonella* microorganisms.

Sizing

Separate from the process of grading, eggs are sorted for size into six weight classes, as shown in Figure 19.7. This is done on the basis of weighing individual eggs. The commercial weighing and packaging of eggs may be automated, as illustrated in Figure 19.8. Within each grade, several sizes are usually available on supermarket shelves.

Size relative to cost per dozen is an important factor to consider when buying eggs. Most eggs are marketed in cartons, on which the minimum weight per dozen, in ounces, is usually listed. This weight can be divided into the price per dozen to determine the cost per ounce of egg. The cost per ounce of each of the sizes of eggs can then be compared to determine which is the best buy.

Another point to consider in buying eggs is the use for which they are purchased. There is no one best size to buy. Large eggs may be preferred for table use, but for cooking purposes price in relation to size may be a more important consideration.

Recipes calling for a specific number of eggs are usually formulated on the basis of the large size. Actually, *measuring* or *weighing* eggs in recipes gives much more uniform results. If jumbo and extra large or small and peewee-sized eggs are used in a recipe, some adjustment should be made, reducing or increasing the number of eggs by one-fourth to one-third for the jumbo and extra large or for the small and peewee sizes, respectively. If a large number of eggs is used in a recipe, the potential for error becomes great.

Safety and Handling

The U.S. Food and Drug Administration (FDA) has designated shell eggs as a potentially hazardous food and recommends that food establishment operators refrigerate and properly cook eggs. Handling and storing eggs properly will

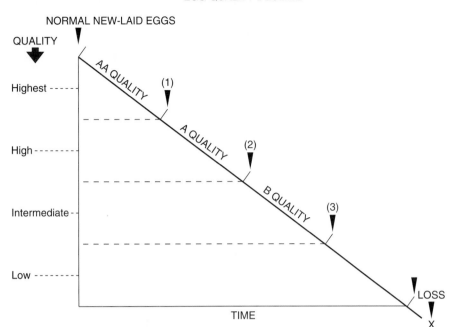

EGG QUALITY DECLINE

NORMAL NEW-LAID EGGS

QUALITY

AA QUALITY

(1)

Highest

A QUALITY

(2)

High

B QUALITY

(3)

Intermediate

Low

LOSS

X

TIME

FIGURE 19.6
The graded quality of eggs declines with the time of holding. (Courtesy of the U.S. Department of Agriculture)

guard against the development of illness resulting from egg products. Salmonellae infection has long been a common concern in relation to eggs and egg products. Foodborne illness caused by eggs contaminated by *Salmonella enteritidis* has been increasing and spreading in recent years.

Salmonella enteritidis may infect the reproductive system of some laying hens, which may lay eggs contaminated with the organism. A possible danger might arise, therefore, from eating raw or lightly cooked eggs, as in eggnogs or very soft-cooked eggs. If *Salmonella* organisms were present in such an egg,

JUMBO 30 OZ.   EXTRA LARGE 27 OZ.   LARGE 24 OZ.   MEDIUM 21 OZ.   SMALL 18 OZ.   PEEWEE 15 OZ.

FIGURE 19.7
Know the eggs you buy. Both size (an indication of quantity) and grade (an indication of quality) should be considered in deciding which eggs to purchase. Six sizes for eggs are shown. Sizing is separate from grading. The weights shown in the illustrations represent ounces per dozen eggs. (Courtesy of the U.S. Department of Agriculture)

FIGURE 19.8

Eggs are handled and processed by automatic in-line scales. Eggs of different sizes are weighed and ejected at different points on the line. (Courtesy of the U.S. Department of Agriculture)

their numbers would likely be small at the time of laying and would probably not create a problem if the product were eaten immediately. The real problems occur with the mishandling of the egg at any place along the line from the hen to the consumer. At warm temperatures, microorganisms can increase rapidly, which is why eggs should *always* be properly refrigerated. Egg products can also be contaminated from sources other than the hen. A few tips on the handling of shell eggs follow [5].

Buy eggs at retail from refrigerated cases only; for foodservice, use only eggs delivered under refrigeration.

Inspect your purchase of eggs and discard any that are broken.

Refrigerate eggs immediately, in cartons or cases, at 4–7°C (40–45°F).

Purchase only the amount of eggs needed for 1–2 weeks.

Be sure your hands and equipment, especially countertops, knives, and cutting boards, are clean before preparing any food, including eggs.

Cook your eggs at least until the whites are completely coagulated and the yolks begin to thicken and are no longer runny. Cook slowly over moderate heat.

In the preparation of cooked foods that incorporate fresh shell eggs, it is best to prepare them individually or in small batches to serve immediately.

Do not leave egg dishes at room temperature for more than one hour, including the time spent for preparation and serving.

It is best never to serve raw or lightly cooked egg dishes to infants, pregnant women, the elderly, or the ill. However, egg products such as commercially prepared frozen, dried, or liquid eggs, for which pasteurization is required, are safe for these individuals. Some foodservice managers prefer to use only pasteurized egg products.

•PRESERVATION

Commercial Cold Storage

To equalize both egg prices and supplies, some of the eggs produced in the United States are placed in commercial cold storage during periods of higher production. Eggs are usually stored at $-1.5°$ to $0°C$ ($29°$ to $32°F$), which is just above their freezing point. To keep well and to retain their quality, only eggs of original high quality should be stored. They remain in desirable condition only if the storage room is well controlled as to humidity (85 to 90 percent), circulation of air, and freedom from objectionable odors. A controlled atmosphere of carbon dioxide or ozone is advantageous in maintaining quality.

Eggs may retain Grade A quality for as long as 6 months in cold storage. If they are of good quality when they are placed in storage and if they are successfully kept under controlled conditions, storage eggs may be of higher quality than many so-called fresh eggs on the market.

Some changes do occur in eggs, as in any other food, during storage. Enzyme action continued over a period of months can result in changes in flavor. These changes need not be objectionable for at least 6 months. Although egg whites become thinner during storage and egg yolks absorb water from the white, for essentially all cooking purposes storage eggs of good quality are entirely satisfactory.

Before being placed in cold storage, eggs may be dipped in light mineral oil [11]. The thin film of oil left on the eggs partially closes the pores in the shell, reducing the loss of moisture and carbon dioxide. If the oiling process is done at the proper time after laying, usually up to twelve hours, the pH of the egg will not rise appreciably on storage. It has been suggested [7] that this control of pH minimizes changes in the egg white proteins, particularly ovomucin and ovalbumin. It also retards the development of increased permeability in the vitelline membrane that surrounds the yolk.

Kitchen Storage

Egg quality deteriorates more rapidly when eggs are kept in a household or institutional foodservice refrigerator than when they are kept under carefully controlled commercial cold storage conditions; however, eggs can be satisfactorily kept under kitchen refrigeration for a few weeks. To retard moisture loss, the eggs should be stored in closed containers. Eggs broken out of the shell can be frozen for longer storage.

Freezing and Drying

Egg breaking, separation, and pasteurization in preparation for freezing or drying are usually done by egg processing plants. After washing and candling, large machines crack open and separate eggs, up to 24,000 per hour for each machine [6]. The safety of eggs preserved by freezing and drying is dependent largely on the sterilization of processing equipment, the maintenance of scrupulous cleanliness throughout the process, and the avoidance of contamination resulting from the introduction of unwholesome eggs into the whole egg mass during processing.

It seems impossible to completely prevent the occurrence of *Salmonella* organisms in liquid egg products unless pasteurization is employed. Pasteurization is therefore required by the federal government for all processed eggs. However, eggs must be pasteurized in such a way that while bacteria are destroyed, the functional properties (whipping and baking performances) are not damaged [16].

The usual pasteurization practice for liquid whole egg involves heat treatment at 60° to 62°C (140° to 143°F) for not less than 3½ minutes. Egg white proteins cannot tolerate the temperatures usually used to pasteurize whole eggs; they become denatured, with consequent decreases in foaming power. Increasing the acidity of the egg whites before pasteurization seems to protect the proteins from damage by heat. The addition of a very small amount of sodium polyphosphate to egg whites and pasteurization at 52° to 55°C (126° to 131°F) for 3½ minutes have also been recommended [17].

The functional properties of raw egg whites are not altered by freezing and thawing. However, frozen egg yolks become viscous and gummy on thawing unless they are mixed with sugar, salt, or syrup before freezing (see Chapter 29 for directions for freezing eggs at home). It has been suggested that the freezing process destabilizes the surface of the tiny lipid-protein particles (lipoproteins) in egg yolk. The fragments that are liberated then aggregate together on thawing to form a mesh-type structure or gel [18]. Whole mixed eggs are often frozen without added salt or sugar; however, because of the presence of the yolk, they probably retain their culinary qualities better when a stabilizer is added. Cooked egg white is not stable to freezing and thawing. The gel structure of the coagulated protein is damaged by ice crystal formation. **Syneresis** occurs on thawing.

Drying is a satisfactory method for preserving eggs, either whole or as separated yolks or whites. Spray-dried egg white and egg yolk have long shelf lives, and their use in food product formulations has increased in recent years. To retain their functional properties, as well as good color and flavor, dried whites require treatment to remove the last traces of glucose. This helps to control the **Maillard** or browning **reaction** during storage. Dried eggs keep best if the initial moisture content is low and if they are kept in a tightly sealed container. Low storage temperatures are also important in maintaining the quality of the dried products.

Dried eggs can be reconstituted before use, or they can be sifted with dry ingredients and extra liquid can be added later to the recipe. General directions for use are to sift prior to measuring and to place lightly in a measuring cup or spoon before leveling off the top with a spatula or straight edge. For reconstitution, dried egg should be sprinkled over the surface of lukewarm water, stirred to moisten, and then beaten until smooth. Reconstituted dried whites are beaten very stiff for most if not all uses.

Liquid Refrigerated Eggs

Liquid eggs, broken out of the shell, are available, generally to food processors, as whole eggs, egg whites, or egg yolks [6]. When these eggs are pasteurized, any *Salmonella* or other pathogenic organisms that may be present are destroyed, but the product is still not sterile. Some microorganisms capable of

Syneresis   a separation or "weeping" of liquid from a gel

Maillard reaction   a special type of browning reaction involving a combination of proteins and sugars as a first step; it may occur in relatively dry foods on long storage as well as in foods heated to high temperatures

causing post-pasteurization spoilage are still present. Consequently, the shelf life of pasteurized, refrigerated liquid eggs is limited. Shelf lives of 12 days at 2°C (36°F) and 5 days at 9°C (48°F) have been reported. Ultrapasteurization, or heating at temperatures up to 68°C (154°F), with subsequent aseptic packaging and refrigerated storage at 4°C (30°F) has been applied on an experimental basis [2].

•EGGS IN FOOD PREPARATION

There are few ingredients in food preparation that are as useful in so many different ways as are eggs. Used alone or in combination with other foods, they may become the major protein dish for a meal. Their color, **viscosity**, emulsifying ability, and coagulability, as well as flavor, make it possible for them to play a variety of roles in cookery processes.

The presence in the yolk of lipoproteins makes the egg yolk especially valuable as an emulsifying agent. (Eggs as emulsifiers are discussed in Chapter 18.) The **surface activity** of the proteins of egg white, in particular, also makes the egg useful in the production of films that hold air and thus create a foam. The leavening of a variety of food mixtures results from this characteristic. An egg white foam used in certain candies also improves the texture by controlling crystallization of sugar.

The ability of egg proteins to coagulate when heated, resulting in thickening or **gel** formation, contributes much to the characteristic properties of such dishes as custards, puddings, and various sauces. The coagulation of egg protein, along with the viscosity of the uncooked egg, is the basis for the use of egg as a binding agent and as a coating to hold crumbs together for crust formation on breaded foods. The coagulation of egg increases the rigidity of cell walls and of crusts in numerous doughs and batters.

The egg's use as a clarifying agent is also dependent on the coagulation of egg proteins. In addition, most dishes to which eggs are added are improved in color and flavor by their inclusion in the mixture.

Egg processing firms are now designing and producing a number of new specialty egg products. Available to some foodservice establishments, for example, are such items as shelled, hard-cooked eggs. Preservation is achieved with careful refrigeration. The *long egg*, an egg roll with the yolk centered for convenient slicing, is also available in both refrigerated and frozen forms. Diced hard-cooked eggs are marketed for use in salad bars, and scrambled eggs and liquid mixes are available in cartons and boilable bags [6]. Egg products on the retail market include frozen liquid quiches, frozen waffle mixes, and Hollandaise sauce.

Heat Coagulation of Egg Proteins

Both egg white and yolk proteins coagulate when heated and, as previously noted, can therefore be used for thickening or gel formation. Upon heating, the egg proteins are **denatured** and then gradually aggregate to form a three-dimensional gel network. The network is stabilized by cross-bonds that include **disulfide linkages** and hydrogen bonding [20].

Egg functions best as a thickener when it is beaten only enough to blend the egg mass smoothly. Beating to the extent of incorporating a considerable

Viscosity resistance to flow as indicated in a thickened consistency

Surface activity the lowering of the surface tension of a liquid because of agents that tend to concentrate at the surface

Gel a colloidal dispersion that shows some rigidity or moldability

Denaturation the unfolding of protein chains to produce a more random arrangement

Disulfide linkages bonding through two sulfur atoms (-S-S-)

amount of air results in the floating of egg foam on the surface of the mixture to be thickened. The following factors affect the heat coagulation of egg proteins.

Concentration and Part of Egg Used

The temperature at which egg proteins coagulate and the time required for coagulation depend in part on the proportion of egg in any mixture. Coagulation does not occur instantaneously but rather proceeds gradually. At a moderate rate of heating, undiluted egg white begins to coagulate and change from a clear mass to an opaque substance at about 60°C (140°F). The egg white gradually becomes completely opaque and more firm as the temperature is increased above 60°C (140°F). At 70°C (158°F), the coagulated mass is fairly firm.

Egg yolk proteins require a slightly higher temperature for coagulation than do those of egg white. Because little color change occurs in egg yolk at the beginning of coagulation, the exact temperature at which thickening starts is more difficult to judge than is the case with egg white. Egg white loses its transparency and becomes opaque white on coagulation. The beginning of coagulation and the thickening of undiluted egg yolk probably occur at about 65°C (149°F). At approximately 70°C (158°F), the yolk loses its fluidity.

The texture of coagulated egg yolk, when it is cooked intact, is crumbly and mealy but solid. When the yolk membrane is ruptured and the stirred yolk is heated, however, the texture of the resulting gel is firm and rubbery. This difference in texture of intact and stirred egg yolk may result from changes that occur in the intricate microstructure of egg yolk with stirring. The tiny discrete granules of the intact yolk may form a highly crosslinked protein network when it is disrupted [28]. To achieve complete coagulation, whole egg must be heated to the temperature required for yolk protein coagulation, since whole egg includes the yolk.

Dilution of egg increases the temperature at which coagulation occurs. Egg diluted with 1 cup of milk coagulates at around 80°C (176°F), although the exact temperature varies with the rate of heating and the presence or absence of other substances in the dispersion.

Time and Temperature

The rate of coagulation and the amount of coagulum formed in a definite time increase with increasing temperature. The character of the coagulum formed when egg white is heated at high temperature is firm, even tough, as compared with the soft, tender, more evenly coagulated product obtained when coagulation takes place at lower temperatures.

The toughness and greater shrinkage of the protein coagulated at a high temperature are the basis for the recommended use of low or moderate temperatures for egg cookery. The temperatures used do not need to be as low as 70°C (158°F), although that temperature, maintained for a sufficient length of time, eventually brings about complete coagulation of egg proteins. If eggs are cooked in water, the water should not boil. Water at a temperature of about 85°C (185°F) will produce a texture that is tender, yet firm. Coagulation at this temperature takes place in a noticeably shorter time than is required at 70°C (158°F).

For an omelet cooked in a skillet over direct heat, the heat should be kept low so that the mass cooks slowly and can be heated uniformly throughout without toughening the bottom layers. The coagulation of a puffy omelet may be finished in a moderate oven. Oven temperatures from 300° to 350°F have been found to be satisfactory for cooking eggs and egg dishes, although there are indications that somewhat higher temperatures are also satisfactory if time is carefully controlled. Placing egg dishes in a pan of water when baking them in the oven helps to protect the egg product from becoming overcooked.

Effect of Rate of Heating

Rapidly heated egg mixtures such as custards coagulate at a higher temperature than similar mixtures that are slowly heated. The fact that the coagulation temperature with rapid heating is very close to the curdling temperature means that a rapidly cooked custard is more likely to curdle than one that is slowly heated. A slowly heated custard can, nevertheless, curdle if it is heated to too high a temperature.

Effect of Added Substances

Egg mixtures containing sugar require a higher temperature for coagulation than do mixtures containing no sugar. The addition of sugar also increases the heat stability of the proteins.

Slightly acid egg mixtures, such as those with added dates or raisins, omelets made with tomato or orange juice, and Hollandaise sauce containing lemon juice, appear to coagulate more rapidly, at a somewhat lower temperature. The coagulum formed is also more firm than that of mixtures with somewhat less acidity. The hardness and cohesiveness of egg white gels have been reported to be minimal at pH 6 and increased as the pH was either decreased to 5 or increased to 9 [29]. Too much acid in egg mixtures may cause curdling. Certain salts, such as chlorides, phosphates, sulfates, and lactates, aid in gel formation in cooked egg mixtures.

Coagulation by Mechanical Beating

As egg whites are beaten, they first become foamy and then form soft moist peaks. With additional beating, the peaks become stiffer, and eventually, with overbeating, the foam becomes dry and may appear to be **flocculated** (Figure 19.9).

Flocculated   separated into small woolly or fluffy masses

Part of the protein in the thin films surrounding each of the air bubbles or cells that make up the structure of a beaten egg white foam is coagulated in the beating process. This provides some rigidity and stabilizes the foam. If the protein becomes overcoagulated, however, the foam takes on a dry, lumpy appearance because of loss of flexibility in the films and the breaking of many air cells. Undesirable effects on both foam volume and stability can be expected when whites are overbeaten. The foam is brittle and inelastic, and large amounts of liquid drain from it on standing. It does not blend well with other food ingredients.

For most uses in food preparation, including the making of soufflés, soft meringues, and puffy omelets and the beating of egg whites with sugar for angel food cakes, egg whites should be beaten to form moderately stiff peaks. The tips should fall over when the beater is withdrawn from the beaten whites. The foam should retain a shiny, smooth surface, and the mass should flow very

FIGURE 19.9

Stages of beating egg white foams. (Photographs by Chris Meister; moderately stiff peaks, courtesy of the U.S. Department of Agriculture)

Egg whites beaten to a foamy stage

Soft peaks

Moderately stiff, but still moist and glossy, peaks

Stiff, dry peaks of overbeaten egg whites

slowly if the bowl is partially inverted. Air cells should be quite fine and of even size. Reconstituted dried egg whites, such as those in angel food cake mixes using a two-stage mixing method, are beaten to a very stiff stage, as indicated in the package directions.

Whole eggs can be beaten much stiffer than might be expected if beating is continued for a long enough time. As a result of the presence of the fat from the yolk, which retards foam formation, there is little danger of overbeating the whole egg.

Egg yolks increase slightly in volume when beaten. They change to a pale lemon color as air is incorporated and the mass may become thick and full of fine cells. It is difficult if not impossible to beat a small quantity of egg yolk thoroughly unless a small dish of narrow diameter and a small egg beater are used.

Because beaten eggs, particularly egg whites, are used in so many cooked dishes, they require proper handling to produce stable foams and retain air cells. Several factors affect the whipping quality of eggs.

Thin and Thick Whites

When thin egg whites are beaten, the character of the resulting foam is different from that produced by beating thick, viscous whites. The foam from thin whites is more fluffy and has less body. Thick whites seem to produce a more stable foam even though thin whites may initially beat to a larger volume. The volume of cooked products, such as angel food cake and meringues, is greater when thick whites are used rather than thin whites.

Temperature

Eggs at room temperature whip more easily, quickly, and to a larger volume than do eggs at refrigerator temperature. This may be due to the lower **surface tension** of the eggs at room temperature.

Surface tension the tension or force at the surface of a liquid that produces a resistance to spreading or dispersing; due to the attraction of the liquid molecules for each other

Type of Beater Used

The type of beater used as well as the fineness of the wires or blades of the beater can affect the size of the air cells that are obtained and the ease with which the eggs are beaten. Thick blades or wires do not divide egg whites as easily as fine wires, and the resulting air cells are therefore larger. All cells become smaller with longer beating regardless of the type of beater used. Egg whisks sometimes give a larger volume of beaten egg mass than do rotary types of beaters but the cells are also larger.

Type of Container in Which Eggs Are Beaten

Bowls with small rounded bottoms and sloping sides are preferable to bowls with large flat bottoms because, in the former, the beater can more easily pick up the egg mass. The size of the bowl must obviously be adapted to the amount of egg to be beaten. If whisks are used for beating egg whites, a large plate or platter is preferable to a bowl for holding the whites because of the over-and-over strokes that are used.

Effect of Added Substances

Fat. Fat, in the form of refined cottonseed oil, has been shown to interfere with whipping when it is present to the extent of 0.5 percent or more. The presence of small amounts of yolk in egg white greatly retards foam formation. This effect is thought to be the result of the fat, probably the lipoproteins, in the egg yolk, which may form a complex with proteins in the white. The directions on packages of angel food cake mix indicate that plastic bowls should not be used for mixing because of the difficulty in removing all fat from the surface of the plastic.

Salt. The addition of a small amount of salt to egg whites (1 gram to 40 grams egg white) has been reported to decrease the volume and stability of the foam and to increase the whipping time [10]. Egg white foams are less elastic when they are beaten with salt than when no salt is added.

Acid. The addition of acid or acid salts to egg white decreases the alkalinity of the white and increases the stability of the egg white foam. The whipping time is increased. A stiff foam and a large foam volume result from addition of acid before or shortly after foaming has started. **Cream of tartar** is frequently added to egg whites before beating to increase the stability of the foam.

Cream of tartar potassium acid tartrate, the partial salt of tartaric acid, an organic acid

Sugar. Sugar retards the denaturation and coagulation of egg proteins and increases the beating time required to attain maximum volume. It is, therefore, important not to add sugar to egg whites before beating is started, but to add it very gradually, possibly 1 to 2 tablespoons at a time, after foaming first occurs. In fact, it is probably best, in the preparation of any sugar-containing egg white foam, to beat the whites to soft peaks before sugar is added, with intermittent beating between the additions of sugar. Otherwise, the beating time is considerably prolonged. The presence of sugar in an egg white foam stabilizes the foam as it forms, greatly decreasing the possibility of overbeating. The texture of the foam is also very fine, with many small air cells, and the surface has a shiny, satiny appearance.

Specific Methods of Egg Preparation

Poached Eggs

Poaching consists of cooking the edible portion of an egg in hot water, milk, cream, or other liquids. To guard against scorching when eggs are poached in milk or cream, the dish should be suspended over hot water. For adequate coagulation of egg proteins, the liquid in which the eggs are poached need not approach the boiling point. However, a temperature of about 85°C (185°F) will still maintain the desirable tender quality of the coagulated egg while requiring less time than when the egg is poached at 70° to 75°C (158° to 167°F). Because the addition of cold eggs to hot liquid immediately lowers the temperature of the liquid, it is possible to have the temperature of the liquid at the boiling point when the eggs are added. The heat can then be regulated to keep the liquid at a simmering temperature of about 85°C (185°F). If the water is not hot enough when the egg is added, the egg white will spread throughout the liquid rather than set quickly and hold its original shape.

The liquid in the pan used for poaching should be deep enough to cover the eggs in order that a film of coagulated white may form over the yolk. Salt and acid added to the cooking water are both aids in coagulation but are not necessary. Two teaspoons of vinegar and 1/2 to 1 teaspoon of salt per pint of water can be effective. Eggs poached in salted water are more opaque white and less shiny than eggs poached in unsalted water. They may also appear puckered or ruffled as they do when they are poached in boiling water. The time required for coagulation depends on the temperature of the water, but at a water temperature of 85°C (185°F), the time required is 4 to 8 minutes. The longer time will, of course, produce a greater degree of coagulation of the yolk so that it will not flow.

There is a wide range of individual preference regarding the desirable characteristics of poached eggs. Many people enjoy a poached egg that is rounded, with a film of coagulated white covering the yolk. The white is completely coagulated but jellylike and tender (Figure 19.4), and the yolk is thick enough to resist flowing. When the cooking time is decreased, the yolk will be more runny.

The freshness of eggs and thickness of whites have considerable influence on the finished product. For example, eggs with thin whites tend to spread out in thin layers and may fragment into pieces when placed in the hot liquid. The technique of adding the egg to the water is also important to the quality of the cooked egg. It is usually desirable to remove the egg from the shell and place it in a small flat dish from which it can easily and quickly be slipped into the poaching water.

Soft-Cooked Eggs

There are several methods for cooking eggs in the shell. The usual objective for soft-cooked eggs is to produce a tender coagulated white and a semiliquid yolk. Water maintained at a boiling temperature for the entire cooking period has a definite toughening effect on that part of the white lying near the shell, even though the time required for coagulation is shorter than when water below boiling is used to cook the eggs. Either of the following two methods can be used to ensure satisfactory tenderness of the coagulated white.

Method I. Allow 1 pint of boiling water for each egg. Add eggs to the boiling water (the temperature of the water will immediately be lowered). Turn off the heat, cover the pan, and allow the eggs to remain in the water for 4 to 6 minutes depending on the degree of coagulation desired.

Method II. Add eggs to water at a simmering but not boiling temperature of about 85°C (185°F). Maintain this temperature for 4 to 6 minutes.

Soft-cooked eggs prepared for those who are pregnant, elderly, very young, or ill should be thoroughly cooked. Foodservice operations serving these groups can use pasteurized egg products safely without having to thoroughly cook them.

Hard-Cooked Eggs

The white of hard-cooked eggs should be firmly coagulated, yet tender. The yolk should be dry and mealy. If the yolk is waxy, it is not sufficiently cooked. The surface of the yolk should be yellow, with no dark green deposit. Hard-cooked eggs can be prepared by either of the methods previously outlined for soft-cooked eggs, but with an extension of the time that the eggs remain in water. The eggs may need to stay in the water for 30 to 40 minutes in method I and 20 to 25 minutes in method II.

One group of researchers [13] compared hard-cooked eggs prepared by two different methods.

Method I. Place the eggs in cold water in a covered pan, bring the water to boiling, remove the pan from the heat, and hold for 25 minutes.

Method II. Carefully place the eggs in boiling water, reduce the heat, and simmer (at 85°C or 185°F) eggs for 18 minutes.

In both methods, the eggs were submerged in cold running water for 5 minutes at the end of the cooking period. The researchers reported that method II produced eggs that were easier to peel and rated higher in all criteria than those prepared by starting with cold water. In another study, boiling for 20 minutes produced hard-cooked eggs that were firmer and exhibited stronger egg odor and more off-flavors than did simmering or steaming methods of cooking [25].

Cooling hard-cooked eggs in cold water immediately after cooking facilitates the removal of the shell. Even so, very fresh eggs (less than 48 hours old) are difficult to peel without considerable white adhering to the shell. The rapid cooling of cooked eggs also aids in the prevention of a dark green deposit, ferrous sulfide (FeS), which tends to form on the outside of the coagulated yolk and detracts from its appearance. Most of the iron in an egg is present in the yolk. Sulfur occurs in about equal amounts in yolk and white, but the sulfur compounds in the white are more labile to heat than those in the yolk. Hydrogen sulfide (H_2S) is therefore easily formed from the sulfur compounds in the white during prolonged heating and forms even more readily when the pH of the egg is markedly alkaline, as in an older egg. Reaction of the iron in the yolk with the hydrogen sulfide from the white produces the greenish ferrous sulfide deposit.

Ferrous sulfide forms very slowly until the yolk reaches about 70°C (158°F) and seldom occurs in fresh eggs cooked 30 minutes at 85°C (185°F). The green color tends to form less in eggs that are cooled rapidly, because the hydrogen sulfide gas is drawn to the lowered pressure at the surface of the cooling egg and thus combines less readily with iron at the surface of the yolk. However, if an egg is cooked 30 minutes in boiling water, the ferrous sulfide will probably form regardless of cooling. Also, in older eggs that are very alkaline, the green color may be produced despite the precautions taken during cooking [1].

In summary, fresh eggs of high quality should be selected for the preparation of hard-cooked eggs. The temperature of the water in which the eggs are cooked should be maintained below the boiling point, and the time of cooking should be no longer than is required to coagulate both the white and the yolk. The eggs should be cooled as quickly as possible after cooking.

Fried Eggs

Because of the difficulty in controlling the temperature of the fat and of the pan, fried eggs can often be somewhat tough, and for this reason are among the preparations requiring the greatest skill. If excess fat is used during the frying of eggs or if the hot fat is dipped with a spoon and poured over the top surface of the eggs as they cook, the eggs may be too greasy to suit many people.

One suggested method of preparation is to use only enough fat to prevent the eggs from sticking to the pan but enough to give the desired flavor. The pan should be sufficiently hot to coagulate the egg white, but not hot enough to toughen it or to decompose the fat. A cover on the pan provides steam, which cooks the top surface of the egg. A small amount of water may be added to the pan just before covering. The water not only furnishes more steam but tends to prevent toughening or hardening of the edges of the eggs. If the underside of a fried egg is brown and the edges crisp and frilled, the pan and fat were probably too hot, unless, as is true for some people, crispness in a fried egg is preferred.

Scrambled Eggs

The whites and yolks are mixed together in the preparation of scrambled eggs. If they are thoroughly mixed, the product has a uniform yellow color. Some people like the marbled effect that is produced by mixing yolks and whites only slightly. About 1 tablespoon of milk is added per egg, along with salt and pepper. The mixture is then poured into a warm skillet containing a small amount of melted butter or margarine.

As the mixture begins to set, an inverted pancake turner may be gently drawn across the bottom, forming large soft curds. Cooking with moderate heat is best.

Frozen scrambled egg mixes are available for foodservice use. Scrambled eggs can be dressed up for lunch or supper by combining them with other items, for example, crumbled bacon, apple, onion, and celery (Figure 19.10).

Shirred Eggs

Shirred eggs are cooked and served in the same dish. The dish is coated with butter or margarine, the eggs are broken into it, and the dish is set directly on the range until the whites are coagulated. The dish is then transferred to a moderate oven to finish cooking. Care must be taken not to overcook and toughen shirred eggs.

Omelets

There are two basic types of omelet: plain or french, and foamy or puffy. The puffy omelet has a more spongy texture than the french omelet because of the greater incorporation of air. The french omelet may be made with or without small amounts of liquid. The liquid used in omelets can be water, milk, cream, or acid juices such as tomato and orange. The omelet can be filled with cheese, a mixture of vegetables, or fruits (Figure 19.11).

PROPORTIONS FOR A FRENCH OMELET

4 eggs	1/2 tsp (3 g) salt
4 Tbsp (59 mL) liquid	fg pepper

Whole eggs are beaten enough to blend white and yolk, then diluted slightly with liquid and seasoned. The mixture is cooked in a greased pan until it is coagulated, after which the omelet is folded (Figure 19.12). To produce more rapid coagulation, a spatula can be used to carefully lift the edges of the egg mass as it

FIGURE 19.10
Apple, bacon, celery, and onion flavor this easy scrambled egg main dish. (Courtesy of the American Egg Board)

FIGURE 19.11

A variety of fillings can be used in a plain omelet. (Courtesy of the American Egg Board)

coagulates, thus allowing the liquid portion on top to flow underneath where it can come in contact with the pan. Another aid is to cover the pan to furnish steam to cook the top surface of the omelet. The omelet should be cooked slowly, keeping the heat low to avoid toughening of the coagulated eggs. The omelet can be considered done when the liquid is thickened but not totally set.

PROPORTIONS FOR A PUFFY OMELET

4 eggs   1/2 tsp (3 g) salt
2 to 4 Tbsp (30 to 59 mL) liquid   fg pepper
1/8 tsp cream of tartar

The cream of tartar is added to the egg whites, which are beaten until moderately stiff. The liquid, salt, and pepper are added to the egg yolks, and the mixture is beaten until it is lemon colored and so thick that it piles. The beaten yolk mixture is folded into the beaten whites, care being taken to blend the mass evenly and yet avoid too much loss of air.

The greased pan in which the omelet is cooked should be hot enough to start coagulation but not hot enough to toughen the coagulated layer in contact with the pan or to brown it excessively. The omelet is cooked slowly until it is light brown underneath.

Several methods can be used to coagulate the top of the foamy omelet.

Method I. Placing a cover on the pan during part of the cooking period forms steam, which cooks the top layer of egg. The cover must not stick to the omelet, as the omelet is likely to collapse when the cover is removed. There is some risk in this method, since a covered pan is hotter than an open pan and overheating may cause the omelet to collapse. If the cover is lifted occasionally and the omelet is cooked successfully by this method, the omelet is usually very tender and moist, partly because it cooks in less time and partly because less evaporation occurs.

FIGURE 19.12
Folding a plain omelet. (Courtesy of the Poultry and Egg National Board)

Method II. When the mass is coagulated to within 1/4 to 1/3 inch of the top, the omelet pan can be placed in a moderate oven to dry the top (Figure 19.13).

Method III. Following method I, the pan can be held in a broiler to dry the top. This method must be used with caution since a broiler flame can very easily overheat the mass and cause it to collapse.

Cook the omelet slowly until it is lightly browned on the bottom.

After drying the top of the omelet in the moderate oven, test it for doneness by inserting a spatula in the center. The spatula should come out clean.

Make a shallow crease across the middle of the omelet.

Fold the omelet over and carefully transfer it to a serving platter.

FIGURE 19.13
Preparation of a puffy omelet. (Courtesy of the Poultry and Egg National Board)

Method IV. The omelet can be cooked in an oven at 300° to 350°F for the entire time.

Crepes

Crepes are thin, tender pancakes containing a relatively high proportion of egg. They can be filled with a variety of items, including fish, meats, poultry, eggs, cheese, vegetables, and fruits (Figure 19.14). Crepes can also be served with sweet, dessert-type fillings.

The thin crepe batter is cooked on medium heat in a seasoned slope-sided omelet or crepe pan. Enough batter is poured in to cover the bottom of the pan; then the pan is tipped or tilted to allow the batter to move quickly over the bottom. Any excess batter is poured off. The crepe is cooked until it is lightly browned on the bottom and dry on the top.

Soufflés

The word *soufflé* is French for *puff*. A soufflé is thus a dish that puffs up spectacularly in the oven (see Figure 20.7). Soufflés are similar to foamy omelets, except that they have a thick white-sauce base and contain additional ingredients such as grated cheese, vegetable pulp, or ground meats. Dessert soufflés are sweet and may contain lemon, strawberry, and chocolate. Because the proportion of egg is slightly lower in soufflés than in omelets, or because of the protection to the egg furnished by the starchy white sauce and some of the additional ingredients used, somewhat less skill is required to make a soufflé than to make a foamy omelet. There is sufficient egg present, however, to

FIGURE 19.14
Chopped hard-cooked eggs and asparagus spears provide the filling for these delicious crepes, which are topped with a cheese sauce. (Courtesy of the American Egg Board)

require application of the basic principles of egg cookery, particularly the need for moderate cooking temperatures. Soufflés are usually baked, although they can be steamed. When they are baked, the dish containing the soufflé mixture should be placed in a pan of hot water to protect against excessive heating.

Custards

A true custard consists only of eggs, milk, sugar, and flavoring. No starchy agent is added. Custards are of two types: the stirred or soft custard, which is given a creamy consistency by being stirred while it is cooking, and the baked custard, which is allowed to coagulate without stirring, thereby producing a gel. There must be enough egg in the baked custard to produce a firm mass when cooked, particularly if the custard is to be unmolded when it is served. The proportion of egg to milk is often the same for baked and stirred custards; however, less egg is used in stirred custard when a thin consistency is desired.

PROPORTIONS FOR CUSTARDS

1 c (237 mL) milk	2 Tbsp (25 g) sugar
1 to 1½ eggs or 2 to 3 yolks	1/4 tsp vanilla or 1/16 tsp nutmeg

(To measure 1/2 egg, mix together white and yolk of whole egg; then divide into two equal portions by measuring 1 Tbsp at a time.)

BAKED CUSTARD

Because the egg is used for thickening, it is beaten only enough to blend the white and yolk well. Sugar can be added to the egg or dissolved in the milk. Milk is usually scalded before being added to the egg mixture. Scalding hastens the cooking and helps retain a mild, sweet flavor, but it does not produce a smoother custard. Flavoring must be added when the mixture is prepared for cooking.

It is best to place the custard cups in a pan of hot water as a protection against overheating, even though a moderate oven temperature may be used (about 350°F). Custards placed in a pan of very hot water can be baked in a 400°F oven for a much shorter time than in a 350°F oven. However, care must be exercised to remove the custard from the oven as soon as it is coagulated to avoid undesirable overcooking.

The baked custard is done when the tip of a knife inserted halfway between the center and outside comes out clean (Figure 19.15). When a custard is overcooked, some clear liquid separates from the gel structure, that is, syneresis occurs. In addition, the custard may appear porous and contain holes, especially on the outer surfaces, when it is unmolded. The top surface may be concave and browned. In an overcooked custard, the egg proteins that form the meshlike gel structure apparently shrink and squeeze out some of the liquid that was held in the mesh.

A baked custard that is overcooked has a porous surface when it is unmolded. Liquid seeps from the gel structure in a process called syneresis.

A baked custard is done when the tip of a knife, inserted into the custard about halfway between the center and the outside, comes out clean.

Unmolded baked custards may be served with fruit sauce.

A stirred custard does not coat the spoon during the beginning stages of cooking.

A stirred custard coats the spoon when it is done and should be cooled quickly to prevent curdling.

FIGURE 19.15
Custards make attractive and nutritious desserts. (Photographs by Chris Meister; baked custard with fruit sauce, courtesy of the Poultry and Egg National Board)

Overheating a stirred custard results in curdling. A very slightly curdled custard may be improved if it is beaten with a rotary beater, but this treatment is of no value for excessively curdled custards. In an overcooked custard, the coagulated proteins shrink and separate out from the more liquid portion of the mixture, giving the appearance of curds. Also, the flavor of an overcooked custard tends to be strong and sulfury.

A stirred custard can be used to create some interesting and delicious desserts. For example, hard meringue shells can be filled with crushed or whole sweetened strawberries or other fruit and the custard poured over the fruit. This can then be crowned with a bit of whipped topping. Or, the custard can be flavored with caramelized sugar and poured into individual serving dishes. Small soft meringues that have been previously baked can be placed on top of the custard.

SOFT CUSTARD

The mixture of egg, milk, and sugar is prepared in the same manner as for baked custard. The vanilla, because of its volatility, is added after the other ingredients are cooked. Custards that are cooked more slowly coagulate more completely at a lower temperature than custards that are cooked rapidly. There is less danger of curdling and both consistency and flavor are better in stirred custards cooked relatively slowly. The total cooking time, in a double boiler, should be 12 to 15 minutes, heating more rapidly at first and then more slowly while stirring thoroughly and rapidly during the entire process.

It is best to keep the water in the lower part of the double boiler under the boiling point, particularly after the custard becomes hot, at 70° to 75°C (158° to 167°F).

Constant stirring is necessary to prevent lumping. Stirring separates the coagulated particles, resulting in a creamy consistency regardless of the amount of egg used. The tendency is to cook a soft custard until it appears as thick as is desired, but caution should be exercised. The custard will be thicker when it is cold. When the custard coats the spoon well (Figure 19.15), it should be removed from the heat and either poured into a cold dish or suspended in cold water in the pan used for cooking.

Meringues

Meringues are of two types: the soft meringue used for pies and puddings, and the hard meringue generally used as a crisp dessert base or as a cookie.

To produce a soft, fine-textured meringue that is tender, cuts easily without tearing, and shows neither syneresis nor **beading** on top of the baked meringue, each of the following items should be considered carefully.

Beading   the appearance of tiny droplets of syrup on the surface of a baked meringue as it stands

1. When the egg whites are partially beaten (possibly to a soft foam), sugar is gradually added, 1/2 to 1 tablespoon at a time, and the beat-

ing is continued until the mixture is stiff but with soft peaks that still tip over.

2. The meringue should be placed on a *hot* filling.
3. The meringue should be baked at 375°F for 12 to 18 minutes, depending on the depth of the meringue.

Heating must be sufficient throughout the soft meringue to destroy any *Salmonella* organisms that may be present in the eggs. Meringues baked at moderate oven temperatures may be slightly sticky, as compared with those baked at high oven temperatures, but the moderate temperature produces an attractive, evenly browned product that is safe to eat. Two particular problems that may be encountered in making soft meringues are weeping, or leaking of liquid from the bottom of the meringue, and beading [9, 12]. Weeping or syneresis apparently results from undercooking the meringue. It can also occur as a result of underbeating the egg whites. Placing the meringue on a hot filling helps to achieve complete coagulation of the egg proteins. Beading is usually attributed to overcooking or overcoagulation of the egg white proteins. It can also result from a failure to dissolve the sugar sufficiently when it is beaten into the meringue.

PROPORTIONS FOR SOFT MERINGUES

1 egg white	1/16 tsp cream of tartar (optional)
2 Tbsp (25 g) sugar	1/8 tsp flavoring (if desired)

PROPORTIONS FOR HARD MERINGUES

1 egg white	1/16 tsp cream of tartar
1/4 c (50 g) sugar	fg salt
1/8 tsp vanilla	

Cream of tartar is added to the egg white, which is beaten until a soft foam begins to form. Flavoring may be added at this point. Sugar is added gradually and beating continued until the mass is very stiff. Portions of the meringue are dropped onto a baking sheet, which may be covered with heavy paper, and shaped into small shells. Meringues are baked at a low oven temperature (about 250°F) for 50 to 60 minutes, depending on the size of the meringues, and then left in the oven with the heat turned off for another hour.

If a temperature lower than 250°F can be maintained for a longer time, the effect is one of drying instead of baking the meringue and produces even better results. Well-insulated ovens that hold the heat for several hours can be preheated, and then turned off entirely.

Desirable meringues of this type are crisp, tender, and white in appearance. It is important that they do not show gumminess or stickiness, which results from underbaking. This may occur either from an oven temperature that is too high or a baking time that is too short. When the baking temperature is too high, the meringues are browned on the outside before the interior is dry enough, and the residual moisture produces stickiness.

Microwave Cooking

One thing that the microwave oven does *not* do successfully is cook an egg in its shell. Steam builds up inside the egg and it bursts. However, eggs can be satisfactorily cooked in several other ways by microwaves. They can be poached in liquid. The liquid is first brought to a boil in a custard cup. Then the broken-out egg is added and cooked for a short time on medium power. The egg should be cooked until the white is opaque but not set. During a standing period of 2 to 3 minutes, the cooking is completed. Broken-out eggs can also be cooked in individual custard cups without liquid, as shirred eggs are. The yolk membrane should be first pierced with a toothpick to help prevent bursting from steam pent up during cooking.

Since the egg yolk contains more fat than the egg white, it attracts more energy and cooks faster. If an egg is microwaved until the white is set, the yolk toughens.

Scrambled eggs are prepared for microwave cooking by mixing melted butter, eggs, and milk and cooking on high power for about half the cooking time before breaking up the set parts and pushing them to the center of the dish. The eggs are stirred once or twice more while the cooking is completed. Again, standing time after cooking is important to finish cooking without toughening the eggs. Scrambled eggs prepared by microwaves are fluffier and have more volume than conventionally scrambled eggs. Omelets, including fluffy omelets, can also be prepared in the microwave oven.

For fried eggs, a browning dish is necessary. The browning dish is preheated on high, and then the eggs are added. The browning dish absorbs enough energy and produces a hot enough surface to brown the eggs lightly. Egg dishes such as quiche can also be prepared using microwaves.

In hospital foodservice, microwaves are often used to reheat food at the point of serving; however, some questions have been raised concerning the lack of uniformity in heating, which results in lack of confidence in the ability of this heating process to sufficiently destroy microorganisms. It has been found, when reheating scrambled eggs in a microwave oven under actual foodservice operating conditions, that temperature variability in the eggs could be controlled within 5°C (9°F) if voltage to the oven and temperature of the food before heating were rigidly controlled [3]. Careful attention to these factors that affect heating is necessary to ensure safety of the food for service to clients.

•EGG SUBSTITUTES

The food industry has responded to the desire of some consumers to have a low-cholesterol egg product by marketing egg substitutes in both liquid and dry forms. Most of the available egg substitute products contain no egg yolk, but have a high concentration of egg white (over 80 percent). To provide yolk-like properties to the egg white mixture, various ingredients are used. These include, in different products, corn oil and nonfat dry milk; soy protein isolate, soybean oil, and egg white solids; and calcium caseinate, nonfat dry milk, and corn oil. A few products on the market do contain small amounts of egg yolk. Most of the egg substitutes are free or almost free of cholesterol and contain considerably less fat than whole egg. The fat in egg substitutes is also more unsaturated.

When compared with fresh whole eggs, egg substitutes have been reported to have less desirable flavor, aroma, and overall acceptability by consumer panelists [8, 19]. Custards made from egg substitute products, however, showed less sag and spread than did whole egg custards. Yellow cakes prepared with egg substitutes were higher in volume than those made with whole eggs, but were less desirable in flavor and overall acceptability.

Egg yolk solids have been extracted with hexane to remove a considerable portion of the fat and cholesterol. One researcher evaluated the sensory quality of a reduced-cholesterol, reduced-fat scrambled egg product containing defatted egg yolks, fresh egg white, skim milk, dextrin, and lecithin [27]. This product contained 84 percent less lipid and 79 percent less cholesterol than does whole egg. Although the mean sensory scores for the defatted yolk product were less than those for the regular scrambled eggs, the scores were equal to or better than the egg substitutes with which it was compared. The field is still open to those who want to develop a better egg substitute.

STUDY QUESTIONS

1. a. Compare the chemical composition of whole egg, egg white, and egg yolk, indicating major differences.
    b. What major protein is found in egg white?
    c. What types of proteins predominate in egg yolk?
2. Describe the following parts of an egg and indicate the location for each.
    a. Cuticle or bloom   f. Thin white
    b. Shell   g. Thick white
    c. Outer membrane   h. Chalazae
    d. Inner membrane   i. Vitelline membrane
    e. Air cell   j. Yolk
3. a. Compare the major characteristics of fresh and deteriorated eggs.
    b. How can freshness best be maintained in eggs during storage?
4. a. List the USDA consumer grades for eggs and describe the major characteristics of each grade.
    b. Describe the process by which eggs are graded.
5. a. Explain why the FDA has designated shell eggs as a potentially hazardous food.
    b. Give several suggestions for the safe handling and preparation of shell eggs.
6. a. Explain why eggs are usually pasteurized before freezing or drying.
    b. What special problem is usually encountered in the freezing of egg yolks and how can this problem be solved?
7. List several different uses for eggs in food preparation.
8. Egg proteins coagulate on heating and can therefore be used for thickening purposes in cooking. Describe the effect of each of the following factors on the temperature of coagulation.
    a. Source of egg protein (white or yolk)
    b. Rate of heating
    c. Dilution

d. Addition of sugar

e. Addition of acid

9. Describe the various changes or stages that occur as egg white is mechanically beaten to a very stiff dry foam.

10. Describe the effect of each of the following on the volume and/or stability of egg white foam.

    a. Thickness of the white

    b. Temperature of the white

    c. Type of beater used

    d. Type of container used

    e. Addition of salt

    f. Addition of acid

    g. Addition of sugar

11. Describe and explain an appropriate procedure for preparing each of the following.

    a. Poached eggs

    b. Soft-cooked eggs in the shell

    c. Hard-cooked eggs in the shell

    d. Fried eggs

    e. Scrambled eggs

    f. Omelets, plain or french and foamy or puffy

    g. Shirred and poached eggs cooked by microwaves

12. a. Describe appropriate procedures for preparing stirred custard and baked custard and explain why each step in the procedures is important.

    b. Why should precautions be taken to avoid overheating custards during preparation? Explain.

13. Describe major differences in preparation and use of soft and hard meringues.

REFERENCES

1. Baker, R. C., J. Darfler, and A. Lifshitz. 1967. Factors affecting the discoloration of hard-cooked egg yolks. *Poultry Science 46*, 664.

2. Ball, H. R., Jr., M. Hamid-Samimi, P. M. Foegeding, and K. R. Swartzel. 1987. Functionality and microbial stability of ultrapasteurized, aseptically packaged refrigerated whole egg. *Journal of Food Science 52*, 1212.

3. Cremer, M. L. 1981. Microwave heating of scrambled eggs in a hospital foodservice system. *Journal of Food Science 46*, 1573.

4. *Egg Grading Manual*. 1990. Agriculture Handbook No. 75. Washington, DC: U.S. Department of Agriculture.

5. *Egg Handling and Care Guide*. 1990. Park Ridge, IL: American Egg Board.

6. *Eggs in Brief, a Guide for Food Processors*. 1985. Park Ridge, IL: American Egg Board.

7. Froning, G. W., and M. H. Swanson. 1964. Oiled versus unoiled eggs for short storage periods. 2. Some chemical and physical changes. *Poultry Science 43*, 494.

8. Gardner, F. A., M. L. Beck, and J. H. Denton. 1982. Functional quality comparison of whole egg and selected egg substitute products. *Poultry Science 61*, 75.

9. Gillis, J. N., and N. K. Fitch. 1956. Leakage of baked soft meringue topping. *Journal of Home Economics 48*, 703.

10. Hanning, F. 1945. Effect of sugar or salt upon denaturation produced by beating and upon the ease of formation and the stability of egg white foams. *Iowa State College Journal of Science 20*, 10.

11. Heath, J. L., and S. L. Owens. 1978. Effect of oiling variables on storage of shell eggs at elevated temperatures. *Poultry Science 57*, 930.

12. Hester, E. E., and C. J. Personius. 1949. Factors affecting the beading and leaking of soft meringues. *Food Technology 3*, 236.

13. Irmiter, T. F., L. E. Dawson, and J. G. Reagan. 1970. Methods of preparing hard cooked eggs. *Poultry Science 49*, 1232.

14. Itoh, T., J. Miyazaki, H. Sugawara, and S. Adachi. 1987. Studies on the characterization of ovomucin and chalaza of the hen's egg. *Journal of Food Science 52*, 1518.

15. Kinner, J. A., and W. A. Moats. 1981. Effect of temperature, pH, and detergent on survival of bacteria associated with shell eggs. *Poultry Science 60*, 761.

16. Kline, L., and T. F. Sugihara. 1966. Effects of pasteurization on egg products. *Baker's Digest 40*, 40 (August).

17. Kohl, W. F. 1971. Pasteurizing egg whites. *Food Technology 25*, 102 (November).

18. Kurisaki, J., S. Kaminogawa, and K. Yamauchi. 1980. Studies on freeze-thaw gelation of very low density lipoprotein from hen's yolk. *Journal of Food Science 45*, 463.

19. Leutzinger, R. L., R. E. Baldwin, and O. J. Cotterill. 1977. Sensory attributes of commercial egg substitutes. *Journal of Food Science 42*, 1124.

20. Margoshes, B. A. 1990. Correlation of protein sulfhydryls with the strength of heat-formed egg white gels. *Journal of Food Science 55*, 1753.

21. Matiella, J. E. and T. C. Y. Hsieh. 1991. Volatile compounds in scrambled eggs. *Journal of Food Science 56*, 387.

22. Meehan, J. J., T. F. Sugihara, and L. Kline. 1962. Relationships between shell egg handling factors and egg product properties. *Poultry Science 41*, 892.

23. Parsons, A. H. 1982. Structure of the eggshell. *Poultry Science 61*, 2013.

24. Shah, D. B., J. G. Bradshaw, and J. T. Peeler. 1991. Thermal resistance of egg-associated epidemic strains of *Salmonella enteritidis*. *Journal of Food Science 56*, 391.

25. Sheldon, B. W. and Kimsey, H. R., Jr. 1985. The effects of cooking methods on the chemical, physical, and sensory properties of hard-cooked eggs. *Poultry Science 64*, 84.

26. Van Elswyk, M. E., A. R. Sams, and P. S. Hargis. 1992. Composition, functionality, and sensory evaluation of eggs from hens fed dietary menhaden oil. *Journal of Food Science 57*, 342.

27. Warren, M. W. and D. R. Davis. 1990. Processing and sensory evaluation of scrambled eggs containing defatted yolk solids. *Journal of Food Science 55*, 583.

28. Woodward, S. A., and O. J. Cotterill. 1987. Texture and microstructure of cooked whole egg yolks and heat-formed gels of stirred egg yolk. *Journal of Food Science 52*, 63.

29. Woodward, S. A., and O. J. Cotterill. 1986. Texture and microstructure of heat-formed egg white gels. *Journal of Food Science 51*, 333.

Milk and
Milk Products*

20

M ilk is the one food for which there seems to be no adequate substitute. It constitutes almost the entire diet for the young of all mammals. Each species produces milk that is especially adapted to the growth of its own young, but milk from one species may be used as food for others. Since animals were domesticated centuries ago, the milk from various species, such as cow, buffalo, goat, and camel, has been used in the diets of people throughout the world. Only cow's milk is of commercial importance in the United States, although small amounts of goat's milk are sold.

A tradition has been established by the dairy industry of minimal modification of milk as it is preserved and handled in market channels. Relatively simple processes and physical separations are used in the manufacture of various dairy products, preserving their natural properties to a large extent. At the same time, however, extensive research has been carried out worldwide on the properties of milk and its products [14]. Because of this research and our considerable knowledge about the nature of milk and its components, many of these isolated components of milk, including its fat, protein, and sugar, are used as ingredients in nondairy foods. There they perform important functions.

•CONSUMPTION TRENDS

When examining the average annual per capita consumption data for dairy products on a milk-equivalent, milkfat basis, it is apparent that consumption has risen from 554 pounds in the early 1970s to 568 pounds in 1989 [28]. Even with this modest increase, however, the average annual per capita consumption of dairy products in 1989 was considerably less than it was during the peak consumption years of 1922 to 1942 (about 800 pounds). The consumption of fluid milk products has declined since 1970, while the consumption of cheese (except cottage types) has markedly increased. Part of the increase in cheese

CHAPTER OUTLINE

Milk products in the title of this chapter refers to those other than butter and ice cream.

421

consumption is due to expanding pizza sales and the use of more convenience-type foods.

Within the fluid milk category, the trend has been toward a significant and steady substitution of lowfat and skim milks for whole milk. In the early 1970s, whole milk accounted for 77 percent of all the fluid milk consumed. By 1989, whole milk made up only 44 percent of the total milk consumption. Several factors have probably contributed to these changes, including the aging of the U.S. population, the increase in snacking and eating out during which soft drinks are likely to be chosen, and heightened concerns about cholesterol and saturated fat in the diet [28].

•COMPOSITION AND PROPERTIES OF MILK

An average percentage composition of whole cow's milk is water, 88; protein, 3.3; fat, 3.3; carbohydrate, 4.7; and ash, 0.7. The quantitative composition of milk varies somewhat in response to several physiological and environmental factors. The breed of the cow, the time of the milking, the feed consumed, the environmental temperature, the season, and the age and health of the cow are all factors that can affect the composition of milk [25].

The most variable component of milk is the fat, followed by protein. Carbohydrate and ash or mineral content vary only slightly. Jersey and Guernsey cattle produce milk with about 5.0 percent fat as compared with about 3.5 percent in Holstein milk. The fat content of pooled market milk is adjusted to a desired level by the dairy processor. Standards for minimum fat content differ somewhat in various states. The composition of some common milk products is given in Appendix C.

Protein

About 82 percent of the protein in milk is *casein*. Most of the remaining 18 percent is classified as *whey protein*, made up principally of *lactalbumin* and *lactoglobulin*. Casein, lactalbumin, and lactoglobulin are not single proteins, but rather are complexes of many closely related protein molecules [25]. For example, there is not just one casein molecule but several, including α-casein, ß-casein, γ-casein, and κ-casein. κ-Casein plays an important role in stabilizing the tiny casein particles in a **colloidal** dispersion.

Colloidal   usually refers to the state of subdivision of dispersed particles; intermediate between very small particles in true solution and large particles in suspension

Casein actually occurs in milk as a colloidal protein-calcium phosphate complex. Very small amounts of other proteins are also present in milk. Casein is classified as a phosphoprotein because of the phosphoric acid that is contained in its molecular structure. At the normal acidity of fresh milk (about pH 6.6) casein is largely combined, through the phosphoric acid part of its structure, with calcium, as calcium caseinate. It is dispersed in the watery portion of milk, called *milk serum*. With the addition of sufficient acid to lower the pH to about 4.6, casein precipitates as a curd. A similar precipitation or coagulation of casein may also be brought about by the addition of an enzyme called *rennin*, or *chymosin*. Rennin, or other milk-clotting enzymes and bacterial cultures that produce lactic acid, is used to coagulate the casein of milk in the making of cheese. We thus have curds (primarily coagulated casein along with entrapped fat globules if whole milk is used) and whey (mainly the whey proteins lactal-bumin and lactoglobulin and the sugar lactose, dispersed in most of the water of milk). Although the whey proteins are not precipitated by acid or rennin, they can be coagulated by heat. They seem to be chiefly responsible for the precipitate that usually forms on the bottom and sides of a container in which milk is heated.

By a process involving **ultrafiltration**, whey protein concentrate (WPC) is produced. On heating, dispersions of WPC can act as gelling agents and may be used in the manufacture of various food products. Beta-lactoglobulin accounts for about 50 percent of total whey proteins and is apparently the principal gelling protein in whey [19, 23]. Whey protein isolates (WPI) are also pro-duced. Whereas WPCs contain 72–76 percent protein, WPIs yield 87–93 per-cent protein. WPIs, as manufactured today, are higher in quality than are most WPCs in terms of composition, sensory attributes, and functional properties [20, 22]. With new technology, however, the quality of WPCs can be improved, making them excellent alternative protein ingredients for the formulated food industry. Whey products, in dried form, have many applications in food pro-cessing, including use in bakery products, prepared mixes, soups, confec-tionary, and margarines [21].

Surplus skim milk is a readily available source of isolated casein and caseinate products. A considerable quantity of caseinates is imported into the United States from New Zealand, Australia, and the European Economic Com-munity. Caseinates are used in such products as imitation cheese, coffee whiteners, dessert toppings, and bakery items [21].

Fat

The fat in milk (milkfat or butterfat) is a very complex lipid. It exists in whole milk as tiny droplets dispersed in the milk serum (watery portion); thus milk is an **emulsion**. The fat globules vary in size; most are very minute yet easily visi-ble under the microscope (see Figure 20.1). To keep the fat globules dispersed in an emulsified form, they are surrounded by a thin film or membrane called the *milkfat globule membrane*. This membrane is composed of a lipid-protein complex and a small amount of carbohydrate [12]. The lipid portion includes both **phospholipids** and **triglycerides**.

Milkfat as a whole is composed primarily of triglycerides. However, in addition to the small amount of phospholipids present, milkfat also contains some **sterols**, chiefly cholesterol. The triglycerides are characterized by the presence of many short-chain, **saturated fatty acids**, such as butyric and caproic acids. These are partly responsible for the relatively low melting point and therefore the soft–solid consistency of butter. When butter spoils as a result of **hydrolysis** of triglyceride molecules, the disagreeable odor and flavor are due primarily to the release of free butyric and caproic acids from the triglyceride molecules.

Some of the fat globules in freshly drawn milk are loosely grouped together in small clusters. Then, as whole, nonhomogenized milk stands, the fat globules tend to form larger and larger clusters. Since fat is less dense than the watery portion of milk, the fat clusters rise to the surface as cream. The size of the dispersed fat globules in milk is decreased by the process of homoge-

Ultrafiltration filtration through an extremely fine filter

Emulsion the dispersion of one liq-uid in another with which it is usually immiscible

Phospholipid a type of fat or lipid molecule that contains phosphoric acid and a nitrogen-containing base along with two fatty acids and a glyc-erol molecule, all linked together chemically

Triglyceride a neutral fat molecule made up of three fatty acids joined to one glycerol molecule through a spe-cial chemical linkage called an *ester*

Sterol a type of fat or lipid mole-cule with a complex chemical struc-ture, for example, cholesterol

Saturated fatty acid a fatty acid with no double bonds between its carbon atoms

Hydrolysis a chemical reaction in which a molecular linkage is broken and a molecule of water is utilized

FIGURE 20.1

Homogenization of milk decreases the size of the dispersed fat particles, as shown in this photomicrograph of evaporated milk. (Courtesy of the Evaporated Milk Association)

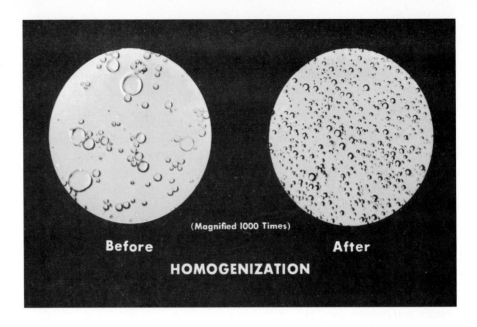

nization. The dispersion is therefore more stable, and the fat no longer rises to the surface on standing. No cream line is formed. Homogenization is discussed later in the chapter.

Fat-soluble vitamins A, D, E, and K are carried in the fat globules. Some yellow fat-soluble carotenoid pigments are also found with the fat and give color to heavy cream and butter.

A decline in milkfat consumption has created a surplus of milkfat in the United States. The application of a technology called *supercritical fluid extraction* (SFE) shows promise for the fractionation or separation of milkfat components into groups with different chemical and physical properties so that the surplus fat can be utilized in new applications [1]. The cholesterol content of milkfat can also be reduced by supercritical fluid processing, as well as by steam-stripping and the use of enzymes [33]. SFE relies on the enhanced ability of a gas to act as a solvent when it is heated above its **critical temperature** and is also compressed so that its **density** increases and *approaches* that of a liquid. Carbon dioxide is the preferred gas in the food industry because it is nontoxic, noncorrosive, nonflammable, low in cost, and readily available.

Critical temperature the temperature above which a gas can exist only as a gas, regardless of the pressure, because the motion of the molecules is so violent

Density mass per unit of volume

Carbohydrate

The chief carbohydrate of milk, lactose or milk sugar, is a disaccharide. On hydrolysis, it yields the monosaccharides glucose and galactose. Lactose is the least sweet and also the least soluble of the common sugars. Because of its low solubility, it may crystallize out and give some food products a sandy texture when it is present in too large an amount. For example, when too much nonfat dry milk, which is high in lactose, is added to ice cream, the less soluble sugar may produce sandiness at the low temperature required for freezing. Lactose separated from milk finds many uses in the food industry. It may be an ingredient in such products as cooked sausages and hams, confections, and infant formulas.

The enzyme *lactase*, normally produced in the small intestine, breaks down lactose into its two component simple sugars. In some people, however, this enzyme is present in insufficient quantity for them to handle more than a very small amount of milk sugar without discomfort. Since lactose is not digested when there is an enzyme deficiency, it remains in the intestine and is broken down by microorganisms, producing gas, cramping, and diarrhea. A deficiency of lactase, producing a lactose intolerance, seems to develop quite frequently, even in early childhood, among certain populations, particularly non-Caucasian peoples. People with lactose intolerance may be able to tolerate small amounts of some fermented milk products, such as yogurt and buttermilk, if much of the lactose in these products has been broken down to glucose and galactose. Aged cheese may also be tolerated.

Since lactase has become available commercially, the dairy industry has produced fluid milks, both whole and low-fat, treated with this enzyme so that the lactose content of the milks is reduced, typically by 70 percent [7, 25]. These milks are sweeter tasting because the lactose has been broken down to the sweeter sugars, glucose and galactose. Lactase is also available for home use in liquid and tablet or capsule form. The lactase can be consumed directly or added to regular milk.

Color

The white appearance of milk is due to the reflection of light by the colloidally dispersed protein casein and by the calcium phosphate salts. Two yellowish pigments contribute to the color of milk—carotenes and riboflavin. The fat-soluble carotenes are found in the milkfat; the riboflavin is water soluble. Depending on the concentration of carotenes, the intensity of color in milk varies. The concentration of carotenes, in turn, depends on the amount of pigment in the feed of the cow and on her ability to change it to the colorless vitamin A molecule. A greenish yellow fluorescent color, particularly noticeable in liquid whey, is due to the presence of riboflavin.

Flavor

The flavor of milk is bland and slightly sweet because of its lactose content. A major flavor sensation of milk is thought to be its particular mouth-feel, which results from the emulsion of milkfat, as well as from the colloidal structure of the proteins and some of the calcium phosphate.

The slight aroma of fresh milk is produced by a number of low-molecular-weight compounds, such as acetone, acetaldehyde, dimethyl sulfide, methyl ketones, short-chain fatty acids, and lactones. Some of the volatile compounds contributing to the flavor of milk are unique to the fatty portion of milk.

Heat processing may affect the flavor of milk, the change in flavor being dependent on the time and temperature of heating. The effect on flavor of heating to pasteurize milk, including the use of ultrahigh temperatures for very short periods, is minimal and tends to disappear during storage. Ultrahigh-temperature sterilized milk tastes very much like conventionally pasteurized milk, although some people may notice a slightly cooked flavor [25].

The off-flavors that sometimes occur in milk may result from the feed consumed by the cow, the action of bacteria, chemical changes in the milk, or the absorption of foreign flavors after the milk is drawn. One chemical off-flavor is called *oxidized* flavor [34]. This flavor can result from the oxidation of phospholipids in the milk. Since traces of copper accelerate the development of oxidized flavor, copper-containing equipment is not used in dairies. An off-flavor may also be produced when milk is exposed to light. This off-flavor, which develops rapidly, involves both milk protein and riboflavin. The amount of riboflavin in milk decreases as the off-flavor develops. Waxed cartons and opaque plastic containers help to protect milk from light.

Acidity

Fresh milk has a pH of about 6.6, which is close to the neutral pH of 7. As milk stands exposed to air, its acidity decreases slightly because of the loss of carbon dioxide. Raw milk, which normally contains some lactic acid-producing bacteria, gradually increases in acidity on storage. Eventually, this results in sour milk when enough lactic acid has been produced from lactose by bacteria in the milk. Pasteurized milk, however, does not generally become sour because the lactic acid bacteria are destroyed during the heating process. Spoilage of pasteurized milk is due usually to the action of putrefactive bacteria that break down proteins in the milk, resulting in a very bitter, unpleasant flavor.

•NUTRITIVE VALUE

Milk is much more than a beverage. Its caloric value and its content of high-quality protein are significant. It is also a rich source of minerals, particularly calcium, and the lactose in milk aids in the absorption of calcium and other minerals from the intestine. Most other foods commonly used in the United States cannot be favorably compared with milk and milk products as good dietary sources of calcium. Without milk or milk products in the diet, very careful planning must be done to meet the recommended dietary allowance for this mineral. Milk is a good source of phosphorus as well as several other minerals, but is a poor source of iron [27]. Young children may become anemic if they remain on an unsupplemented milk diet too long.

All vitamins known to be essential in human nutrition are present in milk to some extent. The vitamin A value varies with the diet of the cow. When fat is removed in the making of skim milk, vitamin A, as well as the other fat-soluble vitamins, are lost with the cream; however, both vitamins A and D are usually added to skim and low-fat milks, and whole milk is commonly fortified with vitamin D.

Thiamin occurs in only fair concentration in milk, but is relatively constant in amount. Riboflavin is present in a higher concentration in milk than the other B vitamins, and its stability to heat makes milk a dependable source of this vitamin. Riboflavin is very unstable to ultraviolet light, which means that milk exposed to light may lose large amounts of this vitamin. Since approximately 38 percent of the riboflavin in the American diet comes from milk and dairy products, it is important to protect the riboflavin in milk. The retention of riboflavin in skim milk placed in blow-molded polyethylene containers and held in a lighted chamber for 5 days has been reported to average 58 percent at the top of the containers compared with 92 percent at the bottom of the containers [26]. Waxed cardboard cartons are protective. The use of a film overwrap for light-permeable milk containers may be helpful in preserving riboflavin while milk is in market channels. New innovations are occurring in milk packaging.

Milk is a good source of the amino acid tryptophan, which is a precursor or provitamin for niacin. Thus, the niacin value of milk is high. Only a small amount of vitamin C is present in raw milk, and approximately 25 percent is destroyed during pasteurization [31]. Milk is therefore not a dependable source of vitamin C.

•SANITATION AND MILK QUALITY

Milk is among the most perishable of all foods because it is an excellent medium for the growth of bacteria. Some of these are harmless, but some may be pathogenic to humans. Quality milk is milk that has been produced, processed, and distributed under rigid sanitary conditions so that it has a relatively low bacterial count, is free from disease-producing organisms, has good flavor and appearance, and is of high nutritive value and satisfactory keeping quality. Various controls and treatments for milk have been instituted to ensure quality in this product. The responsibility for a safe milk supply does not rest solely with the dairy industry, however. It must be shared by public health officials and the consumer.

The Grade A Pasteurized Milk Ordinance is a set of recommendations made by the U.S. Public Health Service—Food and Drug Administration (FDA). This ordinance describes the steps necessary to protect the milk supply. It outlines sanitary practices, which include the following:

Inspection and sanitary control of farms and milk plants

Examination and testing of herds

Employee instruction on good manufacturing practices

Proper pasteurization and processing

Laboratory examination of milk

Monitoring for chemical, physical, and microbial adulterants

The ordinance is revised periodically. Formulated as a guide to states and other jurisdictions responsible for milk quality, this ordinance has been voluntarily adopted by many state and local governments. The majority of people in the United States live in areas where the guidelines of this ordinance are in effect.

Grading

Sanitary codes generally determine the grading of milk. Grades and their meanings may vary according to local regulations unless the pasteurized milk ordinance has been adopted, in which case standards are uniform. Most rigid control is placed on the production and processing of Grade A market milk, the grade supplied to consumers as fluid milk. The Grade A Pasteurized Milk

FIGURE 20.2
USDA shields indicate quality in dairy products. (Courtesy of the U.S. Department of Agriculture)

U.S. Extra Grade is the grade name for instant nonfat dry milk of high quality.

The Quality Approved shield may be used on cottage cheese or other cheeses for which no official U.S. grade standards exist, if the products have been inspected for quality under the USDA's grading and inspection program.

Aseptic packaging   a process that involves sterilizing the product and the package separately, filling the package without recontaminating the product, and sealing

Ordinance recommends that state health or agriculture departments have programs to regularly monitor the milk supply for the presence of unintentional microconstituents, which include pesticide residues, antibiotics, and radioactivity. In addition, the FDA regularly conducts surveys and other monitoring activities [25].

The U.S. Department of Agriculture (USDA) has set quality grade standards for nonfat dry milk and also for butter and some cheeses. In addition, the USDA gives a Quality Approved rating for certain products (Figure 20.2). If a manufacturer uses the USDA grade or the Quality Approved shield on product labels, the plant must operate under the continuous inspection of USDA agents. The grades for regular nonfat dry milk are U.S. Extra and U.S. Standard. For the instantized product, the grade is U.S. Extra. Grading is a voluntary, fee-for-service program.

Pasteurization

Low bacterial count and high standards of production do not always ensure a milk supply that is free from pathogenic organisms. Even under the best sanitary practices, disease-producing organisms may enter raw milk accidentally from environmental and human sources. Therefore, milk is pasteurized as an additional safeguard for the consumer. Pasteurization is required by law for all Grade A fluid milk and milk products that enter interstate commerce for retail sale. The pasteurization process involves heating raw milk in properly approved and operated equipment at a sufficiently high temperature for a specified length of time to destroy pathogenic bacteria [25]. It generally destroys 95 to 99 percent of nonpathogenic bacteria as well. Although milk is not completely sterilized by pasteurization, its keeping quality is greatly increased over that of raw milk.

Individual states may authorize the intrastate distribution of raw milk, generally with rigid specifications. However, health authorities do not advocate its consumption: a number of outbreaks of foodborne illness have resulted from the consumption of raw milk. Home pasteurization or boiling of any milk purchased raw is recommended by public health authorities [25].

Various time and temperature relationships can be used in pasteurization. Milk can be heated to at least 63°C (145°F) and held at this temperature for 30 minutes. This is called the low-temperature longer-time (LTLT) process. A high-temperature short-time (HTST) process that consists of heating milk to at least 72°C (162°F) for 15 seconds is also commonly used. In addition, higher heat, shorter time combinations may be applied.

An ultrapasteurization process involves heating milk to 138°C (280°F) for 2 or more seconds. This product has a longer shelf life than milk pasteurized by other methods. After pasteurization, the milk is cooled rapidly to 7°C (45°F) or lower.

Ultrahigh-temperature processing at 138–150°C (280–302°F) for 2–6 seconds sterilizes the milk. When it is packaged **aseptically** in presterilized containers, this milk may be kept on the shelf without refrigeration for at least 3 months. After it is opened, however, it must be refrigerated.

Various tests can be applied to ascertain the thoroughness of milk pasteurization. For example, measurements can be made of any activity of the enzyme alkaline phosphatase, which is naturally present in milk. If this enzyme is completely inactivated, the milk has been heated sufficiently to destroy any pathogenic microorganisms that might be present. It is also imperative that no raw milk be mixed accidentally with properly pasteurized milk.

The temperatures and times for pasteurization are not sufficient to alter the milk constituents or properties to any significant extent. Whey proteins are denatured only slightly, minerals are not appreciably precipitated, and vitamin destruction is generally minimal. Changes in curd characteristics that occur as a result of pasteurization tend toward the production of a finer curd when milk is digested.

Care of Milk

Fundamentals in the care of fluid milk, whether by producer or consumer, are cleanliness, cold temperature, and the prevention of contamination by keeping the milk covered. So perishable a food as milk should be stored at 7°C (45°F) or below immediately after purchase. Proper containers should be used to protect the milk from exposure to light, which may produce an oxidized off-flavor. The milk container should always be kept closed during storage to prevent the absorption of other food odors and should be returned to the refrigerator immediately after use to prevent warming, which encourages bacterial growth. Milk that has been poured out but not used should never be returned to the original container, because it may contaminate the rest of the milk.

Nonfat dry milk should be stored in moisture-proof packages at a temperature no higher than ordinary room temperature. Dry milk takes up moisture and becomes lumpy and stale if it is exposed to air during storage. Because of the fat content, whole dry milk is not as stable to storage as the nonfat product.

Unopened cans of evaporated milk can be stored at room temperature. Once the can is opened, however, it must be treated as fluid milk and refrigerated. When cans of evaporated milk are stored for several months, they should be turned over periodically to retard the settling out of milk solids.

•MILK PROCESSING

Homogenization

The tendency of the fat globules in whole fluid milk to rise and form a cream line is changed by homogenization. In this process, fat globules are divided into such small particles that they are dispersed permanently in a very fine emulsion throughout the milk serum (see Figure 20.1). Most of the milk marketed in the United States is now homogenized. Cream-line milk is generally not available.

Homogenization consists of pumping milk or cream under pressures of 2,000 to 2,500 pounds per square inch through very small openings in a machine called a *homogenizer*. A film of adsorbed protein or lipoprotein immediately surrounds each of the new globules, acting as an **emulsifier**, and prevents them from reuniting. It is estimated that about one-fourth of the protein of milk is adsorbed on the finely dispersed fat particles of homogenized

Emulsifier a substance that is active at the interface between two immiscible liquids, being attracted somewhat to each liquid; it acts as a bridge between them, allowing an emulsion to form

milk. The increased dispersion of fat imparts richer flavor and increased viscosity to the milk. Homogenization causes the milk proteins to be somewhat more readily coagulated by heat or acid than the nonhomogenized product. Therefore, care must be taken to avoid curdling in the use of homogenized milk in food preparation.

The greatly increased surface exposed in the highly dispersed fat of homogenized milk increases the tendency toward the development of rancidity. Pasteurization before homogenization retards the development of **rancidity**, because it destroys the enzymes that could otherwise attack the more highly dispersed fat.

Rancidity a special type of spoilage in fats that begins with the addition of oxygen to unsaturated fatty acids

Fortification

Fortification is the addition of certain nutrients to milk as a means of improving the nutritional value. The principal form of fortification is the addition of about 400 International Units (IU) of vitamin D per quart. In view of the relationship between vitamin D and calcium and phosphorus absorption and utilization in the body, and because milk is an outstanding source of these minerals, milk is generally regarded as a logical food to fortify with vitamin D. Upon exposure to light, a slight loss of vitamin D from fortified milk has been reported [29].

According to the standards of identity for milk, the addition of vitamin D is optional. However, fortification of skim and low-fat milks with vitamin A is mandatory since vitamin A is present only in the fatty portion of milk. It is particularly important that nonfat dry milk sent to other countries be fortified with vitamin A. Many children in the world do not receive adequate amounts of vitamin A from other sources. Deficiencies are all too common.

•KINDS OF MILK

Milk is marketed in a number of different forms to appeal to the varied tastes and desires of the consuming public. Development of new milk products has been motivated by the desire to improve keeping quality, to facilitate distribution and storage, to make maximum use of by-products, and to utilize surpluses [25]. Cost variations among different forms of milk depend on such factors as supply and demand, production and processing costs, and governmental policies.

Federal standards of identity have been set for a number of milk products that enter interstate commerce. These standards define the composition, the kind and quantity of optional ingredients permitted, and the labeling requirements. The 1990 federal labeling legislation requires that virtually all packaged foods bear nutrition labeling. State and local agencies are encouraged to adopt the federal standards to enhance uniformity.

Fluid Milk

Depending on the milkfat content, fresh fluid milk is classified as *milk*, *low-fat milk*, or *skim milk* and is labeled accordingly.

Whole Milk

The term *milk* usually refers to whole milk. According to federal standards, whole milk packaged for beverage use must contain not less than 3.25 percent milkfat and not less than 8.25 percent milk-solids-not-fat. Milk-solids-not-fat are mostly protein and lactose. Other standards, however, allow the milkfat minimum in whole milk to vary from 3.0 to 3.8 percent. At milk processing plants, the milk from different suppliers is standardized to one fat level by removal or addition of milkfat as necessary.

Whole milk may be canned and is available in this form chiefly for use on ships or for export. It is heated sufficiently to sterilize it and then is put into sterilized cans. It can be stored at room temperature until it is opened.

Low-Fat and Skim Milks

Low-fat milks may contain 0.5, 1.0, 1.5, or 2.0 percent milkfat and are labeled with the appropriate fat level. *Skim* or *nonfat milk* is milk from which as much fat has been removed as is technologically possible. The fat content is less than 0.5 percent. All of these milks contain at least 8.25 percent milk-solids-not-fat. Additional milk-derived ingredients, such as nonfat milk solids, may be added to low-fat milk to increase the viscosity and opacity of the milk and to improve the palatability and nutritive value. If enough nonfat milk solids are added to reach the 10-percent-solids-not-fat level, the product must be labeled *protein-fortified* or *fortified with protein*. Addition of vitamin A to low-fat and skim milk is required for milk shipped in interstate commerce. The addition of vitamin D is optional.

Ultrahigh-Temperature Processed Milk

Ultrahigh-temperature processed (UHT) milk is heated at temperatures higher than those used for pasteurization—138–150°C (280–302°F) for 2–6 seconds. Then, under sterile conditions, it is packaged into presterilized containers, which are aseptically sealed so that spoilage organisms cannot enter. Hydrogen peroxide may be used to sterilize the milk packaging materials. UHT milk can be stored unrefrigerated for at least 3 months, thus representing a considerable savings of energy usually expended for the refrigeration process. After the milk is opened it must be refrigerated, however.

Immediately after processing, UHT milk has a "cooked" and "sulfury" flavor, apparently resulting from the heat denaturation of the whey protein ß-lactoglobulin. This undesirable flavor dissipates as the milk is stored until a maximum flavor potential is reached. Thereafter, as storage continues, off-flavors described as "flat," "lacking freshness," "sweet," and "unclean" may gradually develop. After prolonged storage (up to one year), such flavors as "chalky," "coconut," "rancid," "musty," and "oxidized" may develop [5]. Off-flavors generally are due to chemical and enzymatic activity in the milk and are less pronounced when the milk is held at temperatures lower than ordinary room temperature. The addition of flavorings to the milk masks off-flavors. Low-temperature–inactivation treatments of milk after UHT processing can reduce off-flavors by destroying enzymes responsible for the changes [6]. UHT milk produced in the United States tastes very much like conventionally pasteurized milk [25].

Concentrated Fluid Milk

Evaporated Milk

In the production of evaporated milk, about 60 percent of the water is removed in a vacuum pan at 50° to 55°C (122° to 131°F). A forewarming period of 10 to 20 minutes at 95°C (203°F) is usually effective in preventing coagulation of the protein casein during sterilization. The heat sterilization process occurs after the product is homogenized and canned. In a newer process, the concentrated milk may be heated in a continuous system at ultrahigh temperatures and then canned aseptically. This product is less viscous, whiter, and tastes more like pasteurized milk than does evaporated milk processed by the traditional method. Evaporated milk is fortified with 400 IU of vitamin D per quart.

Federal standards require that evaporated milk contain not less than 7.5 percent milkfat and not less than 25 percent total milk solids. Evaporated skim milk must contain not less than 20 percent milk solids. In this case, both vitamins A and D must be added. Sterilized, canned evaporated milk should keep indefinitely without microbiologic spoilage; however, other changes affect its quality. On long standing, the homogenized fat particles tend to coalesce, thus breaking the emulsion. The solids begin to settle, and the product may thicken and form clots. To retard these changes, stored cans of evaporated and condensed milk should be turned every few weeks. The vegetable gum carrageenan is often added to evaporated milk as a stabilizer.

Sweetened Condensed Milk

To prepare sweetened condensed milk, about 15 percent sugar is added to whole or skim milk, which is then concentrated to about one-third of its former volume. Because the 42 percent sugar content of the finished product acts as a preservative, the milk is not sterilized after canning. Federal standards require 28 percent total milk solids. Whole sweetened condensed milk must contain 8 percent milkfat, while the skim milk product must have not more than 0.5 percent fat.

Browning of condensed milk, as well as of evaporated milk, is probably of the **Maillard reaction** type and occurs during both sterilization and storage. The rate of browning is greater at room temperature and with longer storage time.

Maillard reaction a browning reaction in foods involving many complex chemical changes; in the first stages, a sugar and an amino acid or protein interact

Dry Milk

Nonfat dry milk powder is usually made from fresh pasteurized skim milk by removing about two-thirds of the water under vacuum and then spraying this concentrated milk into a chamber of hot filtered air. This process produces a fine powder of very low moisture content, about 3 percent. Nonfat dry milk may also be produced by spraying a jet of hot air into concentrated skim milk (foam spray-drying).

Regular nonfat dry milk reconstitutes in warm water with agitation. Instant nonfat dry milk disperses readily in cold water. To make the instant product, regular nonfat dry milk is remoistened with steam to induce agglomeration of small particles into larger, porous particles that are creamy white and free flowing. The lactose may be in a more soluble form, particularly on the outside of the particles. Vitamins A and D may be added to nonfat dry milk.

Whole milk or low-fat milk can also be dried. The presence of fat in these products reduces their shelf life, since the fat is subject to oxidation. Packaging under vacuum or with an inert gas increases stability.

Another dried dairy product is buttermilk, which has a rather wide use in commercial flour mixes. It is also available in the retail market. Dried churned buttermilk is an excellent ingredient for use in baked products, because it contains phospholipids that function as emulsifiers.

Dried whey and WPC also have the potential for use in a variety of manufactured foods. WPC can be used as a partial replacer or as a supplement for whole egg or egg white in a number of baked products [2]. The fortification of bread and pasta with WPC can be an economical way to increase nutritional value [30].

When dried milk is reconstituted, the powder is added to water and then shaken or stirred. For use in flour mixtures and some other products, the dry milk can be mixed with dry ingredients and the water added later. The quantity of instant milk powder needed to make 1 quart of fluid milk is usually 1⅓ cups.

Cultured Milk Products

Cultured or **fermented** milks are one of the oldest preserved foods, having been used for centuries. Several hundred different cultured milk products are consumed worldwide [15].

In their preparation, appropriate bacterial cultures are added to the fluid milk. The bacteria ferment lactose to produce lactic acid. A pH between 4.1 and 4.9 is common; this discourages the growth of undesirable microorganisms. Acids, such as lactic and citric, may also be added directly to milk, either with or without the addition of microbial cultures. The development of acidity is responsible for a number of physical and chemical properties that make the fermented products unique. Each bacterial culture produces its own characteristic flavor components. Some protein hydrolysis occurs, apparently contributing to a softer, more easily digested curd.

Health and nutritional benefits have been claimed for various fermented dairy products. *Lactobacillus acidophilus, Lactobacillus reuteri*, and bifidobacteria are normal inhabitants of the intestinal tract, contributing to increased acidity and deterrence of undesirable microbial growth. The addition of safe and suitable microbial organisms to milk products is allowed by the Pasteurized Milk Ordinance. However, additional research is necessary to provide sufficient proof for the FDA to approve label claims for nutritional benefits of fermented milk products [8, 10, 35].

Fermentation the process in which complex organic compounds are broken down to smaller molecules by the action of enzymes produced by microorganisms

Yogurt

Whole, low-fat, and skim milks and even cream can be used to make yogurt. Often, nonfat dry milk solids are added. The nutrient composition of yogurt reflects the nutrient composition of the milk used in its production; however, there does appear to be a considerable increase in folic acid concentration during the fermentation process. Additional calcium is also found in yogurt when milk solids are added [32].

In the production of yogurt, a mixed culture of *Lactobacillus bulgaricus* and *Streptococcus thermophilus* is usually added to the pasteurized milk premix. *Lactobacillus acidophilus* or other strains may also be added to the culture, which is then incubated at 42° to 46°C (108° to 115°F) until the desired flavor, acidity, and consistency are attained. A sharp, tangy flavor is characteristic of yogurt. Two general types of yogurt are manufactured. The set style has a firm gel; stirred yogurt has a semiliquid consistency. Often, yogurt is marketed with sweetened fruit added, producing a sundae-type product. The fruit may be placed on the bottom of the container, or it may be blended throughout the product. Sweetened fruit yogurt is sometimes served as a dessert. Frozen yogurt and frozen yogurt bars containing sugar, stabilizers, and flavorings have also become popular dessert items. They are particularly enjoyed in the hot summer months.

After yogurt has reached the desired flavor and consistency, further bacterial activity is retarded by chilling. The microorganisms are still alive, however, and contain the enzyme *lactase*, which may aid in lactose digestion in people who are lactose intolerant. The lactose content of yogurt is reduced during fermentation, as some lactose is hydrolyzed to the monosaccharides glucose and galactose. When the yogurt premix is enriched with nonfat milk solids, however, the initial level of lactose is actually higher than that of ordinary milk: 6 to 8 percent as compared with 5 percent in milk. During fermentation, the lactose level of yogurt typically falls to about 4 percent [32]. Some yogurt may be heat-treated to destroy the bacterial culture after fermentation is completed, thus extending its shelf life. However, any health benefits that might result from these live microorganisms are also eliminated.

Buttermilk

The term *buttermilk* was originally used to describe the liquid remaining after cream is churned to produce butter. This liquid is still used for the production of dried buttermilk, a baking ingredient. Today, however, fluid buttermilk is a cultured milk. Cultured buttermilk is usually made from pasteurized low-fat or skim milk, with nonfat dry milk solids added. It can also be made from fluid whole milk or reconstituted nonfat dry milk. If it is made from low-fat or whole milk, it really should be called cultured milk or cultured low-fat milk rather than buttermilk.

In the process of manufacturing, a culture of *Streptococcus lactis* is added to the milk to produce the acid and flavor components. The product is incubated at 20° to 22°C (68° to 72°F) until the acidity is 0.8 to 0.9 percent (pH 4.6), expressed as lactic acid [25]. Butter granules or flakes, salt, and a small amount of citric acid may be added to enhance the flavor.

Acidophilus Milks

Low-fat or skim milk may be cultured with *Lactobacillus acidophilus* and incubated at 38°C (100°F) until a soft curd forms. It is called *acidophilus-cultured milk* and has an acid flavor. In another process, a concentrated culture of *L. acidophilus* is grown and then added to pasteurized milk. This product is not acid in taste, and its consistency is similar to that of fluid milk. Acidophilus milk introduces acidophilus bacteria into the intestine, where they are thought to help maintain a proper balance of microorganisms.

Filled and Imitation Milks

Filled Milk

Filled milk is a substitute milk that can be made by combining a fat other than milkfat with water, nonfat milk solids, an emulsifier, color, and flavoring. The mixture is heated, under agitation, and then homogenized. The resulting product appears to be very much like milk [3]. Vegetable nondairy cheese and cultured milk products are produced from filled milk. Thus are created dairylike products that do not contain butterfat or cholesterol. In the past, coconut oil has been the main source of fat in filled milk. However, partially hydrogenated soybean, corn, and cottonseed oils containing approximately 30 percent linoleic acid have been developed for use in filled milk.

Imitation Milk

Imitation milk resembles milk, but it usually contains no milk products per se. Such ingredients as water, corn syrup solids, sugar, vegetable fats, and a source of protein are most often used in imitation milk. Derivatives of milk, such as casein, casein salts, and other milk proteins, may be used as the protein source; soy proteins may also be used. Some imitation milk contains whey products. The vegetable fat is often coconut oil.

Both filled and imitation milks are subject to variable state regulations, but they are not as yet governed by the same rigid sanitation and composition requirements as are pasteurized Grade A milk and milk products. However, filled and imitation milks are subject to the 1990 federal labeling legislation, under which a substitute food must be nutritionally equivalent to its standardized counterpart except that calories and/or fat may be reduced.

People who must eliminate milk from their diet, possibly because of its lactose content, may use lactose-free imitation milks to advantage; however, it is extremely difficult to make a product that matches real milk in nutritional composition. Persons for whom imitation and substitute dairy products make up a major portion of the diet may find it difficult to obtain adequate amounts of all nutrients required for good health [11].

A nonfat dry milk replacer has been designed for use in dry cocoa mixes that are blended with water to make hot chocolate. A whey product is an important ingredient in this replacer.

Some dairy processors use a special seal on their products to emphasize the fact that they are *real* dairy products and not imitation. Figure 20.3 shows this seal, which consists of the word *REAL* enclosed in a symbolic drop of milk.

•MILK IN FOOD PREPARATION

Heating milk to temperature and time combinations more extensive than those used in pasteurization brings about some changes. The changes increase in number and degree with increasing temperature and time of heating. The tendency for milk to curdle is diminished by the use of low or moderate temperatures. You may already have observed that there is less curdling of the milk on

FIGURE 20.3
Sometimes dairy processors put on their packaged products a special symbol which contains the word *REAL*. This emphasizes that these products are not imitation.

scalloped potatoes cooked in a low or moderate oven than when a higher temperature is employed.

The general effect of heat on milk during usual food preparation practices is considered in this section. Preparation of white sauces and cream soups, using heated milk, is discussed in Chapter 13, and preparation of hot chocolate containing milk is covered in Chapter 10.

Effects of Heat

Protein Coagulation

On heating, the whey proteins lactalbumin and lactoglobulin become insoluble or **precipitate**. Lactalbumin begins to **coagulate** at a temperature of 66°C (150°F). The amount of coagulum increases with increasing temperature and time of heating. The coagulum that forms appears as small particles rather than a firm mass and collects on the bottom of the pan in which the milk is heated. This, of course, contributes to the characteristic scorching of heated milk. You can stir the milk while it heats to lessen the amount of precipitate on the bottom, but some scorching may still occur, particularly if a large quantity of milk is heated at one time. One way to prevent scorching is to heat milk over hot water in a double boiler rather than with direct heat.

The protein found in the largest amount in milk, casein, does not coagulate at the usual temperatures and times used in food preparation. Although some of its properties may change slightly, it coagulates only when it is heated to very high temperatures or for a long period at the boiling point. In fact, as long as 12 hours may be required for casein to coagulate when it is heated at a temperature of 100°C (212°F).

Heating periods that produce casein coagulation are shorter when the concentration of casein is increased above that in regular fluid milk. For example, in the sterilization of canned evaporated milk, it is necessary to take certain measures to prevent coagulation of the casein. One such measure is to prewarm the milk prior to its sterilization.

Precipitate   to become insoluble and separate out of a solution or dispersion

Coagulate   to form a clot, a semi-solid mass, or a gel, after initial denaturation of a protein

The coagulation of milk proteins by heat is accelerated by an increase in acidity. It is also influenced by the kinds and concentrations of salts present. The salts in such foods as ham hocks and vegetables are partly responsible for coagulation of casein when these products are cooked in milk.

Effect of Heating on Minerals

The dispersion of calcium phosphate in milk is decreased by heating, and a small part of it is precipitated. Some of the calcium phosphate collects on the bottom of the pan with coagulated whey proteins, and some is probably entangled in the scum on the top surface of the milk.

Film Formation on Heated Milk

The formation of a film or scum on the surface of heated milk is often troublesome, and it is responsible for milk's boiling over the sides of the pan. A certain amount of pressure develops under the film, which forces the film upward, and the milk flows over the sides of the pan. A slight film may form at relatively low temperatures, but this may be prevented by a cover on the pan, by dilution of the milk, or by the presence of fat floating on the surface. As the temperature is increased, a tough scum forms that is insoluble and can be removed from the surface. As soon as it is removed, however, another film forms.

Sometimes, to break up the film, the heated milk is beaten with a rotary-type egg beater. This procedure has limited usefulness because of the continuous formation of fresh film; however, foam formation at the surface appears to aid in preventing a really tenacious scum from forming.

The composition of the film on heated milk is variable. It may contain coagulated protein, with some precipitated salts and fat globules entangled in the mesh of coagulated matter.

Coalescence of Fat Globules on Heating

The layer of fat that may form on milk that has been boiled results from the breaking of the films of protein that surround the fat globules in the unheated milk. The breaking of films of emulsifying agents permits the coalescence of fat globules.

Heating Sugar–Protein Mixtures

When certain sugars and proteins are heated together, browning occurs. This particular nonenzymatic browning is of the Maillard type. Concentrated milk products such as evaporated milk contain substantial amounts of both protein and the sugar lactose and develop some brown color on heating. This reaction may also occur in dried milk stored for long periods. Heating for several hours sweetened condensed milk in the can, which has been placed in a pan of water, results in a brown-colored product of thickened consistency and sweet caramel flavor. This "pudding" is sometimes used as a dessert.

Acid Coagulation

Although the protein casein is not very susceptible to coagulation by heating, it is very sensitive to precipitation on the addition of acid. The acid may be added as such, or it may be produced by bacteria as they ferment milk sugar. The acid curdling of milk is a desirable reaction in the making of such products as cultured buttermilk, yogurt, sour cream, and some cheeses. It is undesirable when it occurs in other food products. Prevention of casein coagulation or curdling is fundamental to the success of such products as cream of tomato soup. Fruit-milk mixtures may also curdle, as you may have noticed when putting cream on fresh fruits or making fruit-milk beverages or sherbets.

What happens when acid is added to milk? The pH, which normally is about 6.6, begins to fall. When it reaches about 4.6, the colloidally dispersed casein particles become unstable. They adhere together and form a coagulum or curd. This probably occurs because the usual negative charge on the casein particles, which causes them to repel each other and remain apart, is neutralized by the acidic hydrogen ion (H^+). A considerable amount of calcium is also released from the casein molecules to the liquid whey. The calcium was bonded through the phosphoric acid groups of casein. The curd then traps the whey in its meshes. The whey, which contains the whey proteins, most of the lactose, and many minerals, is released when the curd is cut or stirred and heated. These processes occur in the manufacture of cheese.

Raw milk ordinarily contains bacteria that ferment lactose and produce lactic acid, thus "souring" the milk and producing a curd. A clean, acidic taste is characteristic. Pasteurized milk does not sour in this way. The heat of pasteurization destroys most of the lactic acid bacteria responsible for the souring process. Instead, pasteurized milk spoils by the action of putrefactive bacteria, which break down the proteins in milk.

Enzyme Coagulation

A number of enzymes from plant, animal, and microbial sources are capable of clotting milk. Rennin or chymosin is such an enzyme. It is found in the stomachs of young animals. Its function is to clot milk prior to the action of other protein-digesting enzymes. The name *chymosin* is derived from the Greek word *chyme*, meaning gastric liquid, and is used in the recommended international enzyme nomenclature [36]. The crude chymosin or rennin enzyme is called *rennet*. Rennet has been used for many years in the preparation of most varieties of cheeses. When the sources of rennet became limited, a number of other nonrennin milk-clotting enzymes were used as rennet substitutes [4]. The FDA has now affirmed that use of the chymosin preparation derived by fermentation from the genetically modified *Aspergillus* mold is GRAS (generally regarded as safe). This is one of the first genetically engineered food products to have been approved.

Since rennet is an enzyme, it requires specific conditions of temperature and acidity for its action. The optimum temperature is 40° to 42°C (104° to 108°F). Refrigerator temperatures retard its action. No action occurs below 10°C (50°F) or above 65°C (149°F). Rennet acts best in a faintly acid medium, and action does not occur in an alkaline environment.

When casein is precipitated by the action of rennet, the calcium is not released to the whey but remains attached to the casein. Therefore, cheese made with rennet is a much better source of calcium than cheese made by acid precipitation alone. Cottage cheese is often made by acid precipitation. From the Table of Composition in Appendix C, it can be noted that cottage cheese is considerably lower in calcium than is cheddar.

The action of the enzyme bromelin from raw or frozen pineapple in preventing the gelation of gelatin is well known. The enzyme digests proteins and hence changes the gelatin to smaller compounds that do not form a gel. The enzyme bromelin also clots milk but later digests the clot. Other enzymes in fruits are probably responsible for some of the curdling action that occurs when milk or cream and certain fruits are combined. All fruits contain some organic acids, but not always in sufficient concentration to cause the curdling of milk. Destroying the enzymes before combining fruit with milk will, of course, prevent curdling caused by enzyme action.

Coagulation by Phenolic Compounds

Some phenolic-type compounds (formerly called *tannins*) are present in fruits and vegetables. In fruits, these compounds are found chiefly in the green stages and are present in a greater amount in some varieties than in others. Seeds and stems may contain significant amounts of phenolic substances. Among vegetables, the roots, pods, some seeds, and woody stems are likely to contain more phenolic compounds than other parts of the plant, although distribution is general throughout the plant. Curdling of milk may occur if phenolic-containing foods, such as potatoes, are cooked in the milk; however, the time and temperature of heating also influence curdling. In addition, the low levels of organic acids present in potatoes contribute to curdling.

Coagulation by Salts

The cause of curdling in foods cooked in milk is likely to be a combination of factors. The salts present in the milk, in the food combined with the milk, or added sodium chloride may also influence coagulation of the casein. Of the meats commonly cooked in milk, ham usually causes more coagulation than chicken, veal, or pork, although these may vary in their action. The high sodium chloride content of ham may be responsible for the excessive curdling that occurs when ham is cooked in milk.

Freezing

When milk or cream is frozen at a relatively slow rate, the film of protein that acts as an emulsifying agent around the fat globules is weakened or ruptured. As a result, the fat globules tend to coalesce. The oily masses that float on top of hot coffee when cream that has been frozen is added to it show the cohesion of fat particles that results from freezing. The dispersion of protein and calcium phosphate is also disturbed by freezing. Both constituents tend to settle out on thawing and standing, thus reducing the whiteness of milk. The effects of freezing are not harmful and do not affect food value.

•CREAM

Types of Cream and Cream Products

Cream is the high-fat, liquid product that is separated from whole milk. According to federal standards of identity, cream must contain not less than 18 percent milkfat.

Several liquid cream products are marketed, including light or coffee cream containing 18 to 30 percent milkfat, light whipping cream with 30 to 36 percent milkfat, and heavy cream or heavy whipping cream with not less than 36 percent milkfat [25].

Half-and-half is a mixture of milk and cream containing not less than 10.5 percent milkfat but less than 18 percent. Very little light or coffee cream is now available as such, half-and-half being commonly used in its place.

The thickness of cream is related to its fat content; it is generally thicker at higher fat levels. Other factors also affect thickness, however. Cream at room temperature is thinner than cream at refrigerator temperature because chilling makes the fat globules firmer, thereby increasing the **viscosity** of the cream. When chilled to a temperature of 5°C (41°F) and held at that temperature for twenty-four to forty-eight hours, cream gradually increases in thickness.

Viscosity resistance to flow; thickness or consistency

Commercial sour cream is a cultured or an acidified light cream. *Streptococcus lactis* organisms are added to the cultured cream, and the product is held at 22°C (72°F) until the acidity, calculated as lactic acid, is at least 0.5 percent [25]. Nonfat milk solids and stabilizing vegetable gums such as carrageenan may be added to sour cream, which can also be produced from half-and-half.

Dried cream, to be used reconstituted to liquid form, has been produced. An instant dry creamed milk made from modified skim milk (calcium reduced), light cream, and lactose has also been manufactured. When it is sprinkled on the surface of a beverage, it disperses quickly.

Cream containing sugar, stabilizers, and flavoring is sold in pressurized containers. When a valve is pressed, a whipped-cream product is emitted as a result of the action of propellant gases.

Many nondairy products for whipped toppings, coffee whiteners, sour cream-type mixtures, and snack dip bases have been developed and marketed. Initially, these were promoted as low-cost substitutes for the more expensive natural dairy products. Many of them, particularly whipped toppings and coffee whiteners, have been gradually accepted on their own merits rather than as substitutes and have taken over the market.

Nondairy whipped toppings often contain sugar, hydrogenated vegetable oil, sodium caseinate, and emulsifiers. They are available in a dry form, which is added to cold milk before whipping, and also in whipped form as a frozen product. The foam is stable and requires only defrosting before use. Nondairy products resembling whipped cream that contain water, vegetable fat, sugar, sodium caseinate, emulsifiers, and vegetable gums are also available in pressurized cans. These products must be refrigerated.

Nondairy coffee whiteners are now widely used in hot beverages. They usually contain corn syrup solids, vegetable fat, a source of protein such as sodium caseinate or soy protein, emulsifiers, and salts.

Surface tension tension created over the surface of a liquid because of the greater attraction of the liquid molecules for each other than for the gaseous molecules in the air above the liquid

Whipping of Cream

A foam is a dispersion of a gas in a liquid. If the foam is stable, there must also be present a stabilizing agent to keep the gas dispersed. Certain conditions are necessary for the foam to form in the first place. A foaming agent must be dispersed in the liquid to lower the **surface tension** of the liquid. This allows the liquid to surround the gas bubbles. The stabilizing agent can then act to keep the gas bubbles separated.

In the whipping of cream, a foam is formed. The liquid is the water in the cream, the gas is air that is beaten in, and the foaming agent that lowers the surface tension of the water is protein that is dispersed in the cream. During whipping, air bubbles are incorporated and surrounded by a thin liquid film containing protein. The foam cells are stabilized by coalesced fat globules. The globules apparently coalesce because much of the milkfat globule membrane surrounding them and keeping them separated has been removed in the whipping process [16]. At the cold temperature of the whipping cream, the fat globules are solid. Because whipping is the first stage of churning cream, the emulsion breaks and butter is formed if whipping is continued too long.

Air bubbles in whipped cream must be surrounded by protein films. Because so much of the protein of homogenized cream is used to surround the increased number of fat globules, little protein remains to surround the air bubbles formed in whipping. Therefore, whipping cream is usually not homogenized. Several factors affect the whipping properties of cream.

Temperature

Cream held at a cold temperature (7°C or 45°F or below) whips better than cream held at warmer temperatures. Above 10°C (50°F), agitation of cream increases the dispersion of the fat instead of decreasing it. In the whipping of cream, the aim is to increase *clumping* of fat particles, and at low temperatures, agitation results in clumping. Lower temperatures also increase viscosity, which increases the whipping properties of cream. The beater and bowl that are used, as well as the cream, should be chilled.

Viscosity

Any condition that increases viscosity increases the whipping property of cream. The effect of temperature on viscosity has already been noted. Higher fat content also increases viscosity and furnishes more fat globules for clumping. Because viscosity increases with aging, the whipping property improves with the aging of cream (see Figure 20.4).

| 35% | 30% | 25% | 20% | | 20% | 25% | 30% | 35% |

FIGURE 20.4

The foam stability of whipped cream increases with increasing fat content of the cream between 20 and 35 percent. Aging of cream also increases the stability of the whipped product. (*left*) Cream whipped soon after separation. (*right*) Cream whipped after aging for 24 hours. Note the smaller amount of leakage from the foam after standing for 18 hours at 4°C (40°F) for creams with higher fat content. (Courtesy of J.C. Hening)

Amount of Fat

A fat content of 30 percent is about the minimum for cream that will whip with ease and produce a stiff product. Increasing the fat up to 40 percent improves the whipping quality of cream, because more solid fat particles are thus available to stabilize the foam (see Figure 20.4).

Amount of Cream Whipped

In whipping large amounts of cream, it is better to do successive whippings of amounts tailored to the size of the whipper used, rather than to whip a large amount at one time. If a very small amount of cream is to be whipped, a small deep bowl should be used so that the beaters can adequately agitate the cream.

Effect of Other Substances

Increased acidity up to the concentration required to produce a sour taste (0.3 percent) has no effect on whipping quality. The addition of sugar decreases both volume and stiffness and increases the time required to whip cream if it is added before whipping. If sugar is to be added, it is best added after the cream is stiff or just prior to serving. If sugar is added just before serving, powdered sugar should be used, since granulated sugar needs more time to dissolve.

Compounds on the market that are said to improve the whipping quality of thin cream have as a common constituent sucrate of lime, a compound formed from sucrose and calcium hydroxide. Used in small amounts, this compound increases viscosity.

The stand-up quality of whipped cream is improved if the cream is whipped as stiff as possible without forming butter, if cream of optimum fat content (about 40 percent) is used, and if the whipped cream is held at a cold temperature (below 10°C or 50°F).

Whipping of Other Milk Products

Evaporated Milk

When evaporated milk is chilled to the ice crystal stage, it will whip to about three times its original volume. This ability to whip is evidently the result of the higher concentration of milk solids in evaporated milk than in fresh whole milk. The protein in the milk acts as a foaming agent and also aids in stabilizing. This foam, however, is not very stable on standing. The addition of acid, such as a small amount of lemon juice (about 1 tablespoon per cup of undiluted milk), helps to stabilize the protein and makes a more lasting foam.

Nonfat Dry Milk

A light and airy whipped product may be produced by the whipping of nonfat dry milk. Equal measures of dry milk and very cold water are usually used, with the dry milk being sprinkled over the surface of the water before whipping. This foam is very unstable but its stability may be increased somewhat by adding small amounts of an acid substance such as lemon juice before whipping.

•LIGHT DAIRY PRODUCTS

The term *light* has been used to refer to decreased levels of sodium, fat, cholesterol, or calories in food products that have been marketed in recent years in response to consumer concerns about nutrition and health. Under the recently promulgated FDA definition of *light*, however, it must mean 33 percent fewer calories or 50 percent of the fat in a reference food (if 50 percent or more of the calories come from fat, reduction must be 50 percent of the fat). *Light in sodium* may be used to describe a product when the sodium content of a low-calorie, low-fat food has been reduced by 50 percent.

Polls indicate that people want light food products, with a majority of respondents indicating that they use them for various reasons related to health [13]. Dairy products are among the most popular light foods, and the dairy industry is responding to the opportunity to develop a variety of these formulated foods. The low-fat milks have been well accepted for several years, of course. Light yogurts are available with no fat using **aspartame** as a sweetener. Frozen desserts may use microparticulated protein or hydrocolloids as fat replacers to qualify as light substitute ice creams. There are also light versions of cheese that are reduced in fat, cholesterol, sodium, or combinations of these [13].

Aspartame a high intensity sweetener with the trade name Nutrasweet™

One of the major problems associated with light dairy products is taste. Panelists who rated high- and low-fat processed American cheese and vanilla ice cream liked the high-fat products better [17]. Despite receiving label information along with the samples, panelists still liked the high-fat ice cream more than the low-fat product. When the panelists knew the fat content of the cheese, however, they tended to like the high-fat product somewhat less and the low-fat cheese somewhat more. The most important determinant of liking in this study was the fat level, regardless of the panelists' level of concern about fat-containing products.

•CHEESE

Cheese is a concentrated dairy food defined as the fresh or matured product obtained by draining the whey (the moisture or serum of the original milk) after coagulation of casein, the major milk protein. Casein is coagulated by acid produced by added microbial cultures and/or by coagulating enzymes, resulting in curd formation. Milk can also be acidified by adding suitable organic acids [25]. The curd may receive further treatment by heat or pressure or by the action of the microbial culture on holding. In the United States, almost all cheese is manufactured from the whole, partly skimmed, or skimmed milk of cows. The pigment carotene is added to give cheese a yellow color when it is desirable.

Most of the cheese consumed in the United States is made commercially. Some consumers, however, may make cottage cheese at home; the USDA has published a bulletin giving instructions on how to do this [18].

The quality of the milk used in cheesemaking is extremely important and is rigidly controlled. Most cheese is made from pasteurized or heat-treated milk. Pasteurization is not a substitute for sanitation but rather an additional safeguard [25].

The manufacture of most cheeses follows similar steps. These include (1) curd formation with acid produced by lactic acid-producing bacteria (a starter culture) and/or a coagulating enzyme; (2) cutting the curd into small pieces to allow the whey to escape; (3) heating the curd to contract the curd particles and hasten the expulsion of whey; (4) draining, knitting or stretching, salting, and pressing the curd; and (5) curing or ripening [25].

Ripening

Ripening refers to the changes in physical and chemical properties, such as aroma, flavor, texture, and composition, that take place between the time of precipitation of the curd and the time when the cheese develops the desired characteristics for its type. Some changes that occur are the formation by bacteria of lactic acid from the lactose; the digestion of the protein by enzymes into end products, including peptides and amino acids; the development and penetration of molds in mold-ripened cheese; the gas formation by certain types of microorganisms used; and the development of characteristic flavor and aroma substances, including those developed from the decomposition of fat by lipase enzymes.

The flavor of ripened cheese results from a blending of the decomposition and hydrolysis products formed from the milk components. The hydrolysis of protein eventually results in free water-soluble amino acids that give the cheese a softer, more pliable texture, as well as improved flavor. The fat of some cheese is hydrolyzed by enzymes, liberating fatty acids. Most of the small amount of lactose that is present in cheese is converted to other compounds. Lactic acid is formed. A characteristic flavor is developed in each particular type of cheese.

The changes that occur in cheese during ripening not only affect flavor and texture but also improve the cooking quality. The increased dispersibility of the protein of ripened cheese contributes to the ease of blending cheese with other food ingredients, particularly for such products as cheese sauce.

Various types of organisms produce distinctive flavors, aromas, and textures in cheeses. The *Penicillium roqueforti* or *Penicillium glaucum* types of molds are responsible for the mottled blue-green appearance of blue, roquefort, gorgonzola, and stilton cheeses. The curd is inoculated with pure cultures of the mold, which penetrate during the curing process.

Camembert cheese is inoculated with two molds: *Oidium lactis*, which covers the cheese in the first stages of ripening, and *Penicillium camemberti*, which grows later. The enzymes produced by the molds penetrate and soften the cheese. Organic acids used as food by the molds gradually disappear, providing a more favorable medium for putrefactive bacteria. The cheese is usually placed in small molds, with the curing agents on the outside surface. They gradually penetrate throughout the cheese during the holding period. Damp caves are used to ripen some types of cheese that depend on mold action for the development of flavor.

Swiss cheese owes its large holes to special gas-forming organisms. These organisms grow and produce carbon dioxide gas during the early stage of ripening, while the cheese is soft and elastic. Limburger cheese owes its characteristic odor to the development of putrefactive bacteria, which are allowed to act over a considerable period. Ordinary cheddar cheese varies widely in flavor and texture depending on the organisms that predominate and the length of time of ripening. *Lactobacilli* and *Streptococcus lactis* organisms play major roles in the ripening of good cheddar cheese. The presence of salt delays bacterial growth, and therefore alters the rate of ripening.

Mild cheeses, such as brick and monterey jack, are allowed to ripen for a shorter period than are strong cheeses, such as parmesan. Blue cheese is usually aged 3 to 4 months but may be aged up to 9 months for more pronounced flavor.

Grades

USDA grade standards U.S. Grade AA and U.S. Grade A have been developed for swiss, cheddar, colby, and monterey cheese. Cheese bearing these grades must be produced in a USDA-inspected and approved plant under sanitary conditions. Graders evaluate the flavor and the texture of the cheese. Some cheese and cheese products not covered by a U.S. grade standard may be inspected and bear a USDA Quality Approved inspection shield on the label. This shield indicates that the cheese has been manufactured in a plant meeting USDA sanitary specifications and is a cheese of good quality.

Composition and Nutritive Value

Cheese is a very concentrated food; 1 pound of cheese may contain the protein and fat of 1 gallon of milk. The protein is of high biologic value, and the fat is largely saturated. Vitamin A is carried in the fat. The addition of salt for flavor generally makes cheese a high sodium food.

The composition of cheese varies widely with the fraction of milk used and the amount of moisture retained. When cheese is made from whole milk, the fat remains with the curd when the whey is drained off. Much of the milk sugar, the soluble salts, and the water-soluble vitamins are drained off in the whey, although even in hard cheeses the whey is never entirely removed. Whey cheeses and concentrated whey added to cheese spreads or cheese foods save some of these valuable nutrients.

Cheese made by rennet coagulation is an excellent source of calcium and phosphorus, whereas that coagulated by acid alone contains less calcium. The reason for this difference in calcium content is that the lower pH or greater acidity produced by adding acid causes the release of more calcium ions (Ca^{2+}) from the phosphate groups that are part of the casein molecule. Much of this released calcium goes into the whey and is not retained in the curd. Cheeses of the cheddar type, made chiefly by rennet coagulation of the milk, may retain up to 80 percent of the original milk calcium. Soft cheeses made by acid precipitation, such as cottage cheese, may retain not more than one-fourth to one-half of the milk calcium.

American cheddar cheese averages, roughly, one-third water, one-third fat, and one-fourth protein. It also contains about 4 percent ash and less than 1 percent carbohydrate, including lactic acid. Cheeses made from low-fat or skim milk are lower in fat content than cheeses made from whole milk. Cheese containing vegetable oil instead of milkfat is also available for those who want to decrease their intake of animal fat.

The moisture content of soft cheese varies from 40 to 75 percent, whereas hard cheeses tend to contain a more nearly uniform amount of water—from 30 to 40 percent. High moisture content is a factor in the perishability of cheese, those with a large amount of moisture being more perishable.

Types of Cheese Products

The groupings of cheeses may be determined by two factors: the amount of moisture in the finished cheese, and the kind and extent of ripening. Based on moisture content, cheese may be classified as soft, semihard, or hard. Based on the kind and extent of ripening, cheese may be classified as strong and sharp, mild, or mold-ripened or bacteria-ripened.

More than 2,000 names have been given to cheeses with somewhat different characteristics, but there are only about ten distinct types of natural cheese.

FIGURE 20.5

Many kinds of cheese are available. To identify the cheeses shown here, see the accompanying labeled drawing. (Courtesy of the American Dairy Association)

Table 20.1 describes the characteristics of some popular varieties of natural cheeses; some of these are shown in Figure 20.5.

Cold-Pack Cheese

Cold-pack or club cheese is made by grinding and mixing together one or more varieties of cheese without the aid of heat. Acid, water, salt, coloring, and spices may be added, but the final moisture content must not exceed that permitted for the variety of natural cheese from which it was prepared. The cheese is packaged in jars or in moisture-proof packages in retail-size units. Cold-pack cheese food is prepared in the same manner as cold-pack cheese, but it may contain other ingredients such as cream, milk, skim milk, nonfat dry milk, or whey. It may also contain pimientos, fruits, vegetables, or meats, and sweetening agents such as sugar and corn syrup.

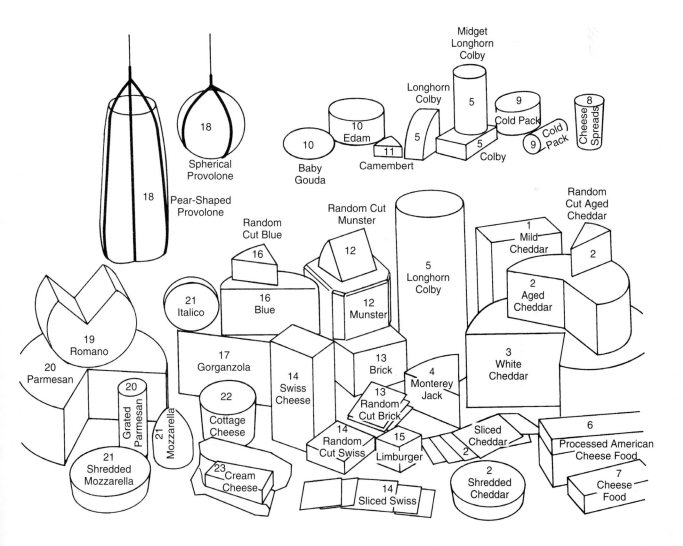

TABLE 20.1
Characteristics of Some Popular Varieties of Natural Cheeses

Kind or Name (place of origin)	Kind of Milk Used in Manufacture	Ripening or Curing Time	Flavor	Body and Texture	Color	Retail Packaging	Use
Soft, Unripened Varieties							
Cottage, plain or creamed (unknown)	Cow's milk skimmed; plain curd, or plain curd with cream added	Unripened	Mild, acid	Soft, curd particles of varying size	White to creamy white	Cup-shaped containers, tumblers, dishes	Salads, with fruits, vegetables, sandwiches, dips, cheese cake
Cream, plain (United States)	Cream from cow's milk	Unripened	Mild, acid	Soft and smooth	White	3- to 8-oz packages	Salads, dips, sandwiches, snacks, cheese cake, desserts
Neufchatel (Nû-shä-tĕl´) (France)	Cow's milk	Unripened	Mild, acid	Soft, smooth, similar to cream cheese but lower in milkfat	White	4- to 8-oz packages	Salads, dips, sandwiches, snacks, cheese cake, desserts
Ricotta (rĭcŏ´-ta) (Italy)	Cow's milk, whole or partly skimmed, or whey from cow's milk with whole or skim milk added; in Italy, whey from sheep's milk	Unripened	Sweet, nutlike	Soft, moist or dry	White	Pint and quart paper and plastic containers, 3-lb metal cans	Appetizers, salads, snacks, lasagna, ravioli, noodles and other cooked dishes, grating, desserts
Firm, Unripened Varieties							
Gjetost* (yĕt´ ŏst) (Norway)	Whey from goat's milk or a mixture of whey from goat's and cow's milk	Unripened	Sweetish, caramel	Firm, buttery consistency	Golden brown	Cubical and rectangular	Snacks, desserts, served with dark breads, crackers, biscuits, or muffins

Name (pronunciation) (Origin)	Kind of Milk	Ripening or Curing Time	Flavor	Body and Texture	Color	Retail Packaging	Uses
Mysost (mü sôst) also called Primost (prēm´-ôst) (Norway)	Whey from cow's milk	Unripened	Sweetish, caramel	Firm, buttery consistency	Light brown	Cubical, cylindrical, pie-shaped wedges	Snacks, desserts, served with dark breads
Mozzarella (mô-tsa-rel´la) (Italy)	Whole or partly skimmed cow's milk; in Italy, originally made from buffalo's milk	Unripened	Delicate, mild	Slightly firm, plastic	Creamy white	Small round or braided form, shredded, sliced	Snacks; toasted sandwiches; cheeseburgers; cooking, as in meat loaf; or topping for lasagna, pizza, and casseroles
Soft, Ripened Varieties							
Brie (brē) (France)	Cow's milk	4–8 weeks	Mild to pungent	Soft, smooth when ripened	Creamy yellow interior; edible thin brown and white crust	Circular, pie-shaped wedges	Appetizers, sandwiches, snacks, good with crackers and fruit, dessert
Camembert (kăm´ ĕm-bâr) (France)	Cow's milk	4–8 weeks	Mild to pungent	Soft, smooth; very soft when fully ripened	Creamy yellow interior; edible thin white or gray-white crust	Small circular cakes and pie-shaped portions	Appetizers, sandwiches, snacks, good with crackers and fruit such as pears and apples, dessert
Limburger (Belgium)	Cow's milk	4–8 weeks	Highly pungent, very strong	Soft, smooth when ripened; usually contains small irregular openings	Creamy white interior; reddish-yellow surface	Cubical, rectangular	Appetizers, snacks, good with crackers, rye, or other dark breads, dessert
Bel Paese† (bĕl pä-ā´-zĕ) (Italy)	Cow's milk	6–8 weeks	Mild to moderately robust	Soft to medium firm, creamy	Creamy yellow interior; slightly gray or brownish surface sometimes covered with yellow wax coating	Small wheels, wedges, segments	Appetizers, good with crackers, snacks, sandwiches, dessert

Kind or Name (place of origin)	Kind of Milk Used in Manufacture	Ripening or Curing Time	Flavor	Body and Texture	Color	Retail Packaging	Use
Brick (United States)	Cow's milk	2–4 months	Mild to moderately sharp	Semisoft to medium firm; elastic, numerous small mechanical openings	Creamy yellow	Loaf, brick, slices, cut portions	Appetizers, sandwiches, snacks, dessert
Muenster (mŭn´stĕr) (Germany)	Cow's milk	1–8 weeks	Mild to mellow	Semisoft; numerous small mechanical openings; contains more moisture than brick	Creamy white interior; yellow-tan surface	Circular cake, blocks, wedges, segments, slices	Appetizers, snacks, served with raw fruit, dessert
Port du Salut (por dü sälü´) (France)	Cow's milk	6–8 weeks	Mellow to robust	Semisoft, smooth, buttery; small openings	Creamy yellow	Wheels and wedges	Appetizers, snacks, served with raw fruit, dessert
Firm, Ripened Varieties							
Cheddar (England)	Cow's milk	1–12 months or longer	Mild to very sharp	Firm, smooth; some mechanical openings	White to medium-yellow-orange	Circular, cylindrical, loaf, pie-shaped wedges, oblongs, slices, cubes, shredded, grated	Appetizers, sandwiches, sauces, on vegetables, in hot dishes, toasted sandwiches, grating, cheeseburgers, dessert
Colby (United States)	Cow's milk	1–3 months	Mild to mellow	Softer and more open than Cheddar	White to medium-yellow-orange	Cylindrical, pie-shaped wedges	Sandwiches, snacks, cheeseburgers
Caciocavallo (kä´chŏ-kä-val´lŏ) (Italy)	Cow's milk; in Italy, cow's milk or mixtures of sheep's, goat's, and cow's milk	3–12 months	Piquant, similar to Provolone but not smoked	Firm, lower in milkfat and moisture than Provolone	Light or white interior; clay- or tan-colored surface	Spindle- or tenpin-shaped, bound with cord, cut pieces	Snacks, sandwiches, cooking, dessert; suitable for grating after prolonged curing

Name	Kind of Milk	Ripening Time	Flavor	Body and Texture	Color	Shapes in Which Sold	Uses
Edam (ē´dăm) (Netherlands)	Cow's milk, partly skimmed	2–3 months	Mellow, nutlike	Semisoft to firm, smooth; small irregularly shaped or round holes; lower milkfat than Gouda	Creamy yellow or medium yellow-orange interior; surface coated with red wax	Cannon ball-shaped loaf, cut pieces, oblongs	Appetizers, snacks, salads, sandwiches, seafood sauces, dessert
Gouda (gou´-dä) (Netherlands)	Cow's milk, whole or partly skimmed	2–6 months	Mellow, nutlike	Semisoft to firm, smooth; small irregularly shaped or round holes; higher milkfat than Edam	Creamy yellow or medium yellow-orange interior; may or may not have red wax coating	Ball-shaped with flattened top and bottom	Appetizers, snacks, salads, sandwiches, seafood sauces, dessert
Provolone (prō-vō-lō´-nē), also smaller sizes and shapes called Provolette and Provoloncini (Italy)	Cow's milk	2–12 months or more	Mellow to sharp, smoky, salty	Firm, smooth	Light creamy interior; light brown or golden yellow surface	Pear shaped, sausage and salami shaped, wedges, slices	Appetizers, sandwiches, snacks, soufflé, macaroni and spaghetti dishes, pizza; suitable for grating when fully cured and dried
Swiss, also called Emmentaler (Switzerland)	Cow's milk	3–9 months	Sweet, nutlike	Firm, smooth, with large round eyes	Light yellow	Segments, pieces, slices	Sandwiches, snacks, sauces, fondue, cheeseburgers
Parmesan (pär´-mĕ-zän´) also called Reggiano (Italy)	Partly skimmed cow's milk	14 months to 2 years	Sharp, piquant	Very hard, granular; lower moisture and milkfat than Romano	Creamy white	Cylindrical, wedges, shredded, grated	Grated for seasoning in soups, vegetables, spaghetti, ravioli, breads, popcorn, used extensively in pizza and lasagna
Romano (rō-mä´-nō), also called Sardo Romano and Pecorino Romano (Italy)	Cow's milk; in Italy, sheep's milk (Italian law)	5–12 months	Sharp, piquant	Very hard granular	Yellowish-white interior, greenish-black surface	Round with flat ends, wedges, shredded, grated	Seasoning in soups, casserole dishes, ravioli, sauces, breads; suitable for grating when cured for about 1 year

TABLE 20.1, *continued*

Kind or Name (place of origin)	Kind of Milk Used in Manufacture	Ripening or Curing Time	Flavor	Body and Texture	Color	Retail Packaging	Use
Sap Sago* (săp´-sä-gō) (Switzerland)	Skimmed cow's milk	5 months or longer	Sharp, pungent, cloverlike	Very hard	Light green by addition of dried, powdered clover leaves	Conical, shakers	Grated to flavor soups, meats, macaroni, spaghetti, hot vegetables; mixed with butter, makes a good spread on crackers or bread
Blue-vein Mold Ripened Varieties							
Blue, spelled Bleu on imported cheese (France)	Cow's milk	2–6 months	Tangy, peppery	Semisoft, pasty, sometimes crumbly	White interior, marbled or streaked with blue veins of mold	Cylindrical, wedges, oblongs, squares, cut portions	Appetizers, salads, dips, salad dressing, sandwich spreads, good with crackers, dessert
Gorgonzola (gôr-gŏn-zō´-lä) (Italy)	Cow's milk; in Italy, cow's milk or goat's milk or mixtures of these	3–12 months	Tangy, peppery	Semisoft, pasty, sometimes crumbly, lower moisture than Blue	Creamy white interior, mottled or streaked with blue-green veins of mold; clay-colored surface	Cylindrical, wedges, oblongs	Appetizers, snacks, salads, dips, sandwich spreads, good with crackers, dessert
Roquefort* (rōk´-fĕrt) or (rōk-fôr´) (France)	Sheep's milk	2–5 months or longer	Sharp, slightly peppery	Semisoft, pasty, sometimes crumbly	White or creamy white interior, marbled or streaked with blue veins of mold	Cylindrical, wedges	Appetizers, snacks, salads, dips, sandwich spreads, good with crackers, dessert
Stilton* (England)	Cow's milk	2–6 months	Piquant, milder than Gorgonzola or Roquefort	Semisoft, flaky; slightly more crumbly than Blue	Creamy white interior; marbled or streaked with blue-green veins of mold	Circular, wedges, oblongs	Appetizers, snacks, salads, dessert

* Imported only.
† Italian trademark—licensed for manufacture in United States; also imported.

Source: Reference 9.

Process Cheese

About one-third of the cheese produced in the United States today is made into pasteurized process cheese and related products. Process cheese is made by grinding and mixing together different samples of natural cheese with the aid of heat and an emulsifying agent. A selected blend of cheese or portions of the same variety selected at different stages of ripeness are used, and the product is pasteurized before packaging. The cheese is ground and heated, and sufficient water is added to replace that lost by evaporation. To aid in producing a uniform blend that melts without separation of fat, an emulsifying agent, such as disodium phosphate or sodium citrate, is added to the ground cheese before heating.

After the cheese is melted, it is run into molds. These are sometimes jars or glasses but are often cardboard boxes lined with metal foil; the wrapper may be of a transparent plastic material. As the cheese hardens, it clings closely to the jar or foil, thus preventing molds from attacking the surface. Pasteurization of the cheese destroys bacteria and enzymes, thus stopping all ripening. Process cheese is also sold in individual slices and can be purchased with individual slices separately wrapped. This extends the shelf life of the cheese.

The quality and flavor of process cheese depend on the quality and flavor of the cheese used to make it. Several varieties of cheese are made into pasteurized process cheeses, including cheddar, swiss, and brick cheese. Convenience, ease of blending in cooked dishes, and the protection offered by the package against spoilage are factors influencing the consumer's choice to use process cheese. The blend of cheeses is chosen to retain as far as possible the characteristic flavor of the type of cheese used; however, the flavor of the process cheese is seldom, if ever, equal to that of the original product. The characteristic differences in texture of the original cheeses tend to be lost, as the texture of process cheese is more or less uniform and soft. The moisture content of process cheese may not exceed 40 percent.

Low-fat (about 8 percent) pasteurized process cheese products in individual slices are also available on the market. These products contain skim milk cheese, water, emulsifier salts, flavorings, and a preservative (sorbic acid).

Process Cheese Foods and Spreads

Pasteurized process cheese food is produced in a manner similar to process cheese except that it contains less cheese. Cream, milk, skim milk, nonfat milk solids or whey, and sometimes other foods, such as pimientos, may be added to it. Cheese food is more mild in flavor, melts more quickly, and has a softer texture than process cheese because of its higher moisture content.

Pasteurized process cheese spread generally has a higher moisture and lower milkfat content than process cheese food. A stabilizer is added to prevent separation of ingredients. It is also generally more spreadable than process cheese food.

Cheese Storage

Soft and unripened cheeses have limited keeping quality and require refrigeration. All cheese is best kept cold. To prevent the surfaces from drying out, the cheese should be well wrapped in plastic wrap or metal foil or kept in the original container if it is one that protects the cheese. Wild molds growing on the surface of cheese are undesirable and must be trimmed off. In the refrigerator, strong cheeses that are not tightly wrapped may contaminate other foods that readily absorb odors.

Freezing is not recommended for most cheeses because, on thawing, they tend to be mealy and crumbly. However, some varieties of cheese can be frozen satisfactorily in small pieces (1 pound or less, not more than 1 inch thick). These varieties include brick, cheddar, edam, gouda, muenster, port du salut, swiss, provolone, mozzarella, and camembert. When frozen cheese is to be thawed, it may be taken from the freezer and placed in the refrigerator for a minimum of 10 days before using it to accomplish what is called *slow thawing*. This helps to avoid the detrimental effects of freezing and aids in preserving the original flavor, body, and texture.

Cheese usually exhibits its most distinctive flavor when it is served at room temperature. An exception is cottage cheese, which should be served cold. The amount of cheese to be used should be removed from the refrigerator about 30 minutes prior to serving [25].

Cheese in Cooked Foods

Cheese is an ingredient in a variety of cooked dishes, adding flavor, color, and texture. Many casserole mixtures use cheese, either as a basic component or as a topping. And what would pizza be without cheese? In addition, a cheese tray combined with fresh fruits and/or vegetable relishes makes an easy snack or a colorful dessert (see Figure 20.6).

A hard cheese, such as cheddar, softens and then melts when it is heated at low to moderate temperatures. Further heating results in the separation of fat and the development of a tough, rubbery curd, which will form long strings when manipulated with a spoon. If the cheese has been heated to the latter stage, it will tend to harden on cooling. Finely dividing the cheese by grating or grinding before combining it with other ingredients facilitates melting without overheating. Cheese sauces should be cooked in a double boiler or over low heat with continuous stirring. Well-ripened cheese and process cheese blend

FIGURE 20.6
Cheese and fresh fruit can appropriately be served either as a snack or as a dessert. This cheese assortment includes a chunk of roquefort or blue, cubes of cheddar, round slices of provolone, wedges of edam, and slices of swiss. (Courtesy of the U.S. Department of Agriculture)

Hot blue cheese and chicken sandwich topped with grated parmesan cheese

Cheese soufflé

Pineapple refrigerator cheesecake containing cottage cheese

FIGURE 20.7
Cheese is used in prepared dishes in a variety of ways, including Welsh rabbit, macaroni and cheese, and cheese omelets. Some unusual and interesting uses of cheese in cooking are shown here. (Courtesy of the American Dairy Association; soufflé, courtesy of Kraft Foods)

better in heated mixtures than mild (less aged) natural cheese and are less likely to produce stringiness.

Welsh rabbit is a thickened cheese sauce with seasonings. It may also contain egg, and is usually served over toast. Cheese soufflé is a combination of white sauce and eggs, with grated cheese to give it flavor. The white sauce used as a basis may vary in consistency or in amount, but soufflés made with a thick sauce base are usually easier for the inexperienced person to make and tend to shrink less after baking. Shrinkage, however, is principally a matter of the temperature and time of cooking. The baking dish containing the soufflé should be placed in a pan of water during baking to avoid overcooking.

Figure 20.7 illustrates several examples of the use of cheese in cooked foods, and Figure 20.8 shows a party salad made with cheese.

FIGURE 20.8

Process cheddar cheese (coarsely shredded), pineapple chunks, and halved seedless grapes are combined in this gelatin party salad. Whipped cream gives it a creamy texture. Sugared grape clusters and mint leaves garnish this fruit-cream mold. (Courtesy of the U.S. Department of Agriculture)

STUDY QUESTIONS

1. Describe present trends in the consumption of dairy products in the United States.
2. What is the average percentage composition of whole cow's milk?
3. Name the following items.
   a. Protein found in milk in largest amount
   b. Two major whey proteins
   c. Major carbohydrate of milk
   d. Two minerals for which milk is considered to be a particularly good source
   e. Vitamin for which milk is a good source that is easily destroyed when milk is exposed to sunlight
4. Explain why milk is classified as an emulsion. Describe how the fat in milk is dispersed.
5. How do opaque containers help to protect milk against the development of off-flavor? Explain.
6. Describe the purpose, process, and resulting product when milk is
   a. Pasteurized
   b. Homogenized
   c. Fortified
7. Briefly describe the major characteristics of each of the following processed milk products.
   a. Whole fluid milk
   b. Skim milk
   c. Low-fat milks
   d. Ultrahigh-temperature processed milk
   e. Evaporated milk
   f. Sweetened condensed milk
   g. Nonfat dry milk, regular and instantized
   h. Dried buttermilk (churned)
   i. Buttermilk (cultured)
   j. Acidophilus milk, acid and sweet
   k. Yogurt
   l. Filled milk
   m. Imitation milk
   n. Whipping cream
   o. Half-and-half
   p. Sour cream
8. a. Explain why it is so important that milk be handled properly, both in processing and in the kitchen.

b. What does the USDA Quality Approved shield mean when it is placed on certain dairy products?

c. What is the Grade A Pasteurized Milk Ordinance?

9. a. What causes milk to scorch when it is heated over direct heat?

b. Which milk proteins coagulate quite easily with heating? Which does not?

10. Suggest ways to prevent or control the formation of a film or scum on the surface of heated milk.

11. a. Which milk protein coagulates easily with the addition of acid?

b. Give examples illustrating when the acid coagulation of milk is desirable and when it is undesirable.

12. a. What is *rennet* and what does it do to milk?

b. What role does rennet play in cheese making?

13. a. Describe what happens when cream is whipped.

b. What conditions should be controlled, and why, if cream is to whip properly?

c. Suggest effective procedures for whipping evaporated milk and nonfat dry milk.

14. Describe the general steps usually followed in the manufacture of cheese.

15. a. What is meant by *ripening* cheese?

b. Describe general changes that may occur during the ripening process.

16. Give examples of each of the following types of cheese.

a. Soft, unripened

b. Firm, unripened

c. Soft, ripened

d. Semisoft, ripened

e. Firm, ripened

f. Very hard, ripened

g. Blue-vein mold-ripened

17. Describe the major characteristics of the following.

a. Cold-pack cheese

b. Process cheese

c. Process cheese food

d. Process cheese spread

18. a. Describe what happens when cheese is heated too long or at too high a temperature.

b. Suggest an appropriate way for preparing a cheese sauce and explain why this method should be effective.

REFERENCES

1. Bhaskar, A. R., S. S. H. Rizvi, and J. W. Sherbon. 1993. Anhydrous milkfat fractionation with continuous countercurrent supercritical carbon dioxide. *Journal of Food Science 58*, 748.

2. Cocup, R. O., and W. B. Sanderson. 1987. Functionality of dairy ingredients in bakery products. *Food Technology 41*, 86 (No. 10).

3. Council on Foods and Nutrition. 1969. Substitutes for whole milk. *Journal of the American Medical Association 208*, 58.

4. Gupta, C. B., and N. A. M. Eskin. 1977. Potential use of vegetable rennet in the production of cheese. *Food Technology 31*, 62 (No. 5).

5. Hansen, A. P. 1987. Effect of ultrahigh-temperature processing and storage on dairy food flavor. *Food Technology 41*, 112 (No. 9).

6. Hill, A. R. 1988. Quality of ultrahigh-temperature processed milk. *Food Technology 42*, 92 (No. 9).

7. Holsinger, V. H., and A. E. Kligerman. 1991. Applications of lactase in dairy foods and other foods containing lactose. *Food Technology 45*, 92 (No. 1).

8. Hoover, D. G. 1993. Bifidobacteria: Activity and potential benefits. *Food Technology 47*, 120 (No. 6).

9. *How to Buy Cheese*. 1974. Home and Garden Bulletin No. 193. Washington, DC: U.S. Department of Agriculture.

10. Hughes, D. B., and D. G. Hoover. 1991. Bifidobacteria: Their potential for use in American dairy products. *Food Technology 45*, 74 (No. 4).

11. Imitation and substitute dairy products. 1983. *Dairy Council Digest 54*, 1 (No. 1).

12. Kanno, C., Y. Shimomura, and E. Takano. 1991. Physicochemical properties of milk-fat emulsions stabilized with bovine milkfat globule membrane. *Journal of Food Science 56*, 1219.

13. Kantor, M. A. 1990. Light dairy products: The need and the consequences. *Food Technology 44*, 81 (No. 10).

14. Kirkpatrick, K. J., and R. M. Fenwick. 1987. Manufacture and general properties of dairy ingredients. *Food Technology 41*, 58 (No. 10).

15. Kroger, M., J. A. Kurmann, and J. L. Rasic. 1989. Fermented milks—Past, present, and future. *Food Technology 43*, 92 (No. 1).

16. Lee, S. Y., and C. V. Morr. 1993. Fixation staining methods for examining microstructure in whipped cream by electron microscopy. *Journal of Food Science 58*, 124.

17. Light, A., H. Heymann, and D. L. Holt. 1992. Hedonic responses to dairy products: Effects of fat levels, label information, and risk perception. *Food Technology 46*, 54 (No. 7).

18. *Making Cottage Cheese at Home*. 1975. Home and Garden Bulletin No. 129. Washington, DC: U.S. Department of Agriculture.

19. Mangino, M. E. 1992. Gelation of whey protein concentrates. *Food Technology 46*, 114 (No. 1).

20. Morr, C. V. 1992. Improving the texture and functionality of whey protein concentrate. *Food Technology 46*, 110.

21. Morr, C. V. 1984. Production and use of milk proteins in food. *Food Technology 38*, 39 (No. 7).

22. Morr, C. V., and E. A. Foegeding. 1990. Composition and functionality of commercial whey and milk protein concentrates and isolates: A status report. *Food Technology 44*, 100 (No. 4).

23. Mulvihill, D. M., and J. E. Kinsella. 1987. Gelation characteristics of whey proteins and beta-lactoglobulin. *Food Technology 41*, 102 (No. 9).

24. *Newer Knowledge of Cheese*. 1992. Rosemont, IL: National Dairy Council.

25. *Newer Knowledge of Milk*. 1993. Rosemont, IL: National Dairy Council.

26. Palanuk, S. L., J. J. Warthesen, and D. E. Smith. 1988. Effect of agitation, sampling location, and protective films on light-induced riboflavin loss in skim milk. *Journal of Food Science 53*, 436.

27. Pennington, J. A. T., E. B. Wilson, B. E. Young, R. D. Johnson, and J. E. Vanderveen. 1987. Mineral content of market samples of fluid whole milk. *Journal of the American Dietetic Association 87*, 1036.

28. Putnam, J. J. 1991. Food consumption, 1970-90. *Food Review 14*, 2 (No. 3).

29. Renken, S. A., and J. J. Warthesen. 1993. Vitamin D stability in milk. *Journal of Food Science 58*, 552.

30. Renz-Schauen, A., and E. Renner. 1987. Fortification of nondairy foods with dairy ingredients. *Food Technology 41*, 122 (No. 10).

31. Rolls, B. A., and J. W. G. Porter. 1973. Some effects of processing and storage on the nutritive value of milk and milk products. *Proceedings of the Nutrition Society 32*, 9.

32. Savaiano, D. A., and M. D. Levitt. 1984. Nutritional and therapeutic aspects of fermented dairy products. *Contemporary Nutrition* (General Mills Nutrition Department) *9* (No. 6).

33. Schroder, B. G., and R. J. Baer. 1990. Utilization of cholesterol-reduced milkfat in fluid milks. *Food Technology 44*, 145 (No. 11).

34. Shipe, W. F., R. Bassette, D. D. Deane, W. L. Dunkley, E. G. Hammond, W. J. Harper, D. H. Kleyn, M. E. Morgan, J. H. Nelson, and R. A. Scanlan. 1978. Off-flavors of milk: Nomenclature, standards, and bibliography. *Journal of Dairy Science 61*, 855.

35. Speck, M. L., W. J. Dobrogosz, and I. A. Casas. 1993. *Lactobacillus reuteri* in food supplementation. *Food Technology 47*, 90 (No. 7).

36. Staff. 1989. Rennet containing 100% chymosin increases cheese quality and yield. *Food Technology 43*, 84 (No. 6).

Meat and Meat Cookery

21

*M*eat is defined as the flesh of animals used for food. The chief meat animals in the United States are cattle, swine, and sheep. Small amounts of rabbit and venison are also consumed in the United States; and in other parts of the world, horse, dog, llama, and camel are used as meat.

•CONSUMPTION OF RED MEAT

Along with poultry and fish, meat plays an important role in meal planning, often being the focus of the menu around which the balance of the meal is planned. But how much meat do Americans really consume? Several sources of data suggest a decline in meat consumption since the 1970s [78]. The U.S. Department of Agriculture (USDA) estimates the meat supply on a per capita basis, using meat production figures adjusted for imports and exports—so-called per capita disappearance data. These figures do not take into account cooking losses and waste. A review of the disappearance data for the years 1970 to 1990 indicates that beef consumption (on a boneless, trimmed-weight basis) in 1990, at 64.0 pounds per person, was at its lowest level since the early 1960s [69]. Per capita consumption of pork was 46.3 pounds, while total red meat consumption was 112.3 pounds per capita.

Some other food consumption data are also available, and, although they are imprecise, they can give us some information about trends in consumption. Responses from 8,327 participants in the 1987–1988 Nationwide Food Consumption Survey by the USDA indicated that meat was consumed on all three days of the survey by 30 to 50 percent of the participants. Only 10 percent of the women and 5 percent of the men reported that they ate no meat on any of the three days. The mean number of servings of meat in three days was about 3.5 (slightly more than one serving per day) for the men and 2.5 to 3.0 (slightly less than one serving per day) for the women [78].

Dietary data were reported for 122 women and 97 men, with a median age of 75 years, who participated in the New Mexico Aging Process Study [35]. The women's mean daily intake of meat was 52.1 grams, while the men's was 78.4 grams. For the women, meat, poultry, and fish supplied 14 percent of total dietary energy, 37 percent of protein, and 20 percent of fat. The fat contribution of these foods may have been lower had lower-fat selections of meat, poultry, and fish been selected.

With food consumption surveys, it is difficult to calculate the actual amounts of meat eaten because so much meat is in mixtures such as burgers, chili, tacos, and tostados. Ground beef patty was the meat product most frequently mentioned in the 1987–1988 USDA survey. Ground beef in a variety of other forms and mixtures also was often mentioned by survey participants [78]. Beef accounts for the largest share of red meat eaten in the United States, followed by pork. Veal and lamb are consumed in relatively small amounts.

•STRUCTURE OF MEAT

As purchased from the market, meat is composed of muscle, connective tissue, fatty or adipose tissue, and bone. The connective tissue is distributed throughout muscle, binding cells and bundles of cells together. It also is present in tendons and ligaments. Depending on the grade and the cut, the amount of fatty tissue varies widely. Although the bone is not eaten, it is an important aid in identifying various cuts of meat.

Muscle Tissue

Muscle has a very complex structure that is important to its function in the living animal, where it performs work by contracting and relaxing. Because the structure and function of muscle fibers do affect the quality and cooking characteristics of meat, it is important to pay attention to the way muscles are put together.

A basic unit of muscle tissue is the muscle fiber or cell. This is a long threadlike cell that tapers slightly at both ends (Figure 21.1). It is very small, averaging about 1/500th inch in diameter and 1 to 2 inches in length. Inside the fiber or cell is an intricate structure. It includes contractile material called

FIGURE 21.1

Tiny muscle fibers or cells are combined to form small bundles.

Muscle fiber

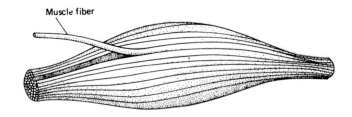

FIGURE 21.2

The muscle fiber or cell consists of many tiny myofibrils held together by the cell membrane. Each myofibril is made up of contractile proteins in a special ordered array, as shown in Figure 21.3.

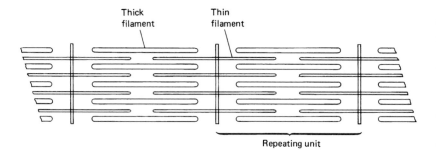

Thick filament   Thin filament

Repeating unit

FIGURE 21.3

Thick and thin, rodlike components or filaments inside the myofibril are composed of protein molecules. Myosin is the protein found in the thick filaments; actin makes up the thin filaments. They are systematically arranged in a cylindrical shape. When muscle contracts, the thin filaments in each repeating unit push together, thus shortening the length of the muscle.

myofibrils, surrounded by the **cytoplasmic** substance called *sarcoplasm* (Figure 21.2). There is also a system of tubules and **reticulum** around each myofibril that plays a key role in initiating muscle contraction. In addition, there are present many **mitochondria** that act as powerhouses to provide energy for the cell in the form of the high-energy compound *adenosine triphosphate* (**ATP**).

If you could look further into the structure of the tiny myofibrils, about 2,000 of which are present in each muscle cell, you would see special proteins. These proteins form thick filaments and thin filaments that are set in an orderly array (Figure 21.3). If you visualize a transverse section cut through the center of a myofibril, it would look something like Figure 21.4. The thick filaments are composed primarily of the protein *myosin*, whereas the thin filaments are made up of another protein called *actin*.

It is thought that when a muscle contracts, the thick and thin filaments slide together, something like a telescope, thus shortening the length of the muscle. As the thick and thin filaments slide together, they apparently form cross-bridges with each other, thus making a new protein in the shortened myofibril called *actinomyosin*. Energy for this process is provided from chemical changes in ATP.

The parallel alignment of the thick and the thin filaments in all of the myofibrils of a cell produces a pattern of dark and light lines and spaces when viewed under a microscope (see Figure 21.5). The thick filaments are present in the dark bands, and the thin filaments extend into the light bands. The pattern continues to repeat itself along the length of the myofibril.

Let us now return to the basic unit, the muscle fiber or cell, and see how these units are built into *larger* bundles and muscles. Each cell or fiber is surrounded by a fine membrane called the *sarcolemma*. Small bundles of the fibers, surrounded by thin sheaths of connective tissue to hold them together, form *primary bundles* (each containing twenty to forty fibers). The primary bundles are then bound together with sheets of connective tissue to form secondary bundles. Secondary bundles bound together by connective tissue form major muscles. The *primary bundles* make up the *grain* of the meat, which may appear to be fine or coarse (see Plate VIII).

Each major muscle in the animal body has been named. Figure 21.6 shows two of the major muscles in a T-bone steak—the *longissimus dorsi*, which runs along the back of the animal, and the *psoas major* or *tenderloin* muscle, which is particularly valued for its tenderness. Plate XIII shows the muscle structure of a pork carcass.

Cytoplasm   pertaining to the protoplasm of a cell, exclusive of the nucleus

Reticulum   a netlike sheath

Mitochondria   sausage-shaped bodies in the cell cytoplasm that contain the enzymes necessary for energy metabolism

ATP   adenosine triphosphate, a compound containing high-energy phosphate bonds in which the body cell traps energy from the metabolism of carbohydrate, fat, or protein; the energy in ATP is then used to do mechanical or chemical work in the body

FIGURE 21.4

Transverse section through a cylindrical myofibril. The large dots represent the thick filaments composed of myosin molecules. The smaller dots represent the thin filaments composed of actin.

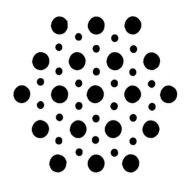

FIGURE 21.5

Representation of a striated muscle showing light and dark bands on the myofibrils (enlarged about 20,000 diameters).

Connective Tissue

As indicated earlier, muscle tissue does not occur without connective tissue, which binds the muscle cells together in various-sized bundles. It also makes up the tendons and ligaments of an animal. Generally, connective tissue has few cells but a considerable amount of extracellular background material called *ground substance*. Running through and embedded in this matrix of ground substance are long, strong fibrils or fibers. Many of these fibrils contain the protein *collagen*. Collagen-containing connective tissue is white. Connective tissue that contains another protein, called *elastin*, is yellow. Although collagen fibers are flexible, they do not stretch as much and are not as elastic as elastin fibers. Very little elastin seems to be present in most muscles, particularly those of the loin and round regions, but a considerable amount of elastin may be present in the connective tissue of a few muscles, including some in the shoulder area. A third type of connective tissue fibril, *reticulin*, consists of very small fibers. This type of connective tissue forms a delicate network around the muscle cells.

In muscles that are used for locomotion by an animal, such as those in the legs, chest, and neck, connective tissue tends to develop more extensively. Less tender cuts of meat usually contain more connective tissue than do tender cuts, although this is not the only factor affecting meat tenderness.

When connective tissue is heated with moisture, some collagen is **hydrolyzed** to produce the smaller gelatin molecule. This change accounts for much of the increase in tenderness that occurs in less tender cuts of meat cooked by moist heat. Heating causes only slight softening of elastin, however.

Hydrolyze   to break a molecular linkage utilizing a molecule of water

FIGURE 21.6

The major muscles in a T-bone steak.

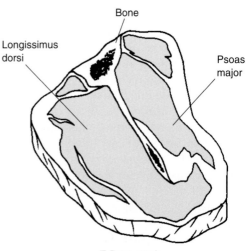

Bone

Longissimus dorsi

Psoas major

T-Bone steak

Fatty Tissue

Special cells contain large amounts of fat for storage in the body. These cells are embedded in a network of connective tissue to form adipose or fatty tissue. Some hard fats, such as beef suet, have visible sheets of connective tissue separating layers or masses of fat cells. Fatty tissue is also supplied with blood vessels. Fatty deposits are found under the skin and around glandular organs. As an animal is fattened, fat cells are deposited between muscles, and finally there is intramuscular distribution to produce the **marbling** of muscle tissue.

The color of fatty tissue changes with age. In older animals, it becomes yellowish instead of white as **carotenoid pigments** accumulate.

Bone

Long shafts of bone are composed chiefly of compact bony tissue. A center canal is filled with yellow marrow. Other bones may be spongy in character and may contain red marrow, which has many blood vessels. Bones or pieces of bone that appear in retail cuts of meat aid in the identification of the cut in regard to its location on the carcass.

•COMPOSITION AND NUTRITIVE VALUE

Meat is composed chiefly of water, protein, fat, and mineral matter. It also contains, in much smaller amounts, vitamins, pigments, and enzymes. Liver contains carbohydrate as glycogen. The amount is variable but usually ranges from 1 to 5 percent.

Fat, Protein, and Water

The percentage of fat in meats varies widely, depending on the breed or biological type of animal, its nutritional state, and the part of the carcass from which the cut is taken. Cuts of meat are now often trimmed of excess fat by meat handlers, and many Americans are increasingly using leaner meats. Although consumers are responding positively to the closely trimmed beef on the market, fat trimming is costly to the meat industry. The industry is therefore attempting to develop genetic lines or biological types of animals that produce lean carcasses [10]. Also, the external fat layer that remains on meat is often not eaten, and thus can be considered waste [71].

Fats from different species and from different parts of the same animal differ to some extent in composition. The more brittle, hard fats of beef and mutton contain higher percentages of **saturated fatty acids**. Softer fats contain more **unsaturated fatty acids**. The high melting point of lamb fat causes it to congeal when it is served unless the meat is very hot. Lard extracted from the fatty tissue around the glandular organs has a somewhat higher melting point than the lard produced from back fat.

With the current public health emphasis on diets lower in fat, there have been recommendations for Americans to reduce their red meat intake. The results of several studies have suggested, however, that moderate amounts of lean red meat, as well as poultry and fish, can be included in a low-fat diet plan

Marbling   the distribution of fat throughout the muscles of meat animals

Carotenoid pigments   fat-soluble, yellow-orange pigments that are produced by plants; may be stored in the fatty tissues of animals

Saturated fatty acids   fatty acids that have no double bonds between carbon atoms; they hold all of the hydrogen that they can attach

Unsaturated fatty acids   fatty acids that have one or more double bonds between carbon atoms; they could hold more hydrogen atoms if these bonds were broken

to lower blood cholesterol levels [60], thereby retaining the valuable contributions that red meats make to the diet in terms of protein, vitamin, and mineral content.

Lean uncooked muscle contains about 75 percent water and about 20 percent protein. In the muscle cells, much of the water is held by the proteins in a gel-type structure. The chief intracellular proteins that take part in the contraction process are myosin and actin. Other proteins, many of which are soluble in water, are present in small amounts. The cell proteins are of excellent nutritional quality. The gelatin formed from connective tissue by cooking has a much lower biologic value. Normal cooking procedures appear to have little effect on protein quality. Excessive heating, however, can decrease the biologic value of meat proteins.

It has been reported that when lean and lean-marbled-with-fat portions of cooked meat were analyzed together, they were found to contain 10 to 21 percent fat and 23 to 32 percent protein [42]. The lean portion or the lean-plus-marble portions of cooked pork contained no more fat than similar portions of beef, veal, or lamb.

Vitamins and Minerals

Meat furnishes valuable amounts of certain vitamins. Lean meats are a good source of thiamin, riboflavin, and niacin, as well as other members of the B complex. Lean pork is particularly rich in thiamin. Liver and kidney are good dietary sources of riboflavin and are richer in niacin than most other tissues. All meats furnish tryptophan, the amino acid that serves as a **precursor** of niacin for the body. Liver is a variable but excellent source of vitamin A. Meat is an excellent source of iron, zinc, and phosphorus. Some copper and other trace minerals are also supplied by meat.

Precursor   a substance that "comes before"; the precursor of a vitamin is a substance that can be used by the body to make the vitamin

Some minerals dissolve in the juices or cooking water of meat, but these can be consumed in gravies. The loss of thiamin in cooking or processing meats appears to be related to the severity of heat treatment. Canned meats usually contain less thiamin than do other cooked or processed meats because of the high temperatures required for sterilization. The average retention of thiamin in cooked meats is about 65 percent. Riboflavin and niacin are more resistant to destruction in cooking than is thiamin and seem to be well retained (see Appendix C for the nutritive value of selected meats).

Pigments

The color of meat comes chiefly from the pigment *myoglobin*. In a well-bled animal, most of the red hemoglobin pigment of the blood is removed. Myoglobin and hemoglobin are similar in chemical structure. Both contain the protein globin and the iron-containing pigment heme, but myoglobin is smaller. Hemoglobin carries oxygen in the bloodstream, whereas myoglobin holds it in the muscle cells. The quantity of myoglobin in muscle increases with age; thus, beef has a darker color than veal. The color of meat also varies with the species of animal from which it is obtained. Pork muscle generally contains less myoglobin than beef muscle and appears lighter in color. Different muscles of the same animal also may differ in color.

When meat is first cut, the myoglobin is in a chemically reduced form and appears purplish red. As it combines with oxygen, or is oxygenated, the myoglobin changes to a bright red pigment called *oxymyoglobin*. Fresh cuts of meat seen in the market show oxymyoglobin on the surfaces that are exposed to air. After a certain period of storage, when **reducing substances** are no longer produced in the tissues, the meat may appear brownish because of the change of myoglobin or oxymyoglobin to an oxidized form, called *metmyoglobin* (see Figure 21.7). Fluorescent light accelerates the formation of metmyoglobin. If further **oxidation** changes take place in fresh meat, a number of greenish compounds may be produced from the breakdown of the heme pigment. The display life of fresh beef has been reported to be extended 2 to 5 days when supplements of vitamin E (alpha-tocopherol), an antioxidant, were fed to beef steers on a long-term basis. Lipid oxidation in the meat was also markedly reduced [4].

Reducing substances chemical molecules that can supply hydrogen or electrons to prevent or reverse oxidation; the reduced state of iron is the ferrous form (Fe^{2+})

Oxidation a chemical change that involves the addition of oxygen or the loss of electrons; the oxidized state of iron is the ferric form (Fe^{3+})

•CLASSIFICATION

Beef

Beef carcasses are classified on the basis of age and sex. A *steer* is a male castrated when young; a *heifer* is a young female that has not yet borne a calf; a *cow* is a female that has borne a calf; a *stag* is a male castrated after maturity; and a *bull* is a mature male that has not been castrated.

Steer carcasses are generally preferred by meat handlers because of their heavier weight and the higher proportion of meat to bone, but steer and heifer carcasses of the same grade are of equal quality. The quality of meat from cows is variable, depending on maturity, but is usually inferior to both steer and heifer meat. Stag meat is not normally marketed in the United States, whereas bull carcasses generally are used in processed meats.

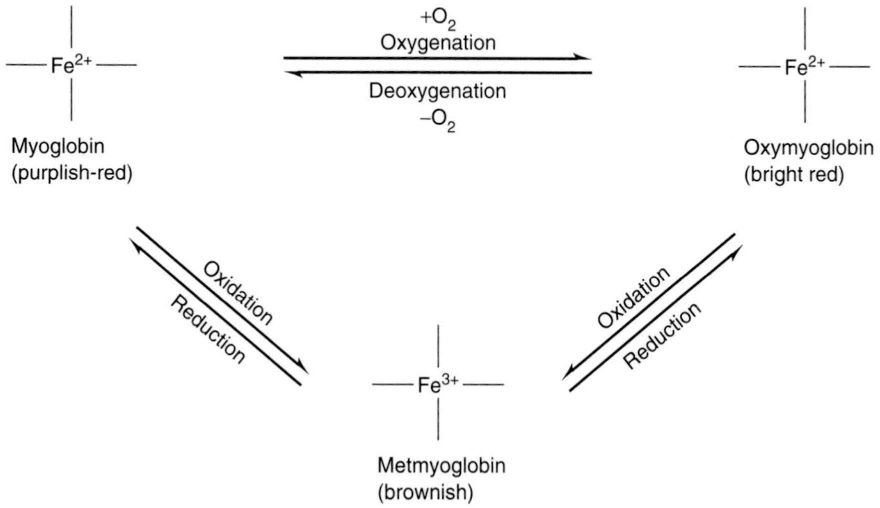

FIGURE 21.7
Some changes that occur in meat pigments.

Veal

Veal is meat from immature bovines. In the wholesale market, veal carcasses are usually from animals of either sex that are at least 3 weeks but less than 3 months of age. They are fed largely on milk or milk products. The term *calf* is applied to animals slaughtered between 3 months and about 8 months of age. The older animals have passed the good veal stage but do not yet possess the properties of good beef. In practice, however, the term *veal* is often used for animals somewhat older than 3 months. The term *baby beef* is sometimes used to refer to meat from animals 8 to 12 months of age.

Lamb and Mutton

Sheep carcasses are classified as lamb and mutton according to the age of the animal. Lamb is obtained from young animals of either sex that are less than 14 months of age, although the exact age at which lamb changes to mutton is somewhat indefinite. Mutton carcasses are those that have passed the lamb stage. The usual test for a lamb carcass is the break joint. The feet of a lamb, when broken off sharply, separate from the leg *above* the regular joint. The break shows four distinct ridges that appear smooth, moist, and red with blood. In mutton, the break comes *in* the true joint, which is below the break joint.

Most of the meat from sheep is marketed as lamb. Relatively little older mutton is sold. The flesh of all carcasses in the mutton class is darker in color than lamb. It is also less tender and has a stronger flavor when it is from animals beyond 2 years of age.

Pork

Pork is the meat of swine. Good-quality pork is obtained from young animals usually 7 to 12 months of age. In young animals there is no distinction in quality or grade because of sex, whereas in older animals sex differences are pronounced. Most of the pork marketed in the United States comes from young animals.

•POSTMORTEM CHANGES AND AGING

Just before an animal is slaughtered, the muscles are soft and pliable. On death, as metabolism in the cells is interrupted, processes begin that lead to a stiffening of the carcass known as *rigor mortis*. Metabolic changes include the accumulation of lactic acid in the muscles, since oxygen is no longer available and circulating blood cannot remove end products of metabolism from the tissues. Therefore the pH decreases. Also, the high-energy compound produced in metabolism in the living animal, ATP, gradually disappears. The muscle becomes contracted as a result of these changes. The muscle proteins (actin and myosin), which form the thin and thick filaments of the myofibrils in the muscle cell, slide or telescope on each other and bond together so that the muscle is no longer extensible.

The time required after the death of the animal for occurrence of the stiffening process is affected by various factors. Rigor mortis begins and is completed relatively slowly when the carcass is held under the usual refrigeration conditions. Both colder and warmer temperatures speed up the development of rigor [27, 87]. The species of animal, its age, and its activity just before slaughter also affect the time of onset of rigor. In large animals, such as cattle, rigor begins more slowly and lasts longer than in smaller animals. It is usually resolved in 24 to 48 hours in beef. If meat is separated from the carcass immediately after slaughter and cooked rapidly before rigor has a chance to develop, it will be tender. However, if the cooking process is slow, rigor may develop during heating and increase toughness in the cooked meat [27, 32].

If the supply of glycogen in the muscle is low at the time of death, as is the case when much activity occurs just before slaughter, less lactic acid is produced from glycogen. The pH of the muscle remains relatively high, above 6.3. The muscle tissue is only slightly acid. In beef, this results in a dark color that is less acceptable in market channels. The muscle tissue also has an increased water-binding capacity and a sticky texture, although it is tender [17, 87].

If meat is allowed to hang under refrigeration for 1 or 2 days after slaughter, it will gradually begin to soften as rigor mortis passes. If it is held still longer, a process of ripening or aging occurs. This results in some increase in tenderness, improvement of flavor and juiciness, better browning in cooking of both lean and fat, and a loss of red interior color at a lower cooking temperature [33]. Aging too long may result in a strong flavor or development of an off-flavor and off-odor. A major reason for the increase in tenderness during aging appears to be a breakdown of proteins in the myofibrils by enzymes [36]. The effect of enzymatic degradation is more pronounced at both high and low muscle pH as compared with an intermediate pH (5.8 to 6.3) [87]. Aging of beef may also produce some breakdown of **mucoprotein**, which is a component of connective tissue [52].

Mucoprotein a complex or conjugated protein containing a carbohydrate substance combined with a protein

Meat is commonly aged at approximately 2°C (36°F). It has been reported, however, that aging sides of beef at 16°C (61°F) produces changes in tenderness more rapidly than aging at 2°C (36°F). The higher temperature and shorter time for aging are sometimes used [66], but some means of retarding microbial growth at the higher temperature is necessary. Aging of meat is a commercial process not accomplished in home kitchens.

Two different methods can be used for the postmortem aging of meat: dry aging is aging meat "as is" under refrigeration, while wet aging involves packaging the meat in a vacuum bag and holding it under refrigeration. When these two methods of aging were compared for short-cut strip loins and ribs of beef, it was found that differences in palatability attributes of cooked steaks and roasts were slight. Scores for tenderness and overall palatability of steaks from wet aging, as judged by trained panelists, were somewhat higher, but both aging treatments provided very palatable products [65]. No significant differences in palatability were detected by consumer panelists. There was, however, one major difference between the two methods: a greater shrink and trim loss was associated with dry aging, making this process more costly and time-consuming.

Beef is the only type of meat that is commonly aged, although some consumers also prefer lamb when it is aged. Beef is usually in market channels for a week to 10 days before the consumer purchases it. It has been suggested that there is little advantage to extending the aging period beyond 10 days [56].

Veal is not improved by aging, and the lack of fat on the carcass results in excessive surface drying. Pork is usually obtained from a young tender animal; thus, toughness is not generally a problem. It has been suggested, however, that the tenderness of pork loin may be increased by aging [28, 70]. In pork, aging may also be complicated by the tendency for relatively rapid development of rancidity in the fat during holding.

•FACTORS AFFECTING TENDERNESS

One of the most valued attributes of meat is tenderness. The grading of meat by USDA standards does not directly measure this characteristic, although the probability that a beef carcass will be tender is greater in a higher grade than it is in a lower grade. Pork and lamb, because they are marketed young, are usually tender. Much more variation exists in beef, and much of the research on tenderness has been concerned with beef cuts.

In studying the tenderness of meat with the use of taste panels, several components of tenderness that are apparent during the biting and chewing of meat have been described. These include the ease with which teeth sink into the meat, or softness, the crumbliness of the muscle fibers, and the amount of connective tissue or the amount of residue remaining after the meat is chewed for a specified time. Each of these components of tenderness may be influenced by various factors operating in the production and preparation of beef and other meats, including, as we have discussed, aging of beef.

Amount of Connective Tissue

It is generally agreed that larger amounts of connective tissue in a cut of meat cause decreased tenderness. The least used muscles of an animal, particularly those in the rib and loin sections, contain less connective tissue than do muscles that are used for locomotion. The muscles of the rib and loin, for example, are more tender than the muscles of the legs and shoulders. As animals mature and become older, more and stronger connective tissue usually forms in muscle tissues. This is undoubtedly a major factor that helps to explain the difference in tenderness between younger and older animals. It has been reported that the decrease in tenderness with age depends on connective tissue strength. The tenderloin muscle, which is not used in locomotion and has little connective tissue, remained tender in animals up to 48 months of age, whereas other muscles with strong connective tissue trebled in toughness [77]. The case of veal is different, however. Although it is a very young animal, there is still a relatively high percentage of connective tissue in the muscles because of the lack of time for development of the muscle itself.

Fat and Marbling

The fattening of animals has long been thought to improve the tenderness of meat. It has been suggested that a layer of subcutaneous fat on a carcass delays chilling of the meat, thereby allowing postmortem metabolic changes that result in greater tenderness [14]. The USDA quality grade standards for beef include an estimation of the amount of marbling (the distribution of fat throughout the muscle). Small but statistically significant decreases in tenderness have been found in beef by expert judging panels as marbling decreased from moderately abundant to practically devoid [79]. Juiciness and flavor also decreased. Untrained consumers in San Francisco and Kansas City gave slightly lower scores for overall desirability of top loin beef steaks as the marbling level decreased. In the same study, consumers in Philadelphia rated the steaks with lesser marbling considerably lower than those well marbled, indicating regional differences [76]. Marbling would appear to have an impact on the eating quality of beef steaks, including tenderness, but sometimes this effect on tenderness may be small.

Ground beef is one of the most popular meat products in the United States. When cooked ground beef patties made from raw meat containing 5, 10, 15, 20, 25, and 30 percent fat were compared, it was noted that the low-fat patties (5 and 10 percent) were firmer in texture, less juicy, and less flavorful than the 20-to-30-percent-fat patties [84]. Objective measurements with the Warner-Bratzler and Lee-Kramer shear instruments also showed decreasing tenderness with decreasing fat content.

Other Factors

Carcasses of beef are sometimes subjected to low-voltage electrical stimulation immediately after slaughter to increase tenderness. The beneficial effects may result from an increase in the rate of postmortem metabolism and a disruption of the myofibrils with accelerated enzymatic breakdown of the muscle proteins [20]. Electrical stimulation and 48 hours of aging were reported to have the same tenderizing effect on both steer and bull carcasses as did a six-day aging period [23].

The hereditary background of the animal, the management of its feeding, and the size of muscle fibers are other factors that affect meat tenderness. Many of these factors are undoubtedly interrelated, and more research is needed to clarify the whole picture of tenderness in meat. For example, pronounced differences in tenderness are apparent among various muscles of the beef carcass. The tenderloin or psoas major and the longissimus dorsi muscles in the rib and loin sections are the most tender; muscles of the round and chuck sections are less tender. These differences in tenderness cannot be completely explained by differences in connective tissue, fat content, or state of muscle contraction [53].

Tenderizing

Because of the lower cost of certain less tender cuts of meat in comparison with more tender pieces, attempts have been made to tenderize the less tender cuts. Grinding and cubing break up the connective tissue and make meat more tender. Tenderizing compounds containing papain, a **proteinase** taken from the papaya plant, bromelin, a similar enzyme obtained from pineapples, or ficin from figs can be applied to the surface of meats prior to cooking. A fork can be used to pierce the meat and allow the compound to penetrate a little further. These enzymes may act on the muscle cell proteins as well as on the connective tissue. Therefore, care must be taken to control excessive action on the meat fibers and prevent the development of a mealy texture. Little enzymatic action

Proteinase an enzyme that hydrolyzes proteins to smaller peptides and amino acids

occurs at room temperature, the optimal temperature for papain activity being 60° to 70°C (140°C to 160°F). This temperature is reached during cooking.

A papain or other enzyme mixture may be injected into the bloodstream of the animal just before slaughter. Theoretically, the enzyme is carried to all parts of the body and is evenly distributed throughout the various retail cuts. The enzyme remains inactive until the meat is heated in cooking. Cuts of meat that are usually classified as less tender can be cooked as tender cuts if the beef animals have received enzyme injections. If the enzyme has not been destroyed in cooking, continued tenderization should occur during standing time after cooking.

•BUYING OF MEAT

American families tend to spend a substantial percentage of their food money on meats. If this amounts to as much as 38 to 40 percent of the food budget, it is quite possible that other important food items, such as milk, fruits, and vegetables, are being neglected. Meats are among the most expensive items of the diet. They are well liked, and many families place undue emphasis on the need for meat in every meal. There is also a lack of information on the part of many consumers as to what determines the price and quality of meats.

A number of laws have been passed and regulations have been published, at both the national and local levels, to protect and inform the consumer with respect to the purchasing of meat and poultry products. The USDA has responsibility at the federal level for the inspection, grading, setting of standards, and labeling of all meat and poultry products. Even the additives that can be used in meat products are regulated by the USDA, using guidelines from the U.S. Food and Drug Administration (FDA).

During the 1950s, the practice of administering compounds with estrogenic activity to beef cattle developed and became fairly common. The purpose for their use was to increase weight gain in the animals with less feed, thus allowing a savings to the cattle industry as well as making earlier marketing possible. Diethylstilbestrol (DES), the most commonly used substance, generated considerable controversy over its safety, and eventually its use was prohibited by federal regulatory agencies. Certain other substances, however, have been approved for use to promote an increased rate of weight gain in calves and heifers. The conditions of their use are prescribed. Some substances are implanted **subcutaneously** in the ear of the animal and may include a mixture of progesterone and estradiol hormones.

Subcutaneous   under the skin

Techniques in biotechnology have been used to produce substances that improve production efficiency in meat- and milk-producing animals. Bovine somatotropin (bST), when given to dairy cows, increases milk production 15 to 20 percent and increases the efficiency with which the cows use feed by about 10 percent. Porcine somatotropin (pST), administered to growing pigs, increases their growth rate by 10 to 20 percent and reduces carcass fat while increasing muscle growth. It also increases their weight gain per unit of feed consumed [19]. Consumer panelists found no difference in acceptability between loin and ham roasts from control or pST-treated animals [68].

The USDA has published standards of identity for some meat products, including corned beef hash: however, for most meat and poultry products, standards of composition have been set. These standards identify the minimum amount of meat or poultry required in a product's recipe. For example, meat pie must contain at least 25 percent meat, beef with gravy or beef with barbecue sauce must contain at least 50 percent beef, and chili con carne must have at least 40 percent meat. Frankfurters and similar cooked sausages must contain no more than 30 percent fat, 10 percent added water, and 2 percent corn syrup. Their labels must clearly indicate the products used in their formulation.

You should be aware of standards and required inspection procedures. Your responsibility to report any infractions that you observe is an important one, since enforcement of regulations at all levels is extremely difficult.

Labeling

While the FDA handles labeling on approximately 70 percent of the food items found in supermarkets, the USDA's Food Safety and Inspection Service approves the labels on the other 30 percent, which are meat and poultry products. Each meat or poultry label must contain the following information:

1. Product name
2. Name and address of producer or distributor
3. Inspection mark (round stamp)
4. List of ingredients, in order from highest to lowest amounts, and net weight
5. Establishment number indicating the plant where the product was processed
6. Handling instructions for products that require special handling to remain safe

Nutrition labeling (discussed in Chapter 2) is mandated for processed meat and poultry products. The USDA has also defined the nutrient content claims that can be used on meat and poultry products. These include the following [25].

1. *Free*: only a tiny or insignificant amount of fat, cholesterol, sodium, sugar, and/or calories
2. *Low*: a product that could be eaten fairly often without exceeding dietary guidelines for fat, saturated fat, cholesterol, sodium, and/or calories; *low in fat* means no more than 3 grams of fat per serving
3. *Lean*: less than 10 grams of fat, 4 grams of saturated fat, and 95 milligrams of cholesterol per serving
4. *Extra Lean*: less than 5 grams of fat, 2 grams of saturated fat, and 95 milligrams of cholesterol per serving (still not as lean as *low*)
5. *Reduced, Less, Fewer*: 25 percent less of a nutrient or calories
6. *Light (Lite)*: one-third fewer calories or one-half the fat or sodium of the original
7. *More*: at least 10 percent more of the Daily Value of a vitamin or mineral per serving
8. *Good Source of*: 10–19 percent of the Daily Value for a particular vitamin, mineral, or fiber

Inspection stamp used on meat
carcasses.

Seal used on prepared meat products.

Government Inspection

All meats entering interstate commerce must be inspected by qualified agents of the USDA's Food Safety and Inspection Service [54]. Animals are inspected alive and at various stages of the slaughtering process. The cleanliness and operating procedures of meat packing plants are also supervised to ensure that meat and meat products are not contaminated or adulterated and that labeling is proper and truthful. If meat carcasses are sound and wholesome, the inspector's stamp (Figure 21.8; see also Figure 4.3) is placed on each wholesale cut of the carcass. This stamp carries numbers that indicate the packer and identify the carcass. If the meat is unsound, it is not permitted to enter retail trade. The Federal Meat Inspection Act also requires that all meat imported into the United States come under the same standards of inspection that are applied to meat produced in the United States.

The Wholesome Meat Act of 1967 requires that state governments have, for meat that is sold within state boundaries, local programs of meat inspection equal to those of the federal government. Otherwise, the federal government will assume the responsibility for inspection. State programs are periodically reviewed to see that satisfactory standards are maintained. This protects the meat-buying public against diseased animals.

The USDA is currently implementing the Hazard Analysis and Critical Control Point (HACCP) system in the meat and poultry inspection process [1]. HACCP is a preventive system, which first determines the most critical points in the process of handling meat and poultry where hazardous products could result, and then controls these points to assure safe, wholesome, and unadulterated commodities. USDA inspectors receive specialized training in this system, and workshops are held for employees in the meat industry.

There is no practical means of inspecting for the presence of the small parasite *Trichinella spiralis*, which may be found in the muscle of approximately one in 1,000 pork carcasses. When consumed, this organism causes *trichinosis*. Regulations for the inspection of meat products containing pork that are usually eaten without cooking require treatment of such products in a way that destroys any live trichinae that may be in the pork muscle tissue. This can be accomplished in one of three ways: heating uniformly to a temperature of 59°C (137°F), freezing for not less than 20 days at a maximum temperature of –15°C (5°F), or curing under special methods prescribed by the USDA. Products such as dried and summer sausage, bologna, frankfurter-style sausage, cooked hams, and cooked pork in casings are among those requiring this treatment.

Much of the meat and poultry slaughtered goes into processed items, including sausages, ham, pizza, frozen dinners, and soups. The federal inspection program is responsible for the safety of these products also. An in-plant inspector monitors the processing operations [54].

Grades and Grading

A program separate from the inspection service is the USDA's system of grading meat. Whereas inspection of meat for wholesomeness is mandatory for all meat as it is slaughtered, grading is voluntary. It is not required that meat be graded to be marketed; however, grading provides a national uniform language for use in the buying and selling of meat. Grades are also useful to the consumer in knowing what quality to expect from purchased meats. The grading program is administered by the Department of Agriculture but the cost of the service is borne by those meat packers who use it.

Quality grades have been established for beef, veal, lamb, and mutton (Figure 21.9). Grades for pork are not intended to identify differences in quality to consumers, as much of the pork is processed before it reaches the retail market. The grades for pork are more concerned with yield than with quality. Pork carcasses and cuts are graded for wholesale trade and for price control on a weight basis, with heavier weights grading lower than lighter weights. Pork, as marketed, is less variable in age and quality than carcasses from other animals.

For beef and lamb, *yield grades* (Figure 21.10) have been established for use along with quality grades. Yield grades are based on *cutability*, which indicates the proportionate amount of salable retail cuts that can be obtained from a carcass (Figure 21.11). Number 1 is for the highest yield and number 5 for the lowest. A large proportion of edible meat is indicated by a relatively large rib-eye area, a thin layer of external fat, and a small amount of fat around the internal organs. The dual system of grading, for both quality and yield, attempts to offer the consumer high-quality meat without excess fat. Both quality and yield grades must be used when beef and lamb are federally graded. Conformation, or shape and build of the animal, is reflected to some degree in the yield grade. A stocky, muscular build usually represents a relatively high proportion of salable meat and receives a high yield grade.

Factors considered in determining the quality grades all have to do with palatability or eating quality. Marbling and maturity are the two major considerations in evaluating the quality of beef. Marbling refers to the flecks of fat within the lean muscle. An optimum thickness of surface fat layer also appears to contribute to palatability [14, 82]. In 1975, the federal standards for grading beef were adjusted so that marbling requirements for prime and choice, the two top grades, are not as high as they were under the previous standards. This reflects the public's apparent desire for lower-fat meats. The meat industry is also experimenting with some new breeds of beef-producing cattle that are considerably lower in fat than the conventional types. Some of these breeds have names that are new to most consumers: *zebu, beefalo, Chianina*, and *limousin*.

The maturity of an animal affects the lean meat texture, the grain generally becoming more coarse with increasing maturity. Fine-textured lean is usually slightly more tender than lean with a very coarse texture. A very mature animal develops changes in connective tissue that contribute to decreased tenderness.

Characteristics of Quality

In a good quality of beef, the lean has a bright red color after the cut surface is exposed to air for a few minutes. It is fine grained and smooth to the touch, and the fat is firm. The chine or backbone is soft, red, and spongy, and shows considerable cartilage. The lean of a poor carcass is darker red in color, is coarse grained, and lacks the smooth, satiny surfaces when it is cut. In a poor-quality carcass the fat is oily or soft in texture, and the bones are white, hard, brittle, and show little or no cartilage.

Good quality in veal is shown by the grayish-pink flesh and a texture that is fine grained and smooth to the touch. The interior fat of good-quality veal is

FIGURE 21.9

U.S. federal meat quality grade stamps are placed within a shield. (Courtesy of the U.S. Department of Agriculture)

FIGURE 21.10

U.S. yield grades identify carcass differences in *cutability*: the percentage yields of boneless, closely trimmed retail cuts from the high-value parts of the carcass. (Courtesy of the U.S. Department of Agriculture)

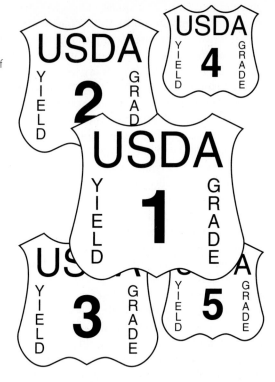

firm and brittle. The bones are red, spongy, and soft and have an abundance of cartilage. Poor quality in veal is characterized by either a very pale or a dark color of the lean and little or no fat distributed throughout the carcass.

Good quality in lamb is shown by the pinkish-red color, fine grain, and smooth cut surfaces of the flesh. The fat of good lamb is firm, flaky, and brittle, and the bones are soft, red, and spongy and show cartilage. Poor quality in lamb is characterized by darker color of the lean, heavier fat layers, and a stronger flavor.

The flesh of good-quality pork is grayish pink and fine grained. The fat of pork should be very firm but not brittle as in other types of meats. The bones are soft, red, and spongy. Pork of poor quality has an excess of fat distributed in the lean tissues as well as on the exterior. The color of the lean is darker, the grain is coarser, and the bones may appear less red and spongy. This is particularly true if the meat is from an animal beyond the optimal age limit.

Grading does not directly measure tenderness. Various studies have produced inconsistent results in relating USDA carcass grades to tenderness. Some researchers have reported that higher grades of beef showed significantly more tenderness than lower grades [49, 65]. Others have not found significant differences, particularly between choice and select grades [81]. The variation in tenderness from one carcass to another within a grade appears to be great.

Quality Grades for Meat

Table 21.1 shows USDA quality grades for beef, veal, lamb, and mutton. Utility and lower grades of meat are rarely, if ever, sold as cuts in retail stores but

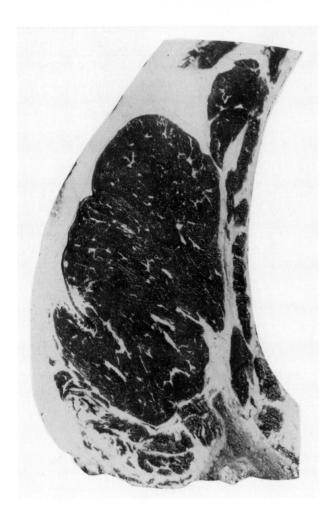

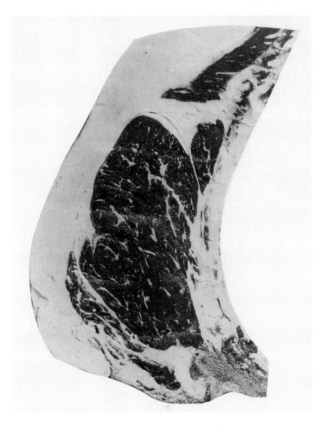

FIGURE 21.11
Beef rib from Yield Grade 2 (*left*). Beef rib from Yield Grade 4 (*right*). (Courtesy of the U.S. Department of Agriculture)

instead are used in processed meat products. The appropriate USDA quality grade mark is applied to meat with a roller stamp that leaves its mark the full length of the carcass.

Because beef can vary so much in quality, it has eight designated grades, with USDA Prime beef being the highest quality. Only about 7 percent of marketed beef is likely to be graded prime, and most of this beef is purchased for use in commercial foodservice. USDA Choice grade beef has slightly less marbling than prime but is still of very high quality. USDA Select grade lacks some of the juiciness and quality of the higher grades, but is usually relatively tender and palatable. USDA Standard beef has a high proportion of lean meat and little fat. It comes from young animals, since the top four grades are all restricted to beef from young animals, and is, therefore, usually fairly tender. USDA Commercial grade beef comes from mature animals and generally requires long cooking with moist heat to tenderize it. It has the full flavor of mature beef.

With the increasing interest in reducing the amount of fat in the diet, a quality grading system for meat that rewards marbling and an external layer of fat on the carcass has sparked some debate. The grading system for meat, par-

TABLE 21.1
USDA Quality Grades for Meat

Beef	Veal	Lamb	Mutton
Prime	Prime	Prime	Choice
Choice	Choice	Choice	Good
Select	Good	Good	Utility
Standard	Standard	Utility	Cull
Commercial	Utility	Cull	
Utility	Cull		
Cutter			
Canner			

ticularly for beef, is likely to be reevaluated in the future. Producing carcasses with considerable fat, then closely trimming the fat from cuts before marketing, is costly to both the meat industry and the consumer.

Cuts of Meat and Identification

As you purchase fresh meat, it is important to have some knowledge about the various retail cuts into which the carcasses are divided and to understand the relative quality characteristics of these cuts. Meat carcasses are first divided into relatively large wholesale or primal cuts, such as the square-cut chuck section of beef. Wholesale cuts are then further divided into smaller retail cuts. Wholesale and retail cuts of beef, pork, veal, and lamb are shown in Figures 21.12, 21.13, 21.14, and 21.15, respectively.

Division into cuts is made in relation to bone and muscle structure. Muscles that are found together in any one retail cut generally have similar characteristics of tenderness and texture. The shapes and sizes of bones and muscles in retail cuts act as guides to identification. Figures 21.16 and 21.17 show basic retail meat cuts that can be identified by their characteristic bone shapes. Since the skeletal structure is similar for all of the meat animals, the basic cuts are similar for beef, pork, veal, and lamb; however, each type of meat carcass is divided in a somewhat different manner.

Some meat cuts are known by different names in various parts of the country. For example, beef top loin steaks are commonly called Delmonico, Kansas City, New York, or strip steaks, and flank steak may be called London broil or minute steak. A cut that is popular in foodservice is the tri tip steak. This cut is the boneless, trimmed single muscle portion of the bottom butt of the sirloin. Because of the confusion created in merchandising by the wide variety of names for retail meat cuts, an industrywide Cooperative Meat Identification Standards Committee was organized by the meat industry. This committee developed standards for the retail meat trade and provided a master list of *recommended* names for retail cuts of beef, pork, veal, and lamb. The list serves all regions of the United States. The recommended retail package label information includes the species or kind of meat, the wholesale cut name, and the specific retail name from the master list. A typical label reads: BEEF CHUCK—BLADE ROAST. Photographs of beef and pork retail cuts are shown in Plates VIII, IX, X, and XI.

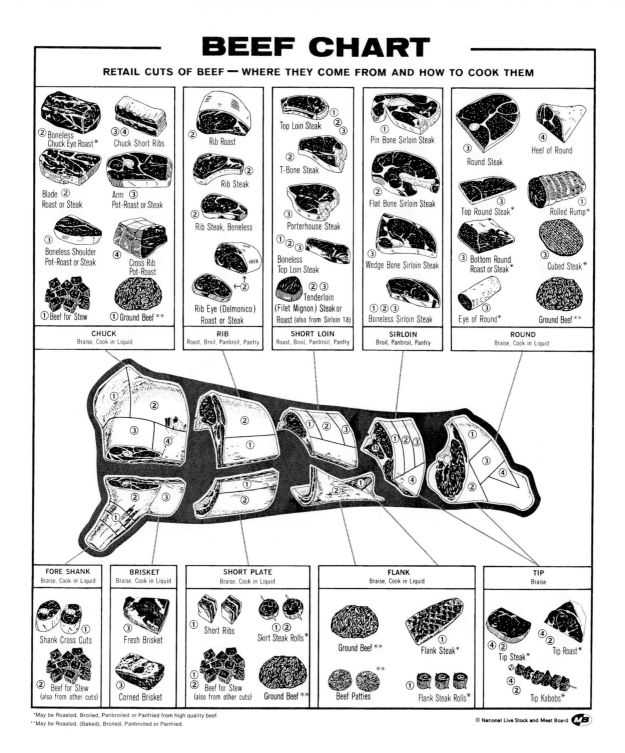

FIGURE 21.12

Wholesale and retail cuts of beef. (Courtesy of the National Live Stock and Meat Board)

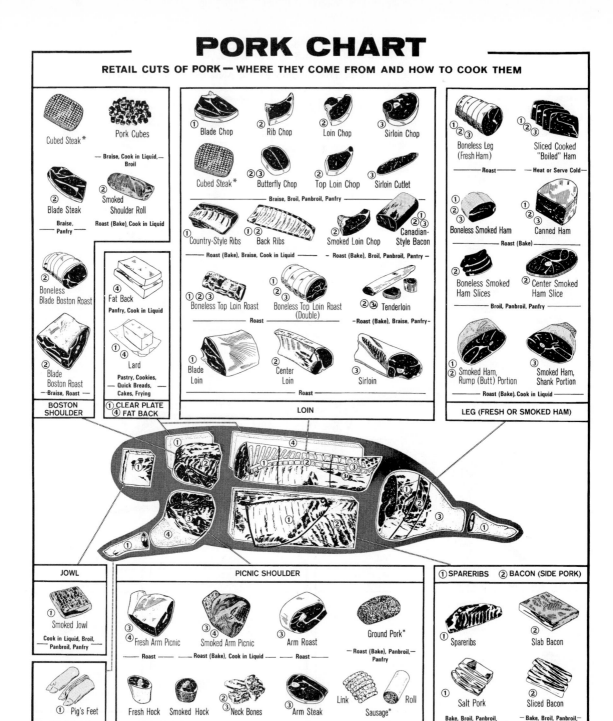

PORK CHART

RETAIL CUTS OF PORK — WHERE THEY COME FROM AND HOW TO COOK THEM

Cubed Steak*

Pork Cubes
— Braise, Cook in Liquid, —
Broil

② **Blade Steak**
Braise, Panfry

② **Smoked Shoulder Roll**
Roast (Bake), Cook in Liquid

② **Boneless Blade Boston Roast**

② **Blade Boston Roast**
— Braise, Roast —

BOSTON SHOULDER

④ **Fat Back**
Panfry, Cook in Liquid

① **Lard**
Pastry, Cookies, — Quick Breads, — Cakes, Frying

① CLEAR PLATE
④ FAT BACK

---

① **Blade Chop**

② **Rib Chop**

② **Loin Chop**

③ **Sirloin Chop**

②③ **Cubed Steak***

②③ **Butterfly Chop**

② **Top Loin Chop**

③ **Sirloin Cutlet**

— Braise, Broil, Panbroil, Panfry —

① **Country-Style Ribs**

①② **Back Ribs**

② **Smoked Loin Chop**

②③ **Canadian-Style Bacon**

— Roast (Bake), Braise, Cook in Liquid —   — Roast (Bake), Broil, Panbroil, Pantry —

①②③ **Boneless Top Loin Roast**

①②③ **Boneless Top Loin Roast (Double)**

②③④ **Tenderloin**

— Roast —   — Roast (Bake), Braise, Panfry —

① **Blade Loin**

② **Center Loin**

③ **Sirloin**

— Roast —

LOIN

---

①②③ **Boneless Leg (Fresh Ham)**
— Roast —

①②③ **Sliced Cooked "Boiled" Ham**
— Heat or Serve Cold —

①②③ **Boneless Smoked Ham**

①②③ **Canned Ham**
— Roast (Bake) —

② **Boneless Smoked Ham Slices**

②③ **Center Smoked Ham Slice**
— Broil, Panbroil, Panfry —

①② **Smoked Ham, Rump (Butt) Portion**

③ **Smoked Ham, Shank Portion**
— Roast (Bake), Cook in Liquid —

LEG (FRESH OR SMOKED HAM)

JOWL

① **Smoked Jowl**
Cook in Liquid, Broil, Panbroil, Panfry

① **Pig's Feet**
— Cook in Liquid, Braise —

PICNIC SHOULDER

③④ **Fresh Arm Picnic**
— Roast —

③④ **Smoked Arm Picnic**
— Roast (Bake), Cook in Liquid —

③ **Arm Roast**
— Roast —

Ground Pork*
— Roast (Bake), Panbroil,— Panfry

Fresh Hock

Smoked Hock
— Braise, Cook in Liquid —

②③ **Neck Bones**
— Cook in Liquid —

③ **Arm Steak**
— Braise, Panfry —

Link   **Roll**
Sausage*
— Panfry, Braise, Bake —

---

① **SPARERIBS**   ② **BACON (SIDE PORK)**

① **Spareribs**

② **Slab Bacon**

① **Salt Pork**

② **Sliced Bacon**

— Bake, Broil, Panbroil, Panfry, Cook in Liquid —   — Bake, Broil, Panbroil, Panfry —

---

*May be made from Boston Shoulder, Picnic Shoulder, Loin or Leg.

© National Live Stock and Meat Board

FIGURE 21.13
Wholesale and retail cuts of pork. (Courtesy of the National Live Stock and Meat Board)

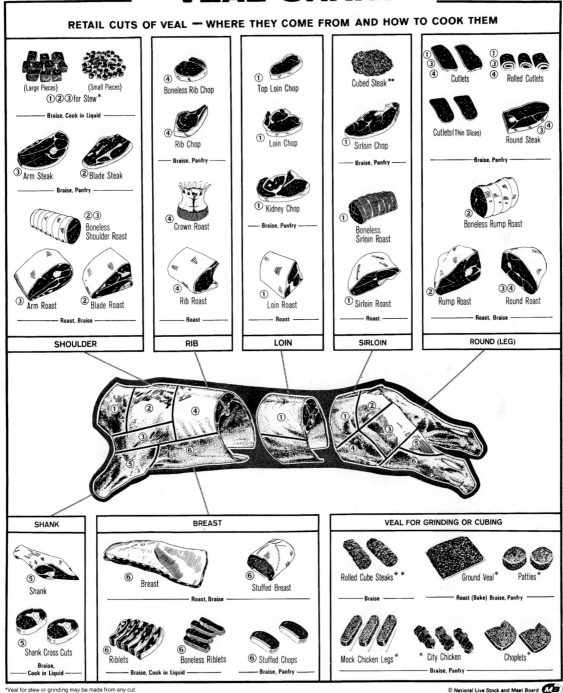

FIGURE 21.14

Wholesale and retail cuts of veal. (Courtesy of the National Live Stock and Meat Board)

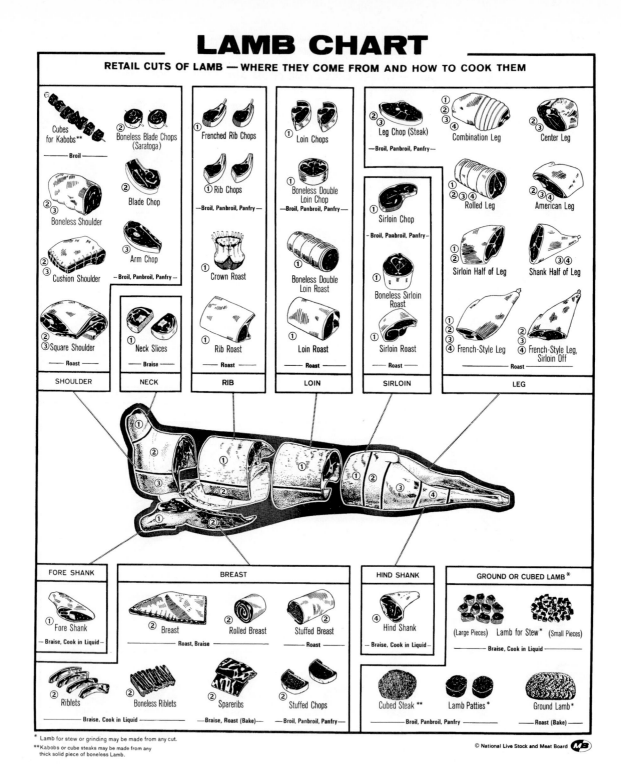

FIGURE 21.15

Wholesale and retail cuts of lamb. (Courtesy of the National Live Stock and Meat Board)

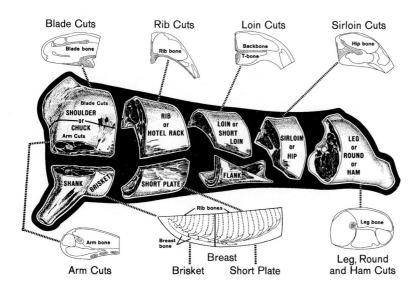

Blade Cuts   Rib Cuts   Loin Cuts   Sirloin Cuts

Arm Cuts   Brisket   Short Plate   Leg, Round and Ham Cuts

Breast

FIGURE 21.16

Seven basic retail cuts of meat. (From Uniform Retail Meat Identity Standards, Industrywide Cooperative Meat Identification Standards Committee, National Live Stock and Meat Board, 1973)

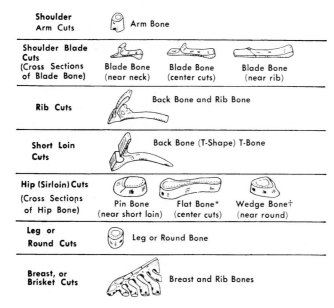

BONES IDENTIFY SEVEN GROUPS OF RETAIL CUTS

Shoulder Arm Cuts	Arm Bone	
Shoulder Blade Cuts (Cross Sections of Blade Bone)	Blade Bone (near neck) Blade Bone (center cuts) Blade Bone (near rib)	
Rib Cuts	Back Bone and Rib Bone	
Short Loin Cuts	Back Bone (T-Shape) T-Bone	
Hip (Sirloin) Cuts (Cross Sections of Hip Bone)	Pin Bone (near short loin) Flat Bone* (center cuts) Wedge Bone† (near round)	
Leg or Round Cuts	Leg or Round Bone	
Breast, or Brisket Cuts	Breast and Rib Bones	

*Formerly part of "double bone" but today the back bone is usually removed leaving only the "flat bone" (sometimes called "pin bone") in the sirloin steak.

†On one side of sirloin steak, this bone may be wedge shaped while on the other side the same bone may be round.

FIGURE 21.17

Basic bone shapes aid in meat cut identification. (From Uniform Retail Meat Identity Standards, Industrywide Cooperative Meat Identification Standards Committee, National Live Stock and Meat Board, 1973)

Beef

Cuts of beef are sometimes classified by most tender, medium tender, and least tender cuts:

Most Tender Cuts	Medium Tender Cuts	Least Tender Cuts
Rib	Chuck	Flank
Short loin	Rump	Plate
Sirloin	Round	Brisket
		Neck
		Shanks

The rib and loin sections lie along the center of the back. Because that part of the body is affected little by the exercise of the animal, the meat is tender. The rib section yields the choicest roasts in the carcass.

The short loin and sirloin are cut into steaks as follows: top loin, nearest the rib, then T-bone, porterhouse, and sirloin. The tenderloin muscle, which lies on the underside of the backbone (between the backbone and kidney fat), forms one eye of meat in the loin steaks. It is very small or even nonexistent in the top loin steak area, but increases in size further back, having maximum size in the porterhouse steaks. The tenderloin may be bought as a boneless cut suitable for roasting or cutting into steaks. It is not removed from high-grade carcasses but from lower-grade carcasses. Because of its tenderness, tenderloin commands a high price.

The medium tender cuts are more easily made tender by moist-heat cookery than are the least tender cuts. In the latter, the connective tissue is more developed.

Veal, Lamb, and Pork

Veal, lamb, and pork carcasses, being smaller than those of beef, are divided into fewer wholesale and retail cuts. The loin of pork is a long cut including both the rib and loin sections. The rib and loin sections of veal, lamb, and pork are cut into chops or roasts. The hind legs are also tender enough for roasts. The individual cuts are identical in general shape and characteristics to similar cuts from beef, but there is less variation in the tenderness of cuts from different sections of the animal. All cuts of young pork of good quality, both fresh and cured, are tender.

Lamb and veal are similar to beef in that neck, shoulder or chuck, breast, and shanks may require some moist heat in cooking for tenderness. Some cuts of lamb are shown in Plate XII. Even the most tender cuts of veal may be improved by some application of moist heat to hydrolyze the collagen in connective tissue. The lack of fat marbling in veal may also affect its tenderness. Larding, which involves inserting strips of fat into lean meat, supplies fat and enhances the flavor. The leg, loin, and rib sections of good-quality veal may be satisfactorily roasted.

Restructured Meat

The market demand today for boneless steak meat that can be prepared rapidly cannot always be met with existing high-quality meat supplies at prices that are seen as reasonable by consumers. One way to help supply this potential market is with the production of restructured meats. *Restructuring* is changing the form of soft tissues, including lean, fat, and connective tissue [46]. The process generally begins with flaking, coarse grinding, dicing, or chopping the meat to reduce the particle size. This is followed by mixing it with small amounts of such substances as salt and phosphates to solubilize muscle proteins on the surface of the meat pieces and to aid in binding the particles together. The meat mass is then formed into the desired shape and size. Through restructuring, less valuable pieces of meat, including lean trimmings, are upgraded. They are used to produce boneless, uniformly sized steak or roast products that resemble fresh intact muscle in flavor, color, and texture.

The composition of restructured meats can be formulated to meet consumer demands, including low-fat items. The meat pieces used may be trimmed of connective tissue to varying degrees [72], and lean meat from grass-fed animals may be used [71].

Variety Meats

Included in the category of variety meats are sweetbreads, brains, heart, tongue, tripe, liver, kidney, and oxtail (Plate XIII). Sweetbreads are the thymus gland of the calf or young beef. This gland disappears as the animal matures. The thymus gland of lamb is sometimes used for sweetbreads but is too small to be of practical value.

The thymus gland has two parts—the heart sweetbread and the throat, or neck, sweetbread. It is white and soft. Brains are also soft and delicate in flavor, and are very tender. Tripe is the smooth lining from the first beef stomach, the honeycombed lining from the second stomach, and the pocket-shaped part from the end of the second stomach. The heart and tongue are much-exercised muscles and therefore are not tender. They, as well as tripe, require relatively long, slow cooking for tenderization. Liver is a fine-textured variety meat. Veal or calf liver, because of its tenderness and mild flavor, is usually preferred to other kinds of liver and for that reason is more expensive; however, livers from all meat animals are high in nutritive value. Kidneys from beef and veal are made up of irregular lobes and deep clefts. Kidneys from veal are more tender and delicate in flavor than those from beef.

Considerations in Buying Meat

There is considerable variation in the percentage of bone, muscle meat, and visible fat among retail cuts. Table 21.2 provides some information about the yield of boneless cooked meat from various cuts. Ground beef yields the largest number of 3-ounce servings per pound of beef; short ribs, bone-in, yield the smallest number of servings. In general, the cost per pound of an edible portion is greatest in those cuts that command the highest prices, and vice versa. However, a number of exceptions occur because of differences in the percentage of bone and fat in the cuts. For example, at the same price per pound, the rump (bone-in) may cost almost double the price of round per pound of edible portions because only about 43 percent of the rump is edible as compared with about 76 percent of round. Also, the price per pound of short ribs would need to be quite low for this cut to be a very economical buy in terms of cooked lean meat yield. Therefore, it is important to recognize that

Kind and Cut of Meat	Number of 3-oz. Servings	Volume, Chopped or Diced (c)
Beef		
Brisket		
Bone-in	2	1–1½
Boneless, fresh or corned	3	1½–2
Chuck roast		
Arm		
Bone-in	2½–3	1½–2
Boneless	3½	2
Blade		
Bone-in	2½	1½
Boneless	3–3½	2
Club or T-bone steak, bone in	2	—
Flank steak, boneless	3½	—
Ground beef	4	—
Porterhouse steak, bone-in	2–2½	—
Rib roast		
Bone-in	2½	1½
Boneless	3	1½–2
Round steak		
Bone-in	3–3½	—
Boneless	3½–4	—
Rump roast		
Bone-in	2½	1½
Boneless	3½	2

cost per pound of meat as purchased is not the sole consideration. Waste is also a factor.

The usual amount to buy per serving is 4 ounces of meat with little or no bone, and 3/4 to 1 pound of meat with a high refuse content. One average pork chop is a serving, as is one to two lamb chops, depending on the size and thickness of the chops. In buying for institutional foodservice, fresh or frozen meat may be ordered as pre-portioned individual servings.

Most of the less expensive cuts of meat are a more economical source of lean than are expensive cuts. Retail prices are determined largely by such factors as tenderness, general appearance, and ease or convenience in cooking. The consumer tends to buy on the basis of these qualities to so great an extent that the loins and ribs, which constitute about one-fourth of the beef carcass, represent about one-half of the retail cost. Neither palatability nor food value corresponds directly to market price. Many of the less expensive, less tender cuts of meat have more flavor than tender cuts and, if properly cooked, are delicious. The food value is similar in both tender and less tender lean meat cuts. Thus, there are many opportunities to save money in the selection of meat cuts.

A maximum fat content of 30 percent by weight has been set for beef ground in federally inspected plants. However, most ground beef is prepared in local supermarkets to maintain freshness. There, it is generally labeled to

Short ribs, bone-in	1½	1	
Sirloin steak			
Bone-in	2–2½	—	
Boneless	2½–3	—	
Veal			
Breast			
Bone-in	2	1–1½	
Boneless	3	1½–2	
Cutlet			
Bone-in	3½	—	
Boneless	4	—	
Leg roast			
Bone-in	2½	1½	
Boneless	3½	2	
Loin chops, bone-in	2½–3	—	
Loin roast			
Bone-in	2½	1½	
Boneless	3½	2	
Rib chops, bone-in	2½	—	
Rib roast			
Bone-in	2–2½	1–1½	
Boneless	3½	2	
Shoulder roast			
Bone-in	2½	1½	
Boneless	3½	2	

* These figures allow no more than 10 percent fat on a cooked bone-in cut and no more than 15 percent fat on a cooked boneless cut.

Source: Used by permission of the U.S. Department of Agriculture.

show the proportion of lean muscle tissue and fatty tissue that has been included.

Cooking yields of ground beef increase with decreasing fat content in the raw product, but tenderness and juiciness generally decrease [13]. Ground beef is the most commonly consumed form of red meat in the United States, and researchers continue to explore ways to produce a palatable product with low fat content [24]. Isolated soy protein has been added to lean ground beef, but it has had little or no success in increasing juiciness [43]. The addition of water, up to 10 percent, with or without added phosphate, has been reported to increase juiciness, tenderness, and overall palatability scores in low-fat ground beef patties (10 percent fat). The low-fat patties with added water scored equal in texture and flavor to those containing 22 percent fat [55]. Combinations of unhydrated dietary fiber (from sugarbeets, oats, or peas), potato starch, and **polydextrose** added to ground beef with 5–10 percent fat content produced cooked patties that were similar in texture to control patties containing 20 percent fat. However, the experimental patties were less juicy than the higher-fat product [83]. An extra-lean ground beef product that contains 11 percent beef stock, hydrolyzed oat flour, and salt is currently being marketed. One fast-food chain features a hamburger that substitutes 9 percent water and 1 percent **encapsulated salt**, carrageenan, and natural beef flavor for a similar amount of beef [18].

Polydextrose a bulking agent often used with nonnutritive sweeteners in manufactured foods

Encapsulated salt sodium chloride encapsulated with partially hydrogenated vegetable oil in order to keep the salt out of solution so it will not interfere with the swelling of gums such as carrageenan

Although the term *hamburger* is usually not used in the retail meat market, federal inspectors make a distinction between ground beef and hamburger. Ground beef has nothing added to it during grinding, whereas hamburger may have a limited amount of loose beef fat and seasonings added during grinding. Ground chuck must come specifically from the chuck area of the carcass, and ground round must come only from the round. Because of marked differences in cost per pound for ground beef, ground chuck, and ground round, ground beef is often the best buy per pound of protein and per pound edible yield: even though the fat content may be highest in ground beef, intermediate in ground chuck, and lowest in ground round, much of the fat in the ground beef is rendered out during cooking.

•CURED MEATS

For centuries, curing has been an important method for preserving meat. At one time, salt (sodium chloride) in comparatively large amounts was the substance used in curing. Today, curing ingredients include sodium nitrite, sugar, and seasonings, in addition to salt. Nitrite reacts with the red pigment of meat, myoglobin, producing nitrosylmyoglobin. This later changes to the characteristic pink color of cured meats during the heating portion of the curing process. The heated pink pigment is called *nitrosyl hemochrome*.

Some controversy has arisen concerning safe levels of nitrite for use in curing meats [26, 85]. Nitrite is toxic when consumed in excessive amounts. In addition, certain cancer-producing substances, called *nitrosamines*, can be formed in food products or in the acid environment of the stomach by reactions between nitrite and **secondary amines**. The FDA has therefore limited the amount of nitrite that can be present in a finished cured product. Nitrite, in addition to fixing color in cured meats, also contributes to the development of characteristic flavor and inhibits the growth of the bacterium *Clostridium botulinum*. This organism has the ability, under suitable conditions, to produce a deadly toxin.

A substitute for nitrite in the curing of meat has been sought for a number of years. Using a multicomponent system that includes a preformed cured meat pigment, an antioxidant system, and an antimicrobial compound, wieners have been produced that reportedly cannot be distinguished from nitrite-cured control wieners [74].

Salt in the curing mixture inhibits the growth of undesirable microorganisms during curing and adds flavor. Because of the interest in decreasing sodium levels in the American diet, attempts are being made to produce processed meats of lower salt content. Phosphates may also be used in curing solutions to decrease shrinkage in meat by retaining moisture.

Ham, bacon, smoked pork-shoulder picnic, and Canadian bacon are commonly cured pork cuts. Corned beef is the cured brisket of beef. Frankfurters and a variety of sausages are also cured products.

The desire to reduce the amount of fat in meats has extended to the cured meat processing industry. **Comminuted** emulsion-type products such as wieners, sausages, and bologna can be produced with reduced fat levels. An increased level of water, along with binders such as starch, cereal, soy flour, soy

Secondary amines derivatives of ammonia (NH_3) in which two of the hydrogen atoms are replaced by other carbon-containing chemical groups

$$\begin{array}{c} R \\ \diagdown \\ NH \\ \diagup \\ R \end{array}$$

Comminute to reduce to small, fine particles

protein concentrate, and nonfat dry milk can be used to produce texture and sensory properties similar to those of the higher-fat products [24].

During the curing process, the curing mixture may be rubbed dry on the outside of a cut of meat, or the meat may be submerged in a solution of the curing ingredients. The rate of diffusion of the ingredients into the meat is, however, slow. The curing ingredients are much more rapidly and uniformly distributed throughout the meat when they are injected internally. In cuts in which the vascular system is still intact, as in hams, briskets, and tongues, the curing solution may be pumped into the arteries. Brine may be injected with needles into other cuts such as bacon. Pumping the curing solution into meat increases the weight of the meat. Federal regulations require that a ham must be "shrunk" back to at least its original fresh weight by the time heating and/or smoking is completed. If it is not, the ham must be labeled *ham, water added* if it contains up to 10 percent added moisture. Hams labeled *country-style* are processed by using a dry cure, slow smoking, and a long drying process. They are firm textured, relatively low in moisture (about 85 percent of the original weight), and always require cooking before eating.

Modern processing techniques are used for most of the ham now on the market. It is no longer necessary to cure ham primarily for preservation purposes, since refrigeration is readily available. Ham is cured today with more interest in flavor and color. Hams are heated or smoked after the injection of curing solution. During this process they are heated to an internal temperature of 60°C (140°F), but they need additional cooking before serving. Hams labeled *fully cooked* are heated to an internal temperature of about 66°C (150°F). No additional cooking is required, but they may be cooked further if desired. Canned hams that have been processed at sterilizing temperatures are also available. All processed products containing pork must be treated so that any trichinae present are destroyed, since this organism causes trichinosis in humans.

More than 200 varieties of sausages and luncheon meats are marketed in the United States. These are made from chopped or ground meat with various seasonings and often contain curing ingredients. Sausages are usually molded in casings, either natural or manufactured, or in metal molds. Recent amendments to the standards of identity for frankfurters and other similar cooked sausages allow low-fat processed meat products to be included. A maximum combination of 40 percent fat and added water is allowed, with the maximum fat content no more than 30 percent. The maximum allowable level of binders, individually or collectively, is 3.5 percent. Sausages containing more than 3.5 percent of the various binders or more than 2 percent of isolated soy protein or caseinate must be labeled *imitation* [24]. However, frankfurters may contain up to 15 percent poultry without special labeling. Turkey is used in the production of a variety of sausages, frankfurters, and luncheon meats, including bologna. Other types of bologna often contain two-thirds beef and one-third pork.

Sausages can be classified as follows:

1. Uncooked
   a. Fresh pork sausage in bulk or encased as links
   b. Fresh bratwurst
   c. Bockwurst

2. Cooked
   a. Bologna (small, medium, and large)
   b. Frankfurters (wieners)
   c. Knockwurst
   d. Liver sausage or Braunschweiger
   e. Miscellaneous loaves
3. Semidry or dry
   a. Salami
   b. Cervelat
   c. Pepperoni

Cured meat pigments tend to be oxidized and to discolor when they are exposed to the lighting of display cases in supermarkets. Vacuum packaging prevents oxygen from coming in contact with the meat. This has increased the shelf life of processed products such as bacon and luncheon meats by controlling the oxidation of pigments and the development of oxidized off-flavors.

•STORAGE OF MEATS

Fresh meats require as cold a storage temperature as other highly perishable foods, including milk, which ideally is below 7°C (45°F). Many meats on the retail market are prepackaged for self-service. The films used for covering the packages of fresh meats are usually permeable to oxygen so that the color of the meat will remain bright red. When they are brought into the kitchen, prepackaged meats can be placed in the refrigerator in their original packages but should be used within a few days or frozen for longer storage. Fresh meat that has not been prepackaged should be removed from the market wrapping and stored loosely wrapped in waxed paper, plastic wrap, or aluminum foil. Meats should not be placed above other foods in the refrigerator, particularly vegetables, unless they are held in a leak-proof container. If bacteria are present on meat and its drippings come in contact with other foods, cross-contamination can occur.

Moist meat surfaces are conducive to bacterial growth. Slight drying of the surface is preferable to bacterial action. Ground meats and variety meats are particularly perishable and should be cooked within 1 to 2 days if they are not frozen. Suggested storage times for some meats are given in Table 21.3. For freezing, meat should be wrapped tightly in moisture/vapor-proof material. The meat may be divided into serving-size portions before freezing. It should be kept frozen at −18°C (0°F) until it is used.

•MEAT COOKERY

In preparing meat for cooking, the outer surfaces may require some cleaning. Because of the soluble constituents and the danger of microbial contamination, however, the surfaces of meat should not be washed in water. A light sponging of surfaces with a clean damp cloth or paper towel is sufficient. Any dried or otherwise undesirable portions may be trimmed off, but it is not necessary to trim off government inspection and grade stamps. Safe vegetable dyes are used in the stamping process. Splinters of bone should be removed.

TABLE 21.3

Suggested Storage Periods to Maintain
High Quality in Beef and Veal

Product	Storage Period	
	Refrigerator [35° to 40°F (2° to 4°C)]	Freezer [0°F (−18°C)]
Fresh meat		
Chops and cutlets	3–5 days	3–4 months
Ground beef or veal	1–2 days	2–3 months
Roasts		
Beef	3–5 days	8–12 months
Veal	3–5 days	4–8 months
Steaks	3–5 days	8–12 months
Stew meat	1–2 days	2–3 months
Variety meats	1–2 days	3–4 months
Cooked meat and meat dishes	1–2 days	2–3 months

Source: Used by permission of the U.S. Department of Agriculture.

Meats generally are more appealing and palatable to most people when they are cooked. Cooked meats are also safer, since flesh foods may contain parasites or the larvae of tapeworms when they are in the raw state. In addition, all raw meats are more or less contaminated with a variety of bacteria, some of which may constitute hazards, particularly if the food is mishandled or undercooked. Ground beef has special potential for harboring pathogens and should therefore always be cooked to an internal temperature of at least 68°C (155°F) in foodservice kitchens and 70°C (160°F) in home kitchens.

It is very important in meat cookery to know the nature of the cut to be cooked and then to choose the proper method for cooking it. Because the meat from most young animals and from the least-exercised muscles of more mature animals is tender, it has a small amount of connective tissue and should be kept tender during cooking. Less tender meats require tenderization during cooking to make them palatable. Distinctive flavors are developed by some methods of cooking.

General Methods

Conventional cooking of meat is divided into dry-heat and moist-heat methods. Dry-heat cookery traditionally includes roasting or baking, broiling, and pan-broiling. Frying can also be included in this classification because fat, not moisture, comes in contact with the surface of the meat during cooking. These procedures are discussed in more detail under "Specific Cooking Methods." Cooking by microwaves is suitable, as are all of the dry-heat methods, for cooking tender cuts of meat. Microwave cooking at low power levels can also be used for less tender cuts of meat.

Moist-heat methods are braising, stewing or cooking in water, and pressure cooking. Simmering temperatures for stewing are sometimes specified on the assumption that the boiling temperature toughens meat; however, there is apparently little difference in the final tenderness of meats cooked in water at simmering or boiling temperatures. The term *fricassee* may be applied to braised meats cut into small pieces before cooking. The braising of large pieces of meat is sometimes called *pot-roasting*. When meats are braised, their surfaces may first be browned using dry heat by pan-broiling or frying.

For many years, dry-heat methods of cooking were generally applied only to tender cuts of meat, while moist-heat methods were thought to be necessary to tenderize all less tender pieces. However, roasting less tender cuts with dry heat can be satisfactorily accomplished using very low oven temperatures and long periods of time [40]. The flavors developed in beef during roasting and broiling seem to be favored by most people over those developed in braising or pot-roasting.

Beef loin, generally considered tender, and bottom round, generally considered less tender, do not respond alike to moist- and dry-heat methods of cooking. Some researchers [12] have found that loin steaks become tougher as they are cooked thoroughly and that moist heat does not seem to tenderize them. Bottom round steaks braised very well done are much more tender than loin steaks cooked in the same way. Although moist-heat methods seem to be unsuitable for tender cuts of meat, dry-heat methods seem to be suitable for both tender and less tender cuts if the time of cooking is adapted. Apparently there is enough water in the meat itself to provide for the hydrolysis of connective tissue during cooking. Additional water, as in braising or stewing, is not necessary for this purpose.

Effect of Heat on Meat

Denaturation a change in a protein molecule, usually by unfolding of the amino acid chains, with a decrease in solubility

Coagulation usually a change in proteins after denaturation, with new bonds being formed between protein chains, resulting in precipitation or gel formation

Heat produces many changes in meat. Studies conducted using small pieces of meat that were heated more quickly and uniformly than large roasts have shown that a decrease in tenderness occurs when the meat reaches from 40° to 60°C (104°F to 140°F). This is followed by a gradual increase in tenderness above 60°C (140°F) or even above 50°C (122°F) in young animals. The original toughening appears to be the result of a shortening of the fibers accompanied by hardening as the proteins **denature** and **coagulate**. The later tenderizing evidently results from the softening of connective tissue and the hydrolysis to gelatin of some collagen in this tissue [8, 41, 51].

The response of an individual muscle to heating apparently depends to some degree on the amount of connective tissue; however, the muscle fibers from different muscles may also react differently toward heat. In one study, researchers heated a tender muscle (longissimus dorsi) and less tender muscles (semitendinosus and semimembranosus) of beef to three different internal temperatures. They found that the tender muscle did not change in tenderness with increasing degrees of doneness, but the two less tender muscles did increase in tenderness with higher internal temperatures [75]. The less tender muscles contained more connective tissue, which was evidently softened with increased temperatures. A different balance between the hardening of muscle fibers and the softening of connective tissue was achieved in the less tender muscles than in the tender muscle.

Fat melts when meat is heated, and the capacity of the muscle proteins to hold water is lessened, thus causing reduced juiciness and tenderness and increased weight loss. The volume of the meat decreases on cooking.

Significant visual color changes occur in heated meat between 60° and 65°C (140° and 150°F) and between 75° and 80°C (168° and 176°F) [9]. Redness decreases as internal temperature increases. The meat pigment myoglobin appears to be denatured around 60°C (140°F), and denaturation of other proteins seems to be complete by 80°C (176°F).

Cooking Losses

Cooking losses, including loss of weight and loss of nutrients, increase gradually with increasing internal temperatures [9]. Weight loss results from the formation of drippings, evaporation of water, and evaporation of other volatile substances. When meat is roasted in an open pan, considerable evaporation of water from the meat surface occurs. However, nutrients and flavor substances are better retained in the meat than when the meat is cooked in water or steam. As water evaporates, minerals and extractives are deposited on the surface of the meat. This probably accounts in part for the pronounced flavor of the outer brown layer in roasted meat.

Fat losses are less consistent than those of other constituents, probably because of the unequal distribution of fat throughout most pieces of meat. Fat on or near the surface is lost to a greater extent than fat in the interior because of the slowness of heat penetration. Not all fat that liquefies is lost, because some of it can and does penetrate to the interior. The fat layer on the outside of meat aids in decreasing water loss by preventing evaporation. Researchers have found that the degree of fat trim on raw beef loin steaks did not significantly affect the sensory characteristics of the cooked meat. However, the fat content of the cooked steak with the fat totally trimmed off was significantly less than the fat content of the steak with regular trim [2]. In cooking ground beef, either as patties or as crumbles, fat losses are greater when the fat content of the raw meat is higher [44]. Ground beef with 20 percent and 30 percent fat in the raw state yields cooked meat with similar fat contents, which are only slightly greater than the fat content of cooked ground beef that contained 10 percent fat in the raw state.

Some researchers [22] compared cooking losses of fabricated ground beef cylinders containing three different levels of fat when they were roasted at 250°, 300°, and 350°F. They found that both total and volatile cooking losses increased as the oven temperature decreased. Longer times were required to cook to the same internal temperature of the meat at the lower oven temperatures. More moisture evidently was evaporated from the surface of the meat during these long periods than when shorter roasting times were used. Loss in total drippings increased with increased fat content of the meat but was not different for the various oven temperatures.

The final internal temperature to which meat is cooked influences total weight losses. Weight loss increases with increasing internal temperature. Total weight loss is usually greater in moist-heat than in dry-heat methods of cooking meat. Top round steaks showed total cooking losses of 27.5 percent when they were cooked by moist heat as compared with 20.6 percent when they were cooked by dry heat [59].

Although some losses of B vitamins, including thiamin, riboflavin, and niacin, occur during cooking, cooked meats are still good sources of these vitamins. Greater vitamin losses occur during braising and stewing than during roasting and broiling, but many are retained in the cooking liquid. Vitamin retention in meats during cooking in water is dependent on the cooking time, with greater losses occurring as cooking continues. In addition to the loss of vitamins by their dissolution in the cooking water, some oxidation may occur. Riboflavin and niacin are more resistant to destruction by heat than is thiamin.

Shrinkage of Meat During Cooking

Shrinkage in cooked meats begins at 50° to 60°C (122° to 140°F) because of the shortening of muscle fibers and coagulation of proteins. There is loss of water and melting of fat. The higher the interior temperature of the meat, the greater the shrinkage. Less shrinkage usually occurs in meats roasted at 300° to 350°F than in meats roasted at higher oven temperatures. Meats roasted for the whole cooking time at a high oven temperature may shrink as much as 40 to 60 percent as compared with 15 or 20 percent at low temperatures. It is wise to consider excess shrinkage in economic terms, since fewer servings can be obtained from meats that have been allowed to shrink excessively during cooking.

Basting

Pouring or spooning liquids such as meat drippings or a marinade over the surface of meat while it is roasting is called *basting*. The major purpose of basting is to keep the surface moist, but the use of a flavorful liquid also enhances the flavor of the cooked meat. If meats are placed in the roasting pan with the fat layer on top, the melted fat flows down over the surface of the roast as it cooks and self-basting occurs.

Salting

When should meat be salted? If the piece of meat is large, it is not possible to salt the interior, because salt does not penetrate a roast to a greater depth than 1/2 inch. Putting much salt on the outer surface may result in too salty an outer layer or salty drippings. The outer layer then also becomes crusty. It is therefore unnecessary to salt a roast before cooking. Salt retards the browning of meat, and for that reason, if for no other, it is best applied to steaks and chops after they are cooked.

Meat loaves cannot be well seasoned unless salt is mixed with the meat before the loaf is shaped. To season small pieces of meat, as in stew, salt may be added to the cooking water. Total losses from the meat seem to be no greater in salted than in unsalted stews.

Although salting a raw or slightly cooked surface of meat draws juice to the surface, it has not been proven that salting meats before or during cooking results in any greater total losses from the meat than would occur if meats were not salted. More information is needed on the effect of salting on cooking losses.

Juiciness

Juiciness is a highly desirable characteristic in cooked meats. Depending on such factors as the quality of the meat, the amount of marbling, and aging, meats differ in their juiciness. Aged meats are usually more juicy than meats that are not aged. The meat from younger animals is often more juicy than that from older animals. The amount of fat in a piece of meat, particularly fat marbled throughout the muscle, may increase the apparent juiciness of meat as it is eaten. In comparing the sensory properties of ground beef patties with three different levels of fat, it was reported that juiciness, as well as tenderness, was associated with the higher amounts of fat [7].

The interior temperature to which meats are cooked affects juiciness, with meats cooked to the rare and medium-done stages being more juicy than well-done meats. In fact, it is difficult to cook meats to a brown interior color without a substantial loss of juiciness.

Meats that are cooked for a long time in moist heat to develop tenderness reach so high an interior temperature that they cannot fail to be dry. If meats are cooked in moisture and are served in the cooking liquid, as Swiss steak is, they may appear to be moist, but that moistness is not juiciness within the meat itself.

Tenderization

Proper cooking contributes to the development of the desirable trait of tenderness in less tender meat and to its preservation in already tender cuts. The tender cuts do not contain large amounts of connective tissue, which may need to be softened by long cooking. Therefore, overcooking of these cuts should be avoided. In fact, long cooking toughens thin cuts.

Adequate tenderization of connective tissue generally occurs with either the application of moist heat or the use of dry heat for extremely long cooking periods at low temperatures. In either case, tenderization results from hydrolysis of the collagen in connective tissue to produce gelatin. A firming effect that may take place in muscle fibers subjected to long cooking is more than counterbalanced by the softening of connective tissue. However, if the meat is not carved across the grain, producing short muscle fiber segments, the long intact muscle fibers that are separated because of connective tissue disintegration may contribute to apparent toughness as the meat is eaten. Proper carving of meat thus contributes to tenderness as the meat is served.

Less tender cuts of beef can be tenderized to some extent by soaking the meat in an acid-containing marinade for 24 to 48 hours before cooking [31, 64]. The tenderizing effect is dependent upon the concentration of acid present. Marinated beef muscles with a pH of 3.25 have been found to be significantly more tender than those with a pH of 4.25 [64]. At the lower pH, the water-binding capacity of the muscle is increased, the total collagen content is reduced, and cooking losses are decreased.

Meat tenderizers increase the tenderness of meat through enzymatic hydrolysis of proteins in the tissue as the meat is heated [21]. (See "Factors Affecting Tenderness" earlier in this chapter.)

Specific Cooking Methods

Roasting or Baking

Historically, the term *roasting* was applied to the cooking of large cuts of meat before an open fire. Today the terms *roasting* and *baking* are used synonymously and apply to the method of placing meat on a rack in an open pan and cooking by the dry heat of an oven. Previously, roasted meats were practically always seared in a hot oven of about 500°F for 20 to 30 minutes, after which the temperature of the oven was reduced to about 300°F for the remainder of the cooking period. Searing produces coagulation of the surface proteins and was formerly believed to prevent the loss of juices and nutrients. It is now fairly certain that searing does not form a pellicle or thin film and does not prevent the loss of interior juices. It may increase total cooking losses because of the high temperature used, although the losses may be chiefly surface losses.

The oven temperature generally recommended for roasting tender cuts of meat is 325°F. As the oven temperature is increased from 300° to 450°F, the cooking time for meats cooked to the same internal temperature is decreased, total cooking losses are increased, and there is decreasing uniformity of doneness throughout the meat (Figure 21.18).

Adequate browning for good flavor and attractive appearance occurs at low constant oven temperatures, particularly if temperatures of 325° and 350°F are used. A higher temperature can be used at the end of the roasting period merely for browning purposes, if desired.

Beef standing rib roast to be cooked at 300°F. Weight 9 lb 10 oz.

Same roast after cooking. Weight after cooking 7 lb 8 oz. Shrinkage 1 lb 1 oz (22 percent). Drippings (good) 1 lb 4 oz.

FIGURE 21.18

Comparison of shrinkage and drippings when roasting is done to the same internal temperature at a constant, low oven temperature, and a constant, high oven temperature. (Courtesy of the National Live Stock and Meat Board)

Meat can also be roasted in a convection oven in which the heated air is constantly recirculated by means of a fan. The cooking process is speeded up in convection ovens and the roasting time is therefore somewhat less than with a conventional oven.

In the past, roasting has been recommended only for cuts of meat that are expected to be tender, and moist-heat methods of cooking have been suggested for less tender cuts. However, studies have shown that less tender cuts of beef are tender and acceptable when they are roasted at oven temperatures of 225° to 250°F [61]. They are more moist and juicy than similar cuts that are braised. The cooking time at the low temperature is considerably extended. If a meat thermometer is used to determine the stage of doneness, the bulb of the thermometer is inserted in the thickest portion of the meat (Figure 21.19). The use of the thermometer is at present the only accurate way to know the interior temperature or stage of doneness of the meat.

If no thermometer is available, meat can alternatively be cooked by minutes per pound (Table 21.4). This is considerably less accurate, however, because pieces of meat of the same weight may vary greatly in shape, thickness, and the proportion of meat to bone. A standing rib roast cooks in less

Beef standing rib roast to be cooked at 450°F. Weight 9 lb 10 oz.

Same roast after cooking. Weight after cooking 6 lb 2 oz. Shrinkage 3 lb 8 oz (36 percent). Drippings (burned) 2 lb 3 oz.

time than a rolled rib roast because the latter is made more compact by boning and rolling. Large roasts of the same general shape as small roasts require fewer minutes per pound.

The usual interior temperatures for beef cooked to various stages of doneness are as follows:

Very rare	55°C (130°F)
Rare	60°C (140°F)
Medium rare	65°C (150°F)
Medium	70°C (158°F)
Well done	75°C (168°F)
Very well done	80°C (176°F)

The color of the interior of the meat changes as the internal temperature increases and the muscle pigments are denatured and coagulated. Bright red or pink gradually changes to grayish pink and finally to grayish brown. The appearance may vary at a specific internal temperature, depending on the particular cut of meat being cooked and on the cooking procedure, especially the length of time required to reach the final temperature. For example, a beef roast may appear less well done when it is cooked to the same internal temperature at a high oven temperature than when it is cooked at a low temperature because of the shorter cooking time at the high temperature. Some unaged beef may still have considerable pink color at 75°C (168°F) and may require cooking to a temperature of 77°C (170°F) or higher to reach a gray stage. Other aged meat that loses its red color at lower temperatures may appear to be overdone when it is cooked to 77°C (170°F).

TABLE 21.4

Approximate Roasting Time for Some Typical Meat Cuts*

Cut	Weight (lb)	Constant Oven Temperature (°F)	Interior Temperature on Removal From Oven (°C)	(°F)	Approximate Time per Pound (min)
Beef					
Standing rib	6–8	300–325	60	140	23–25
			65.5–71	150–160	25–30
			74–76.5	165–170	27–34
Rolled rib	5–8	300–325	60	140	30–32
			65.5–71	150–160	35–38
			74–76.5	165–170	45–48
Rolled rump	4–6	300–325	65.5–76.5	150–170	25–30
Pork (fresh)					
Loin	3–5	325–350	76.5–85	170–185	30–45
Shoulder (cushion)	3–5	325–350	76.5–85	170–185	30–40
Ham (whole)	10–14	325–350	76.5–85	179–185	20–35
Pork (cured)					
Ham (whole)	10–14	300–325	71	160	18–20
Ham (half)	5–7	300–325	71	160	22–25
Picnic shoulder	5–8	300–325	76.5	170	35
Lamb					
Leg	5–8	300–325	79.5–82	175–180	30–35
Shoulder (cushion)	3–5	300–325	79.5–82	175–180	30–35
Shoulder (rolled)	3–5	300–325	79.5–82	175–180	40–45
Veal					
Leg	5–8	300–325	74–76.5	165–170	25–35
Loin	4–6	300–325	74–76.5	165–170	30–35
Rib (rack)	3–5	300–325	74–76.5	165–170	35–40

* If higher or lower temperatures are used for roasting, the times will obviously be somewhat shorter or longer, respectively.

The cooking of fresh pork to a final internal temperature of 80° to 85°C (176° to 185°F) was recommended for many years to ensure destruction of the parasite *Trichinella spiralis*, which might be present in the pork muscle. More recent studies [39], however, have found that pork can be safely cooked to an internal temperature of 77°C (170°F) as long as the cooking method is slow enough to allow relatively uniform heat distribution throughout the piece of meat. The USDA now recommends a final cooking temperature of 71°C (160°F) for medium-cooked pork and 77°C (170°F) for well-done pork. Generally, increased juiciness and decreased cooking losses occur at the lower internal temperatures. Flavor and tenderness appear to be comparable, but some studies have reported increased flavor scores at the higher internal temperatures. A study of consumer preference for pork loins cooked to 71°C (160°F) or 85°C (185°F) found that 57 percent of the 516 participants preferred the pork cooked to 71°C (160°F), but 43 percent preferred the pork cooked to 85°C (185°F) [50]. This study suggests that it may be prudent to offer pork cooked to differing degrees of doneness as is currently the practice for beef.

Veal, lamb, and cured pork are usually cooked to the following internal temperatures:

Veal, well done	74° to 77°C (165° to 170°F)
Lamb, medium	70° to 71°C (158° to 160°F)
Lamb, well done	80° to 82°C (175° to 180°F)
Cured pork, well done	71° to 77°C (160° to 170°F)

Veal, which has a tendency to become very dry during cooking, can be successfully roasted in an open pan if low oven temperatures are used. Larding the roast improves both flavor and juiciness because of the addition of fat.

When meat is wrapped in aluminum foil before roasting, it cooks in a moist- rather than a dry-heat atmosphere. The foil is thought to have an insulating effect on the meat and, for this reason, higher oven temperatures are sometimes recommended for foil-wrapped roasts in comparison with unwrapped roasts. However, this insulating effect may not be present at oven temperatures as low as 200°F [5]. In a comparison of unwrapped and tightly foil-wrapped beef roasts cooked at an oven temperature of 300°F to an internal temperature of 77°C (170°F), the foil-wrapped roasts were found to be less juicy and less tender, and they received lower flavor scores than the unwrapped roasts [30].

After a relatively large roast is removed from the oven, it continues to cook unless it is cut at once. The heat continues to penetrate to the center. The rise in temperature continues for 15 to 45 minutes or longer, depending on the oven temperature at which the meat is roasted, the internal temperature at which the roast is removed from the oven, the size of the roast, and the composition of the meat.

The higher the oven temperature at which the roast is cooked, the greater the increase in internal temperature of the roast after removal from the oven. The lower the internal temperature of the roast when it is removed from the oven, the greater the rise in temperature after removal from the oven. Small, thin roasts may show little or no rise in temperature because of the rapid cooling from the surface. Meat containing much fat and meat having a thick external layer of fat take longer to reach the maximum internal temperature after removal from the oven than does very lean meat.

Broiling and Pan-Broiling

In broiling, meats are cooked with a direct heat source, such as a gas flame, live coals, or an electric element, that emits radiant energy. Broiling is used for relatively thin cuts of meat such as steaks and chops. It is usually done using the broil setting on a range, with the door closed for a gas range and open for an electric range. Steam may accumulate in an electric oven with the door closed, and steam retards browning. A rack for holding the meat out of the drippings is essential, both to keep the meat from stewing in its juices and to prevent burning of the fat.

The source of heat used for broiling is usually constant. However, some variation in temperature is achieved in regulation of the distance of the surface of the meat from the source of radiant heat. The relatively high temperatures usually used in broiling do not seem to toughen the meat, possibly because cooking times are relatively short or because tender cuts of meat are used.

Broiling may be used for relatively thin, less tender cuts of meat if they have been treated with meat tenderizers.

If steaks are very thick, they can be broiled using a thermometer that registers interior temperature, or tested by pulling the fibers in the thickest portion apart to see the color of the juice. A cut is sometimes made next to the bone to determine interior color. Table 21.5 gives the approximate broiling time for some typical cuts. Like the timetable for roasting, it is meant as a guide rather than as a precise statement of time. The distance of the meat surface from the broiling unit is usually 2 to 5 inches. Thicker cuts are placed farther from the heat source than thin cuts are to allow more uniform cooking.

A variation of broiling is pan-broiling. In this case, heat is applied by means of direct contact with a hot surface such as a heavy pan or a grill. The surface of the pan is lightly oiled with a piece of fat meat to prevent the muscle tissue from sticking. As fat accumulates in the pan during cooking, it should be poured off to avoid frying the meat in its own fat.

Tender beef steaks, lamb chops, and ground beef patties are satisfactorily pan-broiled. Veal, because of its lack of fat, does not broil or pan-broil well. Pork chops are tender enough for dry-heat methods of cooking but should be thoroughly cooked. Broiling and pan-broiling, as they are usually practiced, may not ensure that the centers of pork chops reach an appropriate stage of doneness, especially if the chops are very thick.

TABLE 21.5
Approximate Broiling Times for Some Typical Meat Cuts

		Time (min)		
Cut	Average Weight (lb)	Rare	Medium	Well Done
Beef				
Club steak (top loin)				
1 in.	1	14–17	18–20	22–25
1½ in.	1¼	25–27	30–35	35–40
Porterhouse				
1 in.	2	19–21	22–25	26–30
1½ in.	2½	30–32	35–38	40–45
Sirloin				
1 in.	3	20–22	23–25	26–30
1½ in.	4½	30–32	33–35	36–40
Ground beef patty, 1 in. thick by 3½ in. diameter	¼	12–15	18–22	24–28
Lamb				
Loin chops				
1 in.	³⁄₁₆		10–15	16–18
1½ in.	⁵⁄₁₆		16–18	19–22
Rib chops				
1 in.	⅛		10–15	16–18
1½ in.	¼		16–18	19–22
Ground lamb patty 1 in. thick by 3½ in. diameter	¼		18–20	22–24

In one study, the degree of marbling and the level of fat trimmed from beef loin steaks did not significantly affect the sensory properties of the broiled steaks [2]. However, they became increasingly less tender and juicy as they were cooked from the rare to the well-done stage.

In another study, broiling, grilling, and roasting were used to cook ground beef patties of three different fat levels (18.4, 21.5, and 27.0 percent). Differences among the cooked patties in caloric value, fat content, and various vitamins and minerals were found to be too small to be of practical significance, although the cooking yield was slightly lower for the patties with 27.0 percent fat [63].

You can pan-broil bacon by placing the slices in a cold pan and heating them slowly while frequently turning until they are crisp. Much of the fat should be drained off, but the bacon browns more evenly when a small amount of fat is left in the pan.

Frying

Frying has been largely displaced by pan-broiling and broiling as a commonly used method for cooking tender cuts of meat. In pan-frying, only a small amount of fat (enough to form a layer of melted fat 1/4 to 1/2 inch deep) is used; in deep-fat frying, the melted fat is deep enough to cover the food. Fried food requires draining on absorbent paper to remove excess fat. Meats may be dipped in flour or in egg and crumbs before frying. This produces a brown crust on the meat. Frying can also be used to brown meats that are to be braised.

Microwave Cooking

Because the use of microwave ovens has increased in recent years, more meat is being cooked by this method. An important advantage of the microwave oven for cooking meat is that it uses substantially less energy for the same degree of doneness than do conventional methods, cooking in one-third to one-half the time [38]. Convection ovens also conserve energy because lower cooking temperatures and shorter cooking and preheating times are used.

Some early studies involving comparisons of meat cookery using microwave and conventional ovens often found greater cooking losses and somewhat less palatable products with microwave cooking. This was particularly true when less tender cuts of meat were prepared [37, 47]. However, microwave ovens with variable power settings now allow cooking at different energy levels. Cooking top round roasts of beef, particularly from the frozen state, at simmer power levels produces more palatable products than does cooking similar roasts at high power levels. Roasts cooked at the lower power level are often similar in palatability to roasts cooked in conventional ovens [16, 85]. A low power setting has also been reported to produce more palatable pork chops than does a high setting [29].

Microwaves do not heat uniformly. It has been suggested that rapid microwave cooking of pork chops or roasts does not allow the uniform heating necessary to ensure destruction of all trichinae, should they be present, when the meat has an internal temperature in the center of 77°C (170°F). To ensure consistently well-done pork roasts cooked in a microwave oven, one researcher [88] has made the following recommendations:

1. Use a 50 percent or less power level.
2. Use selected roasts weighing 2 kilograms (4.4 pounds) or less—preferably boneless loin, center loin, or blade loin.
3. Allow roasts to stand after cooking, covered with foil, for ten minutes or longer.
4. Make sure the temperature at several locations in the roast registers 77°C (170°F).
5. When the roast is cut, make sure no pink or red meat is evident.

If general recommended procedures for microwave cooking of pork are followed, including proper turning of the meat during cooking and less than high power levels, the temperature throughout should be in excess of that required to destroy any trichinae that are present [6]. Drastic deviations from recommended cooking procedures by either conventional or microwave methods may result in less than safe final temperatures in pork.

Roasts that are about twice as long as they are wide cook well in a microwave oven. Boned and rolled roasts, such as rolled rib roasts, are excellent. Frequent turning and basting with a sauce ensure full flavor and color development of the surface. A rapid-reading thermometer may be inserted in the roast *after it is removed from the oven* to check the degree of doneness. Some special thermometers are available for use inside the microwave oven.

Small pieces of meat, particularly, do not brown when they are cooked in a microwave oven. Various browning elements and special browning grills have been developed by the manufacturers of microwave equipment to solve this problem. The use of browning devices increases fuel consumption by 50 percent or more over cooking by microwaves alone. Total cooking time is also increased [15].

After they come from the microwave oven, roasts of meat should be set aside before carving. Heat is stored inside the product during cooking, and the standby time allows this heat to distribute itself throughout the meat so that proper doneness is achieved. Most roasts require a standby time of 30 to 50 minutes. Standing time is particularly important for less tender cuts of meat to ensure tenderization.

The flavor of microwaved meats may be somewhat different from that of meat cooked by conventional methods. After a comparison of several cooking methods for the preparation of ground beef patties of different fat content, some researchers indicated that they did not recommend microwave cooking of the patties as the method of choice for enhancing sensory properties [7]. Microwave cooking scored lower in this study than broiling or charbroiling on tenderness, juiciness, and flavor intensity.

Using nonwoven, melt-blown polypropylene pads is a simple and effective method of reducing fat in products such as bacon and sausages when they are cooked in a microwave oven [24]. These microwavable pads absorb the fat lost in the cooking process. Since the fat goes into the material and is removed from contact with the meat surface, a larger amount of fat can be withdrawn from the meat than is true with the use of paper towels as absorbants. The material also is hydrophobic and thus aids in retaining moisture in the food being cooked.

Main dishes containing meat often microwave well; they are prepared rapidly and generally result in a flavorful mixture. Microwaving is also particu-

Warmed-over flavor   describes
the rapid onset of lipid oxidation that
occurs in cooked meats during refrigerated storage; oxidized flavors are
detectable after only 48 hours

larly useful for reheating cooked meat and meat dishes, not only because it is rapid but also because it results in minimal **warmed-over flavor** and aroma [34]. Still another convenient use of the microwave oven is for the rapid thawing of frozen meats.

Braising

A moist-heat method of cooking, braising is usually applied to less tender cuts of meat. Browning of the meat surface can be accomplished by first frying, pan-broiling, or broiling. Meats can be braised without added water because steam from the water in the meat itself can provide the moisture needed to hydrolyze the collagen in connective tissue; however, a small amount of water may be added. It is better to add small quantities of water frequently rather than a large amount at one time to retain the brown surface, if the meat was browned before braising began. The pan or kettle is closely covered, and cooking is continued, with the liquid simmering or slowly boiling until the meat becomes tender.

Braising can be done either on the top of the range or in the oven. The cooking time is longer in the oven and more energy is expended. Since the pan is tightly covered, the meat is cooked in a moist atmosphere even though it is cooked in the oven. The time of cooking depends on the character of the meat and the size of the cut, but braised meat is always cooked well done. The term *pot-roasting* is often used to refer to the braising of large cuts of meat such as beef chuck roasts. Swiss steaks are braised beef steaks. (See Plate XIV)

Cuts from the chuck and round of beef are commonly braised. Braising is recommended for veal and pork chops, although pork chops are also effectively cooked by roasting or baking.

Stewing

Stewing is cooking meats in liquid at simmering or slow-boiling temperatures. For brown stew, part or all of the meat may be browned before stewing. This develops flavor as well as color in the stew. If vegetables are used, they should be added just long enough before the stew is to be served so that they are not overcooked.

Pressure Cooking

Cooking meat in a pressure saucepan is a moist-heat method generally used for less tender cuts. Only a relatively short cooking time is necessary because heating produces a temperature higher than that of the usual boiling point of water, which is the temperature used for braising and stewing. The retention of steam within the cooking vessel, which increases the vapor pressure of the water, is responsible for the high temperature. Meats prepared in a pressure saucepan are commonly cooked to a well-done stage. A distinctive steamed flavor can usually be recognized.

Crockery Slow Cooking

Various types of crockery slow-cooking pots are available and are often used for meat cookery. These electric appliances have a low-temperature setting that allows meat and other foods to be cooked for long periods without constant watching. For example, a beef roast can be placed in the cooker with no added liquid, covered, and cooked on the lowest setting for 10 to 12 hours. Meat dishes with added liquid, such as beef stew or Swiss steak, are also satisfactorily cooked in crockery slow cookers. The low setting usually represents a temperature of about 200°F.

Cooking in these covered pots is achieved by moist heat. The long cooking period allows the breakdown of the connective tissue to gelatin in less tender meats, thus increasing tenderness.

Cooking Variety Meats

The choice of a cooking method for variety meats is influenced by the tenderness of the various parts. Heart, kidney, tongue, and tripe all require cooking for tenderness and are braised or simmered. Older beef liver may also require tenderizing by braising. Brains, sweetbreads, and veal or calf liver are tender. They may be cooked by dry-heat methods such as broiling or frying. For variety, they may also be cooked by moist-heat methods. Brains and sweetbreads are delicate tissues that are made more firm and white when they are precooked for about 20 minutes at a simmering temperature in salted, acidulated water. After this preliminary treatment they can be prepared in various ways. Table 21.6 provides suggestions pertinent to the preparation of variety meats.

Cooking Frozen Meats

Frozen meats can be thawed and cooked or cooked without thawing first. The cooking temperature must be lower and the time of cooking increased when the meat is frozen when cooking begins. If pieces of frozen meat are large, the cooking time may be considerably longer than for similar thawed or fresh cuts. Frozen roasts require up to one and a half times as long to cook as unfrozen roasts of the same size. If frozen meats are braised, they may be browned at the end of the braising period rather than at the beginning.

There are no appreciable differences in palatability or nutritive value in meats cooked from the thawed or frozen state. Thawed meats are cooked in the same way as fresh meats. Thawing of frozen meat, particularly large pieces of meat, in the refrigerator is recommended for microbiologic safety.

Meat Flavor

USDA quality grades for meat relate to palatability. In the evaluation of grade, such characteristics as marbling and firmness of the lean cut surface in relation to evidences of carcass maturity or age are considered. It is quite likely that USDA quality grades are related to flavor of the meat because grade indirectly assesses the extent to which flavor compounds are likely to be present in high or low concentrations [80]. For example, carcasses from older and leaner animals and from animals fed little or no grain are assigned low USDA quality grades. These animals are likely to yield meat of less desirable flavor than young, fatter animals fed large quantities of grain and graded higher.

The flavor of meat involves responses from taste and smell or aroma and also sensations from pressure-sensitive and heat-sensitive areas of the mouth. Flavor of meat is developed primarily by cooking; raw meat has little aroma and

TABLE 21.6
Variety Meats

Name	Preliminary Preparation	Cooking Methods
Liver	Liver from young animals should be sliced 1/2 in. thick for best results in retaining juiciness. Remove outside membrane, blood vessels, and excess connective tissue. Wash large pieces before removing membrane.	Broil or pan-broil young liver. Fry or bread young liver. Braise whole piece of older beef liver. Grind and make into liver loaf. (Liver is easier to grind if first coagulated in hot water.)
Kidney	Wash kidneys and remove outer membrane. Lamb kidneys may be split in half and veal kidneys cut into slices. Cook beef kidneys in water for tenderness, changing the water several times.	Young kidneys may be broiled, pan-broiled, made into stew or kidney pie, or ground and made into loaf. Beef kidneys, after being cooked for tenderness, may be cooked in the same way, except that they should not be broiled or pan-broiled.
Sweetbreads and brains	Soak in cold water to remove blood. Remove blood vessels and excess connective tissue. Parboil in salted, acidulated water to make firm and white using 1 tsp salt and 1 Tbsp vinegar per quart of water.	Sweetbreads may be creamed, dipped in egg and crumbs and fried in fat, combined with cooked chicken and creamed or scalloped, or dipped in melted fat and broiled. Brains may be breaded or broiled as suggested for sweetbreads or cut into small pieces and scrambled with eggs.
Heart	Heart is a muscular organ that is usually cooked by moist-heat methods for tenderness. Wash in warm water and remove large blood vessels.	Stuff with bread dressing and braise until tender. May be cooked in water seasoned with salt, onion, bay leaf, celery, and tomato and served hot or cold.
Tongue	Tongue is a muscular tissue that requires precooking in water for tenderness. After cooking, remove the skin and cut out the roots. Smoked or pickled tongue is usually soaked for several hours before cooking.	May be cooked in water, seasoned with salt, onion, bay leaf, and celery. If it is to be served cold, it is more moist when allowed to cool in the water. After it is cooked in water, the tongue may be covered with brown or tomato sauce and braised in the oven. The cooked tongue may be reheated in a sweet pickling solution. For this method, the tongue is best precooked in plain salted water.
Tripe	Fresh tripe is cooked before selling but requires further cooking in water until tender (1 or more hours).	Serve precooked tripe with well-seasoned tomato sauce. Dip in batter and fry in deep fat. Brush with flavorful fat and broil.

only a bloodlike taste. The flavor of boiled meats differs from that of roasted meats.

The chemistry of meat flavor is very complex; many compounds contribute to the characteristic flavor of the cooked product. Some of these flavor compounds are volatile and give rise to odor. One study of the volatile flavor components of fresh beef stew identified 132 different compounds [67].

Although volatile components are possibly the most important part of meat flavor, nonvolatile compounds stimulate taste buds and contribute to the overall flavor complex. The most important taste compounds are inorganic salts, producing a salty taste; sugars, producing a sweet taste; hypoxanthine, contributing some bitterness; organic acids, producing a sour taste; and some nitrogen-containing compounds including nucleotides, amino acids, and peptides. In addition to volatile and nonvolatile components of meat flavor, there are other substances called *flavor potentiators* and *synergists*. Although these substances have no distinctive flavor of their own, they enhance the flavor of other compounds. Flavor potentiators in meat include some amino acids, such as glutamic acid, and certain 5'-nucleotides such as inosinic acid [58].

The feeding management of beef cattle affects the flavor of the meat, particularly the flavor of the fatty portions. Grass- or forage-fed steers have less desirable flavor, characterized as grassy, gamey, and milky-oily, than do those animals finished on grain [48, 57]. Serving temperature also affects perceived meat flavor. Beef steaks tasted at 50°C (122°F) are more flavorful and juicy than similar samples tasted at 22°C (72°F) [62]. Not only the temperature, but also the time a meat product is held before serving can affect flavor. Freshly cooked meat sauce with spaghetti was found to be more flavorful and generally more acceptable to a taste panel than was a similar product held hot on a cafeteria counter for 90 minutes [3].

The study of meat flavor, both boiled and roasted, is important to attempts to learn how to duplicate these flavors in the laboratory. Simulated meat flavors are needed for flavoring meat analogues made from plant proteins. They are also useful in the preparation of various convenience foods. Although a number of simulated meat flavors are available, they cannot completely duplicate the natural flavors; in comparisons by both trained and consumer panels, they have been found to be less desirable [45].

•SOUP STOCK

A stock is a flavored liquid used chiefly in the making of soups. Beef is the most commonly used meat for stock. Veal has too little flavor to be used alone but may be combined with other meats. Lamb and mutton produce excellent broth, but they should be used only when lamb or mutton flavor is desired. The bones and meat from poultry also make desirable broth. Stock for fish soups is made from fish.

In preparing meat for making stock, the more surface of the meat that is exposed to the water, the more flavor that is extracted. This means cutting the meat into small cubes or grinding it through a coarse grinder rather than cooking it in one piece. The meat may be soaked for 1/2 to 1 hour in cold water; then cooking is started and the water is allowed to simmer 3 to 4 hours. Cooking some bone and some fat with the lean meat is thought to improve the flavor.

Vegetables and seasonings should be added during the last hour of cooking to avoid the development of undesirable flavors resulting from the overcooking of some vegetables. When cooking is finished, the stock is poured through a colander to remove the meat, bone, and seasonings. When the stock is cool, the hard fat layer may be removed from the top.

The only difference between brown and white soup stock is that in the making of brown stock, about one-third of the meat cubes are first browned in a skillet. Water may be added to dissolve brown matter from the pan. The browned meat and water are then added to the soup kettle in which the remaining cubes have been placed in cold water.

The meat left from making soup stock retains many of its nutrients. The flavor is lacking, but other flavors from vegetables and condiments may be added so that the meat can be utilized. The meat can be cut into small pieces and served in the soup.

Bouillon is prepared by seasoning a soup stock. *Consommé* is an enriched or double-strength bouillon that has been clarified. It can be made from any kind of stock, although beef is most commonly used. One egg white and one crushed shell per quart of broth accomplish clarification. The broth is heated to the boiling point and boiled for a few minutes, after which it is poured through several thicknesses of cheesecloth to strain out the coagulated egg with its adhering particles. The material that is removed from the soup stock by clarifying is chiefly coagulated protein.

•GRAVY

Gravies or sauces are commonly used as accompaniments to enhance the flavor of meat. The drippings from fried, pan-broiled, or roasted meat and the cooking liquid from stewed or braised meats or poultry can be used to make gravy. Low temperatures for meat cookery usually produce a minimum of brown material. Particularly for the making of gravy, there should be no burned drippings. Gravies and some sauces may be served either thickened or unthickened. *Au jus* gravy goes naturally with roast beef and is unthickened. To thicken gravy, flour or another starch thickener can be added (1½ to 2 tablespoons per cup of liquid) in one of two ways: as a smooth flour and water paste or slurry, or as dry flour stirred into the fat. The latter method is usually preferable when the drippings contain little or no water. Excess fat in the pan should be removed before the flour is added. Once the approximate quantity of gravy desired is determined, 2 tablespoons of fat should be retained for each cup of gravy. When dry flour and fat in the drippings are blended together and cooked for a few minutes, they form a *roux*. Cold liquid can then be mixed gradually with the hot roux until a smooth gravy is formed. Heating is continued, with stirring, until the **starch gelatinizes** and the mixture thickens. Seasonings may then be added.

Starch gelatinization the swelling of starch granules when heated with moisture

In the alternate method of making gravy, a cold slurry of liquid and a thickener, such as flour, are mixed with hot liquid that has been added to the drippings, with constant stirring until the gravy thickens. The liquid used in gravies is usually water, but milk, meat stock, tomato juice, wine, vegetable juice, or other liquids may be used. The richer and more flavorful the drippings, the better the gravy. Gravies should be tasted before serving to make certain that the proper blending of flavors has been achieved.

A great variety of sauces can be served with meats. Sauces may be made from drippings but are often made without any meat components. White sauce (discussed in Chapter 13) may be the basis for some sauces served with meats. Tomato sauces go with meatballs and spaghetti, and mushroom sauce is often served with Swiss steak. Brushing broiled lamb chops with melted butter produces a sauce called *maître d'hôtel* butter.

•CARVING MEAT

509
Meat and Meat Cookery

Successful carving of meat is partly dependent on some knowledge of the anatomy of the cut to be carved. It is important to know something of the location of the joints and the direction in which the muscle fibers run. Insofar as possible, meats should be carved across the grain. Knives for carving should be well sharpened and of good-quality steel that will hold an edge well.

Carving should be done rapidly in order that the meat not become cold. Neatness and economy of cutting are also important. If some parts of the meat are better than others, such parts should be divided among those at the table rather than given to the first ones served. Enough meat to serve all at the table should be carved before the host starts to serve the plates. The slices are arranged neatly on the platter. Before inviting guests to be served a second time, the host should be sure that some meat is carved and ready.

Diagrams showing the techniques for carving certain cuts of meat are shown in Figure 21.20.

Beef Steak

Steak is one of the easiest meats to carve. With the steak lying flat on the platter, the fork is inserted in a suitable position for holding the steak firmly. Steaks from the loin (top loin, T-bone, porterhouse, and sirloin) have the bone separated from the meat before the meat is carved. The knife is allowed to follow the bone closely until the meat is completely separated. The meat is then cut into pieces of a suitable size for serving. Porterhouse and T-bone steaks are usually carved so that each person receives some tenderloin and some outer muscle. Steaks are cut with, rather than across, the fiber.

Standing Rib Roast

A standing rib roast is placed before the carver with the rib side to the left. The carver inserts a fork between two ribs. The knife passes from the outer edge toward the ribs in removing a slice of meat. Slices may vary in thickness, but 1/4 to 3/8 of an inch is desirable. After several slices have been carved, the knife is used to separate the slices from the bone. Each slice is then transferred to the platter.

Rolled Rib Roast

Horizontal slices are cut from the top of a rolled rib roast.

Pot Roasts

Insofar as possible, slices of pot roasts should be cut across the grain. Some cuts used for pot roasts may have fibers running in several directions, in which case it is difficult to carve across the fibers. If the muscles are separated first, cutting across the grain is easier.

Ham

The shank bone of the ham is placed toward the carver's right. The larger muscles of the ham are sliced by cutting straight down from the outer edge to the

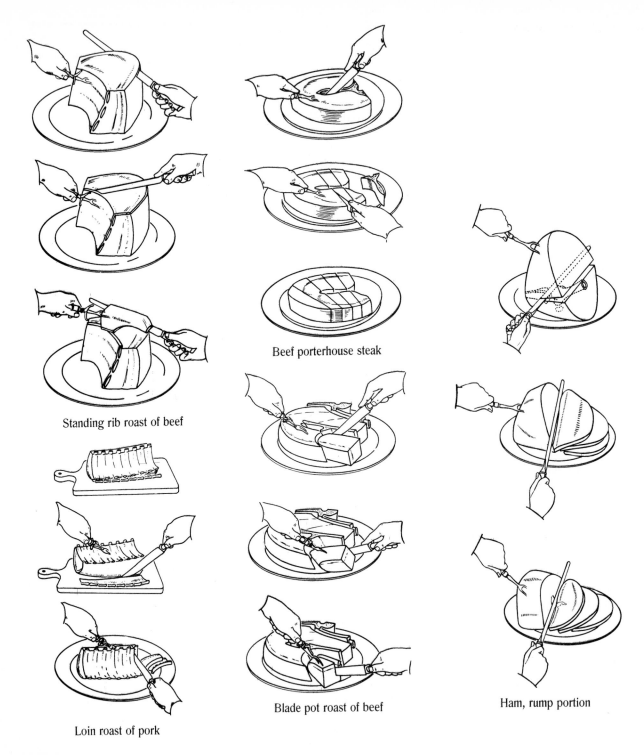

Beef porterhouse steak

Standing rib roast of beef

Loin roast of pork

Blade pot roast of beef

Ham, rump portion

FIGURE 21.20

Techniques for carving various cuts of meat. (Courtesy of the National Live Stock and Meat Board)

leg bone. After several slices have been carved, the knife is inserted in the last opening and is allowed to follow the bone, thus separating slices from the bone. Slices can then be lifted out.

Loin Roasts

A loin roast of pork is carved by cutting slices from the end of the roast. The roast is prepared at the market to make carving easy. The rib section has the backbone sawed loose from the ribs. The backbone is removed in the kitchen before the roast is placed on the platter. Cutting is done close along each side of the rib bone. One slice contains the rib, the next is boneless, and so on.

Leg of Lamb

The cushion of a leg of lamb, which is the most meaty portion, lies below the tail. The carver inserts a fork to bring the cushion into an upright position. Slices are then carved as from ham.

•SOY PROTEINS AND MEAT PROCESSING

The addition of soy ingredients in ground beef products results in reduced shrinkage on cooking and thus higher yields, while generally allowing the product to retain acceptable sensory quality. Soy proteins may also be added for nutritional enhancement. Consumer-acceptable beef patties made with the addition of various soy products are sold on the retail market. Combining textured soy-protein concentrate with a powdered soy concentrate that has emulsifying properties has been reported to produce the highest cooking yields with the greatest nutrient retention in the most economical manner [73]. At high substitution levels, however, soy flavor may be detected. Strong-flavored ingredients such as onions, tomatoes, and chilies can mask the flavor of soy. Soy products may also be used in combination with other substances to improve the flavor and texture of low-fat ground beef products [43].

The soybean is a source of good-quality protein, particularly in combination with some animal protein. Convenience foods produced from these vegetable protein products are marketed frozen, dehydrated, freeze-dried, and canned. An example of one of these foods is hickory-smoked strips, which can be used in place of bacon (Figure 21.21). Bacon-flavored bits for use in salads or combined with eggs and other foods are also made from soy protein. In the preparation of restructured meats, soy protein or wheat gluten products may be used to improve binding properties and to increase the cooking yield because of the higher retention of water.

Tofu or bean curd (see Chapter 15) also offers interesting opportunities to extend meat, fish, and poultry dishes. The texture of this product can vary from soft and creamy to extra firm, broadening its possible uses.

STUDY QUESTIONS

1. Meat is basically muscle tissue containing some fat and bone. Briefly describe what meat is like in structure, including each of the following components in your explanation.
   a. Muscle proteins—myosin and actin
   b. Myofibrils
   c. Muscle fibers
   d. Bundles of muscle fibers (making the grain of the meat)
   e. Muscles (such as tenderloin and rib eye)
   f. Connective tissue
   g. Connective tissue proteins—collagen and elastin
   h. Fat cells, fatty tissues, and marbling
   i. Bone
2. a. List the major and minor components of meat.
   b. The protein content of meat varies with the amount of fat. How much protein is usually present in lean muscle?
   c. What vitamins and minerals does meat provide in significant amounts?
3. Explain why the color of meat may change from a purplish red to a bright red when exposed to air. Explain why meat may turn a brownish color when held too long. What is responsible for the typical cured meat color?
4. a. What is *rigor mortis* and why is it important in a study of meat?
   b. Why is beef aged? What changes occur during aging or ripening of meat?
5. List several factors that may affect tenderness of meat and discuss what effect each factor has on tenderness.
6. Meat and poultry labeling is the responsibility of the USDA.
   a. What must be included on a meat or poultry label?
   b. What nutrient content claims can be made?
7. Explain what the round inspection stamp on meat carcasses implies.
8. a. Why are meats graded and by whom are they graded? Is this a mandatory or voluntary program?
   b. Explain the difference between quality grades and yield grades for meat. What factors are considered in each?
   c. From the following list of quality grade names, indicate which apply to beef, which to veal, and which to lamb.
      (1) Prime   (2) Choice

(3) Select   (7) Cutter
(4) Standard   (8) Canner
(5) Commercial   (9) Cull
(6) Utility   (10) Good

9. a. Name the wholesale cuts of beef and pork.
   b. Name several retail cuts that come from each wholesale cut listed in question a.
   c. Which wholesale cuts of beef are usually tender? Which are less tender?
   d. Be able to identify pictures of each of the following retail cuts of meat.

Beef	*Pork*
Rib steak and roast	Rib chops
Top loin steak	Loin chops
T-bone steak	Blade steak
Porterhouse steak	Ham
Sirloin steak	
Roundsteak or roast	
Blade steak or roast	
Arm steak or roast	
Flank steak	
Brisket	
Short ribs	

10. What are *restructured meats*? What advantages do they offer?
11. Name several variety meats and discuss possible advantages for their use in meal planning.
12. a. Name several cuts of meat that are commonly cured.
    b. What ingredients are usually used in the curing process? Discuss advantages and disadvantages of the use of nitrite as a curing ingredient.
13. Describe appropriate storage conditions for meat in the kitchen.
14. How does heat generally affect muscle fibers? Connective tissue? Explain why this information is important in deciding how to cook tender and less tender cuts of meat.
15. When meat is cooked by any method it usually loses weight. Account for this weight or cooking loss.
16. Describe the usual procedures used in cooking meat by each of the following methods. Indicate whether each is a dry-heat or a moist-heat method. Also suggest several cuts of meat that may appropriately be cooked by each of the methods listed.
    a. Roasting   e. Microwave cooking
    b. Broiling   f. Braising
    c. Pan-broiling   g. Stewing
    d. Frying   h. Pressure cooking
17. In roasting, broiling, and pan-broiling, when should meats be salted and why?
18. Describe how frozen meats may be appropriately handled in preparation for cooking.
19. a. What oven temperatures are most satisfactory when roasting tender cuts of beef? Less tender cuts? Explain why these temperatures are appropriate.
    b. Why should a meat thermometer be used when roasting meat?
20. What types of compounds appear to be important components of meat flavor?
21. Describe appropriate procedures for the preparation of the following.
    a. Soup stock
    b. Gravy
22. Describe several soybean protein products that are available for use in meat processing or as meat extenders in cooking.

REFERENCES

1. Adams, C. E. 1990. Use of HACCP in meat and poultry inspection. *Food Technology 44*, 169 (No. 5).

2. Akinwunmi, I., L. D. Thompson, and C. B. Ramsey. 1993. Marbling, fat trim, and doneness effects on sensory attributes, cooking loss, and composition of cooked beef steaks. *Journal of Food Science 58*, 242.

3. Al-Obaidy, H. M., M. A. Khan, and B. P. Klein. 1984. Comparison between sensory quality of freshly prepared spaghetti with meat sauce before and after hot holding on a cafeteria counter. *Journal of Food Science 49*, 1475.

4. Arnold, R. N., K. K. Scheller, S. C. Arp, S. N. Williams, and D. M. Schaefer. 1993. Dietary alpha-tocopheryl acetate enhances beef quality in Holstein and beef breed steers. *Journal of Food Science 58*, 28.

5. Baity, M. R., A. E. Ellington, and M. Woodburn. 1969. Foil wrap in oven cooking. *Journal of Home Economics 61*, 174.

6. Bakanowski, S. M., and J. M. Zoller. 1984. Endpoint temperature distributions in microwave and conventionally cooked pork. *Food Technology 38*, 45 (No. 2).

7. Berry, B. W., and K. F. Leddy. 1984. Effects of fat level and cooking method on sensory and textural properties of ground beef patties. *Journal of Food Science 48*, 1715.

8. Bouton, P. E., P. V. Harris, and D. Ratcliff. 1981. Effect of cooking temperature and time on the shear properties of meat. *Journal of Food Science 46*, 1082.

9. Bowers, J. A., J. A. Craig, D. H. Kropf, and T. J. Tucker. 1987. Flavor, color, and other characteristics of beef longissimus muscle heated to seven internal temperatures between 55° and 85°C. *Journal of Food Science 52*, 533.

10. Browning, M. A., D. L. Huffman, W. R. Egbert, and S. B. Jungst. 1990. Physical and compositional characteristics of beef carcasses selected for leanness. *Journal of Food Science 55*, 9.

11. Costello, C. A., M. P. Penfield, and M. J. Riemann. 1985. Quality of restructured steaks: Effects of days on feed, fat level, and cooking method. *Journal of Food Science 50*, 685.

12. Cover, S., and R. L. Hostetler. 1960. *Beef Tenderness*. Texas Agricultural Experiment Station Bulletin No. 947. College Station, TX: Texas Agricultural Experiment Station.

13. Cross, H. R., B. W. Berry, and L. H. Wells. 1980. Effects of fat level and source on the chemical, sensory, and cooking properties of ground beef patties. *Journal of Food Science 45*, 791.

14. Dolezal, H. G., G. C. Smith, J. W. Savell, and Z. L. Carpenter. 1982. Comparison of subcutaneous fat thickness, marbling and quality grade for predicting palatability of beef. *Journal of Food Science 47*, 397.

15. Drew, F., and K. S. Rhee, 1979. Microwave cookery of beef patties: Browning methods. *Journal of the American Dietetic Association 74*, 652.

16. Drew, F., K. S. Rhee, and Z. L. Carpenter. 1980. Cooking at variable microwave power levels. *Journal of the American Dietetic Association 77*, 455.

17. Egbert, W. R., and D. P. Cornforth. 1986. Factors influencing color of dark cutting beef muscle. *Journal of Food Science 51*, 57.

18. Egbert, W. R., D. L. Huffman, C. Chen, and D. P. Dylewski. 1991. Development of low-fat ground beef. *Food Technology 45*, 64 (No. 6).

19. Etherton, T. D. 1993. The new bio-tech foods. *Food and Nutrition News 65*, 13 (No. 3).

20. Fabiansson, S., and R. Libelius. 1985. Structural changes in beef longissimus dorsi induced by postmortem low voltage electrical stimulation. *Journal of Food Science 50*, 39.

21. Fogle, D. R., R. F. Plimpton, H. W. Ockerman, L. Jarenback, and T. Persson. 1982. Tenderization of beef: Effect of enzyme, enzyme level, and cooking method. *Journal of Food Science 47*, 1113.

22. Funk, K., and M. A. Boyle. 1972. Beef cooking rates and losses. *Journal of the American Dietetic Association 61*, 404.

23. Gariepy, C., J. Amiot, S. A. Pommier, P. M. Flipot, and V. Girard. 1992. Electrical stimulation and 48 hours aging of bull and steer carcasses. *Journal of Food Science 57*, 541.

24. Giese, J. H. 1992. Developing low-fat meat products. *Food Technology 46*, 100 (No. 4).

25. Gravely, M. H. 1993. Understanding the new meat and poultry labels. *Food News for Consumers 10*, 8 (No. 1–2).

26. Gray, J. I., S. K. Reddy, J. F. Price, A. Mandagere, and W. F. Wilkens. 1982. Inhibition of N-nitrosamines in bacon. *Food Technology 36*, 39 (No. 6).

27. Hamm, R. 1982. Postmortem changes in muscle with regard to processing of hot-boned beef. *Food Technology 36*, 105 (No. 11).

28. Harrison, D. L., J. A. Bowers, L. L. Anderson, H. J. Tuma, and D. H. Kropf. 1970. Effect of aging on palatability and selected related characteristics of pork loin. *Journal of Food Science 35*, 292.

29. Hines, R. C., C. B. Ramsey, and T. L. Hoes. 1980. Effects of microwave cooking rate on palatability of pork loin chops. *Journal of Animal Science 50*, 446.

30. Hood, M. P. 1960. Effect of cooking method and grade on beef roasts. *Journal of the American Dietetic Association 37*, 363.

31. Howat, P. M., L. M. Sievert, P. J. Myers, K. L. Koonce, and T. D. Bidner. 1983. Effect of marination upon mineral content and tenderness of beef. *Journal of Food Science 48*, 662.

32. Jacobs, D. K., and J. G. Sebranek. 1980. Use of prerigor beef for frozen ground beef patties. *Journal of Food Science 45*, 648.

33. Jennings, T. G., B. W. Berry, and A. L. Joseph. 1978. Influence of fat thickness, marbling, and length of aging on beef palatability and shelf-life characteristics. *Journal of Animal Science 46*, 658.

34. Johnston, M. B., and R. E. Baldwin. 1980. Influence of microwave reheating on selected quality factors of roast beef. *Journal of Food Science 45*, 1460.

35. Koehler, K. M., W. C. Hunt, and P. J. Garry. 1992. Meat, poultry, and fish consumption and nutrient intake in the healthy elderly. *Journal of the American Dietetic Association 92*, 325.

36. Koohmaraie, M., S. C. Seideman, J. E. Schollmeyer, T. R. Dutson, and A. S. Babiker. 1988. Factors associated with the tenderness of three bovine muscles. *Journal of Food Science 53*, 407.

37. Korschgen, B. M., R. E. Baldwin, and S. Snider. 1976. Quality factors in beef, pork, and lamb cooked by microwaves. *Journal of the American Dietetic Association 69*, 635.

38. Korschgen, B. M., J. M. Berneking, and R. E. Baldwin. 1980. Energy requirements for cooking beef rib roasts. *Journal of Food Science 45*, 1054.

39. Kotula, A. W., K. D. Murrell, L. Acosta-Stein, L. Lamb, and L. Douglass. 1983. Destruction of *Trichinella spiralis* during cooking. *Journal of Food Science 48*, 765.

40. Laakkonen, E., G. H. Wellington, and J. W. Sherbon. 1970. Low-temperature, long-time heating of bovine muscle. 1. Changes in tenderness, water-binding capacity, pH and amount of water-soluble components. *Journal of Food Science 35*, 175.

41. Leander, R. C., H. B. Hedrick, M. F. Brown, and J. A. White. 1980. Comparison of structural changes in bovine longissimus and semitendinosus muscles during cooking. *Journal of Food Science 45*, 1.

42. Leverton, R. M., and G. V. Odell. 1985. *The Nutritive Value of Cooked Meat*. Oklahoma Agricultural Experiment Station Miscellaneous Publication No. MP-49. Stillwater, OK: Oklahoma Agricultural Experiment Station.

43. Liu, M. N., D. L. Huffman, W. R. Egbert, T. A. McCaskey, and C. W. Liu. 1991. Soy protein and oil effects on chemical, physical and microbial stability of lean ground beef patties. *Journal of Food Science 56*, 906.

44. Love, J. A., and K. J. Prusa. 1992. Nutrient composition and sensory attributes of cooked ground beef: Effects of fat content, cooking method, and water rinsing. *Journal of the American Dietetic Association 92*, 1367.

45. MacLeod, G., and M. Seyyedain-Ardebeli. 1980. Sensory comparisons of the aroma of natural and some simulated beef flavors. *Journal of Food Science 45*, 431.

46. Mandigo, R. W. 1986. Restructuring of muscle foods. *Food Technology 40*, 85 (No. 3).

47. Marshall, N. 1960. Electronic cookery of top round of beef. *Journal of Home Economics 52*, 31.

48. Maruri, J. L., and D. K. Larick. 1992. Volatile concentration and flavor of beef as influenced by diet. *Journal of Food Science 57*, 1275.

49. McBee, J. L., Jr., and J. A. Wiles. 1967. Influence of marbling and carcass grade on the physical and chemical characteristics of beef. *Journal of Animal Science 26*, 701.

50. McComber, D. R., R. Clark, and D. F. Cox. 1990. Consumer preference for pork loin roasts cooked to 160°F and 185°F. *Journal of the American Dietetic Association 90*, 1718.

51. McDowell, M. D., D. L. Harrison, C. Pacey, and M. B. Stone. 1982. Differences between conventionally cooked top round roasts and semimembranous muscle strips cooked in a model system. *Journal of Food Science 47*, 1603.

52. McIntosh, E. N. 1967. Effect of postmortem aging and enzyme tenderizers on mucoprotein of bovine skeletal muscle. *Journal of Food Science 32*, 210.

53. McKeith, F. K., D. L. de Vol, R. S. Miles, P. J. Bechtel, and T. R. Carr. 1985. Chemical and sensory properties of thirteen major beef muscles. *Journal of Food Science 50*, 869.

54. *Meat and Poultry Inspection*. April 1987. FSIS Facts. Washington, DC: U.S. Department of Agriculture.

55. Miller, M. F., M. K. Andersen, C. B. Ramsey, and J. O. Reagan. 1993. Physical and sensory characteristics of low-fat ground beef patties. *Journal of Food Science 58*, 461.

56. Mitchell, G. E., J. E. Giles, S. A. Rogers, L. T. Tan, R. J. Naidoo, and D. M. Ferguson. 1991. Tenderizing, aging, and thawing effects on sensory, chemical, and physical properties of beef steaks. *Journal of Food Science 56*, 1125.

57. Mitchell, G. E., A. W. Reed, and S. A. Rogers. 1991. Influence of feeding regimen on the sensory qualities and fatty acid contents of beef steaks. *Journal of Food Science 56*, 1102.

58. Moody, W. G. 1983. Beef flavor: A review. *Food Technology 37*, 227 (No. 5).

59. Moore, L. J., D. L. Harrison, and A. D. Dayton. 1980. Differences among top round steaks cooked by dry or moist heat in a conventional or a microwave oven. *Journal of Food Science 45*, 777.

60. Morris, D. H. 1991. Meat and dietary guidance. *Food and Nutrition News 63*, 23 (No. 4).

61. Nielsen, M. M., and F. T. Hall. 1965. Dry-roasting of less tender beef cuts. *Journal of Home Economics 57*, 353.

62. Olson, D. G., F. Caporaso, and R. W. Mandigo. 1980. Effects of serving temperature on sensory evaluation of beef steaks from different muscles and carcass maturities. *Journal of Food Science 45*, 627.

63. Ono, K., B. W. Berry, and E. Paroczay. 1985. Contents and retention of nutrients in extra lean, lean and regular ground beef. *Journal of Food Science 50*, 701.

64. Oreskovich, D. C., P. J. Bechtel, F. K. McKeith, J. Novakofski, and E. J. Basgall. 1992. Marinade pH affects textural properties of beef. *Journal of Food Science 57*, 305.

65. Parrish, F. C., Jr., J. A. Boles, R. E. Rust, and D. G. Olson. 1991. Dry and wet aging effects on palatability attributes of beef loin and rib steaks from three quality grades. *Journal of Food Science 56*, 601.

66. Parrish, F. C., Jr., R. B. Young, B. E. Miner, and L. D. Andersen. 1973. Effect of postmortem conditions on certain chemical, morphological and organoleptic properties of bovine muscle. *Journal of Food Science 38*, 690.

67. Peterson, R. J., and S. S. Chang. 1982. Identification of volatile flavor compounds of fresh, frozen beef stew and a comparison of these with those of canned beef stew. *Journal of Food Science 47*, 1444.

68. Prusa, K. J., C. A. Fedler, and L. F. Miller. 1993. National in-home consumer evaluation of pork roasts from pigs administered porcine somatotropin (pST). *Journal of Food Science 58*, 480.

69. Putnam, J. J. 1991. Food consumption, 1070–90. *Food Review 14*, 2 (No. 3).

70. Ramsey, C. B., K. D. Lind, L. F. Tribble, and C. T. Gaskins, Jr. 1973. Diet, sex and vacuum packaging effects on pork aging. *Journal of Animal Science 37*, 40.

71. Rathje, W. L., and E. E. Ho. 1987. Meat fat madness: Conflicting patterns of meat fat consumption and their public health implications. *Journal of the American Dietetic Association 87*, 1357.

72. Recio, H. A., J. W. Savell, R. E. Branson, H. R. Cross, and G. C. Smith. 1987. Consumer ratings of restructured beef steaks manufactured to contain different residual contents of connective tissue. *Journal of Food Science 52*, 1461.

73. Rice, D. R., P. A. Neufer, and E. F. Sipos. 1989. Effects of soy protein blends, fat level, and cooking methods on the nutrient retention of beef patties. *Food Technology 43*, 88 (No. 4).

74. Rubin, L. J., L. L. Diosady, and A. R. O'Boyle. 1990. A nitrite-free meat-curing system. *Food Technology 44*, 130 (No. 6).

75. Sanderson, M., and G. E. Vail. 1963. Fluid content and tenderness of three muscles of beef cooked to three internal temperatures. *Journal of Food Science 28*, 590.

76. Savell, J. W., R. E. Branson, H. R. Cross, D. M. Stiffler, J. W. Wise, D. B. Griffin, and G. C. Smith. 1987. National consumer retail beef study: Palatability evaluations of beef loin steaks that differed in marbling. *Journal of Food Science 52*, 517.

77. Shorthose, W. R., and P. V. Harris. 1990. Effect of animal age on the tenderness of selected beef muscles. *Journal of Food Science 55*, 1.

78. Smiciklas-Wright, H. 1993. Meat as consumed in the U. S. *Food and Nutrition News 65*, 1 (No. 1).

79. Smith, G. C., Z. L. Carpenter, H. R. Cross, C. E. Murphey, H. C. Abraham, J. W. Savell, G. W. Davis, B. W. Berry, and F. C. Parrish, Jr. 1984. Relationship of USDA marbling groups to palatability of cooked beef. *Journal of Food Quality 7*, 289.

80. Smith, G. C., J. W. Savell, H. R. Cross, and Z. L. Carpenter. 1983. The relationship of USDA quality grade to beef flavor. *Food Technology 37*, 233 (No. 5).

81. Tatum, J. D., G. C. Smith, B. W. Berry, C. E. Murphey, F. L. Williams, and Z. L. Carpenter. 1980. Carcass characteristics, time on feed and cooked beef palatability attributes. *Journal of Animal Science 50*, 833.

82. Tatum, J. D., G. C. Smith, and Z. L. Carpenter. 1982. Interrelationships between marbling, subcutaneous fat thickness and cooked beef palatability. *Journal of Animal Science 54*, 777.

83. Troutt, E. S., M. C. Hunt, D. E. Johnson, J. R. Claus, C. L. Kastner, and D. H. Kropf. 1992. Characteristics of low-fat ground beef containing texture-modifying ingredients. *Journal of Food Science 52*, 19.

84. Troutt, E. S., M. C. Hunt, D. E. Johnson, J. R. Claus, C. L. Kastner, D. H. Kropf, and S. Stroda. 1992. Chemical, physical, and sensory characterization of ground beef containing 5 to 30 percent fat. *Journal of Food Science 57*, 25.

85. Voris, H. H., and F. O. van Duyne. 1979. Low wattage microwave cooking of top round roasts: Energy consumption, thiamin content and palatability. *Journal of Food Science 44*, 1447.

86. Wasserman, A. E., J. W. Pensabene, and E. G. Piotrowski. 1978. Nitrosamine formation in home-cooked bacon. *Journal of Food Science 43*, 276.

87. Yu, L. P., and Y. B. Lee. 1986. Effects of postmortem pH and temperature on bovine muscle structure and meat tenderness. *Journal of Food Science 51*, 774.

88. Zimmermann, W. J. 1983. An approach to safe microwave cooking of pork roasts containing *Trichinella spiralis*. *Journal of Food Science 43*, 1715.

Poultry and Fish

22

•POULTRY

The term *poultry* is used to describe all domesticated birds that are intended for human consumption. These include chickens, turkeys, ducks, geese, guinea fowl, squab (young pigeons), and pigeons. Chickens and turkeys are by far the most commonly consumed poultry items in the United States. Poultry is marketed throughout the year in a wide variety of forms, many of which are convenience foods.

Consumption

Poultry production is adaptable to most areas of the world, and it provides a good-quality protein food at a relatively modest cost to supplement the diets of many people. Much of the poultry in the United States is produced with the application of modern management practices. Thousands of birds are sometimes raised under one roof.

In Western countries, the lower fat content of poultry in comparison with red meats has encouraged a trend toward increased consumption of poultry. In 1990, the estimated per capita annual consumption of poultry in the United States was approximately equal to that of beef (64 pounds) on a boneless, trimmed weight basis [34]. The estimated consumption of chicken was 49 pounds, while that of turkey was 14 pounds. It is important to note that these figures do not take into account the quantity of beef and poultry used in pet foods. The use of poultry in pet foods has increased in recent years, especially the less desirable parts, such as necks, backs, and giblets.

Classification and Market Forms

The market forms of poultry have changed over the years. For example, in the early 1960s, whole dressed chicken accounted for 87 percent of chicken sales. Of all the chicken sold in the United States in 1989, however, only 18 percent was in the whole dressed form, while 50 percent was marketed as cut-up parts and 8 percent as boneless, unprocessed chicken [34]. The proliferation of fast-food chains that sell chicken fillet sandwiches and chicken nuggets is partly responsible for these changing market trends.

Poultry is classified on the basis of age and weight in Table 22.1. Ready-to-cook chickens, chilled or frozen, are marketed whole, halved, quartered, and in individual pieces such as breasts, thighs, drumsticks, and wings. Boneless parts are also sold, as are some pieces of skinless chicken. Ground raw chicken is being marketed in increasing quantities. Also available is boned, canned chicken. Many different precooked frozen convenience items are available, such as chicken cannelloni, chicken enchiladas, Mandarin chicken with vegetables (in a savory plum sauce), chicken with fettucini (with mushrooms and spinach in a cream sauce), sweet and sour chicken with rice, and glazed chicken breast (light style), as well as many different brands of fried chicken parts and chicken dinners. Restructured chicken, formed into boneless breaded pieces from chunks of chicken meat, is a popular finger food for dipping into sauces. A complete list of available convenience foods containing chicken would be very long indeed.

No longer just for holidays, turkey has become popular year-round. Turkey is marketed as frozen whole birds and as frozen breasts, which are essentially oven-ready, and also as ground raw turkey. Frozen boneless raw turkey roasts and boneless cooked turkey rolls are convenience items that are available in all white meat, all dark meat, or a combination of both. Canned boned turkey and many frozen turkey products, such as turkey pies, main-dish items, and turkey dinners, are also available.

TABLE 22.1
Poultry Classification

Type	Description	Age	Weight (lb)
Young chicken			
Broiler-fryer	Either sex; tender	9–12 weeks	2–2½
Roaster	Either sex; tender	3–5 months	3–5
Capon	Castrated male; tender	<8 months	4–8
Rock Cornish game hen	Cross of Cornish chicken with another breed; either sex; immature; tender	5–7 weeks	<2
Older chicken			
Baking hen	Female; tender	>10 months	3–6
Stewing hen or fowl	Mature female; less tender	>10 months	3–6
Young turkey			
Fryer-roaster	Either sex; tender	10–12 weeks	4–8
Young hen	Female; tender	5–7 months	8–15
Young tom	Male; tender	5–7 months	>12
Ducks	Either sex; tender	7–8 weeks	3–7
Geese	Either sex; tender	<11 weeks	6–12

Processing Poultry

Many improvements in technology have occurred in poultry processing plants in recent years. Automatic picking machines, which remove feathers from the slaughtered and scalded birds, have been developed and perfected, eliminating much hand labor. Processors eviscerate birds at the processing plant, rather than at the retail market, and then freeze them. The availability of new equipment has continued to mechanize the processing of poultry; for example, a cutting machine that makes possible the cutting up of broilers in the processing plant has greatly decreased labor requirements. Slaughtered, eviscerated poultry are chilled immediately, usually by immersion of the carcasses in chilled water, to control the growth of microorganisms [24].

About 25 percent of chickens leave processing plants with some detectable **Salmonella** bacteria. The U.S. Department of Agriculture's (USDA) Food Safety and Inspection Service has approved the use of trisodium phosphate (TSP) to reduce the incidence of salmonellae on the birds. After inspection and chilling, the chicken may be dipped into a TSP solution. This treatment can reduce to less than 5 percent the number of birds containing salmonellae. It does not affect the flavor, texture, or appearance of the chicken.

Polyphosphates are used in meat and poultry products to improve water binding, texture, color, and flavor. These characteristics are enhanced in ground turkey by the addition of polyphosphates [4, 23].

The use of ionizing radiation for the treatment of raw poultry and poultry products to control and reduce the population of pathogens such as *Salmonella, Campylobacter*, and *Listeria monocytogenes* has been approved by the USDA. Irradiation can be used to treat fresh or frozen, uncooked whole poultry carcasses or parts. Packages must bear an irradiation logo and the statement *treated with radiation* or *treated by irradiation*. They must also be labeled *keep refrigerated* or *keep frozen*. The shelf life of irradiated chicken has been reported to be as long as 15 days compared with about 6 days for unirradiated carcasses, as evidenced by the bacterial counts [20].

Composition and Nutritive Value

The composition and nutritive value of poultry do not differ substantially from those of other meats except that chicken and turkey breast, particularly, are lower in fat and cholesterol and higher in niacin than other lean meats with separable fat removed [38].

The fat of poultry is deposited in the muscle tissue, in thick layers under the skin, and in the abdominal cavity. In **capons**, there is more fat and a more uniform distribution of fat in the flesh than in chickens that have not been castrated. The fat of all types of poultry has a softer consistency and lower melting point than the fat of other meats. Goose and duck are higher in fat than chicken or turkey. Fat of mature birds has a pronounced flavor. Geese, particularly, have a distinctive flavor, which may be objectionable in old birds. The composition of chicken and turkey is given in Appendix C.

The amount of fat in ground chicken influences cooked yield and quality characteristics [42]. In one study, as fat content increased from 5 to 10 percent, cooking losses and moisture/protein ratios of grilled patties increased. Lower-

Salmonellae bacteria, some strains of which can cause illness in humans; because the microorganisms themselves produce the gastrointestinal symptoms, the illness is called a food infection

Capon a male bird castrated when young

FIGURE 22.1

A USDA poultry inspector examines birds in a broiler processing plant to ensure that they are free from disease. (Courtesy of the U.S. Department of Agriculture)

fat patties were harder, springier, less cohesive, and chewier than patties containing higher fat levels.

The light meat of poultry, particularly the breast, has shorter, more tender fibers that are less firmly bound together with connective tissue than those of dark meat. As in mammals, the amount of connective tissue in poultry varies with age; it is more abundant in old birds, especially males.

Buying Poultry

Changes in the efficiency of production and the processing of poultry have greatly increased the supply of poultry meat on a year-round basis. Prices of poultry have become competitive with other meat products, and poultry is a popular item with the American consumer. More and more often, poultry is being chosen in preference to red meats.

In poultry, there is a relatively high proportion of waste from the raw carcass to the cooked bird. The yield of cooked weight for young chickens has been reported to be 65 percent of the raw weight for those that were baked and 73 percent for those that were simmered [29]. Skin, fat, and bone accounted for about 50 percent of the weight of the cooked chicken. Thus, the yield of cooked edible meat from the raw chicken carcass was about 35 percent. Losses vary with the temperature and method of cooking and with the percentage of fat. The high fat content of ducks and geese results in particularly high cooking losses.

Inspection

Federal legislation passed in 1968, the Wholesome Poultry Products Act, is similar to the Meat Inspection Act. It requires that all poultry marketed in the United States be inspected for sanitary processing and freedom from disease. This inspection is performed either by agents of the federal government or by

FIGURE 22.2

U.S. Department of Agriculture inspection mark for poultry. (Courtesy of the U.S. Department of Agriculture)

adequate state systems. The inspection process in a poultry production plant is illustrated in Figure 22.1. The handling of both poultry and meat inspection at the federal level is the responsibility of the Food Safety and Inspection Service of the USDA.

The USDA inspection mark appears in Figure 22.2. Poultry bearing the official mark, often printed on a tag attached to the wing, must come from a healthy flock, be processed under specified sanitary conditions, contain only approved additives, and be properly packaged and labeled. Prepared poultry products, such as canned, boned poultry, frozen dinners and pies, and specialty items, must also be produced with USDA inspection.

The 1990 Nutrition Education and Labeling Act mandates nutrition labels on processed poultry products. As with meat, merchandisers can choose to provide nutrition information on raw, single-ingredient poultry products such as raw chicken legs. This information may appear on labels, posters, pamphlets, or videos in the store. The nutrient content claims that are allowed for poultry are the same as for meat; these are discussed on page 473. The other requirements for a poultry label include the product name, the name and address of the producer or distributor, the inspection mark, the ingredients and net weight, the establishment number identifying the plant where the product was processed, and the handling instructions. After the product leaves the processing plant it comes under the jurisdiction of the FDA, which is responsible for preventing the sale of adulterated food, including poultry.

Grading

In addition to inspecting for wholesomeness, the USDA has developed standards for quality grades. These grades—A, B, and C—are placed on the label in a shield-shaped mark (see Figures 22.3 and 22.4). Signs of quality that are evaluated in grading include conformation or shape of the bird, fleshing, distribution and amount of fat, and freedom from pinfeathers, skin and flesh blemishes, cuts, and bruises.

Many states participate in a grading program, and in such states the official stamp reads *Federal-State Graded*. Grading of poultry is not mandatory but consumers profit by its use. It provides an assurance of quality and class as stated, permits selection of the desired quality for the intended use, and helps in evaluating variable prices. Differences between Grades A and B can be noted by an examination of Figure 22.5.

Characteristics of Age in Poultry

In a young bird, the end of the breastbone is pliable and the wing offers little resistance when it is bent into an upright position. The skin of a young bird is pliable and soft and tears easily. An older bird has a hard, calcified breastbone and may show an abundance of long hairs. Greater weight is not necessarily an indication of age, as some breeds of poultry grow very large. In young birds, sex differences are not significant; however, with increase in age, male birds are inferior in flavor to female birds. Older males are also more tough and stringy and less juicy.

Most poultry sold in retail markets are young tender birds. However, poultry should be purchased with the intended use in mind. The class name sometimes suggests the cooking method, for example, broiler-fryers and roasters.

FIGURE 22.3
The U.S. Department of Agriculture grade shield denotes that poultry has been graded for quality. Poultry must first be inspected for wholesomeness, however. (Courtesy of the U.S. Department of Agriculture)

FIGURE 22.4
The wing tag may include the class name—in this case, Frying Chicken—in addition to the inspection mark and the grade mark. (Courtesy of the U.S. Department of Agriculture)

FIGURE 22.5

Grading for quality is not required by law, but many firms choose to have their poultry graded. U.S. Grade A (*left*) and U.S. Grade B (*right*) young turkeys are shown. (Courtesy of the U.S. Department of Agriculture)

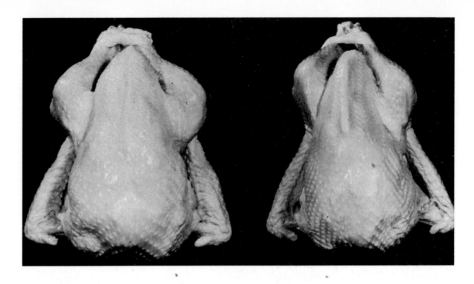

Amount to Buy

Table 22.2 gives the estimated number of servings from a pound of ready-to-cook poultry. Whole chickens usually cost slightly less per pound than those already cut into individual pieces. Figure 22.6 shows a procedure to follow in disjointing whole chickens. As we refer to this figure, perhaps we should ask the question, "What is wrong with this picture?" As you will note, the disjointing of the chicken is being performed on a wooden cutting board. We now recognize that, since wood cannot easily be sterilized, it should not be used for cutting raw poultry: cross-contamination with the cooked product or other foods may occur. The use of a plastic cutting board is recommended.

So that individual preferences for various poultry parts may be satisfied, pieces of all one kind, such as chicken breasts or drumsticks, are often packaged together and sold. As Table 22.2 indicates, more poultry is needed per serving when such pieces as wings or thighs are purchased than when breasts, which contain less bone, are bought. The cost per serving should be compared, in these cases, rather than the cost per pound.

Storage and Handling

Chilled, raw poultry is a very perishable product and should be stored at a refrigerator temperature of 4°C (40°F) or below. Even at refrigerator temperatures, storage time is usually limited to a few days, although irradiation may increase the shelf life. The transparent wrap on prepackaged poultry is designed for refrigerator storage after purchase. In fact, repackaging chicken for short-term storage in the refrigerator may actually increase the bacterial count as a result of the additional handling [10].

Because some poultry carries salmonellae and therefore is contaminated with this food-poisoning organism when it is brought into the kitchen, special precautions in handling are necessary. All surfaces, such as countertops and cutting boards, that come into contact with raw poultry during its preparation for cooking should be thoroughly cleaned and sanitized before other foods are

TABLE 22.2

Number of Servings from a Pound of Ready-to-Cook Poultry

Kind and Class	Approximate Servings of Cooked Meat		Approximate Yield of Cooked, Diced Meat (c)
	Size of Serving	Number of Servings	
Chicken			
Whole			
Broiler-fryer	3 oz without bone	2	1¼
Roaster	3 oz without bone	2¼	1½
Stewing hen	3 oz without bone	2	1¼
Pieces			
Breast halves (about 5¾ ounces each)	1, about 2¾ oz without bone	2¾	
Drumsticks (about 3 ounces each)	2, about 2½ oz without bone	2½	
Thighs (about 3¾ ounces each)	2, about 3 oz without bone	2¼	
Wings (about 2¾ ounces each)	4, about 2¾ oz without bone	1½	
Breast quarter (about 11 ounces each)	1, about 4½ oz without bone	1½	
Leg quarter (about 10¾ ounces each)	1, about 4¼ oz without bone	1½	
Turkey			
Whole	3 oz without bone	2¼	1¼
Pieces			
Breast	3 oz without bone	2¾	1¾
Thigh	3 oz without bone	2¾	
Drumstick	3 oz without bone	2½	
Wing	3 oz without bone	1¾	
Ground	3 oz	3¾	
Boneless turkey roast	3 oz	3¼	
Duckling	3 oz without bone	1	
Goose	3 oz without bone	1¾	

Source: Reference 32.

placed on them. Cutting boards made of wood, which cannot be adequately sterilized, should not be used for cutting up raw poultry. These precautions are necessary to avoid cross-contamination of cooked poultry and other foods prepared on the same surfaces as raw poultry that may be infected with salmonellae. *Salmonella* food poisoning is discussed in Chapter 3.

Poultry should always be cooked to a well-done stage to destroy any food-poisoning organisms that may be present. However, cooked poultry products are ideal for the growth and/or toxin production of any microorganisms with which they may have been contaminated during handling and serving. They should, therefore, always be refrigerated promptly and used within 1 to 2 days. If it is anticipated that cooked poultry will be kept longer than this time, it should be placed in a moisture/vapor-proof wrapping or container and frozen. Stuffing should be removed from cooked poultry and stored separately in a covered container.

FIGURE 22.6

Disjointing a chicken. (Courtesy of the U.S. Department of Agriculture)

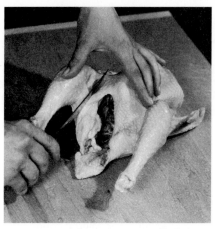

Cut the skin between the thighs and body of the bird.

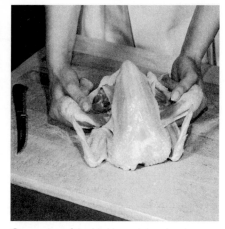

Grasp a leg of the bird in each hand and lift the bird from the table, bending its legs back as you lift. Bend the legs until the hip joints are free.

Remove the wing from the body. Start cutting on the inside of the wing just over the joint. Cut down and around the joint. To make the wing lie flat, either cut off the wing tip or make a cut on the inside of the wing at the large wing joint; cut just deep enough to expose the bones.

Turn the body of the bird over and remove the other leg-and-thigh piece and the other wing in the same way. Separate the thigh and leg at the knee joint. Divide the body by placing the bird on its neck end and cutting through the meat from the back to the tail along the end of the ribs. Then cut along each side of the backbone through the rib joints, then between the backbone and flat bone at the side of the back. Cut the skin that attaches the neck-and-back strip to the breast.

Remove the leg-and-thigh piece from one side of the body by cutting from back to front as close as possible to the bones in the back of the bird.

Locate the knee joint by squeezing the thigh and leg together. Cut through this joint to separate the thigh and leg.

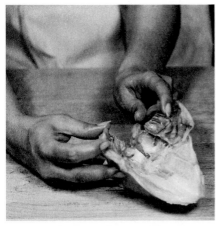

Place the neck-and-back strip, skin side up, on a cutting board. Cut the strip in two just above the spoon-shaped bones in the back. Place the breast, skin side down, on the cutting board. Cut through the white cartilage at the V of the neck as shown.

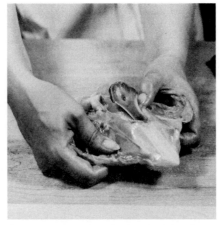

Grasp the breast piece firmly in both hands. Bend each side of the breast back and push up with the fingers to snap out the breastbone. Cut the breast in half lengthwise.

The disjointed chicken. Meaty pieces at left—legs, thighs, wings, breast halves. Bony pieces at right—wing tips, back strip, back, and neck.

Raw as well as cooked poultry can be frozen for longer storage periods. Better flavor and texture are maintained in the uncooked than in the cooked frozen product when they are to be stored for a few months. It is generally not wise to freeze or even refrigerate uncooked, stuffed poultry unless this is done commercially. Stuffed poultry should be cooked immediately on stuffing, because the time required for total cooling and/or freezing is too long. Undesirable microorganisms may grow because stuffings are also excellent media for bacterial growth.

Processed poultry products are popular for use in the foodservice industry since they are uniform in weight, shape, yield, composition, and cooking requirements. Some of these are now being distributed in a precooked form that requires only refrigeration rather than freezing. This is possible because the raw poultry product may be vacuum packaged in a multilaminate film, cooked, and then marketed in the same package. When vacuum-packaged, uncured precooked turkey breast rolls were evaluated for microbiologic stability past 30 days of storage at 4°C (40°F), no colonies of **psychrotrophic** aerobic **bacteria** were detected; however, some **mesophilic** anaerobic **bacteria** were present. These findings indicate that precautions should be taken when serving these precooked poultry products to ensure that they are not temperature abused. This means that they should not be held at higher than refrigerator temperatures for any period that would allow bacteria to multiply. They must always be refrigerated [37].

Psychrotrophic bacteria bacteria that grow best at cold temperatures (cold-loving bacteria)

Mesophilic bacteria bacteria that grow best at moderate temperatures

Cooking Poultry

The fundamental principles of cooking poultry do not differ from those for other meats. Dry-heat methods (broiling, frying, baking, and roasting) are applicable to young, tender birds. Moist-heat methods should be applied to older, less tender birds to make them tender and palatable. Most of the poultry sold on the market today is young and tender and can be cooked by dry-heat methods. As with meat, poultry should not be washed in water before cooking.

Roasting

All kinds of young, tender poultry can be roasted or baked. Poultry roasted whole can be stuffed (Figure 22.7) or unstuffed. Unstuffed poultry cooks more rapidly.

One of the problems associated with roasting whole poultry arises from the necessity of cooking all parts of the bird in one cooking operation even-though some parts are more tender than others. The breast may be over-cooked and dry by the time the legs and thighs are cooked to the desired degree of doneness.

To determine the stage of doneness of large-sized poultry, particularly turkeys, a thermometer can be inserted in the thickest part of the thigh muscle or in the breast muscle. Internal thigh temperatures of 82° to 85°C (180° to 185°F) appear to produce a desired degree of doneness without an objection-able decrease in juiciness [2, 15]. Pop-up timers, which are internal tempera-

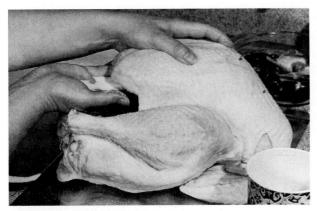

Lightly salt body cavity, if desired.

Fill the body and neck cavities lightly with prepared stuffing; allow about 1/2 cup stuffing for each pound of ready-to-cook poultry.

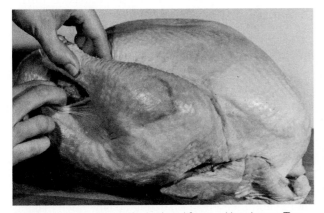

Fold the neck skin over to the back and fasten with a skewer. Turn the wing tips back to rest against the folded neck skin. Tuck the ends of the legs under the band of skin at the tail.

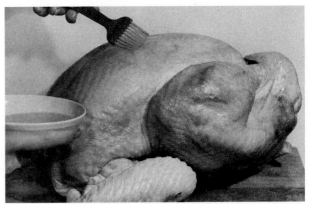

Poultry may be lightly brushed with melted fat before placing it, breast side up, on a rack in an open roasting pan. If poultry browns early in the roasting period, the breast and drumsticks may be lightly covered with aluminum foil or with a thin cloth moistened with fat.

FIGURE 22.7
Preparing a turkey for roasting. (Courtesy of the National Turkey Federation)

ture-indicating devices, are sometimes placed in the breasts of turkeys during processing and are usually set for 85°C (185°F). However, cooking frozen turkeys to an internal temperature, measured in the breast and thigh, of at least 71° ±2°C (160° ±4°F), by both high and low oven temperatures, has also been reported to be satisfactory. This internal temperature was high enough to essentially sterilize the poultry so that no food-poisoning problems would be likely to occur [5].

Variable oven temperatures, within a moderate range, appear to be satisfactory for roasting turkeys. Palatability scores for the tenderness and juiciness of both light and dark meat were found to be similar for turkeys roasted at three different oven temperatures—300°, 325°, and 350°F [12]. Drippings and total cooking losses were also similar at the three temperatures.

An aluminum foil tent is sometimes used to cover the breast of turkeys during roasting to prevent overbrowning. Alternatively, the whole bird can be wrapped in foil, although lower palatability for foil-wrapped turkeys versus open pan-roasted birds has been reported [8]. Palatability is probably similar for birds roasted with the breast either up or down in the roasting rack.

General recommendations for roasting turkey might be an oven temperature of 325°F and an internal temperature in the thigh muscle of 82° to 85°C (180° to 185°F). Table 22.3 is a roasting guide for poultry. The internal temperature of turkey meat, both whole birds and light or dark meat roasts, appears to be a good guide in cooking. The yield and juiciness of cooked meat decrease as the internal temperature increases from 40° to 90°C (104° to 194°F). At the same time, the scores for odor, flavor, and mealiness increase with increasing temperature [16].

Oil is sometimes injected into the breast just below the skin during the processing of turkeys to produce a self-basting effect during cooking. Coconut and palm oils are often used. According to one study [31], the moistness of the breast meat was not affected by self-basting, but a higher proportion of fat appeared in the drippings. In another study [5], however, oil-basted turkeys were considered significantly more juicy and tender than unbasted birds. Injecting fat into the major muscles of the breast has produced a decrease in moisture and an increase in fat in the cooked meat. An analysis of the extracted fat indicated that the fat increase was representative of the injected fat [30].

The yield of cooked meat, fat, and skin from roasted or braised turkeys has been reported [7] to be about 55 percent of the ready-to-cook weight. The cooked lean meat without fat and skin was 46 percent of raw weight for turkeys and 41 percent for chickens.

Convection ovens are often used to bake turkey products, particularly in institutional foodservice. Turkey rolls covered with aluminum foil and placed in an oven of about 225°F took considerably longer to cook than did similar products at 325°F, but used significantly less electrical energy and had higher ratings for juicy mouth-feel [3]. Foodservice managers need to consider the relative importance of time and energy, and their effect on eating quality, when making a decision as to cooking procedure.

Broiling

For broiling, young tender birds are cut into halves, quarters, or smaller pieces. Small young chickens and small fryer-roaster turkey pieces are appropriately broiled.

TABLE 22.3

Timetable for Roasting Poultry

| Kind | Purchased Weight (lb)[a] | Approximate Total Roasting Time at 325°F (hours)[b] | |
		Fresh or Thawed Poultry (32° to 40°F)	Frozen Poultry (0°F or below)[c]
Chickens			
Whole			
Broiler-fryer	2¼–3¼	1¾–2½	2–3
Roaster	3¼–4½	2–3[d]	2½–3½
Capon	5–8½	3–4[d]	
Rock Cornish game hen	1–2	1½–2[d]	
Pieces	¼–¾	1–2½	1–2¾
Ducks	4–6	2½–4[d]	3½–4½
Geese	6–8	3–3½	
Turkeys			
Whole	6–8	3–3½[d]	
	8–12	3½–4½[d]	
	12–16	4½–5½[d]	5½–6½
	16–20	5½–6½[d]	
	20–24	6½–7[d]	7–8½
Halves, whole breasts	5–11	3–5½	4¼–6¼
Quarters, thighs, drumsticks	1–3	2–3½	2–3¾
Boneless turkey roasts	3–10	3–4	

[a] Weight of giblets and neck included for whole poultry.

[b] Cooking time is only approximate; a meat thermometer can be used to help determine doneness of whole turkeys, large turkey pieces, and boneless turkey roasts. The temperature in the inner thigh of whole turkeys and in the center of the thickest part of turkey pieces should reach 180° to 185°F. Turkey roasts are done when the temperature reaches 170° to 175°F in the center. Stuffing temperature should reach at least 165°F.

[c] Unstuffed poultry. Do not use for frozen commercially stuffed turkeys; follow package directions.

[d] Cooking time suggested is for stuffed poultry; unstuffed poultry may take slightly less time to cook.

Source: Reference 32.

The pieces are placed on a slotted grid or rack on the broiler pan. Joints may be snapped so that pieces lie flat. With the broiler rack placed 5 to 6 inches from the flame or heating element, chicken pieces broiled for 20 to 25 minutes on each side should be cooked well done. Turkey pieces require 30 to 35 minutes on each side. Tongs should be used to turn the poultry pieces during broiling.

The flavor and color of broiled poultry may be enhanced by basting during broiling or by applying a coating or breading mixture before cooking. Coating greatly reduces cooking losses not only with broiling but also with other cooking methods [33].

Frying

Pieces of young chickens are frequently fried. In fact, fried chicken has become a popular fast food. The pieces are first coated by being rolled in seasoned flour mixtures, batters, or egg and crumbs [6, 39]. Slow, careful cooking is necessary when pan-frying to prevent overbrowning before the birds are done. Usually, 40 to 60 minutes is required to cook the flesh thoroughly, part of this time with the frying pan covered.

When they are fried in deep fat, pieces of chicken may be steamed almost done before being dipped in flour, batter, or egg and crumbs and then browned in the heated fat. Deep-fat fried chicken may also be coated and fried from the raw state. It is cooked at 165° to 175°C (325° to 350°F) for 20 to 30 minutes, depending on the size of the chicken piece. Pressure deep-fat fryers have been developed especially for the frying of poultry in the food-processing and foodservice industries.

The amounts of batter and breading used on food products has increased in recent years, and breading losses are a problem in the food industry. To improve adhesion of batters to poultry patties or nuggets, hydrocolloids such as xanthan or guar gums may be added to the batter. The increased apparent viscosity of the hydrocolloid-containing batters is positively correlated with batter adhesion [17].

Young chickens may be oven-fried at about 400°F. The pieces are first coated and then placed in a baking pan containing a small amount of oil. The chicken is turned midway through the baking process.

Braising

Braising is cooking in steam in a covered container. The term *fricassee* is often applied to cut pieces of chicken that are braised. Usually, the pieces are browned by first frying them in a small amount of fat. After this, moisture is added and the poultry is simmered in a covered skillet until tender and well done. The pieces of poultry can also first be cooked until they are tender and then fried until brown. A sauce or gravy made from the pan liquor is often served over the poultry pieces. Braising tenderizes older, less tender poultry but is also an appropriate method for cooking young birds.

Stewing

For stewing, birds are usually cut into pieces, although whole birds may be cooked in water seasoned with spices and herbs and vegetables. The poultry should be simmered in a relatively large amount of water until tender.

Microwave Cooking

A small turkey and a plump broiler-fryer are the best poultry choices for microwaving. Older stewing chickens are better simmered by conventional methods.

For microwaving of whole poultry, the ends of the wings and legs should be shielded with foil to prevent overcooking. Turning the birds during the cooking period helps to distribute the heat energy more evenly throughout the product if a turntable is not used. Whole chickens may be cooked the entire time on a high setting. A larger turkey, however, should be cooked on medium after the first 10 to 12 minutes on high, and should be turned several times during cooking.

Microwave cooking is not as effective as conventional cooking for destruction of microorganisms in whole turkeys, in chicken halves, and probably in pieces. In one study, turkeys that had been inoculated with food-poisoning bacteria before cooking were baked in the microwave oven. Roasting to an internal breast temperature of 77°C (170°F) did not completely eliminate the microorganisms [1]. The turkeys in this study contained abnormally high numbers of bacteria, but the possibility of survival of pathogenic microorganisms under more usual conditions should be considered in the handling of turkeys cooked by microwaves. In another study, cooking chicken halves in the microwave oven to an internal temperature of 85°C (185°F) was not sufficient to destroy, in more than 50 percent of the chickens, all *Salmonella* organisms with which the birds had been inoculated [25]. More study is needed in this area.

When poultry pieces are cooked in the microwave oven, they should be arranged with the thickest portions toward the outside of the dish, where they will receive more energy. After half the cooking period, each piece should be turned, unless a turntable is used. Cooking on high for 7 to 8 minutes per pound should be satisfactory; however, it is important to make certain that the poultry is cooked well done throughout. The microwave oven adapts well to the preparation of chicken with various tangy and creamy sauces.

Cooking Skinless Poultry

Poultry carries a layer of fat just under the skin. For those who are following a low-fat diet regimen, it is usually recommended that the skin not be eaten. Individual pieces of poultry such as chicken may have the skin removed either before or after cooking. In the cooking of skinless poultry, a method should be chosen that avoids drying of the skinless surface during the cooking process. For example, skinless pieces of chicken may be dipped in milk or oil and then rolled in fine bread or cereal crumbs, placed in an oiled baking pan, and baked. The crumbs form a crisp coating that acts as a skin. Skinless chicken breasts can also be used to prepare a dinner all in one pot, with potatoes and other vegetables cooked with the seasoned chicken in a covered casserole. Boneless chicken can be poached in chicken stock until tender, cooled, cut into cubes, and combined with celery, sliced mushrooms, garlic, ginger root, and soy sauce to make an Oriental chicken mixture that is served over rice.

Discoloration of Poultry Bones

The bones of frozen young birds are often very dark in color after the birds are cooked. Freezing and thawing break down the blood cells of bone marrow and cause a deep red color to appear. During cooking, the red color changes to brown, although this color change does not affect flavor. Cooking directly from the frozen state has been shown to result in less darkening than rapid or slow thawing, and birds cooked rapidly with microwaves exhibit less darkening than those cooked by other methods [13].

•FISH

There are more than 3,000 different species used for commercial seafoods worldwide and more than 250 in the United States. However, only a few species are well known as edible fish and shellfish in this country, leaving a considerable number of species underutilized.

Minced Fish Products

Included in the technological advances made in the U.S. seafood industry is the production of deboned, minced raw fish from lesser-known species and fillet trimmings. Minced fish has given rise to new families of food products. For example, frozen minced fish blocks are cut into fish sticks and portions. These products can be found on the market in a variety of forms, including crunchy breaded pieces, seafood nuggets, and fish loaf with creamy sauce [28, 35].

A raw material called *surimi* (from the Japanese) offers opportunities for the production of several food items. To prepare surimi, minced fish is first washed to remove fat, blood, pigments, and other undesirable substances, leaving only the myofibrillar proteins of the fish flesh. Then this material is frozen with the addition of **cryoprotectants**, such as sucrose and sorbitol or possibly maltodextrins and polydextrose. These are required because the myofibrillar proteins of fish are labile to denaturation on freezing [27].

Further processing and fiberizing produce an elastic and chewy texture in the product that can be made to resemble that of shellfish [21]. Surimi-based fiberized simulated crab legs are shown in Figure 22.8. Japanese techniques in the production of surimi have been Americanized in recent years, and several plants are presently producing surimi and its analogue products in the United States. Novel snack foods are also produced from surimi [19].

Cryoprotectants substances that offer protection to such sensitive molecules as proteins during freezing and frozen storage

Classification and Market Forms

Two major categories for the classification of fish are vertebrate fish with fins, and shellfish or invertebrates. The former are covered with scales, the latter with some type of shell. Fish with vertebrae are further classified on the basis of their fat content as *lean* or *fat*, lean fish having less than 5 percent fat in their edible flesh. Examples of lean and fat fish are found in Table 22.4.

Shellfish are also of two types: mollusks and crustaceans. The mollusks have a soft structure and are either partially or wholly enclosed in a hard shell that is largely of mineral composition. Examples of mollusks are oysters,

FIGURE 22.8
Surimi-based fiberized crab leg. Surimi is made by a special process from mechanically deboned fish flesh. It is used as an intermediate product for a variety of fabricated seafoods, such as the crab legs shown here. (Reprinted from Lee, C. M. Surimi process technology. *Food Technology*, Vol. 38, No. 11, p. 69, 1984. Copyright© by Institute of Food Technologists.)

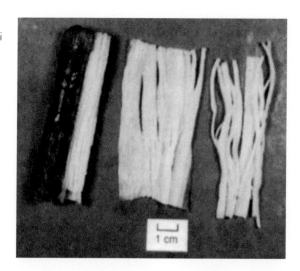

TABLE 22.4

Some Species of Fish

Species	Weight Range (lb)	Usual Market Form	Suggested Preparation Method
Lean saltwater fish			
Bluefish	1–7	Whole and drawn	Broil, bake, fry
Cod	3–20	Steaks and fillets	Broil, bake, fry, steam
Flounder	¼–5	Whole, dressed, and fillets	Broil, bake, fry
Haddock	1½–7	Drawn and fillets	Broil, bake, steam
Hake	2–5	Whole, dressed, and fillets	Broil, bake, fry
Halibut	8–75	Steaks	Broil, bake, steam
Rosefish	½–1¼	Fillets	Bake
Snapper, red	2–15	Drawn, steaks, and fillets	Bake, steam
Whiting	½–1½	Whole, dressed, and fillets	Bake, fry
Fat saltwater fish			
Butterfish	¼–1	Whole and dressed	Broil, bake, fry
Herring	¼–1	Whole	Bake, fry
Mackerel	¾–3	Whole, drawn, and fillets	Broil, bake
Salmon	3–30	Drawn, dressed, steaks, and fillets	Broil, bake, steam
Shad	1½–7	Whole and fillets	Bake
Lean freshwater fish			
Brook trout	¾–8	Whole	Broil, bake, fry
Yellow pike	1½–10	Whole, dressed, and fillets	Broil, bake, fry
Fat freshwater fish			
Catfish	1–10	Whole, dressed, and skinned	Bake, fry
Lake trout	1½–10	Drawn, dressed, and fillets	Bake, fry
Whitefish	2–6	Whole, dressed, and fillets	Broil, bake

clams, abalone, scallops, and mussels. Crustaceans are covered with a crustlike shell and have segmented bodies. Common examples are lobster, crab, shrimp, and crayfish.

The kinds of fish available for food vary widely in different localities. They include both saltwater and freshwater varieties, which differ considerably in flavor and quality. Saltwater fish usually have more distinctive flavors than freshwater fish, and oily fish have more flavor than the lean varieties. Many markets, even those located far from fishing waters, now sell live fish and shellfish.

Fish, fresh or frozen, is marketed in various forms, some of which are shown in Figure 22.9. Whole or round fish are marketed just as they come from the water. Drawn fish have had only the entrails removed, and dressed fish are scaled and eviscerated and usually have the head, tail, and fins removed. Steaks are cross-cut sections of the larger sizes of dressed fish. Fillets are sides of the fish cut lengthwise away from the backbone. A butterfly fillet is the two sides of a fillet. Sticks are uniform pieces of fish cut lengthwise or crosswise from fillets or steaks; however, some breaded, frozen fish sticks may be made from minced fish. Shellfish is marketed in the shell, shucked (removed from the shell), headless (shrimp and some lobster), or already cooked.

FIGURE 22.9

Market forms of fish. (Courtesy of the Bureau of Commercial Fisheries, U.S. Department of the Interior)

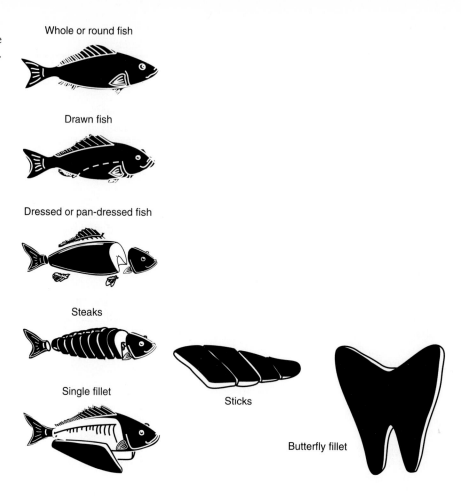

Many convenience items containing fish are now available. In addition to frozen, breaded, precooked fish fillets and sticks, there are a variety of frozen items including creamed fish, fish Florentine, fish soups, fish pies, and fish dinners.

Composition and Nutritive Value

The gross composition of seafood is similar to that of lean meat (see Appendix C). As are meats and poultry, seafoods are valuable sources of good-quality protein, with fish averaging 18 to 20 percent of this important nutrient. Many fish are lower in fat and cholesterol than moderately fat beef. Because of this, public health groups have suggested that the average American would do well from a health standpoint to substitute more fish for red meats in the diet. The U.S. seafood industry has been experiencing a period of growth in recent years because of the increased emphasis on fish.

There is an additional nutritional reason for eating fish on a regular basis. The fat in most fish is very unsaturated. Included among the unsaturated fats in fish oil are ω-3 polyunsaturated fatty acids (PUFA), the most important of which is called *eicosapentaenoic acid* (EPA) (see pages 356–357). The fat in many common fish contains 8 to 12 percent EPA and 30 to 45 percent total ω-3 PUFA [14] (see Table 22.5). This makes fish a very important source of these nutrients, the intake of which is apparently related to a decreased risk of coronary heart disease.

All shellfish have some carbohydrate in the form of **glycogen**. Lobster has less than 1 percent, but abalone, clams, mussels, oysters, and scallops have from 3 to 5 percent. The sweet taste of various shellfish is due to the glucose formed by enzyme action from the glycogen.

Seafoods are important sources of minerals, with oysters being particularly rich in zinc, iron, and copper. Oysters, clams, and shrimp also contain a somewhat higher percentage of calcium than other fish and meats, which are notably low in calcium. Marine fish are a dependable source of iodine. Oysters, clams, and lobster are the highest in iodine of all seafood. Shrimp ranks next, with crab and other ocean fish last in order.

Fat fish contain more vitamin A than lean varieties. Canned salmon is a fair source of vitamin A and a good source of riboflavin and niacin. The presence in raw fish of the enzyme thiaminase, which destroys thiamin, may make the vitamin unavailable if fish is held in the raw state.

Fish protein concentrate or fish flour is produced from dehydrated and defatted whole fish. It appears to be an excellent, concentrated source of high-quality protein and may be used to supplement the breads and cereal products consumed by humans in many parts of the world. The FDA has approved the use of fish protein concentrate made from whole fish as a food additive under prescribed conditions. The making of acceptable crackers containing up to 12 percent fish protein concentrate has been reported [36]. Fish protein concentrate has also been used to enrich noodles that are acceptable to Orientals, especially children [41].

Polyunsaturated fatty acids   fatty acids with two or more double bonds between carbon atoms

ω-3 PUFA   a group of polyunsaturated fatty acids that have the first double bond on the third carbon atom from the end of the carbon chain; also called *n*-3 fatty acids

Glycogen   a complex carbohydrates—a polysaccharide—used for carbohydrate storage in the liver and muscles of the body; sometimes called animal starch

TABLE 22.5
ω-3 (*n*-3) Fatty Acids in Some Fish

Fish	Total oil (wt %)	Total *n*–3 fatty acids (wt % of total oil)
Sea bass	2.9	33.7
Butterfish	2.3	22.2
Atlantic cod	1.1	53.1
Pacific cod	0.9	45.9
Flounder	1.5	37.5
Haddock	1.1	44.3
Halibut	3.1	28.3
Herring	11.2	23.6
Pink salmon	4.2	39.9
Sardines	9.7	43.4
Red snapper	1.2	32.9
Rainbow trout	1.8	30.1
Tuna	7.5	37.6

Source: Reference 14.

Shellfish

The shellfish most commonly marketed in the United States are clams, crab, lobster, oysters, scallops, and shrimp.

Shrimp include the common or white shrimp, which is greenish gray when caught; the brown or Brazilian shrimp, which is brownish red when raw; the pink or coral-colored shrimp; and the Alaska and California varieties, which vary in color and are relatively small. Despite the differences in color in the raw state, cooked shrimp differ little in appearance and flavor. Raw shrimp in the shell are often called *green shrimp*. Shrimp are usually sold with the head and thorax removed.

Shrimp are designated, according to the number required to weigh a pound, as Jumbo, Large, Large Medium, Medium, and Small. The largest size has 15 or fewer shrimp to the pound; the smallest size has 60 or more to the pound. Breaded shrimp, which have been peeled, cleaned, and breaded for frying, are available. Prawns are shrimplike crustaceans that are usually relatively large in size.

Oysters (see Figure 22.10) can be purchased live in the shell, fresh or frozen shucked (removed from the shell), or canned. Live oysters have a tightly closed shell. Gaping shells indicate that they are dead and therefore no longer usable. Shucked oysters should be plump and have a natural creamy color, with clear liquor. Eastern shucked oysters are usually packed in the following commercial sizes: Counts or Extra Large, Extra Selects or Large, Selects or Medium, Standards or Small, and Standards or Very Small. For the Pacific area the designations vary somewhat: size 1 is extra large; size 2, large; size 3, medium; and size 4, small.

The true lobster, or Northern lobster, is found near the shores of Europe and North America in the cold waters of the North Atlantic Ocean. The spiny or rock lobster is nearly worldwide in its distribution. The spiny lobster may be distinguished by the absence of large, heavy claws and the presence of many prominent spines on its body and legs. Figure 22.11 shows both of these lobsters.

Lobsters are a dark bluish green when they are taken from the water but change to a "lobster red" during cooking. Lobsters and crabs must be alive at the time of cooking to ensure freshness. The tail should curl under the body when the live lobster is picked up. Whole lobsters and crabs cooked in the shell are available. They should be bright red in color and have a fresh odor. Frozen lobster tails can be purchased in some markets. The cooked meat, picked from the shells of lobsters and crabs, is marketed fresh, frozen, and canned.

Blue crabs, constituting about three-fourths of all the crabs marketed in the United States, come from the Atlantic and Gulf coasts. Dungeness crabs are found on the Pacific coast from Alaska to Mexico. Both types of crabs are

FIGURE 22.10

Oysters in the shell. (Courtesy of the Bureau of Commercial Fisheries, U.S. Department of the Interior)

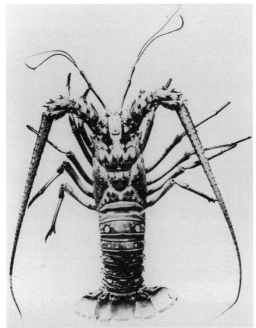

Northern lobster   Spiny or rock lobster

shown in Figure 22.12. Fresh-cooked meat from blue crabs may be packed in several grades: lump meat, or solid lumps of white meat from the body of the crab; flake meat, or small pieces of white meat from the rest of the body; lump and flake meat combined; and claw meat, which has a brownish tinge. Fresh-cooked meat from both the body and claws of Dungeness crabs has a pinkish tinge and is packed as one grade.

Scallops are mollusks similar to oysters and clams except that they swim freely through the water by snapping their shells together. The oversize adductor muscle that closes the shell is the only part of the scallop eaten by Americans. Europeans eat the entire scallop.

Several species of clams are used for food (see Figure 22.13). They are marketed live in the shell, fresh or frozen shucked, or canned. Tightly closed shells indicate that they are alive and therefore usable. Shucked clams should be plump, with clear liquor, and free from shell particles.

Fish Roe

Roe is the mass of eggs from finfish and consists of sacs of connective tissue enclosing thousands of small eggs. It is important that the sacs remain intact, since the eggs cannot otherwise be held together. Although roe is of minor importance in the marketing of fish, available only during spawning season and very perishable, fresh fish roe is well liked by some people. The most highly prized for flavor is shad roe, although in the Great Lakes area, whitefish roe is also popular. Roe from most fish that are commonly consumed can be eaten.

A method of cooking that intensifies flavor is preferable for fish roe. It is usually parboiled for two to five minutes, after which it is dipped in corn meal

Blue crab

Dungeness crab

FIGURE 22.12
The two most common types of crabs available in the United States. (Courtesy of the Bureau of Commercial Fisheries, U.S. Department of the Interior)

or in egg and crumbs and fried. Parboiling aids in thorough cooking of the roe without its hardening by being fried too long.

Caviar, or sturgeon roe preserved in brine, is becoming increasingly scarce because of the low water level of the Caspian sea, where most sturgeon have been produced. Caviar is expensive and is used mainly for making appetizers.

Cured Fish

Although fish may be cured for preservation purposes, the cure often imparts a distinctive flavor of its own that is appreciated for variety. Some hardening and toughening of the outer surface occur when fish is salted, dried, or smoked. Common examples of cured fish are salt cod, mackerel, finnan haddie, and kippered herring. Finnan haddie is haddock that has been cured in brine to which carotene pigment has been added and later smoked. It is preferred lightly cured but does not keep long with a light cure. If finnan haddie is to be kept for some time or shipped long distances, the cure must be stronger. Kippered herring is also lightly brined and smoked. It is often canned to preserve its typical flavor rather than being cured in a heavier brine.

Canned Fish

The principal kinds of canned fish are salmon, tuna, sardines, shrimp, crab, lobster, and clams.

Salmon packing is one of the big industries of the Pacific Northwest. Five principal varieties of salmon are packed, depending on the locality. The five varieties in order of consumer preference are (1) red salmon or sockeye; (2) chinook; (3) coho, medium red or silverside; (4) pink; and (5) chum. The fish

| Steamer | In-shell | Medium chowder | Cherrystone |
| Soft clams | | Hard clams | |

FIGURE 22.13

Clams may be soft- or hard-shelled and are marketed in different sizes. *Littlenecks* and *cherrystones* are dealers' names for smaller-sized hard clams. The larger sizes of hard clams are called *chowders*. The larger sizes of soft clams are known as *in-shells*, and the smaller ones are called *steamers*. (Courtesy of the Bureau of Commercial Fisheries, U.S. Department of the Interior)

with red flesh and high oil content are preferred by consumers although they are the most expensive. The red-fleshed varieties are somewhat higher in vitamin A content.

In the United States, only six species of tuna may be labeled *tuna* when canned: yellowfin, skipjack, albacore, bluefin, Oriental tuna, and little tuna. The related species of bonito and Pacific yellowtail cannot legally be marketed as tuna. Albacore may be labeled *white meat*; the other species are labeled *light meat* tuna. There are three different styles of packing for canned tuna: fancy or solid pack, chunk style, and flake or grated style. Each style can be packed in either oil or water. The normal color of precooked or canned tuna is pinkish. Some fish do not develop the pink color but take on a tan or tannish-green color and are rejected. These fish are referred to in the industry as *green* tuna.

Aquaculture

Aquaculture, or fish farming, is not new. It was apparently practiced in China as early as 2,000 B.C. Extremely rapid growth has occurred in this industry during the past few decades. Aquaculture is now a viable and profitable enterprise worldwide. It will, undoubtedly, continue to grow because of increasing demand for seafood worldwide and diminishing supplies and increasing costs of sea-caught fish and shellfish [18].

Fish farming can be done on land that is unsuitable for other food-producing purposes, such as swamplands or poorly drained lands. Fish convert feed into body tissue more efficiently than do farm animals; they have a lower dietary energy requirement. Also, the percentage of edible, lean tissue in fish is higher than that in beef, pork, and poultry because fish contains less bone, adipose tissue, and connective tissue [18]. Thus, the future of aquaculture looks bright.

Selection and Storage

Freshness

Fresh finfish has firm flesh, a stiff body, and tight scales. The gills are red, and the eyes are bright and unsunken. Pressure on the body does not leave an indentation in the flesh except in the case of fish that has been frozen and thawed. The exterior of fresh fish has little or no slime. Fresh seafood should not smell "fishy." It should smell like a "fresh ocean breeze" [9]. Stale fish, on the other hand, is flabby, and the eyes are dull and sunken. The scales are easily brushed off, the gills are no longer bright red, and the odor is stale or sour.

Frozen fish should be solidly frozen when it is purchased, and there should be no discoloration or brownish tinge in the flesh. It should have little or no odor and should be wrapped in a moisture/vapor-proof material.

Mollusks in the shell should always be alive when they are purchased. The shells of live mollusks will be tightly closed or will close when tapped lightly or iced. Any mollusks that do not close tightly should be thrown away. Seafood should be bought only from reputable dealers [9].

Inspection and Grading

The National Marine Fisheries Service in the U.S. Department of Commerce operates a voluntary seafood inspection and grading program. A fee for the voluntary service is paid by the processor. The U.S. Food and Drug Administration (FDA) also periodically inspects seafood processing plants and, in addition, analyzes samples of seafood, both domestic and imported, for pesticide and industrial chemical residues. Fish products meeting the official standards may carry U.S. inspection and grade labels. In response to Congressional action, the National Marine Fisheries Service has designed and implemented an educational and training program for the seafood industry to upgrade their understanding and acceptance of the Hazard Analysis Critical Control Point (HACCP) concept for the operation and inspection of seafood processing facilities [11].

Quality grades are determined largely on the basis of appearance, uniformity, absence of defects, character (mainly texture), and flavor and odor of the product. Grades for breaded items also consider the amount of edible fish as compared with the amount of breading and the presence of bone in fish sticks. For most items, specific grades are U.S. Grade A, U.S. Grade B, and Substandard.

Seafood Safety

Periodically, the national media have raised questions about the seafood marketed in the United States. Many have asked, "How safe is our seafood supply?" The Centers for Disease Control (CDC) statistics for 1978–1987 indicate that fish and shellfish were responsible for 10.5 percent of all outbreaks of foodborne disease reported to them for that period. However, when the outbreaks were considered in terms of cases (the number of persons affected), seafood was implicated in only 3.6 percent of all cases, while meat and poultry were responsible for more than 6 percent [26]. Approximately 4,000 persons became ill during this period from eating shellfish, while the cause of illness for about 2,000 persons was finfish. These data undoubtedly underestimate the number of actual cases of seafood-related illness, since many incidences of illness go unreported.

What are the causes of seafoodborne illness? In many of the cases reported to the CDC the cause was "unknown" or "unconfirmed." However, there was evidence that a majority of these unconfirmed cases, mostly those from shellfish, were probably due to viruses, particularly the Norwalk virus.

The problem with viruses is probably linked to human populations and waste disposal [26]. Mollusks usually live where rivers and seas meet. Many cities are located near these areas and the waters are more likely to be polluted than are off-shore waters [9].

Another major cause of illness from eating seafood is from bacteria of the *Vibrio* species. These bacteria naturally occur in marine environments and may be a major component of the intestinal flora in marine fish. *Vibrios* are easily destroyed by even modest levels of heat. In fact, disease from both viruses and bacteria in seafood may be prevented by thorough cooking. Shellfish, especially mollusks, should not be eaten raw. Finfish dishes, such as sushi, can be safe for most people to eat if they are made with very fresh fish, commercially frozen at very low temperatures, and then thawed before eating. This kills any parasites that may be present. Parasites, which may be another cause of illness, are also killed by thorough cooking. People with diabetes, liver disease, or immune disorders should not eat even raw finfish since freezing does not kill bacteria [9]. Another cause of seafoodborne illness may be so-called natural toxins, probably derived through the food-chain as certain tropical fish and shellfish feed on toxigenic materials. Chemicals, such as mercury, may also be present in fish in hazardous amounts.

Waste

The refuse of fish is rather high, commonly around 50 percent by weight. In general, the smaller the fish, the higher the percentage of refuse. The waste is composed chiefly of scales, head, and bones, although in some cases the skin, being tough, is also waste. In shellfish, the shell constitutes the chief waste and in some instances runs as high as 60 to 80 percent of the total weight. For example, a lobster weighing 1¼ pounds will yield only about 1/4 pound of edible flesh. The percentage of waste in large lobsters is somewhat less but is still very high. In addition to the shell, clams have a tough portion that must be discarded. The scallop, as it is eaten in the United States, is only the muscle that operates the opening and closing of the shell.

Storage

Fresh fish is extremely perishable and spoils rapidly. After fish is caught, it is stored in ice, or in a frozen salt solution to achieve a somewhat lower temperature, until it is ready for sale [22].

As bacteria decompose fish tissue, a volatile substance called *trimethylamine* is released. Measurement of trimethylamine, for which relatively simple, rapid methods exist, gives an indication of the microbiologic quality of fish [40].

In addition to the delicate structure of fish, which makes bacterial invasion easy, it has been shown that rapid spoilage is partly the result of the high degree of activity of the enzymes present in fish. The low temperatures of the natural environment of some fish may account for the unusual activity of the body enzymes.

Fresh fish must be kept in the coldest part of the refrigerator until it is ready to be cooked. It should be stored in the same wrapper it had in the market. Live mollusks should be refrigerated in containers covered loosely with a clean, damp cloth. Live shellfish should not be stored in airtight containers or in water. Fresh fish must be used no later than two days after purchase [9]. For long-term storage, fish must be frozen.

Preparation

Cooking Finfish

The safest way to thaw frozen seafood is in the refrigerator in its own container. Allow about one day for defrosting [9].

To lend variety to menus, fish may be cooked by either dry- or moist-heat methods. Fish have very little connective tissue, and it is of a kind that is very easily hydrolyzed. The structure of fish is delicate and tender, even in the raw state. Therefore, the use of moist heat for tenderization purposes is not necessary. In fact, one of the chief problems in fish cookery is retention of the form of the fish. This is done by careful handling. If fish is cooked in water, it is usually necessary to tie the piece of fish in cheesecloth or wrap it in parchment paper to prevent it from falling apart during cooking. Because extractives are low in fish, a method that develops flavor, such as frying, broiling, and baking, is often preferred.

Although overcooking is to be avoided, fish must be cooked until thoroughly done. Fish is unpalatable to many people when it is rare and may also be unsafe; for example, fish from some localities may be a source of tapeworm. Fish is fully cooked when the flakes separate easily. It should be tested with a fork in a thick portion, as the outer, thin edges cook more readily than the thicker muscles. About ten minutes of cooking time per inch of thickness is generally recommended for fish fillets.

If two or more fish fillets have been frozen in a package, it is necessary to partially defrost them to separate them for cooking. Individual steaks or fillets may be cooked either thawed or frozen. If they have been thawed, they may be cooked as fresh fish. For partially or wholly frozen fish, the cooking temperature must be lower and the time of cooking longer than for defrosted fish to permit thawing as the fish cooks. Otherwise, ice may remain in the center of the cut even when the outside is thoroughly cooked.

Broiling. Fish to be broiled may be in the form of fillets, steaks, or boned or unboned whole fish (head removed). Unboned whole fish is cut through the ribs along the backbone, allowing it to lie flat. If the skin has been left on, the fish is placed skin side down on the broiler rack. It may later be turned, but turning large pieces of fish is difficult and tends to break the fish apart. Using a relatively low broiling temperature to prevent overbrowning and basting the top surface with fat to keep it moist usually make it possible for fish to be broiled until done without turning.

Baking. Fish fillets may be used for baking, but often whole fish, stuffed and sewed or skewered to prevent loss of stuffing, is baked. It is usually placed in a shallow, open pan and is basted to keep the skin from becoming hard and dry. A moderately heated oven produces the most satisfactory results, especially if the fish is stuffed. Figures 22.14 and 22.15 illustrate methods of baking and oven frying.

Frying. Small whole fish, fillets, or steaks may be fried. Pieces of a suitable size for serving are usually dipped in water, milk, or egg mixed with milk, then in a dry ingredient, such as cornmeal, flour, or fine crumbs. If the fish is to be deep-fat fried, the temperature of the fat should not exceed 196° to 202°C (385° to 395°F) in order that the fish will be cooked done by the time it is browned.

Steaming and Simmering. Fish may be cooked by steaming or simmering. These are closely related methods of cookery, varying in the amount of the

Place steak in a baking dish.

Arrange stuffing on the steak.

Place a second steak on top of the stuffing and brush with melted fat.

Serve baked stuffed halibut steaks with garnishes of parsley sprigs and radishes.

FIGURE 22.14
Preparing baked stuffed halibut steaks. (Courtesy of the Bureau of Commercial Fisheries, U.S. Department of the Interior)

cooking liquid used. Fish to be steamed may be placed on a rack over a boiling liquid with a tight cover on the pan, and cooked until done. Steaming may also be done in the oven in a covered pan, or the fish may be wrapped tightly in aluminum foil. The foil retains moisture, and the fish cooks in an atmosphere of steam. Finnan haddie, which is a cured fish, retains its characteristic flavor particularly well when it is steamed and served with melted butter.

Dip the fish in milk and roll in bread crumbs.

Pour melted fat over the fillets.

Bake the fillets in a shallow baking pan.

Serve the fillets with appropriate garnishes.

FIGURE 22.15
Preparing oven-fried haddock fillets. (Courtesy of the Bureau of Commercial Fisheries, U.S. Department of the Interior)

Fish that is simmered is covered with a liquid and cooked just below the boiling point. The fish holds its form better if it is tied in cheesecloth, wrapped in parchment paper, or placed in a wire basket in the water. Large, firm-fleshed fish are better cooked by this method, as the flesh does not fall apart as readily as less firm or fatty fish. Addition of 3 tablespoons of vinegar or lemon juice and 1½ tablespoons of salt per quart of water seasons fish well. Fish cooked in moist heat is usually served with a sauce.

Microwave Cooking.   Fish can be prepared in a variety of ways using the microwave oven, including soups and chowders, appetizers, and main dishes. Generally, fillets or steaks are arranged in a baking dish, with the thickest portions toward the outside of the dish. They may be brushed with melted butter or lemon juice, covered with waxed paper, and microwaved on medium-high or high. The dish should be rotated halfway during the cooking period unless a turntable is available.

Cooking Shellfish

Shellfish, the flesh of which appears to differ in structure from that of finfish, are much firmer and are easily toughened by high temperatures. Whether the differences are due to the amount and kind of connective tissue is not certain. Nevertheless, in cooking most shellfish, high temperatures and long cooking should be avoided. Moist-heat methods are generally satisfactory, but if the shellfish is cooked in a liquid medium, as in the making of oyster stew, a simmering temperature (82° to 85°C or 181° to 185°F) should be used.

Live lobsters are parboiled in salted water (2 teaspoons salt per quart of water). The water should be boiling when the fish is added but kept at a simmering temperature once the fish has been added. Overcooking toughens the flesh. After parboiling, the flesh is removed from the shell and prepared in any desired manner. The pink coral on the outside adds attractiveness to the lobster meat and should not be discarded. The edible meat is in the claws, which must be cracked to remove the meat, and in the tail. The whole tail may be separated from the body and the segmented shell removed.

Simmering is the basic method of cooking raw shrimp. Depending on the size, the time of cooking is three to five minutes or until the shrimp begin to curl and turn pink. Shrimp can be simmered, the shell removed, and then the sand vein along the back taken out. The sand vein is the intestinal tract located just under the outer curved surface. Alternatively, the shrimp can first be peeled and then simmered. Either way, 1½ pounds of raw shrimp yield about 3/4 pound of cooked ready-to-eat shrimp. The sand vein often remains in canned shrimp and must be removed before this product is used. Large shrimp are often deep-fat fried.

STUDY QUESTIONS

1. Poultry may be divided into several groups with respect to type, age, and sex.
   a. Describe each of the following classes of chickens and turkeys.

Chickens
Broiler-fryer
Roaster
Capon
Rock Cornish hen
Baking hen
Stewing hen or fowl

Turkeys
Fryer-roaster
Young hen
Young tom

    b. Suggest satisfactory methods of cooking each type of poultry listed in question a. and explain why each method is appropriate.

2. a. What does the round USDA inspection mark mean when placed on poultry?

    b. List the USDA grades that may be used on poultry and describe the qualities that are considered in grading.

3. Explain why it is so important to handle poultry properly, both in the raw and in the cooked state.

4. Describe an appropriate method for roasting stuffed and unstuffed turkeys and explain why you would suggest this procedure.

5. Describe general procedures for broiling, frying, braising, stewing, and microwaving poultry.

6. How do fish and shellfish differ? Suggest subclassifications for both fish and shellfish and give several examples from each group.

7. a. Describe five forms in which fish may be sold (market forms).

    b. In what forms may minced fish appear on the retail market?

    c. What is *surimi* and how is it used in the seafood industry?

8. Why has there been emphasis in recent years on increasing the consumption of fish in the American diet?

9. a. Describe typical characteristics of fresh fish.

    b. Suggest appropriate procedures for handling and storing fish and explain why these procedures are necessary.

    c. Explain why shellfish should never be eaten raw.

    d. What are some possible causes of illness when seafood is not properly handled?

10. Describe or identify the following.

    a. Green shrimp

    b. Northern lobster

    c. Spiny or rock lobster

    d. Scallops

    e. Fish roe

    f. Finnan haddie

    g. Tuna

11. List five principal varieties of salmon.

12. Explain why it is appropriate to cook fish with either dry- or moist-heat methods.

13. Describe satisfactory procedures for cooking fish by each of the following methods.

    a. Broiling

    b. Baking

    c. Frying

    d. Steaming

    e. Microwaves

14. What chief precaution should be taken when cooking shellfish and why?

REFERENCES

1. Aleixo, J. A. G., B. Swaminathan, K. S. Jamesen, and D. E. Pratt. 1985. Destruction of pathogenic bacteria in turkeys roasted in microwave ovens. *Journal of Food Science 50*, 873.

2. Bramblett, V. D., and K. W. Fugate. 1967. Choice of cooking temperature for stuffed turkeys. Part I, Palatability factors. *Journal of Home Economics 59*, 180.

3. Brown, N. E., and J. A. Chyuan. 1987. Convective heat processing of turkey roll: Effects on sensory quality and energy usage. *Journal of the American Dietetic Association 87*, 1521.

4. Chambers, L., E. Chambers IV, and J. R. Bowers. 1992. Consumer acceptability of cooked stored ground turkey patties with differing levels of phosphate. *Journal of Food Science 57*, 1026.

5. Cornforth, D. P., C. P. Brennand, R. J. Brown, and D. Godfrey. 1982. Evaluation of various methods for roasting frozen turkeys. *Journal of Food Science 47*, 1108.

6. Cunningham, F. E., and L. M. Tiede. 1981. Influence of batter viscosity on breading of chicken drumsticks. *Journal of Food Science 46*, 1950.

7. Dawson, E. H., G. L. Gilpin, and A. M. Harkin. 1960. Yield of cooked meat from different types of poultry. *Journal of Home Economics 52*, 445.

8. Deethardt, D., L. M. Burrill, K. Schneider, and C. W. Carlson. 1971. Foil-covered versus open-pan procedure for roasting turkey. *Journal of Food Science 36*, 624.

9. Department of Health and Human Services. Get hooked on seafood safety. DHHS Pub. No. (FDA) 92-2258.

10. Gardner, F. A., W. Hopkins, and J. H. Denton. 1980. A comparison of consumer methods of storing chicken broilers at home. *Poultry Science 59*, 743.

11. Garrett, E. P., III, and M. Hudak-Roos. 1991. Developing an HACCP-based inspection system for the seafood industry. *Food Technology 45*, 53 (No. 12).

12. Goertz, G. E., and S. Stacy. 1960. Roasting half and whole turkey hens. *Journal of the American Dietetic Association 37*, 458.

13. Hatch, V., and W. J. Stadelman. 1972. Bone darkening in frozen chicken broilers and ducklings. *Journal of Food Science 37*, 850.

14. Hearn, T. L., S. A. Sgoutas, J. A. Hearn, and D. S. Sgoutas. 1987. Polyunsaturated fatty acids and fat in fish flesh for selecting species for health benefits. *Journal of Food Science 52*, 1209.

15. Hoke, I. M., and M. K. Kleve. 1966. Heat penetration, quality, and yield of turkeys roasted to different internal thigh temperatures. *Journal of Home Economics 58*, 381.

16. Hoke, I. M., B. K. McGeary, and M. K. Kleve. 1967. Effect of internal and oven temperatures on eating quality of light and dark meat turkey roasts. *Food Technology 21*, 773.

17. Hsia, H. Y., D. M. Smith, and J. F. Steffe. 1992. Rheological properties and adhesion characteristics of flour-based batters for chicken nuggets as affected by three hydrocolloids. *Journal of Food Science 57*, 16.

18. Institute of Food Technologists' Expert Panel on Food Safety and Nutrition. 1991. Foods from aquaculture. *Food Technology 45*, 87 (No. 9).

19. Karmas, E., and E. Lauber. 1987. Novel products from underutilized fish using combined processing technology. *Journal of Food Science 52*, 7.

20. Lamuka, P. O., G. R. Sunki, C. B. Chawan, D. R. Rao, and L. A. Shackelford. 1992. Bacteriological quality of freshly processed broiler chickens as affected by carcass pretreatment and gamma irradiation. *Journal of Food Science 57*, 330.

21. Lee, C. M. 1984. Surimi process technology. *Food Technology 38*, 69 (No. 11).

22. Lee, C. M., and R. T. Toledo. 1984. Comparison of shelf life and quality of mullet stored at zero and subzero temperature. *Journal of Food Science 49*, 317.

23. Li, W., J. A. Bowers, J. A. Craig, and S. K. Perng. 1993. Sodium tripolyphosphate stability and effect in ground turkey meat. *Journal of Food Science 58*, 501.

24. Lillard, H. S. 1982. Improved chilling systems for poultry. *Food Technology 36*, 58 (No. 2).

25. Lindsay, R. E., W. A. Krissinger, and B. F. Fields. 1986. Microwave vs. conventional oven cooking of chicken: Relationship of internal temperature to surface contamination by *Salmonella*. *Journal of the American Dietetic Association 86*, 373.

26. Liston, J. 1990. Microbial hazards of seafood consumption. *Food Technology 44*, 56 (No. 12).

27. MacDonald, G. A., and T. Lanier. 1991. Carbohydrates as cryoprotectants for meats and surimi. *Food Technology 45*, 150 (No. 3).

28. Martin, R.E. 1988. Seafood products, technology, and research in the U.S. *Food Technology 42*, 58 (No. 3).

29. Meiners, C., M. G. Crews, and S. J. Ritchey. 1982. Yield of chicken parts: Proximate composition and mineral content. *Journal of the American Dietetic Association 81*, 435.

30. Moran, E. T., Jr. 1992. Injecting fats into breast meat of turkey carcasses differing in finish and retention after cooking. *Journal of Food Science 57*, 1071.

31. Moran, E. T., Jr., and E. Larmond. 1981. Carcass finish and breast internal oil basting effects on oven and microwave prepared small toms: Cooking characteristics, yields, and compositional changes. *Poultry Science 60*, 1229.

32. *Poultry in Family Meals*. 1982. Home and Garden Bulletin No. 110. Washington, DC: U.S. Department of Agriculture.

33. Proctor, V. A., and F. E. Cunningham. 1983. Composition of broiler meat as influenced by cooking methods and coating. *Journal of Food Science 48*, 1696.

34. Putnam, J. J. 1991. Food consumption, 1970-90. *Food Review 14*, 2 (No. 3).

35. Regenstein, J. M. 1986. The potential for minced fish. *Food Technology 40*, 101 (No. 3).

36. Sidwell, V. D., and B. R. Stillings. 1972. Crackers fortified with fish protein concentrate (FPC). *Journal of the American Dietetic Association 61*, 276.

37. Smith, D. M., and V. B. Alvarez. 1988. Stability of vacuum cook-in-bag turkey breast rolls during refrigerated storage. *Journal of Food Science 53*, 46.

38. Stadelman, W. J. 1978. Tenderness, flavor, and nutritive value of chickens. *Food Technology 32*, 80 (No. 5).

39. Suderman, D. R., and F. E. Cunningham. 1980. Factors affecting adhesion of coating to poultry skin, effect of age, method of chilling, and scald temperature on poultry skin ultrastructure. *Journal of Food Science 45*, 444.

40. Wong, K., and T. A. Gill. 1987. Enzymatic determination of trimethylamine and its relationship to fish quality. *Journal of Food Science 52*, 1.

41. Woo, H. C., and A. M. Erdman. 1971. Fish protein concentrate enrichment of noodles. *Journal of Home Economics 63*, 263.

42. Young, L. L., J. M. Garcia, H. S. Lillard, C. E. Lyon, and C. M. Papa. 1991. Fat content effects on yield, quality, and microbiological characteristics of chicken patties. *Journal of Food Science 56*, 1527.

Batters and Doughs

23

Batters and doughs, sometimes called *flour mixtures*, include a large variety of baked products, such as muffins, biscuits and other quick breads, pastry, shortened and unshortened cakes, cookies, and breads. Producing the result that is desired in these flour mixtures is dependent on such factors as accuracy in measurements or weights (Chapter 6), skill in manipulation, control of oven or other temperatures, and knowledge about the kinds and proportions of ingredients used.

A so-called standard product may vary somewhat from one group of people to another, depending on preferences; however, it is important that you learn what characteristics are generally preferred in various baked products and what proportions of ingredients and techniques of mixing might be used to achieve these characteristics. In this chapter, we discuss basic ingredients and their usual effects in baked products, as well as some basic methods of mixing. This information should be useful in learning to produce any desired standard.

•INGREDIENTS

The principal ingredients used in foundation formulas for doughs and batters are flour, liquid, fat, egg, sugar, leavening agent, and salt. Flavoring substances are added to some types of mixtures. A number of additives may be used by commercial bakers and by producers of such manufactured food products as cookies, granola bars, pastries, and various packaged flour mixes. Fat replacers and alternative sweeteners are important ingredients in reduced-fat or reduced-calorie items.

Flour

White wheat flour is defined by the U.S. Food and Drug Administration (FDA) as a food made by the grinding and sifting of cleaned wheat (Figure 23.1). The flour is freed from the bran and germ of the wheat kernel to such an extent that specifications as to moisture, ash, and protein content are met. Flour provides structure and body in baked flour products because of its protein and starch content.

CHAPTER OUTLINE

INGREDIENTS

CLASSIFICATION OF BATTERS AND DOUGHS

GENERAL METHODS FOR MIXING BATTERS AND DOUGHS

STRUCTURE OF BATTERS AND DOUGHS

DRY FLOUR MIXES

BAKING AT HIGH ALTITUDES

a Kernel of Wheat

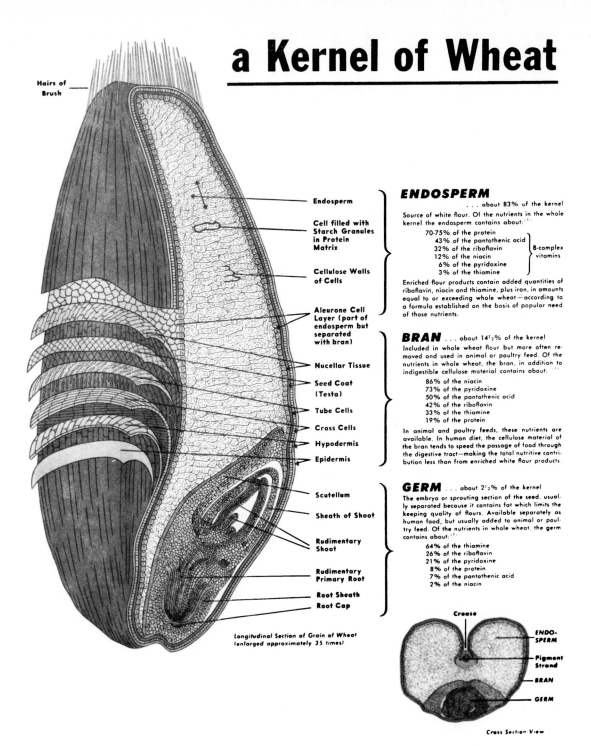

Hairs of Brush

Endosperm

Cell filled with Starch Granules in Protein Matrix

Cellulose Walls of Cells

Aleurone Cell Layer (part of endosperm but separated with bran)

Nucellar Tissue

Seed Coat (Testa)

Tube Cells

Cross Cells

Hypodermis

Epidermis

Scutellum

Sheath of Shoot

Rudimentary Shoot

Rudimentary Primary Root

Root Sheath

Root Cap

Longitudinal Section of Grain of Wheat (enlarged approximately 35 times)

ENDOSPERM
. . . about 83% of the kernel

Source of white flour. Of the nutrients in the whole kernel the endosperm contains about: [1]

70-75% of the protein
43% of the pantothenic acid
32% of the riboflavin — B-complex vitamins
12% of the niacin
6% of the pyridoxine
3% of the thiamine

Enriched flour products contain added quantities of riboflavin, niacin and thiamine, plus iron, in amounts equal to or exceeding whole wheat—according to a formula established on the basis of popular need of those nutrients.

BRAN
. . . about 14½% of the kernel

Included in whole wheat flour but more often removed and used in animal or poultry feed. Of the nutrients in whole wheat, the bran, in addition to indigestible cellulose material contains about: [1]

86% of the niacin
73% of the pyridoxine
50% of the pantothenic acid
42% of the riboflavin
33% of the thiamine
19% of the protein

In animal and poultry feeds, these nutrients are available. In human diet, the cellulose material of the bran tends to speed the passage of food through the digestive tract—making the total nutritive contribution less than from enriched white flour products

GERM
. . . about 2½% of the kernel

The embryo or sprouting section of the seed, usually separated because it contains fat which limits the keeping quality of flours. Available separately as human food, but usually added to animal or poultry feed. Of the nutrients in whole wheat, the germ contains about: [1]

64% of the thiamine
26% of the riboflavin
21% of the pyridoxine
8% of the protein
7% of the pantothenic acid
2% of the niacin

Crease

ENDOSPERM

Pigment Strand

BRAN

GERM

Cross Section View

FIGURE 23.1

The structure of a kernel of wheat. (Courtesy of the Wheat Flour Institute)

Milling

The milling of white flour is a process that involves separating the endosperm from the bran and germ and subdividing it into a fine flour (Figure 23.3). Specific procedures in milling may vary from one mill to another, but the major steps are shown in the simplified chart in Figure 23.2. The three main parts of the wheat kernel are divided approximately as follows: 83 percent endosperm, 14.5 percent bran layers (including the aleurone layer), and 2.5 percent germ [15]. When these parts are not separated, the flour resulting from the milling process is called *whole-wheat*, *entire-wheat*, or *graham* flour.

Many years ago, white flours were made by sifting wheat that had been ground in a stone mill. This method of separation yielded a flour that was generally less white and of poorer baking quality than the flour produced in present-time mills, where the wheat passes through a series of rollers. The first sets of corrugated rolls crush the grain and detach the endosperm from the bran. The portion of the endosperm that is separated and pulverized is sifted after each crushing. The flours resulting from the first siftings are known as *break flours*, of which there are about five streams.

The small pieces of the inner portion of the kernel, which are granulated with difficulty, are known as *middlings*. After their separation from the bran, the middlings are fed through a series of smooth rolls that further reduce the size of the particles and produce fine flour. About six to eight streams of flour are obtained from the rolling and sifting of the purified middlings.

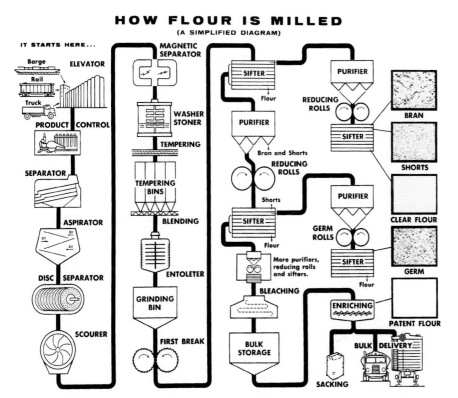

HOW FLOUR IS MILLED
(A SIMPLIFIED DIAGRAM)

FIGURE 23.2

Steps involved in the milling of flour. (Courtesy of the Wheat Flour Institute)

Various grades and types of flours are made from the many streams of flour resulting from the roller process. The streams vary in their protein content. Break flours and those from the last reductions of the middlings are inferior to the other streams of flour for baking purposes.

Because the endosperm represents about 83 percent of the total kernel, about that same amount of white flour should theoretically be obtained by milling. In actual practice, however, only 72 to 75 percent is separated as white flour. The separation of endosperm from bran and germ is neither a simple nor an extremely efficient process. The inner bran layers and the germ are tightly bound to the endosperm, and it is impossible to make a complete separation. The usual 72 to 75 percent extraction produces white flour containing essentially no bran and germ and exhibiting good baking properties. In times of national emergency, the usual percentage of extraction has been increased as a conservation measure. It has been suggested that the regular extraction rate of white flour could be increased up to 80 percent without sacrificing baking quality [19].

A milling method based on separation of flour particles by air currents, called *air classification*, has been developed. The various fractions obtained in this process differ in composition and therefore in baking properties. This method of milling offers promise for the ready production of both high- and low-protein flours for specific uses.

Bleaching and Maturing

Final stages in the production of white flour are bleaching and maturing. What are these two processes and why are they important?

First, let us talk about bleaching. Freshly milled, unbleached flour is yellowish in color, primarily because of the presence of **carotenoid pigments**. If this flour is held for a time, the yellow color becomes lighter. It is *bleached* because the yellow pigments are **oxidized**.

Now, what about the maturing process? When freshly milled flour is used to bake bread, the loaf is of somewhat lower volume and less fine texture than it might be. A loaf with higher volume and finer texture can be made from the same flour after it has been aged. *Aging* involves simply holding or storing the flour for several weeks or months. During this time, not only does the flour lighten because the carotenoid pigments are oxidized, but the baking quality also improves. Baking improvement probably results from chemical changes that occur in the proteins of the flour. These complex chemical changes possibly involve oxidation of some type. From this process, *maturing* of the flour is said to have taken place. Thus, although the aging of white flour brings about both bleaching and maturing, these two chemical processes are separate.

The addition of certain chemical substances to freshly milled flour produces effects similar to aging but in a much shorter period. This saves the cost of storing the flour. The FDA permits the use of specified chemical substances. One of these is benzoyl peroxide, which is primarily a bleaching agent. Chlorine dioxide, chlorine, and acetone peroxides have both a bleaching and a maturing effect. Azodicarbonamide may be added to flour as a maturing agent but does not react until the flour is made into a dough. Flour that has been treated with any of these chemicals must be labeled *bleached*. Both bleached and unbleached flours are available to the consumer on the retail market.

Carotenoid pigments   yellow-orange compounds produced by plant cells and found in various fruit, vegetable, and cereal grain tissues; for example, ß-carotene

Oxidation   a chemical reaction in which oxygen is added or electrons are lost

Classes of Wheat

Wheats may be classified on the basis of the time of planting or the growing season, the color of the kernel, and the hardness or softness of the kernel. Wheats that are planted in the spring and harvested in the fall are called *spring wheats*, whereas those that are planted in the fall and harvested the following summer are called *winter wheats*. Since these wheats remain in the ground all winter, they are grown in areas with relatively mild winters. Some wheat kernels have a reddish appearance and are called *red wheats*, whereas others are white. A hard wheat has a hard, vitreous kernel, whereas a soft wheat appears to be more powdery. Hard wheats are usually higher in protein than are soft wheats, and the protein has more baking strength when flour from this wheat is made into dough. Spring wheats include hard red varieties, hard white and soft white varieties, and durum wheats, which are used only for the production of macaroni products. Winter wheats may be hard, semihard, or soft. Hard winter wheats have a fairly strong quality of protein and are suitable for bread-making purposes.

The geographical areas in which most of the hard spring wheats are produced are the north central part of the United States and western Canada. Hard winter wheats are grown mainly in the middle central states. Soft winter wheat is grown east of the Mississippi River and in the Pacific Northwest. Because climatic and soil conditions affect the composition of wheat, wide variations can be expected within these classes.

Grades of Flour

The miller grades white flour on the basis of which streams of flour are combined. *Straight grade* theoretically should contain all the flour streams resulting from the milling process, but actually 2 to 3 percent of the poorest streams is withheld. Very little flour on the market is straight grade. *Patent* flours come from the more refined portion of the endosperm and can be made from any class of wheat. They are divided into *short patent*, which includes 60 to 80 percent of the total flour streams, *medium patent* with 80 to 90 percent, and *long patent* with 90 to 95 percent. Most patent flours on the market include about 85 percent of the straight flour. *Clear grade* is made from streams withheld in the making of patent flours. Clear-grade flours are used in some commercial flour products such as pancake mixes.

Types of Wheat Flour

It is important to understand the differences in wheat flours in order to use them most effectively. Within certain limits, various types of flour may be interchanged in different recipes by altering the proportions of the nonflour constituents of the mixture. The composition and nutritive value of some wheat flours are given in Appendix C.

Whole-Wheat Flour. Whole-wheat flour may also be called *graham* flour or *entire-wheat* flour. It contains essentially the entire wheat kernel and may be ground to different degrees of fineness. The keeping quality of whole-wheat flour is lower than that of white flour because it contains fat from the germ that may be oxidized on storage. Whole-wheat flour is higher in fiber than is white flour because it contains the bran.

Bread Flour.   Bread flour is a white flour made chiefly from hard wheat. It contains a relatively high percentage of protein that develops into a substance called *gluten* (described in more detail in the next section). Gluten contributes very strong, elastic properties when the flour is made into a dough.

Bread flour has a slightly granular feel when it is touched and does not form a firm mass when pressed in the hand. It may be bleached or unbleached. Bread flour is used by commercial and foodservice bakers for yeast breads and is also available for use in the home kitchen. It produces breads of relatively high volume and fine texture with an elastic crumb.

All-Purpose Flour.   All-purpose flour is sometimes called *family* flour or *general-purpose* flour. It is a white flour usually made from a blend of wheats to yield a protein content lower than that of bread flour. It contains enough protein that it can be used for making yeast bread and rolls under household conditions. Foodservice establishments generally use a bread flour. All-purpose flour is used for making quick breads. The gluten that develops in doughs made from all-purpose flour is less strong and elastic than that produced in bread-flour doughs. All-purpose flour may be used for making pastry, cookies, and certain cakes. It usually has too high a protein content to make a delicate fine-textured cake.

Pastry Flour.   Pastry flour is a white flour that is usually made from soft wheat and contains a lower percentage of protein than is found in all-purpose flour. Its chief use is for baking pastries and cookies, and it is used primarily in commercial baking.

Cake Flour.   Cake flour is prepared from soft wheat. It is so finely milled that it feels soft and satiny and forms a firm mass when pressed in the hand. Cake flour usually contains only the most highly refined streams of flour from the milling process. It is a short patent grade of flour. The protein content of cake flour is very low in comparison with other types of flour. Cake flour is also highly bleached with chlorine [14]. The high starch content and weak quality of gluten produced from cake flour make it desirable chiefly for the preparation of delicate and fine-textured cakes.

Instantized Flour.   Instantized flour is also called *instant, instant-blending,* or *quick-mixing* flour. It is a granular all-purpose flour that has been processed by moistening and then redrying to aggregate small particles into larger particles or agglomerates. The agglomerated particles are of relatively uniform size and do not pack. Therefore, this flour does not require sifting before measuring. It flows freely without dust, is easily measured, and blends more readily with liquid than does regular flour. Some changes should be made in formulas and preparation procedures when this flour is substituted for regular flour in baked products.

An evaluation was made of ten baked products using two brands of instantized flour and a regular all-purpose flour [11]. In general, the volume of instantized flour had to be adjusted by removing two tablespoons per cup of measured flour to ensure a good-quality baked product. Yeast rolls, popovers, and pastry made with instantized flour scored below acceptable quality, however, even when adjustments were made for the amount of flour. Instantized flour is probably most useful when it is blended dry with a liquid, such as in the thickening of gravies and certain sauces.

Self-Rising Flour. Self-rising flour has had leavening agents and salt added to it in proportions desirable for baking. Monocalcium phosphate is the acid salt most commonly added in combination with sodium bicarbonate (baking soda) as leavening ingredients. Self-rising flours are popular for preparing quick breads, such as baking powder biscuits.

Gluten Flour. Wheat flour is mixed with dried extracted gluten to form gluten flour. This flour has a protein content of about 41 percent compared with the 10 to 14 percent protein content of wheat flour. The gluten is extracted by the gentle washing of a flour-and-water dough and is dried under mild conditions to minimize the effects on the baking characteristics of the gluten. Gluten flour is used primarily by the baking industry to adjust the protein level in various doughs.

Gluten

A variety of proteins have been extracted from wheat. Some of these are the more soluble **albumins** and **globulins** that do not appear to play major roles in baking. About 85 percent of the proteins of white flour are relatively insoluble. In early research, the insoluble wheat proteins were separated into two fractions called *gliadin* and *glutenin*. When flour is moistened with water and thoroughly mixed or kneaded, these insoluble proteins form *gluten*. Gluten is primarily responsible for the viscous and elastic characteristics and high loaf volume of wheat flour doughs [4, 9].

Gluten can be extracted from a flour-and-water dough that has been vigorously kneaded by thorough washing with water to remove the starch (Figure 23.4). The moist gluten thus extracted has elastic and cohesive properties similar to those of chewing gum. When gliadin and glutenin are separated from each other, the gliadin is found to be a syrupy substance that can bind the mass together. It has little or no resistance to extension and is responsible for the viscous properties of the dough. The glutenin exhibits toughness and rubberi-

Albumins   simple proteins that are soluble in water

Globulins   simple proteins that are soluble in dilute salt solutions

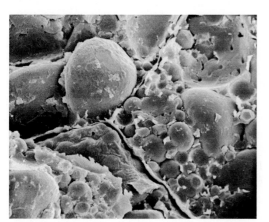

FIGURE 23.3

A scanning electron micrograph (2,100x) of fractured wheat endosperm cells showing small and large starch granules embedded in the cell matrix. (Reprinted from Freeman, T. P., and D. R. Shelton. Microstructure of wheat starch: From kernel to bread. *Food Technology 45*, 165 (No. 3), 1991. Copyright © by Institute of Food Technologies. Photograph supplied by Thomas P. Freeman.)

FIGURE 23.4

Gluten can be extracted from a flour–and–water dough by washing it carefully with cold water to remove the starch. The amounts and characteristics of gluten from various flours can thus be compared. Pictured are samples of unbaked and baked gluten. (*Left*) Cake flour; (*center*) all-purpose flour; (*right*) bread flour. (Courtesy of the Wheat Flour Institute)

Disulfide bond   a bond between two sulfur atoms, each of which is also joined to another chemical group; these bonds often tie protein chains together

ness (Figure 23.5). It resists the extension of the dough and contributes to elasticity. Research on flour proteins has shown that gliadin and glutenin each consist of several components or subunits of different molecular weights. The glutenin molecule is multi-chained and is much larger than the gliadin molecule. High-molecular-weight glutenin molecules may have subunits bound together by the formation of **disulfide bonds** (—S—S—) between the protein chains. Gliadin is made up mostly of single chain molecules of differing sizes that are also linked together by disulfide bonds [7]. Other types of bonds, such as hydrogen bonds, may form intramolecular linkages.

During the mixing of a dough, the long strands of glutenin evidently are aligned in the direction of mixing and interact with gliadin molecules to form a strong elastic uniform film that envelops the starch granules in the mixture (Figure 23.6). An appropriate amount of water must be present to form a dough. Air and carbon dioxide gas bubbles incorporated in the dough produce a foam. Interactions probably also occur in the dough between gluten proteins and lipids and other dough components as well [10]. Wheat-flour dough is a complex but very interesting phenomenon.

In yeast breads, gluten is developed to its maximum strength to make possible a high volume and fine texture. In other baked products, such as shortened cakes, gluten development is retarded to yield a more tender product.

Other Wheat Products

Cracked wheat, although it is not a flour, is used extensively in baking breads and quick breads. It should be soaked in double its volume of water for 24 hours before use. Cracked wheat may be combined in varying proportions with whole-wheat or white flour. Rolled wheat is also used to make cookies and quick breads.

Wheat germ, which contains essentially all of the fat from the wheat kernel, is available as yellowish-tan flakes that have been either toasted or not. It is often vacuum-packed to prevent oxidative changes that may occur in the fat. Wheat germ is a good source of B vitamins, iron, and other nutrients and may be added to both yeast and quick breads. The vitamin potency of wheat germ is not appreciably decreased by baking in the yeast breads that contain it; however, the germ has been found to exert a deleterious effect on the baking quality of flour. For this reason, a relatively strong flour is best used with it. The germ may be substituted to the extent of one-fifth to one-third of the flour.

Defatted wheat germ is also available. It is stable, a good source of protein and fiber as well as certain vitamins and minerals, and may be used in the food industry as a nutritional ingredient for baked products, breakfast cereals, and snack foods.

Flours and Meals Other Than Wheat Flour

Flours other than wheat are used in quick breads as well as in yeast breads.

Rye Flour. Rye flour is obtained by sifting rye meal. It has some gluten-forming properties but it contains chiefly gliadin with only small amounts of glutenin. Therefore, bread made from rye flour, although not necessarily soggy or heavy, is more compact and less elastic than bread made with wheat flour. Some white flour is often combined with rye flour in making bread to yield a lighter, more porous product than is possible with rye flour alone.

Cornmeal and Corn Flour. Cornmeal, a granular product made from either white or yellow corn, is commonly used in several types of quick breads. Its chief protein, *zein*, has none of the properties of the gluten of wheat. If a crumbly product is to be avoided, cornmeal must be combined with some white flour, preferably all-purpose flour, to bind it. Corn flour has the same

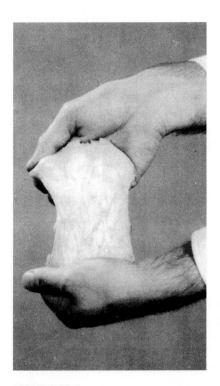

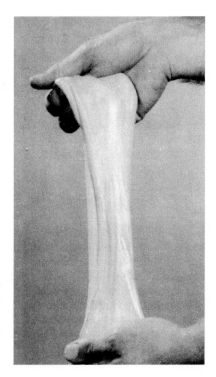

FIGURE 23.5
The different properties of glutenin (*left*), gliadin (*center*), and gluten (*right*). (Courtesy of Baker's Digest and R. J. Dimler)

properties as cornmeal except that it is finer. It is used chiefly in commercial pancake mixes and prepared cereals.

Soy Flour.　Soy flour is made from soybeans, which are legumes. Although soy flour is high in protein, the protein has none of the characteristics of gluten. Soy flour must be used with a strong or moderately strong wheat flour for good results in the baking of breads. An important advantage of using soy flour in baked products is the contribution it makes to the amount and quality of the protein. Soy flour in baked items promotes moisture retention, improves crust color, and extends shelf life. Federal standards for commercial white breads permit the use of 3 percent soy flour as an optional ingredient.

Miscellaneous Flours.　*Buckwheat flour* does not have the same baking properties as does wheat flour. The principal use of buckwheat is in pancakes and waffles. Some of the pancake batters are fermented to increase the flavor.

Triticale flour, made from the cereal that is a cross between wheat and rye, may be used to make yeast bread of satisfactory quality. Its flavor has been reported to be like that of a very mild rye bread [8].

Rice flour is fundamentally rice starch. *Potato flour* is used in some countries and, like rice flour, is chiefly starch.

Amaranth flour, made by grinding the tiny amaranth seed, is used in some areas of Latin America, Africa, and Asia. Amaranth is now being cultivated in limited amounts in the United States. Some interesting historical notes tell us that amaranth grain was a staple cereal during the Mayan and Aztec periods of Central America. On some ceremonial occasions, the seed was ground and shaped with human blood into figures representing gods or revered animals and eaten as part of religious rites. However, to eliminate the established worship rituals, amaranth cultivation was prohibited when Cortez conquered this area in 1519. This grain has therefore been dormant as a popular food crop until relatively recently [18]. Amaranth flour has a high content of the amino acid lysine, which is limited in wheat flour. It may make a valuable nutritional contribution when it is combined in wheat breads, cookies, and other baked products [17].

Leavening Agents

To *leaven* means to "make light and porous." Most baked flour products today are leavened. This is done by incorporation into or formation in the product of a gas that expands during preparation and subsequent heating.

Major Leavening Gases

Three major leavening gases are air, steam or water vapor, and carbon dioxide. In some flour mixtures, one of these leavening gases predominates, whereas in other products, two or three of the gases play important roles.

Air is incorporated into flour mixtures by beating eggs, by folding and rolling dough, by creaming fat and sugar together, or by beating batters. In common practice, some air is incorporated into all flour mixtures.

Because all flour mixtures contain some water and are usually heated so that the water vaporizes, steam leavens all flour mixtures to a certain degree.

Some products leavened almost entirely by steam are popovers and cream puffs. These mixtures have a high percentage of liquid, and baking is started at a high oven temperature, which rapidly causes steam to form. Because one volume of water increases to more than 1,600 volumes when converted into steam, it has tremendous leavening power. The water available for conversion to steam may be added as liquid or as a component of other ingredients, such as eggs. Egg whites contain enough water to furnish two to three times more expansion in baking angel food cakes than does the air that was added by beating. Even stiff doughs, such as pie crust, are partially leavened by steam.

Carbon dioxide may be produced in a flour mixture either by a biological process or by a purely chemical reaction.

Biological Production of Carbon Dioxide

Carbon dioxide is produced by the action of yeast and certain bacteria on sugar. This process is called **fermentation**, and carbon dioxide is a by-product of the overall reaction. Yeast ferments sugar to form ethyl alcohol and carbon dioxide. The alcohol is volatilized by the heat of baking. The fermentation is catalyzed by a mixture of many enzymes produced by the yeast cells. Sugar is usually added to yeast-flour mixtures to speed up fermentation and the production of carbon dioxide gas. If no sugar is used, yeast can form gas slowly from the small amount of sugar that is present in flour. **Maltose** is also produced in flour from the action of **amylase** as it hydrolyzes starch. **Maltase**, an enzyme produced by yeast, then hydrolyzes the maltose to yield glucose, which is available for fermentation by the yeast. The use of yeast in leavening is discussed further in Chapter 25.

Certain bacteria may also produce leavening gas in flour mixtures. One type produces hydrogen and carbon dioxide gases in salt-rising bread. Although the organisms occur normally in the cornmeal used to make the sponge for salt-rising bread, they have also been isolated and put on the market as a starter for this type of bread. Sourdough bread also uses bacteria in producing leavening gas.

Fermentation the transformation of organic substances into smaller molecules by the action of microorganisms; yeast ferments glucose to yield carbon dioxide and alcohol

Maltose a disaccharide or double sugar composed of two glucose units

Amylase an enzyme that hydrolyzes starch to dextrins and maltose

Maltase an enzyme that hydrolyzes maltose to glucose

Chemical Production of Carbon Dioxide

Sodium bicarbonate (baking soda) in a flour mixture gives off carbon dioxide (CO_2) gas when it is heated in accordance with the reaction

$$2NaHCO_3 \;+\; \text{heat} \;\rightarrow\; Na_2CO_3 \;+\; CO_2 \;+\; H_2O$$

| sodium bicarbonate | | sodium carbonate | carbon dioxide | water |

However, the sodium carbonate (Na_2CO_3) residue from this reaction has a disagreeable flavor and produces a yellow color in light-colored baked products. Brown spots may also occur in the cooked product if the soda is not finely powdered or is not uniformly distributed throughout the flour.

To avoid the problem of a bitter, soapy-flavored residue in the baked product, sodium bicarbonate is combined with various acids. The flavor of the residue is dependent on the kind of acid involved in the reaction. The salts formed with many acids are not objectionable in flavor.

Some food substances contain acids and may be combined with soda in flour mixtures, where they release carbon dioxide gas:

1. Buttermilk or sour milk (containing lactic acid)
2. Molasses (containing a mixture of organic acids)
3. Brown sugar (which has a small amount of molasses coating the sugar crystals)
4. Honey
5. Citrus fruit juices (containing citric and other organic acids)
6. Applesauce and other fruits
7. Vinegar (containing acetic acid)

The optimum amount of soda to combine with an acid food in a recipe depends on the degree of acidity of that food. The acid-containing foods listed vary in acidity and yield variable results when combined with soda. However, the usual amount of soda to combine with 1 cup of buttermilk or fully soured milk is 1/2 teaspoon. Less soda is required for milk that is less sour. Because the pronounced flavor of molasses may mask any undesirable flavor resulting from an excess of soda, up to 1 teaspoon of soda is often recommended for use with 1 cup of molasses, but less may be used. The acidity of honey and of brown sugar is too low to allow their use in flour mixtures as the only source of acid to combine with soda.

Cream of tartar is an acid salt (potassium acid tartrate) and may be combined with soda to produce carbon dioxide gas when the mixture is moistened. The salt that is left as a residue in this reaction (sodium potassium tartrate) is not objectionable in flavor. The chemical reaction between cream of tartar and soda is

$$HKC_4H_4O_6 \ + \ NaHCO_3 \ \rightarrow \ NaKC_4H_4O_6 \ + \ CO_2 \ + \ H_2O$$

| cream of tartar | sodium bicarbonate | sodium potassium tartrate | carbon dioxide | water |

Baking powders were developed as one of the first convenience foods. They contain mixtures of dry acid or acid salts and baking soda. Starch is added to standardize the mixture and help stabilize the components so that they do not react prematurely. Baking powders have been classified into different groups or types depending on the acid constituent used; however, not all types are available to the consumer.

The type of baking powder that is generally available for home use is called *SAS-phosphate* baking powder. It is a double-acting baking powder, which means that it reacts to release carbon dioxide gas at room temperature when the dry ingredients are moistened and reacts again when heat is applied in the process of baking. SAS-phosphate baking powder contains two acid substances that each reacts with soda to release carbon dioxide gas at different times in the baking process. One of the acids is a phosphate, usually calcium acid phosphate. This acid salt reacts with soda at room temperature as soon as liquid is added to the dry ingredients. This causes the batter or dough to become somewhat light and porous during the mixing process. The other acid substance is sodium aluminum sulfate (SAS). It requires heat as well as moisture to complete its reaction with soda. Therefore, additional carbon dioxide gas is produced during baking.

The reactions of calcium acid phosphate and baking soda are very complex and difficult to write. A number of different salts are probably produced in this reaction and they may interact with each other.

$$CaH_4(PO_4)_2 \quad + \quad NaHCO_3 \quad \rightarrow \quad \text{insoluble calcium phosphate salts} \quad + \quad \text{soluble sodium phosphate salts} \quad + \quad CO_2 \quad + \quad H_2O$$

calcium acid   sodium   carbon   water
phosphate   bicarbonate   dioxide

Sodium aluminum sulfate apparently reacts in two stages. The first reaction is with water and results in the production of sulfuric acid as heat is applied, after which the sulfuric acid reacts with soda to produce carbon dioxide gas, according to the following equations.

$$(1) \quad Na_2SO_4Al_2(SO_4)_3 \quad + \quad 6H_2O \quad \xrightarrow{heat} \quad Na_2SO_4 \quad + \quad 2Al(OH)_3 \quad + \quad H_2SO_4$$

        sodium aluminum   water   sodium   aluminum   sulfuric
             sulfate   sulfate   hydroxide   acid

$$(2) \quad 3H_2SO_4 \quad + \quad 6NaHCO_3 \quad \longrightarrow \quad 6CO_2 \quad + \quad 6H_2O \quad + \quad 3Na_2SO_4$$

      sulfuric   sodium   carbon   water   sodium
        acid   bicarbonate   dioxide   sulfate

It should be emphasized that *all baking powders are composed of soda plus an acid ingredient*. The carbon dioxide gas (CO_2) comes from the soda. Different acid components may be used. The food industry has available to it a wider variety of baking powders, utilizing various acid components, than does the consumer.

According to federal law, all types of baking powders must contain at least 12 percent available CO_2 gas. Those powders manufactured for home use generally contain 14 percent, and some powders for commercial use have 17 percent available gas. Baking powder containers should always be kept tightly covered to avoid the absorption of moisture that causes the acid and alkali constituents to react prematurely with the loss of some carbon dioxide.

All baking powders leave residues in the mixture in which they are used. The sodium sulfate (Na_2SO_4) residue from the SAS-phosphate baking powder has a somewhat bitter taste that may be objectionable to certain individuals. Some people are more sensitive than others to this bitter taste.

An optimum amount of baking powder is desirable for any baked product. If too much baking powder is used, the cell walls of the flour mixture are stretched beyond their limit, and they may break and collapse. If too little baking powder is present, insufficient expansion occurs, and a compact product results. Use of the minimum amount of SAS-phosphate baking powder that leavens satisfactorily is particularly desirable because of the bitter residue formed with this baking powder. Between 1 and 1½ teaspoons of SAS-phosphate baking powder per cup of flour should be adequate for the leavening of most flour mixtures.

Methods of Adding Baking Powder and Soda

Dry chemical leavening agents, including baking powders, are usually sifted or mixed with the flour. They are not allowed to become wet, and thus begin to release their carbon dioxide gas, until the later stages of the mixing process, when the liquid ingredients are combined with the dry ingredients. It has sometimes been suggested that the soda be mixed with the sour milk or molasses called for in a recipe. This is generally not recommended, however, because leavening gas is more readily lost in this case and it is important to retain as much gas as possible in the flour mixture. Nevertheless, because of the high viscosity of molasses, gas tends to be lost slowly from a mixture of soda and molasses.

It is expected that carbon dioxide gas will be more rapidly lost from a mixture of buttermilk and soda than from a batter made by mixing the soda with dry ingredients and then adding the buttermilk. However, students in laboratory classes have compared the volumes of chocolate cakes containing soda and buttermilk when the soda was either sifted with the dry ingredients or added directly to the buttermilk. They found that when the soda-buttermilk mixture is added immediately to the batter, the volumes of the finished cakes are quite similar. Allowing the soda-buttermilk mixture to stand before adding it to the batter results in a lower cake volume.

Substitutions of Chemical Leavening Agents

Buttermilk and soda may be substituted for sweet milk and baking powder and vice versa in many recipes for baked products. One-half teaspoon of soda and 1 cup of buttermilk or fully soured milk produce an amount of leavening gas almost equivalent to that produced by 2 teaspoons of SAS-phosphate baking powder. Other, approximately equivalent substitutes include 1/2 teaspoon of baking soda plus 1¼ teaspoons cream of tartar and 1/2 teaspoon baking soda plus 1 cup molasses. Sweet milk can be made sour by taking 1 tablespoon of vinegar or lemon juice and adding enough sweet milk to make 1 cup, or by adding 1¾ teaspoons of cream of tartar to 1 cup of sweet milk. An example of making a substitution in a recipe is the following.

ORIGINAL RECIPE

2 c (230 g) flour
1 c (237 mL) sweet milk

3 tsp (9.6 g) SAS-phosphate powder

RECIPE WITH SUBSTITUTION OF SODA AND SOUR MILK

2 c (230 g) flour
1 c (237 mL) buttermilk

1/2 tsp (2 g) soda
1 tsp (3.2 g) SAS-phosphate powder

Fat

The major role of fat in flour mixtures is to tenderize or "shorten" the strands of gluten. This tenderizing effect is produced through formation of layers or masses that physically separate different strands of gluten and prevent them from coming together. To shorten effectively, a fat must have the capacity to coat or spread well and to adhere well to flour particles.

It is difficult to make definite statements concerning the comparative shortening power of various fats because many factors have been shown to modify the effect of fats in different mixtures. For example, the manner in which a fat is distributed in a mixture, the extent of distribution, the temperature of the fat and of the mixture, the presence or absence of **emulsifiers** in the mixture, the type of mixture, and the method and extent of mixing, as well as the method by which the fat itself has been processed, may have an effect on the shortening power of the fat.

Smoothness of the batter and desirable texture in some finished baked products, such as shortened cakes, are related to the emulsification of the fat in the batter. The presence of some **monoglycerides** and **diglycerides** in the fat increases the degree of emulsification of the fat, allowing it to be dispersed in small particles throughout the batter. The addition of emulsifiers to shortened cake batters has been shown to yield cakes of increased volume and finer texture than usually result without the use of emulsifiers.

The *plasticity* of a fat is related to its shortening power. In a plastic fat, some of the **triglyceride** molecules are present in a liquid form and some are crystallized in a solid form. The presence of both solid and liquid phases in the fat means that the fat can be molded or shaped rather than being fractured or broken when force is applied to it. Fats that are more plastic are more spreadable and, presumably, can spread over a greater surface area of flour particles than can less plastic fats. The temperature of fat affects plasticity. At 18°C (64°F), butter is less plastic than at 22° to 28°C (72° to 83°F). At higher temperatures, butter tends to become very soft or to melt completely.

A shortometer is an instrument that measures the weight required to break a baked wafer. Use of the shortometer has enabled a number of tests of the shortening value of fats to be made on pastry. The results of these tests have been somewhat variable but, in many cases, lards have been shown to have more shortening power than most hydrogenated fats, butter, and margarine. Oils that are high in **polyunsaturated fats** usually produce more tender pastries than lards. One explanation that has been offered is that these oils cover a larger surface area of flour particles per molecule of fat than do fats containing a relatively high proportion of **saturated fatty acids**. However, the relationship between the degree of unsaturation and shortening power of fats needs further clarification.

With other proportions and other conditions standardized, the higher the concentration of fat in a mixture, the greater the shortening power. This point deserves consideration in the substitution of one fat for another. Butter and margarines contain approximately 82 percent fat and about 16 percent water. Reduced-calorie spreads that are marketed as substitutes for margarine or butter contain even less fat. Lard, hydrogenated fats, and oils contain essentially 100 percent fat. Disregarding other factors that appear to affect the shortening power of fats, the mere substitution of an equal weight of a fat of higher fat concentration for one of lower concentration affects the tenderness of baked flour mixtures.

Emulsifier   a surface-active agent that acts as a bridge between two immiscible liquids and allows an emulsion to form

Monoglyceride   glycerol combined with one fatty acid; used as an emulsifier

Diglyceride   glycerol combined with two fatty acids; usually present with monoglycerides in an emulsifier mixture

Triglyceride   glycerol combined with three fatty acids; most food fats are triglycerides

Polyunsaturated fats   fats that contain a relatively high proportion of polyunsaturated fatty acids, which have two or more double bonds between carbon atoms; these fatty acids are shaped differently from saturated fatty acids because of the double bonds

Saturated fatty acids   fatty acids that contain no double bonds between carbon atoms and thus hold all of the hydrogen that can be attached to the carbons

Fat in Leavening

Plastic fats appear to play important roles in some flour mixtures in the trapping of air bubbles that later contribute to the texture of the finished product. This role of fat appears to be particularly important in the preparation of shortened cakes. It has been suggested that creaming fat and sugar crystals together and also vigorously beating fat-containing batters cause air cells to be entrapped in the mixture. Fats that incorporate air readily and allow it to be dispersed in small cells are said to have good creaming properties.

Fat Replacers

Surveys of consumer attitudes regarding food have confirmed their concern about the fat content of food products [3]. Interest in reduced-fat baked goods is high. Products such as no-fat cookies, granola bars, and breakfast bars are being marketed. Substances used to replace fat in a flour mixture must mimic the effects of fat on the eating quality of the finished product. This challenges the ingenuity of the food industry as new products are formulated. Cellulose, gums, maltodextrins, modified starches, and polydextrose are carbohydrate-based substances that are used as fat replacers. Protein blends may also be utilized. Specially designed emulsifiers are important components in fat-reduced products since they extend the effects of the fat [13]. However, the fat in many baked product formulas can be reduced at least slightly without jeopardizing the quality of the finished item. Fat replacers are discussed in Chapter 18.

Liquids

Liquids have various uses in flour mixtures. They hydrate the starch and gluten and dissolve certain constituents, such as sugar, salts, and baking powder. It is only when baking powders are wet that the evolution of carbon dioxide gas begins. The typical structure or framework of doughs and batters is not formed until the protein particles become hydrated. The **gelatinization of starch** during baking requires moisture.

Starch gelatinization the swelling of starch granules when heated with water, often resulting in thickening

Various liquids may be used in flour mixtures, including water, potato water, milk, fruit juices, and coffee. The water content of eggs is also a part of the total liquid.

Eggs

Eggs may be used as a means of incorporating air into a batter. The incorporation of air is possible because egg proteins coagulate on beating and give some structure or rigidity to the cell walls surrounding the air bubbles. Egg whites can form a particularly stable foam. As they are beaten, the cell walls become increasingly thinner and more tender up to an optimum point. Beaten egg whites can be carefully folded into a batter, retaining much of the air in the foam.

Lipoprotein a lipid or fatty substance combined with a protein; egg yolk contains lipoproteins that combine phospholipids with protein

Egg yolks add flavor and color to flour mixtures. They also aid in forming emulsions of fat and water because of their content of **lipoproteins**, which are effective emulsifying agents. Because egg proteins coagulate on heating, the addition of eggs to flour mixtures increases the rigidity of the baked product.

Sugar and Other Sweeteners

Granulated sugar is used in many flour mixtures for sweetening purposes. It also contributes to the browning of outer surfaces of baked products. Caramelization occurs at high oven temperatures as the surface of the products becomes dry. In yeast mixtures, sugar is a readily available food for the yeast plant. Sugar has a tenderizing effect because it interferes with the development of gluten in a batter or dough. It may do this by tying up water so that less water is available for the gluten and more manipulation is necessary to develop the gluten structure than when sugar is not present. The volume of many baked flour mixtures is increased by the addition of optimal amounts of sugar, because the gluten mass is tenderized and expands more easily under the pressure of leavening gases. Sugar probably also helps to achieve a fine, even texture in many baked products [12].

The **coagulation** temperature of egg proteins is elevated by sugar. This is especially important in the making of sponge-type cakes containing relatively large amounts of egg. Sugar also increases the temperature at which starch gelatinizes. This is of particular importance in high-sugar products such as cakes.

Brown sugar imparts a distinctive flavor to baked foods and yields products that tend to remain moist longer than those made with granulated sugar. Measured lightly, brown sugar weighs less per cup than granulated sugar. It should be firmly packed in the cup during measurement or be substituted by weight for granulated sugar.

Other sweeteners are sometimes used in baked products. Honey, molasses, and syrups may be used in yeast breads, where they provide distinctive flavors as well as a substrate for yeast fermentation. High-fructose corn syrup has replaced up to 25 percent of the sugar in angel cake without greatly affecting quality characteristics [5]. Crystalline fructose has replaced sucrose (table sugar) in some cakes and cake mixes on the market.

High-intensity or alternate sweeteners, including saccharin, encapsulated aspartame, acesulfame-K, and sucralose, are stable under high temperatures and retain sweetness in baked products. Some of these have a nonsweet aftertaste [16]. A bulking or bodying agent such as polydextrose must be added along with high-intensity sweeteners to substitute for some of sugar's effects on texture. Compensation must also be made for the effect of sugar on the tenderness of the finished product. Again, the food industry faces challenges in formulating no-sugar baked products. Alternate sweeteners are discussed in Chapter 11.

Caramelization the development of brown color and caramel flavor as dry sugar is heated to a high temperature; chemical decomposition occurs in the sugar

Coagulation change in protein, after it has been denatured, that results in hardening or precipitation and is often accomplished by heating

•CLASSIFICATION OF BATTERS AND DOUGHS

Flour mixtures vary in thickness depending largely on the proportion of flour to liquid. Based on thickness, flour mixtures are classified as batters or doughs.

Batters

Batters are classified as pour batters or drop batters. There is considerable variation within each group; some pour batters are very thin, whereas others pour with difficulty. A pour batter contains 2/3 to 1 cup of liquid per cup of flour. A drop batter usually has 1/2 to 3/4 cup of liquid per cup of flour. In batters containing approximately 1 part of liquid to 2 parts of flour, gluten development readily occurs on mixing. Popovers and thin griddle-cake and shortened-cake batters are examples of pour batters. Some drop batters are stiff enough to require scraping from the spoon. Drop batters include muffins, many quick breads, and various kinds of cookies. A batter containing yeast is called a *sponge*.

Doughs

Doughs are thick enough to be handled or kneaded on a flat surface. Most doughs are rolled in the final stages of preparation, although yeast dough is not usually rolled except for the shaping of certain types of rolls. Doughs may be soft (just stiff enough to handle) or stiff. Soft doughs contain about 1/3 cup of liquid per cup of flour. A stiff dough may contain only 1/8 cup of liquid per cup of flour. Examples of soft-dough products include baking powder biscuits, rolled cookies, yeast bread, and rolls. Pie crust is an example of a stiff dough.

•GENERAL METHODS FOR MIXING BATTERS AND DOUGHS

General objectives in the mixing of doughs and batters are uniform distribution of ingredients, minimum loss of the leavening agent, optimum blending to produce characteristic textures in various products, and optimum development of gluten for the desired individual properties.

Many different methods are employed for the mixing of batters and doughs. However, there are three basic methods of mixing that may be adapted for use with a variety of products.

Muffin Method

In the muffin method, dry ingredients are sifted together into the bowl used for mixing. The eggs are lightly beaten and the liquid and melted fat (or oil) are added to the eggs. The liquid ingredients are then blended with the dry ingredients, the amount of stirring depending on the mixture.

For thin mixtures, such as popovers, thin griddle cakes, and thin waffle mixtures, lumping can be prevented by adding the liquid ingredients gradually to the dry ingredients. On the other hand, the overstirring of thicker batters, such as thick waffle mixtures and muffins, can be prevented by the addition of the liquid ingredients all at once to the dry ingredients. Thicker batters are stirred only until the dry ingredients are dampened to avoid an undesirable development of gluten and a resulting decrease in tenderness.

Pastry or Biscuit Method

In the pastry or biscuit method, the dry ingredients are sifted together. Fat is cut in or blended with the dry ingredients, and liquid is then added to the fat-flour mixture. Although this method is used mainly for pastry and biscuits, it is also appropriate for other flour mixtures. The techniques of handling the dough after the addition of liquid differ for pastry and biscuits. Biscuits are generally mixed more thoroughly and are lightly kneaded before they are rolled out and cut into the desired shapes.

Conventional Method

Cakes are mixed by more than one method. The conventional cake method, or simply the conventional method, is usually understood to mean the conventional way in which fat and sugar are creamed together, beaten eggs are added, and dry and liquid ingredients are alternately blended with the fat-sugar-egg mixture. This method may also be used for making cookies and various quick breads as well as other flour products.

Yeast bread, cream puffs, and sponge-type cake are mixed by special methods applicable only to these products. Whatever the method, the optimum amount of manipulation varies with the type of product, with the character and proportion of the ingredients used, and with the temperature of the ingredients.

•STRUCTURE OF BATTERS AND DOUGHS

The structure that develops in batters and doughs varies according to the kind and proportion of ingredients used; however, in all mixtures, except those of high liquid content, the gluten particles, on becoming hydrated, tend to adhere and form a continuous mass that spreads out into a network. Some components of the mixture, such as salts and sugar, are partially or completely dissolved in the liquid. The starch granules from the flour tend to be embedded in the gluten network (Figure 23.6). Other components act as emulsifying agents by separating or dividing the fat in the mixture into particles of varying fineness. The temperature as well as the physical and chemical state of the ingredients partially determines the degree of dispersion of the emulsion. Melted fats or oils may behave differently from solid fats in certain doughs and batters.

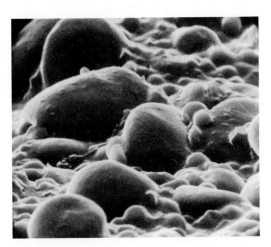

FIGURE 23.6
Scanning electron photomicrograph of a dough sample showing a developed gluten film covering starch granules of variable sizes. (Reprinted from Varriano-Marston, E. A comparison of dough preparation procedures for scanning electron microscopy. *Food Technology 31*, 34 (No. 10), 1977. Copyright © by Institute of Food Technologists.)

The texture of the finished product depends largely on the structure obtained in the mixing of the dough or batter. Texture is a combination of such characteristics as the distribution of cells, the thickness of cell walls, the character of the crumb (elastic, crumbly, velvety, or harsh), and the grain (the size of the cells). Optimum texture cannot be expected to be the same for all products, because of the variation in the kinds and amounts of constituents used. Typical textures for different baked products are discussed along with those products in later chapters. Variations from typical textures and possible causes for variation are also discussed.

When all the factors that affect texture are considered, it is not surprising that products made from the same formula may differ with several bakings. Although a certain degree of control of materials, manipulation, and temperatures is possible, it is difficult in practical baking in the kitchen to always control all factors that play a part in determining the quality of the end products obtained. In industrial operations and in many foodservice establishments, controls are sufficiently precise and reproducible that the same quality product is guaranteed each time. Quality assurance programs are geared to achieve just that.

•DRY FLOUR MIXES

A wide variety of flour-based mixes are marketed. Excellent directions to the consumer in the use of these prepared mixes tend to ensure uniform, good-quality finished products. In addition to flour, they may contain leavening, salt, fat (sometimes powdered shortening), nonfat dry milk, dried eggs, sugar, and flavoring ingredients, such as dried extracts, cocoa, ginger, and dried molasses, depending on the type of mixture. Some mixes are yeast mixtures for making fermented bread or rolls.

A number of additives are used and have contributed to the success of commercial flour mixes. These include various emulsifiers, modified starches, caseinate, gums, cellulose, and whipping aids. A combination of added substances is often necessary in the production of reduced-fat or reduced-calorie mixes that are appearing on the market in increasing numbers.

Mixes are convenient timesavers, and they often cost no more (and sometimes even less) than a similar product prepared in the kitchen. Costs must be determined on an individual basis, however, and are sometimes difficult to compare because of differences in ingredients and yields. (The cost of convenience foods is discussed in Chapter 2.)

A number of mixes may be used in foodservice operations. The savings in labor cost is an important consideration, along with an evaluation of quality, in making decisions regarding the use of dry flour mixes in foodservice establishments.

Various flour mixes can also be made in the home kitchen, saving time by measuring and mixing at least some of the ingredients at one time. (The making of mixes at home is discussed in Chapter 2.) However, because the techniques used in the production of commercial mixes are not available for home use, homemade mixes do not have as long a shelf life. They should be adequately packaged and stored at cool temperatures. Commercial mixes usually contain a leavening acid that dissolves slowly, such as anhydrous monocalcium phosphate or sodium acid pyrophosphate, to prevent the premature reaction of the baking powder during storage. Also, off-flavors do not readily develop in the mixes with these acids.

•BAKING AT HIGH ALTITUDES

Some balancing of ingredients as well as variation of baking temperature may be necessary at high altitudes. Because the atmospheric pressure is less, the leavening gases in baked products meet less resistance and are apt to overexpand, especially during the early part of baking. This overexpansion may stretch the cells to the extent that they break and collapse, producing a coarse texture and decreased volume.

Corrections in recipes that are standardized for use at sea level may involve decreasing the leavening agent or strengthening the cell walls by decreasing the sugar or adding more flour. Increased liquid may also be added because of greater loss by evaporation. Oven temperatures may be increased. However, definite rules cannot be strictly applied in all recipe adjustments because of the varying proportions of ingredients in recipes. Each recipe needs to be tested individually. Agricultural Experiment Stations in the western United States have studied the effects of altitudes up to 10,000 feet on baked products and have developed appropriate adjustments and recipes [2, 6].

Altitude corrections are not necessary for pastry and cream puffs, although yeast products may require shorter rising periods. Muffins and biscuits can usually be made at higher altitudes with little change in recipes, although a slight decrease in baking powder might be desirable above 5,000 feet. Because cakes have a very delicate structure, they are more affected by altitude than most other baked products. The amount of sugar may be decreased and the amount of flour increased in angel food and sponge cakes as altitude increases. The American Home Economics Association, in the *Handbook of Food Preparation*, suggests the adjustments for shortened cakes provided in Table 23.1.

TABLE 23.1
Adjustments for Shortened Cakes

Adjustment	3,000 Feet	5,000 Feet	7,000 Feet
Reduce baking powder			
For each teaspoon, decrease:	⅛ tsp	⅛–¼ tsp	¼ tsp
Reduce sugar			
For each cup, decrease:	0–1 Tbsp	0–2 Tbsp	1–3 Tbsp
Increase liquid			
For each cup, add:	1–2 Tbsp	2–4 Tbsp	3–4 Tbsp

Source: Handbook of Food Preparation, 8th ed. Washington, DC: American Home Economics Association, 1980.

STUDY QUESTIONS

1. a. What is meant by the *milling* of flour?
   b. How is white flour produced?
   c. How is whole-wheat or graham flour produced?
   d. How do hard and soft wheat flours generally differ in characteristics and composition?
   e. Name three grades of white flour and indicate which is usually found on the retail market.

2. For each of the following types of flour, describe general characteristics and uses in food preparation.
   a. Bread flour
   b. All-purpose flour
   c. Pastry flour
   d. Cake flour
   e. Instantized flour
   f. Self-rising flour

3. About 85 percent of the proteins in white wheat flour are relatively insoluble and play an important role in developing the structure of baked products.
   a. Name the two wheat flour proteins that develop into gluten with moistening and mixing or kneading.
   b. Describe the characteristics of wheat gluten and discuss its role in the preparation of baked flour mixtures.

4. a. What is meant by the word *leaven*?
   b. Name three leavening gases that are commonly present in baked products.
   c. Describe several ways in which air may be incorporated into a batter or dough during preparation.
   d. Explain why steam is such an effective leavening gas and name two products that are leavened primarily by steam.

5. Carbon dioxide (CO_2) gas may be produced by biological and by chemical means.
   a. Describe how CO_2 may be produced biologically in baked products.
   b. Describe examples of the chemical production of CO_2 in flour mixtures.

6. Although CO_2 will be released when soda is heated in a moist environment, explain why it cannot satisfactorily be used for leavening in baked products without an accompanying acid.

7. Baking powders always contain at least two active ingredients. Name them. Which one is responsible for the production of CO_2?

8. Name several acid foods that are commonly used with soda in baked products.

9. Generally, the only type of baking powder available to the consumer is SAS-phosphate baking powder.
   a. Explain why this baking powder is called *double-acting*.
   b. Name the active ingredients in this baking powder.
   c. Explain how the active ingredients participate in the production of CO_2 gas.

10. a. How much soda is usually used with 1 cup of buttermilk in a baked product?
    b. How much SAS-phosphate baking powder is usually used per 1 cup of flour to leaven a baked product?

11. Briefly describe the general role of each of the following ingredients in baked flour mixtures.
    a. Fat
    b. Flour
    c. Liquids
    d. Eggs
    e. Sugar

12. Why is it a challenge to produce acceptable baked products that are reduced in fat, sugar, and/or calories? Explain.
13. What are batters? Doughs? Give examples of each.
14. Describe each of the following general methods of mixing batters and doughs and give examples of baked products commonly prepared by each method.
    a. Muffin method
    b. Pastry or biscuit method
    c. Conventional method
15. a. Why do some adjustments need to be made in baked products when they are prepared at high altitudes? Briefly discuss this.
    b. Suggest appropriate adjustments for shortened cakes that are baked at high altitudes when using recipes standardized at sea level.

REFERENCES

1. American Home Economics Association. 1980. *Handbook of Food Preparation*, 8th ed. Washington, DC.
2. Boyd, M. S., and M. C. Schoonover. 1965. *Baking at High Altitude*. University of Wyoming Agricultural Experiment Station Bulletin No. 427. Laramie: University of Wyoming.
3. Bruhn, C. M., A. Cotter, K. Diaz-Knauf, J. Sutherlin, E. West, N. Wightman, E. Williamson, and M. Yaffee. 1992. Consumer attitudes and market potential for foods using fat substitutes. *Food Technology 46*, 81 (No. 4).
4. Butaki, R. C., and B. Dronzek. 1979. Comparison of gluten properties of four wheat varieties. *Cereal Chemistry 56*, 159.
5. Coleman, P. E., and C. A. Z. Harbers. 1983. High fructose corn syrup: Replacement for sucrose in angel cake. *Journal of Food Science 48*, 452.
6. Dyar, E., and E. Cassel. 1958. *Mile-High Cakes: Recipes for High Altitudes*. Colorado Agricultural Experiment Station Bulletin No 404-A. Fort Collins, CO.
7. Il, B., H. Daun, and S. G. Gilbert. 1991. Water sorption of gliadin. *Journal of Food Science 56*, 510.
8. Lorenz, K. 1972. Food uses of triticale. *Food Technology 26*, 66 (No. 11).
9. Ma, C., B. D. Oomah, and J. Holme. 1986. Effect of deamidation and succinylation on some physicochemical and baking properties of gluten. *Journal of Food Science 51*, 99.
10. Mani, K., C. Tragardh, A. C. Eliasson, and L. Lindahl. 1992. Water content, water soluble fraction, and mixing affect fundamental rheological properties of wheat flour doughs. *Journal of Food Science 57*, 1198.
11. Matthews, R. H., and E. A. Bechtel. 1966. Eating quality of some baked products made with instant flour. *Journal of Home Economics 58*, 729.
12. Myhre, D. V. 1970. The function of carbohydrates in baking. *Baker's Digest 44*, 32 (No. 3).
13. Nabors, L. O. 1992. Fat replacers: Options for controlling fat and calories in the diet. *Food and Nutrition News 64*, 5 (No. 1).
14. Ngo, W., R. C. Hoseney, and W. R. Moore. 1985. Dynamic rheological properties of cake batters made from chlorine-treated and untreated flours. *Journal of Food Science 50*, 1338.
15. Pomeranz, Y., and M. M. MacMasters. 1968. Structure and composition of the wheat kernel. *Baker's Digest 42*, 24 (No. 4).
16. Redlinger, P. A., and C. S. Setser. 1987. Sensory quality of selected sweeteners: Unbaked and baked flour doughs. *Journal of Food Science 52*, 1391.

17. Sanchez-Marroquin, A., M. V. Domingo, S. Maya, and C. Saldana. 1985. Amaranth flour blends and fractions for baking applications. *Journal of Food Science 50*, 789.

18. Saunders, R. M., and R. Becker. 1984. Amaranthus: A potential food and feed resource. In Pomeranz, Y., Ed: *Advances in Cereal Science and Technology*, Vol. VI. St. Paul, MN: American Association of Cereal Chemists, Inc.

19. Watson, C. A., W. C. Shuey, R. D. Crawford, and M. R. Gumbmann. 1977. Physical dough, baking, and nutritional qualities of straight-grade and extended-extraction flours. *Cereal Chemistry 54*, 657.

Quick Breads

24

Traditionally, *quick breads* have included a variety of products that can be prepared without the rising or proofing time required by yeast breads. Quick breads are often served warm. Examples of quick breads are popovers, pancakes or griddle cakes, waffles, muffins, biscuits, coffee cakes, and loaf breads made with baking powder as a leavening ingredient. Cream puffs may also be classified with quick breads.

Quick bread ideas and recipes are borrowed from many different ethnic groups. There are Swedish pancakes and pancake balls, Finnish oven pancakes, and German potato pancakes. In many parts of Mexico, flour tortillas are made in the home from a basic flour dough that usually contains baking powder; the dough is rolled into flat circles before being baked on a hot griddle. Sesame turnovers come from Greece; they are made of a pastrylike dough containing a small amount of baking powder and are filled with ground nuts and seeds. The variety of quick breads with ethnic origins is almost limitless.

Table 24.1 provides proportions of ingredients for some basic quick breads. Ingredients are balanced to produce the type of product desired. Structural ingredients, such as flour and egg, are balanced against tenderizing ingredients, primarily sugar and fat, so that the product will have form or structure yet be appropriately tender. The consistency of the batter or dough is generally determined by the ratio of flour to liquid ingredients.

•POPOVERS

Ingredients

Popovers contain a relatively high proportion of liquid, usually milk, and are leavened chiefly by the steam produced in a hot oven in the early stages of baking. They are usually mixed by the muffin method. (The muffin method is described in Chapter 23). Although either pastry or all-purpose flour may be used for making popovers, the crusts are usually more rigid when all-purpose flour is used. Because of the high percentage of moisture in the batter, the gluten particles, on becoming hydrated, tend to float in the liquid. Because the

TABLE 24.1

Proportions of Ingredients for Quick Breads

Product	Flour	Liquid	Eggs	Fat	Sugar	Salt	Baking Powder	Soda
Popovers	1 c	1 c	2–3	0–1 Tbsp		¼–½ tsp		
Cream puffs	1 c	1 c	4	½ c		¼ tsp		
Muffins	1 c	½ c	½–1	1–2 Tbsp	1–2 Tbsp	½ tsp	1½–2 tsp	
Waffles	1 c	⅔ c	1–2	3 Tbsp	1 tsp	½ tsp	1–2 tsp	
Pancakes								
Sweet milk	1 c	⅔ c	1	1 Tbsp	1 tsp	¼–½ tsp	1–2 tsp	
Thick buttermilk	1 c	1 c	1	1–2 Tbsp		¼–½ tsp	¼–½ tsp (optional)	½ tsp
Thick sour cream	1 c	1 c	1			¼–½ tsp	¼–½ tsp (optional)	½ tsp
Biscuits	1 c	Rolled, ⅓ c Dropped, ⅓–⅜ c		2–3 Tbsp		½ tsp	1½–2 tsp	

gluten particles do not adhere to each other sufficiently to form a continuous mass, the batter may be stirred much or little without appreciably affecting the finished product. The batter should be smooth and free from lumps. With so small an amount of flour, the liquid is best added gradually at first until the lumps are stirred out.

Egg is an essential constituent of popovers and gives them structure. The floating gluten particles do not form a mass of sufficient continuity to expand under the pressure of the steam formed during baking. With no egg, the popover is heavy and has a very small volume; with two eggs per cup of flour, enough extensible and coagulable material is furnished to form rigid walls. If the eggs are small or if pastry flour is used, three eggs per cup of flour provide more desirable results than two eggs. Fat serves little purpose in popovers. It tends to float on top of the thin batter, and thus chiefly affects the top crust. If as much as 1 tablespoon of fat is used, the top crust may have a flaky appearance.

Characteristics

Popovers are high rising and usually have irregular shapes. They are hollow, with thick crusty walls (Figure 24.1). Because of the high percentage of liquid in the mixture, the interior is moist but not similar to raw dough. Crusts should not be so brown that their flavor is impaired.

Baking

Muffin pans (preferably deep ones) or heat-resistant glass cups can be used for baking popovers. They are greased to keep the popovers from sticking. When iron pans are used, baking may be speeded up if the pans are prewarmed, because iron requires more time to become hot than does tin or aluminum. Since steam is the chief leavening agent in popovers, a hot oven temperature (450°F) is required to form steam quickly. After 15 minutes at 450°F, the oven is reduced to 375°F for the remainder of the baking time, about 45 minutes. If popovers are baked for the whole time at a hot temperature, the crusts may

FIGURE 24.1
Well-made popovers have a large volume and a moist, hollow interior. (Photographs by Roger P. Smith)

become too brown in the time required to form rigid walls that do not collapse on removal from the oven.

Browning in popovers is apparently produced primarily by the Maillard reaction. The amount of milk sugar or lactose in the mixture is probably sufficient for this reaction to occur. Dextrinization of starch in the flour may also contribute to browning.

Causes of Failure

Probably the chief cause of failure in making popovers is insufficient baking. Popovers are not necessarily done when they are brown and may collapse on removal from the oven if the egg proteins are not adequately coagulated. Popovers will not rise to a sufficient volume unless they are baked in a hot oven for the first part of baking so that steam can quickly be generated. An inadequate amount of egg in the formula may also result in decreased volume.

•CREAM PUFFS

Ingredients and Mixing

Cream puffs contain the same proportion of liquid to flour as do popovers and are also leavened primarily by steam, but they are made with eight times as much fat. Cream puffs are therefore considerably more tender than popovers. A large proportion of egg is used in cream puffs to emulsify the high percentage of fat.

The method of mixing the cream puff batter is unique to this product. The fat is melted in hot water, and the flour is added all at once with vigorous stirring. Heating is continued until the batter is smooth and forms a stiff ball. Gelatinization of the starch occurs during this cooking process. The mixture is then cooled slightly, and the eggs are added (either one unbeaten egg at a time, or one-third of the beaten eggs at one time). Thorough beating is necessary after each addition of egg. The eggs contain lipoproteins that act as emulsifying agents to divide the fat into small particles throughout the mixture. At this stage, the batter is smooth, stiff, and glossy. The egg also plays a role in obtaining a large volume. Egg proteins aid in the stretching process during the first stages of baking and are later coagulated by heat to contribute to the rigid structure of the final product. Even though the cream puff batter is stiff, it can be beaten without danger of toughening the puffs. The high percentage of fat and water in relation to flour interferes with the development of gluten and prevents it from forming a tenacious mass.

Characteristics

Puffs are usually irregular on the top surface, although the surface may vary depending on the consistency of the batter before baking. The walls are rigid but tender because of the high fat content. The center of the puff is hollow and moist. Some of the moist interior strands may be removed, if desired, and the puff dried out in the oven. The crust should have a light golden brown color (Figure 24.2). The hollow center of cream puffs is usually filled. A wide variety of mixtures can be used as fillings, including chicken, tuna, and other types of salads, custards and starch-thickened puddings, flavored and sweetened whipped cream mixtures, and ice cream and other frozen desserts. Smaller puffs are generally used for hors d'oeuvres and larger ones for desserts.

Baking

The cream puff batter is dropped in mounds onto an ungreased baking sheet, allowing some room between mounds for expansion during baking. A high oven temperature (450°F) is necessary to form steam quickly and bring about the puffing or expansion of the batter. The high temperature may be maintained throughout the baking period providing that overbrowning does not occur. The baking time is decreased to about 30 to 35 minutes if a high temperature is used continuously. If 450°F is used for 15 minutes, followed by about

FIGURE 24.2
Cream puffs. (Photograph by Roger P. Smith)

375°F for the remainder of the baking time, about 45 minutes of total baking time will be required. The puffs should feel rigid and should not collapse on removal from the oven. They are not necessarily done when they are brown.

Causes of Failure

As in the making of popovers, one possible cause of failure in making cream puffs is insufficient baking. If the walls of the puffs are not rigid, they will collapse on removal from the oven.

Another possible cause of failure is the excessive evaporation of moisture during the cooking of the paste. This alters the proportions of the ingredients and makes formation of a stable emulsion unlikely. Excessive evaporation may be caused by boiling the water and fat too long before adding the flour, and by overcooking the flour-fat-water mixture. When the emulsion is destabilized, the fat tends to separate from the mixture. The batter appears oily and separated instead of shiny and viscous, and the fat oozes from the puffs during baking. Inaccurate measurements may so increase the percentage of fat in the mixture that the results are similar to those obtained by overcooking.

•PANCAKES

Ingredients

Pancakes, sometimes called griddle cakes, are more variable both in the proportion of flour to liquid and in the characteristics of the finished product than are most flour mixtures. The cooked cakes may be thin and moist or thick and porous according to the proportions of ingredients used (Figure 24.3).

Pancake mixtures contain flour, liquid, a leavening agent, and salt. Egg is usually used but may be omitted. Cakes are more tender if they contain fat, but it is possible to omit fat. Sugar may be used as an aid in browning, because of its caramelization, and may slightly modify the flavor.

FIGURE 24.3
Pancakes or griddle cakes can be made thin and moist (*left*) or thick and porous (*right*).
(Photographs by Chris Meister)

If thick buttermilk or sour cream is used in the cakes, the proportion of flour to liquid may be about one to one. In sweetmilk cakes, 1⅓, 1½, or 1¾ cups of flour may be used per cup of liquid, depending on the type of flour and on the desired thickness of the cake. Shortening can be omitted in cakes made with cream because the cream contains fat.

Pancakes are leavened by carbon dioxide gas produced either from baking powder or from a sour milk and soda combination. Overstirred pancakes may be soggy because of a loss of carbon dioxide during stirring and may show some tunnel formation. Thin batters tend to lose more carbon dioxide gas on standing than do thicker batters. More baking powder may be required if batters are to stand for some time than if they are baked immediately.

Pancakes are usually mixed by the muffin method described in Chapter 23. The stiffer the batter, the less the batter should be stirred, to avoid toughening the cakes by developing the gluten.

Cooking

Seasoned griddles can be used without being greased, particularly if the batter contains 2 or more tablespoons of fat per cup of liquid used. Specially coated cooking surfaces are usually used without being greased.

Much of the success in making pancakes depends on the temperature of the griddle. If the griddle is appreciably below the appropriate temperature, the pancakes cook so slowly that they lose leavening gas. They do not expand sufficiently to produce light, porous cakes. They also do not brown desirably. Browning in pancakes is primarily the result of the Maillard reaction. Too hot a griddle may burn the cakes before they are sufficiently done. Even if the griddle is not hot enough to cause burning, it may produce very uneven browning and a compact texture from too rapid cooking. The temperature of the griddle can be tested by cooking a few drops of batter.

A uniformly heated griddle is essential for the griddle cakes to brown uniformly. Large griddles over small flames may be practically cold in the outer areas. As cakes cook on a griddle of a desirable temperature, bubbles of gas expand and some of them break at the surface. When the edges of the pancakes appear slightly dry, they should be turned. If the entire surface becomes dry, the cakes will not brown evenly on the second side after turning. After being turned, the cakes rise noticeably and become slightly higher in the center. They do not form peaks, however, unless the mixture is very stiff or was greatly overstirred. Pancakes are done when they are browned on the second side. Although pancakes may sometimes be turned a second time provided that they are almost done when turned, more desirable cakes usually result from one turning.

•WAFFLES

Ingredients and Mixing

Waffle mixtures are similar to pancakes except that they contain more egg and more fat. They are leavened by carbon dioxide gas, usually from baking powder. Because tenderness and crispness are desirable characteristics in waffles, a flour of relatively low gluten content and weak gluten quality is a good choice for making them. However, by using a sufficient amount of fat and by avoiding overstirring, a stronger flour can be successfully used. In general, a stronger flour tends to yield a less tender, more breadlike waffle.

The proportion of flour may vary from 1⅓ to 1¾ cups per cup of liquid. If optimum stirring is used with each consistency of batter and if all batters are baked under equally good conditions, there seems to be little difference in the waffles obtained. Thinner batters lose their leavening gas more quickly and it is more difficult, without loss of air, to blend beaten egg whites with batters of thin consistency, but ease of pouring is a point in favor of somewhat thinner batters.

Some waffle mixtures that are to be used as dessert or as shortcake are richer in fat than the proportions suggested in Table 24.1. They often contain sugar and may contain cocoa or molasses. Such mixtures require longer, slower baking than do batters with no sugar in order to be crisp and done without scorching. Caramelization of the sugar contributes to browning.

Waffles of excellent quality usually result when the batter is mixed by a modified muffin method that involves separating the eggs and adding the beaten egg whites last. However, the whole beaten egg may be used successfully in the muffin method for mixing waffles.

Baking

A waffle baker is preheated before the batter is poured on the grids. An automatic heat control with an indicator usually shows when the appliance is ready. The batter may stick to the grids if they are either too hot or insufficiently heated. It is also likely to stick if there is not enough fat in the batter. Waffle grids should be greased, at least for the first waffle, even if they have a nonstick finish. Manufacturer's directions should be followed in preconditioning and using new waffle bakers.

Very thin batters made with 1 cup of flour per cup of liquid are too thin to fill the waffle iron sufficiently to bake the waffle crisp and brown on both sides. Crispness depends partly on the depth of batter that the waffle baker holds. A thicker waffle has a tendency to be less crisp than a thin waffle.

•MUFFINS

Ingredients

Muffins usually contain flour, leavening, salt, sugar, fat, egg, and liquid. Sugar may be omitted and muffins may be made without egg, but better flavor and texture result from including both ingredients. Composite flour blends may be used to extend wheat flour supplies or to enhance nutritional qualities. For example, wheat flour formulations containing peanut, sorghum, cassava, or cowpea flours at levels of 12 to 33 percent have been reported to produce acceptable muffins [1]. There were no significant differences observed between the formulations tested and the control muffins made with 100 percent wheat flour for 22 of 31 sensory, physical, and compositional characteristics.

Muffins are leavened by carbon dioxide gas, usually produced from baking powder. Structure is provided by the flour components, starch and some gluten, and by egg proteins as they coagulate on heating.

Characteristics

A well-made muffin is uniform in texture. However, the grain is usually not very fine and the cell walls are of medium thickness. The surface is lightly browned, has a somewhat pebbly appearance, and is rounded but not peaked. The crumb of the muffin is slightly moist, light, and tender. The muffin breaks easily without crumbling. The flavor is, of course, characteristic of the particular ingredients used, but is usually slightly sweet and pleasant tasting. Figure 24.4 shows a well-made muffin.

Mixing

Muffins are generally mixed by the muffin method. The fat, if it is solid, is melted and combined with the liquid ingredients, including egg, which are then added, all at once, to the dry ingredients. The ratio of flour to liquid in a muffin mixture is approximately two to one.

The amount of stirring is more important for muffins than for most mixtures blended by the muffin method. The gluten forms most readily when a two-to-one ratio of flour to liquid is used and is easily overdeveloped with too much stirring.

Peaks and tunnels tend to form in an overstirred muffin. When a muffin batter is stirred only enough to blend the liquid and dry ingredients, dampening dry flour lumps carefully, the batter appears lumpy and drops sharply from the spoon (Figure 24.5). With continued stirring the batter becomes smooth and tends to string from the spoon (Figure 24.5). An elastic gluten mass begins to form. Moderately overstirred muffins tend to increase slightly in volume, but further stirring results in a decrease in volume. Carbon dioxide gas is probably lost with excessive stirring. A crust then forms on the overmixed muffin during baking before additional carbon dioxide gas is produced by the heat of the oven. As the gas is produced it is forced through the softer center of the muffin and contributes to tunnel formation.

The effects of overmixing a muffin batter can be clearly seen in Figure 24.4. A more compact texture, rather than an open grain, is associated with peaks or knobs and tunnels in the overmanipulated muffin. With extreme overmixing, sogginess may occur and, owing to the loss of much carbon dioxide gas, few tunnels may form.

Muffins containing relatively large amounts of fat may be mixed by the conventional method. Such muffins are more cakelike in texture. They are sweeter and more tender than plain muffins. Because sugar and fat interfere with the development of gluten in the batter, the effects of increased mixing are less pronounced than in a plain muffin, and tunnel formation is less likely [2].

Variations

A great variety of muffins can be made if cornmeal, bran, or whole-wheat flour is substituted for part of the white flour. Nuts, dates, blueberries, apples, other fruits, or bits of crisp bacon may be added to the batter while it is being mixed. Maple syrup muffins are made by substituting maple syrup for half of the milk in the recipe. Preparation of orange-honey muffins calls for placing a teaspoon of honey and a thin slice of fresh orange in the bottom of each baking cup before adding the muffin batter. Or, a teaspoon of jelly can be placed in a half-

Dry ingredients were just dampened.

Additional stirring was done. Some tunnels are beginning to form.

Muffins were overstirred. Tunnels and peaks are apparent.

FIGURE 24.4
External and internal characteristics of muffins made from batters mixed for varying lengths of time.

FIGURE 24.5. (Photographs by Chris Meister)

A properly mixed muffin batter results when dry ingredients are just moistened. The batter appears pebbly, not smooth.

In an overmixed muffin batter, the gluten has partially developed and is smooth and cohesive.

filled muffin cup and then the remainder of the batter added, resulting in a "surprise" muffin.

Bran and cornmeal muffins can tolerate more manipulation without undesirable results than can muffins made entirely of all-purpose wheat flour. Bran interferes with the development of gluten, and cornmeal does not contain gluten proteins. In the making of bran muffins, flavor may be improved by first soaking or hydrating the bran in the liquid before combining it with the other ingredients. The substitution of wheat or corn bran for up to 25 percent of the weight of the flour still allows for an acceptable muffin while increasing the fiber content to a considerable degree [3].

Baking

Pans should be prepared before the muffins are mixed. The batter becomes full of gas bubbles and rises perceptibly if it is allowed to stand in the mixing bowl while the pans are being prepared. Cutting into the batter later to fill muffin pans permits gas to escape and decreases the volume of the finished muffins. The bottoms of the pans should be greased, but the greasing of the side walls is optional. The muffin structure may receive some support from clinging to ungreased sides of the muffin pan as the batter rises in baking; however, muffins may be removed from the pans more easily when the sides are greased.

An oven temperature of 400°F is satisfactory for baking muffins in about 20 to 25 minutes. A product leavened by carbon dioxide gas must be allowed to rise before crust formation occurs. For that reason, a very hot oven must be avoided. A temperature slightly under 400°F is satisfactory if sufficient time is allowed for baking. Browning appears to be chiefly the result of the Maillard reaction, but the caramelization of sugar may also contribute to browning.

•BISCUITS

Ingredients

Biscuits usually contain flour, fat, milk, baking powder, and salt. Soda and buttermilk, either the fresh cultured product or dried churned buttermilk, may be used instead of sweet milk and baking powder for the leavening of biscuits. Dried churned buttermilk contains phospholipids that act as emulsifiers and aid in the fine distribution of fat in baked products. Since cultured buttermilk is usually made from fluid skim or low-fat milk, it does not have the same composition as churned buttermilk.

Characteristics

Rolled baking powder biscuits may be compact and flaky or light and fluffy, depending on how much they are kneaded and how thin the dough is rolled before baking. A well-made biscuit usually has a fairly uniform shape, an evenly browned and tender crust, a tender crumb of creamy color, and good flavor (Figure 24.6). Flakiness is a desirable characteristic of biscuits that have been rolled. Easily separated sheets of dough can be seen when a flaky biscuit is broken open.

Dropped biscuits have slightly more liquid in the recipe and are not kneaded as a soft dough. They are dropped by spoonfuls onto a cookie sheet for baking. The resulting biscuit is usually irregular in shape and slightly coarse in texture, but tender with a crisp crust.

Mixing

Biscuits are mixed by the biscuit or pastry method, which involves cutting a solid fat into the flour, baking powder, and salt mixture before adding milk and stirring. The dough for rolled biscuits should be a soft, rather than a stiff, dry dough. Biscuit dough that is patted or rolled with no preliminary kneading yields biscuits that are very tender and have crisp crusts; however, they are coarse in texture, are small in volume, and have slightly rough surfaces. Kneading lightly, using 10 to 30 strokes (depending on the amount of stirring used to mix the dough), produces a biscuit of fine texture that displays evidence of layering when it is broken open (Figure 24.7). It also rises to a larger volume than an unkneaded biscuit (Figure 24.6). The top crust is smoother and the general external appearance is better in slightly kneaded biscuits than in unkneaded ones. Kneading past the optimum amount produces a compact, toughened biscuit.

FIGURE 24.6
The proper amount of kneading improves the volume and quality of baking powder biscuits. The biscuit on the left was prepared from unkneaded dough; the one on the right was made from dough kneaded 15 times before rolling and cutting. (Photograph by Chris Meister)

FIGURE 24.7

Steps in making rolled biscuits. (Courtesy of General Foods, Inc.)

Make soft, dry dough.

Knead dough lightly.

Roll to about 1/2-inch thickness.

Cut and transfer to baking sheet.

The flakiness of a biscuit results from the distribution of fat particles coated with dough. The fat melts on baking and leaves spaces between the sheets of dough.

For variation in the preparation of biscuits, cooked bacon chips, grated cheese, chopped chives, or other herbs may be added to the flour mixture before the liquid. Grated orange rind may also be added to the flour mixture, and a sugar cube soaked in orange juice can be placed on top of the biscuit before baking.

Baking

The baking sheet requires greasing for dropped biscuits but not for rolled ones. Rolled biscuits can be placed on the baking sheet about 1 or 1½ inches apart if crusty biscuits are desired. Otherwise, no space need be allowed between biscuits. A hot oven (425° to 450°F) for 8 to 10 minutes is satisfactory for baking biscuits. The hot oven produces steam that aids in separating sheets of dough as the fat melts. Biscuits may stand for at least an hour before baking without loss of quality.

STUDY QUESTIONS

1. For each of the following products, describe (1) the usual ingredients, (2) the usual method of mixing, and (3) any special precautions to be observed in their preparation or potential problems to be avoided.
   a. Popovers
   b. Cream puffs
   c. Pancakes
   d. Waffles
   e. Muffins
   f. Biscuits
2. What characterizes a quick bread?

REFERENCES

1. Holt, S. D., K. H. McWatters, and A. V. A. Resurreccion. 1992. Validation of predicted baking performance of muffins containing mixtures of wheat, cowpea, peanut, sorghum, and cassava flours. *Journal of Food Science 57*, 470.
2. Matthews, R. H., M. E. Kirkpatrick, and E. H. Dawson. 1965. Performance of fats in muffins. *Journal of the American Dietetic Association 47*, 201.
3. Polizzotto, L. M., A. M. Tinsley, C. W. Weber, and J. W. Berry. 1983. Dietary fibers in muffins. *Journal of Food Science 48*, 111.

Yeast Breads

25

Consumer demand for bakery products has increased in recent years. Annual per capita consumption of flour in the United States rose by 10 pounds between 1985 and 1990 [9]. Since the 1980s, bakery wholesalers have been confronting new competition from in-store bakeries, retail bakeries, and foodservice retailers who bake goods on their premises. Many new bakery products have been introduced into U.S. markets, and items such as bagels and pita bread, which were once considered to be strictly specialty items, are now enjoying great popularity. In any supermarket with an in-store bakery, one is likely to find a wide variety of breads and rolls, including such breads as honey wheat, crushed wheat, branola, oatnut, 12-grain, 7-grain, sour dough, dark rye, light rye, pumpernickel rye, light oatmeal, light stone-ground wheat, and Roman meal, as well as the usual white, whole-wheat, and French breads. In addition, five or six different kinds of English muffins and four or five different types of bagels may be offered.

Foodservice outlets, from fast-food units to up-scale restaurants, are selling large quantities of sandwiches, all of which have as a major component breads, buns, or rolls. One National Restaurant Association survey of 50 menus reported that the number of sandwiches listed had increased by 55 percent between 1984 and 1989 [9].

The making of bread has become a very large industry. Most Americans buy bread rather than make it at home. From many sources we hear that traditional home cooking is losing out to fast-foods and convenience foods in our busy and changing society. We should all hope that home cooking does not become a lost art, however. It has been suggested that the rewards of cooking extend beyond the benefits of providing healthy foods for the body. Cooking may also nourish the spirit, providing quality companionship with family and friends as both preparation and eating are shared [7]. And the making of bread at home can be a particularly rewarding experience if you take the time to develop a certain amount of skill. Hot homemade bread can make any ordinary meal a special one. In low-income families, for whom a higher-than-average consumption of cereal products may be advisable, home production of bread is one way to increase bread consumption.

Well-made baker's bread is of uniform quality but its moisture content is generally high, especially for white bread; often it is extremely compressible. A good-quality homemade bread is often conceded to be superior in flavor and in eating quality, particularly when it is very fresh. Because of differences in ingredients available to the consumer and the commercial baker, however, homemade bread tends to stale more rapidly than does the commercial product.

•CHARACTERISTICS OF YEAST BREADS

The texture of bread should be fine, the cell walls thin, and the grain uniform. Cells tend to be slightly elongated rather than round, although the shape of the cell varies. The crumb is elastic and thoroughly baked so that it does not form a gummy ball when it is pressed between the fingers. The fresh crumb should spring back quickly when it is touched with the finger (Figure 25.1).

A well-shaped loaf of bread has a rounded top and is free from rough, ragged cracks on the sides. The **shred** on the sides of the loaf where the dough rises is smooth and even. Careful and uniform shaping of the loaf and placing the shaped dough in the center of the baking pan contribute to the production of a well-shaped baked loaf of bread. However, abnormalities in shape have numerous causes in addition to problems created by the way the dough is shaped. Such factors as the stiffness of the dough, the strength of the gluten, the extent of **fermentation** and **proofing**, the baking temperature, and the position in the oven may all affect the shape of the loaf as well as its volume and texture. Bread of good quality is light, having a large volume in relation to the weight of the loaf.

If a loaf has been allowed to proof too long before being placed in the oven, the cells overexpand and collapse somewhat. This may result in a loaf of bread that is flat or sunken on top and has overhanging eaves on the sides, somewhat like a mushroom shape. The texture of such a loaf is coarse, with an open grain and crumbly character (Figure 25.2). If a loaf has not proofed long enough before being placed in the oven, it may have wide cracks on the sides after baking because the crust structure will have set before sufficient expansion of the loaf has occurred. The texture may be somewhat compact and coarse (Figure 25.3).

Shred   the area on the sides of a loaf of bread, just above the pan, where the dough rises in the oven before the crust is formed; a desirable shred is even and unbroken

Fermentation   the transformation of organic substances, such as simple sugars, into smaller molecules by the action of microorganisms

Proofing   the last rising of bread dough after it is molded into a loaf and placed in the baking pan

FIGURE 25.1
Bread of relatively high volume and fine texture can be made using all-purpose flour.

FIGURE 25.2
A loaf of bread that has proofed too long in the pan before being baked. The texture is open and coarse, and "eaves" are seen on the sides of the loaf.

•INGREDIENTS

The essential ingredients for yeast-leavened dough are flour, liquid, yeast, and salt. Other constituents, mainly sugar and fat, affect texture and flavor. Additives are also used commercially in the baking of bread and rolls. These include oxidants and vital wheat gluten, which strengthen the dough and assist in the retention of leavening gas [10].

Yeast

Yeast has been the leavening agent for baking bread for thousands of years, although it has been produced industrially for only about 150 years [23]. It is a microscopic one-celled plant (shown in Figure 25.4) that undergoes **metabolic** activity in dough, affecting the functional properties of the dough and the quality of the bread. Among the metabolites are amino acids, which are necessary for the activity of the yeast and also serve as important sources of bread flavor **precursors** [3]. The yeast produces carbon dioxide, which makes the dough light or leavened. Carbon dioxide results from the breaking down of simple sugars in the series of chemical reactions in fermentation. Many enzymes, produced by the yeast cells, are responsible for these metabolic processes, which

Metabolic having to do with any of the chemical changes that occur in living cells

Precursor a forerunner or predecessor such as a molecule that later develops into a flavor molecule

FIGURE 25.3
A loaf of bread that did not rise sufficiently in the pan before being baked. A ragged crack appears on the end and side where the dough rose unevenly during the process of baking. The volume is relatively low and the texture rather coarse.

FIGURE 25.4
Photomicrograph of baker's yeast, *Saccharomyces cerevisiae*. The yeast cell in the lower right-hand corner is in the process of reproducing by budding; a new daughter cell is being created. (Courtesy of Universal Foods Corporation)

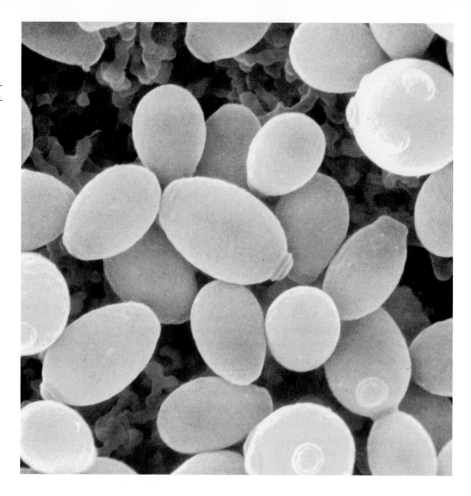

yield ethyl alcohol and various additional flavoring substances, as well as carbon dioxide.

The species of yeast that is used in making bread, often called baker's yeast, is *Saccharomyces cerevisiae*. Strains of this microorganism are carefully selected, grown, and sometimes cross-bred to produce a final product with desirable characteristics for baking. (Fermentation by yeast is also discussed in Chapter 25.)

Types of Yeast

Baker's yeast is marketed as *compressed yeast, active dry yeast*, and *instant quick-rising active dry yeast*. Compressed yeast is produced from a blend of wet yeast cells and emulsifiers that is extruded and then cut into a block form in a variety of sizes. It is perishable and must be kept refrigerated. When it is held at room temperature for more than several hours it loses leavening activity. A fresh sample is creamy white in color, is moist but not slimy, crumbles easily, and has a distinctive odor. When stale, the yeast becomes brownish and may develop a strong unpleasant odor. Because compressed yeast undergoes minimal processing, it is the most consistent in quality of all the baker's yeasts.

It is still *the* leavening agent for the baking trade [6]. Very little compressed yeast is to be found on the retail market, however.

Compressed yeast must be softened in lukewarm liquid (29°C [85°F]) so that it will blend with other dough ingredients. It may be softened either in a small amount of water or in the total amount of liquid used in the dough.

Active dry yeast is prepared from a yeast strain selected for its ability to retain activity when it is dried. The moist yeast is extruded into fine, cylindrical strands that are dried over a 6-hour period at 25° to 45°C (75° to 110°F) under a continuous process. For consumer use, the large dense granules are usually ground and packaged, with the exclusion of oxygen, in glass jars, metal cans, or foil pouches. Active dry yeast has much better storage stability than compressed yeast. It may be stored for up to a year when packaged properly [6]. Packages of dry yeast are usually dated, after which time the optimal activity is not guaranteed. The conditions that contribute to loss of viability in the yeast are mainly air, moisture, and warm temperatures.

Before it can be added to a dough mix, active dry yeast must be rehydrated 5 to 10 minutes in water at 43° to 46°C (110° to 115°F). This allows proper reconstitution of the yeast without a loss of cell contents. The temperature of rehydration is critical. Water above 54°C (130°F) kills the yeast; cool water can shock the yeast particles, causing them to leach out some of the cell contents. This may result in a "slackened" dough that flows in the pan when proofed [6].

The development of instant quick-rising active dry yeast in recent years has been made possible because of new advances in genetics and drying technology [23]. A specially selected strain of *Saccharomyces cerevisiae* is used, and drying is done in special equipment that allows very rapid dehydration. No loss of optimal activity occurs in the drying process. The instant yeast consists of cylindrical and porous, rod-shaped particles that are very fine and light with a large surface area. They therefore rehydrate very rapidly. In fact, they rehydrate so rapidly that they can be mixed with the dry ingredients of a dough and need not be softened separately in liquid [6]. Doughs containing instant active dry yeast rise substantially faster than doughs containing the same amount of regular active dry yeast (Figure 25.5). Quick-rising active dry yeast works well in automatic bread-making machines. When yeast is added to the pan of an automatic bread-making machine, it should be placed in or near the flour. It should not come into contact with liquid or salt, especially when the timer is being used to delay the mixing and baking of the bread.

The same properties of instant quick-rising active dry yeast that are responsible for its ease of rehydration also contribute to its high instability in air. It is packaged in vacuum or in the presence of nitrogen gas with oxygen excluded to preserve its activity. After 4-oz. jars are opened, the unused portion of the yeast should be protected by resealing the jar and storing it in the refrigerator [23].

Starters

A *starter* is some of the **sponge** from a previous baking saved for future use (to replace yeast). It has sugar added as food for the yeast plant and should be used frequently (once or twice a week) to keep the yeast cells alive and to prevent undesirable flavor changes. Sourdough starters may be prepared initially

Sponge   the mixture of liquid, yeast, sugar, and part of the flour to make a thin batter that is held at a lukewarm temperature to allow yeast activity for a period before the remaining ingredients are added to form a dough

FIGURE 25.5

Bread dough containing quick-rising yeast (*left*) rises substantially faster than dough containing the same amount of regular active dry yeast (*right*). Both doughs proofed for 15 minutes at 100°F (38°C). (Reprinted from Trivedi, N. B., E. J. Cooper, and B. L. Bruinsma. Development and applications of quick-rising yeast. *Food Technology*, Vol. 38, No. 6, p. 51, 1984. Copyright © by Institute of Food Technologists.)

by mixing equal volumes of milk or water and flour and exposing the mixture to air so that wild yeast cells will inoculate it. After 2 to 5 days, the mixture should be sour and bubbly and ready to use in a variety of recipes. Both wild yeasts and bacteria probably contribute to the formation of gas and flavor substances in sourdough starter.

Liquid yeast usually is made from potato water, sugar, and yeast. Like starter yeast, it must be used frequently to avoid spoilage. Both starter and liquid yeast are more uncertain sources of yeast cells than compressed and dry yeast. Their chief advantages are convenience and economy in families in which bread is baked frequently or where markets are not easily accessible for the purchase of yeast; however, a sourdough starter may be used because of its flavor.

Amount of Yeast to Use

The amount of yeast to be used may be altered within limits according to the amount of time to be used for the bread-making process. Small amounts of yeast, such as 1/4 to 1/3 cake or package per 1 cup liquid, are satisfactory when the yeast is given enough time to activate. With small amounts of yeast, a sponge method of mixing permits more rapid growth of yeast. Excess yeast causes an undesirable odor and flavor in bread. Coarse texture, gray color of crust and crumb, and loaves of distorted shapes may also result from a great excess of yeast and too rapid fermentation. Bread can be made in about 2½ hours using 1 cake or package of yeast per 1 to 1¼ cups of liquid. The use of quick-rise active dry yeast can shorten the rising time even further. For ordinary use, however, the smallest amount of yeast that will serve the purpose is desirable.

The carbon dioxide gas produced during yeast fermentation causes the bread dough to expand or rise. Ethyl alcohol is volatilized during baking. By-products of the fermentation reaction also include many flavor substances. Organic acids, amino acids, and other substances produced during fermentation participate in complex reactions that result in characteristic bread flavor.

Flour and Liquid

Wheat flour is unique in that it has the components necessary to produce bread of high volume and fine texture with a cohesive, elastic crumb. This is because the flour provides the proteins that, when hydrated and mixed, produce gluten. Gluten is responsible for extensibility and elasticity in the dough. (Gluten is discussed in Chapter 23.) After the gluten structure has been expanded by gas cells, heat coagulates the gluten proteins and sets the structure. Because of the weakening effect of fermentation on gluten, the flour best adapted to the making of bread is one of strong gluten quality. A weak gluten becomes so highly dispersed that a bread of poor volume and quality is likely to result. If soft wheat flours are used for bread, variations in proportions, method, and technique are necessary to obtain a good product.

A high-protein bread flour is used in commercial bread making. Bread flour is also available in retail markets for use in home kitchens. It usually has a dough conditioner such as **potassium bromate** added to it. Acceptable bread can also be prepared using all-purpose flour.

Potassium bromate an oxidizing substance often added to bread dough to strengthen the gluten of strong or high-protein flour

It has been suggested by some baking analysts that the baking performance of flour generally has decreased in the last 25 years [10]. Although some scores on laboratory tests of baking quality appear to have declined over the past decade, the relationship between laboratory tests and flour performance in production is complex, and two lots of flour with the same lab analysis rating may bake quite differently in a commercial operation. Among the factors that may have contributed to the change in flour performance are genetics of the developed wheat varieties and changes in milling practices. There has also been a decline in the average level of protein in the wheat crop. Bakers today more routinely than they did in the past use additives to strengthen the desirable characteristics of the dough.

Liquid is essential in bread dough to hydrate flour proteins and contribute to the development of gluten. In addition, it is essential for the partial gelatinization of starch, which makes an important contribution to bread structure [11]. Other components are also dissolved or dispersed in the liquid. The liquid used in making bread may be milk, water, potato water, or whey. If the liquid is milk, it should be scalded. Heating destroys certain enzymes and changes some proteins so that an undesirable softening of the dough does not occur during fermentation.

Dry milk used by commercial bakers has been heat-treated. A small quantity of mashed potato may be added to bread dough. Potato water and cooked potato introduce gelatinized starch into the mixture. This favors fermentation and also enhances the keeping quality and flavor of the baked bread. Milk and whey increase the nutritive value of bread to some extent.

Approximately 3/4 of a pound or 3 cups of flour are required to make a pound loaf of bread. The amount depends chiefly on the **hydration capacity** of the flour proteins. Strong flours with a high protein content have a higher hydration capacity than do flours of lower protein content, and the quantity of high-protein flours required is slightly smaller. Thus, the amount of liquid used in making bread varies with the hydration capacity of the gluten-forming proteins in the flour. For good bread flours, about 60 to 65 percent of the weight of the flour as liquid gives a dough of the best consistency. In terms of mea-

Hydration capacity the ability of a substance, such as flour, to absorb water

surements, 65 percent of the weight of the flour is approximately 1 cup of water for a 1-pound loaf.

Weak flours have a low imbibition capacity and therefore require a lower percentage of moisture. If milk is used instead of water, a slightly higher proportion of it is needed because of the 12 to 14 percent of milk solids present.

Beyond the amount of liquid required to achieve maximum loaf volume, additional absorption of water produces a less tenacious or more tender gluten. This results in decreased loaf volume. Too small a proportion of moisture may not provide enough water for optimal gluten development and may result in decreased loaf volume of the finished bread.

Sugar

Although it is not an indispensable ingredient in a bread formula, sugar plays several roles in bread making. It increases the rate of fermentation by providing readily available food for yeast so that the bread rises in a shorter period. If larger amounts of sugar are used, however, as in sweet rolls, the action of the yeast is somewhat repressed, and the fermentation and proofing periods must be longer. Flavor (primarily sweetness), texture, and browning are also affected by the use of sugar, although the browning of bread is primarily the result of the Maillard reaction. Sugar in bread dough comes from three sources: that present in the flour, that produced by the action of enzymes hydrolyzing starch, and that added as an ingredient [17].

For loaf breads, 2 teaspoons to 1½ tablespoons of sugar per 1-pound loaf are common amounts used. Doughs for rolls usually contain slightly more sugar—about 2 to 4 tablespoons per cup of liquid used.

Fat

Fat is used in commercial bread making to facilitate the handling of the dough, to increase the keeping quality of the bread, and to improve loaf volume and texture [15]. The tenderness of the bread is also increased. Liquid oils do not perform the same functions that allow an increase in volume as do solid shortenings. However, commercial bakers can combine various conditioners and softeners with liquid oil and produce a bread of acceptable quality [8].

For loaf breads, 1 to 1½ tablespoons of fat per 1 pound loaf are sufficient to improve tenderness, flavor, and keeping quality. Two to four tablespoons or more per cup of liquid may be used in roll dough for increased tenderness.

Salt

Salt is added to bread dough for flavor, but it also has other effects. Salt retards yeast fermentation and therefore increases the time required for bread dough to rise. Salt has a firming effect on gluten structure. Bread made without salt is often crumbly in texture and may easily become overlight.

The amount of salt usually considered to produce good flavor in bread is approximately 1 teaspoon per 1 pound loaf. An excess of salt should be avoided from the standpoint of both texture and flavor. Because of the public health emphasis on using salt and sodium only in moderation, recommendations have been made to reduce the sodium content of processed foods. Salt is the highest contributor of sodium in the American food supply. In one study, a panel of 40 untrained judges found both white and wheat breads acceptable when salt was reduced by 50 percent of the normal level [25]. It would therefore appear that the usual level of salt might be reduced in bread without sacrificing quality or acceptability.

•MIXING AND HANDLING

Two basic methods of mixing yeast bread are the straight-dough method and the sponge method. The batter method may also be used for some breads.

Straight-Dough Method

In the mixing of yeast bread by the straight-dough method, the liquid is generally warmed with the sugar, salt, and softened fat. If scalded milk is used, it must be cooled to the proper temperature before yeast is added. Yeast may be softened in a small amount of warm water and added to the liquid mixture, or it may be softened in the total liquid. The temperature of the liquid used for softening should be appropriate for the type of yeast used. Instant quick-rising dry active yeast does not need to be softened in liquid and may be stirred with part of the flour.

About a third of the flour is then blended with the liquid ingredients and vigorously mixed. Beating the batter blends ingredients uniformly and starts the development of gluten. It also incorporates air cells. The remainder of the flour is added gradually to form a dough that is then transferred to a floured board for kneading. The dough is kneaded (see "Kneading") until it has a smooth, satiny outside surface.

The kneaded dough is next placed in a clean mixing bowl and allowed to rise until it is at least doubled in bulk, after which it is lightly punched down. It may then either be allowed to rise a second time or be molded into loaves or rolls. If special bread mixers are available, the entire mixing process can be done by machine.

The number of times the dough should be allowed to rise in the fermentation period varies with the strength of the flour. Doughs made from strong gluten flours may be allowed to rise more times than doughs made from flours with lower protein content before the dough is placed in the pans. Weak glutens tend to become too highly dispersed with too long a fermentation period. More thorough mixing of the bread alters the quality of the gluten so that a shorter fermentation time gives as good a volume and quality of loaf as may be obtained by a shorter preliminary mixing and a longer fermentation period (more risings). Satisfactory bread can be made at home with only one rising period, if either all-purpose flour or bread flour is used.

When rapid-rising yeast is used, it is possible to let the dough rest for about 10 minutes after kneading in lieu of a rising period. The dough is then molded and placed in a pan to proof before baking.

Sponge Method

In the sponge method, a sponge consisting of liquid, sugar, yeast, and part of the flour is mixed as in the straight-dough method. When the mixture has stood until it is light and full of gas bubbles, it is then made into a dough by the addition of slightly cooled melted fat, salt, and the remainder of the flour. The dough is kneaded and allowed to rise until it is at least double its original volume, after which it is molded and placed in baking pans.

Batter Method

Breads may be made from batters containing less flour than doughs contain. The straight-dough method is modified to eliminate the kneading and shaping steps. The batters are allowed to rise at least once in the bowl and/or in the baking pan. These unkneaded breads usually have a more open grain and uneven surface than kneaded breads and lack the elasticity of the crumb; however, they require less preparation time.

Automatic Bread Machines

Machines are available that will accomplish the total bread-making process automatically for one loaf of bread. Ingredients are placed in the pan and the timing cycle is set according to the manufacturer's instructions. At the scheduled time, the loaf of bread will be mixed, proofed, and baked. If you desire, you can plan to return home and find fragrant odors of baking bread permeating your kitchen. Rapid-rise yeast is well suited for use in bread machines.

Kneading

Kneading of bread dough is essential for the development of strong elastic gluten strands from flour of relatively high protein content. Skillful handling of the dough ball is necessary at the beginning of kneading. The mass may rather easily be collected into a ball of dough that, with proper handling, tends to remain smooth on the outer surface in contact with the board. All wrinkles and cracks are best kept on the side in contact with the hands to minimize the tendency for the dough to stick to the board. Wet spots on the outside surface may require frequent coating with flour until the dough becomes elastic enough to knead easily.

The kneading movement is a rhythmical one in which the fingers are used to pull the mass over into position for kneading and the lower part of the hand is used for applying pressure to the dough. Forcing the fingers into the dough or using too heavy a pressure tends to keep the mass of dough sticky and difficult to handle. (See Figures 25.6 and 25.7.)

FIGURE 25.6
Dough development. (*left*) Dough barely mixed; (*center*) dough partially developed; (*right*) dough developed. (Courtesy of the Wheat Flour Institute)

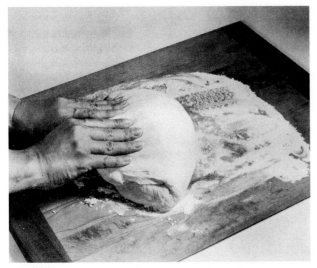

FIGURE 25.7
Steps in kneading dough. (Courtesy of Fleischmann's Yeast)

Fold the dough over from the far side toward you.

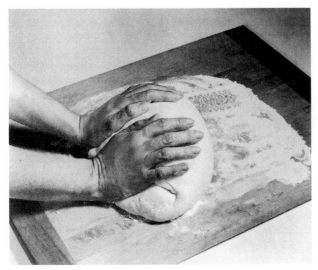

Firmly push the dough away, using the heels of the hands.

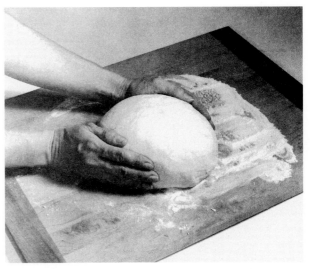

Turn the ball of dough one-quarter of a turn and repeat the steps from the first folding.

Kneading should be thorough. It is unlikely that bread dough will be overkneaded by hand. Various mixers are available with motors powerful enough to mix bread dough completely, thus eliminating the necessity of kneading by hand. The manufacturers' directions should be followed in the use of these mixers. After fermentation has been completed, doughs should be handled lightly to avoid pressing together the thin filaments of gluten that are formed.

Care must be used during kneading to avoid the incorporation of excess flour into the mixture, which results in too stiff a dough. With the development of a good kneading technique, it is surprising how little flour need be used on a board for the handling of any kind of dough. Later handling can be

599

done with practically no flour because of the increased extensibility of the dough after fermentation.

During the kneading process, the swollen particles of the proteins *gliadin* and *glutenin* adhere to each other and become aligned in long elastic strands. Starch granules from the flour are entrapped in the developing gluten. The development of gluten during kneading is important to provide structure and strength for the dough and the finished loaf of bread.

•FERMENTATION AND PROOFING

Fermentation occurs primarily during the rising periods in the preparation of yeast breads. It is catalyzed by many different enzymes from the yeast cells and is a complex process. Additional enzyme action also occurs in bread dough. A starch-splitting enzyme called *amylase* is present in the flour and may also be added in commercial bread making. This enzyme catalyzes the hydrolysis of starch to dextrins and maltose. Gelatinized starch is more easily broken down by amylase than is uncooked starch. Therefore, mixing some cooked potato in the dough favors amylase action. There may also be some action of proteases in bread dough. These enzymes hydrolyze proteins to peptides and amino acids. If the proteases are too active, they may hydrolyze too much of the protein and produce harmful effects, such as poor texture and decreased volume. Slight action of protease may be beneficial.

Acidity increases in bread dough during fermentation. The increase in acidity is attributed largely to the carbon dioxide, but organic acids, chiefly acetic and lactic, are also formed. Advantageous effects of a certain degree of increased acidity are the promotion of fermentation and amylase activity and the holding in check of some unwanted organisms.

The changes in gluten quality during fermentation are attributed partly to the increased acidity. Greater dispersion of the gluten with loss of elasticity and tenacity occurs as acidity increases. The action of proteases may possibly be a factor in the softening of the gluten, although this is not well understood. The stretching of the dough under the pressure of gas also appears to have a modifying effect on the gluten.

The optimum amount of fermentation varies with flours of different gluten strength and of different amylase activity. Bread must be baked before gluten strands become so thin and weak that they break, thus allowing carbon dioxide gas to escape. Overfermentation with excessive loss of gas results in poor **oven spring** and is likely to produce a loaf that is flat or sunken on top.

Oven spring the rapid increase in volume in a loaf of bread during the first few minutes of baking

Overfermented bread has a coarse grain and thick cell walls. It may also have a sour odor and flavor and a crust that does not brown well. The volume is small and the loaf is heavy and compact. Weak glutens are more easily overfermented than are strong glutens, which not only tolerate but require more fermentation to yield bread of a good quality. Underfermentation produces bread that has thick cell walls and is heavy, small in volume, and less tender than bread that has fermented sufficiently to bring about a desirable dispersion of the gluten.

Fermentation can take place over a wide range of temperatures, but the best flavor is probably developed at 26° to 32°C (79° to 90°F). Cold inhibits yeast activity, and a temperature of about 55°C (130°F) destroys yeast plants. Warm temperatures may favor the growth of organisms that produce undesirable flavors in bread.

Dough that is exposed to air develops a crust or film that must later be thrown away to avoid the formation of heavy streaks throughout the dough. To avoid crust formation, a proofing cabinet should be used. If one is not available, the bowl containing the dough may be placed in a pan of warm water and then covered with another pan of the same size. The vaporization of moisture from the surface of the water maintains a humidity that keeps the bread surface from drying out. Alternatively, the surface of the dough may be lightly greased and the bowl covered with a plastic wrap. Fermentation is usually continued until the dough has risen to 2 to 2½ times its original volume.

After the dough has undergone fermentation and is molded into a loaf and placed in a baking pan, it is allowed to rise again. This final rising in the pan is called *proofing*. Proofing should be terminated when the loaf has approximately doubled in size and the dough does not spring back when it is lightly touched. In foodservice establishments, proof boxes with temperature and humidity controls are used for both fermentation and proofing of bread dough.

•COMMERCIAL PROCESSES

Numerous technological advances have been made in the baking industry. Many processes used in commercial bread making are, of course, very different from procedures used in the home kitchen. Some foodservice establishments bake their own bread; others may prepare only hot breads such as rolls, biscuits, and muffins. The equipment used for bread making in most foodservice kitchens is less automated than that usually found in large commercial bakeries.

Pure yeast cultures and standardized ingredients, including a number of chemical additives, are available to commercial bakers. Powerful mixers, fermentation rooms, dough dividers, and automatic proofing, baking, and wrapping systems are used. Through the 1940s, the predominant bread-making system in the United States was a sponge and dough system. Since then, several alternative methods have been developed. These include a conventional straight-dough method, a continuous dough process, and a short-time bread-making system. Short-time doughs involve a single mixing step and little or no bulk fermentation of the dough before panning. Short-time breads are generally made with warmer doughs, more yeast, and higher levels of oxidants than are used in the preparation of conventional doughs [24]. High-speed mixing of doughs substitutes to some degree for the fermentation period. Addition of oxidizing and/or reducing agents also helps to develop the dough with less fermentation required. Shortening the fermentation period in commercial bread production results in large savings in time and labor costs.

Dough Conditioners

Dough conditioning formulations are commonly added to yeast doughs. They were once used sparingly or not at all but today are often used at their legal limits [10]. These include oxidizing agents that act on the gluten structure to produce a better handling dough and a higher quality bread. Gluten may be envisioned as a coiled protein that contains a number of disulfide bonds (-S-S-) linking parts of the molecule together in order to provide more strength and rigidity (see Figure 25.8) [22]. During mechanical mixing, many of these bonds are broken and the gluten becomes more expanded and relaxed so that it may be stretched by the leavening gases. The gluten is "developed" and becomes more extensible and elastic. To maintain this expanded structure, however, new linkages need to reform, strengthening the expanded gluten structure. This is the role played by oxidizing dough conditioners. Many of the sulfhydryl groups (-SH) formed during dough development are oxidized back to disulfide linkages to lock the new structure in place. Finer texture, better volume, and a softer crumb result.

The U.S. Food and Drug Administration (FDA) has approved several oxidizing substances for use as dough conditioners. These include potassium bromate, ascorbic acid, calcium iodate, azodicarbonamide, and calcium peroxide. Potassium bromate may be added to bread flour sold on the retail market. A number of emulsifiers such as lecithin, mono- and diglycerides, diacetyl tartaric esters of mono- and diglycerides, and sodium stearoyl lactylates are also used. Bread dough is a very complex system, and emulsifiers interact with a number of components in the dough to achieve their effects on volume and crumb softness. In addition, yeast nutrients such as monocalcium phosphate and calcium sulfate may be used in commercial bread making.

Amylase an enzyme that breaks down or hydrolyzes starch

Protease an enzyme that hydrolyzes protein

Addition of certain enzymes, including **amylases** and **proteases**, to flours or doughs can initiate improvements such as retardation of staling, enhancement of bread crust color, and softer crumb. Most of the enzymes that are commercially available for use in bakery processing come from fungi and bacteria [5].

•BAKING BREAD

Conventional Baking

As heat is applied to the bread during baking, gas production and expansion are greatly accelerated. This results in a sharp rising of the dough for the first few minutes of the baking period. The rapid increase in loaf volume is called *oven spring*. The temperature of the interior of the loaf gradually rises until a temperature is reached that destroys yeast plants and enzymes and stops fermentation. Alcohol is volatile and is almost completely driven off during the baking of bread. The maximum temperature of the interior of the loaf is approximately the boiling point of water. However, as moisture evaporates from the exterior surface and crust formation occurs, the temperature of the crust becomes higher than that of the crumb.

Gluten undergoes a gradual change in properties over a rather wide range of temperatures—50° to 80°C (122° to 175°F)—and finally becomes firm as it coagulates. Partial gelatinization of starch occurs during baking. Starch absorbs only about one-third of its weight of water at room temperature, but because it constitutes about four-fifths of flour, it is responsible for about half the total water absorption of flours when they are made into dough. As the gluten loses water during baking and the starch swells with the imbibition of additional water during heating, at least a partial gelatinization of the starch is

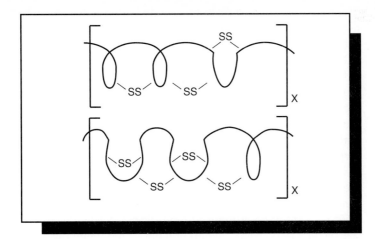

FIGURE 25.8
Gluten molecules. (Reprinted from
Tieckelmann, R. E. and R. E. Steele.
Higher-assay grade of calcium perox-
ide improves properties of dough.
Food Technology, Vol. 45, No. 1, p.
108, 1991. Copyright © by Institute of
Food Technologists.)

Proposed structure of gluten
molecules.

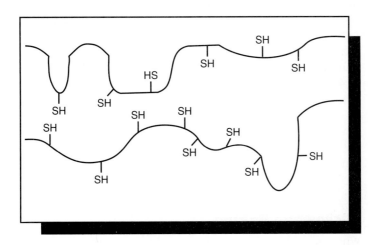

Expanded and relaxed gluten molecules after mechanical mixing.

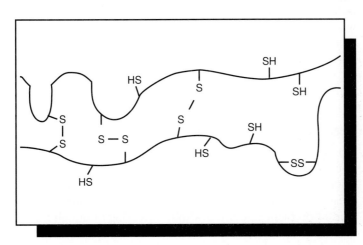

Formation of new linkages by chemical oxidation to strengthen the
expanded gluten structure.

made possible [12]. In fresh bread, the gluten holds less and the starch holds more water than in the uncooked dough. The partially gelatinized starch contributes to bread structure as it is embedded within strands of coagulated gluten proteins.

The Maillard reaction appears to be chiefly responsible for the brown crust color in baked bread. The browning reaction probably also contributes to bread flavor. Browning of bread, as with other baked products, is influenced by the type of pan used. Pans with dark or dull finishes absorb heat more readily than do bright shiny ones that reflect heat. Therefore, the surfaces of bread in contact with dull or dark pans brown more readily and uniformly.

Greasing the bottoms of pans is an aid in removing the baked bread from the pan. The greasing of side walls is optional, but a somewhat larger volume of loaf may result from allowing the dough to cling to the side walls while rising.

Baking temperatures and times vary according to the type of dough and size of mass to be baked. Whether a hot or moderate oven is used at the beginning depends on the extent of rising before the bread is placed in the oven. Bread that has risen approximately double its bulk should go into a hot oven (400° to 425°F) to set the structure of the bread and prevent too much rising in the oven. Bread that has risen less than double its bulk may be allowed to continue rising in the oven by the use of a more moderate oven temperature (375° to 400°F). The oven temperatures should be hot enough to avoid overfermentation in the oven before yeast destruction occurs. Too hot an oven, however, sets the bread before optimum oven spring occurs, thus reducing the final volume and affecting the texture.

One-pound loaves can bake for 35 minutes at 400°F. Alternatively, they can bake for about 15 minutes at 425°F and for an additional 30 to 45 minutes at 375°F.

Microwave Baking

White bread is generally not acceptably cooked by microwaves because of the lack of crust formation; however, relatively dark breads, such as rye and whole wheat, have been satisfactorily prepared in the microwave oven with very little additional heating in a hot conventional oven. Yeast dough may be proofed in the microwave oven fairly well, speeding up the rising. Brown-and-serve rolls are successfully prepared by the use of microwaves. They are browned in a hot conventional oven before being served.

Frozen Yeast Doughs

Frozen bread dough that is already shaped into a loaf is marketed at the retail level. The dough is thawed at room temperature and allowed to rise before baking. This convenience food allows one to have the aroma of freshly baked bread in the kitchen without the mixing and kneading processes. The most significant problem associated with the freezing of dough is how to maintain the viability and gassing power of frozen yeasts. The longer the active fermentation time undergone by yeast before freezing, the less stable the yeast is to freezing. Thus, the addition of yeast at the end of mixing, a reduction in proofing time, and an increase in yeast amount are possible aids in producing acceptable frozen doughs. The addition of extra wheat gluten and oxidants, as well as other additives, may also help to ensure yeast viability and baking strength. The possibility of using yeast strains other than *Saccharomyces cerevisiae* in frozen doughs has been suggested [2].

•ROLLS

Rolls usually contain somewhat larger amounts of fat and sugar than are generally found in bread. Eggs may also be added, although satisfactory roll dough can be made without eggs. The eggs may be beaten lightly and added in the early stages of dough making. Because an egg adds about 3 tablespoons of liquid, either the liquid should be decreased by that amount or extra flour should be added to form a dough that can be handled.

Rolls usually require 20 to 25 minutes of baking at 425°F. Pan rolls require a longer baking time than do single rolls separated on a baking sheet or in muffin pans. A pan of rolls may require almost as much baking time as a pound loaf of bread.

Although any roll dough can be held in the refrigerator for 1 or 2 days before baking, refrigerator rolls are probably best made from a dough of slightly different proportions from plain rolls. For refrigerator rolls, only a moderate amount of yeast is used to avoid overfermentation, and slightly more than the usual amount of sugar is added to serve as food for the yeast during the approximately 1-week period that the dough may be held before baking. The rolls may or may not contain egg. When the rolls are first mixed they are kneaded and allowed to undergo one fermentation, after which they are punched to release gas and stored closely covered at refrigerator temperature to be used as needed. If the dough rises appreciably during holding, it is punched from time to time to release gas. When it is needed, part of the dough is removed from the refrigerator, shaped into rolls, and allowed to rise in a warm room until it doubles in bulk. This may require 2 to 3 hours, depending on the temperature of the dough and the room. Rolls can be formed into a variety of shapes and sizes (Figure 25.9 and Plate XVI).

•WHOLE-GRAIN AND VARIETY BREADS

Contrast in the flavor and texture of breads is made possible by the use of a variety of grains in various forms (Figure 25.10). Flours, meals, and flakes can all be used. Whole-grain flours contain essentially all of the vitamins and minerals, as well as fiber, present in unmilled grain and thus offer nutritional advantages over highly milled flours. The importance of incorporating whole grain products into the diet on a regular basis has been emphasized by public health authorities.

Other nutritive ingredients may be added to breads to meet the needs of particular groups. For example, some researchers developed a bread formulation designed to supply the elderly with essential nutrients that are often deficient in their diets. With the use of whey, a nutritive yeast product, and low-fat cheese, an acceptable bread was formulated that increased the calcium, thiamin, and riboflavin content 1.2, 2.0, and 1.2 times, respectively, over that of the best-liked commercial bread [14].

FIGURE 25.9
Rolls can be formed into many different shapes. (Courtesy of Fleischmann's Yeast®)

The consumption of variety breads in the United States has been increasing in recent years, while the sale of white bread has been declining, and now represents a substantial part of the total bread market. Four slices of most variety breads furnish appreciable amounts of minerals and vitamins to help meet daily nutritional needs [19, 20].

Whole-Wheat Bread

Whole-wheat bread is prepared with whole-wheat flour. All of the flour in the bread may be whole wheat, or varying proportions of white and whole-wheat flour may be used. The procedure for mixing, fermenting, and baking whole-wheat dough is similar to that described for white bread dough, although the kneading does not have to be as extensive. The small particles of bran in whole-wheat flour interfere with the development of gluten. Even extensive kneading does not overcome this effect. The volume of the finished loaf of whole-wheat bread is therefore usually somewhat less than that of white bread. If the whole-wheat flour is very finely ground, however, the volume of the bread made from this flour may approach that of white bread. Commercial breads containing some white and some whole-wheat flour are labeled *wheat bread* instead of *whole-wheat bread*, which is made entirely of whole-wheat flour.

FIGURE 25.10
Examples of variety breads include, in the center, Bavarian rye; to the lower left of this loaf, an onion bagel; and continuing clockwise around the circle, a dark round loaf of pumpernickel; a three-seed loaf containing sesame seed, cottonseed, and linseed; oat bran fiber bread; apple cinnamon bread with frosting on top; honey wheat bread; and pita bread. Pita is a flat round piece that opens up like a pocket when it is cut and can be filled with a variety of sandwich fillings. (Photograph by Chris Meister)

High-Fiber Breads

With an emphasis on the need for increased fiber in the diets of most Americans, the baking industry has developed ways of adding extra bran to breads without sacrificing quality [16, 21]. Vital wheat gluten and certain conditioners can be used to counteract the deleterious effects of up to 15 parts of bran per 85 parts of flour. Bran flakes or prepared bran cereals may be used at home as added ingredients in wheat bread or rolls to provide additional fiber.

A survey of breads marketed in one local area suggests that there are considerable differences in the amounts of dietary fiber found in specialty breads and breads labeled *wheat bread*. The fiber content ranged from 0.5 gram to about 2.0 grams per slice. Whole-wheat bread contains about 1.5 grams of dietary fiber per slice [13].

Use of Flours Other Than Wheat

Some wheat flour is needed in all yeast breads to provide gluten for bread structure and lightness. Flours milled from grains other than wheat may be combined with wheat flour to give varied and flavorful baked products. Of all the grains, rye flour comes closest to wheat in terms of gluten-forming properties, but rye flour alone does not make a light loaf of bread. Rye yeast bread generally contains some wheat flour. Approximately equal portions of rye and wheat flour yield good results.

The germ of wheat or other grains is a good source of protein, vitamins, and minerals. However, the germ contains a **reducing substance** that has a detrimental effect on bread volume. Heat treatment inactivates this substance. Heat-treated wheat germ may be added to bread in amounts of up to 15 percent of the weight of the flour with no deleterious effect on bread volume.

Soy flour increases the protein content of breads and has been used commercially to make high-protein breads. Additives are commonly used by commercial bakers to overcome the adverse effects of soy flour on the absorption, mixing, and fermentation of dough. However, bread containing about 1/3 cup of soy flour to 5 cups of all-purpose flour can be satisfactorily made at

Reducing substance a molecule that has an effect opposite that of an oxidizing agent; hydrogen or electrons are gained in a reaction involving a reducing substance

home. This bread can be made higher in protein by the use of extra nonfat dry milk solids.

Other grains that may be used in bread making, in combination with wheat flour, include oatmeal, cornmeal, barley flakes, and buckwheat flour. Molasses and honey are often used as the source of sugar in whole-grain breads to contribute flavors that blend well with whole-grain products. The relatively coarse textures and dark colors of some of the specialty breads lend variety to meals.

•STALING OF BREAD

Staling refers to all of the changes that occur in bread after baking. These include increasing firmness of the crumb, decreasing capacity of the crumb to absorb moisture, loss of flavor, and development of a leathery crust. Changes that can be detected in the laboratory in the starchy portion of bread have led to the conclusion that starch is somehow responsible for staling. It is also possible that the **amylopectin** fraction of starch is more involved in staling than is **amylose**. The complex processes related to staling are not fully understood even though they have been studied for many years [4]. Fat in the bread formula helps to retard staling. Emulsifiers added by commercial bakers have a similar effect.

If stale bread is reheated to 50° to 60°C (122° to 140°F) or above, the staling is reversed and the bread regains many of the characteristics of fresh bread. The soluble fraction of the starch that decreased during staling is increased. The process can be reversed several times until the bread has lost too much moisture. In the practical application of this freshening process, moisture may even be supplied if rolls are covered with a slightly dampened cloth or paper toweling during heating. Freezing also seems to reverse the staling process. Freezing combined with heating to thaw the frozen product brings about considerable freshening of stale bread products. This process can be quickly accomplished in a microwave oven. Caution must be exercised, however, to avoid the dehydrating effect of microwaving too long. Bread stales more rapidly when it is held at refrigerator temperatures than it does when it is stored at room temperature.

•SPOILAGE OF BREAD

Bread spoils most commonly by molding. Any mold spores in the dough are destroyed in baking, so mold growth on baked bread comes from contamination of the loaf after baking. Conditions favorable to mold growth are moisture and warm temperatures. Commercially, sodium or calcium propionate is added to the bread dough as an antimolding additive and is quite effective. In warm, humid weather, however, even bread containing this additive is likely to mold if it is held for more than a few days at room temperature. Refrigeration retards mold growth but also speeds up the staling process. Bread should be frozen if it is not to be used within a few days.

Rope is a bacterial contamination that can originate in the flour bin or in the various constituents used to make the bread. The spores of this bacterium

Amylopectin   a fraction of starch with a highly branched and bushy type of molecular structure

Amylose   a fraction of starch in which the molecules are generally long chains of glucose linked together

are not destroyed in baking, and within a few days the interior of the loaf becomes sticky and may be pulled into "ropes" of a syrupy material. The odor of the loaf becomes foul and somewhat like the aroma of overripe melons. Bread is inedible when rope has developed extensively. The cure consists mainly of eliminating the source of the bacteria, although acidifying dough to a pH of 4.5 or lower will prevent rope development. Sour milk or buttermilk may be substituted for one-fourth to one-half of the total liquid, or approximately 1 tablespoon of distilled vinegar per quart of liquid may be added. This does not change the flavor of the bread. Calcium or sodium propionate that is added to bread to retard molding is also effective in preventing rope.

Bread may be packaged in a plastic film under a modified atmosphere, which in most cases is carbon dioxide alone or in combination with nitrogen gas. This limits the loss of moisture and microbial growth to extend the shelf life of the bread. The carbon dioxide also has an anti-staling effect, possibly due to a change in the ability of amylopectin to bind water in the bread [1]. Shelf-stable *meal, ready-to-eat* (*MRE*) bread is preserved by controlling water activity, pH, oxygen content, and initial microbial load [18].

STUDY QUESTIONS

1. Describe desirable characteristics of yeast bread.
2. Explain the role played by each of the following ingredients in the making of yeast bread.
   a. Yeast
   b. Flour
   c. Liquid
   d. Sugar
   e. Fat
   f. Salt
   g. Dough conditioners
3. Compare the similarities and differences among compressed yeast, dry active yeast, and instant quick-rising dry active yeast as they are used for the preparation of yeast breads.
4. Compare bread flour and all-purpose flour in terms of mixing, handling, and expected outcome in the making of yeast bread.
5. What steps are involved in mixing yeast bread by the straight-dough method? The sponge method? The batter method?
6. Explain why kneading is such an important step in the preparation of yeast bread at home.
7. What is meant by *fermentation* of yeast dough and by *proofing*? What important things occur during these processes?
8. a. Describe changes that occur during the baking of yeast bread.
   b. What is meant by *oven spring*?
   c. Why is it important to bake bread at precisely the right time after proofing in the pan?
9. How do ingredients and their proportions generally differ between rolls and bread?
10. a. What changes occur as bread stales?
    b. Which component of bread appears to be responsible for staling?
    c. How can somewhat stale bread be refreshened?
11. a. Give suggestions as to how to store bread appropriately.
    b. What is *rope* in bread, and how can it be controlled?

REFERENCES

1. Avital, Y., C. H. Mannheim, and J. Miltz. 1990. Effect of carbon dioxide atmosphere on staling and water relations in bread. *Journal of Food Science 55*, 413.

2. Baguena, R., M. D. Soriano, M. A. Martinez-Anaya, and C. Benedito de Barber. 1991. Viability and performance of pure yeast strains in frozen wheat dough. *Journal of Food Science 56*, 1690.

3. Collar, C., A. F. Mascaros, and C. Benedito de Barber. 1992. Amino acid metabolism by yeasts and lactic acid bacteria during bread dough fermentation. *Journal of Food Science 57*, 1423.

4. D'Appolonia, B. L., and M. M. Morad. 1981. Bread staling. *Cereal Chemistry 58*, 186.

5. Dziezak, J. D. 1991. Enzymes: Catalysts for food processes. *Food Technology 45*, 78 (No. 1).

6. Dziezak, J. D., Ed. 1987. Yeasts and yeast derivatives: Definitions, characteristics, and processing. *Food Technology 41*, 104 (No. 2).

7. Gentry, M. 1993. Editor's Note. *Newsletter, American Institute for Cancer Research Issue 41*, p. 3.

8. Hartnett, D. I., and W. G. Thalheimer. 1979. Use of oil in baked products—Part I: Background and bread. *Journal of the American Oil Chemists' Society 56*, 944.

9. Harwood, J. 1991. U.S. Baking industry responds to consumers. *Food Review 14*, 39 (No. 2).

10. Harwood, J. 1991. U.S. flour milling on the rise. *Food Review 14*, 34 (No. 2).

11. Hoseney, R. C., D. R. Lineback, and P. A. Seib. 1978. Role of starch in baked foods. *Baker's Digest 52*, 11 (No. 4).

12. Marston, P. E., and T. L. Wannan. 1976. Bread baking. *Baker's Digest 50*, 24 (No. 4).

13. Patrow, C. J., and J. A. Marlett. 1986. Variability in the dietary fiber content of wheat and mixed-grain commercial breads. *Journal of the American Dietetic Association 86*, 794.

14. Payton, S. B., R. E. Baldwin, and G. F. Krause. 1988. Bread formulation designed for the elderly using response surface methodology. *Journal of Food Science 53*, 302.

15. Pomeranz, Y. 1980. Molecular approach to breadmaking—An update and new perspectives. *Baker's Digest 54*, 26 (No. 1).

16. Pomeranz, Y. 1977. Fiber in breadmaking. *Baker's Digest 51*, 94 (No. 5).

17. Pomeranz, Y., and K. F. Finney. 1975. Sugars in breadmaking. *Baker's Digest 49*, 20 (No. 1).

18. Powers, E. M., and D. Berkowitz. 1990. Efficacy of an oxygen scavenger to modify the atmosphere and prevent mold growth on Meal, Ready-to-Eat pouched bread. *Journal of Food Protection 53*, 767.

19. Ranhotra, G., J. Gelroth, F. Novak, and R. Matthews. 1985. Minerals in selected variety breads commercially produced in four major U.S. cities. *Journal of Food Science 50*, 365.

20. Ranhotra, G., J. Gelroth, F. Novak, and R. Matthews. 1985. B vitamins in selected variety breads commercially produced in major U.S. cities. *Journal of Food Science 50*, 1174.

21. Shogren, M. D., Y. Pomeranz, and K. F. Finney. 1981. Counteracting the deleterious effects of fiber in bread making. *Cereal Chemistry 58*, 142.

22. Tieckelmann, R. E., and R. E. Steele. 1991. Higher-assay grade of calcium peroxide improves properties of dough. *Food Technology 45*, 106 (No. 1).

23. Trivedi, N. B., E. J. Cooper, and B. L. Bruinsma. 1984. Development and applications of quick-rising yeast. *Food Technology 38*, 51 (No. 6).

24. Wu, J. Y., J. I. Maningat, J. G. Ponte, Jr., and R. C. Hoseney. 1988. Short-time breadmaking systems. Effect of formulation, additives, temperature, and flour quality. *Journal of Food Science 53*, 535.

25. Wyatt, C. J. 1983. Acceptability of reduced sodium in breads, cottage cheese, and pickles. *Journal of Food Science 48*, 1300.

Cakes and Cookies

26

Although a wide variety of formulations are included in the class of baked products called *cakes*, these recipes can usually be classified into two major groups: shortened cakes or cakes containing fat, and unshortened cakes or cakes with no fat. A third category might be added—the chiffon cake, which has characteristics of both shortened and unshortened cakes. A chiffon cake usually contains a larger proportion of egg than does a shortened cake, a proportion similar to that found in unshortened cakes. It does contain fat in the form of oil.

Among the fat-reduced bakery items that are now appearing on the market in larger numbers are low-fat or no-fat cakes and cake mixes. These cakes are similar to shortened cakes in general characteristics but have been formulated with various fat replacers.

Cookies differ in a number of ways from cakes. Fine texture and velvety crumb are less prominent characteristics of cookies than of cakes, and often, less skill is required to prepare them. Special skills are required to make certain types of cookies, such as rolled cookies or meringue-type cookies; the inexperienced person may find the preparation of these products very challenging.

•SHORTENED CAKES

Types and Characteristics

Shortened cakes are of two types: pound cake and standard shortened cake. The pound cake, as commonly prepared, has no added leavening agent except for the air incorporated in the creaming of the fat and sugar and in the beaten eggs. Steam has been found to be responsible for about half the expansion during baking provided that the air cells are retained. Theoretically, the moisture evaporates into the air cells and the vapor expands during baking. In commercial pound cakes, improved textures have resulted from the addition of a small amount of baking powder.

The standard shortened cake is leavened chiefly by carbon dioxide gas from baking powder or from soda and buttermilk. Air incorporated into the plastic fat or into the beaten eggs or egg whites also aids in leavening the mixture.

The textures of the two types of shortened cakes are different. Pound cakes have a close grain and are somewhat compact in character, yet they are very tender (Figure 26.1). They should not be heavy or soggy, but they lack the soft, light, velvety crumb of a well-made shortened cake. A good standard shortened cake has a fine grain, cells of uniform size, thin cell walls, and a crumb that is elastic rather than crumbly (see Figure 26.4). Crusts should be thin and tender. Top crusts should be smooth or slightly pebbly and have top surfaces that are only slightly rounded.

Proportions of ingredients vary widely for ordinary shortened cakes. Mixtures may be classified as lean or rich depending largely on the relationship of fat and sugar, the tenderizing ingredients, to the ingredients that give structure, flour and egg. One has only to study recipe books and experiment a little with the many proportions given for cakes to realize that numerous variations are possible. Maximum and minimum quantities doubtless exist for most of the essential ingredients for cake, but all of these are not yet known. Specific ingredients can be increased or decreased within certain limits without producing undesirable results.

Change in proportion often requires change in manipulation. The optimum amount of stirring that produces the best results from one set of proportions or a definite quantity of mixture usually cannot be applied to another set of proportions or a smaller or larger quantity of mixture.

FIGURE 26.1
A cherry pecan pound cake. Originally, pound cakes contained approximately one pound each of the main ingredients: eggs, butter, flour, and sugar. (Courtesy of the American Egg Board)

Ingredients

Usual ingredients in a standard shortened cake include sugar, fat, egg, liquid, a leavening agent, salt, and flour. A proper balance between the tenderizing effects of sugar and fat and the firming or structural effects of flour and egg is particularly important in shortened cakes [14].

Sugar

Sugar adds sweetness to a shortened cake, but it also has an important effect on texture and volume. It interferes with gluten development from the flour and has a weakening effect on the structure of the cake. It probably affects gluten development because it attracts and holds water that would otherwise be absorbed by the gluten proteins. Only when the proteins of flour become sufficiently hydrated to adhere to each other is gluten produced. Gelatinized starch is an important part of the structure of a cake. Sugar delays gelatinization of the starch, raises the temperature at which the starch gelatinizes, and causes a decrease in the viscosity of the batter in the early stages of baking [11].

It has been suggested that the resistance to movement of a cake batter during baking, referred to as *cohesive forces*, influences the development of the structure of the finished cake. Various ingredients affect these cohesive forces in different ways. Sugar, added in increasing amounts up to an optimum quantity, decreases the cohesive forces and allows the batter to move more freely. The volume of the cake therefore increases [18]. As sugar is increased in a formula, stirring must also be increased to develop the gluten sufficiently to overcome the weakening effects of excess sugar. Without increased stirring, an increase in the percentage of sugar in a cake causes the cake to fall and to have a coarse texture and thick cell walls. Both crust and crumb are gummy. The crust may appear rough, sugary, and too brown (Figure 26.2).

Sucrose or table sugar is the sugar that is most commonly used in cakes; however, successful layer cakes can be made with glucose or fructose substituted for sucrose if the sugar/water ratio in the batter is adjusted to achieve a desirable starch gelatinization temperature [2]. The temperature at which

FIGURE 26.2
A cake containing too much sugar may fall in the center and have a coarse, gummy texture.

starch gelatinizes in cake batters appears to be an important factor in determining cake volume and contour. More fructose and glucose than sucrose are required in the formula to attain the same starch gelatinization temperature. Cakes made with fructose also tend to be darker because the browning (Maillard) reaction is more pronounced.

High-fructose corn syrup has become an important alternative sweetener in place of sucrose for such products as beverages and soups. The use of this sweetener in baked products has been tested. Acceptable cakes have been made with 50 and 75 percent of the sucrose replaced with high-fructose corn syrup using all-purpose flour in the recipe [15]. Although the cakes with the corn syrup were more brown and of somewhat lower volume, the adverse effects on sensory quality were slight.

Egg

The optimum amount of egg in a given mixture produces finer cells and thinner cell walls than are obtained with a lower or higher percentage of egg. The volume of the cake is also likely to be larger. Although the way the eggs are added may modify the effects, an excess of egg gives a rubbery, tough crumb. When beaten egg whites are added last, the effects of increased egg are less noticeable. The cohesive forces in a baking cake batter are increased as egg white is added in increasing amounts [18].

Fat

Increasing the fat in a shortened cake increases tenderness. Fat weakens structure and tends to decrease volume when it is added beyond optimum amount. Cohesive forces decrease with increasing amounts of fat [18].

In substituting a shortening containing 100 percent fat for butter or margarine (which are 82 percent fat) in a formula that has a fairly high fat content, it is best to use only 82 percent as much fat. Fat of good creaming quality yields a cake of better texture than do soft or liquid fats unless the methods of mixing are altered. In comparing various fats, butter has been reported to make cakes that scored highest for tenderness and velvetlike texture, whereas hydrogenated shortening produced cakes with the highest rating for evenness of grain [14]. Decreasing by half the amount of oil added to a commercial yellow cake mix batter did not appreciably change the appearance, moistness, flavor, or overall acceptability of the baked cake [3]. This achieved a reduction in calories and fat content with no decrease in quality.

In addition to tenderizing, plastic fats aid in incorporating air into the batter. Most hydrogenated fats contain some inert gas as they are marketed. Creaming fat and sugar together adds additional air bubbles to the fat. It has been suggested that the air bubbles incorporated into fat during creaming act as a base for the distribution of leavening gas (carbon dioxide, particularly) during mixing and baking. Additional research with microscopic studies on freeze-dried cake batters showed that the air bubbles were not necessarily incorporated into the fat but were distributed throughout the watery phase of the batter [19]. The fat probably still plays an important role, however, in the trapping of air bubbles in a batter mixture.

Interest in reduced-fat and reduced-calorie foods has led to the development of fat replacers for cakes [22]. One such product is a dry, free-flowing powder, which can be incorporated into both cake mixes and batters, that contains a mixture of emulsifiers, pregelatinized modified starch, and guar gum, with nonfat dry milk as a carrier for the other ingredients. The replacer allows air to be entrapped in the batter, similar to the way in which shortening entraps air.

An instantized modified high-amylose starch has been developed specifically for use in reduced-fat bakery products. It is designed to aid in the aeration of the batter. This, in turn, increases batter viscosity and entraps air during the baking process, resulting in a fine texture. The shelf life is also extended. All of the fat or oil in a cake can be replaced by one of these systems containing modified starches, gums, emulsifiers, and stabilizers. Acceptable ratings have come from the sensory evaluation of many of the resulting cakes. No-fat cake mixes are available for use in foodservice establishments. Light cake mixes containing reduced amounts of shortening, with gums, modified starch, and emulsifiers to compensate, are sold on the retail market. Fat may be reduced by up to 50 percent and calories by about 20 percent.

Emulsifiers

Emulsifying agents in cake batter cause the fat to be distributed more finely throughout the mixture and allow the cake formula to carry more sugar than flour. Shortenings that contain small amounts of emulsifiers are often called *high-ratio* shortenings because of the higher ratio of sugar to flour that is possible with their addition. When optimum amounts of an emulsifier are used, the cohesive forces in the cake batter are decreased, the batter moves or flows more readily because the viscosity is decreased during the early part of the baking period before the structure sets, and the volume of the finished cake is increased [11]. The emulsifier may interact with the starch as it gelatinizes. A fine and even texture is the result in the finished cake (Figure 26.3).

Emulsifiers are commonly added to shortenings that are to be used for making cakes. Hydrogenated shortenings on the retail market often contain small amounts (about 3 percent) of mono- and diglycerides. Polysorbate 60 (about 1 percent) is also frequently used in commercial emulsified shortenings. A larger variety of emulsifiers are available to commercial bakers [6]. In foodservice operations, prepared baking mixes containing emulsified shortening are used to a considerable extent [13].

FIGURE 26.3
The volume and quality of a shortened cake improve when an emulsifier is used. (Courtesy of *Food Engineering* and C. D. Pratt, Atlas Powder Company. Photograph by R. T. Vanderbilt Company.)

Baking Powder

Too little baking powder in a cake produces a compact, heavy product. Increasing the baking powder increases cake volume until the optimum quantity is reached. Beyond that, volume decreases and the cake falls. A coarse texture and a harsh gummy crumb may also result from an excess of baking powder. Cake made from SAS-phosphate powder may be disagreeably bitter if large amounts are used. Less baking powder is needed to produce the best volume and texture when more air is incorporated into the cake by means of the creamed fat-sugar mixture or the beaten egg whites.

Flour

Too little flour has the same effect on a cake as an excess of fat or sugar. The structure is weak and the texture is coarse. The cake may fall. Excess flour, on the other hand, produces a compact, dry cake in which tunnels form readily. Tunnels, however, may form in a cake of good proportions if the mixture is overmanipulated or is baked at too high a temperature.

Flour contributes structure to shortened cakes. Cakes made with all-purpose flour are generally lower in volume and have a coarser texture than similar cakes made with cake flour. Cake flour used in making high-ratio cakes, containing more sugar than flour, must be treated with chlorine gas to produce high-quality cakes [16]. Chlorine not only bleaches pigments in the flour, but it also oxidizes some of the proteins, destroys the normal gluten-developing properties of the flour, and interacts with the starch. Apparently some of the lipids in the flour are also affected [9]. Since cake batter is a complex system, the chlorine-treated flour undoubtedly reacts with other formula components to produce the texture and volume of the final product [16]. In the making of cakes with cake flour, the gelatinized starch is probably more important to structure than is the small amount of gluten developed. The gelatinization of the starch helps to convert a fluid phase into a solid, porous structure.

Liquid

The liquid ingredient in cakes dissolves the sugar and salt and makes possible the reaction of baking powder. It disperses the fat and flour particles and hydrates the starch and protein in the flour, allowing both starch gelatinization and gluten development. Liquid provides some steam, which helps to leaven the cake. Various liquids may be used, including milk, water, and fruit juices. Too much liquid produces a moist cake of low volume.

Chocolate Cakes

Because of the starch content of cocoa and chocolate, a smaller percentage of flour than that used in a yellow cake produces a more desirable chocolate cake. With the same proportions of flour, fat, and sugar that are used in plain shortened cakes, chocolate cake batters tend to be undesirably stiff and the cakes are dry, with a tendency to crack on top. Chocolate cake recipes usually contain relatively high percentages of sugar or fat or both, however, and the proportion of flour may approach that usually used in other shortened cakes. Cocoa has a greater thickening effect than chocolate because the percentage of starch in cocoa is about 11 percent as compared with 8 percent in chocolate. From the standpoint of flavor, color, and thickening effect, best results are usually obtained by using about two-thirds, by weight, as much cocoa as chocolate in a recipe. This amounts to about 3 to 3½ tablespoonfuls of cocoa as a substitute for 1 ounce of chocolate.

The acidity of chocolate is not sufficiently high to necessitate the use of soda unless buttermilk is used in the cake mixture. The color of chocolate cakes gradually changes from cinnamon brown to a mahogany red as the acidity decreases and the alkalinity increases. Devil's food cakes, which are characteristically mahogany red, contain enough soda to produce an alkaline pH in the batter. The characteristic chocolate flavor is decreased with increasing amounts of soda, and thus greater alkalinity, in a chocolate cake.

Proportions of Ingredients

Salt is used in cakes for flavor, and only small amounts are needed. A very satisfactory plain standard cake has, by measure, one-third as much fat as sugar, two-thirds as much milk as sugar, and about three times as much flour as liquid, as in the following example of a cake formula.

Sugar 1½ c	Eggs 2
Fat 1/2 c	Salt 1/2 tsp
Milk 1 c	Baking powder 3 tsp
Cake flour 3 c	Flavoring 1 tsp

In foodservice, recipes designed for household use are often adjusted for quantity production. Various methods may be used for making this adjustment, including multiplying the weight of each ingredient by a certain factor. The factor is determined by dividing the desired yield by the yield of the current recipe. These calculations can be done quickly on a computer, and such software programs are available. Five german chocolate cakes, in quantities serving 60, were prepared with formulations that were generated from a household recipe. Several different computer programs were utilized to perform the calculations for the same home-sized recipe. The cakes were then evaluated for quality characteristics [12]. Because significant differences were found among the cakes, foodservice managers using computers for recipe adjustment were encouraged to test product quality for each adjusted recipe to be sure that the new recipe would produce the same product as the original recipe. The five computer programs used for this study gave somewhat different ingredient quantities and these differences appeared to affect quality.

Mixing

A variety of methods can be used to combine the ingredients in shortened cakes. Four commonly used methods are described here.

Conventional Method

The conventional method consists of creaming a plastic fat, adding the sugar gradually to the fat with continued creaming, adding the egg or egg yolks to the fat–sugar mixture, and beating until the mixture is well blended and very light. The dry ingredients are sifted together and are added alternately with the milk in about four portions. The egg whites may be beaten separately until stiff but not dry and quickly folded into the batter at the end of mixing to avoid excessive loss of gas.

Flavoring extract may be added to the creamed mixture, to the milk, or when the dry and liquid ingredients are being added. The conventional method of mixing is more time consuming than the other methods described here. It should produce a fine-textured cake and may be conveniently used for mixing cakes by hand.

Conventional Sponge Method

The conventional sponge method is used in lean cake mixtures, in which the amount of fat is not sufficient to produce a light creamed mass when all the sugar is added to the fat. To avoid the dry, crumbly character of the fat–sugar mixture, about half of the sugar is reserved to be beaten with the eggs until the mixture is very stiff. The rest of the sugar is creamed with the shortening. The liquid and dry ingredients are added alternately to this sugar–fat mixture. The beaten egg–sugar mixture is then folded into the batter at the end of mixing. Note, however, that a surprisingly large amount of sugar can be creamed with a small or moderate amount of fat if the fat is at the most favorable temperature for creaming, 24°C to 29°C (75° to 85°F), and if the addition of sugar is gradual. A good cake can be made from oil by the use of the conventional sponge method.

Muffin Method

In the muffin method, the eggs, milk, and melted fat are mixed together and added all at once to the sifted dry ingredients. This method is simple and rapid and is particularly useful for lean formulas for which the cake is to be eaten while still warm.

Quick-Mix Method

The quick-mix method is known by several other names, including *single-stage, one-bowl,* and *one-mix.* It requires a change in the proportions of ingredients from those that are satisfactory for the conventional method of mixing. Higher proportions of sugar and liquid are used with the quick-mix method, and the shortening should contain an emulsifying agent. All of the ingredients, particularly the fat, should be at room temperature so that the ingredients can be readily dispersed. Use of this method is difficult when mixing is to be done by hand. An electric mixer is desirable; however, commercial cake mixes, which are designed for the one-bowl method of mixing, may be mixed by hand if the number of mixing strokes, rather than time, is used as the measure. The quick-mix method used with an appropriate formula yields a fine-grained, tender, moist cake of good volume that remains fresh for a relatively long period.

The mixing of the batter can be completed in two stages (Figure 26.4).

STAGE I

Sift all dry ingredients into the bowl used for mixing. Add all fat, *part* of the liquid, and flavoring or add all fat, liquid, and flavoring. Beat for a specified time.

STAGE II

Add unbeaten eggs or egg whites and the remaining liquid if part of the liquid was withheld in the first stage. Beat for a specified time.

In some recipes, the baking powder may be omitted from the first stage and stirred in quickly (all by itself) between the two stages. For uniformity of blending, both the sides and the bottom of the bowl should be scraped frequently during mixing.

Effects of Under- and Overmanipulation

It appears that the amount of mixing needed to produce the best cake texture varies with the proportions of ingredients and the quantity of batter. The temperature of the ingredients is also a factor, as is the quantity of baking powder and the time at which the baking powder is added.

The thoroughness of creaming the fat–sugar mixture affects the extent of subsequent mixing. Thorough creaming makes possible a wider range in the amount of mixing that will produce a good texture. A good creamed mixture is light and spongy but has enough body to prevent an oily, pasty, or frothy mass. When eggs are added to the creamed fat and sugar, the mass becomes softer but should retain enough air to remain light. When the fat–sugar mixture separates into large flecks or curds on the addition of eggs, the resulting cake usually has a coarser texture than does a cake produced from an uncurdled batter. A more stable emulsion may result from adding eggs gradually to the fat–sugar mixture. The use of a shortening containing an emulsifier, such as mono- and diglycerides, also aids in forming a stable emulsion.

Mixing a cake batter barely enough to dampen the dry ingredients may yield a cake of good volume, but the texture is coarse and the cell walls are thick. The optimum amount of stirring produces a cake of optimum volume, uniform texture, small cells, and thin cell walls. Stirring beyond the optimum amount tends to produce a compact cake of smaller volume. The texture may be fine, but tunnels are likely to be formed. When cakes are greatly overstirred, they become heavy or soggy. Cakes stirred close to the optimum amount tend to be slightly rounded on top. As stirring is increased, peaks tend to form and the side walls of the cake are not as high as those in cakes stirred the optimum amount. If cakes are cut or broken where the peaks occur, long tunnels will be found. Certain rich mixtures may show a concave surface if they are understirred.

The fact that cake mixtures contain more sugar and fat than most other flour mixtures decreases the tendency for toughness to result from stirring. Gluten development is retarded by sugar and fat. But more than the optimum amount of stirring may appreciably toughen cakes, especially those made from lean mixtures and from flours of stronger gluten quality.

Preparation of Pans

If the baking pans are prepared before the cake batter is mixed, the batter can then be transferred to them immediately after mixing. Allowing the batter to stand in the mixing bowl more than 15 to 20 minutes before placing it in the baking pans is undesirable, since transfer of the batter at this point may have adverse effects on the volume and texture of the baked product.

Pans may be greased on the sides and bottoms, or the sides may be left dry. If the sides of the pan are not greased, the cake volume may be somewhat greater because the cake structure is supported by clinging to the sides. Flour-

1. Grease the bottom and sides of the pan and dust with flour before beginning to mix the cake.

2. Add shortening, two-thirds of the liquid, and flavoring to the blended dry ingredients.

3. Blend in a mixer at low speed to moisten ingredients. Beat 2 minutes; scrape the bottom and sides of the bowl often. Undermixing gives a coarse texture.

4. Add the remaining liquid and unbeaten eggs. Beat 2 minutes longer; scrape the sides and bottom of the bowl often.

5. Pour the batter into prepared pans. The batter should be divided evenly between the layer pans.

FIGURE 26.4

One-bowl, two-stage method of mixing a shortened cake. (Courtesy of Kitchens of Betty Crocker, General Mills, Inc.)

ing the greased bottom of the pan is an aid in removing the cake from the pan, but the flour coating should be light. An alternative procedure is to cut a piece of paper, waxed or unwaxed, to fit the bottom of the pan. After the paper is in place in the greased pan, it is greased on the top surface, which will come in contact with the cake.

6. Place the pans on the middle rack at least 1 inch from the sides of the oven. The pans should not touch.

7. After minimum baking time, touch the center lightly. If no imprint remains, the cake is done. Or insert a wooden pick in center; if it comes out clean, the cake is done.

8. Allow the cakes to cool 10 minutes on the wire racks before removing them from the pans. If the cakes are left in the pans too long, they will steam and become soggy.

9. The finished cake has a moist, velvety crumb and good volume.

Baking

Baking Temperatures

The oven temperatures commonly used for baking shortened cakes range from 350° to 375°F. The optimal temperature may vary with the cake formula. Some data indicate that plain cakes increase in volume and in total cake scores (including such characteristics as texture, tenderness, velvetiness, and eating quality) up to 365°F but decrease at 385°F. Chocolate cakes, which have often been baked at lower temperatures than other shortened cakes on the theory that chocolate scorches easily, also show increased volume and total cake scores when they are baked at higher temperatures—loaf cakes at 385° to 400°F and layer cakes at 400°F. High temperatures are sometimes not recommended because of excessive browning and humping of the top. The browning of cakes is apparently the result of both the Maillard reaction and the caramelization of sugar.

The better results obtained with higher temperatures would seem to indicate that a more rapid coagulation of cake batter in relation to the rate of gas formation and gas expansion prevents the collapse of cells. Such collapse results in coarse grain and thick cell walls in the baked cake.

If dark, dull pans are utilized, the cake will brown more readily and uniformly than when bright, shiny pans are used. The shiny pans tend to reflect heat while the dull pans absorb it more easily.

Cooling the Cake Before Removal from the Pan

It is recommended that cakes not be removed from the pan until the interior reaches a temperature of about 140°F. At this point, they have usually become firm enough to handle without damage to the structure of the cake. Allowing the baked cake to stand about 10 minutes before removal from the pan is usually sufficient for this temperature to be reached.

Microwave Baking

Flour mixtures do not form a brown crust when they are cooked by microwaves. Since cakes are usually frosted, the lack of crust formation is of less importance from the standpoint of appearance for cakes than for some other baked products. However, the flavor associated with browning is not developed. A browning unit in the microwave oven may aid in browning the top surface of the cake. Waxed paper laid over the surface of cake batters before cooking gives them a smooth surface.

When double layers of cakes were baked in a combination microwave/convection oven using 10 percent microwave power, they were rated equal or near equal to similar cakes baked in a conventional oven [21]. The microwave/convection-baked cakes were rated slightly lower than the conventional cakes for crust color, moistness, and total sensory score when only single layers were baked.

Many cake mixes are satisfactorily cooked in a microwave oven. Rich, moist mixes with pudding added are excellent for microwaving. Because microwaved cakes rise higher than conventionally baked cakes, the pans should be filled no more than one-third to one-half full. Starting the cake at 50 percent power and finishing it at high power result in a more even top than does cooking on high for the entire period. The top of a microwaved cake may be slightly moist when done, but this will evaporate during standing time out of the oven. A number of cake mixes designed especially for the microwave oven are marketed. Special pans for use in the microwave oven are packaged with the cake mixes (Figure 26.5).

•UNSHORTENED CAKES

Unshortened cakes are of two types: white angel food, which is made from egg whites, and yellow sponge, which is made from the whole egg.

Angel Food Cake

Angel food cakes are often made using commercial mixes in which the egg white foam is stabilized by the addition of a whipping aid; however, good-quality cakes can also be made at home using fresh egg whites. Without the incorporation and retention of air, proper expansion and a typical texture do not develop in the baking of unshortened cakes. Air accounts for approximately half of the leavening in angel food cakes. But steam also plays an important role in the leavening of this product. Steam that is formed from the vaporization of the water of egg white brings about two or three times the expansion in baking angel food cake as is accounted for by the expansion of air.

Characteristics

A desirable angel food cake is porous or spongy, is of large volume, and has thin cell walls (Figure 26.6). Tenderness and moistness are also important characteristics. The size of the cells varies, but the grain is generally more open and less fine than that of good-quality shortened cakes.

Ingredients

The ratio of sugar to flour in the following cake formula is an appropriate one for tenderness yet not high enough to cause the collapse of the cake.

FIGURE 26.5
Special pans must be used to bake cakes in microwave ovens. These plastic pans are used to bake cake and brownie mixes engineered especially for the microwave oven. The layer cake at the top of the picture was baked in the round pan at the left. The frosted cake in the center may be baked and served in the same pan. The round pan at the right was used to bake a bundt cake. (Photograph by Chris Meister)

Eggs whites 1 c	Cream of tartar 1 tsp
Sugar 1¼ c	Salt 1/4 tsp
Cake flour 1 c	Flavoring 1 tsp

Egg Whites. Egg whites incorporate air as they are beaten to form a foam. Important in stabilizing the foam is the coagulation of egg proteins by the mechanical forces of beating. (See Chapter 19 for a discussion of beating eggs.) Fresh eggs are preferable to older eggs for making angel food cakes because the fresh whites are thicker and produce a more stable foam. Good-quality angel food cakes may be prepared using frozen or dried egg whites [8]. In addition to the important role of egg white proteins in foam formation and stabilization, some proteins in egg white are coagulated by heat and give structure to the baked cake.

Flour. Cake flour, because of its low percentage of protein, its weak quality of gluten, and its fine granulation, produces a more tender, delicate angel food cake than does flour of stronger gluten quality. Flour increases the strength of the cake crumb and contributes to the structure. As the amount of sugar is increased, the flour also, within certain limits, must be increased to provide a satisfactory ratio of sugar to flour so that sufficient structure is maintained in the cake.

Sugar. Sugar has a stabilizing effect on the egg white foam and allows more beating without overcoagulation of the egg white proteins. Sugar also sweetens the cake and aids in browning. The higher the percentage of sugar in the formulation, the greater the tendency toward development of a sugary crust.

Sugar interferes with gluten development and therefore tends to produce a more tender and fragile cake when it is used in increasing amounts. Sugar elevates the coagulation temperature of egg proteins and, if it is used in excess, may retard coagulation to such an extent that the cake collapses. In addition, the temperature for starch gelatinization is increased by sugar, and that structure of the cake for which gelatinized starch is responsible is affected by increasing amounts of sugar.

A fine granulated sugar is usually used in making angel food cakes; however, 25 percent of the sugar may be replaced by high-fructose corn syrup with little effect on the physical or sensory characteristics of the cake [5].

Cream of Tartar. Cream of tartar is an important constituent of angel food cake because of its beneficial effect on color, volume, and tenderness. The anthoxanthin pigments of flour are yellowish in an alkaline medium but are white in an acid or neutral medium. Also, the Maillard or browning reaction between sugars and proteins is less likely to occur in an acid than an alkaline medium. Therefore, the addition of cream of tartar (an acid salt) produces a cake that is more white than yellow or tan. Cream of tartar, as an acid substance, also stabilizes the egg white foam so that there is time for heat to penetrate and bring about coagulation without collapse of the foam. Large air cells and thick cell walls (coarse grain) are the effects of an unstable foam that has partially collapsed. Cream of tartar prevents extreme shrinkage of the cake during the last part of the baking period and during the cooling period. Cream of tartar also produces a more tender cake. The optimal proportion is about 1 teaspoon per cup of egg whites.

Mixing

The whites can be beaten with an electric mixer, a rotary beater, or a wire whisk. The whisk usually produces a somewhat larger volume of cake but the cells are also larger. Egg whites should not be overbeaten. This contributes to dryness and a lack of extensibility in the films surrounding the air bubbles. The air cells break and collapse, which results in a cake of low volume, thick cell walls, and coarse texture. The whites should be stiff but the peaks and tails that form should bend over slightly instead of standing rigid and upright.

Egg whites beat more easily to a foam of large volume when they are at room temperature than when they are beaten at a lower temperature. Therefore, eggs to be used in angel food cake should be removed from the refrigerator some time before they are to be beaten. Cream of tartar is added to the egg whites, and they are beaten until a foam begins to form. Sugar may be beaten into the whites as they are being whipped, or it may be folded in after the egg whites are completely beaten. In the first case, the sugar is added gradually as for meringue, starting after the cream of tartar is added. Beating the sugar into the whites is known as the *meringue* method and is preferable if an electric mixer is used. Beating some sugar into the egg white foam seems to have a greater stabilizing effect on the cake than folding all of the sugar in with the flour. Regardless of the method used for adding sugar, about 2 tablespoons of sugar at a time are sifted over the surface of the egg whites. Adding either sugar or flour in too large portions results in the loss of air and often in the uneven blending of the sugar or flour.

After the sugar is added, the flour is gently folded into the mixture. If an electric mixer is being used, it should be turned down to the lowest speed setting. Part of the sugar may be reserved to be mixed with the flour. The flour mixed with some sugar unquestionably folds into the mixture more easily, but usually a better cake is obtained when as much of the sugar as possible is added to the egg white foam before the addition of any flour. Thorough mixing of the sugar with the egg white produces a mixture into which the flour blends easily.

The number of strokes needed by different individuals for folding the flour varies. Thorough blending is necessary, but overmanipulation results in a loss of air and in decreased tenderness.

The flavoring extract may be added after the whites are partially beaten. Adding the extract at this stage allows it to become thoroughly distributed without the necessity for overmanipulation later. In no case is it desirable to add extract at the end of mixing because the extract is either incompletely blended with the batter or extra manipulation is needed to blend it uniformly. Alternatively, extract may be added while sugar or flour is being folded into the mixture. The salt may be added toward the end of the beating of the foam and before the addition of flour, because salt may have a slight destabilizing effect on the egg white foam if it is added earlier.

Preparation of Pans

Pans are not greased for either type of sponge cake. It is desirable to have the mixture cling to the sides of the pan until it is coagulated by the heat of the oven. After baking, the pan is inverted and allowed to stand until the cake is thoroughly cooled. This gives the delicate cake structure a chance to set with the least amount of strain placed on it.

Baking Temperatures

Baking at 350°F has been found to result in a more tender and moist angel food cake of larger volume and thinner cell walls than baking at lower temperatures [1]. A wide range of oven temperatures would appear to be satisfactory, however, if the minimum time required to bake the cake is used. Longer baking tends to toughen the cake whatever the temperature, but greater toughening occurs with longer baking at higher temperatures.

Angel food cakes made from commercial mixes and baked at 350° and 375°F scored higher in all quality characteristics than did those baked at 400° and 425°F [7]. Compact layers formed as a result of partial collapse of the structure after the cakes baked at 400° and 425°F were removed from the oven. It has been suggested that baking angel food cakes made from commercial mixes initially at 375°F and then lowering the temperature to 350°F, 325°F, and finally 300°F at 10-minute intervals yields tender baked cakes of very high volume.

When the baking cake begins to shrink, it may be tested with a toothpick or cake tester. If moist or sticky crumbs cling to the tester, the cake must be baked longer.

Sponge Cake

Ingredients

The usual ingredients and proportions for yellow sponge cake are as follows.

Eggs 6	Water 2 Tbsp
Sugar 1 c	Lemon juice 1 Tbsp
Cake flour 1 c	Grated lemon rind 1 Tbsp
Salt ¼ tsp	(lightly measured)

Mixing

Yellow sponge cakes can be made by either separated or whole egg methods. In the whole egg method, the eggs are beaten until they are foamy. The water, lemon juice, and lemon rind are then added, and the mixture is beaten until it is as stiff as possible. (This mixture can be made very stiff.) The sugar is added gradually and beaten into the mixture. The flour and salt are mixed together and then sifted over the surface, about 2 tablespoons at a time, and folded into the egg mixture until all is well blended.

This method is desirable when a very small recipe is prepared. It produces a cake no better than that produced by a method in which egg whites and yolks are separated, but it is difficult to beat one or two separated egg yolks as thoroughly as they should be beaten for best results.

In one separated egg method, the egg yolks are partially beaten. The sugar, salt, water, lemon juice, and lemon rind are added, and the whole mass is beaten until it is very stiff. The flour is folded lightly into the mixture, after which the stiffly beaten egg whites are folded in [4]. Alternatively, the stiffly beaten mixture of yolks, sugar, water, lemon juice and rind, and salt is combined with the beaten egg whites before the flour is folded into the mixture.

In a meringue method, the sugar is boiled with about three-fourths the volume of water to 118°C (244°F). It is then poured gradually over the beaten egg whites with constant stirring until a stiff meringue is formed. The egg yolks, lemon juice, lemon rind, and salt are beaten together until very stiff. The yolk mixture is folded into the whites, and the flour is then gradually folded in.

Certain types of emulsifiers may be used by commercial bakers of sponge cakes. These allow the use of a simplified one-stage mixing procedure and result in a lighter cake of uniform grain, greater tenderness, and longer shelf life.

Baking

Baking temperatures for sponge cakes are similar to those used for angel food cakes. Sponge cakes are toughened by overbaking.

•COOKIES

Classification

Cookies are of six basic types. (1) *Rolled cookies*, when baked, may form either a crisp or a soft cookie depending on the proportions of the ingredients and the degree of doneness. (2) *Dropped cookies* are made from a stiff batter that may be dropped or scraped from the spoon. (3) For *bar cookies*, a cake-type mixture is baked in a thin sheet and later cut into bars or squares. (4) *Pressed cookies* are made from an extra-rich stiff dough that is pressed through a cookie press into various shapes. (5) *Molded cookies* are made from a stiff dough that is shaped into balls, bars, or crescents and sometimes flattened before baking. (6) So-called *icebox* or *refrigerator cookies* are made from a mixture so rich in fat that the dough is difficult if not impossible to roll; it is chilled in the refrigerator to harden the fat and is then sliced from the roll or mold and baked (Figure 26.7).

FIGURE 26.7

Several types of cookies are illustrated in this photograph. Beginning at the bottom center of the tray with the rolled bear cookies and proceeding clockwise, there are two kinds of bar cookies, drop cookies, pressed spritz cookies, Bavarian refrigerator cookies, and molded crescent cookies. (Photograph by Chris Meister)

Ingredients

Formulas for cookies are at least as varied as are those for cakes. In general, the same ingredients that produce good cakes also produce good cookies; however, cake flour is usually not used in cookies because few cookies have a soft, velvety crumb or the texture of good sponge or shortened cakes. All-purpose flour is satisfactory for most cookies.

Crisp cookies are usually made from a mixture that is rich in fat or sugar or both. Many rolled cookie recipes call for very little or no liquid. Because high volume is not desired in rolled cookies, the mixtures contain little or no leavening agent other than air incorporated into the creamed fat–sugar mixture.

Cookies are a major snack item in many countries of the world. Particularly in countries where wheat flour is imported while other flours are abundant, a composite flour may be utilized in the making of cookies. Cookies prepared from formulas containing 50:45:5 or 50:40:10 parts of wheat flour, rice flour, and defatted soy flour were found to be acceptable by both trained and consumer panels in Brazil [10]. These cookies were baked in a microwave oven as an alternative method for preventing nutrient degradation from extensive browning.

Cookie aroma is unique. Some of the volatile flavor compounds of cookies are formed during processing. For example, nonenzymatic (Maillard) browning reactions produce flavor compounds in the baking of cookies. Some of these sweet aroma compounds have been characterized [17]. However, a wide range of aromatic compounds are added to cookies during preparation, making the study of the final flavor profile more difficult. Extraction methods have been developed for the analysis of cookie aroma [20].

Mixing and Handling

The conventional method is used for mixing most cookies, but beaten egg whites are seldom added last. Cookies of the sponge type are made by sponge cake methods.

Doughs for rolled cookies are usually as soft as can be handled and rolled. Stiffer doughs and those rehandled and rerolled give dry, compact cookies. Many cookie mixtures must be chilled to facilitate rolling. Rolling only a portion of the dough at one time prevents continued rerolling. All trimmings can then be collected at the end for rerolling. Rolling between sheets of heavy waxed paper is sometimes done, but the usual method is to roll the dough on a floured board. Care must be used to avoid incorporating much extra flour into the dough while rolling it and to avoid having the cookie covered with excess flour when it is ready for baking. If excess flour is on the surface of the cut cookie dough, it will remain on the cookie after baking and mar the external appearance and flavor. A pastry cloth and stockinet-covered rolling pin may also be used for rolling cookies.

The thickness of rolled dough ready for cutting is usually 1/8 or 3/16 of an inch. If the dough is to be used for cutouts, especially large ones, it is good to roll it to a 1/4 inch thickness. In the removal of cut cookies from the board to the baking sheet, the use of the side, rather than the end, of a spatula usually avoids marring the shape of the cookie. Sticky cookie dough and dough that is rolled tightly to the board are difficult to remove by any method.

Dropped cookie mixtures vary in consistency depending on the finished product desired. Some mixtures are meant to be spread into a round flat cookie of about 3/8 to 1/2 inch thickness after baking. Such mixtures produce softer cookies than does the average rolled dough. Other dropped cookies are meant to hold their form. Judgment and experience with the recipe are necessary if too stiff or too soft a mixture is to be avoided. A mixture that is stiff enough to hold its form almost completely while baking usually produces a dry, breadlike cookie that may crack on top while baking. A cookie that only partially holds its shape during baking is usually of a more desirable texture and eating quality and has a better appearance. The type of mixture partially determines how stiff it can be without producing undesirable results. A mixture very rich in fat can be stiffer than a leaner mixture. Practically all mixtures will be stiff enough to require scraping rather than dropping from the spoon if they are expected to hold their form fairly well. Flour of strong gluten quality tends to produce a dry, breadlike drop cookie, particularly if the mixture is very stiff before baking.

Baking

Baking sheets rather than cake pans are more efficient for baking most cookies, since there are no high side walls to interfere with the circulation of heat. Cookies baked in pans with high sides may cook until they are done, but their tops may be only slightly browned or not at all. Bar cookies are usually baked in pans with sides, however. Baking sheets require no greasing for rolled or refrigerator cookies, which are rich in fat, but do require greasing for dropped cookies or cookie bars. Cookie dough should be put on cool cookie sheets since the dough will melt and spread if it is placed on a hot pan. You may want to bake a test cookie first to be sure that the consistency of the dough is just right.

Rolled cookies spread little in baking, so little space is needed between them. Icebox cookies spread somewhat more, and dropped cookies must have space to spread.

A number of cookie doughs ready for baking are marketed in the refrigerated state. The dough is spooned or molded into balls and baked. A recent addition to the market is cookie dough in the form of little balls or pieces that are frozen and packaged. This allows you to bake only part of the package, if you wish. Ready-to-bake brownies are also available, as either frozen or refrigerated doughs, for both microwaving and conventional baking.

Some restaurants with buffet-type service bake cookies on a continuous basis for customer consumption. The dough is previously prepared but baked where customers can see the process and smell the aroma.

STUDY QUESTIONS

1. Shortened cakes are of two types. Name them and describe distinguishing characteristics of each.
2. Describe the usual role and the effect of an excessive amount of each of the following ingredients in the production of a shortened cake.
   a. Sugar   d. Baking powder
   b. Egg   e. Liquid
   c. Fat   f. Flour
3. What role is played by an emulsifier in a shortened cake batter and what effect does it have on the finished product?
4. Briefly describe each of the following methods for mixing a shortened cake and explain advantages or disadvantages of each method.
   a. Conventional
   b. Conventional sponge
   c. Muffin
   d. Quick-mix
5. Describe the effects of under- and overmixing a shortened cake batter. What factors affect the desirable amount of mixing to be done?
6. Why is it important to prepare the pans for a shortened cake batter before the batter is mixed? Explain.
7. Suggest an appropriate temperature for baking a shortened cake and explain why this temperature is recommended.
8. Why should a shortened cake be allowed to stand for about 10 minutes after baking before removal from the pan?
9. a. Name and describe characteristics of two types of unshortened cakes.
   b. What is a *chiffon cake*?
10. Describe the usual role of each of the following ingredients in angel food cake.
    a. Egg whites
    b. Sugar
    c. Cream of tartar
    d. Flour
11. a. Describe appropriate methods for mixing angel food and sponge cakes.
    b. Point out precautions that should be taken in the mixing of unshortened cakes to ensure finished cakes of good quality.
12. Suggest appropriate baking temperatures for angel food and sponge cakes.
13. How should angel food and sponge cakes be cooled after baking and why?
14. a. Describe six basic types of cookies.
    b. Suggest some precautions that are necessary in the preparation of rolled cookies of good quality.
    c. What types of baking pans are generally recommended for cookies and why?

REFERENCES

1. Barmore, M. A. 1936. *The Influence of Various Factors Including Altitude in the Production of Angel Food Cake*. Colorado State University Experiment Station Technical Bulletin No. 15.

2. Bean, M. M., W. T. Yamazaki, and D. H. Donelson. 1978. Wheat starch gelatinization in sugar solutions. II. Fructose, glucose, and sucrose: Cake performance. *Cereal Chemistry 55*, 945.

3. Berglund, P. T., and D. M. Hertsgaard. 1986. Use of vegetable oils at reduced levels in cake, pie crust, cookies, and muffins. *Journal of Food Science 51*, 640.

4. Briant, A. M., and A. R. Willman. 1956. Whole-egg sponge cakes. *Journal of Home Economics 48*, 420.

5. Coleman, P. E., and C. A. Z. Harbers. 1983. High fructose corn syrup: Replacement for sucrose in angel cake. *Journal of Food Science 48*, 452.

6. Ebeler, S. E., L. M. Breyer, and C. E. Walker. 1986. White layer cake batter emulsion characteristics: Effects of sucrose ester emulsifiers. *Journal of Food Science 51*, 1276.

7. Elgidaily, D. A., K. Funk, and M. E. Zabik. 1969. Baking temperature and quality of angel cakes. *Journal of the American Dietetic Association 54*, 401.

8. Franks, O. J., M. E. Zabik, and K. Funk. 1969. Angel cakes using frozen, foam-spray-dried, freeze-dried, and spray-dried albumen. *Cereal Chemistry 46*, 349.

9. Gaines, C. S., and J. R. Donelson. 1982. Contribution of chlorinated flour fractions to cake crumb stickiness. *Cereal Chemistry 59*, 378.

10. Gonzales-Galan, A., S. H. Wang, V. C. Sgarbieri, and M. A. C. Moraes. 1991. Sensory and nutritional properties of cookies based on wheat–rice–soybean flours baked in a microwave oven. *Journal of Food Science 56*, 1699.

11. Kim, C. S., and C. E. Walker. 1992. Changes in starch pasting properties due to sugars and emulsifiers as determined by viscosity measurement. *Journal of Food Science 57*, 1009.

12. Lawless, S. T., M. B. Gregoire, D. D. Canter, and C. S. Setser. 1991. Comparison of cakes produced from computer-generated recipes. *School Food Service Research Review 15*, 23 (No. 1).

13. Lawson, W. 1985. *Standards for Fats and Oils*. Westport, Conn.: Avi Publishing Company, Inc.

14. Matthews, R. H., and E. H. Dawson. 1966. Performance of fats in white cake. *Cereal Chemistry 43*, 538.

15. McCullough, M. A. P., J. M. Johnson, and J. A. Phillips. 1986. High fructose corn syrup replacement for sucrose in shortened cakes. *Journal of Food Science 51*, 536.

16. Ngo, W., R. C. Hoseney, and W. R. Moore. 1985. Dynamic rheological properties of cake batters made from chlorine-treated and untreated flours. *Journal of Food Science 50*, 1338.

17. Nishibori, S., and S. Kawakishi. 1990. Effects of dough materials on flavor formation in baked cookies. *Journal of Food Science 55*, 409.

18. Paton, D., G. M. Larocque, and J. Holme. 1981. Development of cake structure: Influence of ingredients on the measurement of cohesive force during baking. *Cereal Chemistry 58*, 527.

19. Pohl, P. H., A. C. Mackey, and B. L. Cornelia. 1968. Freeze-drying cake batter for microscopic study. *Journal of Food Science 33*, 318.

20. Prost, C., C. Y. Lee, P. Giampaoli, and H. Richard. 1993. Extraction of cookie aroma compounds from aqueous and dough model system. *Journal of Food Science 58*, 586.

21. Stinson, C. T. 1986. A quality comparison of devil's food and yellow cakes baked in a microwave/convection versus a conventional oven. *Journal of Food Science 51*, 1578.

22. Waring, S. 1988. Shortening replacement in cakes. *Food Technology 42*, 114 (No. 3).

Pastry

27

Pastries are products made from doughs containing moderate to large amounts of fat and mixed in such a way as to produce flakiness. Note the following three examples.

1. Plain pastry or pie crust is used to make all types of tarts, turnovers, and dessert pies—including single- and double-crust fruit pies (Figure 27.1); custard-type pies baked in the shell; and soft starch-thickened cream pies and gelatin-based chiffon pies in which the fillings are added after the pie shells are baked.
2. Plain pastry is also used as a carrier of high-protein foods to be served as a main dish: various types of meat, poultry, and fish pies with single or double crusts; patty shells to hold chicken à la king and similar types of creamed mixtures; and quiches, which are pies that can be made with a variety of ingredients, such as bacon, ham, swiss cheese, mushrooms, onions, and other vegetables, baked in a custard-type filling (Figure 27.2).
3. Puff pastry—flaky layers of light, buttery dough—is used to make crisp, sugar-glazed and cream-filled french pastry or flaky sweet rolls called *danish pastry* (Figure 27.3). Puff pastry is made by rolling chilled butter in a well-kneaded flour-and-water dough; then folding and rerolling several times to make many thin layers of dough separated by thin layers of butter. During baking, the butter melts and permeates the dough.

This chapter focuses on the making of plain pastry.

•CHARACTERISTICS OF PLAIN PASTRY

Good-quality pastry is tender but does not break too easily when it is served. It is flaky, with a blistered surface, is slightly crisp, evenly and lightly browned, and pleasantly flavored.

FIGURE 27.1
A lattice-top fruit pie. (Courtesy of Sun-Maid Raisin Growers of California)

FIGURE 27.2
A quiche that contains fresh sliced mushrooms, sliced green onions, and shredded swiss cheese. The custard base is made with eggs and light cream or milk. (Courtesy of the American Egg Board)

FIGURE 27.3
Puff pastry can be utilized to produce a variety of tantalizing products. In the center front is an apple turnover; behind this, the thin flakes of the pastry can be seen in elephant ears; three creme-filled french pastries are on the right; and at the top of the picture is a small danish pastry. (Photograph by Chris Meister)

Flakiness

Flakiness is described as thin layers of baked dough separated by open spaces (Figure 27.4). Some factors that have been found to affect flakiness are (1) the character of the fat used (solid versus melted or liquid fat), (2) the consistency of solid fat, (3) the type of flour used, (4) the proportion of water, (5) the degree of mixing, (6) the method of mixing, and (7) the number of times the dough is rolled.

Flakiness is thought to result from a process in which small particles of fat are coated with moistened flour or dough and then flattened into thin layers when the dough mixture is rolled out. On baking, the fat melts, is absorbed by the surrounding dough, and leaves empty spaces between thin layers of the baked dough.

Solid fats yield a flaky crust more easily than do melted or liquid fats; however, flaky pastry can be produced with melted fats or oils. Liquid fats generally tend to blend more completely with flour. They may yield a very tender and crumbly crust when they are used in the same proportion as solid fats.

Firm fats that remain in layers when they are rolled yield a flakier crust than do soft fats. The method used in making puff pastry, in which the fat is reserved to be rolled between the layers of dough, increases flakiness. Merely rerolling increases flakiness, but unless the percentage of fat in the mixture is high, rerolling may also develop the gluten sufficiently to increase toughness. Rerolling as a means of increasing flakiness is valuable chiefly for puff pastry.

A regular pastry flour may yield a very flaky crust, but flakiness increases with the strength of gluten. Toughness may also increase with the use of a stronger flour unless additional fat is used and greater care is taken in manipulation.

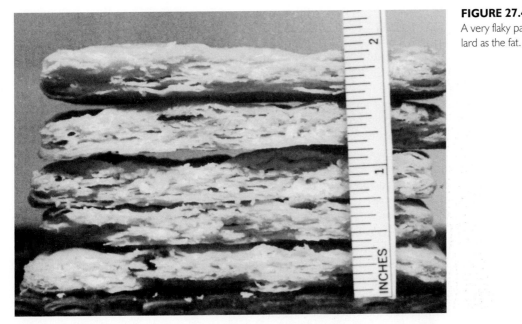

FIGURE 27.4

A very flaky pastry can be made with lard as the fat.

Tenderness

Because tenderness is one of the most desirable characteristics of good pastry, it requires at least as much consideration as flakiness. Yet some of the factors that produce flakiness tend to decrease tenderness and vice versa. Tenderness is at a maximum when the fat spreads over the flour particles, interferes with the hydration of gluten proteins in the flour, and thus decreases the formation of gluten strands. If the fat blends too thoroughly with the dough, the crust is too tender to handle and tends to be crumbly. Adjustments in both ingredients and techniques of mixing and handling must be made so that both flakiness and tenderness are achieved in the baked pastry.

•INGREDIENTS IN PLAIN PASTRY

Plain pastry contains only a few ingredients—flour, fat, salt, and water. Either pastry or all-purpose flour can be used; pastry flour requires less fat for optimum tenderness and is used primarily by commercial bakers. Because of the larger amount of gluten formed with all-purpose flour, about 1/3 cup of fat per cup of flour may be needed to produce a tender crust. This proportion is also dependent on the kind of fat used and the skill of the handler.

The amount of water required for plain pastry varies with the hydration capacity of the flour, the amount and type of fat, the temperature of the ingredients, and the individual technique of handling. An excessive amount of water added in the making of pastry dough allows the hydration and development of more gluten than is desirable for optimum tenderness. Toughness of pastry is therefore increased by too much water in the dough. Too little water produces a dry dough that is crumbly and difficult to handle. The amount of liquid should be sufficient to barely form a dough; the dough should not be wet and sticky [5].

Fat is responsible for the tenderness of pastry because it spreads over the particles of flour and retards their hydration. Fats vary in their tenderizing properties [4]. Liquid oils spread more than do plastic fats and usually have greater tenderizing power. Reduction of the level of soybean or safflower oil in pie crust results in a product that compares favorably in quality characteristics with pie crust made with a standard level of shortening [1]. Softer plastic fats spread more readily than harder fats. Butter and margarine contain only about 82 percent fat and therefore have less tenderizing power than 100 percent fats such as lard and hydrogenated shortening when substituted on a weight basis. A cup of lard weighs more than a cup of hydrogenated shortening because the shortening has been precreamed and contains an inert gas to make it lighter. In addition to the role of fat in tenderizing, plastic fats, in particular, play an important part in the development of flakiness in pastry.

Plain pastry is leavened primarily by steam, which is produced by baking in a hot oven. Leavening in plain pastry is not extensive, however.

Very hard fat, direct from the refrigerator, and iced water are not necessary in the making of pastry. The fat should be cold enough to be firm rather than pasty or oily but plastic enough to be measured accurately and to blend with the flour. In warm weather, some chilling of fat may be necessary. Likewise, some chilling of water may be required, but both water and fat at room temperature produce good results.

•TECHNIQUES OF MIXING

Fat can be cut into the flour with a pastry blender or with a knife or spatula. It can even be lightly blended with the fingers. Electric mixers or food processors can also be used both to mix the fat with the flour and to mix the liquid with the fat–flour mixture in the final stages of dough preparation. A reasonably uniform blending of fat with flour produces a more uniformly tender crust. Fat particles may vary in size. Those who favor a relatively coarse division of fat in the flour-and-salt mixture do so on the theory that flakiness is increased by the rolling of larger fat masses into thin layers.

Unless sufficient water is added, the baked crust will be too tender and crumbly; however, too much water toughens the pastry. Gluten forms to a greater than desirable extent when water is used in excessive amounts [3].

Several methods of mixing pastry, other than the traditional pastry method shown in Figure 27.5, have been suggested. A satisfactory pastry product can be obtained by using any one of these methods.

A modified method of mixing pastry has been developed in which 1/4 cup of a 2-cup portion of flour is reserved to be mixed with liquid to form a paste. After the fat and the remainder of the flour have been combined as described, the paste is added all at once and blended with the fat–flour mixture.

In the hot water method of mixing pastry, solid fats can be melted by stirring them into boiling water; this mixture is then stirred into the flour and salt. If oil is used as the fat, it can be shaken with water and added in a similar manner. Alternatively, the oil can be sprinkled over the flour-salt mixture followed by stirring to disperse the oil. The water can then be added as in the traditional method. Pastry made by the hot water and oil methods may be somewhat less flaky than pastry made by the traditional method.

Pastry can also be made by a modified puff pastry method: about 2 tablespoons of the fat–flour mixture are removed before the liquid is added. After the pastry has been rolled out, this fat–flour mixture is sprinkled over the dough. The dough is rolled up like a jelly roll and cut into two pieces. One piece is placed on top of the other, and they are then rerolled for the pie pan. This method tends to increase flakiness in pastry.

•ROLLING PASTRY

Pastry can be rolled as soon as it has been mixed, but allowing the dough to stand for a few minutes increases the extensibility or elasticity of the dough, making it easier to handle and to roll. For ordinary pie crust, the dough is rolled to about 1/8 inch thickness. Enough flour is required for the board to keep the crust from sticking, but the minimum amount should be used to avoid toughening the pastry. Occasional lifting of the crust while rolling also tends to prevent sticking. The dough can be rolled on a canvas-covered board, into which a small amount of flour has been rubbed, or between two layers of waxed paper. Crusts that are rolled very thin become too brown when they are baked as pie shells and break in handling or in serving. If they are used for fruit pies, they may break during baking and allow juices to flow out.

Crusts are rolled into a circular shape. The dough for a lower crust or a pie shell should be about 1 to 2 inches greater in diameter than the top of the

FIGURE 27.5

Preparation of pastry. (Courtesy of Kitchens of Betty Crocker, General Mills, Inc.)

1. After the flour and salt are measured and mixed together in the bowl, the shortening is cut with a pastry blender.

2. Sprinkle the water, a tablespoonful at a time, over the flour–fat mixture.

6. Divide dough approximately in half; round up larger part on lightly floured cloth-covered board.

7. Roll out not quite 1/8 inch thick.

pan, which allows for variable pan depth (Figure 27.5). To avoid excessive rolling of dough, which toughens the pastry, each crust is rolled separately. For future use, the rolled pastry can be frozen before baking [2], or the baked shells can be frozen.

Although pie shells tend to shrink somewhat in baking, excessive shrinkage can be prevented if the dough is not stretched when it is fitted into the pan. Preparing enough dough to make a rim or a frilled edge is also an advantage if shrinking occurs. Overdevelopment of the gluten by rerolling may result in greater shrinkage during baking than occurs when gluten is not developed to an appreciable extent.

The formation of large blisters in pastry shells during baking can be prevented by forcing air from under the dough while fitting the dough into the pan and by pricking the dough adequately with a fork before baking. Crusts in which fillings are to be cooked are never pricked.

3. Mix lightly with a fork until all the flour is moistened.

4. Gather the dough together with your fingers and press into a ball.

5. A canvas-covered board and a stockinet-covered rolling pin prevent the pastry from sticking while being rolled out.

8. Keep the pastry circular and roll it about 1 to 2 inches larger than the pie pan.

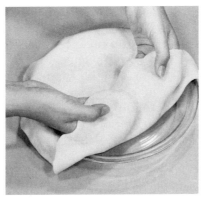

9. Fold the pastry in half. Quickly transfer to a pie pan and unfold.

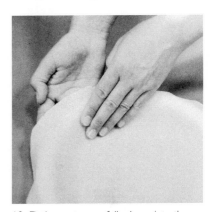

10. Fit the pastry carefully down into the pan. Avoid trapping air underneath the dough. Trim off the overhanging edges. Place the filling in the pastry-lined pan. Roll out the other part of the dough for the top crust.

Top crusts for fruit pies are less likely to break under the pressure of steam if small openings are made near the center for the escape of steam. Large gashes should be avoided since they are unattractive and permit the loss of juices. Top crusts adhere more closely to lower crusts if the latter are moistened before the crusts are pressed together.

•BAKING

Plain pastry that is baked prior to the addition of the filling is baked at a hot oven temperature (425° to 450°F). This allows rapid production of steam, which separates the layers of dough formed as the fat particles melt. Baking is continued until the surface is delicately browned, which probably occurs chiefly as a result of the Maillard reaction.

Baking temperatures are adjusted according to the type of filling in pastry shells. The filling must be adequately cooked before the crust becomes too brown. Soaking of bottom crusts by fruit and custard fillings sometimes creates problems in baking.

Preventing Soaked Crusts

Many methods have been suggested and tried for the prevention of soaked crust in fruit, custard, and pumpkin pies. Some methods—partially baking the crust, coating the crust with raw egg white, or heating the crust until the egg white is coagulated—have no value. A partially baked crust becomes more soaked than one that is not baked. It also tends to be heavy or soggy. Raw egg white, being soluble in water, blends with the filling, thus offering no protection against the soaking of the crust.

So how can the crusts be protected? For fruit pies, you can coat the upper surface of the lower crust with melted butter, use a hot oven temperature for the first 15 minutes of baking, and thicken the filling before placing it in the pastry-lined pan. Thickening the filling has the added advantage of letting you know the precise consistency of the juice before the pie is baked.

For custard and pumpkin pies, the problem of soaked crusts is even more difficult to solve. The lower baking temperatures required for egg mixtures prolong the baking time and permit increased soaking before the pie is done. A method that has been suggested to improve the crusts of custard pies is chilling the pastry for 1 hour before adding the filling, and using a high oven temperature (450°F) for the first 10 minutes of baking. Increasing the percentage of egg in the mixture (three eggs per pint of milk) lowers the coagulation temperature of the egg proteins and increases the ease of coagulation for the mixture. Scalding the milk used for the filling also shortens coagulation time. A coagulated custard does not penetrate the crust as readily as an uncooked mixture. An overcooked custard may exude sufficient water to produce a very wet crust.

Using the Microwave Oven

Microwaved pastry is tender, flaky, and puffy, but it does not brown. A few drops of yellow food coloring can be added to the dough, or the pastry can be brushed with egg yolk before microwaving. A one-crust pastry shell is cooked on high power for about 6 or 7 minutes, the dish being rotated one half turn after 3 minutes. Alternatively, the pastry shell can be baked in a conventional oven and the filling cooked in a microwave oven. Commercial pie filling mixes are easily prepared by mixing the packet contents with milk and cooking on a high-power setting for 2 to 3 minutes with periodic stirring.

The bottom crust of a two-crust pie can be cooked by microwaves on a medium setting for 5 to 6 minutes, the uncooked filling added, the top crust put in place, and the pie cooked again. The pie should be turned midway in the cooking period. If a broiling unit is not available for browning, the pie can be finished by baking for 10 to 15 minutes in a hot conventional oven. Meringues can be cooked by microwaves but must be browned in a conventional heating unit.

Prepared Pie Crust

Partially prepared pie crust is available on the market in several forms. Ready-to-bake pie crust in aluminum pie pans is sold as a frozen product. Instructions generally suggest that the dough be thawed before baking. However, if the product is to be used in the preparation of a fruit pie, it should be filled with the fruit and put in to bake without being thawed. Rolled sheets of pie crust, enclosed in plastic sheets and folded, are sold as refrigerated dough. They should be allowed to warm to the degree that they are pliable before being unfolded and placed in a pie pan for baking. Pie crust is also marketed as a dry mix that needs only the addition of water to form a dough that can be rolled and placed in pie pans.

STUDY QUESTIONS

1. Describe desirable characteristics of good-quality pastry.
2. Describe the role of each of the following ingredients in the preparation of good-quality pastry.
   a. Flour
   b. Fat
   c. Water
3. a. Suggest an appropriate ratio of fat to flour for making pastry.
   b. Explain how the type of fat and the type of flour used might affect these proportions.
4. a. Describe several procedures for mixing pastry.
   b. What techniques of mixing are likely to produce the most flaky pastry and why?
5. Describe a satisfactory procedure for making pastry with oil. How does this pastry compare with one made with a solid fat?
6. What is the effect of each of the following on tenderness of pastry?
   a. Type of fat used
   b. Type of flour used
   c. Technique of mixing and handling
7. Suggest an appropriate temperature for baking plain pastry and explain why this temperature may be recommended.
8. How might one prevent or minimize the soaking of bottom crusts of custard and fruit pies during baking?

REFERENCES

1. Berglund, P. T., and D. M. Hertsgaard. 1986. Use of vegetable oils at reduced levels in cake, pie crust, cookies, and muffins. *Journal of Food Science 51*, 640.
2. Briant, A. M., and P. R. Snow. 1957. Freezer storage of pie shells. *Journal of the American Dietetic Association 33*, 796.
3. Hirahara, S., and J. I. Simpson. 1961. Microscopic appearance of gluten in pastry dough and its relation to the tenderness of baked pastry. *Journal of Home Economics 53*, 681.
4. Matthews, R. H., and E. H. Dawson. 1963. Performance of fats and oils in pastry and biscuits. *Cereal Chemistry 40*, 291.
5. Miller, B. S., and H. B. Trimbo. 1970. Factors affecting the quality of pie dough and pie crust. *Baker's Digest 44*, 46 (No. 1).

Food Preservation and Packaging

28

Food preservation has been practiced for thousands of years, but marked changes have occurred in the processes applied as civilization has developed and become industrialized. In early historic times, people learned to dry their supplies of fresh meat and fish in the sun and to store food for the cold winter months. Later they discovered how to smoke and salt these products to extend the time that the foods remained edible.

In the early days of America, particularly on the frontiers, a precise schedule of work was necessary to harvest crops of fruits, vegetables, and grains at just the right time. Much labor was also expended in preserving excesses of these crops, often in root cellars and granaries, for later use when nothing could be grown. When animals were slaughtered, they had to be processed quickly. To decrease the likelihood of rapid spoilage, this was usually done in cool weather. Canning had not yet been discovered in the very early days of America. That came later, beginning in France about 1810. Much time was required by members of a household, particularly the housewife, for preparing and preserving food.

Today it is very different. The basic food preservation methods used in early years are still utilized. Added to them, however, is a whole arsenal of technology for ensuring the availability of a large variety of high-quality foods throughout the year. The future may also bring the development of novel nonthermal preservation methods that use such technologies as high-electric field pulses, oscillating magnetic field pulses, and high-pressure treatments [24].

Much of the processing and initial treatment for the preservation of foods in Western countries is done by the food industry. Consumers, as well as food-service managers, are becoming very used to purchasing canned, frozen, fermented, dried, portioned, and packaged foods for only short-term storage in their kitchens. The freezer and the microwave oven form a duo that is widely used for the final storage and then rapid heating of the processed and preserved foods that are purchased.

Despite these trends in commercial preservation and packaging of foods, there are still many places in America, particularly in rural areas and smaller towns, where home gardens are popular and the excess produce is canned, frozen, or dried for future use. Thus, a brief discussion of home canning and freezing techniques is provided in the following chapter. In this chapter, some recently developed techniques for food preservation and packaging are described. The basic causes of food spoilage and general methods of food preservation are also discussed.

•CAUSES OF FOOD SPOILAGE

When foods spoil, they become inedible or hazardous to eat because of chemical and physical changes that occur within the food. The two major causes of food spoilage are the growth of microorganisms, including bacteria, yeasts, and molds, and the action of **enzymes** that occur naturally in the food. Additional causes of food spoilage are nonenzymatic reactions, such as oxidation and **desiccation**, mechanical damage, such as bruising, and damage from insects and rodents.

Although microorganisms can cause food spoilage, they also have important advantageous roles in food preservation and processing. For example, certain cheeses, such as Roquefort and Camembert, are ripened by molds; other cheeses are ripened by bacteria. Production of some Oriental foods, including soy sauce, requires fermentation by molds. Yeast is an essential ingredient in bread and many other baked products. The brewing industry also relies on yeast. Buttermilk, yogurt, sauerkraut, and fermented pickles owe their special desirable flavors to bacterial action. (Some basic characteristics of molds, yeasts, and bacteria are described in Chapter 3.)

Enzymes are present in any food that has been living tissue, such as meat, fish, fruits, and vegetables. They are also present in milk and eggs. Unless undesirable enzyme action is controlled or the enzymes are destroyed (usually by heating), they may be responsible for unwanted chemical changes in preserved foods. (General characteristics of enzymes are discussed in Chapter 5.)

Proper packaging of food plays an important role in controlling food spoilage resulting from desiccation, bruising, and damage by insects and rodents. Oxidation of fats may also be retarded to some degree by appropriate packaging, as well as by the control of environmental conditions and the addition of antioxidants. Edible films or coatings, composed of polysaccharides, proteins, lipids, or combinations of these substances, may be used as vehicles for incorporating antioxidants onto the surface of foods [12]. New technologies are bringing dramatic changes to the world of food packaging, some of which are discussed later in this chapter.

•GENERAL METHODS OF FOOD PRESERVATION

All methods used for preserving foods are based on the general principle of preventing or retarding the causes of spoilage—microbial decomposition, enzymatic and nonenzymatic chemical reactions, and damage from mechanical causes, insects, and rodents. When the growth of microorganisms is only retarded or inhibited, preservation is temporary. When spoilage organisms are completely destroyed and the food is protected so that no other microorganisms are permitted to reinfect it, more permanent preservation is achieved.

Enzymes protein molecules produced by living cells that act as organic catalysts and change the rate of a reaction without being used up in the process

Desiccation the process of drying as moisture is lost

No method of food preservation improves the original quality of a food product. If a preserved food is to be of satisfactory quality, then fresh, flavorful produce at an optimal stage of ripeness or maturity must be used.

Preservation by Temperature Control

Either cold or hot temperatures can be used to produce an environment unfavorable to microbial growth.

Cold Temperatures

Cold temperatures mainly inhibit the growth of microorganisms, although some destruction of microbial cells does occur at very low temperatures. With chilling, the length of time that the food remains wholesome varies with the temperature employed and with the type of food being chilled. It also depends on the type of packaging, including modified-atmosphere packaging and vacuum cooking–packaging, which extend the effective period of refrigerated storage for food.

In most refrigerators, maintenance of a temperature of 7° to 10°C (45° to 50°F) preserves many foods for only a few days. In cold-storage warehouses, the time is increased. Here the temperature is lower and the humidity is controlled, both conditions favoring preservation. Control and monitoring of gases in the atmosphere of the cold-storage facility (controlled-atmosphere storage) are also used in some cases to retard ripening or maturation changes that decrease the storage life of fresh produce.

Freezing can preserve foods for long, but not indefinite, periods of time provided that the quality of the food is good to begin with and the temperature of storage is well below the actual freezing temperature of the food. For the highest retention of both flavor and nutritive value in frozen foods, the freezer should be maintained at no higher than –18°C (0°F) [16]. Care must be exercised in the marketing of frozen foods to ensure that they are held at freezing temperatures at all times as they move through the various market channels to the consumer.

The action of enzymes already present in the tissues is retarded at freezing temperatures. In certain products such as vegetables, however, enzyme action may still produce undesirable effects on flavor and texture during freezer storage. The enzymes, therefore, must be destroyed by heating the vegetables in hot water or steam, a process called *blanching*, before they are frozen. The market for refrigerated and frozen foods has expanded greatly in recent years. The success of the microwave oven and its penetration into the majority of American homes have had much to do with stimulating this market, particularly that of ready-to-eat foods [2].

Thermal Processing

Hot temperatures preserve by destroying both microorganisms and enzymes. Yeasts, molds, and enzymes are readily destroyed at the boiling temperature of water. The heating must be maintained long enough to permit all parts of the food to reach the necessary temperature. Heat penetration is sometimes slow in such foods as partially ripe pears or peaches. Bacteria are less readily destroyed than are yeasts, molds, and enzymes, the vegetative or active cells

Spore   an encapsulated, resistant form of a microorganism

Botulism   a disease resulting from consumption of a deadly toxin produced by the anaerobic bacterium *Clostridium botulinum*

Retort   pressure canning equipment used in commercial canning operations to process low-acid foods at high temperatures

Pasteurization   a mild heat treatment that destroys many, but not all, vegetative microorganisms

Sterilization   the complete destruction of microorganisms in a medium

being more readily destroyed than **spore** forms. Many bacterial spores, including spores of *Clostridium botulinum*, are very resistant to heat. Care must be exercised in the heat processing of canned food to assure destruction of bacterial spores. The leading cause of **botulism** in the United States is the consumption of inadequately processed home canned foods.

Canning as a method of food preservation involves essentially the complete destruction of microorganisms and their spores, as well as enzymes, by the use of high temperatures, followed by sealing of the container to prevent recontamination of the food (Figure 28.1). The food in this case is essentially sterilized.

Retort pouches or packages have been developed as flexible packaging for thermoprocessed foods (see Figure 28.4). Lightweight pouches with a thin cross section improve the quality of sterilized packaged food because of the decreased time required for complete heat penetration. Energy savings also result. The weight of the packages is much less than that of metal cans and lids. The ease of transporting is thus increased while the expense is decreased [30].

Pasteurization of food products involves the use of temperatures lower than those required for **sterilization**. Foods that are often pasteurized include milk, fruit juices, and eggs that are to be frozen or dried. All pathogenic microorganisms, but not all of the other microorganisms present, are destroyed by pasteurization. This results in a more limited or temporary preservation period than do sterilization and canning.

Preservation by Moisture Control

Drying

One of the oldest methods of preserving foods involves the removal of moisture until the product is dry. As practically applied, the food is dried in the sun or by air currents and artificial heat until the moisture content of the food is reduced to a level that inhibits the growth of microorganisms. The actual per-

FIGURE 28.1

Bottled green beans are sealed so that recontamination by microorganisms cannot occur. (Courtesy of the Ball Brothers Company)

centage of moisture varies but is usually under 30 percent. Some dehydrated foods, such as dried potato slices, contain only 2 to 3 percent moisture. Many commercially dried fruits with an intermediate moisture content, about 15 to 35 or 40 percent, have low enough water activity for preservation yet are pleasant to eat directly without rehydration [11].

Some foods can be easily dried at home. These include most garden vegetables, fruits, and garden herbs such as parsley and oregano. Drying can be done in driers especially designed for this purpose, in the oven, or, in sunny climes, in trays placed in the sun. Vegetables, with few exceptions, should be **blanched** before drying to stop the action of enzymes that produce undesirable changes in texture and flavor during storage. Dried vegetables that have been blanched also dry more easily and retain more vitamins. Light-colored fruits, such as apples, apricots, and peaches, are of better quality when they are sulfured before drying to prevent darkening. This involves exposing the fruit to the fumes of burning sulfur.

Blanch   to immerse in hot water or steam for a short time and then cool quickly in cold water

Freeze-Drying

In the process of freeze-drying, the food product is first frozen and then placed in a vacuum chamber, to which a small amount of heat is applied. Under the reduced pressure of the vacuum, the ice in the frozen food changes directly to water vapor (sublimes) and is carried away by the circulating heated air. The moisture content of the food is thus reduced. The food remains frozen through most of the drying period. It does not get warm as does food that is subjected to ordinary drying processes. Fresh flavors and textures are therefore better preserved by freeze-drying than by sun-drying or other procedures of artificial drying without vacuum. It is also possible, on a commercial basis, to use microwaves rather than a conventional heat source in the freeze-drying process [29].

The time for freeze-drying depends on the product and its thickness. It usually requires 10 to 20 hours, and the moisture content of the final product is 1 to 4 percent. Oxidation during freeze-drying is curbed by the low oxygen tension maintained and sometimes by the breaking of the vacuum with an inert gas rather than air.

By conventional drying methods, the satisfactory drying of meat is limited to ground or extremely thin strips. By freeze-drying, steaks and chops 1/2 to 1 inch thick can be processed. Roasts require a longer drying period, thus presenting cost and technical problems. The freeze-drying of food is a relatively expensive process.

The food industry is interested in freeze-drying for two principal reasons: transportation and storage costs are reduced (the weight of the dried product is about one-third that of the original food), and refrigeration is not required. To illustrate these advantages: Sir Edmund Hillary took 300 pounds of freeze-dried items on his Himalayan mountain-climbing expedition. The products reconstituted to 1,200 pounds and included ham, chicken, chops, steaks, fruits, and vegetables. Although refrigeration is not required, freeze-dried products do tend to deteriorate with long storage unless they are properly packaged.

Some fruits are very successfully freeze-dried to 5 to 8 percent moisture levels. Apricots are light in color, hydrate rapidly, and have a fresh flavor. Some strawberries have been held for long periods without a change in flavor. The browning of fruits that are freeze-dried can be prevented by treatment with sulfur dioxide.

Freeze-dried coffee, dried by both conventional and microwave methods, is marketed. Freeze-dried fish salad mixes are available for institutional use. A number of freeze-dried foods for individual use are sold in sporting goods outlets and are used by campers and hikers.

Freeze-dried meats are very similar to fresh meats in flavor and color, but they may be somewhat tougher and drier. Tenderness is improved if the meat is hydrated in 2 percent brine or if proteolytic enzymes are added to the hydrating liquid.

Use of Preservatives

Adding chemical substances called *preservatives* to a food product is another method of inhibiting the growth of undesirable microorganisms. Common preservatives, sometimes called *household preservatives*, include acids, salt, sugar, spices, and smoke. It is the phenols in wood smoke that seem to exert the major preservative action. Vinegar contains acetic acid and is commonly used, along with salt, to pickle vegetables (Figure 28.2). In pickle and sauerkraut fermentations, lactic and other organic acids are produced over a period by friendly bacteria present on the vegetables. Not only does the acid prevent microbial growth, but additional flavor substances are also produced by the bacteria. Sugar in large amounts is used in the production of jellies, jams, and preserves (Figure 28.3). It acts as a preservative by binding the moisture necessary for microbial growth and activity.

Spices inhibit bacterial growth to some degree but vary in their effectiveness. Ground cinnamon and cloves are more valuable than nutmeg and allspice in quantities that can be used without marring flavor. However, spices themselves are often responsible for introducing bacteria into foods. Oils of spice are sterile and have a more inhibitory effect on microbial growth than do ground spices.

FIGURE 28.2
A mixture of salt, vinegar, and water is poured over cucumbers and dill to make dill pickles. (Courtesy of the U.S. Department of Agriculture)

FIGURE 28.3
A good-quality jelly is stiff enough to hold its shape yet is delicate and tender. The jelly is preserved by its content of approximately 65 percent sugar.

A number of preservatives are used as food additives and must be approved for use by the U.S. Food and Drug Administration (FDA). Thorough testing for safety is required before approval is given. Sodium benzoate, used in very small amounts in some margarines, and sulfur dioxide, used to prevent the discoloration of dried fruits such as apricots, apples, and pears, are examples of preservatives that may be added to foods. An antioxidant is a special type of preservative that inhibits the spoilage of fats because of a nonenzymatic oxidative process. The FDA has approved nisin, or *bacteriocin*, a polypeptide antibacterial substance, for use in some pasteurized cheese spreads. It is active only against gram-positive bacteria and is approved for use to inhibit the growth of *Clostridium botulinum* spores. The bacterium *Streptococcus lactis* produces this antibiotic [6, 31].

Preservation by Ionizing Radiation

Ionizing radiation is a type of radiation used to preserve foods to a greater or lesser degree. Treated foods are commonly called *irradiated foods*.

Energy exists in the form of waves and is defined by its wavelength. Shorter wavelengths have higher energy. Ionizing radiation has high enough energy to change atoms in the irradiated food by removing an electron to form an **ion**. However, it does not have enough energy to split atoms in the food and cause it to become **radioactive**. The sources of radiation allowed for food processing include cobalt-60 and cesium-137 as sources of gamma rays, accelerated electrons, and X rays (see Figure 8.1 for the electromagnetic spectrum showing these rays in relation to visible light and microwaves). At the dosages allowed, the radiation cannot make food radioactive [7].

Absorbed radiation is measured in units called *grays*. In the past, the term *rad* was commonly used; it stands for *radiation absorbed dose*. A gray, then, is the level of energy absorbed by a food from ionizing radiation that passes through the food in processing. One gray equals 100 rads. One thousand grays equals one kilogray [3].

Food is irradiated for a number of reasons. Low doses, less than one kilogray, inhibit sprouting of tubers, delay ripening of some fruits and vegetables, control insects in fruits and stored grains, and reduce the problems of parasites in products of animal origin. Medium doses, 1 to 10 kilograys, control patho-

Ion an electrically charged atom or group of atoms; the electrical charge results when a neutral atom or group of atoms loses or gains one or more electrons; loss of electrons results in a positively charged ion

Radioactive giving off radiant energy in the form of particles or rays, such as alpha, beta, and gamma rays, by the disintegration of atomic nuclei (the central part of atoms)

TABLE 28.1

Food Irradiation in the U.S.

Product	Purpose of Irradiation	Dose Permitted (kGy)	Date of Rule
Wheat and wheat powder	Disinfestation of insects	0.2–0.5	8/21/63
White potatoes	Extend shelf life	0.05–0.15	11/1/65
Spices and dry vegetable seasoning	Decontamination or disinfestation of insects	30 (max.)	7/5/83
Dry or dehydrated enzyme preparations	Control of insects and microorganisms	10 (max.)	6/10/85
Pork carcasses or fresh noncut processed cuts	Control of *Trichinella spiralis*	0.3 (min.) 1.0 (max.)	7/22/85
Fresh fruits	Delay maturation	1	4/18/86
Dry or dehydrated aromatic vegetable substances	Decontamination	30	4/18/86
Poultry	Control of illness-causing microorganisms such as *Salmonella*	3	5/2/90

Source: Reference 3.

genic microorganisms responsible for foodborne illness and extend the shelf life of refrigerated foods. Doses greater than 10 kilograys are not used for foods other than spices and dried vegetable seasonings. High doses *could* be used to destroy all microorganisms without the effects on food produced by heat sterilization [7]. These dosages are not allowed, however, at the present time.

The FDA must approve any irradiated food before it is marketed. Table 28.1 lists food products that have been approved. Petitions for the irradiation of other foods, including seafood products and beefsteaks, are being considered by the FDA. Irradiated foods marketed for consumers must be labeled with an official logo and the statement *treated with radiation* or *treated by radiation*. Market tests indicate that consumers will try irradiated food.

Radiation preservation of food is considered to be a cold process because there is only a slight rise in the temperature of the food being irradiated. The dose of radiation that a food receives depends on the time of exposure to the source of radiation—often the manmade **radioisotope** cobalt-60, which generates **gamma rays**. Usually the cobalt-60 is contained in a lead-lined chamber and the food is conveyed into and out of the chamber on a moving belt. The speed of the conveyor belt determines the amount of exposure. The dose of radiation that a food receives must be sufficient to produce the desired effect but not enough to exceed legal limits [25].

The irradiation of food does not generally cause major changes in flavor, texture, color, and composition. However, some chemical reactions do occur in the food. The FDA must make certain that none of the compounds that may be produced is harmful. Some of the reactions in irradiated food are similar to those occurring in food when it is heated by conventional means [25]. Most of the research reported on irradiated foods indicates that nutrient retention in these foods is comparable to that of heat-processed foods [18].

Radioisotope   an artificially created radioactive isotope of a chemical element that is normally nonradioactive

Gamma rays   one of three kinds of rays emitted by radioactive substances

•PACKAGING OF FOOD

A revolution has occurred in recent years in the food packaging industry. The packaging technologies developed during the past two decades far outnumber those developed in the previous two or three hundred years. These innovations in food packaging, along with new food processing technologies, have resulted in greater convenience for the consumer, less flavor loss during processing, and savings on materials and energy costs [26].

Functions of Food Packaging

The main function of a food package is to contain the food product, then to protect it from contamination and spoilage until it reaches the consumer. In addition, the food package also acts as a form of communication in its labeling function. In containing the food, it separates it into units of a particular size and weight. This may allow ease in handling and convenience and is also a marketing tool. Appropriate packaging minimizes reactions that affect the stability or the shelf life of the food products. Water vapor and oxygen are always present in the environment around foods and can affect the stability of packaged food products. The package provides a barrier to these gases. It may act in some cases to keep moisture in the food and thus prevent desiccation or drying. In other cases, it prevents moisture from entering the package and being absorbed by the food. The permeability of the package to light may also affect the stability of the food.

Deterioration from microbial decomposition depends on the presence of microorganisms in the food and on the environmental conditions conducive to their growth in the packaged product. Both temperature and moisture content can affect the microbes' potential for growth and activity. Proper packaging keeps microbial contamination at a minimum.

Food packaging may also allow energy and cost savings when the product is reheated and served in its original package. This is often of particular benefit in foodservice operations. The results of a survey of foodservice administrators revealed that many respondents perceived food packaging information as being useful and beneficial in making decisions concerning food procurement [5].

The shelf life of packaged food products is affected by physical or mechanical factors. For example, damage to the package in shipping, insect infestation, and failure of the package seal may all affect food quality and stability [13].

Regulatory Requirements

The FDA considers the compatibility of food and its packaging to be a safety issue. The package is a potential source of chemical substances for the food product. Migration of substances from packaging materials does occur and cannot be completely eliminated. Therefore, the packaging materials are legally considered to be food additives and require premarket safety evaluation and approval by the FDA [17]. Testing is extensive and thorough to assure safety.

The tray at the left is a retortable package used for shelf-stable meat and vegetable dishes. The light plastic cover in front can be placed on the tray after it is opened. The box in the center is a paperboard container for individual servings of frozen foods. It can be heated in either a microwave or a conventional oven. At the top is a microwave sleeve in which a pastry-type product can be microwaved to preserve crispness. The metal can at the top right is made of only two pieces and is seamless. At the lower right are examples of microwavable plastic trays used for many frozen entrees.

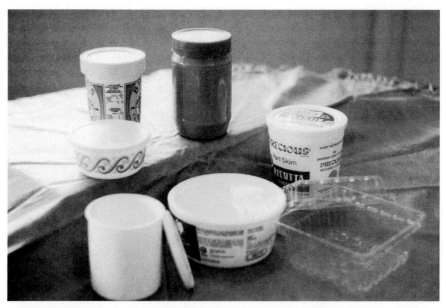

A variety of light plastic materials are used to package such items as ready-made frostings, soft margarines, frozen desserts, peanut butter, soft cheeses, baked products, and whipped toppings.

Retail and institutional-sized retort pouches and cans of comparable capacity.

Packaging Materials

A variety of packaging materials are available for use with different food products (Figure 28.4). Plastics, manufactured by a number of **thermoforming** technologies, have taken over an increasingly larger share of the container market. The packaging industry is the largest user of plastics. Fewer glass and metal containers are being utilized as plastics become more popular. A number of products, including **aseptic-packaged**, hot filled, dry-filled–no process, frozen, and retorted foods, are the result of innovations in packaging [4].

Thermoforming the application of heat in the formation of a product

Aseptic packaging packaging a product that is free of microorganisms; product and package are sterilized separately before packaging

Paper

Paperboard trays, transparent to microwave energy, were developed for use in microwave ovens, but they can also withstand up to 400°F in conventional ovens. A heat-resistant plastic resin is applied to solid, bleached sulfate board, which is formed into trays of various shapes and sizes. These containers can be used for **shelf-stable foods**, refrigerated foods, and frozen foods [5].

Rectangular paperboard cartons, laminated with aluminum and/or polyethylene, can be used for the aseptic packaging of products such as fruit juices and drinks [23]. They are made in various sizes. An assortment of products, including dry cereals, cake mixes, rice mixes, macaroni and cheese, and so on, are packed in paperboard cartons. In some cases, inner linings hold the product.

Shelf-stable foods foods that can be stored at room temperature

Plastics

Plastics are **organic polymers** with variable chemical compositions and physical properties. A number of different fabrication processes are used to produce

Organic polymers large carbon-containing molecules made up of many small molecules linked together

the many types and shapes of both rigid and flexible packages used by the packaging industry. Most applications involve several types of resins. Structural polymers such as polyethylene and polypropylene provide mechanical properties at low cost. Barrier polymers such as polyvinylidene chloride (PVDC) and ethylene vinyl alcohol (EVOH) provide protection against transfer of gases such as oxygen through the package. Adhesive resins bond the structural and barrier resins together. In flexible packaging, heat-seal resins provide closure for the package [9]. Polyethylene terephthalate (PET) is a durable packaging material with good barrier properties and impact resistance. PET containers are widely used for carbonated beverages, pourable dressings, edible oils, peanut butter, and other products [20].

Plastic films have been used in *skin packaging* for a number of years (see Figure 28.5). In skin packaging, the individual products are placed on a substrate, such as a large piece of corrugated board or box board, that has been previously treated with a special coating. The plastic film is preheated, draped over the product and the board, and tightly drawn down around each individual product. The coating on the substrate fuses with the heated film to secure the product between the film and the substrate. After cooling, the substrate is cut into individual packages. The use of skin packaging has been suggested as a means to give rigidity and physical support to flexible retort pouches so that potential damage to the pouch is lessened during shipping [10].

Metals

The traditional metal can is made of steel with a thin coating of tin. It generally is cylindrical and comprises three pieces. The two ends are attached to the cylinder, which has a soldered seam. Tin-free steel cans have now been developed and the side seam may be cemented or welded instead of soldered, decreasing concern about potential lead contamination. The National Food Processors Association has recommended that food manufacturers cease the production, packing, and distribution of foods in lead-soldered containers.

Two-piece cans, with the base and cylinder in one piece, are manufactured; these cans have fewer seams, are more durable, lighter in weight, stack better on shelves, and can be produced more inexpensively than the traditional three-piece cans. The two-piece can can also be shaped as a tray. This allows more rapid heat penetration during processing and thereby reduces heating time [5].

Aluminum cans are produced for such products as beverages. Aluminum foil, both alone and with other laminated materials, is also used for packaging foods.

Combinations of Materials

A combination of two or more materials can provide improved functional properties for food packages. Several films can be laminated together, each layer contributing specific characteristics. For example, containers for aseptic packaging may be fabricated with aluminum foil as a barrier material and polypropylene or polyethylene as heat-sealing and food contact surfaces. Since foil needs to be protected from mechanical damage, paperboard is often utilized as the outer layer of this laminate. These packages act as barriers to moisture, oxygen, light, and microorganisms, and they have the necessary strength and heat seal-

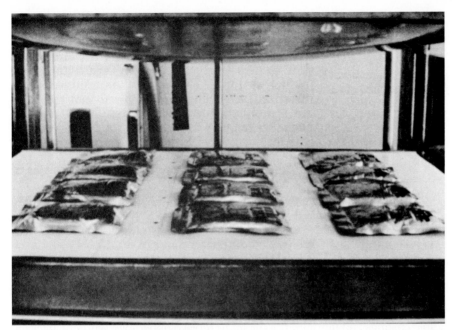

FIGURE 28.5
Skin packaging can be used to protect retort pouches in handling and shipping. (Reprinted from Friedman, D. Skin packaging retort pouches. *Food Technology 39*, 106 (No. 5), 1985. Copyright © by Institute of Food Technologists.)

Film (*top*) is lowered over the pouches on a substrate pad.

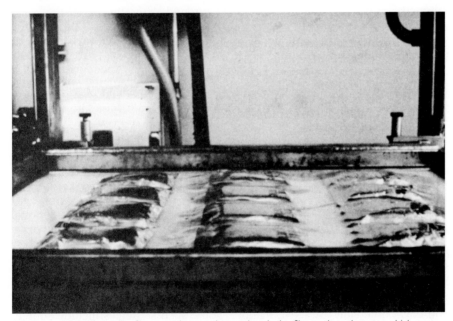

A vacuum tightly draws the film over the pouches and seals the film to the substrate, which may then be cut into individual packages.

ability [27]. Individually portioned fruit drinks are often marketed in such packages.

The flexible retort pouch is another example of a package using a combination of materials. It typically consists of three laminated materials held together by adhesives. The outer layer is polyester, which provides strength; the middle layer is aluminum foil, which provides a barrier to moisture, gas, and light; and the inner layer is polyolefin (polyethylene or polypropylene), which provides a good heat seal.

The retort pouch is thin and permits sterilizing temperatures to be reached more quickly throughout it than does the traditional can. Thus, the processed product is fresher and firmer. The sealed pouch, which can be stored on the shelf, may be heated in boiling water in preparation for serving. The pouch is easily opened by cutting with scissors or tearing across the top [5].

The retort pouch is a successful product in the Far East and to a lesser degree in Europe. In North America, however, the consumer more often uses frozen boil-in-the-bag products than shelf-stable thermoprocessed foods packaged in retort pouches [8].

Edible Films and Coatings

Edible coatings and films are not meant to replace nonedible, synthetic packaging materials for prolonged storage of foods. They can, however, act as adjuncts for improving overall food quality and extending shelf life. The desired characteristics of the edible film depend on the food product and its primary type of deterioration. For example, if the food is a manufactured product high in polyunsaturated fat, a film extremely resistant to the entrance of oxygen would be desirable to avoid the early development of rancidity. If the product is a fresh fruit or vegetable, however, the film would need to retard moisture loss but allow some permeability of oxygen and carbon dioxide gases as the plant cells continue to respire [21].

Zein a protein found in corn

Potential edible films include polysaccharides such as pectin, starch, cellulose, and vegetable gums; gelatin, **zein**, and possibly other proteins; edible waxes; and combinations of these substances. As fabricated foods become more prevalent, the use of edible films and coatings is likely to increase.

Packaging Waste Management

As we evolve into a "throw-away" society, we are producing waste from packaging, as well as from other sources, at a faster rate than we are finding solutions to deal with it [1]. Landfills are quickly being filled up. Industries and legislatures alike are facing the challenge of handling solid waste in an economical and environmentally attractive manner. Some such strategies include source reduction, or eliminating unnecessary packaging and using lighter-weight materials; recycling, which provides another source of raw materials and decreases the waste going to landfills; incineration, burning waste properly without causing air pollution; and landfilling—the least desirable method but the most commonly used. The success of these strategies will depend on communication between industry and government, the creation of markets for recycled goods, the development of effective disposal systems, and public support of recycling programs.

Aseptic Packaging

Aseptic processing involves sterilization of the food product, sterilization of the package or container in which the food will be placed, filling the sterilized container with the sterilized food in an environment in which sterility is maintained, and sealing the container to prevent subsequent contamination. Aseptic processing was developed in the 1940s. Since 1981, when the use of hydrogen peroxide for the sterilization of packaging materials was approved by the FDA, this process has rapidly gained popularity in the United States. Superheated steam or dry hot air may be used to sterilize aseptic packages, as well as hydrogen peroxide in combination with heat or ultraviolet light [19]. Hydrogen peroxide together with heat or ultraviolet radiation treatment is commonly used for the sterilization of paper-based packaging.

Food products to be aseptically packaged are pumped through heat exchangers of various types, then into a holding tube, and finally into a cooling section before being packaged. Aseptic packaging of low-acid foods containing particulates requires demonstration of sterility at the center of the food particles, based on a defined microbiological procedure and a mathematical model [22]. Destruction of any ***Clostridium botulinum*** spores present must be ensured.

Aseptic sterilization and packaging has several advantages over in-container sterilization, the process that is used in conventional canning. Processing conditions are independent of container size and therefore very large containers can be used. The process is highly automated, resulting in higher productivity. It is also more energy efficient and less expensive. Packaging costs are less for many container types. Aseptic processing yields higher-quality foods than traditional procedures requiring longer heating. Transport and storage costs are also less than those for frozen foods since refrigeration is unnecessary [27].

Modified-Atmosphere Packaging

Modified-atmosphere packaging (MAP) may be defined as the enclosure of food products in gas-barrier materials, in which the gaseous environment has been changed or modified. The modification may slow respiration rates of fresh produce, reduce microbial spoilage, and retard spoilage due to enzymatic reactions with the end result of extending the shelf life of the food [14, 28]. The gaseous atmosphere within the package usually contains a reduced amount of oxygen and increased amounts of carbon dioxide and nitrogen.

Modification of the gas mixture may be accomplished by two different methods: vacuum packaging and gas packaging. Vacuum packaging involves packaging the product in a film with low oxygen permeability, removing air from the package, and sealing it **hermetically**. Oxygen in the headspace is reduced to less than one percent. Carbon dioxide, if it is produced from tissue and microbial respiration, eventually increases to 10–20 percent within the headspace. Low oxygen and elevated carbon dioxide extend the shelf life of fresh meat by inhibiting the growth of aerobic microorganisms. The meat must be kept refrigerated. Although this works well for fresh and processed meat products, it cannot be used for crushable items such as pizza, pasta, and baked products [28].

Clostridium botulinum   a spore-forming, anaerobic bacterium that can produce a very potent toxin that causes botulism

Hermetic   completely sealed so as to keep air or gas from getting in or out

The technique in gas packaging involves removing air from the package and replacing it with a mixture of nitrogen, oxygen, and carbon dioxide. The pressure of gas inside the package is maintained approximately equal to the external pressure. Nitrogen is an inert gas that does not affect the food and has no antimicrobial properties. It is used chiefly as a filler to prevent package collapse in products that can absorb carbon dioxide. Oxygen is generally avoided except for products that continue to respire after packaging, such as fruits and vegetables. It is also used with fresh meat to maintain the red color associated with good-quality meat. Carbon dioxide is bacteriostatic and fungistatic. Its effect depends on several factors, including the microbial load, gas concentration, temperature, and packaging film permeability. Table 28.2 gives some examples of gas mixtures for selected foods [28].

Gas packaging is being used to extend the shelf life of fresh pasta, cheese, peanuts, pecans, prepared salads, sandwiches, and certain gourmet foods. In addition to increased shelf life, the advantages of MAP in these cases include increased market area, lower production and storage costs, and fresh appearance.

Some disadvantages of MAP are the initial high cost of equipment and the potential growth of organisms of public health significance. Particularly when there is temperature abuse, thus making carbon dioxide less effective, there may be a danger of the growth of microorganisms capable of causing illness [28]. A safety concern with MAP is whether or not it will inhibit microorganisms that might warn consumers of spoilage while either allowing or promoting the growth of pathogens. It is essential to assure that such organisms as *Clostridium botulinum* do not grow in these products [15]; thus, they must be kept refrigerated.

Sous vide is a French term meaning *under vacuum*. Sous-vide processing technology involves the slow, controlled cooking of foods in sealed, evacuated, heat-stable pouches or trays so that the natural flavors are retained, quick chilling, and cold storage at 0–3°C. These refrigerated products with extended shelf life can be reheated in a boiling water bath or in a microwave oven. The major microbiological hazard associated with this processing technology is the potential growth and toxin production of *Clostridium botulinum*. Other organisms of public health concern include pathogenic strains of *E. coli, Salmonella, Staphylococcus, Listeria*, and *Yersinia* species. These organisms

TABLE 28.2

Gas Mixtures for Selected Food Products

Product	Temperature (°C)	Gas Concentration (%)		
		Oxygen	**Carbon Dioxide**	**Nitrogen**
Fresh meat	0–2	70	20	10
Cured meat	1–3	0	50	50
Cheese	1–3	0	60	40
Apples	4–6	2	1	97
Tomatoes	5–10	4	4	92
Baked products	Room temperature	0	60	40
Pizza	Room temperature	0	60	40

Source: Reference 28.

should all be destroyed during the heating process. However, a hazard analysis and critical control point (HACCP) approach at all stages of sous-vide processing and handling is essential to promote a reasonable degree of confidence in product safety [28]. The risks involved in temperature abuse continue into the kitchen. Refrigerator temperatures should always be 4°C (40°F) or lower.

STUDY QUESTIONS

1. Describe several basic causes of food spoilage.
2. Why are enzymes of some concern in preserving foods? Explain.
3. For each of the following general principles of food preservation, describe a specific method of preserving food.
   a. Use of low temperatures
   b. Use of high temperatures
   c. Reduction of moisture
   d. Addition or development of acid
   e. Addition of large amounts of sugar
4. a. What is meant by *ionizing radiation*?
   b. Describe uses of low-dose ionizing radiation in the preservation of foods.
   c. Why might some members of the public be concerned about the safety of irradiated foods? How could these concerns be addressed?
5. a. Describe several functions of food packages.
   b. Why does the FDA consider food packaging materials to be food additives?
   c. Briefly describe and give examples of how each of the following materials can be used in packaging.
      (1) Paper
      (2) Plastics
      (3) Metals
      (4) Combinations of plastic and metal
      (5) Edible films and coatings
6. What is *aseptic packaging* and what advantages does it have for food products?
7. a. Describe what is meant by *modified-atmosphere packaging*.
   b. What types of foods may benefit from a modified atmosphere and why? Explain.
   c. What two methods may be employed for the modification of the gaseous atmosphere in a package? Describe them.
   d. Describe the sous-vide processing of food. What precautions must be exercised in its processing and handling?

REFERENCES

1. Anonymous. 1990. Packaging waste management. *Food Technology 44*, 98 (No. 7).
2. Anonymous. 1988. Ready-to-eat foods usage tied to microwave ovens. *Food Engineering International 13*, 23 (No. 4).
3. Blumenthal, D. 1990. Food irradiation. Department of Health and Human Services Publication No. (FDA) 91-2241.
4. Cabes, L. J., Jr. 1985. Plastic packaging used in retort processing: Control of key parameters. *Food Technology 39*, 57 (No. 12).
5. Clausen, S., M. J. A. Barclay, and L. C. Wolf-Novak. 1986. Food packaging: A consideration for procurement. *Journal of the American Dietetic Association 86*, 362.
6. Delves-Broughton, J. 1990. Nisin and its uses as a food preservative. *Food Technology 44*, 100 (No. 11).

7. Derr, D. D. 1993. Food irradiation: What is it? Where is it going? *Food and Nutrition News 65*, 5 (No. 1).

8. Downes, T. W. 1989. Food packaging in the IFT era: Five decades of unprecedented growth and change. *Food Technology 43*, 228 (No. 9).

9. Eidman, R. A. L. 1989. Advances in barrier plastics. *Food Technology 43*, 91 (No. 12).

10. Friedman, D. 1985. Skin packaging retort pouches. *Food Technology 39*, 105 (No. 5).

11. Gee, M., D. Farkas, and A. R. Rahman. 1977. Some concepts for the development of intermediate moisture foods. *Food Technology 31*, 58 (No. 4).

12. Giese, J. 1993. Packaging, storage, and delivery of ingredients. *Food Technology 47*, 54 (No. 8).

13. Gilbert, S. G. 1985. Food/package compatibility. *Food Technology 39*, 54 (No. 12).

14. Hintlian, C. B., and J. H. Hotchkiss. 1986. The safety of modified atmosphere packaging: A review. *Food Technology 40*, 70 (No. 12).

15. Hotchkiss, J. H. 1988. Experimental approaches to determining the safety of food packaged in modified atmospheres. *Food Technology 42*, 55 (No. 9).

16. Institute of Food Technologists' Expert Panel on Food Safety and Nutrition. 1986. Effects of food processing on nutritive values. *Food Technology 40*, 109 (No. 12).

17. Institute of Food Technologists' Expert Panel on Food Safety and Nutrition. 1988. Migration of toxicants, flavors, and odor-active substances from flexible packaging materials to food. *Food Technology 42*, 95 (No. 7).

18. Institute of Food Technologists' Expert Panel on Food Safety and Nutrition. 1983. Radiation preservation of foods. *Food Technology 37*, 55 (No. 2).

19. Ito, K. A., and K. E. Stevenson. 1984. Sterilization of packaging materials using aseptic systems. *Food Technology 38*, 60 (No. 3).

20. Kern, C. L., Jr. 1989. High-performance polyester for food and beverage packaging. *Food Technology 43*, 93 (No. 12).

21. Kester, J. J., and O. R. Fennema. 1986. Edible films and coatings: A review. *Food Technology 40*, 47 (No. 12).

22. Kim, H., and I. A. Taub. 1993. Intrinsic chemical markers for aseptic processing of particulate foods. *Food Technology 47*, 91 (No. 1).

23. Lisiecki, R., A. Spisak, C. Pawloski, and S. Stefanovic. 1990. Aseptic package addresses a variety of needs. *Food Technology 44*, 126 (No. 6).

24. Mertens, B., and D. Knorr. 1992. Developments of nonthermal processes for food preservation. *Food Technology 46*, 124 (No. 5).

25. Rogan, A., and G. Glaros. 1988. Food irradiation: The process and implications for dietitians. *Journal of the American Dietetic Association 88*, 833.

26. Schwartz, P. S. 1985. Regulatory requirements for new packaging materials and processing technologies. *Food Technology 39*, 61 (No. 12).

27. Smith, J. P., H. S. Ramaswamy, and B. K. Simpson. 1990. Developments in food packaging technology. Part 1: Processing/cooking considerations. *Trends in Food Science & Technology 1*, 107 (No. 5).

28. Smith, J. P., H. S. Ramaswamy, and B. K. Simpson. 1990. Developments in food packaging technology. Part 2: Storage aspects. *Trends in Food Science & Technology 1*, 111 (No. 5).

29. Sunderland, J. E. 1982. An economic study of microwave freeze-drying. *Food Technology 36*, 50 (No. 2).

30. Tuomy, J. M., and R. Young. 1982. Retort-pouch packaging of muscle foods for the Armed Forces. *Food Technology 36*, 68 (No. 2).

31. Wagner, M. K., and L. J. Moberg. 1989. Present and future use of traditional antimicrobials. *Food Technology 43*, 143 (No. 1).

Food Preservation by Freezing and Canning

29

•FREEZING

The consumer-oriented frozen food industry developed between the 1930s and the 1950s, with Clarence Birdseye one of the pioneers in this era [5]. Since then, there have been many improvements. Researchers have studied the freezing process itself in an attempt to understand and minimize the effects on food quality at each stage in the production of frozen foods [16]. Equipment for rapid freezing and widespread availability of freezers in both home and institutional kitchens have led to considerable growth in the frozen food industry. A large assortment of frozen foods is marketed. The sweeping success of the microwave oven has also contributed to growth in the industry [1]. Many frozen ready-to-eat entrées, meals, and snacks, accompanied by instructions for reheating in the microwave oven, are available.

The frozen food industry continues to work at improving the quality of frozen foods. For example, research concerning the properties and possible applications of "antifreeze" proteins as agents to prevent the growth of large ice crystals during frozen storage may in the future be applied to certain frozen foods. Antifreeze proteins are **glycoproteins** found in fish from southern polar oceans, but they also can now be synthesized chemically or by genetic engineering [6].

Producers of frozen foods are concerned with maintaining quality as the food moves through the transport and distribution systems, where it must *always* be held at low temperatures [2]. Various devices called *time-temperature indicators* (TTIs) have been developed and are being tested as possible means of monitoring and controlling critical temperatures during the storage, handling, and distribution of frozen and refrigerated foods [18].

The extent to which home freezing is practiced depends on individual circumstances and objectives. Produce, for example, must be available at advantageous prices in the market or from home gardens to make freezing an economical practice. However, the freezer contributes to efficient management in meal planning and preparation, and it has the advantage of allowing quantity buying with less frequent purchasing. It also provides convenience in the temporary storage of prepared foods made in larger quantities than are to be consumed immediately.

Glycoproteins proteins composed of amino acid chains with a carbohydrate moiety, such as a galactose derivative, attached at certain points

The Freezing Process

Freezing is the change in physical state from liquid to solid that occurs when heat is removed from a substance. When foods are frozen, they undergo a phase change of liquid water into solid ice. The water molecules reduce their motion and form an organized pattern of crystals. There are three stages in the freezing process:

1. The temperature of the food is lowered to freezing.
2. Ice crystals begin to form. This is the freezing point, and the temperature required varies with the product to be frozen. For water, the freezing temperature is 0°C (32°F). As ice crystals form from water, the remaining water becomes more concentrated with solute, lowering the freezing point still further. This is a continuous process, but the zone of maximum crystal formation in frozen foods is –4° to –0.5°C (25° to 31°F).
3. After ice formation ceases, the temperature of the frozen product is gradually lowered to the necessary storage temperature.

In a frozen food product, the activity of microorganisms is negligible. Enzymatic processes may continue, although at a reduced rate. Fast freezing and low storage temperatures are favorable for holding enzyme action at a minimum and for the best retention of nutrients. Most vegetables are **blanched** before freezing to destroy enzymes so that enzymatic action does not produce off-flavors and undesirable texture changes during frozen storage. When the secondary changes in flavor and texture resulting from blanching are unacceptable, such as in freezing strawberries or other fresh fruits, chemicals such as vitamin C (ascorbic acid) may be added to control some of the enzymatic reactions [16]. After thawing, the growth of microorganisms may occur at a rapid rate.

Blanch to heat for a few minutes by immersing in boiling water, surrounding with steam, or applying microwaves

The first commercial method of freezing foods was the slow freezing process sometimes called *sharp freezing*. In this method, foods are placed in refrigerated rooms ranging from –4° to –29°C (25° to –20°F), and large pieces of food or large containers of food require many hours or days to freeze. Quick–freezing methods have also been developed. When lower temperatures are used, –32° to –40°C (–25° to –40°F), the time of freezing is greatly reduced over that required in sharp freezing. Other factors that aid in hastening freezing are small masses of foods, contact with freezing coils or metal plates, and rapidly moving currents of frigid air. Figure 29.1 shows the relative differences in time of freezing by quick- and slow-freezing methods. The freezing of food in most home freezers is a relatively slow process.

The process of freezing rapidly at very low temperatures (–60°C or lower) is called *cryogenic freezing*. In cryogenic freezers, which use liquid nitrogen or carbon dioxide, the food is cooled so quickly that many tiny ice crystals form simultaneously, producing a much smaller number of large crystals. Tiny ice crystals have a less damaging effect on plant and animal cells than do large crystals.

Changes During Freezing, Storage, and Thawing

Changes may occur in many foods that are to be frozen as they are held before freezing. Careful handling, transportation, and storage procedures must be

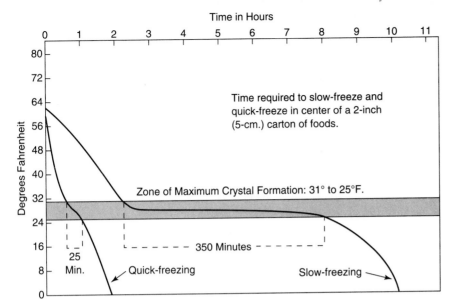

FIGURE 29.1
Diagram showing some differences between quick and slow freezing. (Courtesy of Frosted Foods Sales Corporation)

used before and during preparation for freezing if quality loss is to be minimized [16]. Crops should be harvested at the optimal stage of maturity and the produce frozen before the sugar content is reduced or undesirable enzyme activity develops. Such care greatly increases the chances that high-quality frozen produce will result. Still a number of changes do occur on the freezing of food, holding it in frozen storage, and thawing it.

Formation of Ice Crystals

Ice crystals formation, changes occurring during frozen storage, and later thawing all affect the texture of many frozen foods. The effects of freezing depend partly on the nature and state of the material that is frozen. Vegetable and fruit tissues, in particular, decrease in firmness with freezing and thawing. Whether or not plant tissues are blanched may affect the way ice crystals form in the tissues. For example, in unblanched tissue, the cell walls are intact and the exchange of water through **osmosis** is possible. If the freezing rate is slow, significant amounts of water may translocate from within cells into the extracellular medium. The formation of ice crystals in extracellular spaces causes injury to the cells. On thawing, not all of the moisture is reabsorbed by the cells.

With rapid freezing, more and smaller ice crystals are formed within cells. These also cause damage to cell structures, although the damage is less when the crystals are small. The loss of water held in the cells (turgor) as the cells are ruptured during freezing is probably responsible for much of the loss of firmness in frozen and thawed plant tissues.

As the temperature is reduced during freezing and more ice crystals form, the concentration of dissolved substances in the unfrozen medium increases and the viscosity of this unfrozen portion increases. At some temperature, dependant upon the composition of the system, the viscosity of the unfrozen matrix becomes so high that molecular motion is greatly inhibited. Unfrozen water molecules can then no longer migrate to join ice crystals.

Osmosis the movement of water through a semipermeable membrane; as ice crystals form extracellularly, the concentration of solute in this area is increased and water then moves out of the cell in an attempt to equalize the solute concentration

Other reaction rates become very slow. The temperature at which this transformation takes place is called the *glass transition temperature* (T_g). Frozen storage stability is greatest at or below T_g temperature. This information should be valuable in optimizing storage conditions for particular frozen products as researchers develop methods of modifying T_g [16].

Enzyme Action

Enzymes are present in all living tissue. Respiration, catalyzed by many enzymes, continues in fruits and vegetables after they are severed from the growing plant. It reduces sugar content, which accounts for the loss of sweetness in such vegetables as peas and corn.

Other enzymatic changes also occur. Unless the enzymes responsible for undesirable chemical changes are destroyed before foods are frozen, the foods may show various undesirable color, flavor, and texture changes during freezing, storage, and thawing. Freezing inhibits enzyme action somewhat, but it does not destroy the enzymes.

Vegetables are blanched before freezing to inactivate enzymes that may cause browning, destruction of chlorophyll and carotenoid pigments, or development of unpleasant flavors during storage [15]. In addition, blanching shrinks the vegetable tissues so that they pack more easily, expells air so that the potential for oxidation is lessened, and decreases the microbial load. From the standpoint of both overcooking and loss of soluble nutrients, however, the blanching operation should be as short as possible.

Light-colored fruits, such as peaches and apples, are particularly susceptible to **enzymatic oxidative browning** in both the fresh and frozen states. The addition of sugar or syrup to the fruit before freezing it aids in the retention of color, although darkening may occur if the fruits are held too long. Sugar also aids in preventing marked flavor changes and loss of the natural aroma. The addition of vitamin C to the syrup is also effective in preventing browning; it acts as an **antioxidant**. Citric and other organic acids may be effective for some fruits as well by lowering the pH enough to interfere with the activity of the browning enzymes.

Nonenzymatic Oxidation

Nonenzymatic oxidation of fatty materials in frozen foods may also occur. Residual oxygen is usually present in frozen foods. The fat of pork is particularly susceptible to oxidation and the development of rancidity. Bacon does not keep well in frozen storage. Antioxidants may be added to some products commercially to control unwanted oxidation.

Desiccation

If food products to be frozen are not properly packaged with **moisture/vapor-proof material**, they tend to lose moisture by **sublimation**. Some of the ice changes directly to water vapor without going through the liquid state, and the water vapor collects as frost inside the package and/or inside the freezing compartment. **Desiccation** or dehydration thus occurs.

The term *freezer burn* as applied to frozen foods refers to dehydration resulting in discoloration, change in texture, and off-flavors. This condition is

Enzymatic oxidative browning the discoloration produced in some light-colored substances in plant tissue by the enzyme polyphenol oxidase when the tissue is cut or injured

Antioxidant a substance that interferes with the oxidation process

Nonenzymatic oxidation an oxidation reaction that occurs spontaneously and is not catalyzed by enzymes, for example, oxidation of fats that results in rancidity

Moisture/vapor-proof materials materials that are relatively impermeable to water vapor and other gases; they are desirable for frozen foods to minimize the loss of moisture, particularly from sublimation

Sublimation a solid, such as ice, goes directly to the vapor state (water vapor) without going through the liquid state; in the freezer, sublimed water may collect as frost

Desiccation drying out

often observed in frozen poultry and other flesh foods as brownish dehydrated areas. Proper packaging is important in the control of freezer burn.

Activity of Microorganisms

Microorganisms are usually present in frozen foods. Their activity is negligible, however, as long as the storage temperature remains below $-9°$ to $-12°C$ ($16°$ to $10°F$). The microorganisms become active at warmer temperatures. They may begin to multiply rapidly as soon as defrosting occurs. It is very important that frozen foods be held at optimal, nonfluctuating storage temperatures and be used as soon as they are defrosted.

Selection of Foods for Freezing

Success in freezing depends to a considerable degree on the kinds and varieties of foods selected for freezing. Local agricultural experiment stations are usually able to furnish advice concerning the kinds and varieties of locally grown fruits and vegetables that are best adapted to freezing preservation. The fruits that are least changed in freezing preservation include red tart cherries, cranberries, currants, gooseberries, blueberries, and raspberries. Strawberries and peaches yield frozen products superior to those preserved by other methods. Loganberries, boysenberries, blackberries, dewberries, pineapples, melons, apples, and plums also yield good frozen products.

Although citrus fruits do not freeze well, their juices freeze quite satisfactorily, as do apple cider and other fruit juices. Some fruit juices are concentrated by partial freezing, the ice crystals being removed by straining. Some vegetables do not freeze satisfactorily. These include green onions, lettuce and other salad greens, radishes, and raw tomatoes.

Fruits and vegetables should be frozen at the proper stage of maturity. Vegetables should be harvested while they are young and tender, and fruits should be at their optimal stage of ripeness for best flavor, color, and texture. Meats and poultry to be frozen should be of high quality. Fish deteriorates so rapidly that it is best frozen as soon as possible after it is caught.

Techniques for Freezing

Fruits

Detailed instructions for the freezing of fruits and vegetables are provided in a U. S. Department of Agriculture (USDA) bulletin [10]. Figure 29.2 shows a procedure for the freezing of sliced peaches.

Mixing juicy fruits with dry sugar draws out the juices to form a syrup. Alternatively, the fruit can be covered with a sugar syrup. Most fruits require sugar or syrup treatment to protect against enzymatic changes during freezing and storage. Blanching changes the fresh flavor and texture characteristics of fruits and is thus not commonly used. Blueberries and cranberries yield satisfactory products when they are frozen without sugar or syrup or scalding. Strawberries can be frozen whole, but they retain their best color and flavor in sliced form in sugar or syrup packs.

When syrups are used, they are prepared and chilled prior to packing. Vitamin C may be added to the syrup to control browning of the fruit—approx-

1. Select mature peaches that are firm-ripe, with no green color in the skins. Allow 1 to 1½ pounds for each pint to be frozen. Wash the peaches carefully and drain.

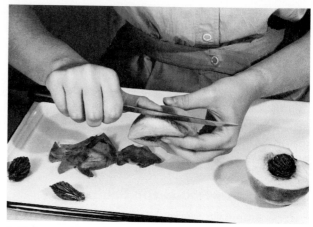

2. Pit the peaches and peel them by hand for the most attractive product. Peaches peel more quickly if they are dipped first in boiling then in cold water, but they may have ragged edges after thawing.

FIGURE 29.2
Steps involved in the freezing of peaches at home. (Courtesy of the U.S. Department of Agriculture)

3. Pour about 1/2 cup of cold syrup into each pint container. Slice the peaches directly into the container.

4. Add syrup to cover the peaches. Leave 1/2 inch of headspace at the top of wide-mouth containers like these, to allow for expansion of the fruit during freezing.

5. Put a small piece of crumpled waxed paper on top of the fruit to keep it down in the syrup. The syrup should always cover the fruit to keep the top pieces from changing color and flavor.

6. Wipe all sealing edges clean for a good seal. Screw the lid on tight. Label with the name of the fruit and the date of freezing. Put the sealed containers in the coldest part of the freezer. Leave a little space between containers so that air can circulate freely. Store the frozen fruit at −18°C (0°F) or below.

imately 1/2 teaspoon of crystalline vitamin C per quart of syrup. Commercial products containing vitamin C are also available for use in retarding the browning of frozen fruit. Syrup concentrations usually vary from about 30 to 70 percent sugar, although lower concentrations may be preferred from both a flavor and nutritive standpoint.

Vegetables

Most vegetables yield products of the best quality and flavor when they are frozen on the day they are harvested. If immediate freezing is impossible, adequate refrigeration is necessary. The speed at which the vegetables go from garden to freezer is one of the most important factors affecting quality in frozen products. The stage of maturity is also important. For those vegetables that change rapidly in maturity, such as peas, corn, snap beans, lima beans, soybeans, and asparagus, 1 or 2 days may mean the difference between a young tender vegetable and one that is tough and of poor quality.

Figure 29.3 shows the steps involved in the freezing of snap beans. Washing, draining, and sorting of the vegetable usually precede trimming and cutting. To avoid undesirable enzymatic changes, which adversely affect color, flavor, and texture during freezing and frozen storage, most vegetables require blanching to inactivate enzymes. Blanching can be done in boiling water, in steam, or by the application of microwaves. Water-soluble constituents are better retained in steam blanching, but efficient steaming equipment is sometimes difficult to obtain for home use. What is necessary is a tightly closed container that holds enough rapidly boiling water to form steam and a rack to hold the vegetable above the water level. If boiling water is used, the water should be of such a volume that the boiling does not stop when the vegetable is placed in the water. Wire racks are ideal containers to hold the vegetable. At least 1 gallon of water per pound of vegetable is needed, and more might be desirable.

Important as the blanching process is, it should not be overdone. The shortest possible time needed to inactivate enzymes should be used to avoid both actual cooking and the loss of water-soluble nutrients. Small quantities of a vegetable are blanched at one time so that all pieces will be quickly, thoroughly, and uniformly heated. After it is blanched, the vegetable must be cooled *quickly* in cold running water or ice water to about 10°C (50°F). Chilling is necessary to avoid overheating and to maintain quality. Fully as much time is required for thorough chilling as for blanching.

Prompt freezing is very important in the freezing preservation of foods, particularly vegetables. The sooner vegetables are frozen after blanching, the better the product is likely to be.

Meat, Fish, and Poultry

Meats to be frozen are usually cut into pieces of a suitable size for cooking. The pieces may be steaks, chops, roasts, ground meat, cubes for stews, or other forms. Removal of the bone conserves freezer space. Fish can be boned and packed as fillets or steaks. Poultry can be dressed and left whole for roasting or cut into pieces. Giblets are usually wrapped in parchment and placed inside of whole roasters and broilers. Only high-quality fresh meat products should be frozen.

Careful wrapping or packaging with recommended packaging materials is essential in protecting the products from oxidation and desiccation. More infor-

1. Select young, tender, stringless beans that snap when broken. Allow 2/3 to 1 pound for 1 pint of frozen vegetable. Wash thoroughly.

2. Cut the beans into 1- or 2-inch pieces, or slice them lengthwise.

3. Put the beans in the blanching basket, lower the basket into boiling water, and cover. Heat 3 minutes. Keep heat high under the water.

4. Plunge the basket of heated beans into cold water to stop the cooking. It takes about as long to cool vegetables as to heat them. When the beans are cool, remove them from the water and drain.

FIGURE 29.3

Steps involved in the freezing of snap beans at home. (Courtesy of the U.S. Department of Agriculture)

mation on the freezing of meat, fish, and poultry is found in USDA bulletins [8, 11] and in bulletins obtained from county agricultural extension agents.

Eggs

Frozen egg whites seem to lose none of the quality needed for culinary uses; however, yolks become gummy and gelled on thawing because of an irreversible change involving the lipoproteins. To be usable, a stabilizer such as sugar, syrup, or salt must be added to yolks. Mixed whole eggs usually have a small amount of stabilizer added because they contain the yolk, but they have been successfully frozen without a stabilizer.

5. Pack the beans into bags or other containers. A stand to hold the bags makes filling easier. A funnel helps keep the sealing edges clean. Seal and freeze.

When freezing eggs at home, about 1 tablespoon of sugar or corn syrup or 1/2 teaspoon of salt can be blended with 1 cup of egg yolk before freezing. The use of a small container that makes possible the thawing of only the amount of egg needed is recommended. Defrosted eggs usually have a relatively high bacterial count and deteriorate very rapidly after defrosting.

Prepared Foods

Many different frozen prepared foods and meals that require only reheating are marketed. Packaging technologies that allow direct heating in the microwave oven or boiling in the bag in which the product was frozen contribute to the wide variety of available choices. Prepared foods that require only thawing, including a variety of baked products, are usually brought into the kitchen for only short-term storage.

Many prepared foods can also be frozen in the kitchen for convenience and efficiency. Instructions for freezing combination main dishes are provided in a USDA bulletin [7]. Various casseroles, main dish items, and plated meals can be prepared in quantity and frozen for future use.

Programs to provide meals for homebound elderly people often involve the preparation and delivery of single meals one to five days a week. Some programs, however, have elected to offer supplementary meals. Plated meals prepared on-site but not served immediately may be frozen, decreasing cost and waste in preparation. Freezing practices in such programs have been investigated in a study of time–temperature relationships during the freezing of packaged meals. Similar meals were frozen in a refrigerator–freezer unit, an upright freezer, and a walk-in freezer [19]. Meals packaged in individual divided foil containers were positioned either individually or stacked three deep on the freezer shelf. The temperature during the freezing process was recorded in the center meal.

These investigators found that the temperature in the refrigerator–freezer was –11°C (12°F), in the upright freezer it was –26°C (–15°F), and in the walk-in freezer it was –23°C (–9°F). The time that the meals spent in the danger zone,

7–60°C (45–140°F), after placement in the freezer was longer in the refrigerator–freezer than in the other freezing units and was much longer in all of the freezers for the stacked meals than for the single layer. The time in the danger zone was about half as long for pot roast as for oven-baked chicken. It was concluded that freezers that maintain temperatures above –18°C (0°F) may have difficulty freezing meals within a two-hour period. It was also concluded that stacked meals take considerably longer to exit the danger zone than those that are placed in a single layer. Employees who work in feeding programs for the elderly may need to be trained in the proper handling of food to be frozen [19].

Baked products can be frozen either before or after baking. The storage life of unbaked batters and doughs is usually less than that of the baked products. If frosted or iced cakes are to be frozen, they might be frozen first without wrapping to prevent the wrapping material from sticking to the frosting, and then wrapped and returned to the freezer.

Frozen bread doughs can be made from the usual formulations, provided that the level of yeast is increased to 4 or 5 percent. A short fermentation period is desirable before freezing. If a satisfactory product is to result, sufficient yeast viability must be maintained during freezing and freezer storage to produce adequate amounts of carbon dioxide gas.

Certain foods do not freeze well at home, although commercial processes and materials may produce satisfactory results. For example, cooked egg whites toughen and become rubbery, mayonnaise tends to separate as the emulsion breaks, starch-thickened sauces tend to weep as starch retrogradation occurs, and fried foods often change in flavor when they are reheated.

Containers

Containers for freezing foods can be made of glass, metal, plastic materials, paper or fiber board, and certain moisture/vapor-proof transparent materials and should have tight-fitting lids or closures. A container that is ideal for freezer use has been described as one that is both airtight to prevent oxidation and moisture/vapor-proof to prevent dehydration. Of course, liquid tightness is necessary for use with liquid foods, such as sugar and syrup packs for fruits.

Freezer space is usually such that cube-shaped containers permit the most efficient use of storage space. It is obvious that rigidity in a container prevents crushing of the products. If containers are of such a material as to permit thorough cleaning, they may be reused. Moisture/vapor-proof bags are satisfactory if little handling is required.

Pliable moisture/vapor-proof bags should have as much air as possible removed from them and should be twisted and tightly closed. Immersing the lower part of the bag and its contents in water while packaging such irregularly shaped items as whole poultry may aid in removing air by the pressure of the water on the bag. Boil-in-the-bag containers are available for home use in freezing prepared foods. These bags may be heat-sealed before freezing.

The size of the container used is important because many frozen foods should not be held after defrosting (see Table 29.1). Containers larger than 1/2 gallon or 5 pounds are not recommended because of the slow rate of freezing.

For dry packs, the cartons can be almost completely filled before freezing. Syrup packs, or juicy products such as sliced strawberries mixed with sugar, should have about 10 percent headspace to allow for expansion of the contents during freezing.

Servings	Size of Container
1 or 2	½ pt
4	1 pt
8	1 qt

Use and Management of the Home Freezer

A freezer can be a convenience in many ways, but careful planning should go into its selection and use. The needs in each situation differ, and freezer use should be adapted to individual conditions and preferences. A freezer is a considerable investment and should be kept full or nearly full all of the time to minimize the cost per unit of food stored. For example, as the stock of frozen garden vegetables and fruits diminishes, it may be possible to buy large quantities of commercially frozen products at a savings. However, it should be remembered that the quality of frozen foods is not maintained indefinitely, but decreases with time. Suggested maximum storage periods for maintaining good quality in commercially frozen foods that are stored in kitchen freezers are provided in Table 29.2.

Time can be saved by doubling or tripling recipes when they are being prepared if they are suitable for freezing. The frozen products can be conveniently served on busy days. Advance planning in meal preparation and entertaining may be simplified with the use of a freezer. An accurate inventory of frozen foods should be kept. All foods should be stored no higher than –18°C (0°F) to maintain palatability and nutritive value. Accurate and effective temperature control is therefore very important. If a freezer stops running and remains off for an extended period, several alternatives are possible to keep the food from spoiling. If it is available, enough dry ice may be added to the freezer to maintain below-freezing temperatures for a few days. Or, the food may be put into insulated boxes or wrapped in newspapers and blankets and rushed to a freezer-locker plant. If the freezer will be off only a few hours, it should simply be kept tightly closed.

Sometimes frozen foods are partially or completely thawed before it is discovered that the freezer is not operating. Although partial thawing and refreezing reduce the quality of most foods, partially thawed foods that still contain ice crystals or foods that are still cold (about 4°C or 40°F) can usually be safely refrozen. Ground meats, poultry, and seafood should not be refrozen if they have thawed completely because bacteria multiply rapidly in these foods. Each package of meat, vegetable, or cooked food should be carefully examined. If the food is thawed and the color or odor is questionable, the food should be discarded since it may be dangerous.

•CANNING

Canning involves, first, the application to foods of temperatures high enough to destroy essentially all microorganisms present, both vegetative cells and spores, and second, the sealing of the heated product in sterilized airtight con-

TABLE 29.2

Suggested Maximum Home-Storage Periods to Maintain Good Quality in Commercially Frozen Foods

Food	Approximate Holding Period at −18°C (0°F) (months)	Food	Approximate Holding Period at −18°C (0°F) (months)	Food	Approximate Holding Period at −18°C (0°F) (months)
Fruits and vegetables		Pies (unbaked)		Cooked chicken and turkey	
Fruits		Apple	8	Chicken or turkey dinners (sliced meat and gravy)	6
Cherries	12	Boysenberry	8		
Peaches	12	Cherry	8		
Raspberries	12	Peach	8	Chicken or turkey pies	12
Strawberries	12			Fried chicken	4
Fruit juice concentrates		*Meat*		Fried chicken dinners	4
Apple	12	Beef			
Grape	12	Hamburger or chipped (thin) steaks	3	*Fish*	
Orange	12			Fillets	
Vegetables		Roasts	12	Cod, flounder, haddock, halibut, pollack	6
Asparagus	8	Steaks	12		
Beans	8	Lamb			
Cauliflower	8	Patties (ground meat)	3	Mullet, ocean perch, sea trout, striped bass	3
Corn	8				
Peas	8	Roasts	12		
Spinach	8	Pork, cured	2	Pacific Ocean perch	2
		Pork, fresh		Salmon steaks	2
Frozen desserts		Chops	4	Sea trout, dressed	3
Ice cream	1	Roasts	8	Striped bass, dressed	3
Sherbet	1	Sausage	2	Whiting, drawn	4
		Veal			
Baked goods		Cutlets, chops	4	*Shellfish*	
Bread and yeast rolls		Roasts	8	Clams, shucked	3
White bread	3	Cooked meat		Crabmeat	
Cinnamon rolls	2	Meat dinners	3	Dungeness	3
Plain rolls	3	Meat pie	3	King	10
Cakes		Swiss steak	3	Oysters, shucked	4
Angel	2			Shrimp	12
Chiffon	2	*Poultry*			
Chocolate layer	4	Chicken		*Cooked fish and shellfish*	
Fruit	12	Cut up	9	Fish with cheese sauce	3
Pound	6	Livers	3	Fish with lemon butter sauce	3
Yellow	6	Whole	12		
Danish pastry	3	Duck, whole	6	Fried fish dinner	3
Doughnuts		Goose, whole	6	Fried fish sticks, scallops, or shrimp	3
Cake type	3	Turkey			
Yeast raised	3	Cut up	6	Shrimp creole	3
		Whole	12	Tuna pie	3

Source: Courtesy of the U.S. Department of Agriculture.

tainers to prevent recontamination. The degree of heat and the length of heating vary with the type of food and the kinds of microorganisms likely to occur. Fruits and tomatoes that are sufficiently acid are successfully canned at the temperature of boiling water. The time of boiling depends on the degree of acidity, the consistency of the product, the method of preparation, and other factors. Vegetables and meats, which are relatively low in acid, must be heated to temperatures higher than that of boiling water at atmospheric pressure. This involves the use of a pressure canner. Because bacterial spores that may be present are more resistant to heat under conditions of low acidity, the time of heating necessary to destroy them at the temperature of boiling water would likely be several hours. The food would be rather unpalatable after such a prolonged cooking period. Moist heat evidently destroys microorganisms by coagulating proteins. It destroys enzymes in a similar manner.

Historical Highlights

The history of canning begins at about 1795, when the French government offered a prize for the development of a new method of preserving food from one harvest to the next. Nicolas Appert, a Parisian confectioner, worked many years on such a process and finally, in 1809, he successfully preserved some foods by sealing them with corks in glass bottles and heating them for various lengths of time [4]. Appert received a cash award (12,000 francs) for his accomplishment.

From these crude beginnings, with contributions from many workers along the way, has come the modern canning industry, with cans being produced, filled, sealed, and processed by the millions. The tin canister was first developed in England in about 1810, the **retort** for pressure canning was developed in Philadelphia around 1874 [9], Pasteur's work with microorganisms in about 1860 began a study of the true causes of food spoilage, and the process of canning was approached on a scientific basis at about the turn of the twentieth century.

Various types of batch and continuous retorts are used in commercial canning (Figure 29.4). Some retorts agitate or rotate the cans during processing in order to increase the rate of heat penetration and to aid heat distribution [12]. Commercial canning also includes methods that employ higher temperatures and shorter time periods than are used in traditional commercial canning. **Aseptic canning** (discussed in Chapter 28) is also practiced, preserving a fresher flavor for many food products. The variety of equipment available for commercial canning provides the industry with the flexibility it needs to develop and produce unique food products and to select various packaging options. Semi-rigid and flexible packages, such as the **retort pouch**, can be readily handled to produce shelf-stable foods. In all cases of commercial canning, careful written documentation of temperature distribution during processing must be maintained [14].

Although much of our canned food is now produced commercially, some people still can or bottle foods at home for various reasons, including palatability, economy, and the satisfaction derived from do-it-yourself projects. For those who must restrict their intake of salt and sugar, products may be canned without the addition of these substances. Canning tomatoes from backyard gardens appears to be one of the more popular home food preservation activities.

Retort commercial equipment used for pressure canning

Aseptic canning a process in which the food material and the container are sterilized separately, and the container is filled without recontamination

Retort pouches flexible laminated packages made of special materials that withstand high-temperature processing in a commercial pressure canner called a *retort*

FIGURE 29.4
Various types of commercial retorts
are available. (Reprinted from Kimball,
R. N., and T. L. Heyliger. Verifying the
operation of steam retorts. *Food Technology 44*, pp. 102–103 (No. 12),
1990. Copyright © by Institute of
Food Technologists.)

Batch agitating retorts, such as the Orbitort, produce product agitation by rotating the containers.

Methods for Home Canning

High-quality products should always be selected for canning. Recommended procedures should be followed to ensure safe products that do not spoil on storage. Detailed steps to be followed in home canning are given in USDA bulletin No. 539, *Complete Guide to Home Canning* [3].

Packing

Only glass jars are generally available for home canning. Foods can be packed into the jars either raw or hot (Figure 29.5).

In the *raw-pack method* of canning, the uncooked food is packed into the container and the container is filled with boiling liquid. Some headspace should be left in the top of the container before sealing. Usually 1/2 to 1 inch of headspace is suggested. This allows for the expansion of the jar contents during heating. Glass jars are only partially sealed before processing at the necessary temperature for the recommended time.

In the *hot-pack method* of canning, the food is heated in syrup, water, steam, or extracted juice before being packed into containers. With the hot-pack method, the temperature of the food should be at least 77°C (170°F) when it is packed in the container.

The raw-pack method may have an advantage over the hot-pack method in that large pieces of fruit, such as peach halves, or fragile berries can be placed in jars so that they present an attractive appearance and are closely packed. The hot-pack method may be advantageously used for some foods because it helps to drive out air, wilts or shrinks plant tissues, allows closer packing, and slightly shortens the processing time. The initial temperature of the food is relatively high and heat penetration is more rapid than when food is

Continuous rotary sterilizers provide continuous handling of containers at up to 600 cans per minute.

packed cold. Pears, apples, and pineapples have a more attractive translucent appearance when they are prepared by the hot-pack than by raw-pack method. Also, more fruit can be fit into the container.

Processing

The processing of canned fruits, vegetables, and meats is done after these foods have been packed into containers by either hot- or raw-pack methods as described previously. The processing may be accomplished in a boiling water bath for acid fruits and acid tomatoes. For vegetables, meat, fish, and poultry, which are low in acid, the use of a pressure canner is essential. A higher temperature is required with these products for the complete destruction of bacterial spores. Of particular concern is the destruction of the spores of *Clostridium botulinum*. These spores can vegetate and, under the anaerobic conditions that are found in the sealed cans, may produce a deadly toxin that causes **botulism** when consumed, even in very small amounts. In low-acid foods such as vegetables and meats, the temperature of boiling water is not sufficient to assure spore destruction. A pressure canner, in which higher temperatures can be attained, must be used in the canning of these products.

Botulism a serious illness resulting from consumption of food containing the toxin produced by *Clostridium botulinum* bacterial spores that are not destroyed in processing and vegetate on storage in an anaerobic environment

Boiling-Water Bath.

Processing by means of a boiling-water bath requires a large boiling-water canner (Figure 29.6). The canner must be deep enough so that at least 1 inch of briskly boiling water will be above the tops of the jars during processing. A fitted lid covers the canner. A rack keeps jars an inch or less above the bottom, thus avoiding breakage and allowing even circulation of heat underneath the jars. Unless the bath has a removable holder for jars, a lifter of some kind is necessary for placing jars into and removing them from the boiling water.

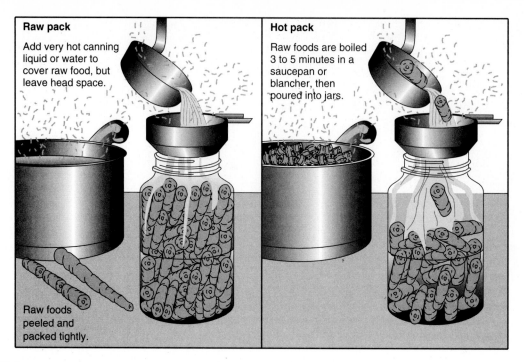

Raw pack

Add very hot canning liquid or water to cover raw food, but leave head space.

Raw foods peeled and packed tightly.

Hot pack

Raw foods are boiled 3 to 5 minutes in a saucepan or blancher, then poured into jars.

FIGURE 29.5

Bottles can be filled by either the raw-pack or the hot-pack method, as illustrated. (Courtesy of the U.S. Department of Agriculture)

The canner should be filled halfway with water. For raw-packed foods, preheat the water to 60°C (140°F); for hot-packed foods, 82°C (180°F). Load the filled jars, fitted with lids, into the canner rack and use the handles to lower the rack into the water, or fill the canner one jar at a time. Add more boiling water so that the water level is at least one inch above the jars tops. Heat on high until the water boils vigorously. Cover the canner and lower the heat to maintain a gentle boil throughout the processing period [3].

Some varieties of tomatoes now being grown in the United States, including Garden State, Ace, 55VF, and Cal Ace, are lower in acid content than tomatoes that were commonly produced in previous years. These tomatoes are likely to have pH values above 4.6 and are considered to be low-acid foods. If they are to be canned as acid foods in a boiling-water canner, they must be acidified with lemon juice or citric acid to a pH of less than 4.6. Properly acidified tomatoes can be processed in a boiling-water canner. Alternatively, low-acid tomatoes must be processed in a pressure canner, as are other vegetables and meat products. Some other local varieties of tomatoes may be too low in acid to be processed in a boiling-water bath. County Cooperative Extension Service offices should be contacted for the latest information on low-acid tomato varieties.

Pressure Canning. If temperatures higher than 100°C (212°F) are necessary for processing, a pressure canner must be used. The boiling point of a liquid such as water varies with the atmospheric pressure over its surface. As the

Boiling water should extend 2 inches above the surface of the jars.

A lifter is desirable for placing jars into and removing them from the boiling water.

FIGURE 29.6
Processing by means of the boiling-water bath. (Courtesy of the Ball Brothers Company)

atmospheric pressure is decreased with higher altitudes, the boiling point of the liquid is decreased. In a pressure canner, the water vapor or steam that is produced when the water is heated to its normal boiling point is captured inside the pan with its tightly sealed cover, thus increasing the pressure over the surface of the water in the pressure canner. This raises the boiling point of the water. Temperatures higher than the usual boiling point of water can thus be achieved.

Pressure canners in the past were constructed of heavy metal with clamp-on or turn-on lids. They had a dial gauge to indicate pressure (Figure 29.7). Most pressure canners of today are lightweight, thin-walled kettles with turn-on lids. Their essential features are a *rack* to hold jars off the bottom, a *vent port* (steam vent or petcock) that is left open for a few minutes to drive out air

FIGURE 29.7
A pressure canner is necessary to obtain temperatures higher than 100°C (212°F). (Courtesy of National Presto Industries, Inc.)

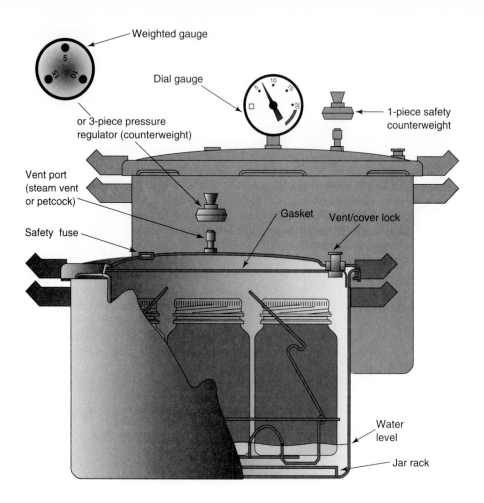

FIGURE 29.8

Essential parts of a pressure canner. Also note the water level in the canner. (Courtesy of the U.S. Department of Agriculture)

Weighted gauge

Dial gauge

or 3-piece pressure regulator (counterweight)

1-piece safety counterweight

Vent port (steam vent or petcock)

Safety fuse

Gasket

Vent/cover lock

Water level

Jar rack

and fill the compartment with steam and then closed with a *counterweight* or *weighted gauge*, and a *safety fuse* or *valve* through which steam may escape if too high a pressure develops within the canner (Figure 29.8). The pressure canner is used primarily to provide a high temperature for the destruction of heat-resistant microorganisms and their spores in a shorter time than is possible at the boiling temperature of water.

To operate the pressure canner, put 2–3 inches of water in the canner and then place filled jars on the rack, using a jar lifter. Space the jars to permit circulation of steam. Fasten the canner lid securely, assuring that the gasket is clean and in place. Leave the petcock open or the weight off the vent port and heat on high until steam flows from the port or petcock. Allow a steady stream of steam to exit from the canner for 10 minutes before closing the petcock or placing the weight on the vent port. The steam drives air out of the canner as completely as possible. This is said to *exhaust* the canner. If the air is not removed, the air in the canner contributes a partial pressure along with the steam and the temperature inside the canner will not be as high as when all of the pressure comes from steam. The food may therefore be underprocessed. Canners are not equipped with thermometers that show the exact interior temperature, so it is very important that the canner be properly exhausted. Table

29.3 shows temperatures that are obtainable in a pressure canner at different pressures, provided that no air remains in the canner.

Pressure will build up during the first 3–5 minutes after closing the vent port. Start the timing process when the pressure gauge shows the desired pressure or when the weighted gauge begins to wiggle or rock. Regulate the source of heat to maintain a steady pressure on the gauge. Rapid and large fluctuations in pressure during processing will cause liquid to be lost from the jars. Weighted gauges should jiggle periodically or rock slowly throughout the process. They allow the release of tiny amounts of steam each time they move and thus control the pressure precisely. They do not require constant watching.

When the processing time is completed, turn off the heat and remove the canner from the heat source, if possible. Let the canner depressurize. *Do not force the cooling process*. Cooling the canner with cold water or opening the vent port or petcock before the canner is depressurized will cause loss of liquid from the jars and the seals may fail. After the canner is depressurized, remove the weight from the vent port or open the petcock, unfasten the lid, and open the canner carefully.

Immediately after processing in either the boiling-water canner or the pressure canner, jars that were not tightly closed before processing, as is proper when using self-sealing lids, should now be tightly closed. Sealing occurs automatically with cooling. A vacuum is gradually produced as the jars cool.

The temperature most commonly used for home canning of low-acid foods is 116°C (240°F), corresponding to a pressure of 10 pounds per square inch. However, it has been reported that a higher pressure (15 pounds) and thus a shorter processing time also gives satisfactory results in terms of texture, color, and flavor of vegetables. Asparagus, peas, and strained squash were the vegetables tested [13].

Internal canner temperatures are lower at higher altitudes. Adjustments must therefore be made to compensate. If the pressure canner has a pressure gauge, the canner should be checked for accuracy at the beginning of each season. Checking is often done locally through the County Cooperative Extension Service or the home service department of a utility company. The amount and direction of error in the pressure gauge should be noted on a tag tied to the canner. An adjustment should then be made whenever the canner is used. Weighted-gauge canners cannot be adjusted for altitude. Therefore, at altitudes above 1,000 feet, they must be operated at canner pressures of 10 instead of 5 pounds per square inch or 15 instead of 10 pounds, as indicated in the USDA bulletin [3].

TABLE 29.3

Temperatures Obtainable at Different Pressures in a Pressure Cooker

Pressure (lb)	Temperature	
	°C	°F
5	109	228
10	116	240
15	121	250
20	126	259
25	131	267

Containers for Canning

Containers for commercially canned foods may be made of tin-plated steel (tin cans) or of glass. Tin-free steel cans have also been produced. Tin cans are of two types: plain and lacquered. The latter may be coated with the bright, or R, lacquer suitable for all red-colored foods containing anthocyanin pigment and for pumpkin and squash. If anthocyanins are canned in plain tin they fade and become bluish. Pumpkin and squash tend to corrode plain tin. The dull, or C, lacquer is best not used with acid foods or with meats that contain much fat, as both acid and fat may cause the lacquer to peel. This makes the food unsightly, although it is harmless. The dull, or C, lacquer is used for corn, succotash, and other sulfur-containing foods to prevent dark deposits of tin or iron sulfide on the food and on the can. Tin sulfide, which is brown, and iron sulfide, which is black, are not harmful but detract from the appearance of the food.

Commercial canning in metal has a number of advantages over glass: breakage is eliminated, cans are always sealed before processing, heat penetration is more rapid than with glass, the cans may be rapidly cooled after processing by being plunged into cold water, and the cans are generally less expensive. Special flexible packages, such as retort pouches, may also be used for commercial canning to produce shelf-stable foods not requiring refrigeration. These packages are less expensive to process and ship, after the initial expense by the food processor for the necessary processing equipment or modification of conventional equipment [17, 20]

The jars generally available in the United States for home canning are heat-resistant glass jars with self-sealing lids (Figure 29.9). The self-sealing closure for a canning jar has a composition ring in the lid that becomes soft when heated and then hardens, forming a seal on the edge of the jar top when it becomes cold. New lids are required for self-sealing jars each time the jars are used, but the screw bands may be reused over a long period. The lids are placed briefly in boiling water prior to use according to the manufacturer's directions.

For low-acid vegetables and for meats, jars no larger than quart size are recommended because of the danger of poor heat penetration in larger jars. The pint size is usually advised for corn, shell beans, and lima beans, in which heat penetration is slow.

Heat Penetration

Heat penetration during canning is affected by such factors as the size of the container, the material from which the container is made, the initial temperature of the food when the processing is started, the temperature used for processing, the fullness of the pack, and the character of the food. Heat penetration is more rapid in smaller containers and in tin than in glass. Starchy vegetables and closely packed leafy vegetables transmit heat poorly. Colloidal starch solutions retard heat penetration more than concentrated sugar solutions. Heat penetration is more rapid if the food is hot when the processing is started and if a higher temperature is used for processing. In general, the higher the processing temperature, the shorter the required heating time.

FIGURE 29.9

The most commonly used closure for canning jars is the metal screw band and metal self-sealing lid. Sealing occurs on the top edge of the jar. (Courtesy of the U.S. Department of Agriculture)

Obtaining a Partial Vacuum

A partial vacuum in the sealed jar is important in the canning of food. It maintains an effective seal and inhibits oxidative changes. A partial vacuum is created when the air within the jar exerts less pressure outward than the atmosphere exerts on the outside of the jar. A vacuum is produced as a result of several events during the canning process. First, food is heated. The application of heat causes internal gases to expand. When the food is heated in the jar, the gases escape through the partially sealed lid. This process is called *venting*. The formation of an effective vacuum depends largely on venting.

After processing is completed and the jar is removed from the canner, sealing occurs. With self-sealing devices the complete sealing takes place automatically as the softened sealing compound hardens on cooling. During cooling, the contents of the jar contract, leaving a space in the top that is less dense than the atmosphere pressing down on the outside of the lid. Thus, a partial vacuum is formed to aid in keeping the seal tight.

Obtaining an Effective Seal

A good seal is essential in canned foods. All jars should be examined for nicks or rough places on the sealing surfaces that might interfere with a good seal. Lids should fit well. Care should be taken to remove small bits of food from the top of the jar before closing the container since they interfere with the formation of a complete seal.

After the jars have cooled for 12–24 hours, the screw bands may be removed and the jars tested for a complete seal. If the center of the lid is either flat or bulging, it is probably not sealed. It should be concave, that is, pulled down slightly in the center. When the lid is tapped with the bottom of a teaspoon, it should give a ringing rather than a dull sound.

Handling After Processing

Proper handling and storage of canned food are important in maintaining its quality. When glass jars with self-sealing lids are thoroughly cool and have sealed, the screw bands should be removed and rinsed clean so that they can be used again. If they are left on the jars they may stick or rust, making removal difficult. The outside of the jars should be wiped clean of any residual syrup or other material. Containers should be labeled to show the contents and date of processing.

Canned foods should be stored in a cool, dry, dark place. At cool storage temperatures the eating quality and nutritive value are better maintained. Glass jars, particularly, should be stored in a dark place because light causes fading and discoloration of plant pigments. Properly canned foods may be safely stored for several years, but the quality of the food gradually decreases, especially if storage temperatures are relatively high.

If low-acid and tomato foods have not been canned according to the recommendations of the USDA, they should be boiled for 10 minutes after opening the can and before tasting any of the food contained in it. For altitudes at and above 1,000 feet, one additional minute should be added per 1,000 feet.

This recommendation is for safety in case *Clostridium botulinum* organisms have survived and produced toxin in the sealed jar [3]. Botulism has occurred most commonly from the use of home-canned products.

STUDY QUESTIONS

1. Discuss differences in methods used, rate and time of freezing, and size of resulting ice crystals between slow freezing and quick freezing.
2. Describe several undesirable changes that may occur during freezing, frozen storage, or thawing of frozen foods.
3. a. Explain why vegetables should be blanched before freezing.
   b. Give several suggestions for carrying out the blanching process to ensure that it will accomplish its purpose satisfactorily.
4. What is *freezer burn* and how can it be prevented in frozen foods?
5. How does freezing control the causes of food spoilage and thus preserve foods?
6. Discuss several points that should be considered in selecting foods for freezing.
7. What are two important roles, in addition to sweetening, that are played by sugar or syrup packs in freezing fruits?
8. What general procedures should be followed in the freezing of meat, fish, and poultry?
9. What differences are there between the procedures for freezing egg whites and egg yolks? Why are these different procedures necessary?
10. a. Why should containers and wrappers used on frozen foods be moisture/vapor-proof?
    b. Why should headspace be left in containers when freezing foods?
11. List several things that should be considered if you are to make the most effective use of your freezer.
12. Describe some pertinent events in the history of canning that are associated with each of the following names and dates.
    a. Appert, 1809
    b. 1810
    c. 1874
    d. Pasteur, 1860s
13. Distinguish between the raw-pack and the hot-pack methods of packing canned foods and discuss advantages of each.
14. Explain why fruits and high-acid tomatoes can be safely canned in a boiling-water bath while vegetables and meat products must be canned in a pressure canner. What might botulism have to do with your explanation?
15. a. Describe the essential parts of a pressure canner and explain their functions.
    b. Why is it important to completely *exhaust* a pressure canner before closing the petcock and building up pressure?
    c. Suggest a possible explanation for the loss of liquid from jars processed in a pressure canner.
16. a. Of what materials are "tin" cans usually made? Why are their inside surfaces sometimes lacquered with R or C enamel?
    b. Describe self-sealing lids commonly used on bottled produce and explain how they work.
    c. What steps should be taken to ensure that an effective seal is formed in bottled produce?
17. List several factors that may affect the rate of heat penetration as canned foods are processed.
18. Explain how a partial vacuum is formed in canned foods. Why is it important that this occurs?

REFERENCES

1. Anonymous. 1988. Ready-to-eat foods usage tied to microwave ovens. *Food Engineering International 13,* 23 (No. 4).

2. Bramsnaes, F. 1981. Maintaining the quality of frozen foods during distribution. *Food Technology 35,* 38 (No. 4).

3. *Complete Guide to Home Canning.* 1989. Agriculture Information Bulletin No. 539. Washington, DC: U.S. Department of Agriculture.

4. Corcos, A. 1975. A note on the early life of Nicolas Appert. *Food Technology 29,* 114 (No. 5).

5. Farkas, D. F. 1981. New concepts for expanding and improving frozen preservation techniques. *Food Technology 35,* 63 (No. 3).

6. Feeney, R. E., and Y. Yeh. 1993. Antifreeze proteins: Properties, mechanism of action, and possible applications. *Food Technology 47,* 82 (No. 1).

7. *Freezing Combination Main Dishes.* 1976. Home and Garden Bulletin No. 40. Washington, DC: U.S. Department of Agriculture.

8. *Freezing Meat and Fish in the Home.* 1977. Home and Garden Bulletin No. 93. Washington, DC: U.S. Department of Agriculture.

9. Goldblith, S. A. 1972. Controversy over the autoclave. *Food Technology 26,* 62 (No. 12).

10. *Home Freezing of Fruits and Vegetables.* 1980. Home and Garden Bulletin No. 10. Washington, DC: U.S. Department of Agriculture.

11. *Home Freezing of Poultry and Poultry Main Dishes.* 1975. Home and Garden Bulletin No. 70. Washington, DC: U.S. Department of Agriculture.

12. Kimball, R. N., and T. L. Heyliger. 1990. Verifying the operation of steam retorts. *Food Technology 44,* 100 (No. 12).

13. Lazaridis, H. N., and E. H. Sander. 1988. Home-canning of food: Effect of a higher process temperature (121°C) on the quality of low-acid foods. *Journal of Food Science 53,* 985.

14. Park, D. J., L. J. Cabes, Jr., and K. M. Collins. 1990. Determining temperaure distribution in rotary, full-immersion, hot-water sterilizers. *Food Technology 44,* 113 (No. 12).

15. Poulsen, K. P. 1986. Optimization of vegetable blanching. *Food Technology 40,* 122 (No. 6).

16. Reid, D. S. 1990. Optimizing the quality of frozen foods. *Food Technology 44,* 78 (No. 7).

17. Roop, R. A., and P. E. Nelson. 1982. Processing retort pouches in conventional sterilizers. *Journal of Food Science 47,* 303.

18. Taoukis, P. S., B. Fu, and T. P. Labuza. 1991. Time-temperature indicators. *Food Technology 45,* 70 (No. 10).

19. Thole, C., and M. B. Gregoire. 1992. Time-temperature relationships during freezing of packaged meals in feeding programs for the elderly. *Journal of the American Dietetic Association 92,* 350.

20. Williams, J. R., J. F. Steffe, and J. R. Black. 1981. Economic comparison of canning and retort pouch systems. *Journal of Food Science 47,* 284.

Weights and Measures

SYMBOLS FOR MEASUREMENTS

tsp	=	teaspoon	cc	=	cubic centimeter
Tbsp	=	tablespoon	mL	=	milliliter
fg	=	few grains	L	=	liter
fl oz	=	fluid ounce	oz	=	ounce
c	=	cup	lb	=	pound
pt	=	pint	μg	=	microgram
qt	=	quart	mg	=	milligram
gal	=	gallon	g	=	gram
			kg	=	kilogram
			mm	=	millimeter
			cm	=	centimeter
			m	=	meter

Equivalents

			Common Use
1 gram	=	0.035 ounce	
1 ounce	=	28.35 grams	30 grams
4 ounces	=	113.40 grams	125 grams
8 ounces	=	226.80 grams	250 grams
1 kilogram	=	2.2 pounds	
1 kilogram	=	1000 grams	
1 pound	=	0.454 kilogram	
1 pound	=	453.59 grams	450 grams
1 liter	=	1.06 quarts	
1 liter	=	1000 milliliters	
1 quart	=	0.946 liter	0.95 liter
1 quart	=	946.4 milliliters	950 milliliters
1 cup	=	236.6 milliliters	240 milliliters
1/2 cup	=	118 milliliters	120 milliliters

1 fluid oz	=	29.57 milliliters	30 milliliters
1 tablespoon	=	14.8 milliliters	15 milliliters
1 teaspoon	=	4.9 milliliters	5 milliliters
1 inch	=	2.54 centimeters	2.5 centimeters
1 centimeter	=	0.4 inch	
1 yard	=	0.914 meter	

METRIC CONVERSIONS

		Multiply by
Length	inches to centimeters	2.5
	feet to centimeters	30
	yards to meters	0.9
Volume or Capacity	teaspoons to milliliters	5
	tablespoons to milliliters	15
	fluid ounces to milliliters	30
	cups to liters	0.24
	cups to milliliters	237
	quarts to liters	0.95
	gallons to liters	3.8
Mass or Weight	ounces to grams	28
	pounds to grams	454
	pounds to kilograms	0.45

COMMON MEASUREMENTS USED IN FOOD PREPARATION

3 tsp	=	1 Tbsp	10⅔ Tbsp	=	2/3 c
16 Tbsp	=	1 c	2 c	=	1 pt
4 Tbsp	=	1/4 c	4 c	=	1 qt
8 Tbsp	=	1/2 c	4 qt	=	1 gal
12 Tbsp	=	3/4 c	2 Tbsp	=	1 fl oz or 1/8 c
5⅓ Tbsp	=	1/3 c	8 fl oz	=	1 c or 1/2 pt

APPROXIMATE NUMBER OF CUPS IN A POUND OF SOME COMMON FOODS

2¼ c granulated sugar	2 c butter or margarine
4 c all-purpose flour	4 c grated cheese

WEIGHTS AND MEASURES FOR SOME FOOD INGREDIENTS

All-purpose flour, sifted	1 lb	= 4 c	115 g per c
Whole-wheat flour, stirred	1 lb	= 3⅓ c	132 g per c
SAS-phosphate baking powder	14 oz	= 2½ c	3.2 g per tsp
Baking soda	1 lb	= 2⅓ c	4 g per tsp
Granulated sugar	1 lb	= 2¼ c	200 g per c

Brown sugar, packed	1 lb	= 2¼ c	200 g per c
Salt	1 lb	= 1½ c	288 g per c
Margarine	1 lb	= 2 c	224 g per c
Hydrogenated fat	1 lb	= 2⅓ c	188 g per c
Oil	1 lb	= 2⅙ c	210 g per c
Eggs, fresh whole	1 lb	= 1¾ c	248 g per c

Some Ingredient Substitutions

For:	Substitute:
1 tablespoon flour (thickener)	½ tablespoon cornstarch, potato starch, or arrowroot starch, or 1 tablespoon quick-cooking tapioca
1 cup sifted all-purpose flour	1 cup unsifted all-purpose flour minus 2 tablespoons
1 cup sifted cake flour	⅞ cup or 1 cup minus 2 tablespoons sifted all-purpose flour
1 cup sifted self-rising flour	1 cup sifted all-purpose flour plus 1½ teaspoons baking powder and ½ teaspoon salt
1 cup honey	1¼ cups sugar plus ¼ cup liquid
1 cup corn syrup	1 cup sugar plus ¼ cup liquid
1 cup butter	1 cup margarine or ⅞ cup hydrogenated shortening or ⅞ cup lard
1 ounce chocolate	3 tablespoons cocoa plus 1 tablespoon fat
1 ounce semisweet chocolate	½ ounce baking chocolate plus 1 tablespoon sugar
1 cup buttermilk	1 cup plain yogurt
1 teaspoon baking powder	¼ teaspoon baking soda plus ⅝ teaspoon cream of tartar or ¼ teaspoon baking soda plus ½ tablespoon vinegar or lemon juice

Standard Can Sizes

Can Size	Contents (c)	Average Net Weight
8 oz.	1	8 oz
Picnic	1¼	11 oz
No. 300	1¾	15 oz
No. 303	2	16 oz
No. 2	2½	1 lb 4 oz
No. 2½	3½	1 lb 13 oz
No. 3 cylinder	5¾	46 fl oz
No. 10	13	6 lb 10 oz

Source: American Home Economics Association. 1993. *Handbook of Food Preparation,* 9th ed. Washington, D.C.: American Home Economics Association.

Temperature Control

OVEN TEMPERATURES

Temperatures for cooking can be most accurately controlled when a thermostat or a thermometer is used. Modern ovens have thermostat-controlled heat. They may be checked occasionally with a portable oven thermometer if there is some question about the accuracy of the thermostatic control.

Temperature Range for Ovens

Very low	250°–275°F
Low	300°–325°F
Moderate	350°–375°F
Hot	400°–425°F
Very hot	450°–500°F

THERMOMETERS FOR OTHER USES

Thermometers are available for reading the temperature of deep fats, sugar syrups, and meats. In taking the temperature of hot fats or of boiling sugar syrups, the bulb of the thermometer should be fully submerged but should not touch the bottom of the utensil. In reading the scale, the eye should be level with the top of the mercury column.

Meat thermometers have a short scale, up to about 100°C (212°F). The bulb is small, and the thermometer is inserted so that the bulb rests in the center of the roast or the muscle being roasted. The thermometer should be inserted so that its position in the oven is convenient for reading the scale.

CONVERTING CELSIUS TEMPERATURES TO FAHRENHEIT

Formulas

$1.8 \times °C = °F - 32$

or

$$°C = (°F - 32) \times 5/9$$
$$°F = (°C \times 9/5) + 32$$

The first formula given for temperature conversion can be used either for changing Celsius to Fahrenheit or Fahrenheit to Celsius simply by inserting the *known* temperature in the appropriate place in the formula and then solving the equation for the unknown.

Conversion Table

°F	°C	°F	°C
50	10.0	200	93.3
60	15.6	210	98.9
70	21.1	212	100.0
80	26.7	215	101.7
90	32.2	220	104.4
100	37.8	230	110.0
110	43.3	235	112.8
120	48.9	240	115.6
130	54.4	245	118.3
140	60.0	248	120.0
150	65.6	250	121.1
160	71.1	252	122.2
170	76.7	255	123.9
180	82.2	260	126.7
190	87.8	270	132.2

Nutritive Value of Selected Foods

APPENDIX

C

TABLE C.I

Vegetables

Vegetable	Approximate Measure	Weight (g)	Food Energy (kcal)	Water (%)	Protein (g)	Carbohydrate (g)	Calcium (mg)	Iron (mg)	Vitamin A Value (IU)	Vitamin A Value (RE)	Thiamin (mg)	Riboflavin (mg)	Ascorbic acid (mg)
Leaves													
Cabbage, raw, finely shredded	1 c	70	15	93	1	4	33	0.4	90	9	0.04	0.02	33
Lettuce, raw, crisphead	¼ head	135	20	96	1	3	26	0.7	450	45	0.06	0.04	5
Spinach, frozen cooked	1 c	190	55	90	6	10	277	2.9	14,790	1,479	0.11	0.32	23
Vegetable–fruits													
Peppers, green, sweet, raw	1 pod	74	20	93	1	3	3	0.6	390	39	0.06	0.04	95
Squash, winter, baked, cubes	1 c	205	80	89	2	18	29	0.7	7,290	729	0.17	0.05	20
Tomatoes, raw	1	123	25	94	1	5	9	0.6	1,390	139	0.07	0.06	22
Flowers and stems													
Asparagus, cooked from raw, cut	1 c	180	45	92	5	8	43	1.2	1,490	149	0.18	0.22	49
Broccoli, cooked from raw, cut	1 c	155	45	90	5	9	71	1.8	2,180	218	0.13	0.32	97
Cauliflower, cooked from raw	1 c	125	30	93	2	6	34	0.5	20	2	0.08	0.07	69
Celery, raw, outer stalk	1 stalk	40	5	95	Trace	1	14	0.2	50	5	0.01	0.01	3

Vegetable	Approximate Measure	Food Weight (g)	Energy (kcal)	Water (%)	Protein (g)	Carbohydrate (g)	Calcium (mg)	Iron (mg)	Vitamin A Value (IU)	Vitamin A Value (RE)	Thiamin (mg)	Riboflavin (mg)	Ascorbic acid (mg)
Bulbs, roots, tubers													
Beets, cooked, diced	1 c	170	55	91	2	11	19	1.1	20	2	0.05	0.02	9
Carrots, cooked from raw, sliced	1 c	156	70	87	2	16	48	1.0	38,300	3,830	0.05	0.09	4
Potatoes, peeled after boiling	1	135	115	77	2	27	11	0.4	0	0	0.14	0.03	18
Sweet potatoes, boiled, peeled	1	151	160	73	2	37	32	0.8	25,750	2,575	0.08	0.21	26
Seeds and pods													
Snap beans, cooked from frozen	1 c	135	35	92	2	8	61	1.1	710	71	0.06	0.10	11
Corn, sweet, cooked from raw	1 ear	77	85	70	3	19	2	0.5	170	17	0.17	0.06	5
Peas, green, cooked from frozen	1 c	160	125	80	8	23	38	2.5	1,070	107	0.45	0.16	16
Peas, split, dry, cooked	1 c	200	230	70	16	42	22	3.4	80	8	0.30	0.18	0
Beans, dry, cooked Pinto	1 c	180	265	65	15	49	86	5.4	Trace	Trace	0.33	0.16	0

Source: *Nutritive Value of Foods*. Home and Garden Bulletin No. 72. Washington, DC: U.S. Department of Agriculture, 1991.

693

TABLE C.2

Fruits and Fruit Juices

Fruit	Approximate Measure	Weight (g)	Food Energy (kcal)	Water (%)	Protein (g)	Carbohydrate (g)	Vitamin A Value (IU)	(RE)	Ascorbic Acid (mg)
Apples, raw, unpeeled	1 medium	138	80	84	Trace	21	70	7	8
Apricots, raw	3 apricots	106	50	86	1	12	2,770	277	11
Avocados, raw, California	1 avocado	173	305	73	4	12	1,060	106	14
Bananas, raw, without peel	1 banana	114	105	74	1	27	90	9	10
Blueberries, raw	1 c	145	80	85	1	20	150	15	19
Cantaloupe, raw	½ medium	267	95	90	2	22	8,610	861	113
Grapefruit, medium White	½	120	40	91	1	10	10	1	41
Pink or red	½	120	40	91	1	10	310	31	41
Grapefruit juice, frozen concentrate diluted with 3 parts water	1 c	247	100	89	1	24	20	2	83
Grapes, raw, Thompson	10 grapes	50	35	81	Trace	9	40	4	5
Oranges, raw	1 orange	131	60	87	1	15	270	27	70
Orange juice, fresh	1 c	248	110	88	2	26	500	50	124
canned, unsweetened	1 c	249	105	89	1	25	440	44	86
frozen concentrate, diluted with 3 parts water	1 c	249	110	88	2	27	190	19	97
Peaches, raw	1 medium	87	35	88	1	10	470	47	6
Pears, raw	1 pear	166	100	84	1	25	30	3	7
Pineapple, raw, diced	1 c	155	75	87	1	19	40	4	24
Raspberries, red, raw	1 c	123	60	87	1	14	160	16	31
Strawberries, raw, capped	1 c	149	45	92	1	10	40	4	84
Tangerines, raw	1 medium	84	35	88	1	9	770	77	26
Watermelon, raw, wedge, with rind and seeds	4 × 8 in.	482	155	92	3	35	1,760	176	46

Source: Nutritive Value of Foods. Home and Garden Bulletin No. 72. Washington, DC: U.S. Department of Agriculture, 1991.

TABLE C.3
Meat, Fish, and Poultry

Meat	Approximate Measure (oz)	Weight (g)	Food Energy (kcal)	Water (%)	Protein (g)	Fat (g)	Iron (mg)	Thiamin (mg)
Beef, cooked								
Cuts braised, simmered, or pot roasted								
Lean and fat	3	85	325	43	22	26	2.5	0.06
Lean only	2.2	62	170	53	19	9	2.3	0.05
Ground beef, broiled								
Lean	3	85	230	56	21	16	1.8	0.04
Regular	3	85	245	54	20	18	2.1	0.03
Roast, oven-cooked								
Relatively fat, such as rib								
Lean and fat	3	85	315	46	19	26	2.0	0.06
Lean only	2.2	61	150	57	17	9	1.7	0.05
Relatively lean, such as eye of round								
Lean and fat	3	85	205	57	23	12	1.6	0.07
Lean only	2.6	75	135	63	22	5	1.5	0.07
Lamb, cooked								
Leg, roasted								
Lean and fat	3	85	205	59	22	13	1.7	0.09
Lean only	1.6	73	140	64	20	6	1.5	0.08
Liver, beef, fried	3	85	185	56	23	7	5.3	0.18
Pork, fresh, cooked								
Chop, loin, broiled								
Lean and fat	3.1	87	275	50	24	19	0.7	0.87
Roast, rib								
Lean and fat	3	85	270	51	21	20	0.8	0.50
Lean only	2.5	71	175	57	20	10	0.7	0.45
Veal, cooked, bone removed								
Roast, rib, medium fat	3	85	230	55	23	14	0.7	0.11
Poultry								
Chicken, breast, fried, batter-dipped								
Flesh with skin	4.9	140	365	52	35	18	1.8	0.16
Chicken, drumstick, fried, batter-dipped								
Flesh with skin	2.5	72	195	53	16	11	1.0	0.08
Chicken, canned, boneless	5	142	235	69	31	11	2.2	0.02
Turkey, roasted, flesh only								
Dark meat	3	85	160	63	24	6	2.0	0.05
Light meat	3	85	135	66	25	3	1.1	0.05
Fish								
Haddock, breaded, fried	3	85	175	61	17	9	1.0	0.06
Tuna, canned in oil								
Drained solids	3	85	165	61	24	7	1.6	0.04
Tuna, canned in water								
Solids and liquid	3	85	135	63	30	1	0.6	0.03
Flounder, baked	3	85	80	78	17	1	0.3	0.05
Salmon, baked	3	85	140	67	21	5	0.5	0.18

Source: Nutritive Value of Foods. Home and Garden Bulletin No. 72. Washington, DC: U.S. Department of Agriculture, 1991.

TABLE C.4

Dairy Products

Product	Approximate Measure	Weight (g)	Food Energy (kcal)	Water (%)	Protein (g)	Fat (g)	Carbohydrate (g)	Calcium (mg)	Vitamin A (IU)	Vitamin A (RE)
Fluid milk										
Whole, 3.3% fat	1 c	244	150	88	8	8	11	291	310	76
Nonfat (skim)	1 c	245	85	91	8	Trace	12	302	500	149
Low-fat, 2% fat, nonfat milk solids added, less than 10 g of protein per cup	1 c	245	125	89	9	5	12	313	500	140
Buttermilk	1 c	245	100	90	8	2	12	285	80	20
Canned										
Evaporated, unsweetened whole	1 c	252	340	74	17	19	25	657	610	136
Condensed, sweetened	1 c	306	980	27	24	27	166	868	1,000	248
Dry, nonfat, instant	1 c	68	245	4	24	Trace	35	837	1,610 (added)	483
Yogurt, plain (from partially skimmed milk with added milk solids)	1 c	227	145	85	12	4	16	415	150	36
Cream										
Half-and-half	1 c	242	315	81	7	28	10	254	1,050	259
Light, coffee or table	1 c	240	470	74	6	46	9	231	1,730	437
Heavy whipping	1 c	238	820	58	5	88	7	154	3,500	1,002
Cheese										
Cheddar	1 oz	28	115	37	7	9	Trace	204	300	86
Creamed cottage, 4% fat (curd not pressed down), large curd	1 c	225	235	79	28	10	6	135	370	108

Source: Nutritive Value of Foods. Home and Garden Bulletin No. 72. Washington, DC: U.S. Department of Agriculture, 1991.

TABLE C.5
Cereal Products

Product	Approximate Measure	Weight (g)	Food Energy (kcal)	Water (%)	Protein (g)	Carbohydrate (g)	Iron (mg)	Thiamin (mg)	Riboflavin (mg)	Niacin (mg)
Wheat										
Bread, whole-wheat	1 slice	25	70	29	3	13	1.0	0.08	0.06	1.1
Bread, white, enriched	1 slice	25	65	37	2	12	0.7	0.12	0.08	0.9
Bulgur, uncooked	1 c	170	600	10	19	129	9.5	0.48	0.24	7.7
Cream of Wheat, quick, enriched, cooked	1 c	244	140	86	4	29	10.9	0.24	0.07	1.5
Flour, whole-wheat	1 c	120	400	12	16	85	5.2	0.66	0.14	5.2
Flour, all-purpose, enriched	1 c	125	455	12	13	95	5.5	0.80	0.50	6.6
Flour, cake or pastry, enriched	1 c	96	350	12	7	76	4.2	0.58	0.38	5.1
Raisin bran	1 oz	28	90	8	3	21	3.5	0.28	0.34	3.9
Shredded wheat	1 oz	28	100	5	3	23	1.2	0.07	0.08	1.5
Wheaties	1 oz	28	100	5	3	23	4.5	0.37	0.43	5.0
Macaroni, cooked enriched	1 c	130	190	64	7	39	2.1	0.23	0.13	1.8
Noodles (egg), enriched, cooked	1 c	160	200	70	7	37	2.6	0.22	0.13	1.9

TABLE C.5, *continued*

Product	Approximate Measure	Weight (g)	Food Energy (kcal)	Water (%)	Protein (g)	Carbohydrate (g)	Iron (mg)	Thiamin (mg)	Riboflavin (mg)	Niacin (mg)
Corn										
Cornmeal, whole-ground, dry	1 c	122	435	12	11	90	2.2	0.46	0.13	2.4
Cornmeal, degermed, enriched, cooked	1 c	240	120	88	3	26	1.4	0.14	0.10	1.2
Corn tortillas	1	30	65	45	2	13	0.6	0.05	0.03	0.4
Cornflakes										
plain	1 oz	28	110	3	2	24	1.8	0.37	0.43	5.0
sugar covered	1 oz	28	110	3	1	25	1.8	0.37	0.43	5.0
Oats										
Oatmeal or rolled oats, cooked	1 c	234	145	85	6	25	1.6	0.26	0.05	0.3
Rice										
white, enriched, cooked										
regular	1 c	205	225	73	4	50	1.8	0.23	0.02	2.1
instant	1 c	165	180	73	4	40	1.3	0.21	0.02	1.7
brown	1 c	195	230	70	5	50	1.0	0.18	0.04	2.7

Source: Nutritive Value of Foods. Home and Garden Bulletin No. 72. Washington, DC: U.S. Department of Agriculture, 1991.

TERMS USED IN COOKERY

Baste. To spoon liquid over food as it cooks. The liquid may be drippings from the food itself.

Beat. To make a mixture smooth using a brisk motion that has an up-and-down movement.

Blanch. To apply boiling water or steam for a few minutes.

Blend. To mix two or more ingredients thoroughly.

Boil. To cook in water at a boiling temperature.

Braise. To cook meat or poultry slowly in a covered utensil in a small amount of liquid or in steam.

Bread. To roll in bread crumbs before cooking

Broil. To cook by direct exposure to radiant heat.

Brown. To produce a brown surface on a food by the use of relatively high heat.

Caramelize. To heat sugar until a brown color and characteristic flavor develop.

Chop. To cut into pieces using a sharp knife or other tool.

Clarify. To clear a liquid of all solid particles.

Cream. To mix one or more foods, usually fat and sugar, until smooth and creamy.

Crumb. To coat or top with crumbs, such as topping a casserole dish.

Cut in. To distribute solid fat throughout dry ingredients using two knives or a pastry blender.

Dice. To cut into small cubes.

Dot. To place small particles at intervals on a surface, as to dot with butter.

Dredge. To sprinkle or coat with flour or other fine substance.

Fold. To combine by using two motions, cutting vertically through the mixture and turning the mixture over and over.

Fricassee. To cook by braising; usually applied to fowl, rabbit, or veal cut into pieces.

Fry. To cook in fat. Pan-frying is to cook to doneness in a small amount of fat; deep-fat frying is to cook submerged in hot fat.

Grind. To reduce to small particles by cutting or crushing mechanically.

Knead. To manipulate by pressure alternated with folding and stretching, as in kneading a dough.

Lard. To place fat on top or insert strips of fat in uncooked lean meat or fish to give flavor and prevent drying of the surface.

Leaven. To make lighter by use of a gaseous agent such as air, water vapor, or carbon dioxide.

Level off. To move the level edge of a knife or spatula across the top edge of a container, scraping away the excess material.

Marinate. To let lie in a prepared liquid for a period for tenderizing and seasoning purposes.

Melt. To liquefy by use of heat.

Mince. To divide into very small pieces by chopping or cutting.

Mix. To combine ingredients.

Oven spring. The rapid increase in volume of yeast bread during the first few minutes of baking.

Pan-broil. To cook uncovered on a hot surface, pouring off fat as it accumulates.

Panning. The cooking of a vegetable in a tightly covered skillet, using a small amount of fat but no added water.

Pare. To cut off an outside covering such as skins of vegetables.

Peel. To remove outside coverings.

Poach. To cook in a hot liquid. The food is carefully handled to retain its form as in poaching an egg.

Pot-roast. To cook large pieces of meat by braising.

Proofing. The final rising period before baking for yeast doughs that have been molded.

Render. To melt fat and remove from connective tissue using low heat.

Retort pouch. A flexible laminated package that withstands high-temperature processing in a commercial pressure canner called a *retort*.

Roast. To cook, uncovered, by use of dry heat.

Roux. A thickening agent made by heating a blend of flour and fat. It may be white or brown and is used in making sauces and gravies.

Sauté. To cook quickly in a small amount of hot fat; a partial cooking process.

Scald. To heat milk or other liquids just below the boiling point.

Sear. To coagulate or brown the surface of meat by the application of intense heat for a brief period.

Sift. To separate the fine parts of a material from the coarse parts by use of a sieve.

Simmer. To cook in liquid at about 85°C (185°F). The liquid may show slight movement or bubbling, but the bubbles tend to form slowly and to break below the surface.

Steam. To cook in direct contact with steam in a closed container. Indirect steaming may be done in the closed top of a double boiler.

Steep. To extract flavor or color at a temperature below the boiling point of water.

Stew.   To simmer in a small to moderate quantity of liquid.

Stir.   To mix food materials with a circular motion.

Toast.   To brown by means of dry heat.

Truss.   To secure the wings and legs of a bird with pins or twine.

Whip.   To rapidly beat such mixtures as gelatin dishes, eggs, and cream to incorporate air and increase volume.

TERMS USED IN FOOD SCIENCE

Acid.   Sour-tasting compound containing hydrogen that may be ionized or replaced by positive elements to form salts.

Acrolein.   Irritating substance formed by the decomposition of glycerol at high temperatures.

Alkali.   Substance having the ability to neutralize an acid.

Amino Acid.   Organic molecule containing both an amino group ($-NH_2$)

and an acid group ($-\overset{\overset{\textstyle O}{\|}}{C}-OH$); the basic building block of proteins.

Amylase.   Enzyme that breaks down or hydrolyzes starch.

Amylopectin.   Highly branched-chain fraction of starch.

Amylose.   Straight-chain fraction of starch.

Antioxidant.   Substance that retards oxidative rancidity in fats by becoming oxidized itself and stopping a chain reaction.

Aroma.   Distinctive fragrance or odor.

Astringent.   Shrinking or contracting of tissues in the mouth to produce a puckery effect.

Boiling point.   Temperature at which the atmospheric pressure is equal to the vapor pressure of a liquid and an equilibrium is established.

Brownian movement.   The pushing to and fro of comparatively large molecules, such as those in a colloidal dispersion, by the rapidly moving small molecules of the dispersing medium (usually water in food products).

Buffer.   Substance that resists change in acidity or alkalinity.

Carbohydrates.   Organic compounds containing carbon, hydrogen, and oxygen; simple sugars and polymers of simple sugars.

Catalyst.   Substance that affects the rate of a chemical reaction without being used up in the reaction.

Coagulation.   Usually refers to a change in or denaturation of a protein that results in hardening or precipitation. Often accomplished by heat or mechanical agitation.

Colloid.   Usually refers to the state of subdivision of dispersed particles; intermediate between very small particles in true solution and large particles in suspension. Proteins and pectins are usually colloidal.

Crystallization.   Process of forming crystals that result from chemical elements solidifying with an orderly internal structure.

Denaturation.   Changing of a protein molecule, usually by the unfolding of the chains, to a less soluble state.

Dextrinization.   Breakdown of starch molecules to dextrins by dry heat.

Dextrins. Polysaccharides resulting from the partial hydrolysis of starch.

Disaccharide. Carbohydrate made up of two simple sugars (monosaccharides) linked together. Table sugar (sucrose) is a disaccharide.

Disperse. To distribute or spread throughout some other substance.

Disperse phase. Separated or particle component in a dispersion.

Dispersion. System composed of dispersed particles in a dispersion medium.

Dispersion medium. Continuous medium in which particles are dispersed.

Emulsifier. Surface-active agent that acts as a bridge between two immiscible liquids and allows an emulsion to form.

Emulsion. Dispersion of one liquid in another with which it is usually immiscible.

Enzyme. Organic catalyst produced by living cells that changes the rate of a reaction without being used up in the reaction.

Ester. Chemical combination of an alcohol and an organic acid. Fats are esters of glycerol and three fatty acids.

Fatty Acids. Organic acids made up of chains of carbon atoms with a carboxyl group $(-\overset{\overset{\textstyle O}{\|}}{C}-OH)$ on one end; three fatty acids combine with glycerol to make a triglyceride.

Fermentation. Transformation of organic substances into smaller molecules by the action of a microorganism; yeast ferments glucose to carbon dioxide and alcohol.

Foam. Dispersion of a gas in a liquid.

Gel. Colloidal dispersion that shows some rigidity and keeps the shape of the container in which it has been placed.

Gelatinization. Swelling and consequent thickening of starch granules when heated in water.

Glycerol. Three-carbon organic compound (an alcohol) that combines with fatty acids to produce fats (triglycerides).

Gluten. Elastic, tenacious substance formed from the insoluble proteins of wheat flour during dough development.

Gram. Basic unit of weight in the metric system; 28.35 grams equal 1 ounce and 453.59 grams equal 1 pound.

Gustatory. Having to do with the sense of taste.

Homogenize. To break up particles into small, uniform-sized pieces. Fat in milk may be homogenized.

Hydration. Process of absorbing water.

Hydrogenation. Process in which hydrogen is combined chemically with an unsaturated compound such as an oil. Hydrogenation of oil produces a plastic shortening.

Hydrolysis. Chemical reaction in which a molecular linkage is broken and a molecule of water is utilized. Starch is hydrolyzed to produce glucose; water is a necessary component of the reaction.

Hydrophilic. Attracted to water.

Hygroscopic. Tending to absorb water readily.

Immiscible. Not capable of being mixed.

Inversion. Breakdown of sucrose to its component monosaccharides, glucose and fructose.

Irradiation. Process in which food is exposed to radiant energy.

Kilocalorie. Amount of heat required to raise the temperature of 1 kilogram (1000 grams) of water 1°C; a unit of energy.

Kinetic energy. Energy created by the very rapid movement of small molecules or ions in a liquid.

Lecithin. Fatty substance containing two fatty acids esterified to glycerol along with phosphoric acid and a nitrogen-containing compound; a phospholipid.

Maillard reaction. Browning reaction involving combination of an amino group ($-NH_2$) from a protein and an aldehyde group ($-\overset{\overset{\textstyle H}{\textstyle |}}{C}=O$) from a sugar, which then leads to the formation of many complex substances.

Minerals. Inorganic substances; noncarbon compounds; ash.

Monoglyceride. Glycerol esterified to one fatty acid.

Monosaccharides. Simple sugars, for example, glucose, fructose, and galactose.

Olfactory. Having to do with the sense of smell.

Opaque. Not reflecting or giving out light; not clear.

Organic. Pertaining to carbon compounds.

Osmosis. Movement of water through a semipermeable membrane from an area of low concentration of solute to an area of higher concentration to equalize the osmotic pressure created by differences in concentration.

Oxidases. Enzymes that catalyze oxidation reactions.

Oxidation. Gain in oxygen or loss of electrons.

Pasteurization. Mild heat treatment to destroy vegetative microorganisms; not complete destruction of microbes.

Pectin. Polysaccharide composed of galacturonic acid subunits, partially esterified with methyl alcohol, and capable of forming a gel.

pH. Expression of degree of acidity. On a scale from 1 to 14, 7 is neutral, 1 is most acid, and 14 is most alkaline or least acid.

Photosynthesis. Formation of carbohydrates in living plants from water and carbon dioxide by the action of sunlight on the green chlorophyll pigment of the leaves.

Plasticity. Ability to be molded or shaped.

Polyphenols. Organic compounds that include as part of their chemical structures an unsaturated ring with more than one $-OH$ group on it. These compounds are implicated in certain types of oxidative enzymatic browning in foods.

Polysaccharides. Complex carbohydrates containing many simple sugars (monosaccharides) linked together. Starch and pectins are polysaccharides.

Polyunsaturated fatty acid. Fatty acid that has two or more double bonds between carbon atoms. A polyunsaturated fat is one that contains a relatively high proportion of polyunsaturated fatty acids.

Reduction. Gain of hydrogen or gain of electrons.

Rennet. Crude extract from calf stomach containing the enzyme rennin.

Rennin. Enzyme from the stomach that clots milk.

Retrograde. Close association of amylose molecules in a starch gel during aging.

Saturated fatty acid.   Fatty acid that has no double bonds between its carbon atoms and thus holds all of the hydrogen it can hold. A saturated fat is one that contains a relatively high proportion of saturated fatty acids.

Saturated solution.   Solution containing all of the solute that it can dissolve at that temperature.

Sol.   Pourable colloidal dispersion that has not yet set into a gel.

Solubility.   Amount of a substance that will dissolve in a specified quantity of another substance.

Solute.   Substance to be dissolved in another substance (called the solvent).

Solution.   Mixture resulting when a solute is dissolved in a solvent.

Solvent.   Substance that will dissolve another substance (called the solvent).

Spore.   Encapsulated, resistant form of a microorganism.

Sterilize.   To destroy microorganisms by heating with steam or dry heat or by boiling in liquid for 20 to 30 minutes.

Substrate.   Substance on which an enzyme acts or the medium on which microorganisms grow.

Supersaturated solution.   Solution that has dissolved more solute or dispersed substance than it can ordinarily hold at a particular temperature. The solution is formed by being heated and slowly cooled without disturbance.

Syneresis.   Separation or weeping of liquid from a gel.

Tactile.   Having to do with the sense of touch.

Toxin.   A poison, usually a protein, formed by microorganisms.

Translucent.   Shining or glowing through; partly transparent.

Viscosity.   Resistance to flow.

Volatile.   Readily forming a vapor or gaseous phase.

Volatilization.   Process of becoming volatile.

Whey.   Liquid portion of milk remaining after the curd, which is chiefly the protein casein, is precipitated.

Index